Schott's
Almanac

2011

Although those who concern themselves with details are regarded as folk
of limited intelligence, it seems to me that this part is essential, because
it is the foundation, and it is impossible to erect any building or establish
any method without understanding its principles. It is not enough to
have a liking for architecture. One must also know stone-cutting.
– MARÉCHAL DE SAXE, *Les Rêveries*, 1756

Schott's Almanac 2011 ™ · Schott's Almanac ™
Schott's Annual Astrometer ™ © 2010

© BEN SCHOTT 2010 · All rights reserved

Published by Bloomsbury Publishing Plc., 36 Soho Square, London, W1D 3QY, UK

www.benschott.com
You can follow the (t)witterings of the editor at @benschott

1 2 3 4 5 6 7 8 9 10

The moral right of Ben Schott to be identified as the author
of this work has been asserted by him in accordance with
the Copyright, Designs and Patents Act, 1988.

Cover illustration by Alison Lang. © Ben Schott 2010. All rights reserved.
Portraits by Chris Lyon. © Ben Schott 2006–10. All rights reserved.
The table of PMs on pp.264–65 was first published in *The Times*; grateful thanks are extended to *Facts About the British Prime Ministers*, Englefield, Seaton, & White (The H. W. Wilson Co., NY).
Many of the words of the year were first published on the *Schott's Vocab* blog on nytimes.com.
The credit ratings data on p.231 were first published, in a modified form, in the *New York Times*.
Other illustrations © Ben Schott 2010. All rights reserved.

NOTE · Information included within is believed to be correct at the time of going to press. Neither the author nor the publisher can accept any responsibility for any error or subsequent changes.

The paper this book is printed on is certified by the © 1996 Forest Stewardship Council A.C. (FSC). It is ancient-forest friendly. The printer holds FSC chain of custody SGS-COC-2061

FSC
www.fsc.org
MIX
Paper from responsible sources
FSC® C018072

ISBN 978-0-7475-9951-7

A CIP catalogue record for this book is available from the British Library. Designed & typeset by BEN SCHOTT. Printed in Great Britain by CLAYS Ltd, ST IVES Plc.

Also by BEN SCHOTT

Schott's Original Miscellany
Schott's Food & Drink Miscellany
Schott's Sporting, Gaming, & Idling Miscellany
Schott's Miscellany Diary (with Smythson)

Schott's Almanac

2011

· *The book of things past and the song of the future* ·

Conceived, edited, and designed by

BEN SCHOTT

Assistant Editors
Claire Cock-Starkey & Bess Lovejoy

Sports Editor · Richard Album

Researcher · Iona Macdonald

BLOOMSBURY
LONDON · BERLIN · NEW YORK · SYDNEY

Preface

Completely revised and updated, *Schott's Almanac 2011* is the sixth annual edition in the series [see p.5]. ❦ This year saw a transformation in the way we consume data. The ubiquity of portable computer hardware and the popularity of social-networking software fused, so that many of us are now 'always on', ever alert to the buzz or flash of new input. The effect this 'dopamine dependency' has on our ability to comprehend information (not least books) is the subject of much debate, and some are urging 'digital detox' to 'degauss' the brain. Yet, if this avalanche of data is unstoppable, then 'slow food' filters – like the hardback almanac – may be ever more vital. ❦ The C21st almanac is necessarily different from some of its distinguished predecessors, which were published in times when the year was defined by considerations astronomical, ecclesiastical, or aristocratic. By exploring high art and pop culture, geopolitics and gossip, scientific discovery and sporting achievement, *Schott's Almanac* endeavours to describe the year as it is lived, in all its complexity and curiosity.

— *Schott's* is an almanac written to be read.

--------------------- THE ALMANAC'S YEAR ---------------------

In order to be as inclusive as possible, the *Schott's Almanac* year runs until mid-September.

Data cited in *Schott's Almanac* are taken from the latest sources available at the time of writing.

--------------------- ERRORS & OMISSIONS ---------------------

Every effort has been made to ensure that the information contained within *Schott's Almanac* is both accurate and up-to-date, and grateful acknowledgement is made to the various sources used. However, as Goethe once said: 'error is to truth as sleep is to waking'. Consequently, the author would be pleased to be informed of any errors, inaccuracies, or omissions that might help improve future editions.

Please send all comments or suggestions to the author, care of:
Bloomsbury Publishing Plc, 36 Soho Square, London, W1D 3QY
or email *editor@schottsalmanac.com*

The author is grateful to the readers who sent in comments on the 2010 edition. Notable corrections and clarifications are included in the Errata section on p.352.

	2005–06	2006–07	2007–08	2008–09	2009–10	2010–11
Person of the year	Saparmurat Niyazov & Turkmenistan's final years of bizarre rule	M. Ahmadinejad & the provocative realpolitik of Iran	Vladimir Putin: the resurgence of Russia on the world stage	Hu Jintao: Beijing's triumphant games & Sichuan's tragic quake	Peter Mandelson: New Labour's midwife & mortician	The Mili·Cleg·Eron – the effortless rise of a new class of politician
Object of the year	Camera phones: citizen reporters & the end of photo-journalism?	The St George Cross: football, fascism, & an icon of England	The demise of the incandescent light bulb & the vital 'wife test'	The hand: Iraqi voting stains, iPhone gestures, & historic handshakes	The tweets of Twitter: the rise (and fall?) of a social-networking fad	The roof over our head – at risk from natural and man-made disasters
Substance of the year	Sudan 1: a ubiquitous red dye at the centre of a mass food scare	Oseltamivir phosphate – Tamiflu & the threat of avian flu H5N1	Polonium 210 & the strange death of Alexander Litvinenko	Honey: the curious & concerning decline of the honey bee	H_2O: droughts, deluges, water wars, & taps running dry	Unobtainium – from the fiction of Avatar to the fact of 'conflict minerals'

Contents

Chronicle

Time destroys the speculation of men, but it confirms nature.
— MARCUS TULLIUS CICERO (106–43 BC)

——— SOME AWARDS OF NOTE ———

Time magazine Person of the Year [2009] · BEN BERNANKE

In a time of rabid partisanship, it's a tribute to Bernanke's basic desire to try to do the right thing that Obama aides don't seem worried about handing a Republican the keys to the economy for the next four years.

Tipperary International Peace Prize......Edward Kennedy & Jean Kennedy Smith
Woodrow Wilson Award for Public Service.......................Condoleezza Rice
Robert Burns Humanitarian Award.....................................Habib Malik
Australian of the Year... Professor Patrick McGorry [expert in adolescent mental health]
BP Portrait Award...Daphne Todd
Car of the Year [*What Car?*] ....Volkswagen Polo
Loo of the Year [2009]...McDonald's
International Engine of the Year............ Volkswagen 1·4-litre TSI Twincharger
Whisky of the Year ,,,Sazerac Rye
Charity Awards · overall winner...................Community Service Volunteers
Sandwich Designer of the Year .... Thomas Allen · Buckingham Foods
Barrister of the Year [*The Lawyer*].............. Michael Brindle QC, Fountain Court
Annual Ernest Hemingway Look-Alike Award.......................Charles Bicht
Slimming World Man of the Year............... Stuart Howells [lost 79kg · 12st 5lbs]
Pet Slimmer of the Year...........................Amber the cat [lost 1·23kg · 2·6lbs]
Lollipop Person of the Year [Kwik Fit · 2009]...............................John Foley
Rears of the Year .... Fiona Bruce · Ricky Whittle [actor, *Hollyoaks*, &c.]
Pier of the Year... Boscombe Pier
Airline of the Year [Skytrax]..................................Asiana Airlines [S Korea]
Pantone Colour of the Year...Turquoise
Celebrity Mum of the Year [Tesco] ....Tana Ramsay
Top Tea Place [UK Tea Council] ....The Black Swan Tea Room, North Yorkshire

——— PLAIN ENGLISH CAMPAIGN · 2009 ———

Lord Mandelson won the 'Foot in Mouth' award for this remark on MPs' expenses:

Perhaps we need not more people looking round more corners but the same people looking round more corners more thoroughly to avoid the small things detracting from the big things the Prime Minister is getting right.

———— MISC. LISTS OF 2010 ———— ——2011 WORDS——

MOST PICTURESQUE
BRITISH STREETS
*according to the Google
Street View Awards*
The Shambles, York
Royal Crescent, Bath
Grey Street, Newcastle
New College Lane,
Oxford
Pen Cei, Aberaeron

MOST COMMON
PASSWORDS
*according to an analysis
of 32 million by Imperva*
123456
12345
123456789
Password
iloveyou
princess
rockyou
1234567
12345678
abc123

SUBJECT OF
MOST CONSUMER
COMPLAINTS
to Consumer Direct
[1] *second-hand cars
from independent traders*
[2] *televisions*
[3] *mobile agreements*
[4] *mobile hardware*
[5] *laptops, notebooks, &c.*

MOST POPULAR
PLACES TO HAVE SEX
*(other than the bedroom)
according to Cosmo*
1 ....shower or bath
2 ....a car
3 ... childhood bedroom
4 . pool or body of water
5 ....woods

BEST PUB MEALS
according to OnePoll
1 ....steak & chips
2 .... roast beef
3 ....fish & chips
4 . cheeseburger & chips
5 ....lasagne

GREATEST INVENTION
according to Tesco Mobile
1 .... wheel
2 .... aeroplane
3 ....light bulb
4 ....internet
5 .... personal computer
6 ....telephone
7 .... penicillin
8 ....iPhone
9 ...... flushing lavatory
10...combustion engine

GREATEST DRUMMER
OF THE PAST 25 YEARS
according to Rhythm
[1] Joey Jordison
(Slipknot, Rob Zombie)
[2] Mike Portnoy
(Dream Theater)
[3] Gavin Harrison
(Porcupine Tree)
[4] Neil Peart (Rush)
[5] Dave Grohl (Nirvana,
Them Crooked Vultures)

GREATEST TV/FILM
CHARACTER *of the past
20 years, according to
Entertainment Weekly*
1 ....Homer Simpson
2 ....Harry Potter
3 .....Buffy the V. Slayer
4 .... Tony Soprano
5 . (Heath Ledger's) The Joker
6 ...Rachel from *Friends*
7 ..Edward Scissorhands
8 ....Hannibal Lecter

The following words
celebrate anniversaries
in 2011, based upon the
earliest cited use traced
by the venerable *Oxford
English Dictionary*:

{1511} *playbook* (a
volume containing the text
of plays) · {1611} *ABC*
(to speak the alphabet) ·
bumhole (the bottom or
anus) · {1711} *dumb-bell*
(the exercise apparatus)
· *ketchup* (the sauce) ·
lipogram (a composition
omitting certain letters)
· {1811} *Armageddon*
(the place of the final battle
at the Day of Judgement)
· {1911} *jinx* (someone
or something which
brings bad luck) · *maths*
(colloquial abbreviation for
mathematics) · {1921}
Abominable Snowman
(the Yeti) · *Chaplinesque*
(characteristic of Charles
Spencer 'Charlie' Chaplin
[1889–1977]) · {1931}
Filofax (the loose-leaf
filing system) · *Lindy Hop*
(the Afro-American dance
originating in Harlem, New
York) · {1941} *bad-mouth*
(to speak ill or deprecate)
· {1951} *backasswards*
(J.D. Salinger's backasswards
corruption of ass-backwards)
· *fast food* (McEating) ·
{1961} *Eurocrat*
(a burEaUcrat) · {1971}
romcom (a romantic
comedy film) · {1981}
poindexter (American slang
for an overly studious nerd)

———— SOME SURVEY RESULTS OF NOTE · 2009–10 ————

%	*of British adults, unless stated*	source & month
96	think >60s today are 'much younger in spirit than previous generations'	[ICM; Apr]
94	have little to no trust in political parties	[ICM; Feb]
92	believe bringing a laptop on holiday won't cause arguments	[YouGov/Softwareload; Jul]
91	of women prefer a man with a few flaws to a 'perfect' man	[OnePoll; Feb]
86	of men are nagged by their 'other halves'	[OnePoll; Jun]
82	of students in the UK were satisfied with their course	[National Student Survey; Aug]
81	of internet users would go elsewhere if a once-free site started charging	[KPMG; Jul]
80	of Tube users have experienced overcrowding discomfort	[Lond. Assembly; Dec '09]
76	agree the BBC is a national institution we should be proud of	[ComRes; Nov '09]
75	of 16–24s 'couldn't live' without the internet	[YouthNet; Oct '09]
73	of Londoners support the city hosting the 2012 Olympic Games	[Ipsos Mori; Jul]
73	support assisted suicide for the terminally ill [see p.111]	[BBC; Jan]
71	believe the world's climate is changing (compared to 91% in 2005)	[Cardiff University; June]
68	of people have abandoned a slow-moving queue	[Barclays; Aug]
68	of Pakistanis have an unfavourable view of the US	[Pew Research Center; Jul]
64	believe the war in Afghanistan is unwinnable	[ComRes; Nov '09]
63	of Scots believe immediate action is required on climate change	[Ipsos Mori; Nov '09]
60	of 18–34s feel lonely 'often' or 'sometimes'	[Mental Health Foundation; May]
59	believe the government should not be funding 'faith schools'	[ICM; Jun]
58	of men lie to their friends about having seen classic films	[Orange; Oct '09]
55	dunk biscuits into their tea or coffee	[OnePoll; Feb]
50	of <35s do not know how to rewire a plug	[Halifax Home Insurance; Aug]
49	of 8–15-year-olds save at least half their pocket money	[Halifax; Dec '09]
47	of 14-year-olds in England report having been bullied	[DCSF; Nov '09]
45	of final-year students view their career prospects as 'very limited'	[High Flyers; May]
44	think Britain is becoming 'less tolerant' of religion	[ComRes; Feb]
43	agreed there should be no legal restrictions on wearing a burka	[ComRes; Jan]
42	of girls wish they could spend more time with their fathers	[Nat. Family Week; Apr]
41	of Americans believe Jesus Christ will return by 2050	[Pew Research Centre; Jun]
37	support building new nuclear power stations in the UK	[Ipsos Mori; Nov '09]
35	of women keep a 'trophy' pair of jeans they hope to fit into again	[Special K; Dec '09]
33	of mothers don't consider their 'mum friends' real friends	[The Baby Website; May]
28	of Brits view the internet as a good place to find a relationship	[BBC; Feb]
27	'strongly agree' they have good relationships with their neighbours	[YouGov; Feb]
23	of Scots believe a women is 'partly responsible' for a rape if drunk	[Cello MRUK; Jun]
22	of drivers admit to not wearing their seat belts	[Esure; Jun]
22	agree 'a woman's place is in the home'	[Reuters/Ipsos; Jan]
20	have sent a racy text message to the wrong person	[SellMyMobile.com; Jul]
18	get less than 5 hours' sleep on an average week night	[YouGov; May]
14	think slapping children is an unacceptable means of punishment	[Children's Soc; Jul]
14	disapprove of unmarried couples cohabiting	[NatCen; Jan]
7	believe the Royal family is the best role model for a strong family	[YouGov; Feb]
6	of girls wish they could spend more time with their mothers	[Nat. Family Week; Apr]
6	spend >1 hour a day on social networking sites while at work	[MyJobGroup; Aug]
2	trust banks more now than they did five years ago	[ICM; Feb]

———————————— WORDS OF THE YEAR ————————————

NOPENHAGEN & FLOPENHAGEN · two terms reflecting fears (now confirmed) that the Copenhagen climate talks would not succeed [see p.27]. *Also* CONSTIPAGEN.

SECOND TREMOR · the lawlessness and looting that followed Chile's February earthquake [see p.21].

POST-CLASS UPPER CLASS · journalist Michael Woolf's description of the Tory party under David Cameron who – alongside Boris Johnson, &c. – challenged the assumption that the 'posh' no longer have a place in British politics.

SHARP-ELBOWED MIDDLE CLASS · Cameron's semi-joking reference to people like him and his wife who 'get in there and get all the [public] services'.

SHOWMANCE · a showbiz romance faked for public relations purposes.

WINTER WHAMMY · the causes of unusually high domestic heating bills – a bitter winter and rising fuel costs.

PAEDO POUND · allegation that some companies make products to profit from the sexualisation of young children: e.g., padded bikini tops for 7-year-olds.

SNOO-BO · portmanteau for a threatened duet between Susan Boyle (SuBo) and rapper Snoop Dogg [see p.143].

GENERATION R · those who kept their jobs during the recession but took on more responsibility for the same pay.

MAGIC PUDDING SOLUTION · the Australian PM's ironic nickname for solutions to climate change that rely on magically self-replenishing funds.

SHINY FLOOR SHOWS · bold, brash light entertainment TV shows, such as *Strictly Come Dancing*.

GLAMAZON GRANDMOTHERS · fashion-following grannies.

THE NEW MIX · a model for US economic recovery driven by exports and investment rather than consumption and housing.

PLAYBOUR · the increasingly blurred distinction between online play and labour, e.g., Google's Image Labeler.

SWOFTIES · Single Women Over Fifty.

WOCIAL · the (awkward) combination of working and socialising – 'the brunch of the business world'.

WOMINNOVATION · innovations (e.g., the pill) that benefit women.

DIVORCE CLUSTERING · the increased incidence of divorce among those whose friends or family are divorced.

MEDIA STACKING · using two (or more) forms of media simultaneously – e.g., surfing the net while watching TV.

DURCHMERKELN · 'to Merkel through' · a German phrase for Chancellor Angela Merkel's hesitant approach to the Greek economic collapse.

OH MY LADY GAGA · a bizarre version of OH MY GOD that became popular among China's young netizens.

SUICIDE CUISINE · unhealthy (fast) food. *Also* GASTROGROTESQUERIE.

SBNR · Spiritual But Not Religious.

—————— WORDS OF THE YEAR cont. ——————

FAKELAKI, ROUSFETI & 4-4-2 SYSTEM · terms associated with Greece's culture of bribery [see p.32], identified by Marcus Walker in the *WSJ*. FAKELAKI is Greek for 'little envelopes' of payola; ROUSFETI are expensive political favours; 4-4-2 SYSTEM is a soccer allusion to tax: 40% to the corrupt official, 40% one keeps, 20% paid to the state. *Also* GREEK STATISTICS · (EU)phemism for 'creative accounting'.

DOGLERS · dogless dog-lovers who ogle other people's pooches.

TOP HAT, TOP KILL, & JUNK SHOT · three mooted means of halting the Deepwater Horizon spill [see p.22].

NEO-FRUGALISTS · thrifty young consumers who are happy to buy secondhand, barter, or defer a purchase.

ODYSSEY YEARS · the period in a person's twenties before careers and relationships have settled.

EQUAL-OPPORTUNITY PESTS · vermin – such as bedbugs – which afflict the entire socio-economic spectrum.

GREYCATION · holidays made possible by the participation of grandparents.

THE SAUDI ARABIA OF LITHIUM · the idea that Afghanistan could be to lithium as Saudi Arabia is to oil [see p.186].

PUBLICY · when the public, not the private, is the default state – for politicians, businesses, and even individuals.

AIDWASHING · the charge that rich nations may be repackaging existing aid as 'green aid' to avoid giving more money to the developing world.

SEXSOMNIA · a sleep disorder where sufferers engage in sexual activities while sleeping.

HUG-ME · the most popular languages spoken in Mumbai: ^{H}indi, ^{U}rdu, ^{G}ujarati, ^{M}arathi, and ^{E}nglish.

RE-FRESHMAN · a mature student embarking on a second degree.

DATING DOWN · seeking a relationship with someone less successful.

ABCD · an initialism that describes the most marketable segments of the Indian mobile market – Astrology, Bollywood, Cricket, and Devotion.

MATE CRIME · crimes against the disabled by those posing as 'friends'.

VAPING · puffing on 'e-cigarettes'.

iPOD OBLIVION · the inattentiveness of those engrossed with iPods, &c.

LINNER & DUNCH · portmanteau terms for late-afternoon dining.

SELECTARIAN · one who exercises meticulous choice over what they eat.

THE TIGER RECESSION · the economic consequence for golf of Woods's withdrawal from the game [see p.303].

NO HOMO · a bizarre disclaimer used by rappers (&c.) to ensure that their words or deeds are not mistaken as gay.

HEAVAGE · male cleavage – an exposed (and often buffed) chest.

INCIDENTALOMAS · tumours discovered by accident during medical exams.

──────── WORDS OF THE YEAR cont. ────────

GOLDILOCKS DEVICES · Web-browsers (e.g., Apple's iPad) which are between smartphones and laptops.

AVATARDS · fervent fans of James Cameron's movie *Avatar*.

TWILLIONAIRE · Twitterers with >1m followers. *Also* TWITTICIDE · those who abandon their tweeting. *Also* TWITGRIEF · condensed expressions of grief posted on Twitter.

2KX · abbreviation for the year 2010.

FOODOIRS & CHICKEN LIT · memoirs and novels centred around food. *Also* LAY-OFF LIT · books relating to the effects of the economic downturn.

CARNISM · term given to the psychological disconnect which allows people to eat some animals while remaining resolutely sentimental about others.

DRIP PRICING · online pricing tactic where the total cost is revealed only at the end of a long process and after (compulsory) add-ons have been included.

SAS · Single, Attractive, and Successful.

1549ers · nickname used by passengers on Flight 1549, which crashed into the Hudson River in January 2009.

SPLINTERNET · a fragmented internet – the consequence of proprietary hardware and software, private networks, and content gated behind logins.

THE ERMINTRUDE EFFECT · looking like a ruminant when eating watercress.

MAMILS · Middle-Aged Men In Lycra · a disturbing by-product of cycling.

GENERATION XD · the youngest generation that has never known life without the internet. [Generation X + D(igital)]

MEOW MEOW · nickname for the drug mephedrone (aka 4-MMC) – a 'herbal high' implicated in a number of deaths.

HUS-BEEN · a husband who follows in the wake of his successful wife.

FOOD CLIMATE LABELS · see p.225. *Also* PAW PRINTS · see p.229.

HOURGLASS SYNDROME · stress and frustration caused by slow computers.

i-DOSING · online audio tracks which supposedly trigger a 'digital high'.

AU-TAN · an autumnal tan – more subtle than the usual lurid orange fake tans.

BILLIONAIRE BLING-MOBILES · flash 'supercars' (brought over to Britain).

PAR-DONS · people who divide their time between Par[is] and [Lon]don.

COFFEE NAME · an alias given when ordering at a coffee shop to avoid the bother of spelling one's real name.

NONSULTATION · a specious public consultation on decisions already made.

VELCRO PARENTS · who cling on.

DOUBLE-DIP · when exiting recession is a prelude to a new economic downturn.

SPOT-FIXING · manipulating a specific event in a sports match (e.g., no-balls in cricket) as part of a betting scam.

[See also pp.64–65, p.198, & pp.252–53]

——————— OBJECT OF THE YEAR · THE ROOF ———————

Humans have sought shelter since they first crawled into caves, and a 'roof over your head' remains one of life's essentials. Yet, events around the world this year highlighted the fragility of shelter, even in the wealthiest of societies. ❧ Some of the year's most harrowing images were of houses swept away by floods (Cumbria, Pakistan) or pulverised by earthquakes (Haiti, Chile, China). The numbers left homeless by these disasters (c.1·5m in China, c.2m in Haiti, c.5m in Pakistan) are almost incomprehensible. After the Haiti quake [see p.20], >1m endured the rainy season in hastily constructed tarp-roofed shacks. Port-au-Prince alone had >500 camps, where residents without doors or locks fought against theft and rape, as well as exposure and disease. Relief agencies constructed 'T-shelters' from bamboo and steel – though, despite their name (T=temporary), these structures are built to last, recognition that many Haitians will not enjoy secure housing for years. ❧ Many of those spared nature's wrath were nonetheless forced to confront the fragility of their shelter. As housing markets slumped across the West, some warned that the 'iron law' of house price growth was cracked, so that home ownership was no longer a nest egg guaranteed to appreciate. In August, the Chartered Institute of Housing declared that Britain's 'golden age of home ownership' was over, and called for an end to the 'right-to-buy, wrong-to-rent' mentality. ❧ Although many mortgagers have, thus far, been cushioned by sustained, historically low interest rates, RealtyTrac estimated that >1m US homes would be foreclosed on in 2010, and Britain's National Housing Federation predicted that those who bought at the boom's height in 2007 may not escape negative equity until 2014. (It is darkly ironic, in light of this year's floods, that those in negative equity are said to be 'under water'.) ❧ Disturbingly, the fragility of shelter in the West is not necessarily linked to supply. Europe's house building boom (in Spain construction grew by >187% between 1996–2006) created such a glut, that unfinished 'ghost estates' scar many a landscape (Ireland has c.300,000 vacant properties). In April, the *Guardian* estimated that the UK's c.450,000 empty homes could house 25% of those on council waiting lists. ❧ While declining birth rates in E Europe have led to 'perforated cities' – abandoned conurbations crumbling into 'feral wastelands' – booming populations elsewhere are straining the supply of housing. China alone needs c.40bn m^2 of new commercial and residential floor space by 2030. Also, the UN estimates that the number of slum-dwellers worldwide will rise from 827m today, to 889m in 2020. ❧ Faced with the need for quick and cheap shelter, a range of innovative solutions have emerged. Some are ingenious, such as the re-purposing of shipping containers to house students (France), refugees (Gaza), prisoners (New Zealand), soldiers (Afghanistan), schools (Jamaica), or entire villages (Haiti). Others are more elemental, such as the emergence across the US of small, informal 'tent cities', where the newly homeless band together. ❧ It is curious that shelter became one of the year's defining issues because of disasters both natural and man-made (though the US housing collapse has been described as a tsunami). It seems likely that in the years to come, the most basic human requirement – a roof over one's head – will be taken less and less for granted.

———————————— SIGNIFICA · 2010 ————————————

Some (in)significa(nt) footnotes to the year. ❦ A man in Benxi, China, attempted to rob a restaurant by threatening to blow himself up unless staff handed over the contents of the till. However, when the police arrived they discovered that the 'explosives' packed around the man's chest were, in fact, sausages. ❦ 300 Lebanese chefs prepared two tonnes of hummus in a successful bid to seize the Guinness World Record from the title-holder, Israel. The chefs argued their victory supported the claim that hummus was a Lebanese dish, and they said that

their next endeavour would be to create the world's largest serving of tabbouleh. ❦ Due to a typo, President Obama signed a law requiring all American rail passengers carrying firearms to be locked in boxes for the duration of their journey. The Bill should have stipulated that it was the firearms that needed to be locked away. ❦ The general manager of the Chilean mint was sacked after thousands of 50 Peso coins were discovered to have been stamped with the word 'CHIIE'. The coins had been circulating since 2008. ❦ Police in Malmö, Sweden, arrested two men in their fifties for stealing seven left-footed shoes from displays at a shopping centre. After questioning, the thieves admitted that they had planned to continue their spree in Denmark, where shops customarily display right-footed shoes. ❦ French philosopher Bernard-Henri Lévy was obliged to admit that a source cited in his 2010 book, *On War in Philosophy*, did not exist. The Paraguayan thinker, Jean-Baptiste Botul, was revealed to be the creation of satirical French journalist Frédéric Pagès, who regularly gathers friends in Paris to discuss Botul's school of thought – 'Botulism'. ❦ Shop owners in Mexico reported that the economic downturn had altered women's underwear choices in late 2009. According to Mexican custom, the colour of panties worn on New Year's Eve can, during the following year, bring luck in money, health, or love. In 2009, yellow underwear (for luck with money) outsold red underwear (for luck with love; the traditional best-seller) by two to one. ❦ Residents in Morriston, Swansea, were amused by the erection of a bilingual road sign which included an unfortunate translation error. The English element of the sign read: 'No entry for heavy goods vehicles. Residential site only', while the Welsh half read: 'I am not in the office at the moment. Send any work to be translated.' ❦ Residents of Georgia scurried to petrol stations and banks after a fake TV newscast reported a Russian invasion. Despite a warning at the beginning of the programme, parts of the country were plunged into panic, and paramedics reported a surge in incidents of heart attack. ❦ A long-simmering territorial dispute between India and Bangladesh ended peacefully after oceanographers confirmed that the contested island of New Moore had sunk beneath the Bay of Bengal. 'What these two countries could not achieve from years of talking, has been resolved by global warming,' said a scientist at the University of Calcutta. ❦ Figures from the Insolvency Service found that 35,682 people were declared insolvent in England and Wales during the first three months of 2010 – the highest level since records began in 1960. ❦ Staff at a New Zealand funeral home confronted a man who attended several funerals a week in order to eat the free food. Staff said the man, dubbed the 'Grim Eater', was polite and well-dressed, but clearly did not know the deceased, and thought nothing of packing food to take home. ❦

—————————— SIGNIFICA · 2010 cont. ——————————

An Australian publisher was forced to reprint 7,000 copies of the cookbook *Pasta Bible* after a recipe for tagliatelle with sardines and prosciutto accidentally called for 'freshly ground black people', instead of 'freshly ground black pepper'. ❦ During the oil disaster in the Gulf of Mexico [see p.22], US hairdressers sent thousands of pounds of hair to the Gulf region to be crafted into homemade oil booms. The clippings, which are highly absorbent, were stuffed inside tights and stockings during 'Boom-B-Q' parties. ❦ French MPs submitted a bill to repeal a 1799 law prohibiting women in Paris from wearing trousers. Previous attempts to strike down the law had been unsuccessful, despite exemptions in 1892, for women 'holding the reins of a horse', and in 1910, for women 'on a bicycle or holding it by the handlebars'. ❦ A JetBlue flight attendant made the year's most dramatic exit from a job (or anywhere else). After an alleged dispute with a passenger on a plane that had landed in New York, the attendant took to the public address system with a stream of invective, grabbed two beers, opened a door, slid down the emergency slide, and ran across the tarmac. He was later arrested and charged with criminal mischief and reckless endangerment. ❦ Members of a WeightWatchers group in Växjö, Sweden, who had gathered to share how much weight they had lost over Christmas, were astonished when the floor of their meeting room collapsed; fortunately, no one was hurt. ❦ A Gloucestershire collector purchased at auction Winston Churchill's dentures for £15,200. The teeth were sold by the family of Churchill's dental technician, who revealed that the former PM used to throw them across the room when angry. ❦ A medical student in Australia was rescued from muggers when a student at a ninja training school saw the attack and called in his classmates. The martial arts students chased down the would-be thieves while clad in their all-black ninja uniforms: 'I've never seen guys running that fast,' said the school's instructor. ❦ An activist group was criticised by the French government after it posted online a video in which a French official promised to repay Haiti the 90m gold Francs the former slave colony had paid for its freedom in the C19th. The 'official' was revealed to be an actor, and the video – posted on a hoax website that mimicked that of France's foreign ministry – was created by a group calling itself the Committee for the Reimbursement of the Indemnity Money Extorted from Haiti (CRIME). ❦ An Australian café in the town of Mildura made the best of a plague of locusts by offering the insects as a special pizza topping. The town's mayor promised that the bugs would taste 'as good as olives or anchovies', though he admitted to disliking both. ❦ The mayor  of Worthing, England, apologised after he and his wife dozed off during a performance of *Bugsy Malone* by local 11-year-olds – apparently reducing some of them to tears. The couple, who were seated in the front row, blamed medication and a packed schedule for their inadvertent nap. ❦ Iranian officials issued a catalogue of acceptable 'Islamic' haircuts, and warned that young men who sported 'decadent Western' styles, such as ponytails or spikes, would be obliged to have new conservative cuts, or be forced to pay stiff fines. ❦ Householders in Shitterton, England, each donated £20 for a new town sign to be carved from marble. The 1½-tonne sign was designed to deter thieves, who had apparently found many previous versions of the sign irresistible. ❦

--------------------------- THE GENERAL ELECTION ---------------------------

Confounding expectations that 2010 would see Britain's first 'internet election', the traditional media, notably TV, dominated the 4-week campaign. The most consequential innovation was the 3 televised leaders' debates [see p.19] which gave the Lib Dems equal billing with Labour and the Tories – thrusting Nick Clegg into the limelight, and creating the (temporary) phenomenon of 'Cleggmania'. The second major TV moment was 'bigotgate' – when, just over a week before polling, Brown was caught by a Sky News microphone castigating a Labour voter with whom he had just chatted as a 'bigoted woman' [see p.32]. These televisual highlights were compounded by a resolutely anti-Brown press. Most of Fleet Street came out for Cameron [pictured], and the pro-Labour *Guardian* and *Observer* advocated voting Lib Dem. Only the *Mirror* stuck by Brown – but even this loyal title advocated tactical voting to 'save Britain from a Tory nightmare'. ❦ As the results rolled in, many opinion polls, and the exit poll, were vindicated. Parliament was hung: the Tories had won the most seats and votes, but no overall majority; Labour avoided coming third, but suffered its worst result since 1918; and the Lib Dems, despite the hype and hope of Cleggmania, actually *lost* 5 seats [see p.17]. ❦ Thereafter, confusion reigned. Brown announced that he was constitutionally obliged to remain as PM until a workable coalition had been formed, but suggested that the Tories were entitled to negotiate first with the Lib Dems. However, it soon emerged that the Lib Dems were in simultaneous talks with Labour to form a 'progressive alliance'. On 10 May, in a last-ditch attempt to facilitate a Lib-Lab pact by removing his unpopularity from the equation, Brown promised to step down as Labour leader by the autumn conference. However, a day later, Brown was forced to admit defeat and he resigned as PM, paving the way for a Cameron-led Con-Lib deal. The scope of this deal surprised even the most seasoned commentators. Talk of a 'confidence and supply' arrangement (where the Lib Dems would support Tory manifesto pledges and budgets) proved spectacularly timid when, on 12 May, in No. 10's 'rose garden', Cameron and Clegg announced Britain's first power-sharing coalition in *c*.70 years. Cameron appointed Clegg as Deputy PM, and gave the Lib Dems 4 other Cabinet seats [see p.255]. Additionally, the two parties published a long list of agreed policies, including: an emergency budget [see p.235]; scrapping the proposed 1% NI rise; banking reform and taxation; guaranteed NHS spending rises; a pledge not to join the euro; fixed 5-year parliaments; and the scrapping of ID cards. Of the many policies agreed, the most controversial were the Tories' plans for immediate cuts; the renewal of Trident (opposed by most Lib Dems); a referendum on the Alternative Vote for general elections (opposed by many Tories, including Cameron); and a cap on extra-EU immigration (ridiculed by Clegg during the election). ❦ Cameron and Clegg's willingness to compromise so comprehensively led some to hail their agreement as revolutionary, and others to dismiss it as unworkable. ❦ Meanwhile, in the aftermath of defeat, and Brown's resignation, the Labour party began the drawn-out process of electing a new leader [see p.18].

——————— 2010 GENERAL ELECTION RESULTS ———————

Party	seats	won	lost	±	votes	%	±%
Conservative	305	100	4	+96	10,683,577	36·0	+3·6
Labour	258	4	94	−90	8,601,349	29·0	−6·2
Liberal Democrat	57	8	13	−5	6,827,312	23·0	+1·0
Democratic Unionist Party	8	0	1	−1	168,216	0·6	−0·3
Scottish National Party	6	0	0	0	491,386	1·7	+0·2
Sinn Féin	5	0	0	0	171,942	0·6	−<0·1
Plaid Cymru	3	1	0	+1	165,394	0·6	−<0·1
SDLP	3	0	0	0	110,970	0·4	−0·1
Green	1	1	0	+1	284,823	1·0	−<0·1
Alliance Party	1	1	0	+1	42,762	0·1	+<0·1
UK Independence Party	0	0	0	0	917,581	3·1	+0·9
British National Party	0	0	0	0	564,003	1·9	+1·2
Ulster Con. & Unionists	0	0	1	−1	102,361	0·3	−0·2
English Democrats	0	0	0	0	63,299	0·2	+0·1
Respect	0	0	1	−1	33,251	0·1	−0·2
Traditional Unionist Voice	0	0	0	0	26,300	0·1	–
Christian Party	0	0	0	0	17,417	0·1	–
Ind. Cmty and Health Concern	0	0	1	−1	16,150	0·1	−<0·1
Trade Unionist & Socialist Cltn.	0	0	0	0	13,989	<0·1	–
Scottish Socialist Party	0	0	0	0	3,157	<0·1	–
Independent	1	1	1	0	229,021	0·8	+0·4

The 2010 UK turnout was 65·1% (3·7% up on 2005). The highest turnout was in East Renfrewshire (77·3%); the lowest was Manchester Central (44·3%). Turnout in Tory constituencies was on average 7·4% higher than in those with Labour MPs.

% share of vote	Conservative 36·1	Labour 29·0	Lib Dem 23·0	Other 11·9

The 'swing' from Labour to Conservative was 5%. ❦ In total, 1,873 candidates lost their deposits: 4 Tories, 7 Labour, 2 Lib Dems, and 1,860 others. ❦ 117 (18%) seats changed party hands, compared with the notional 2005 results. ❦ A record 4,133 candidates stood in the 2010 election: 3,773 for one of the 129 parties, and 337 independents and the Speaker [see p.18]. 20·8% of the candidates (861) were women; and 80·2% (3,272) were men. ❦ Of all those elected in 2010, 64% had been MPs in the last Parliament. (Five MPs returned from previous Parliaments, including Stephen Twigg.) The remaining 227 candidates (35%) had no prior Commons experience – a consequence, at least in part, of so many MPs standing down after 'expensegate', and the fear that the generous pensions allocated to ex-MPs would be scrapped in the new fiscal climate. Some 145 sitting MPs decided not to stand again. ❦ The average age of those elected was 50 (51 in 2005); the youngest MP, Pamela Nash (Lab; Airdrie & Shotts) was 25; the oldest, Sir Peter Tapsell (Con; Louth & Horncastle), was 80. (Sir Peter became Father of the House.) ❦ Operation Black Vote reported that 26 MPs elected in 2010 (4%) were from minority ethnic groups. ❦ The Sutton Trust reported that at least 20 MPs were Old Etonians. [Source: House of Commons Library]

—— ELECTION RACES ——

The Speaker John Bercow [see p.253] easily held Buckingham, despite a number of challenges, including one from UKIP's Nigel Farage who, coincidentally, was injured in a plane crash on the day of the poll. On 18 May, MPs re-elected Bercow as Speaker, notwithstanding a few voices of dissent. ❦ Luton South, previously the seat of Margaret Moran (who was embarrassed during 'expensegate') was held by Labour. The TV presenter Esther Rantzen was one of a number of independents who failed to dent Labour's vote. ❦ Caroline Lucas became the Green Party's first MP, taking Brighton Pavilion from Labour. ❦ Despite the Tory's 'castration strategy' [see p.252], Ed Balls kept his Morley & Outwood seat, although with a much reduced majority. ❦ The 'colourful' Lib Dem Lembit Öpik lost Montgomeryshire to the Tories – 'perhaps it was my brand of politics which people weren't too keen on,' he said. ❦ The British National Party failed in its bid to take Barking: Nick Griffin came third, behind Labour's Margaret Hodge and Simon Marcus for the Tories; Griffin's share of the vote fell by 1·7% from 2005. Hodge told the BNP to 'get out and stay out'. ❦ Sinn Féin held Fermanagh & South Tyrone by just 4 votes. ❦ Multi-millionaire Tory Zac Goldsmith overturned a 3,700 Lib Dem majority to take Richmond Park. ❦ Former Home Sec. Jacqui Smith – who had earlier been humiliated by her husband's expense claim for porn – lost her Redditch seat to the Tories. ❦ Charles Clarke, another former Home Sec. and Labour 'big beast', narrowly lost Norwich South to the Lib Dems. ❦ The Thirsk & Malton election was postponed to 27 May, after the death of the UKIP candidate John Boakes on 22 April. The Tories held the seat.

—— LABOUR LEADERSHIP ——

Gordon Brown's resignation as Labour leader [see p.16] paved the way for a contest that would set the direction of the party in opposition to the Con-Lib coalition. After a number of high-profile candidates ruled themselves out (including Harriet Harman, Alan Johnson, and Jack Straw), six MPs announced their candidature. However, only five received the required 33 nominations from Labour MPs, and the left-winger John McDonnell withdrew.

Candidate	age	nominations	Oxbridge	ex-Cabinet
Diane Abbott	47	33	C	N
Ed Balls	43	33	O	Y
Andy Burnham	40	33	C	Y
David Miliband	44	81	O	Y
Ed Miliband	40	63	O	Y

Abbott aside†, the social and ideological uniformity of the candidates was striking [see p.38] and, as almost everyone joked, it was a safe bet that the next leader would be called 'Ed', or 'Miliband', or both. ❦ Throughout the summer, the media reported on each twist of the contest, from internecine squabbles and the size of campaign donations to the all-important endorsements of party elders and trades union. However, it quickly became clear that Abbott and Burnham were out of the picture and, despite a series of successful attacks on the coalition, Balls was also trailing. At the time of writing, it seemed inevitable that the next Labour leader would be one of the brothers Miliband.

† An outspoken MP on the far left of the party, Abbott only secured her 33 nominations at the very last minute with the support of her opponent David Miliband. This led some to claim she was only on the ballot for reasons of 'tokenism'.

——THE PRE-ELECTION PARTY LEADER DEBATES——

15 APRIL · MANCHESTER
Channel: ITV · *Host:* Alistair Stewart
Podium position: Clegg · Cameron · Brown
Peak viewers: 9·9m

The first debate was a clear victory for Clegg, and the Lib Dems soared in the polls which followed. In part this was due to the novelty of Clegg's equal billing, but he also managed adroitly to suggest that *real* change meant ending the duopolistic status quo. Cameron performed well, kept his cool, and was impressive on the NHS. His closing words, calling for the triumph of (Tory) hope over (Labour) fear, were perhaps his finest. Brown appeared more natural than some had predicted, and he was as pointed in his attacks on Cameron as he was diligent in praising the Lib Dems (much to Clegg's surprise). Brown even got one of the evening's few laughs – albeit with a weak, prepared dig at Cameron's airbrushed posters. There were no real gaffes and few defining moments – except for the instant catchphrase prompted by Brown's wooing of Clegg: 'I agree with Nick'.

22 APRIL · BRISTOL
Channel: Sky · *Host:* Adam Boulton
Podium position: Cameron · Clegg · Brown
Peak viewers: 4·1m

The received wisdom before the second debate was that Clegg would struggle to keep his lead, Cameron needed to sharpen his performance, and Brown had much to prove. In fact, all three leaders performed well – although the prior week's Lib Dem love-bombing was noticeably absent. Clegg stuck to his line on change – but was attacked for his policy on Trident; Cameron deployed the line "if I were your Prime Minister …" – but was challenged on his party's Euroscepticism; and Brown played up his experience – but was discomfited when asked to defend Labour leaflets that misrepresented Tory policy. The tactic of claiming the high ground by accusing the other parties of petty bickering was neutralised by being deployed by all three leaders. Instant post-debate polls placed Cameron and Clegg as the tied winners, with Brown, as in the previous debate, third.

29 APRIL · BIRMINGHAM
Channel: BBC1 · *Host:* David Dimbleby
Podium position: Cameron · Clegg · Brown
Peak viewers: 8·4m

The final debate was set against the backdrop of Brown's 'bigot' blunder the day before [see p.32], though the PM frankly addressed his gaffe in his opening remarks. Cameron attempted to remain positive throughout – dodging Brown's attacks and declining to return fire. As before, Brown took the most negative approach – warning voters about the risks of voting Tory or Lib Dem. Clegg's attempt to portray himself as an honest broker was undermined by his newfound second-place position in the polls – which itself prompted more scrutiny of Lib Dem policy, not least on the economy. Although the debate's focus was the economy, little new information on tax or cuts was forthcoming. Indeed the final debate seemed only to confirm the brave new status quo established by the first debate. The instant polls had Cameron first, Clegg close(ish) second, and Brown trailing third.

─── HAITI EARTHQUAKE ───

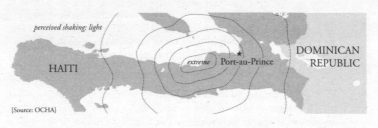

perceived shaking: light

HAITI

extreme Port-au-Prince

DOMINICAN
REPUBLIC

[Source: OCHA]

On 12/1/2010, at 16:53 local time, a 7·0 Richter earthquake struck 25km south-west of Haiti's capital, Port-au-Prince. The quake was the most intense to hit the nation in >200 years. It killed *c*.230,000, wounded >300,000, and left >1·5m homeless. ❦ Haiti is the poorest nation in the W hemisphere, and few of its buildings were constructed to withstand a quake. The tremors destroyed the Port-au-Prince Cathedral, the National Assembly, the Presidential palace, the tax office, the central bank, the main jail, the UN headquarters, scores of hospitals and schools – as well as acres of residential housing. Haitian President René Préval described the devastation as 'unimaginable'. ❦ For days after the quake, chaos gripped the already unstable country. Amid a series of powerful aftershocks, and the near-total absence of authority, survivors slept in streets littered with corpses. Rescue teams operated with the barest of supplies, as hospitals and morgues overflowed. Most of the nation lacked power and phone services, further frustrating attempts to disseminate information to the outside world. Nevertheless, the global response was swift and generous: within a week world governments had pledged *c*.$1bn in aid, and international charities rushed to send money, assistance, and supplies. Sadly, the distribution of aid was hindered by damage to Haiti's far-from-sophisticated infrastructure: Port-au-Prince's port was severely damaged, as was the city's airport control tower, and many overland routes were blocked. Delays were compounded by a confused chain of command and the threat of civil unrest. ❦ Assuming the dominant security role, the US took control of the port and airport – sparking criticism from some foreign powers and aid agencies, who accused America of prioritising their personnel over humanitarian aid. The American presence became even more controversial on 26/1, when Haiti charged 10 US Baptist missionaries with allegedly attempting to 'smuggle' 33 Haitian children into the Dominican Republic. ❦ Amid the tragedy, the media spotlighted a handful of miraculous rescues from the rubble, including a man saved after being trapped for 12 days, a girl saved after 15 days, and a man apparently rescued after 4 weeks. Yet, on 22/1, the Haitian government called off the search for survivors, and turned its focus to providing shelter for the *c*.1·3m living in spontaneous settlements around Port-au-Prince [see p.13], as well as those around the country scarred by the quake. ❦ At the time of writing, the Haitian government estimated it would need $11·5bn for long-term reconstruction, and $9·9bn had been pledged by the end of a major UN donor conference in March. The government also estimated that it would take some three years simply to remove all the debris the quake had generated.

———— OTHER SIGNIFICANT NATURAL EVENTS ————

Cumbria Flooding

In 11/2009, severe rains swept across the UK and Ireland. Seathwaite recorded the UK's highest-ever daily rainfall: 314·4mm in the 24 hours prior to 0:45 GMT on 20/11. Cumbria was hardest hit, with >1,000 homes and businesses destroyed. 16 bridges in the county were damaged or collapsed, including the Northside Bridge in Workington, which swept PC Bill Barker to his death as he tried to clear traffic on 20/11. On 21/11, rescue personnel evacuated *c.*500 people from the rising waters, including *c.*300 from Cockermouth, and *c.*50 from Keswick. Gordon Brown pledged £1m for flood victims, while the Cumbria Flood Recovery Fund raised £2·4m. Total damage was estimated at *c.*£100m, and residents said the physical and psychological toll of the 'biblical' floods would take years to fix.

Chile Quake

On 27/2/10, at 3:34am local, an 8·8 magnitude quake struck central Chile. *c.*500 were killed, >500,000 homes were destroyed, and major roads, bridges, ports, and airports all suffered severe damage. Although the quake tied for the 5th most powerful recorded anywhere since 1900, strict building codes and a well-trained populace (evidence of a long history of earthquakes) minimised casualties. Nonetheless, >20 aftershocks >5·0 kept nerves on edge, and a 'second tremor' of looting and disorder coursed through the worst-hit areas. Michelle Bachelet, in the last days of her presidency, declared a 'state of catastrophe' and sent troops to maintain order, for the first time since the Pinochet dictatorship. Incoming President Sebastián Piñera (whose inauguration was jolted by an aftershock) vowed to raise the >$30bn the country would need to rebuild.

Qinghai Quake

On 14/4/10 at 7:49am local, a 7·1 magnitude earthquake struck Yushu County in China's Qinghai province. >2,600 people were killed, *c.*12,000 injured, and >150,000 homes destroyed. The Chinese government quickly mounted a major relief effort, but faced difficult conditions in the disaster zone, which lay 13,000ft above sea level, in a rugged region bordering Tibet. In fact, Tibetan monks were among the first on the scene, despite reports that the Chinese authorities sought to restrict their role. Nevertheless, crews of monks and soldiers working together in near-freezing temperatures and with a critical lack of heavy machinery pulled >1,000 survivors from the rubble. China has vowed to rebuild the politically sensitive area (the birthplace of the Dalai Lama), but has said this will take at least 3 years.

China Floods

From May–August 2010, China suffered its heaviest rainfall in a decade. The deluge led to floods and landslides that left *c.*3,900 dead or missing, >1m homes destroyed, and *c.*$30bn of damage across the country. In all, >400m people in half the nation's provinces were affected. The most concentrated casualties occurred in August, when mudslides killed >1,400 in the NW province of Gansu. In late August, rains also caused the Yalu river (the border between China and N Korea) to overflow, leaving *c.*15,000 families in N Korea homeless, and further raising fears for the impoverished nation – where deforestation and food shortages have left the land, and its people, especially vulnerable to floods.

For information on other natural disasters of the year, see p.20 and p.74.

GULF OF MEXICO OIL SPILL

On 20·4·10, at 21:49, explosions ripped through the Deepwater Horizon oil rig off the Louisiana coast in the Gulf of Mexico. 11 crew were killed, *c.*17 injured, and, as the rig sank, crude oil from the Macondo well gushed unchecked into the sea. ❧ As days and weeks passed, the public watched in horror and frustration as BP, the well's owners, failed to stem the flow of oil with a series of complex manoeuvres (many of which had memorable names, like 'top hat', 'junk shot', and 'top kill'). A 'spill cam' at the leak's source, *c.*5,000 ft down, broadcast the haemorrhage live, 24/7. Meanwhile, *c.*4,000 boats converged to attack the spill using skimmers, controlled burns, (controversial) chemical dispersants, and other techniques. ❧ A series of PR gaffes (notably by BP CEO Tony Hayward) fuelled public anger, as did allegations of inadequate maintenance, management, and government oversight. ❧ By the time the well was capped – 86 days after the explosions – *c.*4·9bn barrels of crude had spilled into the Gulf. BP reported that it had spent $8bn on its response, though the full cost of the disaster was likely to be significantly higher. Scientists said it would take several seasons to begin to understand the toll of the spill on the Gulf's complex eco-systems. Local fishing and tourism operators wondered if their businesses would ever recover. ❧ At the time of writing, civil and criminal investigations into the disaster were ongoing, and a number of lawsuits had been launched. ❧ Below is a timeline of key events:

20·04	*an eruption of oil and gas caused explosions aboard the rig, killing 11*
22·04	*the $560m Deepwater Horizon rig sank, and an 8km oil slick appeared*
25·04	*a plan to activate the well's 'blowout preventer' failed*
30·04	*a controversial freeze on new offshore drilling was announced in the US*
05·05	*the smallest of the three leaks from the well was plugged*
07·05	*a containment dome was lowered over the main leak, but it clogged with ice*
11·05 & 12·05	*BP, Halliburton, and Transocean execs appeared before Congress*
26·05	*BP began a 'top kill' procedure to plug well with drilling mud*
29·05	*BP announced the 'top kill' had failed*
30·05	*Hayward told a* Today Show *reporter, 'I'd like my life back'*
01·06	*the US govt said it had opened civil and criminal investigations*
03·06	*a cap was successfully placed over the well, limiting the flow of oil*
16·06	*BP agreed to a $20bn escrow fund for damage claims*
18·06	*BP said Hayward would step down from day-to-day spill oversight*
19·06	*Hayward was criticised for taking time off to watch a yacht race*
15·07	*a new cap on the well halted the flow of oil for the first time in 86 days*
27·07	*Hayward was replaced as CEO by Managing Director Robert Dudley*
04·08	*BP said pumped-in drilling mud had brought the well to a 'static condition'*
19·09	*the US government declared that the well had been sealed*

─────────── DERRICK BIRD & RAOUL MOAT ───────────

On Wednesday 2 June, 2010, Derrick 'Birdy' Bird, a 52-year-old taxi driver, murdered 12 and injured 11 during a *c.*3-hour 'shooting spree' in his home county of Cumbria. ❦ Bird's first victim was his twin, David, who he shot dead in Lamplugh during the early hours. Bird subsequently drove to Frizington where, at *c.*10:20, he killed Kevin Commons (60), his family's solicitor. At *c.*10:30, in nearby Whitehaven, Bird killed fellow cabbie, Darren Rewcastle (43) and wounded several others. Alerted to the attacks, the police scrambled armed officers and warned locals to stay indoors. (The Sellafield nuclear plant, from which Bird had been sacked for theft in 1990, was 'locked down'.) Bird drove south to Egremont where he killed Susan Hughes (57) and retired Sellafield security officer Kenneth Fishburn (71), and wounded several others. Bird drove on to Carleton Woods where he killed Isaac 'Spike' Dixon (65). In Wilton, Bird killed Jennifer Jackson (68) and her husband James (67). Bird wounded another before driving to Gosforth, where he killed Garry Purdham (31). Driving south, Bird killed James Clark (23) and, reaching Seascale at *c.*11:30, he wounded two others and killed Michael Pike (64) and Jane Robinson (66). Bird drove near to the hamlet of Boot, injuring several people en route, before abandoning his car. At 13:40, Bird's body was discovered in nearby woods; he had shot himself in the head. ❦ Although it appeared that Bird had known some of his victims and shot others indiscriminately, the absence of a suicide note or 'hit list' meant that the motive behind Britain's third-deadliest gun massacre would

Derrick Bird

never be known. ❦ Described as affable and with a wide circle of friends, Bird was said also to have a paranoic 'dark side' exacerbated by drink. After his death, rumours circulated about unpaid taxes, disagreements over an inheritance, feuds with fellow taxi drivers, and an 'obsession' with young female prostitutes he met in Thailand. ❦ Inevitably, questions were asked as to whether Bird should have held a licence for the shotgun and .22 telescopic rifle he used in his attack. However, the newly elected PM David Cameron warned against reflex demands for new laws. ❦ A month after Bird's attack, a second shooting dominated the news. On 3 July, 2 days after his release from an 18-week prison sentence, the 37-year-old panel-beater and bouncer, Raoul Moat shot and wounded his ex-partner Samantha Stobbart (22) and killed her boyfriend Chris Brown (29). The next day, Moat shot and critically injured PC David Rathband (42). (Moat had posted on Facebook, 'Just got out of jail, I've lost everything, my business, my property and to top it all off my lass has gone off with someone else. Watch and see what happens'.) After a 7-day manhunt involving >200 officers, Moat was cornered in a 6-hour standoff which ended, reportedly, when he fatally shot himself. At the time of writing, investigations into the incident were ongoing – and a number of people were assisting the police with their enquiries. ❦ Many questioned what impact the saturation media coverage of the Bird shootings and the Moat manhunt had on Moat himself – not least because Moat reportedly threatened to murder a member of the public for each piece of 'inaccurate' reporting about him.

—————————— UK ECONOMIC INDICATORS ——————————

The latest ONS data revealed that, while the unemployment rate for the 3 months to June 2010 fell by 49,000, to 2·46m, the number of people unemployed for >12 months increased by 33,000 to 796,000 – the highest figure since 1997. Below are the number of men and women unemployed in the UK since New Labour:

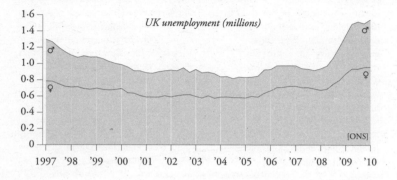

The GfK NOP 'consumer confidence barometer' gives a sense of the public mood:

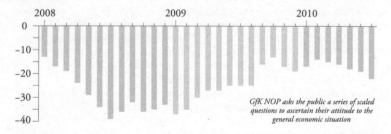

GfK NOP asks the public a series of scaled questions to ascertain their attitude to the general economic situation

As the global economy remained unstable, investors continued their 'flight to safety' – not least in the form of gold. Charted below is the rising price of 'shining dawn':

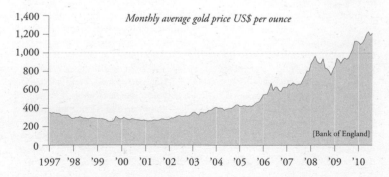

——————— UK ECONOMIC INDICATORS cont. ———————

Below are data for the quarterly annual percentage change in UK house prices:

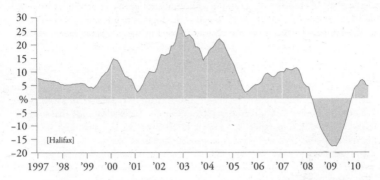

Charted below are the monthly changes in a 3-year fixed-rate mortgage, since 1997:

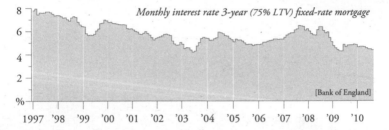

Charted below are Halifax data for average national house prices, average national earnings, and (in parentheses) the price-to-earnings ratio, for 1997–2009:

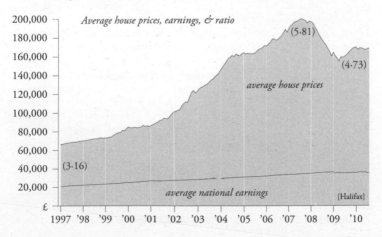

THE WORLD CUP FINAL

11 July 2010 · Soccer City, Johannesburg · Attendance: 84,490

SPAIN 1–0 NETHERLANDS (AET)

Thanks to the octopus we are champions … I feel very happy, and to have scored such an important goal for everybody, to make millions of people happy. That is priceless.
— ANDRES INIESTA, Spain's No. 6

Spain won its first World Cup in an ugly and brutal final – defeating a Dutch side that had betrayed its 'total football' heritage[†]. Spain's victory was the first time a European country had won the World Cup outside of Europe. The Netherlands' defeat was its third World Cup final failure (q.v. 1974 & 1978). The spine of the Spanish side came from Barcelona: Puyol and Xavi recreated their best form, and Iniesta scored the winning goal in extra time. Yet the poor quality of the final reflected the disappointing nature of the tournament as a whole, which produced only flashes of top-class football and few notable games. It seems likely that the 2010 World Cup will be remembered primarily for Paul the Octopus [see p.230] and the damn vuvuzela [see p.298].

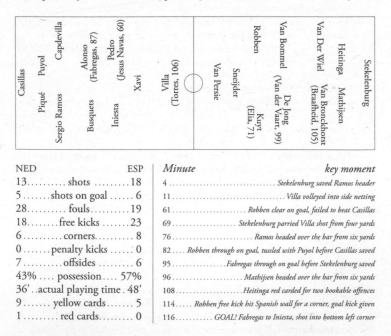

NED		ESP	Minute	key moment
13	shots	18	4	*Stekelenburg saved Ramos header*
5	shots on goal	6	11	*Villa volleyed into side netting*
28	fouls	19	61	*Robben clear on goal, failed to beat Casillas*
18	free kicks	23	69	*Stekelenburg parried Villa shot from four yards*
6	corners	8	76	*Ramos headed over the bar from six yards*
0	penalty kicks	0	82	*Robben through on goal, tussled with Puyol before Casillas saved*
7	offsides	6	95	*Fabregas through on goal before Stekelenburg saved*
43%	possession	57%	96	*Mathijsen headed over the bar from six yards*
36'	actual playing time	48'	108	*Heitinga red carded for two bookable offences*
9	yellow cards	5	114	*Robben free kick hit Spanish wall for a corner, goal kick given*
1	red cards	0	116	*GOAL! Fabregas to Iniesta, shot into bottom left corner*

† The Dutch were much criticised for an aggressive physicality which led English ref Howard Webb to brandish 14 yellow cards, including 2 for Holland's Johnny Heitinga (leading to his dismissal). Webb was criticised by both sides: the Spanish said he had failed to protect their players, and the Dutch said he had erred in not awarding them a corner, moments before the decisive winning goal. The legend Johann Cruyff lamented: 'It hurts me that Holland chose an ugly path to aim for the title.'

—————————— COPENHAGEN CLIMATE TALKS ——————————

The UN Climate Change Conference was held in Copenhagen, Denmark, between 7–18 December 2009. The conference's goals were to negotiate a successor to the Kyoto Treaty, and to coordinate global strategy on reducing emissions. Climate activists hoped the summit would produce the world's first legally binding global treaty limiting emissions. Ultimately, however, corralling 192 nations to agree on what the *Economist* called 'the hardest political problem the world has ever had to deal with' proved too much. ❦ The UN called for the summit to set 'ambitious' emissions targets for developed countries, as well as 'nationally appropriate' targets for developing countries, alongside aid commitments to help the latter adapt to climate change. Britain negotiated as part of the EU, which committed to a 20% cut in emissions by 2020 (compared to 1990 levels), and a 30% cut if other countries made 'sufficiently ambitious' commitments. Such commitments proved scarce, however, and even before the summit began there were signs that negotiations would founder. On 15/11, world leaders dampened expectations by announcing that the Copenhagen talks would provide only an interim, non-binding pact. The conference itself was stymied by a range of logistical problems, including long queues and security snafus. Negotiations were also hindered by historical antagonisms, a general distrust of America (which had refused to ratify Kyoto), and China's perceived intractability. A flow of leaks also served to undermine what trust had been established. ❦ On 14/12, talks were suspended for several hours when the G77-China bloc withdrew from negotiations over concerns it had been sidelined. By the time government leaders arrived on 18/12, the conference was 'in crisis', in the words of UN Environment Programme director Achim Steiner. Finally, a series of last-minute meetings between the US, China, India, Brazil, and S Africa forged a compromise deal that – while far from the conference's lofty goals – ensured leaders did not go home empty-handed. Among other points, the Copenhagen Accord agreed:

climate change is one of the greatest challenges of our time · deep cuts in global emissions are required according to science ... so as to hold the increase in global temperature below 2 degrees Celsius · new and additional resources ... approaching $30bn for the period 2010–12 ... [and] $100bn a year by 2020 to address the needs of developing countries will be mobilised

However, the Accord failed to establish a plan for global emission cuts, merely asking nations to submit non-binding plans to the UN by 31/1. And, after an all-night session, the conference agreed only to 'take note' of the Accord – leaving its legal status unclear. Britain's then Climate Secretary, Ed Miliband, called the deal 'definitely worth saving', though others were less charitable. The G77's head negotiator, Lumumba Stanislaus Di-Aping, said the deal had 'the lowest level of ambition you can imagine'. Indeed, the failure of the talks to agree a binding deal led many to question whether the UN framework held any hope. By June 2010, only 76 nations had submitted emissions pledges, and analysts said these would not hold warming below 2°C. In August, UN Sec.-General Ban Ki-moon said negotiators at Copenhagen's follow-up, the UN Climate Change Conference 2010 in Cancún, were likely also to fail to reach a global deal on emissions. Nonetheless, Ban emphasised that climate change remained 'the greatest collective challenge we face as a human family'.

———————————— AFGHANISTAN ————————————

Because Afghanistan's August 2009 elections were tainted by violence, intimidation, and fraud, the country's election commission was obliged to order a run-off between the incumbent Hamid Karzai and his opponent Abdullah Abdullah. However, in October, Abdullah withdrew his candidacy, citing insufficient anti-fraud measures, and weeks later Karzai was sworn in for a second presidential term. In December, President Obama announced a 'surge' of 30,000 US troops (bringing the total to *c.*100,000). At the same time he pledged to 'begin the transfer of [American] forces out of Afghanistan in July of 2011' – thereby setting the clock ticking on an 'Afghanistan endgame'. ❦ Hopes that Karzai might reverse the country's political paralysis were frustrated in January 2010, when the Afghan parliament rejected more than two-thirds of his cabinet nominees. Meanwhile, the country's security situation was described as 'perilous', and experts warned that insurgents could launch attacks 'with impunity'. ❦ In February, >15,000 Nato and Afghan troops, led by US Marines, launched Operation Moshtarak – a major offensive to push the Taliban out of areas of Helmand where poppy cultivation and the insurgency were most intense. Opinions differ as to the success of Moshtarak – though the UN concluded in August that the operation had 'not resulted in increased protection for the local population', and that 'the Taliban's violent intimidation of civilians has become the defining protection concern in the area'. World opinion was far from reassured by Karzai's February decree in which he took control of the country's electoral commission. ❦

In June, Obama was forced to sack his Afghanistan commander, Gen. Stanley McChrystal, after *Rolling Stone* published a story that quoted the general mocking the American administration. Obama replaced him with Gen. David Petraeus (who masterminded the 2007 Iraq 'surge'), but insisted, 'this is a change in personnel, not a change in policy'. ❦ In Britain, the mounting military death toll did little to persuade the public that the Afghanistan war was 'winnable'. The Wiltshire town of Wootton Bassett continued to be the focus of public remembrance – as the bodies of the fallen were driven through the town from RAF Lyneham – and there was increased concern about the rate of non-fatal injuries. In July, the British Limbless Ex-Servicemen's Assoc. reported that 28 soldiers had suffered amputations since January: 11 single amputees, 12 double, and 5 triple [see p.291]. ❦ Visiting Afghanistan soon after becoming PM, David Cameron called 2010 a 'vital year' for the occupation, though he ruled out sending additional forces and said, 'no one wants British troops to stay … for a day longer than is necessary'. ❦ Below are the UK military and civilian casualties from Operation Herrick [as of 15/8/10 · Source: MoD]:

CASUALTIES	438
very seriously injured/wounded	221
seriously injured/wounded	217
FIELD HOSPITAL ADMISSIONS	4,211
wounded in action	1,429
disease or non-battle injury	2,782
AEROMED EVACUATIONS	3,761
FATALITIES (as at 15/8/10)	331
killed in action	262
died of wounds	34
other	35

──────── OTHER MAJOR STORIES IN BRIEF ────────

Iran's Nuclear Programme

Negotiations on Iran's nuclear programme continued in 2009/10 with seemingly little progress. In late September 2009, Tehran caused international alarm by admitting to the development of a nuclear plant near Qom. In October, Iran soothed anxieties by agreeing to export much of its uranium for processing – but backed out of the deal weeks later. In February 2010, tensions rose again when President Ahmadinejad said Iran had succeeded in enriching uranium to 20% (enough for a medical reactor, but not for a weapon), and declared his nation was a 'nuclear state'. In the same month, an International Atomic Energy Agency (IAEA) report cited evidence that Iran was developing a nuclear warhead. In May, Iran agreed to transport about half its (known) uranium to Turkey for storage, in exchange for enriched uranium from other countries. However, experts warned that the deal would leave Iran with enough material for a weapon and, on 9/6, the UN Security Council imposed a new round of sanctions. Throughout 2010, IAEA reports said Iran was expanding its activities and restricting access by inspectors. Tehran continued to insist that its nuclear programme was peaceful, and that any evidence to the contrary was fabricated.

Climategate & the IPCC

In November 2009, a cache of emails and other documents was stolen from the University of East Anglia's Climatic Research Unit (CRU) and posted online. Climate change 'sceptics' claimed that the cache contained evidence that scientists had manipulated data, limited access to the CRU temperature database (one of the most important), and sought to discourage publications by opponents – all in an attempt to support claims of global warming. For months, the media debated whether 'climategate' was a major scientific scandal or a storm in a teacup. However, by July 2010 three independent reviews had cleared the scientists of any wrongdoing – although questions were asked about transparency and openness. ❦ In a related development, the Intergovernmental Panel on Climate Change (IPCC) also came under scrutiny when, in late 2009, errors were discovered in its landmark 2007 assessment, including a mistaken date forecast for the melting of the Himalayan glaciers. However, in August an independent review of IPCC procedures found that the panel's assessments were generally sound, though changes to encourage accuracy and transparency were recommended.

Edlington Attacks

On 22/1/2010, two brothers, aged 11 and 12, were given indeterminate sentences (with 5-year minimums) for the horrific torture of two boys, aged 9 and 11. For 90 minutes on 4/4/2009, on wasteland in Edlington, S Yorkshire, the young victims (who are uncle and nephew) were assaulted with rocks, sticks, barbed wire, and broken glass. They were made to eat dirt and nettles, burned with a cigarette, stripped naked and forced to perform sexual acts, and repeatedly threatened with death. Some of this torture was filmed on a mobile phone, the footage of which drew gasps of shock when it was replayed in court. The attackers said that their assault was motivated by having 'nowt to do', and admitted that they only ceased their torture when their arms began to ache. ❦ The trial judge, Mr Justice Keith, said, 'the fact is this was

—————— OTHER MAJOR STORIES IN BRIEF cont. ——————

prolonged, sadistic violence for no reason other than that you got a real kick out of hurting and humiliating them'. ❦ After the trial, Doncaster Council offered an 'unqualified apology ... for the admitted failings which led to this terrible incident'. An official report said that 9 separate agencies had failed 31 times over 14 years to intervene in the family lives of the two young attackers.

The Chilcot Inquiry

The public hearings of the Iraq Inquiry, chaired by Sir John Chilcot, began on 24/11/2009 and ran, off and on, until 30/7/2010. Some 130 people were questioned by the 6-strong committee, including 'star' witnesses such as Tony Blair, Alastair Campbell, Hans Blix, Gordon Brown, Gen. Sir Richard Dannatt, David Miliband, Sir John Scarlett, and Lord Goldsmith. ❦ Blair's 6-hour appearance was eagerly anticipated – not least by anti-war protesters, who were disappointed that the former PM entered and exited the inquiry in secret. Blair gave a vigorous defence of his decision to topple Iraq's regime, denied he had entered into a 'covert' deal with George W. Bush, and said that he would take the same decisions again. When asked by Chilcot whether he had any regrets, Blair replied: 'Responsibility, but not a regret for removing Saddam Hussein. I think that he was a monster.' ❦ The inquiry is set to report in late 2010, or 'possibly later'.

Catholic Church Abuse Scandals

In late 2009 and 2010, a series of abuse scandals rocked the Catholic Church in America and across Europe. In Ireland, a government report released in November 2009 found systematic collusion between the police and clergy in covering up abuse cases and complaints in the Dublin Archdiocese. The report led to the resignation of several bishops, and vows by the government and the Church to make amends. In March 2010, the scandal erupted anew after the head of the Irish Church, Cardinal Sean Brady, was revealed to have been present at a 1975 abuse inquiry at which alleged victims were sworn to silence; he denied any wrongdoing. On 20/3, the Pope sent a letter to Irish parishioners expressing 'shame and remorse', though some victims' groups said his apology did not go far enough. ❦ In March, the *New York Times* revealed that, during the 1990s, the Vatican body responsible for handling abuse cases, then led by Cardinal Ratzinger, did not defrock a priest accused of molesting *c.*200 deaf boys in Wisconsin. Reports showed the accused had appealed personally to the Cardinal for leniency, though there was no record of a response. ❦ In Germany, the press reported that, while Archbishop of Munich, the Pope had unknowingly allowed an accused molester to be transferred to Munich for therapy. The priest later returned to work with children, and was not stripped of his duties until March 2010. ❦ 2010 also saw abuse-related allegations, investigations, and resignations in Austria, Belgium, Italy, Switzerland, and the Netherlands. ❦ Throughout the year, the Vatican vehemently denied that the Pope had been directly involved in any of the events in question. Initially, Church officials were criticised for statements that seemed to associate child abuse with homosexuality. Later in the year, the Vatican appeared to take a more conciliatory stance. In April, the Church published an online guide for bishops investigating cases of abuse, which urged them to

─────── OTHER MAJOR STORIES IN BRIEF cont. ───────

report allegations to the civil authorities when so required by law. In July, the Vatican released new procedures designed to speed up abuse investigations – although many were angered when the ordination of women priests was listed as a 'more grave delict' [offence], alongside paedophilia and heresy. ❦ Critics accused the Vatican of being tone-deaf to the issue of abuse, and claimed the scandals compromised the Church's moral authority. Others argued that Benedict XVI had done more than any other Pope to address abuse within the Church, and questioned the media's relentless focus on the issue.

Parliamentary Expenses
In February 2010, 3 Labour MPs and a Tory peer were charged with false accounting under section 17 of the Theft Act 1968. The charges – vehemently denied by each of the accused – related to expenses they had allegedly claimed as parliamentarians. In March, all four pleaded not guilty and were remanded on bail. In June, Mr Justice Saunders rejected a submission that the issue was covered by 'parliamentary privilege', ruling: 'I can see no logical, practical or moral justification for a claim for expenses being covered by privilege; and I can see no legal justification for it either.' All four were given leave to appeal. ❦ In May, a fourth Labour MP was charged with false accounting, and in July a Tory peer was charged with the same offence; both denied any wrongdoing. ❦ The cases continue.

Protests in Thailand
In the spring of 2010, battles between anti-government protesters and the Thai military killed 88 and wounded >1,800 in Bangkok. The violence pitted 'red-shirt' supporters of exiled Thai PM

Thaksin Shinawatra against anti-Thaksin 'yellow-shirts'. According to news analysts, the 'red-shirts' were largely drawn from the rural poor, while the 'yellow-shirts' belonged mainly to the urban middle class. In March, Thailand's supreme court convicted Thaksin *in absentia* of concealing his wealth and abusing his office, and seized $1·4bn of his assets. The move galvanised tens of thousands of Thaksin's supporters, who took to the streets to call for fresh elections. In a gruesome display, on 16/3, protesters splashed blood on government buildings. By early April, protesters had set up an encampment in Bangkok's downtown shopping area. On 10/4, a military attempt to disperse the camp left *c*.25 dead. Reconciliation plans were offered by both sides, and rejected in turn. Clashes on the perimeter of the camp intensified, and after repeated warnings, the military stormed the site on 19/5. In response, protesters set buildings across the city ablaze. However, red-shirt leaders surrendered within hours, urging their followers to do the same. After mass arrests, the fighting died down and protesters returned home, their demands unmet, and the political stability of the country in doubt.

Eyjafjallajökull & Air Travel
On 14/4/2010, an eruption beneath Iceland's Eyjafjallajökull glacier sent vast plumes of volcanic ash miles into the sky. (The BBC's pronunciation is *AY-uh-fyat-luh-YOE-kuutl[-uh]*.) Within 24 hours, as winds carried the ash cloud south, the entirety of UK airspace was closed – an unprecedented move that left millions stranded at home and abroad. Over the next few days, countries across Europe introduced similar restrictions, and airlines launched test

———— OTHER MAJOR STORIES IN BRIEF cont. ————

flights to explore the effects of the ash on jet engines. Inevitably, media reporting combined stories of hardship with tales of Phileas Fogg-esque adventure. The government's response, doubtless influenced by the looming election, was to pledge Royal Navy support to ferry Brits across the Channel. But, by day four, BA's CEO had attacked the blanket ban as 'unnecessary', and the Air Transport Assoc. estimated that airlines were losing 'at least $200m a day'. On 20/4, against a backdrop of intense industry pressure, the Civil Aviation Authority lifted its blanket no-fly ban after engine manufacturers agreed 'increased tolerance levels in low ash density areas'. The cancellation of *c*.100,000 flights took some time to clear, and subsequent minor airspace closures reminded the public of the fragility of air travel.

Bigotgate

One of the defining incidents of the general election occurred a week before polling, when PM Gordon Brown met Gillian Duffy – a 65-year-old lifelong Labour supporter – during an informal 'walkabout' in a Rochdale street. After a frank but amicable debate with Duffy on the deficit, immigration, education, &c. Brown got into his car and drove away. Unbeknownst to him, his Sky News radio-mic was still live, and it captured his remarks about Duffy: '*That was a disaster. ... Should never have put me with that woman. Whose idea was that?* ... [Aide: What did she say?] *Everything. She's just this sort of bigoted woman who said she used to be Labour. It's just ridiculous.*' Alerted to his gaffe, Brown made six apologies over the following six hours, including visiting Duffy's home to apologise in person – after which he (smilingly) described

himself as a 'penitent sinner'. ❦ Despite being replayed ceaselessly by the media, Brown's indiscretion was not as disastrous as it might have been. In part this was due to his bullish performance in the third leaders' debate the next day [see p.19]. Yet there was also a sense that the public's opinion of Brown and its cynicism towards the political class could hardly sink any lower [see p.38].

Toyota Recalls

In late 2009 and 2010, Toyota issued >15 safety recalls relating to sticking accelerator pedals, troublesome floor-mats, and other issues, variously blamed for 'unintended accelerations' and implicated in several accidents. *c*.10m vehicles were affected by these recalls – leading to criticism of Toyota's response and prompting a series of investigations and lawsuits. In April, the US government fined Toyota $16·4m, the maximum possible, for concealing information about defects that may have caused the acceleration issues. Toyota continued to issue recalls throughout 2010, although a US government report in August said that many of the acceleration issues may in fact have been caused by 'driver error'.

Greece Debt Crisis

Escalating fears that Greece was near bankruptcy were formally acknowledged on 8/12/09, when Fitch became the first of the major ratings agencies to downgrade the country's credit rating [see p.231]. Over the months that followed, the Greek government, led by George Papandreou, launched a series of austerity measures, including: higher taxes, a public sector pay freeze, deep cuts in services, and a clampdown on the country's culture of corruption and tax evasion. In response, strikes

──────── OTHER MAJOR STORIES IN BRIEF cont. ────────

and demonstrations swept the country, in some cases escalating to fatal rioting. Fearing that 'Aegean contagion' would hit other weak eurozone economies, the EU negotiated hard to agree a rescue package. Despite widespread unease (not least in fiscally conservative Germany), on 2/5/10, the EU announced a 3-year €110bn bailout in return for radical cuts to Greece's deficit. Yet, even this unprecedented injection of liquidity failed to calm the markets – or the Greek protesters, who promptly stormed the Acropolis. ❦ The vulnerability of Greece inevitably focused attention on other weak eurozone economies – including Spain, Portugal, Ireland, and Italy – and led some to speculate on the long-term future of the common currency.

Korean Ship Sinking

On 26/3/10, the S Korean warship *Cheonan* was sailing near the disputed inter-Korean maritime border when an explosion tore the vessel in two, killing 46 sailors. Though the source of the explosion was initially unclear, in May S Korea released a multinational report that blamed a N Korean torpedo. Pyongyang denied any involvement in the incident, and threatened 'ruthless punishment' if it was held accountable. The South retaliated by cutting almost all trade ties with its neighbour, banning N Korean merchant ships from its waters, resuming propaganda broadcasts at the border, and re-designating N Korea as its 'principal enemy'. In July, a UN Security Council statement condemned the attacks, but did not name N Korea as the culprit (reportedly due to pressure from Russia and China). In late July, the US imposed additional sanctions against Pyongyang, and began joint military exercises in the South. The crisis brought relations between the two Koreas to a new nadir, and presented a further impediment to multinational efforts aimed at ending the 'hermit' North's nuclear ambitions.

Mazher Mahmood – the 'Fake Sheikh'

Several of this year's most dramatic scoops were reported by the *News of the World*'s Investigations Editor, Mazher Mahmood. The 'Fake Sheikh', as Mahmood is known (on account of one of his disguises), was responsible for allegations about Sarah Ferguson [see p.277], John Higgins [see p.316], and the Pakistani cricket team [see p.309]. For obvious reasons, little is known about Mahmood – though his methods are not without their critics. In January, the *News of the World* reported that, with the jailing of a council official, 'Maz' had brought his 250th 'villain' to justice. 'His extraordinary haul is almost enough to fill Dorchester prison', the paper noted.

Gaza Flotilla Raid

On 31/5/10, Israeli commandos raided a flotilla of aid ships bound for Gaza. 9 Turkish activists were killed, sparking an international outcry. The flotilla, organised by the Free Gaza Movement and the Turkish group Insani Yardim Vakfi, was carrying *c.*10,000 tons of aid to Gaza in contravention of Israel and Egypt's blockade of the Hamas-controlled territory. Israeli warships intercepted the flotilla shortly before midnight, while the boats were in international waters. Five ships were taken with little resistance, but the largest ship, the *Mavi Marmara*, was the site of a bloody confrontation. Both sides accused the other of instigating the violence, and both claimed their response had been self-defence. After an hour of

——————— OTHER MAJOR STORIES IN BRIEF cont. ———————

battle with knives, bats, and guns, nine activists had been killed and *c.*40 people wounded. The boats were escorted to a nearby Israeli base and *c.*600 passengers arrested (most were released 2/6). Turkey, once Israel's strongest Muslim ally, recalled its ambassador and sharply condemned the raid, demanding compensation, an international inquiry, and an apology. Large protests broke out in the Middle East, as the UN said the situation in Gaza was 'not sustainable' – a position supported by the US and UK. On 17/6, Israel announced 'adjustments' to the Gaza land blockade, later clarified to include a list of materials banned from the territory, rather than a list of goods allowed in. Israel initially rejected an international inquiry, and instead launched an internal investigation with two foreign observers. However, in August, Israel agreed to participate in a UN investigation into the raid – the first time Israel had agreed to such an inquiry involving its military.

Kyrgyzstan Violence

In mid-June 2010, clashes between ethnic Uzbeks and Kyrgyz in southern Kyrgyzstan killed >200 (perhaps as many as 2,000), and displaced *c.*400,000. While tensions between the Kyrgyz and Uzbeks had long simmered, analysts said the overthrow of then-President Kurmanbek Bakiyev in April 2010 contributed to the June violence. After Bakiyev's deposal, groups in his traditional southern strongholds began organising resistance against the interim government. Criminal groups, fuelled by the drugs trade, and local gangs exploited this unrest, leading to clashes that broke out on 10/6 in Osh, Jalalabad, and other cities. Disturbingly, witnesses reported that gunmen in Kyrgyz army uniforms oversaw much of the violence, which some speculated was designed to allow Bakiyev to return, a charge he denied. Amidst the unrest, *c.*10,000 ethnic Uzbeks streamed into neighbouring Uzbekistan, while thousands fled to refugee camps that became plagued by hunger and disease. Many returned (allegedly under duress) in time for a referendum on 27/6. This vote approved a new constitution, lending some legitimacy to the interim government, but reports of ongoing violence continued to test residents' faith in their government, the military, and each other.

Russian Spy Ring

On 27/6/10, 10 Russian spies were arrested in raids in Boston, New York, New Jersey, and Virginia. These 'illegals' had undertaken long-term, 'deepcover' assignments – cultivating an all-American life while covertly spying for the Russian intelligence agency *Sluzhba Vneshney Razvedki* (SVR). All 10 were initially charged with conspiracy to act as unlawful agents (some were also charged with money laundering), but not with espionage, since none had gathered any classified information. On 8/7, all 10 pleaded guilty, and were sentenced to time already served. That evening, in a scene out of le Carré, the spies were swapped for 4 supposed Western agents held in Russia. Observers said the incident's swift conclusion showed that America and Russia were serious about 'resetting' relations, if not yet friendly enough to stop spying on each other.

N Ireland Devolution & Violence

On 4/2/10 the leaders of N Ireland's power-sharing government agreed to transfer policing and justice powers from London to Belfast. Control of

—————— OTHER MAJOR STORIES IN BRIEF cont. ——————

the criminal justice system had been one of the most contentious issues of the peace process, and disputes on the matter threatened to undermine the country's fragile coalition. On 9/3, the N Ireland Assembly approved a deal to create a locally controlled Justice Ministry with powers over the country's courts, prisons, probation board, and forensic science agency. This new Ministry assumed power on 12/4, with Justice Minister David Ford at the helm. As part of this deal, the agreement also called for the creation of a working group to address management of the annual Protestant parades. However, in July, the Orange Order rejected proposals offered by the working group, and marches on 12/7 were marred by some of the worst violence in years. *c.*82 police officers were injured in Belfast, while Londonderry and Lurgan saw smaller disturbances. The clashes came amid a year of heightened dissident Republican violence, including a series of assaults, shootings, and attempted bombings which resulted in at least one death. However, in May, the Independent Monitoring Commission concluded that, 'while the threat from [the Real IRA] is dangerously lethal, it is also politically marginal'.

Pakistan Flooding

On 22/7/10 Pakistan's worst flooding in *c.*80 years began when the banks of the Indus overflowed in Baluchistan Province. Torrential monsoon rains soon unleashed floods throughout the country's north-west and south, leaving *c.*20% of the country underwater. >1,700 were killed, >2,700 injured, and 1·3m rescued. The devastation created a humanitarian catastrophe, with >4·6m left homeless, >10m in need of food, and vast swathes of the country's

cropland and infrastructure destroyed. Citizens trapped in ravaged villages without food, or left exposed to violence and disease in makeshift camps, protested angrily at their government's response – raising fears for the country's fragile political stability. Such concerns were particularly pronounced in the volatile north-western Khyber-Pakhtunkhwa Province, which was still attempting to rebuild after a major 2009 offensive against the Taliban. In the north-west and elsewhere, officials expressed concern that the disaster would distract resources from the fight against insurgents, and boost support for radical groups who provided food and shelter. Foreign donors exhausted by a year of natural disasters [see pp.21–21] were slow to contribute aid and, as of early September, only 64% of the $460m requested by the UN had been provided. Officials said it could take $15bn and 5 years for Pakistan to rebuild – though others warned that the country had been set back decades.

WikiLeaks

The whistle-blowing website *WikiLeaks* had two major scoops in 2010 – both of which tested the boundary between free speech and national security. In April, the site posted video footage, purportedly from a US Apache helicopter, that appeared to show the killing of civilians (including 2 Reuters journalists) by the US military in Baghdad, in 2007. In July, the site posted >76,000 classified US military incident and intelligence reports relating to the war in Afghanistan. (Extracts from these documents were also published by the *Guardian*, the *New York Times*, and *Der Spiegel*.) The July leak, described as one of the largest in history, was condemned by the Pentagon for endangering national security, the lives

————— OTHER MAJOR STORIES IN BRIEF cont. —————

of troops, and the security of informants in Afghanistan. Though the material contained few major revelations, it included previously undisclosed reports of civilian deaths, and allegations that Pakistan and Iran had assisted the Taliban. ❦ In May, an American soldier was charged with distributing classified information; he denied any wrongdoing. *WikiLeaks* refused to identify its sources, and argued that the dissemination of even highly sensitive data was an essential part of democratic transparency.

The Stig

The media's obsession with the identity of The Stig (*Top Gear*'s white-helmeted 'tame racing driver') intensified in August 2010 when the BBC sought an injunction to halt the publication of the autobiography of ex-F3 driver, Ben Collins. The book's publisher, Harper-Collins, said it was 'disappointed that the BBC has chosen to spend licence fee payers' money to suppress this book'. *Top Gear*'s executive producer said his team had 'worked bloody hard for many years to make the Stig something worth caring about, and that includes protecting it from a bunch of chancers'. On 1/9, a judge refused an injunction and, at the time of writing, the publication of *The Man in the White Suit* by Ben Collins looked set to go ahead.

Lola, the Cat in the Bin

In August, while strolling down a Coventry street, 45-year-old bank worker Mary Bale stopped to stroke a passing 4-year-old cat (named Lola) before inexplicably dropping the feline in an adjacent wheelie bin and walking off. After 15 hours in the bin, Lola's meows alerted her owners who, realising they had caught her incarceration on CCTV, posted the footage online to identify the culprit. Inevitably, the story went 'viral'. (One of the many YouTube clips of Bale's act has been viewed >1·4m times.) Faced with an astonishing outpouring of public vitriol (a Facebook group calling for her death was taken down), Bale made a public apology: 'I cannot explain why I did this, it is completely out of character and I certainly did not intend to cause any distress to Lola or her owners.' At the time of writing, the RSPCA was investigating the incident, and Lola was reported to be 'fine'.

New Labour Memoirs

Labour's electoral failure [see p.16] was swiftly followed by the memoirs of New Labour's triumvirate. First out of the gate (too soon for some) was Peter Mandelson's mischievously titled *The Third Man*. 'The book should be read by anyone remotely interested in politics, psychiatry and theatre,' said Steve Richards in the *Independent*, though in the *Observer* Andrew Rawnsley concluded, 'Having spent more than 500 pages in his slippery company, the reader doesn't feel that he has met the real Peter Benjamin Mandelson'. ❦ Blair's memoir, *A Journey*, may have dropped the more messianic definite article (its original title was *The Journey*), yet it was still the most hyped book of the year. Days before its release, Blair pledged to donate his *c*.£4·6m advance and all his royalties to the Royal British Legion – a decision both praised for its generosity and damned for its cynicism. *A Journey* contained little new. No one was surprised by Blair's justification of the Iraq war, or by the detail of his antagonistic relationship with Brown. Eyebrows were raised, however, that his greatest regrets seemed to be the fox hunting ban and the Freedom of Information Act. In the *Spectator*, Fraser Nelson

———— OTHER MAJOR STORIES IN BRIEF cont. ————

concluded: 'This memoir is not about score-settling, or making money. It's not about self-vindication … he's using his memoirs to build Blair Inc.' Sales of *A Journey* were described as 'unprecedented' – though Blair cancelled several events because of concerns about anti-war protests. (Bookshops reported that *A Journey* had been re-shelved by customers as 'fiction' and 'true crime'.) ❦ The final book [released after the publication of this volume] was Brown's account of the economic crisis, for which he was (partly) the cause and (partly) the cure. No one expected the ex-Chancellor's book to equal the spin of Mandelson's or the success of Blair's, not least because, according to *Private Eye*, the sales of Brown's last three books totalled 5,002, 816, and 32 [sic].

US Combat Missions in Iraq

On 31/8/2010, Barack Obama declared the end of US combat missions in Iraq. The President said it was time to 'turn the page' on the *c*.10-year conflict that had cost the US alone *c*.4,421 lives, >$1 trillion, and an unquantifiable sum in goodwill. Obama promised Iraq America's ongoing support, but he encouraged the country's leaders 'to move forward with a sense of urgency to form an inclusive government that is just, representative, and accountable'. Despite Obama's declaration that 'Operation Iraqi Freedom is over', *c*.50,000 US troops remain in the country to 'advise and assist' Iraqi security forces and to engage in counter-terrorism operations. Indeed, a week after the president's address, 2 US soldiers were killed and 9 were wounded during a fire-fight inside an Iraqi army base near Baghdad.

William Hague

On 1/9/2010, the Foreign Secretary William Hague issued a frank personal statement with a detailed refutation of press and internet innuendo that he was a homosexual, that his marriage was 'in trouble', and that he had an inappropriate relationship with a 25-year-old man he had appointed as his special adviser. Hague confirmed stories that he had shared twin hotel rooms with this man during the general election campaign, but said, 'neither of us would have done so if we had thought that it in any way meant or implied something else'. In a bid to end the 'continued and hurtful speculation' about his sexuality and marriage, Hague also disclosed that his and his wife Ffion's desire for children had been frustrated by a series of miscarriages.

Benedict XVI's State Visit to Britain

The Pope's state visit to Britain (16/9–19/9/2010) was enthusiastically welcomed by the faithful, and vociferously opposed by those dismayed at its cost (*c*.£12m) and angered by the Vatican's stance on issues from contraception to child abuse. ❦ Despite an inauspicious start (when a Papal aide likened Britain to a 'third world country'), BXVI was greeted by large crowds in Edinburgh, Glasgow, London, and Birmingham. In a sermon at Westminster Hall, he addressed directly the issue of paedophilia in the Church, expressing 'deep sorrow to the innocent victims of these unspeakable crimes'. Yet, his central message was to attack 'atheist extremism' and 'aggressive forms of secularism' that challenge 'traditional values and cultural expressions'. Because of fears of assassination – or an attempted citizen's arrest – security was especially tight. (6 men arrested in connection with an alleged plot against the Pope were all released without charge.) On the final day of his visit, BXVI beatified Cardinal John Henry Newman.

—— PERSON OF THE YEAR · THE MILI·CLEG·ERON——

The person of 2010 is a political composite: the *Mili·Cleg·Eron* is a well-schooled, Oxbridge-educated, London-centric, white, married, heterosexual, 40-something male. The *Mili·Cleg·Eron* has never depended on benefits, earned minimum wage, or lived in council housing. The *Mili·Cleg·Eron* has never run a business, worked in a hospital, walked the beat, taught in a school, served in the military, or laboured in agriculture, manufacturing, or construction. The *Mili·Cleg·Eron* has, however, toiled at the coalface of journalism, PR, and research before segueing into office. Confident, polished, dark-suited, managerial (not ideological), and urban (not urbane) – the *Mili·Cleg·Eron* is now running Britain, and is likely to do so for the foreseeable future. ❦ The *Mili·Cleg·Eron* represents a range of individuals: David Cameron, Nick Clegg, much of the Cabinet and Shadow Cabinet, and 4 out of 5 of Labour's leadership candidates – 2 of whom are Milibands. (The fifth candidate, Diane Abbot, her gender and ethnicity aside, still fits much of the bill.) ❦ In 2010, the long-observed 'disconnect' between MPs and voters was stretched ever wider. A range of issues urgent to voters (not least immigration) is disdained by the political class – as Brown's accidental 'bigotgate' candour showed [see p.32] – making promises of a 'national conversation' about the 'big society' even more tenuous. Fearful of this gulf, the *Mili·Cleg·Eron* repeats the empty phrase 'what I hear on the doorstep', and stages photo-shoots doing 'normal' things, like watching football on TV. ❦ The *Mili·Cleg·Eron*'s rise has revivified Britain's obsession with class. Labelling both Cameron and Clegg 'posh', commentators attempted to parse exactly how posh each was. (According to Ben Macintyre, Cameron is 'Eton-Oxford-country-clubby-cutglass-shooting party sort of posh' whereas Clegg is 'Westminster-Cambridge-metropolitan-foreign-glottalstop-trustfund sort of posh'.) Cameron's description of himself as one of the 'sharp-elbowed middle classes' amused some, to whom being a millionaire Old Etonian married to an aristocrat hinted at certain upper-class credentials. To others, the 'sharp-elbowed' element rang true, reflecting a view that politicians are on the make – either by maximising their expenses, or by monetising their experiences (to the tune of millions in the case of Tony Blair). As the *Mili·Cleg·Eron* took office, Labour's old guard took to the airwaves to plug memoirs in which they came (almost)° clean about the feuds they had spent years vehemently denying. Inside Westminster, such duplicity is part of the game; outside, it reinforces the belief that politicians just don't 'get it'. ❦ One could argue that the *Mili·Cleg·Eron*'s ascendancy is temporary and that (like the Con-Lib coalition) it will falter if the economy struggles and the cuts bite. Or, it could be that Britain is coming to terms with a new political elite, described by Michael Woolf as 'the post-class upper class'. ❦ In 1973, Margaret Thatcher famously erred when she said, 'I don't think there will be a woman prime minister in my lifetime'. But for everything that has changed in Britain in the intervening 37 years, it is notable that the dominance of the *Mili·Cleg·Eron* means that a female, ethnic-minority, gay, or proudly working-class prime minister seems as unlikely now as then.

─── SCHEMATIC · WORLD EVENTS OF NOTE · 2009–10 ───

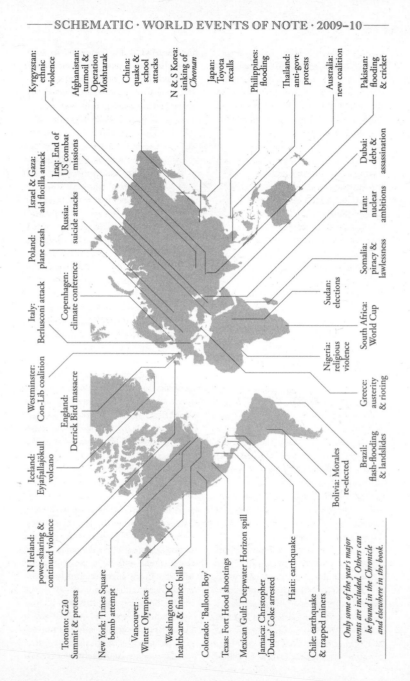

Kyrgyzstan: ethnic violence

Afghanistan: turmoil & Operation Moshtarak

China: quake & school attacks

N & S Korea: sinking of *Cheonan*

Japan: Toyota recalls

Philippines: flooding

Thailand: anti-govt protests

Australia: new coalition

Pakistan: flooding & cricket

Iraq: End of US combat missions

Israel & Gaza: aid flotilla attack

Russia: suicide attacks

Poland: plane crash

Copenhagen: climate conference

Italy: Berlusconi attack

Dubai: debt & assassination

Iran: nuclear ambitions

Somalia: piracy & lawlessness

Sudan: elections

South Africa: World Cup

Nigeria: religious violence

Greece: austerity & rioting

Westminster: Con-Lib coalition

England: Derrick Bird massacre

Iceland: Eyjafjallajökull volcano

Bolivia: Morales re-elected

Brazil: flash-flooding & landslides

N Ireland: power-sharing & continued violence

Toronto: G20 Summit & protests

New York: Times Square bomb attempt

Vancouver: Winter Olympics

Washington DC: healthcare & finance bills

Colorado: 'Balloon Boy'

Texas: Fort Hood shootings

Mexican Gulf: Deepwater Horizon spill

Jamaica: Christopher 'Dudus' Coke arrested

Haiti: earthquake

Chile: earthquake & trapped miners

Only some of the year's major events are included. Others can be found in the Chronicle and elsewhere in the book.

————— IN BRIEF · SEPTEMBER – OCTOBER 2009 —————

The daily chronicle below picks up from the 2010 edition of Schott's Almanac.

SEPTEMBER 2009 · {11} Police announced they were investigating reports that an MI6 agent was complicit in the torture of a non-British man. {12} 4 children were made seriously ill and 8 hospitalised after an E. coli outbreak traced to a Surrey farm. ☞ RIP @ 81, Larry Gelbart, writer of M*A*S*H. {13} An 8-year-old girl known to the local authorities was found hanged at her home in Nottinghamshire. {14} 3 men found guilty of conspiring to blow up transatlantic flights with liquid bombs were jailed for 32–40 years. {15} RIP @ 57, Patrick Swayze. ☞ RIP @ 65, Keith Floyd [see p.61]. {16} UK unemployment rose to 2·47m. {17} Obama announced he was shelving plans for an E Europe-based missile shield; Russia welcomed the move. {18} Chief Medical Officer Sir Liam Donaldson warned that swine flu could rise again after an estimated 5,000 cases were reported in a week. {19} The Lib Dem conference opened in Bournemouth. {21} Honduran President Manuel Zelaya, who had been ousted in a coup 3 months previously, returned to the capital, Tegucigalpa. {22} French police forcibly closed 'the jungle' – a camp of illegal immigrants in Calais; >278 were arrested. ☞ At a UN climate summit in New York, President Hu Jintao announced that China would improve energy efficiency and attempt to curb the rise in CO₂ emissions. {23} PM Gordon Brown told the UN that Britain could cut its Trident subs from 4 to 3. {24} Data from India's

Angela Merkel

This country has been kidnapped by the military forces. – ousted Honduran President MANUEL ZELAYA

Chandrayaan probe indicated the presence of water on the Moon. {25} Iran admitted to the UN that it had built a concealed second nuclear plant; the UN demanded instant access to the site and threatened further sanctions. {26} >50 died and thousands were left homeless after flooding engulfed Manila. {27} As >300,000 people fled, rescuers in Manila attempted to help those stranded on roofs; *c.*80% of the city was under water. ☞ Iran test-fired 2 short-range missiles and announced it would test a long-range missile. ☞ Germany went to the polls. {28} German Chancellor Angela Merkel was returned to power but sought a new ruling coalition with the FDP. ☞ A 14-year-old girl died after she was given the cervical cancer vaccine, raising concerns over the jab's safety. {29} Brown attempted to start Labour's comeback by stating the party could 'change the world again' at his conference speech in Brighton. ☞ The girl who died after having the cervical cancer jab had a 'serious underlying medical condition', according to the NHS, which said the jab was unlikely to have caused her death. ☞ Many died and hundreds were missing after a tsunami caused by an underwater quake hit Samoa. {30} >75 died and hundreds were homeless after a powerful earthquake hit Padang on the Indonesian island of Sumatra. ☞ The *Sun* announced it would back the Tories at the next election [see p.136].

OCTOBER · {1} Angela Allen, Colin Blanchard, and nursery worker Vanessa George were convicted of a number of sexual assaults

— IN BRIEF · OCTOBER 2009 —

against children. ❦ The death toll in the Sumatran earthquake rose to >1,100. {3} 67% of the Irish voted in favour of the Lisbon Treaty, 16 months after they had rejected it. ❦ International aid began to arrive in Sumatra. {4} Socialists swept to power in Greece, after a snap election. ❦ A Taliban attack in E Afghanistan killed 8 US and 2 Afghan soldiers. {5} 2 teenage girls (14 & 15) died after jumping hand-in-hand from the Erskine Bridge, near Glasgow. {6} BA announced it was cutting 1,700 jobs. {7} Bones found by the M5 in Gloucestershire were confirmed to belong to 25-year-old Melanie Hall, who went missing in 1996. ❦ Italy's highest court overturned the immunity granted to Silvio Berlusconi. {8} Royal Mail workers voted to strike over job security. {9} Obama was awarded the Nobel Peace Prize [see p.66]. {10} The Territorial Army was ordered to suspend training for 6 months to cut costs. ❦ Polish President Lech Kaczyński signed the Lisbon Treaty, leaving only the Czech Rep., to ratify it. {11} RIP @ 33, Boyzone's Stephen Gately [see p.61]. {12} Sir Thomas Legg's review into the past 5 years of MPs' expenses reported; among other headlines, Brown was asked to repay £12,415 he had claimed for cleaners. ❦ >41 died in a militant attack in NW Pakistan. {13} 14 senior Tories were asked to pay back money claimed as expenses. {14} Brown announced he would send 500 more troops to Afghanistan. {15} >40 died in militant attacks in Pakistan, including >26 in attacks on police academies in Lahore. ❦ Rescuers in Colorado, US, followed an untethered weather balloon for 2 hours after it was reported a 6-year-old

Silvio Berlusconi

boy might have been trapped inside; the balloon was found to be empty, and the boy was discovered hiding in his parents' attic. {16} >11 died in a bomb attack in Peshawar, Pakistan. ❦ Controversial Dutch MP Geert Wilders arrived in Britain after a banning order against him was lifted. {17} The Pakistani army launched an offensive against the Taliban in S Waziristan. ❦ Gately's funeral was held in Dublin. {18} Jenson Button became Formula One World Champion after securing 5th place in Brazil [see p.307]. ❦ >31 died in a terrorist attack on Revolutionary Guards in SE Iran. {19} The Colorado sheriff investigating the 'balloon boy' incident said it was a hoax planned by the boy's parents. ❦ >100,000 people fled their homes in S Waziristan as the Pakistani army continued their offensive against the Taliban. ❦ RIP @ 89, Ludovic Kennedy [see p.61]. {20} After international pressure, Afghanistan's Independent Election Commission announced a run-off vote between President Karzai and Abdullah Abdullah. ❦ The Catholic Church announced new rules to allow Anglicans to join Rome while retaining their own distinct religious identity: the move was seen as an attempt to woo those disaffected by the C of E's stance on women bishops. {21} Frontline NHS staff became the first Britons to be given the swine flu vaccine. {22} Anti-fascist activists gathered outside BBC TV Centre to protest against the appearance on *Question Time* of BNP leader Nick Griffin. ❦ British postal workers went on strike. {23} Britain's GDP was reported to have contracted for 6 consecutive quarters, indicating the deepest recession since

> *It has been determined that this is a hoax, that it was a publicity stunt.*
> — Colorado Sheriff, JIM ALDERDEN

——————— IN BRIEF · OCTOBER – NOVEMBER 2009 ———————

figures were first recorded. ❦ Postal workers announced 3 more days of strikes. {24} The BNP's *Question Time* appearance seemed to have boosted its electoral appeal; a YouGov poll showed that 22% would 'seriously consider' voting BNP. {25} Coordinated suicide bombs in Baghdad killed >155 and injured >500. {26} The trial of former Bosnian Serb leader Radovan Karadžić opened in the Hague; Karadžić refused to leave his cell, claiming he had had insufficient time to prepare his defence. ❦ 4 teenagers aged 14–17 were arrested after a homophobic attack on a 22-year-old trainee policeman in Liverpool. {27} 8 US soldiers died in a Taliban bombing in S Afghanistan. ❦ A British couple, Paul and Rachel Chandler, were seized by Somali pirates as they sailed near the Seychelles. {28} 5 UN workers died when the Taliban launched an attack on a guest house in Kabul, Afghanistan. {29} Footballer Marlon King was jailed for 18 months after he broke the nose of a young woman who had spurned his advances. {30} Prof David Nutt, head of the Advisory Council on the Misuse of Drugs, was 'sacked' after criticising the govt's drug policy. ❦ Somali pirates demanded a £4·3m ransom for the Chandlers. ❦ ≥118 died in a car bomb in Peshawar, Pakistan. {31} The govt said that Lloyds, RBS, and Northern Rock would be broken up, and several new banks would be created.

Mahmoud Abbas

Karadžić is making the world and justice ridiculous.
– ADMIRA FAZLIC, Bosnian war survivor

NOVEMBER · {1} Abdullah Abdullah announced he would not stand in the presidential run-off against Hamid Karzai after demands to counteract election fraud were not agreed. {2} 2 members of the Advisory Council on the Misuse of Drugs resigned in protest at the sacking of Prof Nutt; Nutt said: 'My sacking has cast a huge shadow over the relationship of science to policy.' ❦ >30 died in a suicide attack in Rawalpindi, Pakistan. ❦ Heavy rain caused serious flooding across N & E Scotland. {3} The Czech Rep. ratified the Lisbon Treaty, thereby bringing it into law [see p.273]. ❦ Simon Mann, the British mercenary jailed for his part in a failed coup in Equatorial Guinea, was pardoned and released. {4} 5 British soldiers serving in Helmand were killed by an Afghan policeman they had been training. {6} >13 died and >30 were injured when an American soldier went on the rampage at Fort Hood, Texas, USA. ❦ BA announced it would axe 1,200 jobs worldwide. ❦ Postal unions called off pre-Christmas strikes. ❦ Palestinian Authority President Mahmoud Abbas announced he would not stand for re-election in January. {7} Details of the Fort Hood shooting emerged; the gunman was a Muslim army psychiatrist, Major Nidal Malik Hasan, who reportedly did not want to be deployed to Afghanistan. ❦ 8 Afghans working with US troops were killed by a Nato air strike. {8} 2 British soldiers died in Afghanistan as the nation marked Remembrance Sunday. ❦ Obama's Bill to provide affordable health care to 96% of Americans narrowly passed the Senate. ❦ >91 died in El Salvador after rain and flooding. {9} Germany celebrated the 20th anniversary of the fall of the Berlin Wall. ❦ The mother of a British soldier killed in Afghanistan publicly criticised Brown for writing a 'hastily scrawled insult' of

IN BRIEF · NOVEMBER 2009

a condolence letter which misspelled her family name; the PM apologised for the error and his handwriting. {10} >24 died and >100 were injured after a suicide attack in Charsadda, Pakistan. ❦ Lloyds Banking Group announced it would axe 5,000 jobs. {11} The war dead were mourned at Armistice Day services [see p.282]. {13} Labour's Willie Bain won the (previous day's) Glasgow NE by-election, with a majority of 8,111. {14} Storms hit the UK, causing flooding across Wales and S England. {15} A 52-year-old man was arrested in connection with hundreds of sex attacks on the elderly across SE London. {16} RIP @ 79, Edward Woodward. {17} Easyjet announced its full-year profits had fallen 50% as a result of fuel costs. {18} In the Queen's Speech, Brown introduced Bills he hoped would set the election agenda, including plans to help pay for elderly care, and proposals to rein in bankers; Cameron accused him of 'desperately trying a few tricks to try and save his own skin'. ❦ Controversy raged when France beat Ireland to a place in the World Cup after Thierry Henry appeared to handle the ball setting up the winning goal. {19} Belgian PM, Herman van Rompuy, was named the first permanent European Council President. ❦ The RAF rescued c.200 people stranded by flooding in Cockermouth, Cumbria. {20} The body of PC Bill Barker, 44, was found; he had been swept into the Derwent when a bridge collapsed during the flooding in Cumbria. {21} >500 people were evacuated from their homes in Cumbria as the flooding continued and local bridges were declared unsafe. {22} An experienced canoeist, Chris Wheeler,

Jedward

I will be honest, it was a handball ... but I'm not the referee.
– THIERRY HENRY

46, died on the fast-flowing River Dart, Dartmoor. ❦ Urgent safety checks were made on all 1,800 bridges in Cumbria after 6 collapsed in the floods; thousands were cut off from basic facilities. ❦ A 400lb bomb was defused after it was left outside the Belfast Policing Board HQ by dissident Republicans. ❦ John & Edward (i.e., Jedward) were voted off *X Factor* [see p.122]; Katie Price quit *I'm A Celebrity ...* after she was nominated for a 7th consecutive 'bush tucker trial'. {23} A plot by dissident Republicans to murder a policeman in Fermanagh was foiled. ❦ >46 died in political violence on the Philippine Island of Mindanao. {24} The Chilcot Inquiry into the Iraq invasion opened in London. {26} The FTSE 100 saw its greatest fall since March over concerns about Dubai's liquidity. ❦ The bookseller Borders went into administration in the UK. {27} A Moscow–St Petersburg train crashed, killing >25 and injuring many more. ❦ Tiger Woods was found semi-unconscious after a car crash near his Florida home [see p.303]. ❦ Threshers announced the loss of 2,140 jobs. {28} It was revealed that a bomb caused the Russian train crash. {29} Brown urged Pakistan to do more to find Osama bin Laden. ❦ 57% of Swiss voters backed a controversial referendum to ban the construction of minarets in the country. {30} It emerged that 5 British sailors taking part in a Bahrain–Dubai yacht race had been detained on 25 Nov, after allegedly straying into Iranian waters. ❦ Brown announced he would deploy 500 more troops to Afghanistan. ❦ A 4-year-old boy was mauled to death by a dog at his grandmother's house in Liverpool.

——— IN BRIEF · DECEMBER 2009 ———

DECEMBER · {1} Foreign Sec. David Miliband pressed the Iranian govt to release the 5 British yachtsmen. ❦ Carwyn Jones was named the new Welsh Labour leader and First Minister in the Welsh Assembly. {2} The Taliban announced it would escalate the war in Afghanistan after Obama pledged a surge of 30,000 troops. ❦ RIP @ 75, *Coronation St* actress Maggie Jones. {3} ❦ The 5 British yachtsmen were freed by Iran. {4} Corus announced it would close a factory in Teeside, putting 2,000 jobs at risk. ❦ >40 died and >80 were injured

Amanda Knox

after militants attacked a mosque in Rawalpindi, Pakistan. ❦ Nato announced that 7,000 extra troops from 25 countries would be deployed to Afghanistan to support Obama's surge. ❦ American student Amanda Knox and her Italian ex-boyfriend Raffaele Sollecito were found guilty by an Italian court of the murder of British student Meredith Kercher; Knox was sentenced to 26 years, Sollecito to 25. ❦ >109 were killed and >140 injured after a blast caused by fireworks at a nightclub in Perm, Russia. {6} Bolivian President Evo Morales was re-elected for a further 5 years. {7} The UN summit on climate change opened in Copenhagen [see p.27]. ❦ A British soldier was killed in Afghanistan, taking 2009's toll to 100. ❦ Richard Wright won the Turner Prize [see p.171]. ❦ >36 died and hundreds were injured in 2 explosions in Lahore, Pakistan. {8} >127 died in a series of car bombs across Baghdad. {9} In his Pre-Budget Report, Darling announced that National Insurance would increase by 0·5% from 2011; imposed a 1% public sector pay cap; and introduced a tax on

I feel like I'm floating, just floating around, and I just feel like jelly.
– JOE McELDERRY

bank bonuses >£25,000. {10} Obama accepted his Nobel Peace Prize in Oslo [see p.66]. {11} The EU announced £6·5bn in aid to help poorer nations with climate change. {12} The Danish police were criticised after detaining *c.*900 protesters at the Copenhagen climate summit. {13} Italian PM Berlusconi spent the night in hospital after he was attacked by a man in the crowd at a rally in Milan; Berlusconi suffered a broken nose and broken teeth after he was hit in the face with a model of Milan Cathedral. ❦ Brown went on an overnight visit to Afghanistan to boost troop morale and meet with President Karzai. ❦ 17m watched Joe McElderry win the *X Factor* [see p.122]. {14} Dubai reported that Abu Dhabi had given it $10bn to help pay down debt. ❦ Iran announced it would put on trial 3 Americans who had crossed over the Iraqi border. ❦ BA cabin crew voted for a 12-day strike over Christmas. {15} 2 British and 2 Afghan soldiers were killed trying to foil a suicide bomb attack on a busy market in Helmand. {16} Serial killer Peter Tobin (already serving life for murdering Vicky Hamilton, 15, and Angelika Kluk, 23) was given another life sentence for the murder of Dinah McNicol, 18. ❦ Developing nations boycotted the Copenhagen talks for 9 hours, complaining that the West was not taking seriously compensation negotiations. {17} BA won a high court injunction banning the planned 12-day cabin crew strike. ❦ A Turkish Kurd was jailed for the 'honour killing' of his 15-year-old daughter. ❦ >80 MPs challenged expenses repayment requests. {18} Snow blanketed much of SE England; travel chaos ensued. ❦ A deal of sorts

—— IN BRIEF · DECEMBER 2009 – JANUARY 2010 ——

was reached at Copenhagen [see p.27]. ❦ The *Arbeit Macht Frei* ('Work Sets You Free') sign from Auschwitz was stolen; the Polish and Israeli govts reacted with dismay. ❦ After 27 years, Terry Wogan hosted his last Radio 2 breakfast show. {19} Eurostar trains broke down in the Channel Tunnel due to inclement weather; hundreds were stranded. ❦ Chris Hollins won *Strictly Come Dancing* [see p.122]. {20} Eurostar services remained suspended for engineering investigations. ❦ RIP @ 32, Brittany Murphy. {21} 5 men were arrested in Poland after the Auschwitz sign was found; it had been cut into 3 pieces. ❦ Brown, Cameron, and Clegg agreed to the first-ever TV election debates [see p.19]. ❦ Further snow caused travel chaos across Britain. ❦ Thousands of Iranians took to the streets of Qom, turning the funeral of cleric Grand Ayatollah Hoseyn Ali Montazeri into an anti-govt protest. {22} A British soldier was killed in a suspected 'friendly fire' incident in central Helmand. ❦ >90 died across Europe as a result of cold weather. {23} 2 further MPs were reported by police to the CPS regarding their expenses. {24} Obama's health care Bill passed the Senate. {25} The Queen used her Christmas message to pay tribute to those killed in Afghanistan [see p.278]. ❦ A Nigerian man, claiming to be working for al-Qaeda, allegedly attempted to blow up a flight from Amsterdam–Detroit; it was reported he had explosives in his underwear. {26} Iranian forces and anti-govt protesters clashed in Tehran. {27} Obama ordered a review of air security after it emerged that the 'underwear bomber' was 'known' to US intelligence. ❦ >4 died and >300 were arrested during violence in Tehran. ❦ {28} Home Sec. Alan Johnson revealed that the 'underwear bomber' was on a UK watch-list. {29} The British govt reacted with dismay after it emerged China had executed a British citizen, Akmal Shaikh, 53. ❦ Further snow fell across Wales and England. {30} Peter Moore, a hostage in Iraq for >2 years, was released. ❦ 7 Americans working for the CIA were killed in a bomb attack in Khost Province, Afghanistan. {31} Status Quo's Rick Parfitt and Francis Rossi were awarded OBEs [see p.281].

Nick Clegg

J ANUARY 2010 · {1} >88 died in a suicide attack at a volleyball match in NW Pakistan. ❦ Brown called for a world summit to discuss the radicalisation of Yemen. ❦ The nephew of Iranian opposition leader Mir Hossein Mousavi was killed during protests in Iran. {2} A Somali man armed with a knife and an axe broke into the home of Danish cartoonist Kurt Westergaard who, in 2005, had drawn a caricature of the Prophet Muhammad; the Somali was shot and arrested, Westergaard was unharmed. {3} Brown announced that full-body scanners would be introduced at British airports [see p.207]. {4} The US introduced tougher screening for those flying in from 14 'risky' countries. ❦ The world's tallest building (828m) opened in Dubai; at the last minute it was renamed Burj Khalifa after the ruler of Abu Dhabi, who had helped Dubai pay off $10bn in debts. {5} It was reported that the man who killed 7 CIA agents in Afghanistan was a Jordanian double-agent working for al-Qaeda. {6} Former Cabinet ministers Geoff Hoon

You start off rebellious, a teenager in a band, but you end up being part of the establishment. – FRANCIS ROSSI, OBE

IN BRIEF · JANUARY 2010
---

and Patricia Hewitt attempted to unseat Brown by calling for a secret leadership ballot; a noticeably slow trickle of support for Brown eventually quashed the plot. ❦ Continued freezing weather closed schools and caused travel chaos across Britain. {7} Concerns were raised as to the security of Britain's gas supply during the cold weather. ❦ Brown dismissed the Hoon/Hewitt plot as a 'storm in a teacup'. ❦ Jonathan Ross announced he would quit the BBC [see p.128]. {8} A N Irish policeman was seriously injured when a bomb exploded under his car in County Antrim.

Jonathan Ross

❦ The Togo football team was attacked by rebels in Angola on their way to the African Cup of Nations; 3 non-players were killed. ❦ N Ireland's First Minister Peter Robinson attempted to secure his position after lurid allegations about his wife's relationship with a 19-year-old man were reported. {9} 31-year-old Sukhwinder Singh was stabbed to death after chasing 2 muggers in E London. {10} The *Sunday Mirror*'s defence correspondent, Rupert Hame, was killed by a roadside bomb in Afghanistan; a US marine also died in the incident. ❦ It was reported that Iris Robinson, the wife of N Ireland's First Minister, was receiving 'acute psychiatric treatment' as revelations about her private life continued. {11} Peter Robinson announced he would step down for 6 weeks to clear his name. {12} A powerful 7·3 earthquake hit Haiti, causing massive devastation to the capital, Port-au-Prince [see p.20]. ❦ Alastair Campbell appeared before the Chilcot Inquiry; he robustly defended the govt's actions in the run-up to the Iraq invasion. ❦ Islam4UK, a radical Islamist group, was banned under counter-terror legislation. ❦ The first non-jury trial in England and Wales for 350 years opened at the Royal Courts of Justice. {14} The Red Cross estimated that >50,000 might have died in the Haiti quake [see p.20].

❦ Obama announced a tax to recoup the $117bn ploughed into US banks during the financial crisis. ❦ RIP @ 59, soul singer Teddy Pendergrass. {15} Survivors of the Haiti quake expressed frustration as aid agencies struggled to import supplies. ❦ Bosch announced it would close a factory in S Wales, cutting 900 jobs. {16} 2 British soldiers were killed by a roadside bomb in Helmand. {17} Ban Ki-moon visited Haiti. {18} The Taliban launched attacks on Kabul, killing >5 and injuring >70. ❦ >2,000 US marines arrived in Haiti. {19} Cadbury confirmed it had accepted a takeover bid from US food giant Kraft. ❦ >149 died in 2 days of religious conflict between Christians and Muslims in Jos, Nigeria. {20} Republican Scott Brown took Edward Kennedy's Massachusetts seat, eliminating the Democrat Senate majority and putting Obama's health care reform in jeopardy. ❦ The Court of Appeal freed Munir Hussain, who had been jailed for attacking a burglar who had terrorised his family. ❦ A woman who 'euthanised' her disabled son with heroin was jailed for life. {21} 400,000 Haitian refugees were relocated from Port-au-Prince to tented villages outside the capital. {22} The UK terror threat level was raised to 'severe'; Home Sec. Alan Johnson denied there was a specific threat [see p.117]. ❦ 2 brothers who sadistically tortured 2 young boys in Edlington were sentenced to be held

I defend every single word of the dossier.
I defend every single part of the process.
— ALASTAIR CAMPBELL

──── IN BRIEF · JANUARY – FEBRUARY 2010 ────

indefinitely; Doncaster Council apologised for the many mistakes that had left the brothers free to carry out the attack [see p.29]. ❦ As the deadline imposed by Obama to close Guantánamo Bay passed, a US task force reported that 47 detainees should be held indefinitely without trial. {23} A 23-year-old man was rescued from the rubble of a collapsed supermarket in Haiti, 11 days after the quake. ❦ RIP @ 80, actress Jean Simmons. {24} A Haitian govt minister said that the quake death toll was >150,000 in Port-au-Prince alone. ❦ An audio tape purportedly by Osama Bin Laden was received by al-Jazeera; Bin Laden claimed responsibility for the foiled Christmas Day 'underwear' plot, and warned of future attacks. {25} Crisis talks were held in Belfast in an attempt to prevent the collapse of power-sharing at Stormont. ❦ Iraq executed 'Chemical' Ali Hassan al-Majid for his part in the attack on Halabja. ❦ A Lebanese plane heading to Ethiopia crashed in bad weather, killing all 90 on board. {26} The UK economy exited recession; the economy grew 0·1% in the last 3 months of 2009. {27} Talks in N Ireland over the devolution of policing collapsed. {28} A UN summit in London on the future of Afghanistan agreed that £87m could be spent on recruiting Taliban fighters. ❦ RIP @ 91, J.D. Salinger [see p.61]. {29} Tony Blair appeared at the Chilcot Inquiry [see p.30]. ❦ Toyota announced it would recall c.1·8m cars across Europe due to faults [see p.32]. {30} China imposed a number of sanctions on the US after it emerged America had agreed a $6·4bn weapons deal with Taiwan. ❦ There were calls for John Terry to be stripped of the England

captaincy after a series of lurid allegations about his private life. {31} 3 weeks after the Haiti quake, the UN began a major push to deliver food to Port-au-Prince. ❦ Roger Federer beat Andy Murray in the final of the Australian Open to take his 16th Grand Slam.

Peter Robinson

FEBRUARY · {1} 2 British soldiers were killed by roadside bombs in Afghanistan. ❦ >41 Shia pilgrims were killed by a female suicide bomber in Baghdad. ❦ Israel revealed it had reprimanded 2 senior army officers over the use of white phosphorus during an attack on the UN Gaza compound in 2009. {2} The Pope urged British bishops to fight the UK's Equality Bill with 'missionary zeal', arguing the proposals 'violated natural law'. {3} *L'Homme Qui Marche I* by Alberto Giacometti was sold at auction for a record £65,001,250. ❦ DUP leader Peter Robinson returned as First Minister. {4} It was revealed that £1·1m of MPs' second homes repayments claimed between 2004–08 would have to be repaid. ❦ 10 US missionaries in Haiti were charged with child abduction after they allegedly attempted to take 33 children out of the country, reportedly to found an orphanage. {5} The DPP announced that 3 Labour MPs and a Tory peer would be charged under the Theft Act with regard to their expenses claims; all denied any wrongdoing [see p.31]. ❦ BAE was ordered to pay £286m in fines to the US and UK authorities after an investigation into its business practices. ❦ Fabio Capello stripped John Terry of the England captaincy over allegations concerning his private life; Rio Ferdinand replaced Terry.

I felt the house dancing around me.
I didn't know if I was up or down.
– EMMANUEL BUSO, Haiti survivor

───────── IN BRIEF · FEBRUARY 2010 ─────────

{6} RIP @ 89, actor Ian Carmichael. ❦ The G7 said it would cancel Haiti's debt. ❦ The Irish National Liberation Army declared it would decommission its weapons. {7} Toyota announced a recall of the Prius after concerns about the car's brakes. ❦ RIP @ 82, John Dankworth [see p.61]. {8} Met Police Commander Ali Dizaei was sentenced to 4 years in jail for misconduct and perverting the course of justice. {9} Kraft announced it would close Cadbury's Bristol factory with the loss of *c*.400 jobs. {10} David Miliband lost an appeal to prevent the release of details of the alleged torture of Binyam Mohamed. {11} RIP @ 40, Alexander McQueen [see p.61]. {12} >15,000 Nato troops took part in Operation Moshtarak, an offensive to push the Taliban out of Helmand. ❦ 21-year-old Georgian Olympic luger, Nodar Kumaritashvili, died while practising in Vancouver; his team vowed to compete in his memory, and officials began an investigation into track safety [see p.317]. ❦ 8 Iraqis were arrested in connection with the 2003 deaths of 6 Royal Military Police officers in Majar al-Kabir. {13} A British soldier died during Op. Moshtarak. {14} 12 Afghan civilians were killed when a Nato rocket missed its target during Op. Moshtarak. ❦ The BNP voted to change its whites-only membership rules after the party was threatened with an injunction by the Equality & Human Rights Commission. ❦ RIP @ 89, Dick Francis [see p.62]. {15} >18 died when 2 trains collided in Belgium. {16} Dubai released the passport photos of 11 Europeans wanted in connection with the 20 January murder of al-Mabhouh. ❦ The MoD announced

Tiger Woods

that a British soldier killed in S Afghanistan may have been killed by 'friendly fire'. {17} SOCA launched an investigation into how fake passports were used in the murder of Mahmoud al-Mabhouh; Israel denied any responsibility. {18} After >10 years in power, Niger's President Mamadou Tandja was toppled by a coup, throwing the uranium-rich nation into chaos. ❦ January's economic figures revealed that the govt had borrowed a further £4·3bn. {19} Tiger Woods read a carefully worded statement to a hand-picked group of journalists; he apologised for his infidelities and said he would return to therapy. ❦ Former Cabinet minister James Purnell announced he would step down as an MP at the next election. ❦ In Vancouver, Britain's Amy Williams won gold in the skeleton [see p.317]. {20} Downing St denied claims in a new book by journalist Andrew Rawnsley that Brown bullied staff [see p.252]. ❦ >32 died after flooding hit Madeira. {22} >33 Afghan civilians travelling in a convoy were killed by a UN air strike in Uruzgan province. {23} A bomb exploded outside a courthouse in Newry, N Ireland; the police said it was a 'miracle' that no one was killed, since they had only been given a 17-minute warning. ❦ After weeks of tabloid intrigue, Cheryl Cole announced she was separating from her husband, Ashley. {24} 2 men were killed by an avalanche in Glencoe, Scotland. ❦ Toyota's president Akio Toyoda apologised for the faults that had caused 8·5m vehicles to be recalled. ❦ A killer whale caused the death of his trainer during a live show at SeaWorld, Orlando. {25} The DPP released new guidelines for cases of assisted suicide [see

We recognise legal reality ... and now, for one thing, they can't call us racist any more. – NICK GRIFFIN

─────── IN BRIEF · FEBRUARY – MARCH 2010 ───────

p.111]. {26} >17 died in a suicide attack on Kabul. ☙ Portsmouth became the first Premier League club to go into administration [see p.300]. {27} >214 died when an earthquake hit Chile; tsunami warnings were issued [see p.21]. {28} >50 died after storms swept W Europe; in France, flooding in the Vendée and Charente-Maritime regions killed >45. ☙ The Winter Olympics ended [see p.317].

MARCH · {1} RIP @ 71, Rose Gray [see p.62]. ☙ Conservative Party Deputy Chairman Lord Ashcroft revealed he had 'nom-dom' tax status. {2} BBC DG Mark Thompson announced that BBC 6 Music and BBC Asian Network faced closure [see p.138]. ☙ Jon Venables, one of the murderers of James Bulger, was returned to jail for breaking the terms of his release. {3} RIP @ 96, Michael Foot [see p.62]. {4} US-Turkish relations were strained when Congress voted to recognise as genocide the killing of >1m Armenians in Turkey during WWI. {5} Brown appeared before the Chilcot Inquiry; he backed the invasion and said that, as Chancellor, he had adequately funded the military. {6} Brown visited British troops in Afghanistan; the Tories called the move a 'cynical' ploy to deflect attention from his Chilcot appearance. ☙ Icelandic voters rejected a proposal to repay Britain and the Netherlands £3·4bn after the collapse of Icesave. {7} >35 were killed as Iraq went to the polls in the 2nd elections since the invasion. {8} Kathryn Bigelow's *The Hurt Locker* was the big winner at the Oscars [see p.156]. ☙ >500 people died after clashes between Christians and Muslims in Jos, Nigeria.

Kathryn Bigelow

The colonial attitude is still going strong. The UK should come to its senses.
– A. GUNNARSSON, former Icelandic MP

{9} Stormont voted overwhelmingly to devolve policing and justice powers to N Ireland. ☙ Israel announced the building of 1,600 new homes in disputed E Jerusalem. {10} 2 British women made pregnant >18 times by their abusive father received an apology from the agencies who failed to protect them; a serious case review discovered that, despite contact with >28 different agencies and >100 members of staff over 35 years, no action had been taken to protect the girls. ☙ RIP @ 38, *Lost Boys* actor Corey Haim. {11} Transport Sec. Lord Adonis announced plans for a high-speed Birmingham–London rail link. {12} BA cabin crew announced a 3-day strike from 20 March. ☙ 39 died in suicide blasts in Lahore. {14} >100,000 'red shirt' protesters attended an anti-govt rally in Bangkok [see p.31]. ☙ David Beckham tore his left Achilles tendon, ending his World Cup hopes. {15} Labour MP Ashok Kumar was found dead at his home; police said his death was not suspicious. ☙ The separation of Kate Winslet and Sam Mendes was announced. {16} It was reported that 2 teenagers had died after taking the 'legal high' mephedrone. {17} The govt requested advice on whether to ban mephedrone. ☙ Brown admitted erroneously telling the Chilcot Inquiry that spending on defence rose in 'real' terms every year under Labour: 'I do accept … that in one or two years defence expenditure did not rise in real terms.' {18} 2 army bomb disposal experts, Staff Sgts Olaf Schmid and Kim Hughes, were awarded the George Cross for bravery in Afghanistan; Schmid's award was posthumous. {19} 6 Birmingham City Council social workers were sacked over failings

─────── IN BRIEF · MARCH – APRIL 2010 ───────

of their children's services dept. {20} BA cabin crew began a 3-day strike. ❦ RIP @ 84, Harry Carpenter [see p.62]. ❦ A volcano near the Eyjafjallajökull glacier in Iceland erupted [see p.31]. {21} It was reported that 3 former Labour ministers – Stephen Byers, Patricia Hewitt and Geoff Hoon – had been covertly filmed offering to assist in influencing govt policy in exchange for payment; all denied any wrongdoing. ❦ Sarkozy's party, the UMP, performed badly in France's regional elections, winning 36% of the vote. ❦ The US Congress approved Obama's landmark health care reform.

Alistair Darling

{22} It was announced that David Cameron's wife, Samantha, was pregnant. {24} Chancellor Darling unveiled his Budget [see p.234]. ❦ Portugal's credit rating was downgraded. {25} Prince Charles visited troops in Afghanistan. ❦ Rail unions announced a 4-day strike from 6 April. {26} A S Korean Navy ship sank following an explosion near a disputed maritime border with N Korea. ❦ *The Times* and *Sunday Times* announced they would start charging for online content from June. ❦ 2 bombs exploded in Khalis, Iraq, killing *c.*42; Ayad Allawi won the Iraq election by a narrow margin. [27] Iraqi PM Nuri Kamal al-Maliki contested the election results; the death toll in the Khalis bombings rose to 59. {28}

When we checked some of the [election] papers we found a large percentage were forged. – NOURI AL-MALIKI

Obama visited Afghanistan and met with President Karzai and US troops. {29} 2 female suicide bombers attacked the Moscow Metro during the morning rush hour, killing *c.*38 and injuring >60. ❦ The Home Sec. announced he would seek to ban mephedrone and other 'legal highs' on advice from the Drugs Advisory Council. ❦ Alistair Darling, George Osborne,

& Vince Cable appeared on a Channel 4 'Chancellors debate'. {30} An Iranian nuclear scientist, missing since June 2009, was reported to have defected to the US; he later denied this. {31} 2 suicide bombers killed *c.*12 in Dagestan, a province in Russia's N Caucasus region. ❦ Heavy snow hit Scotland and N Ireland, causing travel chaos. ❦ Yasir Arman, Sudan's leading opposition candidate, withdrew from the presidential race blaming the conflict in Darfur and vote-rigging concerns.

APRIL · {1} >6 Sudanese opposition parties announced an election boycott. ❦ Afghan President Karzai accused foreign election observers of fraud in last year's disputed elections. ❦ A British soldier was killed in Helmand. ❦ A planned rail strike was banned by the High Court. {2} Israel launched air strikes on 'weapon sites' in Gaza. {3} In a radio interview, the Archbishop of Canterbury said that the Catholic Church in Ireland had lost 'all credibility' as a result of its handling of child sex abuse allegations; he later apologised. ❦ In Iraq, 25 people thought to have links with Sunni militias opposed to al-Qaeda were killed. ❦ Eugene Terre'Blanche was killed by 2 workers on his S African farm, apparently over a wage dispute. ❦ Tens of thousands of anti-govt protesters in Thailand gathered in Bangkok's main shopping area, demanding elections. {4} S African President Zuma called for calm following Terre'Blanche's death. ❦ 3 suicide car bombs in Baghdad killed >40. ❦ RIP @ 91, Alec Bedser, England bowler. {5} WikiLeaks released a military video which appeared to show US forces

IN BRIEF · APRIL 2010

killing 12, including 2 Reuters staff, in Baghdad in July 2007. ❦ >40 died in a suspected suicide attack at a political rally in NW Pakistan. {6} A series of bombs in Baghdad killed *c*.50. ❦ Brown announced a general election for 6 May [see p.16]. ❦ RIP @ 70, Corin Redgrave [see p.62]. {7} Flash floods and landslides killed >95 in Rio de Janeiro. ❦ The President of Kyrgyzstan fled the capital following anti-govt protests that killed >40. ❦ The Thai govt declared a state of emergency after protesters stormed the parliament [see p.31]. {8} US and Russia signed a nuclear arms reduction treaty. ❦ A landslide in Rio's Morro Bumba slum killed *c*.200. ❦ Opposition leaders in Kyrgyzstan claimed they had seized power, and called for President Bakiyev to resign. {9} Kyrgyzstan held a day of mourning for those killed in the protests. {10} Many of Poland's senior officials, including President Lech Kaczyński, died when their plane crashed in Russia [see p.63]. ❦ >20 died and hundreds were injured in Thailand when troops tried to disperse anti-govt protesters. {11} Polling began in Sudan's first election in >20 years. {12} A car bomb exploded outside MI5's N Ireland HQ shortly after justice and policing powers were transferred to Belfast; the Real IRA claimed responsibility. ❦ 47 world leaders met in Washington for a nuclear security summit. ❦ {13} The Kyrgyz interim govt stripped Bakiyev of his immunity and gave him a day to resign. ❦ The Red Cross announced that 8 of its staff had been kidnapped in DR Congo. ❦ The FSA fined two former Northern Rock executives and banned them from working in finance. {14} An earthquake in Qinghai

Gordon Brown

The Polish state must function and will function.
– Polish PM, DONALD TUSK

province, China, killed >400 and injured thousands. ❦ Brown admitted he had erred by not introducing tougher banking regulations when Chancellor. ❦ Iceland's Eyjafjallajökull glacier volcano erupted for the 2nd time in a month; *c*.800 people were evacuated as ice melted and water levels rose. {15} Bakiyev resigned and left Kyrgyzstan. ❦ A cloud of ash from Iceland's volcanic eruption forced the closure of British and European airspace [see p.31]. ❦ Rescue teams arrived in China's earthquake-stricken Qinghai province [see p.21]. ❦ Party leaders sparred in the first of 3 TV debates [see p.19]. {16} Mephedrone was made illegal. ❦ Goldman Sachs and one of its traders were accused of fraud by the US SEC; all denied any wrongdoing. {18} The death toll in China's earthquake rose to >1,300. {19} A partial recount of Iraq's election was ordered. {20} Airspace restrictions were lifted over parts of Europe. ❦ The FSA announced it would investigate Goldman Sachs. ❦ Inflation rose to 3·4% in March. {21} 11 people were missing, feared dead, following an explosion at the Deepwater Horizon oil rig in the Gulf of Mexico. [see p.22] ❦ UK unemployment hit 2·5m. ❦ Airspace across most of Europe, and all British airports, reopened; Transport Sec. Lord Adonis admitted authorities had been 'too cautious'. ❦ The Pope promised 'church action' on child sex abuse scandals. {22} The Deepwater Horizon oil rig sank after burning for 36 hours; officials warned of a potential oil spill. ❦ The ONS reported that UK borrowing reached £163·4bn in the last fiscal year. ❦ Catholic bishops in England & Wales apologised to sex-abuse victims;

—————— IN BRIEF · APRIL – MAY 2010 ——————

a German bishop, alleged to have beaten children at a Catholic children's home in the 1970s and '80s, resigned. ❦ Brown, Cameron, and Clegg appeared in the 2nd TV debate. ❦ 5 grenades exploded among 'red-shirt' protesters in Bangkok, killing 1 and injuring >75. {23} Greece requested the activation of a joint EU-IMF debt rescue package. ❦ A Belgian bishop resigned after admitting the sexual abuse of a boy. ❦ >58 died in a series of bombs across Baghdad. {24} A leak was discovered at the site of the Deepwater Horizon rig. {25} RIP @ 82, author Alan Sillitoe [see p.63]. {26} Sudan's incumbent president, Omar al-Bashir, was declared the winner of elections. {27} The Met Police released a report saying that it could 'reasonably be concluded that a police officer struck the fatal blow' which killed Blair Peach in 1979. ❦ The Ukrainian govt approved extending the lease for a Russian naval base. ❦ World markets fell after Greece's credit rating was reduced to 'junk' and Portugal's was downgraded. {28} Spain's credit rating was downgraded, causing further market turmoil. ❦ In Guangdong Province, China, 15 primary school pupils and their teacher were injured by a man who attacked them with a knife. {29} The US Coast Guard said oil from Deepwater Horizon was leaking 5× faster than first estimated; Louisiana declared a state of emergency. ❦ Brown, Cameron and Clegg appeared in the final TV debate [see p.19]. ❦ In Jiangsu Province, China, a man stabbed *c*.25 nursery pupils and 3 teachers. {30} Oil from the Deepwater Horizon spill was reported to have reached Louisiana's shores; the US halted all new drilling in

Eyjafjallajökull

BP is responsible for this leak.
BP will be paying the bill.
— BARACK OBAMA

the Gulf of Mexico. ❦ 5 pupils at a nursery in Shandong, China, were injured by a man who attacked them with a hammer before killing himself.

MAY · {1} In Athens, thousands of Greeks protested against govt austerity measures. ❦ A car bomb was found in Times Square, New York. {2} Eurozone members approved a joint EU-IMF bailout for Greece. ❦ Obama said BP would be liable for cleaning up the Deepwater Horizon spill. ❦ RIP @ 67, actress Lynn Redgrave [see p.62]. {3} Pakistani citizen Mohammad Ajmal Amir Qasab, the sole surviving gunman from the 2008 Mumbai terror attacks, was found guilty of murder and other charges by an Indian court. ❦ United Airlines and Continental announced a merger that would create the world's largest airline. {4} A US citizen was arrested in New York, on a Dubai-bound plane, in connection with the attempted Times Sq bombing [see p.207] ❦ Flights were grounded for several hours in Scotland, N Ireland, and Ireland due to fresh volcanic ash. ❦ Public sector workers in Greece went on strike; Communist Party protesters stormed the Acropolis. ❦ The Court of Appeal ruled that the govt could not rely on secret evidence to defend itself against a claim by 6 former Guantánamo Bay detainees. {5} 3 died in Athens after protesters firebombed a bank. ❦ Flight disruptions continued across Scotland, N Ireland, and Ireland. {6} UK voters went to the polls in general and local elections. ❦ Mumbai gunman Qasab was sentenced to death. ❦ Nigerian president Umaru

——— IN BRIEF · MAY 2010 ———

Yar'Adua died; acting president Good-luck Jonathan replaced him. ❦ Markets fell amid continuing fears over Greece. {7} The general election resulted in a hung parliament [see p.16]. ❦ World stock markets fell on fears that the EU could not contain the Greek crisis. {8} Flights to Europe and N America were disrupted by volcanic ash. ❦ Efforts to use a 'containment dome' to collect oil from the Deepwater spill failed. {9} RIP @ 92, singer Lena Horne. ❦ >12 died and >80 were trapped in 2 explosions at a Russian coal mine. {10} The EU agreed a £650bn stability package to prevent Greek debt contagion. ❦ The Unite union confirmed 4 5-day BA strikes. ❦ A mass grave was discovered in Serbia, containing the bodies of *c.*250 Kosovo Albanians. ❦ >100 died in a series of seemingly coordinated attacks across Iraq. {11} Fabio Capello named his 30-man World Cup squad. ❦ Execs from BP, Transocean, and Halliburton testified at a Senate hearing on the Deepwater explosion. ❦ David Cameron became PM [see p.16]. ❦ Airports in N Africa and Spain were closed by volcanic ash. {12} A man stabbed to death 7 children and 2 adults at a nursery in Shaanxi province, China; *c.*20 other kids were injured. ❦ A plane crashed just short of the runway in Tripoli, Libya, killing 103; a young boy was the only survivor. ❦ David Miliband announced he would stand as Labour leader. {13} The search for 24 people still missing after the Russian mine explosions was called off due to fears of more explosions; the death toll rose to 66. ❦ The Thai govt called on red-shirt protesters to leave their encampment in Bangkok. {14} Live rounds were fired as Thai troops

Thaksin Shinawatra

We will take resolute counter-actions against North Korea. – S Korean President, LEE MYUNG-BAK

clashed with anti-govt protesters; >8 died and >100 were injured. ❦ Shares fell across Europe and the euro fell amid fears about the eurozone debt bailout. {15} Ed Miliband confirmed he would stand as Labour leader. {16} An election recount in Iraq confirmed Ayad Allawi's victory. ❦ Airports across Britain were closed by volcanic ash. {17} George Osborne announced an emergency budget for 22 June. ❦ BA won a High Court ruling preventing strikes. {18} A suicide attack on a Nato convoy in Kabul killed *c.*18. ❦ UK inflation hit 3·7% in April. ❦ 2 Pakistani citizens arrested but not charged during an anti-terror operation in England in April 2009 won an appeal against their deportation. ❦ 2 British children were found dead in a Spanish hotel room; their mother was detained by police. {19} The partner of a British woman arrested in Spain on suspicion of murdering her 2 children appeared in a British court to face charges of child rape. ❦ Ed Balls, Andy Burnham, and John McDonnell said they would stand as Labour leader. {20} Diane Abbott announced she would stand as Labour leader. ❦ The Tories and Lib Dems unveiled further details of their coalition deal. ❦ The Court of Appeal overturned the High Court's injunction on strike action by BA cabin crew. ❦ The London 2012 Olympic mascots were unveiled. ❦ Paintings worth *c.*£430m were stolen overnight from the Paris Museum of Modern Art. ❦ S Korea accused N Korea of being responsible for the sinking of the *Cheonan* on 26 March. ❦ The US Senate passed a landmark financial regulatory bill. {21} BA reported annual losses of £531m. ❦ The Thai PM Abhisit Vejjajiva

─────────── IN BRIEF · MAY – JUNE 2010 ───────────

claimed that order had been restored in his country. {22} A plane crashed after landing at Mangalore airport, India; 158 of the 166 on board died. ❧ Talks between BA and Unite ended after protesters stormed the meeting. ❧ The Foreign Sec. William Hague, Dev. Sec. Andrew Mitchell, and Defence Sec. Liam Fox arrived in Afghanistan for talks with Afghan leaders. {23} The *News of the World* released footage showing the Duchess of York appearing to offer 'access' to Prince Andrew in exchange for £500,000 [see p.277]. ❧ Jamaica declared a state of emergency after supporters of a 'gang leader' wanted by the US, Christopher 'Dudus' Coke, barricaded an area of Kingston and clashed with police. {24} Osborne revealed the details of his £6·2bn spending cuts. ❧ BA cabin crew began a 5-day strike. ❧ The US announced it would participate in joint naval exercises with S Korea, putting pressure on N Korea. ❧ Two boys (10 and 11) were found guilty of the attempted rape of an 8-year-old girl. {25} S Korea announced it would cut ties with N Korea over the sinking of the *Cheonan*. ❧ Security forces in Jamaica stormed Christopher 'Dudus' Coke's stronghold in Kingston. {26} The death toll in Jamaica rose to >44; Coke's whereabouts remained unknown. ❧ Facebook

People think that we don't care about privacy, but that's not true.
– MARK ZUCKERBERG, Facebook

revealed changes to its privacy settings, following complaints. ❧ BP announced it would attempt a 'top kill' manoeuvre aimed at stemming the oil spill [see p.22]. ❧ Body parts thought to belong to Suzanne Blamires were found in the River Aire in W Yorkshire; police questioned a man suspected of killing her and two other women, Shelley Armitage and

Sarah Ferguson

Susan Rushworth; all three women were prostitutes. {27} A man was charged with the murder of 3 women; remains found in the River Aire were confirmed as belonging to Suzanne Blamires. ❧ Home Sec. Theresa May said ID cards would be scrapped. {28} A train collision in E India killed >70; Maoist saboteurs were blamed. {29} Treasury Chief Sec. David Laws apologised after it emerged he had claimed expenses to rent rooms from his partner, a move he said was motivated by a desire to keep private his homosexuality; Laws agreed to pay back £40,000, and he referred himself to the Parliamentary Standards Commissioner. ❧ RIP @ 74, Dennis Hopper [see p.63]. ❧ The UK came last in the Eurovision Song Contest; Germany won [see p.148]. ❧ BP said its 'top kill' manoeuvre had failed. {30} David Laws resigned as Chief Sec. to the Treasury. ❧ BA cabin crew began a 5-day strike. {31} 9 people, 8 of whom were Turks, were killed when Israeli forces stormed a flotilla of ships carrying aid to Gaza [see p.33].

JUNE · {1} The UN Security Council called for an investigation into Israel's raid on the flotilla of aid ships. ❧ A tropical storm killed *c*.179 in Central America. ❧ The leader of al-Qaeda in Afghanistan, Mustafa Abu al-Yazid, was reported to have been killed in a drone attack on 22 May. {2} Japan's PM Yukio Hatoyama resigned. ❧ In W Cumbria, taxi driver Derrick Bird murdered 12 people and injured 11, before killing himself [see p.23]. {3} Deepwater oil was reported to be nearing Florida's beaches. {4} Naoto Kan became PM of Japan. ❧ The euro fell to a 4-year

——————— IN BRIEF · JUNE 2010 ———————

low against the $ amid fears that Hungary was facing a Greek-style debt crisis. {5} BA cabin crew began a 5-day strike. ✤ 2 British soldiers were reported to have been killed in Helmand. ✤ Israeli soldiers boarded an Irish aid ship bound for Gaza. {7} An Indian court convicted 8 of causing 'death by negligence' in relation to the 1984 Bhopal disaster. {8} China said that 3 of its citizens had been shot by a N Korean border guard. ✤ Spanish public sector workers striked over austerity measures. {9} The UN Security Council approved new sanctions against Iran over its nuclear programme. ✤ 4 Nato soldiers died when their helicopter was shot down in Helmand. ✤ Funerals were held in Cumbria for the victims of Derrick Bird. ✤ Abbott, Balls, Burnham, and the Miliband brothers secured enough nominations for the Labour leadership ballot; John McDonnell withdrew. {10} Cameron visited Afghanistan and said that an increase in British troops was 'not remotely on the UK agenda'. {11} Nelson Mandela missed the opening of the World Cup following the death of his 13-year-old granddaughter. ✤ A judge ruled that 3 Labour MPs and 1 Tory peer could not claim 'parliamentary privilege' over alleged expenses fraud [see p.31]. ✤ >45 were reportedly killed and hundreds injured in ethnic clashes between Kyrgyzs and Uzbeks in S. Kyrgyzstan. {12} England drew its opening World Cup game against the US, 1–1 [see p.298]. {13} The death toll in Kyrgyzstan rose to >100; tens of thousands of Uzbek refugees fled to Uzbekistan. {14} Obama visited the Gulf Coast for the 4th time since the Deepwater explosion. {15} The Saville Inquiry into Bloody

David Petraeus

I extend my sincerest apology for this profile. It was a mistake reflecting poor judgement. – STANLEY McCHRYSTAL

Sunday exonerated those killed by British soldiers on 30 January 1973; Cameron apologised for the deaths, calling them 'unjustified and unjustifiable' [see p.67]. {16} UK unemployment rose to 2·47m in the 3 months to April. ✤ Flash floods in the S of France killed ≥19. ✤ BP agreed to create a $20bn compensation fund. {17} BP chief exec Tony Hayward was criticised for a 'lack of candour' at a Congressional hearing into the Deepwater spill. ✤ Israel announced it would ease its land blockade of Gaza. {18} In Utah, Ronnie Lee Gardner became the first American in 14 years to be executed by firing squad. ✤ A British soldier was killed in Helmand. ✤ The death toll in Kyrgyzstan rose to c.2,000. {19} The UN announced a £48m appeal to help 400,000 people displaced by fighting in Kyrgyzstan. {20} Flooding in S. China was reported to have killed >130 and forced the evacuation of 800,000. {21} The MoD confirmed the death of the 300th British casualty in Afghanistan. ✤ It was revealed that Jon Venables, one of James Bulger's killers, had been charged with possessing and distributing child pornography. {22} Osborne revealed his 'austerity budget' [see p.235]. ✤ Jamaican police arrested Chrisopher Coke. {23} Gen. Stanley McChrystal was dismissed as commander of US forces in Afghanistan, after his criticisms of the Obama regime were published by *Rolling Stone*; he was replaced by Gen. David Petraeus. ✤ US BP exec Robert Dudley took over the handling of the Deepwater crisis from Tony Hayward. ✤ 3 British soldiers were reported to have died in Helmand. {24} 4 British soldiers were reported to have died in a road

—— IN BRIEF · JUNE –JULY 2010 ——

accident in Helmand. ❦ In Spain, 12 people were killed and >14 injured after being hit by a train. ❦ At Wimbledon, John Isner beat Nicolas Mahut in the longest-ever pro tennis match [see p.314]. {25} The US Congress approved a major financial regulation reform bill. {26} Cameron and Obama met for talks in Canada. {27} At the G20 in Toronto, world leaders agreed to cut govt deficits by half by 2013; >500 protesters were arrested following clashes with police. ❦ England lost to Germany in the World Cup [see p.298]. {28} Home Sec. Theresa May announced a temporary limit on non-EU migrants allowed into the UK before the introduction of a permanent cap in April 2011. ❦ US authorities revealed 10 suspected Russian spies had been arrested in America. ❦ RIP @ 82, Nicolas Hayek, founder of Swatch. {29} The *Guardian* reported leaked govt data that showed cuts would result in the loss of 1·3m jobs over 5 years. {30} Taliban insurgents attacked a Nato air base in E Afghanistan. ❦ Justice Sec. Ken Clarke said 'radical reform' of the prisons system was needed and announced a 're-habilitation revolution'. ❦ The Office for Budget Responsibility predicted the loss of >600,000 public sector jobs by 2016.

C. 'Dudus' Coke

In tomorrow's world we must all work together as hard as ever if we are truly to be united nations. – ELIZABETH II

JULY · {1} 9 of the suspected Russian spies appeared in court; the FBI said that one had admitted ties to the 'service'. ❦ Charles Saatchi announced he would donate to the nation >200 works from his collection. {2} In Pakistan, *c*.42 were killed by suicide bombers at a Sufi shrine; *c*.175 were injured. ❦ RIP @ 75, Beryl Bainbridge. ❦ The family of Sakineh Mohammadi Ashtiani, a 43-year-old Iranian woman sentenced to death by stoning, launched a campaign to quash her 'bogus' conviction for adultery. {3} >200 died in the DR Congo after an overturned oil tanker exploded in a village; some of those killed were attempting to collect leaking fuel. ❦ The Treasury warned Cabinet ministers to prepare for 40% cuts. ❦ Serena Williams won her 4th Wimbledon title [see p.314]. ❦ Police in Northumbria began a search for Raoul Thomas Moat, who was suspected of shooting his ex-girlfriend and killing her lover [see p.23]. {4} A policeman was shot in Northumbria by Raoul Moat. ❦ Rafael Nadal won his 2nd Wimbledon title. {5} The govt announced a further £1·5bn in cuts, including scrapping Labour's school building programme; Nick Clegg announced a referendum on electoral reform for 5 May 2011. {6} Netanyahu and Obama met for talks at the White House. ❦ The Queen addressed the UN General Assembly for the first time since 1957. {7} The Defence Sec. Liam Fox announced that UK forces would hand control of Sangin, Helmand, to the US. {8} The 10 Russian spy suspects pleaded guilty to conspiracy; a 'spy swap' was arranged with Russia. ❦ Anti-terror 'stop and search powers' were scrapped. {9} A suicide bomber in Yakaghund, Pakistan, killed >50 at a meeting of tribal elders and local officials. {10} Raoul Moat shot himself following a 6-hour stand-off with police [see p.23]. ❦ The Yakaghund death toll rose to >100. {11} Officials announced that ≥14 Afghan police officers had been killed in targeted attacks in N Afghanistan. ❦ Spain won the World Cup [see p.26]. {12} In the Ugandan capital, Kampala,

>74 died in twin bombings targeted at people who had gathered to watch the World Cup final; a Somali militant group claimed responsibility. ❦ An Iranian judicial official said that Ashtiani's death by stoning would not be 'implemented for the time being'. ❦ Switzerland decided against extraditing Roman Polanski to the US to face charges of sexual abuse. ❦ 3 police officers were shot during rioting in Belfast. ❦ An Israeli military investigation into the attack on a Gaza aid flotilla blamed the violence on poor planning and intelligence. {13} BP began installing a new cap on the Deepwater well. ❦ A renegade Afghan soldier killed 3 British troops and injured 4 others in Helmand. ❦ France's lower house voted in favour of banning women from wearing face-covering veils in public. ❦ 82 police officers were reported to have been injured in the violence in Belfast. {14} UK unemployment fell to 2·47m. {15} BP announced that oil had stopped spilling from the Deepwater well. {16} A judge ruled that the Yorkshire Ripper, Peter Sutcliffe, should never be released from prison. ❦ 5 companies were ordered to pay fines of >£10m over the 2005 Buncefield oil depot explosion. {17} 4 British soldiers were reported to have been killed in Afghanistan. {18} Defence Sec. Liam Fox announced his aim to withdraw all British troops from Afghanistan by 2014. {19} >60 were killed when 2 trains collided in E India. {20} At a conference in Afghanistan, Western leaders supported President Karzai's plans for Afghan forces to take control of security by 2014. ❦ The former head of MI5, Baroness Manningham-Buller, told the Chilcot Inquiry that

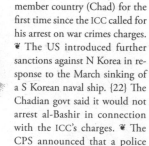
Tony Hayward

What country has ever arrested a sitting head of state?
– A.M. BACHIR, Chadian politician

the Iraq war had 'undoubtedly' increased the terrorist threat to Britain; she also said that prior to the war, the threat to the UK from Iraq was 'very limited'. {21} Sudanese President Omar al-Bashir travelled to an International Criminal Court member country (Chad) for the first time since the ICC called for his arrest on war crimes charges. ❦ The US introduced further sanctions against N Korea in response to the March sinking of a S Korean naval ship. {22} The Chadian govt said it would not arrest al-Bashir in connection with the ICC's charges. ❦ The CPS announced that a police officer filmed during the G20 protests pushing Ian Tomlinson to the ground shortly before he died would not face charges. ❦ BNP leader Nick Griffin was barred from attending the Queen's garden party, despite having been previously invited in his capacity as an MEP. {23} Jon Venables was jailed for child pornography. ❦ The UK economy was reported to have grown faster than expected, April–June 2010. ❦ A Dutch court fined an oil trader €1m for illegally exporting toxic waste to the Ivory Coast in 2006. {24} BP announced it would begin drilling off the coast of Libya. ❦ A search began in Afghanistan for 2 US soldiers the Taliban claimed to have kidnapped. ❦ 19 were killed and >300 injured in a stampede at the Love Parade music festival in Duisburg, Germany. {25} RIP @ 61, Alex Higgins [see p.63]. ❦ A Nato air strike in Helmand was reported to have killed >45 civilians. ❦ Many thousands of secret military documents concerning the war in Afghanistan were made public by the website, *WikiLeaks* [see p.35]. {26} Duch, the Khmer Rouge

—— IN BRIEF · JULY – AUGUST 2010 ——

prison chief who presided over Tuol Sleng prison, was found guilty of committing crimes against humanity by a UN-backed tribunal in Cambodia; he was sentenced to 35 years (reduced to 19 for being held illegally and for time already served). ❦ Pakistan denied allegations contained in the *WikiLeaks* documents that its intelligence agency had assisted Taliban insurgents in Afghanistan. {27} BP confirmed that Tony Hayward would step down by 1 October; the company announced quarterly losses of $17bn. ❦ Former UN weapons inspector Hans Blix told the Chilcot Inquiry: 'Some people maintain that Iraq was legal. I am of the firm view that it was an illegal war.' {28} 152 people died in a plane crash near Pakistan's capital Islamabad. ❦ Home Sec. Theresa May called for the end of ASBOs. ❦ Speaking in India, Cameron said Pakistan must not be allowed 'to look both ways and [be] able, in any way, to promote the export of terror'. {29} Cameron defended his 'frank' remarks about Pakistan, saying that he was not accusing the govt of promoting terrorism, but 'people within Pakistan'. ❦ Osborne stated that funding for the renewal of Trident must come from the MoD budget. {30} A coroner at the inquest into the Potters Bar rail crash warned that people were still at risk on UK railways. ❦ Greece mobilised its army and navy to ease a fuel crisis caused by striking lorry drivers. {31} It was reported that Soham murderer Ian Huntley would sue the prison service for failing in its duty of care following attacks on him by other inmates. ❦ The MoD announced that UK troops had found and destroyed a cache of bomb-making

Naomi Campbell

The fire destroyed everything. It is an enormous tragedy.
– DMITRY MEDVEDEV

materials during an operation in S Afghanistan. ❦ >400 people were killed in flooding in Afghanistan and Pakistan.

AUGUST · {1} In Pakistan, the death toll from flooding reached >1,100. {2} Rescue workers in Pakistan struggled to reach *c.*27,000 people stranded by the flooding; cholera was reported. ❦ BP announced it would attempt finally to seal the Deepwater well. ❦ Rockets reportedly fired from Egypt hit Jordan and Israel; 1 person was killed and 3 injured in Aqaba, Jordan. ❦ Obama announced that US strategy in Iraq would shift 'from a military effort led by our troops to a civilian effort led by our diplomats'. ❦ The Food Standards Agency said it would investigate claims that a farmer was selling milk produced by the offspring of a cloned cow. ❦ Russia declared a state of emergency in 7 regions as emergency services struggled to contain forest fires; 34 people were reported to have died. {3} Shortly before arriving in Britain, Pakistan's President Asif Ali Zardari said he believed the international community was 'in the process of losing the war against the Taliban'. ❦ 5 were killed in a border clash between Israel and Lebanon. ❦ The Food Standards Agency announced that meat from the offspring of a cloned cow had entered the food chain last year. {4} BP said that the 'static kill' manoeuvre on the Deepwater Horizon well was going well. ❦ Iran denied reports that an attempt had been made to assassinate President Ahmadinejad. {5} Naomi Campbell testified at the war crimes trial of Charles Taylor. ❦ Russia banned the export of

IN BRIEF · AUGUST 2010

grain for 6 months after wildfires and drought destroyed crops. ❦ BP pumped concrete into the Deepwater Horizon well. ❦ Wyclef Jean announced he would run in Haiti's presidential election. {6} Cameron and Zardari had formal talks at Chequers; they called the relationship between Britain and Pakistan 'unbreakable'. ❦ Flooding in Pakistan spread south, affecting *c.*12m; the death toll was estimated at >1,600. ❦ The US reported July job losses of 131,000 – twice as high as expected. {7} 10 aid workers were reported to have been killed in N Afghanistan. {8} >43 died in explosions at a market in Basra; reports differed on whether they were caused by a car bomb or a malfunctioning generator. ❦ After some confusion, Cameron ruled out a proposal to scrap free milk for <5s. ❦ Landslides in Gansu, China, were reported to have killed >127. {9} Netanyahu testified at an inquiry into the 31 May attack on the Gaza aid flotilla. ❦ The death rate in Moscow was reported to be twice its usual as the city suffered the combined effect of a heat wave and toxic smoke from nearby wildfires. ❦ Presidential elections were held in Rwanda. {10} The death toll in Gansu rose to >700. ❦ Suicide bombers attacked a guest house in Kabul, killing two Afghans. ❦ David Cameron defended plans to use private credit rating firms to tackle benefit fraud. {11} 8 Iraqi soldiers were killed in an attempted raid in the north of the country. ❦ 1,117 deaths were confirmed in Gansu; heavy rain threatened to cause further landslides. ❦ Rwanda's incumbent President, Paul Kagame, was re-elected with 93% of the vote; a number of opposition parties had been

B. Netanyahu

blocked from participating. {12} BAA staff voted in favour of a strike over pay. ❦ It was announced that 4 police officers would face prosecution over the December 2003 assault of terror suspect Babar Ahmad. ❦ Pakistan's President Asif Ali Zardari visited one of the areas affected by the country's worst-ever flooding. {13} The MoD confirmed that two British soldiers had been killed in Afghanistan. {14} Three children were injured by a bomb in Lurgan, N Ireland. {15} Fresh flooding hit Pakistan; Ban Ki-moon said: 'I have witnessed many natural disasters around the world, but nothing like this.' {17} >60 Iraqi soldiers and recruits died in a suicide bombing in Baghdad. ❦ Michael Douglas revealed he was beginning treatment for throat cancer. ❦ *c.*20 people were injured when a train hit a lorry in Suffolk. {18} Two 11 year-old boys found guilty of the attempted rape of an 8-year-old girl were given a three-year supervision order. {19} The A-level pass rate rose for the 28th year; 8% were awarded the new A* grade. {20} Israel and Palestine agreed to resume direct peace talks. {21} Loading fuel at Iran's first nuclear power station, in Bushehr, began. {22} Elections in Australia produced a hung parliament. ❦ After 17 days, 33 men trapped in a collapsed Chilean mine were discovered to be alive; rescue workers said it would take *c.*4 months to free them. {23} Video footage emerged of a middle-aged woman stroking a cat on a suburban street before dumping the animal in a wheelie bin. {24} An investigation concluded that the Catholic church, police and the British government colluded in covering up a priest's involvement in the 1972 Claudy

I think we had some straight talk, and we became friends.
– ASIF ALI ZARDARI

─────── IN BRIEF · AUGUST – SEPTEMBER 2010 ───────

bombings. ❦ A record 69·1% of GCSE pupils received a grade C or higher. ❦ Samantha Cameron gave birth to a girl, Florence [see p.121]. {25} >50 died in a string of bomb attacks across Iraq. ❦ Police found the body of an MI6 officer, Gareth Williams, inside a hold-all in the bath of his London flat. {26} Asil Nadir returned to the UK to face fraud charges, 17 years after he left the country; he denied any wrongdoing. {27} A UN draft report said killings in the 1993–2003 conflict in the DR of Congo could be classified as genocide. {28} Culture SoS Jeremy Hunt indicated that the BBC would face further cuts. ❦ *c.*50 insurgents attacked a Nato base in Afghanistan; there were no coalition casualties. {29} 4 Pakistani cricketers were questioned by police after the *News of the World* published allegations of a betting scam; all denied any wrongdoing [see p.309]. ❦ Sujawal, a town of *c.*250,000 in S Pakistan, was submerged by floods. {30} In Chile, work began on a rescue shaft to free the 33 trapped miners. {31} 4 Israeli settlers were killed by Hamas gunmen near Hebron. ❦ The General Medical Council ruled that the doctor who cut the lip of a rugby player during the 2009 'bloodgate' scandal could continue to practise medicine. ❦ Barack Obama announced the end of the US combat missions in Iraq [see p.37].

Tony Blair

Estamos bien, en el refugio, los 33.
(All 33 of us are fine in the shelter.)
– Note from the trapped Chilean miners

he was gay [see p.37]. {2} Israeli, Palestinian, and US leaders began peace talks in Washington. ❦ 13 people were rescued from the sea after an explosion at an oil rig in the Gulf of Mexico; the rig was not in production. {3} A US Middle East envoy said talks between Israeli and Palestinian leaders had been 'constructive'. {4} New Zealand suffered a 7·0 magnitude earthquake; despite 'widespread damage' to buildings, no deaths were reported. ❦ Protesters threw shoes and eggs at Blair at a book event in Dublin. {5} It was revealed that *c.*6m people had under or overpaid taxes under the PAYE system over the last 2 years; *c.*1·5m owed an average of £1,500 each. {6} *Daybreak*, Adrian Chiles and Christine Bleakley's new morning show, debuted on ITV. ❦ Tube workers began a 24-hour strike over plans to scrap 800 ticket-office jobs. {7} The 70th anniversary of the start of the Blitz was commemorated. ❦ >1m protested in France against plans to raise the age of retirement from 60 to 62. {8} A BP report blamed the Deepwater explosion on a 'sequence of failures involving a number of different parties'. ❦ RIP @ 77, David Cameron's father, Ian. ❦ {10} A US pastor who had threatened to burn copies of the Koran on the anniversary of 9/11 backed down, but not before ≥1 had died in rioting in Afghanistan and elsewhere. ❦ *Big Brother 2* winner Brian Dowling won *Ultimate Big Brother*. ❦ Osborne revealed plans to cut welfare spending by a further £4bn. {11} The 9th anniversary of the 9/11 attacks was commemorated across America.

SEPTEMBER · {1} Tony Blair's memoirs were published [see p.36] ❦ Three bombs exploded during a procession of Shia Muslims in Lahore, Pakistan; >25 were killed and *c.*170 injured. ❦ Foreign Sec. William Hague issued a personal statement denying rumours that

The daily chronicle will continue in the 2012 edition of Schott's Almanac.

SOME GREAT LIVES IN BRIEF

KEITH FLOYD
28·12·1943–14·9·2009 (65)

The epitome of the bon viveur chef (and the less-than-competent businessman), Floyd rescued TV cookery from banality with his irresistible, wine-fuelled, bow-tied, gravel-voiced rakishness. Bankruptcy and a chequered personal life did little to quell the man who was the first and best of a new breed of larger-than-life celebrity foodies.

STEPHEN GATELY
17·3·1976–10·10·2009 (33)

A member of the ballad-prone Irish band Boyzone, Gately helped his group rack up six No. 1s and four bestselling albums. In 1999, he became the first member of a boy band to reveal his homosexuality, in the pages of the *Sun*. Fans were undeterred by his announcement, and Gately went on to enjoy a successful solo career that included TV and stage performances. Sadly, his untimely death led to a row over homophobia in the press [see p.125].

LUDOVIC KENNEDY
3·11·1919–18·10·2009 (89)

A writer, thinker, and broadcaster of depth and integrity, 'Ludo' combined a high-profile TV career with a passionate advocacy of his liberal (and Liberal) beliefs. He fought miscarriages of justice (including Derek Bentley, the Birmingham Six, and the Guildford Four), campaigned against capital punishment, and championed choice with regard to euthanasia. He was knighted in 1994.

CLAUDE LÉVI-STRAUSS
28·11·1908–30·10·2009 (100)

A hugely influential French anthropologist, Lévi-Strauss re-shaped Western views of 'primitive' cultures by focusing on the universal structures that underpin myth-making, kinship, and other aspects of village life. Works such as the memoiristic *Tristes Tropiques* (1955) were beloved by the 1970s counterculture, though his ideas fell from fashion with the rise of 'post-structuralists' like Derrida and Foucault.

J.D. SALINGER
1·1·1919–27·1·2010 (91)

Though Salinger published only a handful of books, his 1951 chronicle of alienated adolescence, *The Catcher in the Rye,* became one of the most important novels of C20th America. Yet the devotion of his fans was not reciprocated, and in later life Salinger shunned the public eye, retiring to New Hampshire to focus on meditation and macrobiotics. He is said to have written 15 further novels, though he also spent much of his later life in legal battles to protect his much-cherished privacy.

JOHN DANKWORTH
20·9·1927–6·2·2010 (82)

Dankworth was one of the first true stars of British jazz. He found fame as a saxophonist and composer, worked alongside legends like Ella Fitzgerald and Oscar Peterson, defined the sound of swinging '60s cinema, and was a tireless advocate of music's power to defy genres. He married Cleo Laine in 1958, and in 2006 became the first British jazz musician to be knighted.

ALEXANDER MCQUEEN
17·3·1969–11·2·2010 (40)

The 'dark genius' of British fashion, McQueen was famous for his theatricality, sending models down the runway drenched in blood, or towering on claw-shaped stilettos. His imagination and technical skill drew fans from Isabella Blow to Lady Gaga, and a stint

———————— SOME GREAT LIVES IN BRIEF cont. ————————

designing for Givenchy brought finan-cial success. Despite once declaring, 'I'm not interested in being liked', many of his designs were influential – like the low-rise 'bumsters' that sparked a decade-long trend in trousers [see p.182].

DICK FRANCIS
31·10·1920–14·2·2010 (89)

Francis uniquely combined two utterly divergent careers. As a National Hunt jockey he rode >300 winners, and as a writer of equine-themed crime fiction he sold *c.*60 million books. The intrigue of both worlds combined in 1956 when Francis mysteriously failed to win the Grand National when Devon Loch, the Queen Mother's horse, belly-flopped just 50 yards before the finish.

ROSE GRAY
28·1·1939–28·2·2010 (71)

In 1987, aged 48, self-trained chef Rose Gray co-founded London's River Café with her friend Ruth Rogers. By 1998, the restaurant had a Michelin star, and its owners had helped rejuve-nate simple and seasonal British/Ital-ian food. In addition to championing the River Café style in books and on TV, Gray helped launch the careers of luminaries like Jamie Oliver and Hugh Fearnley-Whittingstall.

MICHAEL FOOT
23·7·1913–3·3·2010 (96)

Foot's ill-fated leadership of the Labour party (1980–83) may have caused the SDP schism and heralded the zenith of Thatcherism, but it did little to dent the reputation of one of the left's most respected and admired par-liamentarians. A writer, scholar, and orator of passion and conviction, Foot remained, in the words of *The Times*, 'the best-loved socialist of his time'.

HARRY CARPENTER
17·10·1925–20·3·2010 (84)

Although his commentary on a range of sports combined flair and expertise, for generations of fight-fans Carpenter was simply 'the voice of boxing'. He will be remembered for the special rela-tionships he enjoyed with Muhammad Ali and Frank Bruno, the latter for ever associating him with the unlikely catch-phrase – 'Know what I mean, 'Arry?'

CORIN REDGRAVE
16·7·1939–6·4·2010 (70)
LYNN REDGRAVE
8·3·1943–2·5·2010 (67)

A member of the third generation of the Redgrave theatrical dynasty, Corin Redgrave was known equally for his acting and his ardent devotion to left-wing politics. He flourished in the 1960s, memorably in 1962's *Chips With Everything*, before taking a break to devote himself to politics. His re-emergence in the 1990s led to a string of roles playing authority fig-ures in works from Shakespeare to Pin-ter, and a successful cinematic turn in *Four Weddings and a Funeral* [1994]. ❦ Despite her pedigree, Lynn Redgrave (Corin's younger sister) once said she was just an actor trying to make a liv-ing. After early acclaim playing the title role in *Georgy Girl* [1966], she moved on to Broadway and American TV – where audiences admired her wit but critics found her unfocused. She re-vived her critical reputation with films such as *Gods and Monsters* [1998], as well as by writing and performing plays that drew upon her celebrated family.

MALCOLM MCLAREN
22·1·1946–8·4·2010 (64)

Pop Svengali, agent provocateur, and irrepressible self-publicist, McLaren was a pioneer of the lucrative symbiosis of fashion and music. Famously, he formed The Sex Pistols from the boutique ('Sex') that he ran with his partner Vivienne Westwood, parlaying the punk band's success and notoriety into a lifelong career as a cultural iconoclast.

LECH KACZYŃSKI
18·6·1949–10·4·2010 (60)
As President of Poland from 2005 until his death in a plane crash, Kaczyński was a conservative who championed his country's interests while tussling with Moscow, Brussels, and Berlin. A former law professor, justice minister, and Mayor of Warsaw, he was known for a tough anti-crime stance, which was crystallised in the Law and Justice party he founded in 2001 with identical twin brother Jaroslaw Kaczyński – who ran unsuccessfully to replace him after his death.

ALAN SILLITOE
4·3·1928–25·4·2010 (82)
Inevitably called a 'kitchen sink' writer and grouped with the 'Angry Young Men' (both titles he rejected), Sillitoe championed an unvarnished approach to post-war working-class life. His first two (and best-known) works – *Saturday Night and Sunday Morning* and *The Loneliness of the Long Distance Runner* – set the tone for a lifetime in literature.

DENNIS HOPPER
17·5·1936–29·5·2010 (74)
Once one of Hollywood's leading wild men, Hopper danced with his demons during the 1960s and '70s, then overcame them to become one of the most prolific actors of the 1980s and '90s. He will be forever remembered as the biker Billy in 1969's counterculture classic *Easy Rider* (which Hopper also co-wrote and directed) – although his performances as the gas-huffing psycho in *Blue Velvet*, and the alcoholic father in *Hoosiers* (both 1986), among many others, made Hopper one of the iconic faces of late-C20th cinema.

LOUISE BOURGEOIS
25·12·1911–31·5·2010 (98)
Bourgeois' disquieting sculptures drew on a rich store of unresolved family issues, from the fleshy red latex of *The Destruction of the Father* (1974) to her giant steel spider *Maman* (1999). Ignored as an artist until the latter half of her life, Bourgeois rose to fame in the 1960s and '70s amid increased interest in female art; she remained a beacon of originality until her death.

JOSÉ SARAMAGO
16·11·1922–18·6·2010 (87)
In a career spanning 30 years and some 30 books, Saramago explored the perils of modern life and the sorrows of the human condition – sweetening both with touches of fantasy. In 1998 he became the first Portuguese-language writer to win the Nobel Prize for Literature, a reward for such international best-sellers as *Baltasar and Blimunda* (1982), *The Stone Raft* (1986), and *Blindness* (1997).

ALEX 'HURRICANE' HIGGINS
18·3·1949–24·7·2010 (61)
Snooker's 'greatest player' and 'the people's champion' had another apt nickname – hurricanes are awesome to observe at a distance, but devastating to experience up close. Sinking as many drinks as balls, Higgins turned the staid and suited game on its head, but at a heavy cost to his mental and physical wellbeing. The statistics fail to do justice to a man described by Steve Davis, no less, as snooker's 'only true genius'.

The World

The World is a book, and those who do not travel read only a page.
— AUGUSTINE OF HIPPO (354–430)

————— INTERNATIONAL WORDS OF NOTE —————

Selected vocabulary from the year's more unusual international stories: ❦ In Eastern Europe, press reports highlighted the growth of *perforated cities* – (sub)urban areas pockmarked by wastelands as a consequence of declining birthrates, &c. ❦ In Switzerland, the appointment of women to three top government posts focused attention on the term *Rabenmutter* ('raven mother'), used to disparage working mums. ❦ In Australia, the press noted a growing number of *kangatarians* – people who forego eating all meat except kangaroo, citing ethical and ecological concerns. (Others suggested the label *vegeroos*.) ❦ In Chile, residents who survived the country's February earthquake began referring to unsound buildings that still looked safe as *casas de mentira* – 'houses that lie'. ❦ In Germany, nostalgia for the country's erstwhile Communist east was labelled *ostalgie* – a portmanteau of *ost* (east) + *nostalgie* (nostalgia). ❦ In the Philippines, nationalistic fashionistas fond of wearing the country's map on clothing and accessories were dubbed *fashionalistas*. ❦ In Iraq, pundits began referring to the government as an *Iraqracy* – a state somewhere between democracy and autocracy. (The term was reportedly coined by US Army General David Petraeus.) ❦ In Hong Kong, protesters opposed to Chinese plans for a high-speed national rail network were nicknamed *the four antis*, because they were said by their critics to be 'anti-authority, anti-government, anti-establishment, and anti-tradition'. ❦ In southern China, a terrible drought was nicknamed *The Panzhihua Pain*, after a flower that grows in the region (Panzhihua is also the name of a city in the area). ❦ In Thailand, troops sympathetic to the country's 'red-shirt' protesters were called *watermelon soldiers* – a reference to their green uniforms and 'red' hearts [see p.31]. ❦ In America, the press reported on *crop mobs* of *agricurious* young people who converge on farms to volunteer for seasonal labour. ❦ In southern Sudan, commentators began using the bleak phrase *pre-failed state* to describe the region, a reference to its independence referendum planned for 2011. ❦ In Rwanda, open-air community courts used to try those accused of participating in the country's 1994 genocide were labelled *gacaca courts* (*gacaca* derives from the Kinyarwanda word for 'grass' or 'lawn'.) ❦ In Tibet, 20 sherpas scaled Mt Everest to retrieve years-worth of corpses and rubbish from the *Death Zone* – the altitude at which there is insufficient oxygen for normal human function. ❦ In France, a trend towards upscale halal products was said to be driven by the *beurgeois* – a play on *beur*, French slang for a person of N African descent. ❦ In

———— INTERNATIONAL WORDS OF NOTE cont. ————

Russia, a temporary ban on US poultry raised national pride, after years during which the country had been flooded with American chicken parts dubbed *Bush legs*. ❧ Young people in Japan reportedly became fond of the verb *obamu*, a pun on Barack Obama's name that means 'to persevere with optimism'. ❧ In Mexico, oligarch Carlos Slim Helú's prodigious business holdings led columnists to dub the country *Slimlandia* [see also p.239]. ❧ In Italy, a brand of mozzarella seized by authorities because of its puzzling tendency to turn bright blue was nicknamed *Smurf cheese*. ❧ Police in Amsterdam hoped to combat anti-Semitic attacks by dressing officers in Jewish garb and deploying them as *decoy Jews*. (The city's police also uses *decoy prostitutes*, *decoy gays*, and *decoy grannies*.) ❧ In S Korea, the Seoul government launched a parenting programme called *Sesalmaul* – a portmanteau combining *sesal* (a three-year-old) + *maul* (village). The neologism is based on a Korean proverb that says: 'The habits acquired by a three-year-old will last until she's 80.' ❧ The *New York Times* described the rise of *flashblooding* – a trend in some African countries where heroin addicts inject themselves with blood from other users in an attempt to share the high. ❧ The press reported that hard-working young graduates living crammed together on the outskirts of major cities in China are nicknamed *the ant tribe*. ❧ Germany's intelligence agencies founded *HATIF* – a help-line for those who want to escape radical Muslim groups. *Hatif* is Arabic for telephone, and the acronym stands for *Heraus Aus Terrorismus und Islamistischem Fanatismus*, or 'Leaving Terrorism and Islamist Fanaticism'. ❧ In Nigeria, a commentator described the country's political environment as driven by the 'philosophy of *Nsikology*' – mutually assured destruction likened to the behaviour of captive crabs (*nsiko*) trying to escape a soup pot. ❧ In Japan, a criminal trial drew attention to the widespread use of *wakaresaseya*, or 'splitter uppers' – professionals hired to begin affairs or dig up past misdeeds as grounds for divorce or job dismissal. ❧ In China, reports highlighted the plight of *shengnü* – 'leftover ladies' – independent, well-paid career women uninterested in marriage or unable to find husbands comfortable with their success. The group is also called *3S Women*, because they are Single, usually born in the Seventies, and said to be Stuck. ❧ The Scottish National Party threatened to lodge an official complaint against the German advertising association over the common use of the phrase *Schotten Preise* ('Scottish prices') to denote bargains and discounts. ❧ In Tanzania, women who use skin-lightening cream in the hope of attracting Chinese husbands were dubbed *the Michael Jacksons*. ❧ A (disputed) report suggesting that Pakistan led the world in online searches for pornography gave rise to the nickname *Pornistan*. ❧ In France, an MP in favour of the nation's proposed ban on full-face Islamic veils described the garb as *walking coffins*. ❧ In Japan, efforts to encourage working fathers to care for their children led the press to spotlight the rise of stay-at-home dads known as *iku-men* – a play on the Japanese for child-rearing: *iku-ji*. ❧ Survivors of the Haitian earthquake used the term *Goudou Goudou* as an onomatopoeic description of the tremors that caused so much damage and killed so many.

Further details on these, and other, stories can be found at schott.blogs.nytimes.com.

———————— NOBEL PEACE PRIZE ————————

The 2009 Nobel Peace Prize was awarded to BARACK H. OBAMA (1961–)

*for his extraordinary efforts to strengthen international
diplomacy and cooperation between peoples*

Barack Hussein Obama was born in Honolulu, Hawaii, in 1961, to a mother from Kansas and a father from Kenya. His early years were peripatetic; he moved to Indonesia in 1967, but returned to Hawaii in 1971 to finish school. He began college in LA in 1979, and finished in New York in 1983, earning a degree from Columbia. After college, he worked as a community activist in the churches and housing projects of Chicago's South Side, but left in 1988 to pursue a degree from Harvard Law School. There, he was elected the first black president of the prestigious *Harvard Law Review* – providing early evidence of his ability to break racial barriers. He then served in the Illinois State Senate from 1997–2004, leaving that year to become a US Senator. It was also in 2004 that Obama experienced what many commentators call his 'breakthrough', when he delivered the keynote address at the 2004 Democratic Convention. His rhetorical prowess and personal charm wowed the crowd and impressed many in politics and the media. And, while his Senate legislative record over the next few years was relatively undistinguished, Obama built a following that coalesced around him as a symbol and agent of 'change' – a concept that would become his

Barack Obama

defining leitmotif. After just over two years in the Senate, Obama announced a run for the Presidency. Amid widespread disappointment with the war in Iraq and concern for the economy at home, the US was eager to replace George W. Bush. Aided by powerful speeches, a mastery of social media, and undreamt-of levels of fund-raising, Obama rode a wave of optimism into the White House. On 4 November, 2008, he was elected the 44th President. ❦ Despite this momentum, Obama's Nobel win came as a surprise. Even his staunchest supporters on the Left felt the prize was premature; the Right was considerably less charitable. According to a CNN poll, only 19% of Americans thought Obama deserved the prize. The Nobel committee maintained that Obama's commitment to dialogue and multilateralism had ushered in a 'new climate in international politics'. Yet, the new President himself seemed unconvinced, calling his achievements 'slight' in his Nobel lecture. Paradoxically, he used this speech to outline his approach to war, in light of his recent decision to 'surge' troops into Afghanistan. While his lecture was generally well received, Obama was criticised for spending barely 24 hours in Oslo – perhaps cognisant that he still had much to prove.

In November 2009, Iranian human rights lawyer Shirin Ebadi said her 2003 Nobel Peace Prize medal had been taken from a Tehran bank on orders of Iran's Revolutionary Court. Iran claimed Ebadi owed taxes on her Nobel winnings, but an outraged Norway demanded the return of the prize, saying it was the first time authorities had seized a Nobel medal. The medal was returned a month later.

──────────── STATE APOLOGIES ────────────

In June 2010, Prime Minister David Cameron apologised on behalf of the British government for the events of 30 January 1972 – 'Bloody Sunday' – when 14 people in Northern Ireland were shot dead by British troops. Cameron announced that a 12-year inquiry, headed by Lord Saville, had found that none of those killed had posed a threat; that no warning had been given before shots were fired; that fleeing protesters and those helping the wounded were among those shot; and that many soldiers had lied afterwards about their actions. Cameron told the House of Commons: 'What happened should never, ever have happened. The families of those who died should not have had to live with the pain and hurt of that day, and a lifetime of loss. Some members of our armed forces acted wrongly. The government is ultimately responsible for the conduct of the armed forces. And for that, on behalf of the government – indeed on behalf of our country – I am deeply sorry.' ❧ While statements of government contrition were once a rarity, the latter half of the C20th saw a stream of public apologies, beginning after WWII and escalating after the Cold War. Below are some recent state apologies of note:

Apology from …	to	year	for
Serbia	victims	2010	*1995 Srebrenica massacre*
Japan	Korea	2010	*colonial rule 1910–45*
UK	victims	2010	*Thalidomide drug scandal*
UK & Australia	victims	2010 & 2009	*child migrants scheme*
Peru	Afro-Peruvians	2009	*abuse & discrimination*
Canada	native peoples	2008	*residential school system*
Australia	Aborigines	2008	*historic mistreatment*
Germany	Namibians	2004	*massacre of Herero people*
Croatia/Serbia-Mon.	citizens	2003	*'evils' of 1991–95 war*
Belgium	Congolese	2002	*1961 assassination of Congo PM*
Japan	leprosy patients	2001	*confinement in sanatoriums*
Germany	homosexuals	2000	*Nazi persecution*
Indonesia	East Timorese	2000	*rights abuses during occupation*
US	Native Americans	2000	*wrongs by Bureau of Indian Affairs*
Belgium	Rwandans	2000	*failures during genocide*
Queen Elizabeth	South Africans	1999	*Second Boer War*
Germany	Jews	1999	*Holocaust*
US	victims	1997	*Tuskegee syphilis study*
UK	Irish	1997	*indifference during potato famine*
Japan	victims	1995	*aggression during WWII*
France	Jews	1995	*Vichy collaboration*
Queen Elizabeth	Maori	1995	*seizure of land in New Zealand*
Austria	Jews	1994	*Holocaust*
South Africa	blacks	1993	*apartheid*
US	Native Hawaiians	1993	*overthrow of Hawaiian kingdom*
Japan	victims	1992	*use of wartime 'comfort women'*
Chile	victims	1991	*crimes of Pinochet regime*

[Sources include the book *The Sins of the Nation and the Ritual of Apologies* by Danielle Celermajer.]

WARS & SEVERE CRISES

There were 365 conflicts around the globe in 2009, according to Germany's Heidelberg Institute for International Conflict Research. Of these, 31 were fought with the use of 'massive violence', including seven wars and 24 'severe crises'. These 31 conflicts are listed below:

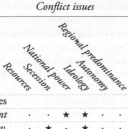

Conflict issues

WARS

Country	parties	Resources	Secession	National power	Ideology	Regional predominance	Autonomy
Afghanistan	Taliban, government	·	·	★	★	·	·
Israel	Hamas, Islamic Jihad, other groups, Israeli gov.	·	★	·	★	·	·
Pakistan	Taliban, various tribes	·	·	·	★	·	★
Pakistan	various Islamist militants, government	·	·	★	★	·	·
Somalia	rebel groups, government	·	·	★	★	·	·
Sri Lanka	Tamil Tiger rebels, government	·	★	·	·	·	·
Yemen	al-Houthi rebels, government	·	·	·	★	·	★

SEVERE CRISES

Country	parties	Resources	Secession	National power	Ideology	Regional predominance	Autonomy
Chad	various rebel groups, government	★	·	★	·	·	·
Colombia	FARC militants, government	★	·	·	★	·	★
DR Congo	FDLR rebel group, government	★	·	·	·	·	★
Ethiopia	ONLF rebels, government	★	·	·	★	·	·
India	Naxalites, government	·	·	·	★	·	·
Iran	Kurdish nationalist groups, government	·	·	·	·	★	·
Iraq	al-Qaeda insurgents, government	·	·	★	★	·	·
Iraq	other insurgents, government	·	·	★	★	·	·
Mexico	drug cartels, government	★	·	·	·	·	★
Burma/Myanmar	rebels, military groups, gov.	·	★	·	·	·	·
Nigeria	Boko Haram militants, government	·	·	·	★	·	·
Nigeria	various rebel groups, government	★	·	·	·	★	·
Pakistan	Sunni groups, Shiite groups	·	·	·	★	·	★
Peru	Shining Path rebels, government	★	·	·	★	·	★
Philippines	Abu Sayyaf militants, government	·	★	·	★	·	·
Philippines	MILF militants, government	★	·	·	★	★	·
Russia	Islamist rebels in Chechnya, government	·	★	·	★	·	·
Russia	Islamist rebels in Ingushetia, government	·	★	·	★	·	·
Saudi Arabia	al-Houthi rebels, government	·	·	·	★	·	★
Sudan (Darfur)	rebels, government, Janjaweed	★	·	·	·	·	★
Sudan	various ethnic groups	·	·	·	·	·	★
Thailand	Muslim separatists, government	·	★	·	★	·	·
Turkey	Kurdish militants, government	·	·	·	·	★	·
Uganda	Lord's Resistance Army rebels, government	★	·	★	·	·	·

According to the Institute, a SEVERE CRISIS is a conflict 'in which violent force is used repeatedly in an organized way'. The Institute defines a WAR, in part, as a conflict in which violent force is used 'in an organized and systematic way …[and the] extent of destruction is massive and of long duration'.

— MILITARY SPENDING —

The world spent $1,464bn funding militaries in 2008 – 2·4% of global GDP – according to the Stockholm International Peace Research Institute. Since 1999, all regions of the world have increased military spending, though Europe has done so less rapidly:

2008 spend (2005 $bn)	'99–'08 ±%
Africa............. 20·4	.........+40
Americas........... 603	..........+64
Asia & Oceania 206	..........+52
Europe.............. 320	..........+14
Middle East .... 75·6	..........+56
TOTAL............1,226	..........+45

The nations with the highest spending:

2008 spend (2008 $bn)	% of total
USA.................. 607	.... 41·5
China (est.)...........84·9	.........5·8
France ....65·7	.........4·5
UK...................65·3	.........4·5
Russia (est.) ....58·6	.........4·0

—— ARMS TRADE ——

The US, Russia, Germany, France and UK have been the biggest suppliers of conventional arms since the end of the Cold War, according to the Stockholm International Peace Research Institute. Below are the largest arms suppliers and their primary recipients, 2004–08:

Supplier	% global share	top recipients
USA	31	S Korea
		Israel
		UAE
Russia	25	China
		India
		Algeria
Germany	10	Turkey
		Greece
		S Africa
France	8	UAE
		Singapore
		Greece
UK	4	USA
		India
		Chile

——— DRUG USE WORLDWIDE ———

155m–250m adults aged 15–64 used an illicit drug in 2008 (3·5–5·7% of the global population), according to the UN Office on Drugs and Crime *World Drug Report 2010*. 11m–21m injected drugs, while 16m–38m were said to be 'problem drug users'. The report noted a recent shift away from cocaine and opiate use towards abuse of amphetamine-type stimulants and prescription drugs. Below are the high and low estimates for the number of drug users in various world regions:

(millions)	cannabis	opiates	cocaine	amphetamines	ecstasy
Africa	28–53	0·7–3	1–3	2–5	0·4–2
Americas	38–40	2·3–2·4	9–9·1	5–5·8	3–3·2
Asia	32–65	6–13	0·4–2	4–37	2–16
Europe	29–30	3·3–3·8	4·5–4·9	2·5–3	3·8–4
Oceania	2–3	0·12–0·15	0·33–0·39	0·4–0·6	0·8–0·9
WORLD	129–191	13–22	15–19	14–53	10–26

The report also noted a decline in the cocaine market in the US, although not in Europe, where the number of cocaine users doubled between 1998 and 2008. Globally, the retail cocaine market is worth $88bn, compared to $65bn for opiates, $32bn for trafficking in persons, and $1bn for illegal firearms.

──────────────── EXECUTIONS ────────────────

At least 714 people were known to have been executed in 2009, according to data released by Amnesty International in 2010. Unlike in previous years, Amnesty International chose not to release an estimate of executions in China, saying that figures based on public information would serve only to under-represent grossly the true number of those killed. Totals for Malaysia and North Korea were also not released. The 18 countries known to have executed people in 2009 are listed below:

Iran .... >388	Sudan.......... >9	Libya .... >4	China.... unknown
Iraq .... >120	Vietnam ...... >9	Bangladesh 3	Malaysia. unknown
Saudi Arabia..>69	Syria .... >8	Thailand........ 2	N Korea . unknown
USA 52	Japan 7	Botswana........ 1	[58 nations have the
Yemen .... >30	Egypt .... >5	Singapore........ 1	death penalty.]

──────────── STATE OF WORLD HUMAN RIGHTS ────────────

Amnesty International's 2010 *State of the World's Human Rights* focused on human rights abuses in 159 countries during the previous year. The report argued that many nations fail to hold human rights abusers to account, and found that Asian countries performed especially poorly in 2009. Among other cases, the report spotlighted migrant abuse in Korea, Japan, and Malaysia; mistreatment of civilians in Pakistan living along the Afghan border; and political violence in the Philippines. Overall, the Amnesty report documented the following human rights abuses:

Torture or ill-treatment.. 111 *countries*	Restrictions on free speech 96
Unfair trials 55	Prisoners of conscience 48

──────────── CORRUPTION PERCEPTIONS INDEX ────────────

Somalia and Afghanistan[†] are seen as the most corrupt nations in the world, according to the Corruption Perceptions Index released by Transparency International in 2009. The Index gauged the extent of public sector and government corruption, which was defined as 'the abuse of entrusted power for private gain'. Countries were scored between 0 (seen to be highly corrupt) and 10 (perceived to have low levels of corruption). The top and bottom-scoring nations appear below:

Most corrupt		*Least corrupt*	
1 .. Somalia............................ 1·1		1 .. New Zealand.................... 9·4	
2 .. Afghanistan..................... 1·3		2 .. Denmark........................ 9·3	
3 .. Myanmar......................... 1·4		3 .. Singapore .... 9·2	
4 .. Sudan .... 1·5		4 .. Sweden.......................... 9·2	
5 .. Iraq............................... 1·5		5 .. Switzerland..................... 9·0	

† A UN study found Afghans paid £1·5bn in bribes between autumn 2008–2009, about ¼ of the country's official GDP. The average bribe was £98, in a country where GDP per capita is £260 a year.

———————— DEVELOPMENT AID · 2009 ————————

In 2009, net development aid contributed by the Development Assistance Committee (a group of the world's major donors) rose 0·7% from 2008 to $119·6bn, according to the Organisation for Economic Co-operation and Development. In total, development aid accounted for 0·31% of the combined gross national income of Committee countries. A breakdown of 2009 development aid is below, with nations ranked by the share of their gross national income devoted to such aid:

Country	aid $m	% income			
Sweden	4,546	1·12	France	12,431	0·46
Norway	4,086	1·06	Germany	11,982	0·35
Luxembourg	403	1·01	Canada	4,013	0·30
Denmark	2,810	0·88	Austria	1,146	0·30
Netherlands	6,425	0·82	New Zealand	313	0·29
Belgium	2,601	0·55	Australia	2,761	0·29
Finland	1,286	0·54	Portugal	507	0·23
Ireland	1,000	0·54	US	28,665	0·20
UK	11,505	0·52	Greece	607	0·19
Switzerland	2,305	0·47	Japan	9,480	0·18
Spain	6,571	0·46	Italy	3,314	0·16
			Korea	816	0·10

Top recipients of UK aid			
Iraq	£353m	Pakistan	144	Sudan	110
India	339	Tanzania	141	Mozambique	109
Afghanistan	178	Ethiopia	140	DR Congo	107
		Bangladesh	140	[2008 data; net bilateral dev. aid]

———————— ASYLUM LEVELS & TRENDS · 2009 ————————

377,200 applications for asylum were recorded by the UN High Commissioner for Refugees (UNHCR) in 2009, an increase of just 100 applications from 2008. While total applications remained nearly the same, there were significant changes in the origin and destination of asylum seekers. Notably, applications from Iraqi citizens fell by 40% compared to 2008, while those from Afghanistan rose by 45%. The top nations of origin for applicants, and the top nations that received claims, are below:

Origin	applications	'08–'09 ±%	Recipient	applications	'08–'09 ±%
Afghanistan	26,803	+45	US	49,020	–1
Iraq	24,341	–40	France	41,980	+19
Somalia	22,558	+3	Canada	33,250	–10
Russia	20,367	0	UK	29,840	–5
China	20,100	+16	Germany	27,650	+25

Asylum applicants are those seeking formal recognition of refugee status. The UNHCR collects data on asylum applications in 44 industrialised countries, including nations in the EU, as well as Albania, Australia, Bosnia and Herzegovina, Canada, Croatia, Iceland, Japan, Korea, Liechtenstein, Macedonia, Montenegro, New Zealand, Norway, Serbia, Switzerland, Turkey, and the United States.

—————————— GROUP OF ? ——————————

The Group of 77 (G77) drew headlines in late 2009, when the bloc temporarily withdrew from Copenhagen climate summit talks [see p.27] over concerns it had been left out of the negotiations. The move focused attention on the host of 'G' coalitions that play a part in world politics. The origins of such groups lie in the oil crisis of the 1970s, when US, European, and later Japanese finance ministers began meeting in the White House library for informal discussions on economic matters (the officials became known as the 'Library Group'). In 1975, the group was established as the G6 (France, the US, Britain, Germany, Japan, and Italy). Other 'G' groups include:

G7 · *est. 1976* · The G6 + Canada

P8 · *est. 1994* · G7 + Russia (known as 'the political 8'; met alongside G7)

G8 · *est. 1998* · The G7 + Russia

G8+5 · *est. 2005* · G8 + Brazil, China, India, Mexico, and South Africa

G20 · *est. 1999* · Finance officials of the G8 + 11 other major economies + the EU

G77 · *est. 1964* · A UN subset of 77 developing nations

G24 · *est. 1971* · A chapter of the G77 formed to coordinate monetary and development issues

G2 · *unofficially proposed* · US + China

G3 · *unofficially proposed* · G2 + EU

The EU has participated in G7/G8 meetings since 1977, but is not included in the 'G number' because it is not a sovereign state. ☞ In 2009 it was announced that the G20 would take over economic discussions from the G8.

—————————— WALLS AROUND THE WORLD ——————————

In November 2009, celebrations around the world marked the 20th anniversary of the fall of the Berlin Wall, which stood 1961–1989. While the fall of this wall was greeted with jubilation, a number of other countries have since erected new barriers, or failed to tear old walls down. Below are some of the walls dividing peoples:

Location	erected	description
West Bank	2002	*'security barrier' separating Israelis and Palestinians*
N. Ireland	1969	*'peace lines' separating Catholics and Protestants*
Saudi Arabia	2009	*£1·8bn fence planned to encircle the entire nation*
Ceuta & Melilla	1990s	*designed to prevent immigration from Africa*
Cyprus	1964	*'green line' separating Greeks & Turks; reopened 2003*
Pakistan/Iran	2007	*built in Balochistan to stem black market, militants*
Rio de Janeiro	2009	*built around 13 favelas to protect a nearby forest*
US/Mexico	1991	*£1·5bn metal barrier to deter illegal immigrants*
India/Pakistan	1980s	*built by India to combat terrorism; covers c. ½ border*
Korean border	1953	*4km-wide strip that divides N & S Korea*
Western Sahara	1980	*2,700km wall built by Moroccans to keep out Sahrawi*
Botswana/Zimbabwe	2003	*built by Botswana to halt cattle disease, immigration*

[Source: BBC Mundo] In December 2009 the BBC reported that Egypt had begun constructing a 10–11km wall along its border with Gaza. The wall is made of bomb-proof, super-strength steel and extends 18 metres below the surface; it is designed to halt the smuggling of both goods and people.

——— POST-COMMUNISM CONTENTMENT ———

Although people who live in the former 'Iron Curtain' states of Eastern Europe generally approve of their country's transition from communism to capitalist democracy, they are less enthusiastic than they once were, according to a 2009 survey released by the Pew Global Attitudes Project. Below are the percentages of people in the countries canvassed who approved of the transition, in 1991 and 2009:

% approve of change to capitalism				*% approve of change to multiparty system*			
Nation	1991	2009	± %	Nation	1991	2009	± %
Czech Rep.	87	79	–8	East Germany	91	85	–6
East Germany	86	82	–4	Czech Rep.	80	80	0
Poland	80	71	–9	Bulgaria	76	52	–24
Hungary	80	46	–34	Lithuania	75	55	–20
Lithuania	76	50	–26	Hungary	74	56	–18
Bulgaria	73	53	–20	Ukraine	72	30	–42
Slovakia	69	66	–3	Slovakia	70	71	+1
Russia	54	50	–4	Poland	66	70	+4
Ukraine	52	36	–16	Russia	61	53	–8

The survey also discovered that while majorities in several countries believed that people had been economically better off under communism, the self-reported sense of 'life satisfaction' had increased since 1991 in every single country surveyed:

% who said people were economically 'worse off' compared to communism				*% who rated themselves 'satisfied' with life (7–10 on a 10-point scale)*			
Nation			2009	Nation	1991	2009	± %
Hungary			72	Poland	12	44	+32
Ukraine			62	Slovakia	13	43	+30
Bulgaria			62	Russia	7	35	+28
Lithuania			48	Czech Rep.	23	49	+26
Slovakia			48	Lithuania	13	35	+22
Russia			45	Ukraine	8	26	+18
Czech Rep.			39	Bulgaria	4	15	+11
Poland			35	Hungary	8	15	+7
Germany			[not asked]	Germany	44	47	+3

According to the Pew, many residents of former Eastern Bloc countries agree on the main problems their nations face. The top issues cited as 'very big problems' were[†]:

Country	top problem (% who agreed)		
Bulgaria	corruption (76)	Lithuania	corruption (78)
Czech Republic	corruption (71)	Poland	corruption (58)
East Germany	illegal drugs (50)	Russia	illegal drugs (54)
Hungary	corruption (76)	Slovakia	crime (55)
		Ukraine	corruption (70)

† Problems aside from the economy.

———————————— DISASTERS OF THE DECADE ————————————

The 2004 Indian Ocean tsunami was the deadliest natural disaster of the decade (2000–2009), according to data released in 2010 by the UN International Strategy for Disaster Reduction and the Centre for Research on Epidemiology of Disasters (CRED). Tabulated below are the five deadliest disasters of the decade:

Disaster	people killed	Disaster	people killed
Asian Tsunami, 2004	226,408	*Sichuan earthquake*, 2008	87,476
Cyclone Nargis, 2008	138,366	*Pakistan earthquake*, 2005	73,338
		Heat waves in Europe, 2003	72,210

In contrast to 2010 [see p.21], no 'mega-disasters'† occurred in 2009. According to CRED, 328 natural disasters were recorded, which killed 10,443 people, affected 112·8m others, and caused $34·9bn of damage. 2009's deadliest disasters were:

Disaster	month(s)	people killed‡
Earthquake, Indonesia	September	1,195
Flood, India	July–September	992
Typhoon Morakot (Kiko), Taiwan	August	630
Typhoon Pepeng (Parma), Philippines	October	539
Tropical storm Ondoy (Ketsana), Philippines	September	501
Extreme temperature, Australia	January–February	347
Flood, India	September–October	300
Earthquake, Italy	April	295
Hurricane Ida, El Salvador	November	275
Extreme temperature, Peru	May–August	274

Earthquakes were the deadliest type of disaster between 2000–09, causing 60% of disaster deaths. † Defined as disasters that kill >10,000 people or cause losses worth >$10bn. ‡ Death tolls include missing persons. ❦ According to the UK Department for International Development, between 1900–2004, 94% of disasters and 97% of disaster-related fatalities occurred within developing countries.

———————————— DEVELOPING CITIES & FLOODS ————————————

Manila, Alexandria, and Lagos are the cities in the developing world whose populations may be most vulnerable to the worsening storms and rising seas associated with climate change, according to a 2009 report by the Centre for Global Development. The report analysed coastal 'inundation zones' in 84 developing nations as they may look in 2100, based on a one-metre sea level rise and 10% increase in the intensity of a 1-in-100-year storm. The cities with the largest exposed populations were:

City	increase in pop. exposed to floods by 2100	City	increase in pop.
Manila, Philippines	3,438,334	Karachi, Pakistan	1,417,639
Alexandria, Egypt	2,723,464	Aden, Yemen	1,235,473
Lagos, Nigeria	2,121,263	Jakarta, Indonesia	836,130
Monrovia, Liberia	1,751,428	Port Said, Egypt	672,210
		Khulna, Bangladesh	635,950
		Calcutta, India	547,004

——————AIDS & HIV——————

The number of new HIV infections and HIV/Aids-related deaths has fallen significantly in the past decade, thanks to prevention efforts and better access to anti-retroviral drugs. According to the World Health Organization and the Joint UN Programme on HIV/Aids (UNAIDS), new HIV infections have fallen by 17% in the past eight years, while deaths related to Aids have fallen by >10% in the last five years. However, the lower number of Aids deaths means that, cumulatively, more people are living with HIV/Aids than in previous years. The number of people living with and dying from HIV/Aids around the world in 2008 is below:

	2008 infections	*2008 deaths*	*No. with HIV*	*% with HIV†*
Sub-Saharan Africa	1·9m‡	1·4m	22·4m	5·2
South and SE Asia	280,000	270,000	3·8m	0·3
East Asia	75,000	59,000	850,000	<0·1
Latin America	170,000	77,000	2·0m	0·6
North America	55,000	25,000	1·4m	0·4
W. & Cent. Europe	30,000	13,000	850,000	0·3
E. Europe & Cent. Asia	110,000	87,000	1·5m	0·7
Caribbean	20,000	12,000	240,000	1·0
Mid. East & N. Africa	35,000	20,000	310,000	0·2
Oceania	3,900	2,000	59,000	0·3
WORLD	2·7m	2m	33·4m	0·8

60m people have been infected with HIV since the beginning of the epidemic, and some 25m people have died – equivalent to about half the population of England. However, the spread of HIV appears to have peaked in 1996. [Source · UNAIDS, 2009] † Among adults. ‡ 72% of all cases diagnosed in 2008. ✱ In October 2009, the US lifted a rule banning those with HIV/Aids from entering the country without a waiver from Homeland Security. In April 2010, China also lifted decades-old travel and entry restrictions on those with the disease. Yemen, Oman, and others continue to ban HIV/Aids sufferers.

——————— INFECTIOUS DISEASES ———————

The global number of official cases of various infectious diseases reported in 2008, according to data released by the World Health Organization (WHO) in 2010:

Malaria 172,997,420	Pertussis [whooping cough] 151,568
Tuberculosis 2,654,410	Tetanus 16,628
Mumps 536,698	Diphtheria 7,088
Measles 281,972	Neonatal tetanus 6,658
Leprosy 248,983	Japanese encephalitis 5,071
Cholera 190,130	Polio myelitis [2009] 1,733
Rubella [German measles] 179,622	Plague [2009] 958

Approximately 1·3m people died of tuberculosis in 2008, according to the WHO, with most of the dead in Southeast Asia. Nearly 1m people died of malaria, mostly children in Africa – a child there dies of the disease every 45 seconds. Tuberculosis is the seventh leading cause of death in the world.

―――――――――――――― WOMEN'S HEALTH ――――――――――――――

Aids is the leading cause of death for women of childbearing age around the globe, according to a survey of women's health released by the World Health Organization in 2009. Below are the top causes of death for women at some key stages of life:

Age 0–9	*% of deaths*	*Age 15–44*	*% of deaths*
Lower respiratory infections	17·6	Aids	19·2
Diarrhoeal diseases	15·9	Maternal conditions†	14·6
Prematurity/low birth weight	10·5	Tuberculosis	6·4
Neonatal infections	10·1	Self-inflicted injuries	4·7
Birth asphyxia/birth trauma	7·6	Road traffic accidents	3·7

Age 10–19		*Age ≥60*	
Lower respiratory infections	8·9	Ischaemic heart disease	19·2
Road traffic accidents	5·6	Stroke	17·5
Self-inflicted injuries	5·5	Chronic obstruct. pulm. disease	8·2
Tuberculosis	4·5	Lower respiratory infections	5·3
Fires	3·8	Diabetes mellitus	3·3

Data are from 2004. † 99% of maternal deaths occur in developing countries.

―――――――――――― PREGNANCY AND ABORTION ――――――――――――

Unplanned pregnancies and abortions have decreased globally since 1995, according to a 2009 Guttmacher Institute report. Below are the estimated rates of pregnancy and unplanned pregnancy per 1,000 women (15–44) in 1995 and 2008:

(per 1,000 women)	*pregnancy rate* 1995	2008	*unplanned pregnancy rate* 1995	2008
World	160	134	69 (43%)	55 (41%)
More-developed world†	108	90	59 (55%)	42 (47%)
Less-developed world‡	173	143	71 (41%)	57 (40%)

According to the Guttmacher Institute, increased contraceptive use has contributed to the decrease in unwanted pregnancies and abortions. The chart below shows the percentage of married women (15–49) who used contraception in 1990 and c.2003:

% of women using contraception	1990	c.2003		1990	c.2003
			Africa	17	28
			Asia	57	68
World	54	63	Latin America	62	71
More developed world†	66	67	Europe	66	68
Less developed world‡	52	62	North America	71	72

† The 'more developed world' includes Australia, Europe, Japan, New Zealand, and North America. ‡ The 'less developed world' includes Africa, Asia (excluding Japan), Central America, Oceania (not Australia or New Zealand), and South America. All data are the most recent available in the report.

———————— GLOBAL HUNGER ————————

One in seven people around the world failed to get enough food to meet their basic needs in 2009, according to a report released by the United Nations Food and Agriculture Organization (FAO). In total, some 1·02bn went hungry – the highest number since record-keeping began in 1970. The FAO attributed the rising number of hungry people to higher food prices compounded by lower incomes, and noted that the recent global recession had added *c.*100m people to the tally of the world's hungry. Below is a breakdown of hunger around the world:

Region	*No. hungry (m)*		
Asia and the Pacific	642m	Latin America & the Caribbean	53m
Sub-Saharan Africa	265m	Near East and North Africa	42m
		Developed countries	15m

The Global Hunger Index, released by the International Food Policy Research Institute in 2009, also measured levels of hunger in nations around the world. Countries were assessed on three measures (percentage of the population who did not consume sufficient calories; prevalence of underweight children under five years old; and infant mortality rates), and were assigned a score on a 0–100 scale. The six countries in the list below were found to have 'extremely alarming' levels of hunger:

DR Congo	*score* 39·1	Sierra Leone	33·8
Burundi	38·7	Chad	31·3
Eritrea	36·5	Ethiopia	30·8

Data for the Index were collected 2002–07. Some nations facing severe hunger (including Afghanistan, Iraq, and Somalia) were omitted due to lack of data. Kuwait was found to have made the most progress reducing hunger since 1990, while the Dem. Rep. of the Congo made the least.

———————— WEIGHT AROUND THE WORLD ————————

A January 2010 *Reader's Digest* poll of 16,000 citizens in 16 countries revealed the nations in which people are most and least obsessed with how much they weigh:

Nation in which the most people ...	*(%)*
Had tried to lose weight at least once	Finland (83)
Had tried to lose weight because of doctor's orders	Mexico (46)
Had taken diet pills	China (37)
Said they wanted their husbands to lose weight (*of wives*)	US (51)
Said they wanted their wives to lose weight (*of husbands*)	India (48)
Blamed their genes for their weight	Russia (70)
Said being overweight could interfere with career advancement	India (67)
Said excess weight interfered with their sex lives	Australia & Mexico (tie; 52)
Said there was too much emphasis on weight	Brazil (83)

64% of respondents in the UK said they had tried to lose weight at least once, and 34% said they wanted their spouse to slim down. 55% said they felt society places too much emphasis on weight.

———————————— MOST POPULOUS COUNTRIES ————————————

India is projected to overtake China as the globe's most populous nation in 2025, according to US Census Bureau data released in 2009. China's population is expected to peak at 1·4bn in 2026, earlier than demographers anticipated, as a result of declining fertility. The most populous nations in 2010 and 2025 are estimated below:

2010		2025	
1 .... China	1·330bn	1 .... India	1·396bn
2 .... India	1·173bn	2 .... China	1·394bn
3 .... United States	310m	3 .... United States	357m
4 .... Indonesia	242m	4 .... Indonesia	278m
5 .... Brazil	201m	5 .... Brazil	231m
6 .... Pakistan	177m	6 .... Pakistan	217m
7 .... Bangladesh	158m	7 .... Nigeria	197m
8 .... Nigeria	152m	8 .... Bangladesh	192m
9 .... Russia	139m	9 .... Ethiopia	140m
10 ... Japan	126m	10 ... Mexico	130m

———————————————— MEGA-REGIONS ————————————————

Some of the world's largest cities are outgrowing their former boundaries and becoming interlinked mega-regions, according to the UN-HABITAT *State of the World Cities 2010/2011*. Economic growth and rapid urbanisation have created at least 40 of these so-called 'endless cities', which are said to account for 66% of the world's economic activity. Some of the mega-regions highlighted in the report include:

Mumbai–Delhi corridor...*population c.*180m
Hong Kong-Shenzen-Guangzhou, China....................................... 120m
Nagoya-Osaka-Kyoto-Kobe, Japan........................ 60m (projected by 2015)
São Paulo–Rio de Janeiro, Brazil 43m
Greater Ibadan-Lagos-Accra (West Africa) corridor *c.*20m

According to the UN report, there are now more people living in cities than living in rural areas.

———————————— WORLD BIRTH & DEATH RATES ————————————

Births	*time unit*	*deaths*	*change*
132,397,530	*per* YEAR	56,167,829	+76,229,701
11,033,128	*per* MONTH	4,680,652	+6,352,475
362,733	*per* DAY	153,884	+208,848
15,114	*per* HOUR	6,412	+8,702
252	*per* MINUTE	107	+145
4·2	*per* SECOND	1·8	+2·4

[Source: US Census Bureau, 2010 · Figures may not add up to totals because of rounding.]

THE RED LIST · 2009

The World Conservation Union (IUCN) publishes an annual 'Red List' of plant and animal species under threat – classifying them according to the following scheme:

Least Concern (LC) → *Near Threatened (NT)* → *Vulnerable (VU)* → *Endangered (EN)* → *Critically Endangered (CR)* → *Extinct in the Wild (EW)* → *Extinct (EX)*

47,677 species were included on the 2009 Red List, of which 17,291 (36%) were considered threatened with extinction. Of these, 9,075 were listed as Vulnerable, 4,891 as Endangered, and 3,325 as Critically Endangered. Below are some of the species whose status declined since the 2008 list, and the threats these species face:

Species	status change	threatened by
Kihansi Spray Toad	CR→EW	dam construction; chytridiomycosis
Hooded Grebe	NT→EN	climate change, salmon & trout in private lakes
Popondetta Blue-eye	LC→VU	human population growth
Samoana attenuata	EN→CR	the carnivorous snail Euglandina rosea
Toussaintia orientalis	VU→EN	forest loss

GLOBAL BIODIVERSITY LOSS

In May 2010, the UN announced that efforts to halt biodiversity loss had fallen short of a major target. In April 2002, 191 parties to the Convention on Biological Diversity committed themselves to 'significantly reducing' biodiversity loss by 2010, and to 21 subsidiary goals designed to encourage conservation and reduce environmental pressures. These aims were later endorsed by the World Summit on Sustainable Development, and incorporated into the UN Millennium Development Goals. However, in May 2010 the UN's *Global Biodiversity Outlook 3* revealed that the three main components of biodiversity (genes, species, and ecosystems) were all in decline, while the five pressures driving biodiversity loss (habitat change, over-exploitation, pollution, invasive species, and climate change) were constant or increasing. None of the 21 subsidiary goals had been fully met. While the news came as little surprise, it was a sobering addition to the UN's International Year of Biodiversity, meant to 'raise awareness about the crucial importance of biodiversity' during 2010.

NUMBER OF SPECIES WORLDWIDE

11m species of living things exist on Earth, according to a 2009 report from the Australian Biodiversity Information Service. The number of species that have been described (reported in the literature) and the total estimated to exist are listed below:

Taxonomic group	described	estimated
Chordates	64,788	80,500
Invertebrates	1,359,365	6,755,830
Plants	310,129	390,800
Fungi	98,998	1,500,000
Others	c.66,307	2,600,500
TOTAL	1,899,587	11,327,630

[c.18,000 new species are described per year]

―――――――――――― UNCONTACTED TRIBES ――――――――――――

About 100 'uncontacted' tribes still exist across the world, according to the tribal rights group Survival International. While the existence of these tribes has been documented (rendering the term 'uncontacted' somewhat equivocal), members of these tribes have never met with authorities, have never been studied, and, in general, resist contact with the outside world. The tribes are clustered in S America, India, and New Guinea, and face two main threats: Western diseases (to which they have little or no immunity), and violence (often from loggers, ranchers, or settlers). Many of these tribes are disappearing, taking with them unique languages [see p.81] and cultures. According to Survival International, the following tribes are closest to extinction:

Awá, Brazil   *300 people left (60 uncontacted), threatened by loggers & ranchers*
Ayoreo-Totobiegosode, Paraguay   *numbers unclear, land bulldozed by ranchers*
Envira River Indians, Peru   *fleeing into Brazil because of mahogany & cedar loggers*
Napo-Tigre Indians, Peru   *live between the Napo and Tigre rivers,*
                               threatened by multinational oil companies building wells
Rio Pardo Indians, Brazil   *probably <50 people left, on the run from loggers*

Listed below are some of the other uncontacted peoples around the world:

BRAZIL · Hi-merimá
Jururei · Kawahiva of Rio Pardo
Korubo · Massacó · Piripkura
Tsohom djapá · Uncontacted peoples
of Envira and Tarauacá rivers

PERU · Cacataibo · Isconahua
Mashco-Piro · Mastanahua

Matsigenka · Murunahua · Nanti
Pananujuri

ECUADOR · Waorani

INDIA · Sentinelese[†]

PAPUA · Korowai

† Anthropologists have labelled the Sentinelese the 'world's most isolated tribe'.

―――――――――――――― PEAK THEORIES ――――――――――――――

Peak theory, first proposed by US geophysicist M. King Hubbert in 1956, argues that extraction of finite natural resources (e.g., fossil fuels) follows a bell-shaped curve, in which new discoveries increase production until a maximum peak is reached, at which point production slows. The growing demand for natural resources has led to a number of theories forecasting the approximate date at which mankind will begin running out of its most precious commodities, including the following:

Coal   *peak usually forecast >100 years away, though new estimates are sooner*
Oil   *most hotly debated peak; some say it was reached in 1970, as Hubbert forecast*
Water   *overuse can produce peaks in some areas, such as China and the Middle East*
Gold   *one 2009 industry prediction said we may have reached the peak already*
Tuna   *sushi demand in Japan has driven tuna past its peak, analysts say*
Uranium   *some argue the peak occurred in the 1980s, others predict c.2035*

————————— LANGUAGES OF THE WORLD —————————

6,909 languages are spoken throughout the globe, according to the 2009 *Ethnologue*, a catalogue of the world's living languages that is produced by SIL, a faith-based organisation studying the world's lesser-known languages. (The *Ethnologue* defines a 'living language' as one passed parent to child as the language of daily communication.) Below are the world's most-spoken tongues by number of native speakers:

Language	speakers				
Chinese	1,213m	Portuguese	178	Vietnamese	69
Spanish	329	Russian	144	Marathi†	68
English	328	Japanese	122	French	68
Arabic	221	German, Std	90	Korean	66
Hindi	182	Javanese	85	Tamil	66
Bengali	181	Lahnda†	78	Italian	62
		Telugu†	70	Urdu	61

473 languages are classified by *The Ethnologue* as 'nearly extinct' – i.e., 'only a few elderly speakers are still living'. 182 of such languages come from the Americas, 152 come from the Pacific, 84 come from Asia, 46 from Africa, and nine from Europe. The nine European languages listed as being on the verge of extinction are:

Krimchak (from Ukraine) · Liv (from Latvia) · Pite Saami (from Norway)
Pite Saami (from Sweden) · Romano-Greek (from Greece) · Ter Saami (from the Russian
Federation) · Ume Saami (from Sweden) · Vod (from the Russian Federation)
Wymysorys (from Poland)

The *Ethnologue* also revealed the most and least linguistically diverse countries, based on Greenberg's Diversity Index, which measures the probability that two people chosen at random have different mother tongues. A Greenberg value of 1 means no one in the nation speaks the same language, while a value of 0 means everyone speaks the same tongue. The most and least linguistically diverse nations are:

MOST DIVERSE				LEAST DIVERSE			
No. nation	index	languages		No. nation	index	languages	
1 … P. New Guinea	0·990	830		1 … Vatican State	0·000	1	
2 … Vanuatu	0·974	114		2 … Saint Helena	0·000	1	
3 … Solomon Isls	0·967	71		3 … North Korea	0·000	1	
4 … C. African Rep.	0·959	82		4 … Falkland Isls	0·000	1	
5 … D. Rep. Congo	0·948	217		5 … B.I. Ocean Ter.	0·000	1	
6 … Tanzania	0·947	129		6 … Haiti	0·000	2	
7 … Cameroon	0·946	279		7 … Cuba	0·001	4	
8 … Chad	0·944	133		8 … Samoa	0·002	2	
9 … India	0·940	445		9 … South Korea	0·003	4	
10 … Mozambique	0·932	53		10 … Rwanda	0·004	5	

25 languages die out each year, according to linguist Claude Hagège's 2009 book *On the Death and Life of Languages*. This means half the world's *c.*5,000 living languages could be extinct by 2100.
† Lahnda is spoken primarily in Pakistan and India, Telugu in India and Malaysia, and Marathi in India.

THE PLANETS

Symbol	Name	Diameter km	No. of moons	Surface gravity m/s^2	Rings?	Distance from Sun ×10^6 km	Mean temp. °C	Day length hours
☿	Mercury	4,879	0	3·7	N	57·9	167	4,222·6
♀	Venus	12,104	0	8·9	N	108·2	457	2,802·0
⊕	Earth	12,756	1	9·8	N	149·6	15	24·0
♂	Mars	6,794	2	3·7	N	227·9	−63	24·6
♃	Jupiter	142,984	63	23·1	Y	778·4	−110	9·9
♄	Saturn	120,536	60	9·0	Y	1,426·7	−140	10·7
♅	Uranus	51,118	27	8·7	Y	2,871·0	−195	17·2
♆	Neptune	49,532	13	11·0	Y	4,498·3	−200	16·1

In May 2010, one of the dark belts that encircle Jupiter disappeared from view, puzzling astronomers. Images from the Hubble telescope later showed the belt was merely hiding behind ammonia clouds.

PLANETARY MNEMONIC

M any Mercury V ery Venus E ducated Earth M en Mars J ustify Jupiter S tealing Saturn U nique Uranus N inth Neptune

THE CONTINENTS

Continent	area km^2	est. population	population density
Asia	44,579,000	3,959m	88·8
Africa	30,065,000	910m	30·3
North America	24,256,000	331m	13·6
South America	17,819,000	561m	31·5
Antarctica	13,209,000	(Summer: 20k tourists & 3k scientists; winter: 1k scientists)	
Europe	9,938,000	729m	73·4
Australia	7,687,000	33m	4·3

THE OCEANS

Oceans make up *c.*70% of the globe's surface. The five oceans are detailed below:

Ocean	area km^2	greatest known depth at	depth
Pacific	155,557,000	Mariana Trench	11,033m
Atlantic	76,762,000	Puerto Rico Trench	8,605m
Indian	68,556,000	Java Trench	7,258m
Southern	20,327,000	South Sandwich Trench	7,235m
Arctic	14,056,000	Fram Basin	4,665m

———————— A WORLD OF SUPERLATIVES ————————

Highest capital city	La Paz, Bolivia	3,636m
Highest mountain	Everest, Nepal/Tibet	8,850m
Highest volcano	Ojos del Salado, Chile	6,908m
Highest dam	Nurek, Tajikistan	300m
Highest waterfall	Angel Falls, Venezuela	979m
Biggest waterfall (volume)	Inga, Dem. Rep. of Congo	43,000m³/s
Lowest point	Dead Sea, Israel/Jordan	*c.*-400m
Deepest point	Challenger Deep, Mariana Trench	*c.*-11,033m
Deepest ocean	Pacific	average depth -4,300m
Deepest freshwater lake	Baikal, Russia	1,637m
Largest lake	Caspian Sea	370,886km²
Largest hot desert	Sahara	9,065,000km²
Largest island	Greenland	2,166,086km²
Largest country	Russia	17,098,242km²
Largest population	China	1·3bn
Largest monolith	Uluru, Australia	345m high; 9·4km base
Largest landmass	Eurasia	*c.*54,000,000km²
Largest river (volume)	Amazon	28bn gal/min
Largest peninsula	Arabian	2,590,000km²
Largest rainforest	Amazon, South America	6·7m km²
Largest forest	Northern Russia	5,000,000 km²
Largest atoll	Kwajalein, Marshall Islands	16·39km²
Largest glacier	Lambert Glacier, Antarctica	96km×400km
Largest concrete artichoke	Castroville, USA	6m×4m
Largest archipelago	Indonesia	17,508 islands
Largest lake in a lake	Manitou, on an island in Lake Huron	104km²
Largest city by area	Hulunbuir, China	250,000km²
Smallest country	Vatican City	0·44km²
Smallest population	Vatican City	826 people
Smallest republic	Republic of Nauru	21km²
Longest beach	Cox's Bazar, Bangladesh	129km
Longest coastline	Canada	202,080km
Longest mountain range	Andes	*c.*8,900km
Longest suspension bridge	Akashi-Kaikyō, Japan	1,990m
Longest rail tunnel	Seikan, Japan	53·9km
Longest road tunnel	Lærdal, Norway	24·5km
Longest river	Nile	6,695km
Tallest inhabited building	Burj Khalifa, UAE	828m
Most land borders	China & Russia	14 countries
Most populated urban area	Tokyo, Japan	36·1m
Most remote place	Tibetan plateau	3 weeks to nearest city
Least populous capital city	Ngerulmud, Palau	pop. 391
Warmest sea	Red Sea	Average temp. *c.*25ºC
Longest bay	Bay of Bengal	*c.*2,000km
Largest banknote	Brobdingnagian bills, Philippines	14"×8½"

Unsurprisingly, a degree of uncertainty and debate surrounds some of these entries and their specifications.

——————— MOST PROSPEROUS COUNTRIES ———————

Finland is the most prosperous nation in the world, according to a 'Prosperity Index' released by think tank The Legatum Institute in 2009. The Index measured material wealth and 'quality of life' in the following nine areas: economic fundamentals; entrepreneurship; democratic institutions; education; health; safety; governance; personal freedom; and social capital. The top and bottom-scoring countries were:

#	nation	high marks in …	#	nation	low marks in …
1	Finland	*safety, governance*	104	Zimbabwe	*econ. fundamentals*
2	Switzerland	*democratic inst.*	103	Sudan	*democratic inst., safety*
3	Sweden	*entrepreneurship, social cap.*	101	Yemen	*econ. fundamentals*
4	Denmark	*governance, freedom*	101	C. Afr. R.	*entrepreneurship, health*
5	Norway	*education, safety, freedom*	100	Cameroon	*governance*

The United Kingdom came 12th – though rated highly for entrepreneurship and innovation, the nation scored lower on measures of health, safety and security, and education. See also p.85.

——————— MOST LIVEABLE CITIES ———————

A 2010 survey by the consultancy Mercer ranked the cities below as having the world's best living conditions, based on housing, schools, politics, and other factors:

1	Vienna, Austria	4	Vancouver, Canada [tie]
2	Zurich, Switzerland	4	Auckland, Australia [tie]
3	Geneva, Switzerland	6	Düsseldorf, Germany

——————— ENVIRONMENTAL PERFORMANCE INDEX ———————

Iceland does a better job of protecting its environment than any country in the world, according to the 2010 Environmental Performance Index by researchers at Yale and Columbia Universities. The Index ranked countries based on environmental public health, air quality, water resources, biodiversity, and other factors. Below are the nations at the top and bottom of the ranking, and scores for some nations of note:

Rank	country	index score	notable for …
1	Iceland	93·5	*high marks in water, health, climate change*
2	Switzerland	89·1	*high marks for biodiversity, forests, water*
3	Costa Rica	86·4	*high marks for forests, fisheries, biodiversity, water*
14	UK	74·2	*high marks for forests, air; lower for climate change*
44	Ireland	67·1	*high marks for forests, air, water; low for biodiversity*
50	Australia	65·7	*high on forests, fish, agriculture; low on climate change*
61	US	63·5	*high on forests, health; low on emissions*
121	China	49·0	*low on air pollution, emissions, ecosystem vitality*
123	India	48·3	*low on agriculture, air pollution, biodiversity*
163 (last)	Sierra Leone	32·1	*low on biodiversity, air, and water*

— DEVELOPMENT INDEX —

The UN Human Development Index annually ranks 182 countries by health, life expectancy, income, education, and other measures. The 2009 ranking was:

Most developed	Least developed
1 . . . . Norway	182 . . . . Niger
2 . . . . Australia	181 . . . . Afghanistan
3 . . . . Iceland	180 . . . Sierra Leone
4 . . . . Canada	179 .C. African Rep.
5 . . . . Ireland	178 . . . . Mali
6 . . . . . Netherlands	177 . . . Burkina Faso
7 . . . . Sweden	176 . . . . . DR Congo
8 . . . . France	175 . . . . Chad
9 . . . . . . Switzerland	174 . . . . . . Burundi
10 . . . . Japan	173 . . Guinea-Bissau

— PEACE INDEX —

The Global Peace Index, released by the Institute for Economics and Peace, ranks 149 nations on 23 measures of internal and external peace, including military spending, rates of violent crime, and respect for human rights. According to the 2010 Index, the most and least peaceful countries were:

Most peaceful	Least peaceful
1 . . . . New Zealand	149 . . . . Iraq
2 . . . . Iceland	148 . . . . Somalia
3 . . . . Japan	147 . . . . Afghanistan
4 . . . . Austria	146 . . . . Sudan
5 . . . . Norway	145 . . . . Pakistan
6 . . . . Ireland	144 . . . . Israel

— NOTES TO THE GAZETTEER —

The gazetteer on the following pages is designed to allow comparisons to be made between countries around the world. As might be expected, some of the data are tentative and open to debate. A range of sources has been consulted, including the CIA's *World Factbook*, Amnesty International, HM Revenue and Customs, &c.

Size km²	*sum of all land and water areas delimited by international boundaries and coastlines*
Population	*July 2010 estimate*
Flying time	*approximate travelling time from London Heathrow to capital city;*
	will vary depending on route and connecting flight, as well as direction travelled, &c.
GMT	*based on capital city; varies across some countries; varies with daylight saving*
Life expectancy at birth	*in years; 2010 estimate*
Infant mortality	*deaths of infants <1, per 1,000 live births, per year; 2010 estimate*
Median age	*in years; 2010 estimate*
Birth & death rates	*average per 1,000 persons in the population at midyear; 2010 estimate*
Fertility rate	*average theoretical number of children per woman; 2010 estimate*
HIV rate	*percentage of adults (15–49) living with HIV/AIDS; mainly 2007 estimate*
Literacy rate	*%; definition (especially of target age) varies; mainly 2003 estimate*
Exchange rate	*as at June 2009 (Financial Times)*
GDP per capita	*($) GDP on purchasing power parity basis/population; from 2009*
Inflation	*annual % change in consumer prices; years vary, generally from 2009*
Unemployment	*% of labour force without jobs; years vary, generally from 2008/9*
Voting age	*voting age; (U)niversal; (C)ompulsory for at least one election; entitlement varies*
Military service	*age, length of service, sex and/or religion required to serve vary*
Death penalty	*(N) no death penalty; (N*) death penalty not used in practice;*
	(Y) death penalty for common crimes; (Y*) death penalty for exceptional crimes only
National Day	*some countries have more than one; not all are universally recognised*

—— GAZETTEER · ALGERIA – SOUTH KOREA · [1/4] ——

Country	Size (km²)	Population (m)	Capital city	Phone access code	Phone country code	Flying time (h)	GMT
United Kingdom	243,610	61·3	London	00	44	—	n/a
United States	9,826,675	310·2	Washington, DC	011	1	7h50	–5
Algeria	2,381,741	34·6	Algiers	00	213	2h45	+1
Argentina	2,780,400	41·3	Buenos Aires	00	54	15h45	–3
Australia	7,741,220	21·5	Canberra	0011	61	25h	+10
Austria	83,871	8·2	Vienna	00	43	2h20	+1
Belarus	207,600	9·6	Minsk	810	375	4h40	+2
Belgium	30,528	10·4	Brussels	00	32	1h	+1
Brazil	8,514,877	201·1	Brasilia	00	55	16h	–3
Bulgaria	110,879	7·1	Sofia	00	359	3h	+2
Burma/Myanmar	676,578	53·4	Naypyidaw	00	95	13h	+6½
Cambodia	181,035	14·8	Phnom Penh	001	855	14h	+7
Canada	9,984,670	33·8	Ottawa	011	1	7h45	–5
Chile	756,102	16·7	Santiago	00	56	17h	–4
China	9,596,961	1·3bn	Beijing	00	86	10h	+8
Colombia	1,138,914	44·2	Bogota	009	57	13h	–5
Cuba	110,860	11·5	Havana	119	53	12h	–5
Czech Republic	78,867	10·2	Prague	00	420	1h50	+1
Denmark	43,094	5·5	Copenhagen	00	45	1h50	+1
Egypt	1,001,450	80·5	Cairo	00	20	4h45	+2
Estonia	45,228	1·3	Tallinn	00	372	4h	+2
Finland	338,145	5·3	Helsinki	00	358	3h	+2
France	643,427	64·1	Paris	00	33	50m	+1
Germany	357,022	82·3	Berlin	00	49	1h40	+1
Greece	131,957	10·7	Athens	00	30	3h45m	+2
Haiti	27,750	9·2	Port-au-Prince	00	509	20h30	–5
Hong Kong	1,104	7·1	—	001	852	12h	+8
Hungary	93,028	9·9	Budapest	00	36	2h25	+1
India	3,287,263	1·2bn	New Delhi	00	91	8h30	+5½
Indonesia	1,904,569	243·0	Jakarta	001	62	16h	+7
Iran	1,648,195	67·0	Tehran	00	98	6h	+3½
Iraq	438,317	29·7	Baghdad	00	964	14h30	+3
Ireland	70,273	4·3	Dublin	00	353	1h	0
Israel	22,072	7·4	Jerusalem/Tel Aviv	00	972	5h	+2
Italy	301,340	58·1	Rome	00	39	2h20	+1
Japan	377,915	126·8	Tokyo	010	81	11h30	+9
Jordan	89,342	6·4	Amman	00	962	6h	+2
Kazakhstan	2,724,900	15·5	Astana	810	7	8h15	+6
Kenya	580,367	40·0	Nairobi	000	254	8h20	+3
Korea, North	120,538	22·8	Pyongyang	00	850	13h45	+9
Korea, South	99,720	48·6	Seoul	001	82	11h	+9

——————— GAZETTEER · KUWAIT – ZIMBABWE · [1/4] ———————

Country	Size (km²)	Population (m)	Capital city	Phone access code	Phone country code	Flying time (h)	GMT
United Kingdom	243,610	61·3	London	00	44	—	n/a
United States	9,826,675	310·2	Washington, DC	011	1	7h50	−5
Kuwait	17,818	2·8	Kuwait City	00	965	6h	+3
Latvia	64,589	2·2	Riga	00	371	2h45	+2
Lebanon	10,400	4·1	Beirut	00	961	4h45	+2
Liberia	111,369	3·7	Monrovia	00	231	12h	0
Lithuania	65,300	3·5	Vilnius	00	370	4h	+2
Malaysia	329,847	26·2	Kuala Lumpur	00	60	12h25	+8
Mexico	1,964,375	112·5	Mexico City	98	52	11h15	−6
Monaco	2	30·5k	Monaco	00	377	2h	+1
Morocco	446,550	31·6	Rabat	00	212	5h45	0
Netherlands	41,543	16·8	Amsterdam	00	31	1h15	+1
New Zealand	267,710	4·3	Wellington	00	64	28h	+12
Nigeria	923,768	152·2	Abuja	009	234	6h15	+1
Norway	323,802	4·7	Oslo	00	47	2h	+1
Pakistan	796,095	177·3	Islamabad	00	92	10h	+5
Peru	1,285,216	29·9	Lima	00	51	15h15	−5
Philippines	300,000	99·9	Manila	00	63	15h	+8
Poland	312,685	38·5	Warsaw	00	48	2h20	+1
Portugal	92,090	10·7	Lisbon	00	351	2h30	0
Romania	238,391	22·2	Bucharest	00	40	3h15	+2
Russia	17,098,242	139·4	Moscow	810	7	4h	+3
Rwanda	26,338	11·1	Kigali	00	250	11h20	+2
Saudi Arabia	2,149,690	29·2	Riyadh	00	966	6h15	+3
Singapore	697	4·7	Singapore	001	65	12h45	+8
Slovakia	49,035	5·5	Bratislava	00	421	3h30	+1
Slovenia	20,273	2·0	Ljubljana	00	386	3h30	+1
Somalia	637,657	10·1	Mogadishu	00	252	12h45	+3
South Africa	1,219,090	49·1	Pretoria	00	27	11h	+2
Spain	505,370	40·5	Madrid	00	34	2h20	+1
Sudan	2,505,813	42·0	Khartoum	00	249	12h	+3
Sweden	450,295	9·1	Stockholm	00	46	2h30	+1
Switzerland	41,277	7·6	Bern	00	41	2h	+1
Syria	185,180	22·2	Damascus	00	963	6h30	+2
Taiwan	35,980	23·0	Taipei	002	886	14h30	+8
Thailand	513,120	66·4	Bangkok	001	66	14h20	+7
Turkey	783,562	77·8	Ankara	00	90	5h15	+2
Ukraine	603,550	45·4	Kiev/Kyiv	810	380	3h25	+2
Venezuela	912,050	27·2	Caracas	00	58	11h30	−4½
Vietnam	331,210	89·6	Hanoi	00	84	13h45	+7
Zimbabwe	390,757	11·7	Harare	00	263	12h50	+2

───── GAZETTEER · ALGERIA – SOUTH KOREA · [2/4] ─────

Country	Male life expectancy	Female life expectancy	difference	Infant mortality	Median age	Birth rate	Death rate	Fertility rate	Adult HIV rate	Literacy
United Kingdom	76·7	81·8	−5·1	4·8	40·5	10·7	10·0	1·7	0·2	99
United States	75·8	80·8	−5·0	6·1	36·8	13·8	8·4	2·1	0·6	99
Algeria	72·6	76·0	−3·5	26·8	27·1	16·7	4·7	1·8	0·1	70
Argentina	73·5	80·2	−6·7	11·1	30·3	17·8	7·4	2·3	0·5	97
Australia	79·3	84·3	−4·9	4·7	37·5	12·4	6·8	1·8	0·2	99
Austria	76·7	82·7	−6·0	4·4	42·6	8·7	10·1	1·4	0·2	98
Belarus	65·3	76·9	−11·7	6·3	38·8	9·8	13·8	1·3	0·2	100
Belgium	76·2	82·7	−6·5	4·4	42·0	10·1	10·5	1·7	0·2	99
Brazil	68·7	76·0	−7·3	21·9	28·9	18·1	6·4	2·2	0·6	89
Bulgaria	69·7	77·2	−7·4	17·3	41·6	9·4	14·3	1·4	0·1	98
Burma/Myanmar	62·2	66·9	−4·7	50·8	26·5	19·5	8·2	2·3	0·7	90
Cambodia	60·4	64·7	−4·3	53·0	22·5	25·8	8·0	3·0	0·8	74
Canada	78·7	84·0	−5·3	5·0	40·7	10·3	7·9	1·6	0·4	99
Chile	74·3	81·0	−6·7	7·5	31·7	14·5	5·9	1·9	0·3	96
China	72·5	76·8	−4·2	16·5	35·2	12·2	6·9	1·5	0·1	91
Colombia	71·0	77·8	−6·9	16·9	27·6	17·8	5·2	2·2	0·6	90
Cuba	75·4	80·1	−4·7	5·7	37·8	11·0	7·3	1·6	0·1	100
Czech Republic	73·7	80·5	−6·7	3·8	40·4	8·8	10·8	1·3	0·1	99
Denmark	76·1	81·0	−4·9	4·3	40·7	10·4	10·2	1·7	0·2	99
Egypt	69·8	75·1	−5·3	26·2	24·0	25·0	4·9	3·0	0·1	71
Estonia	67·7	78·8	−11·0	7·2	40·2	10·4	13·5	1·4	1·3	100
Finland	75·6	82·8	−7·1	3·5	42·3	10·4	10·2	1·7	0·1	100
France	77·9	84·4	−6·5	3·3	39·7	12·4	8·7	2·0	0·4	99
Germany	76·4	82·6	−6·2	4·0	44·3	8·2	11·0	1·4	0·1	99
Greece	77·2	82·5	−5·3	5·1	42·2	9·3	10·6	1·4	0·2	96
Haiti	59·7	63·1	−3·5	58·1	20·5	28·7	8·4	3·7	2·2	53
Hong Kong	79·2	84·9	−5·6	2·9	42·8	7·5	6·9	1·0	0·1	94
Hungary	69·5	78·1	−8·6	7·7	39·7	9·4	12·9	1·4	0·1	99
India	65·5	67·6	−2·1	49·1	25·9	21·3	7·5	2·7	0·3	61
Indonesia	68·5	73·7	−5·2	28·9	27·9	18·5	6·3	2·3	0·2	90
Iran	69·9	73·0	−3·1	34·7	27·6	17·3	5·8	1·7	0·2	77
Iraq	68·9	71·7	−2·8	43·2	20·6	29·4	4·9	3·8	0·1	74
Ireland	75·8	81·2	−5·5	5·0	35·3	14·1	7·7	1·9	0·2	99
Israel	78·7	83·1	−4·4	4·2	29·3	19·5	5·5	2·7	0·1	97
Italy	77·4	83·5	−6·1	5·4	43·7	8·0	10·8	1·3	0·4	98
Japan	78·9	85·7	−6·8	2·8	44·6	7·4	9·8	1·2	0·1	99
Jordan	78·6	81·3	−2·6	17·0	21·8	27·1	2·7	3·4	0·1	90
Kazakhstan	62·9	73·8	−10·9	25·0	29·9	16·7	9·4	1·9	0·1	100
Kenya	58·3	59·3	−1·0	53·5	18·8	35·1	9·3	4·4	6·7	85
Korea, North	61·5	66·9	−5·4	50·2	33·9	14·6	10·6	1·9	—	99
Korea, South	75·6	82·3	−6·7	4·2	37·9	8·7	6·2	1·2	0·1	98

—————— GAZETTEER · KUWAIT – ZIMBABWE · [2/4] ——————

Country	Male life expectancy	Female life expectancy	difference	Infant mortality	Median age	Birth rate	Death rate	Fertility rate	Adult HIV rate	Literacy
United Kingdom	76·7	81·8	−5·1	4·8	40·5	10·7	10·0	1·7	0·2	99
United States	75·8	80·8	−5·0	6·1	36·8	13·8	8·4	2·1	0·6	99
Kuwait	76·6	79·2	−2·6	8·8	26·4	21·6	2·3	2·7	0·1	93
Latvia	67·3	77·8	−10·5	8·6	40·4	9·9	13·6	1·3	0·8	100
Lebanon	73·3	76·4	−3·1	16·4	29·4	15·1	6·5	1·8	0·1	87
Liberia	55·1	58·1	−3·0	76·4	18·4	38·1	10·9	5·2	1·7	58
Lithuania	70·2	80·3	−10·1	6·5	39·7	9·2	11·3	1·2	0·1	100
Malaysia	70·8	76·5	−5·7	15·4	25·1	22·1	5·0	2·9	0·5	89
Mexico	73·5	79·2	−5·7	17·8	26·7	19·4	4·8	2·3	0·3	91
Monaco	85·8	93·9	−8·1	1·8	48·9	7·0	8·0	1·5	—	99
Morocco	72·6	78·9	−6·3	28·6	26·5	19·4	4·7	2·2	0·1	52
Netherlands	76·9	82·3	−5·4	4·7	40·8	10·3	8·8	1·7	0·2	99
New Zealand	78·5	82·5	−4·0	4·9	36·8	13·8	7·1	2·1	0·1	99
Nigeria	46·5	48·1	−1·6	93	19·1	36·1	16·3	4·8	3·1	68
Norway	77·4	82·9	−5·5	3·6	39·7	10·9	9·3	1·8	0·1	100
Pakistan	63·8	67·5	−3·7	65·3	21·2	25·1	7·1	3·3	0·1	50
Peru	69·1	73·0	−3·9	27·7	26·4	19·0	6·1	2·3	0·5	93
Philippines	68·5	74·5	−6·0	19·9	22·7	25·7	5·1	3·2	0·1	93
Poland	71·9	80·1	−8·2	6·7	38·2	10·0	10·1	1·3	0·1	100
Portugal	75·1	81·9	−6·8	4·7	39·7	10·1	10·7	1·5	0·5	93
Romania	69·2	76·4	−7·2	22·1	38·1	10·4	11·9	1·4	0·1	97
Russia	59·5	73·2	−13·7	10·3	38·5	11·1	16·0	1·4	1·1	99
Rwanda	56·1	58·9	−2·8	65·6	18·6	37·3	10·2	5·0	2·8	70
Saudi Arabia	74·4	78·7	−4·3	11·2	21·6	28·2	2·5	3·8	0·01	79
Singapore	79·5	84·9	−5·4	2·3	39·6	8·7	4·8	1·1	0·2	93
Slovakia	71·7	79·7	−8·0	6·7	37·3	10·6	9·6	1·4	0·1	100
Slovenia	73·5	81·0	−7·5	4·2	42·1	8·9	10·7	1·3	0·1	100
Somalia	48·1	51·9	−3·8	107·4	17·6	43·3	15·2	6·4	0·5	38
South Africa	50·1	48·3	1·8	43·8	24·7	19·6	17·0	2·3	18·1	86
Spain	76·9	83·7	−6·8	4·2	41·5	9·5	10·1	1·3	0·5	98
Sudan	51·6	53·5	−1·9	78·1	19·3	33·3	12·3	4·4	1·4	61
Sweden	78·7	83·4	−4·7	2·7	41·7	10·1	10·2	1·7	0·1	99
Switzerland	78·1	84·0	−5·9	4·1	41·3	9·6	8·7	1·5	0·6	99
Syria	72·1	77·0	−4·9	16·1	21·5	24·4	3·7	3·0	0·1	80
Taiwan	75·3	81·2	−5·9	5·3	37·0	9·0	6·9	1·2	—	96
Thailand	71·0	75·8	−4·8	16·9	33·7	13·2	7·2	1·7	1·4	93
Turkey	70·4	74·2	−3·8	24·8	28·1	18·3	6·1	2·2	0·1	87
Ukraine	62·6	74·7	−12·1	8·7	39·7	9·6	15·7	1·3	·1·6	99
Venezuela	70·7	77·0	−6·3	21·1	25·8	20·3	5·1	2·5	0·7	93
Vietnam	69·5	74·7	−5·2	21·6	27·4	17·3	6·0	1·9	0·5	90
Zimbabwe	48·0	47·1	0·9	30·9	17·8	31·6	14·9	3·7	15·3	91

Country	Currency	Currency code	£1 =	GDP per capita $	Inflation %	Unemployment %	Fiscal year end
United Kingdom	Pound=100 Pence	GBP	—	35,200	2·2	7·6	5 Apr
United States	Dollar=100 Cents	USD	1·5	46,400	−0·3	9·3	30 Sep
Algeria	Dinar=100 Centimes	DZD	110·6	7,000	5·7	10·2	31 Dec
Argentina	Peso=100 Centavos	ARS	5·8	13,800	7·7	8·7	31 Dec
Australia	Dollar=100 Cents	AUD	1·7	38,800	1·8	5·6	30 Jun
Austria	euro=100 cent	EUR	1·2	39,400	0·4	4·8	31 Dec
Belarus	Ruble=100 Kopecks	BYR	4,469·3	11,600	13	1·0	31 Dec
Belgium	euro=100 cent	EUR	1·2	36,600	0	7·9	31 Dec
Brazil	Real=100 Centavos	BRL	2·6	10,200	4·2	8·1	31 Dec
Bulgaria	Lev=100 Stotinki	BGN	2·3	12,600	1·6	9·1	31 Dec
Burma/Myanmar	Kyat=100 Pyas	MMK	9·5	1,100	6·5	4·9	31 Mar
Cambodia	Riel=100 Sen	KHR	6,223·8	1,900	−0·7	3·5	31 Dec
Canada	Dollar=100 Cents	CAD	1·5	38,400	0·3	8·3	31 Mar
Chile	Peso=100 Centavos	CLP	786·6	14,700	1·5	9·6	31 Dec
China	Renminbi Yuan=100 Fen	CNY	10·1	6,600	−0·7	4·3	31 Dec
Colombia	Peso=100 Centavos	COP	2,800·10	9,200	4·2	12·0	31 Dec
Cuba	Peso=100 Centavos	CUP	1·5	9,700	4·3	1·7	31 Dec
Czech Republic	Koruna=100 Haléru	CZK	30·9	25,100	1·5	8·1	31 Dec
Denmark	Krone=100 Øre	DKK	8·9	36,000	1·3	4·3	31 Dec
Egypt	Pound=100 Piastres	EGP	8·4	6,000	11·8	9·4	30 Jun
Estonia	Kroon=100 Sents	EEK	18·7	18,700	−0·1	13·8	31 Dec
Finland	euro=100 cent	EUR	1·2	34,900	0	8·5	31 Dec
France	euro=100 cent	EUR	1·2	32,800	0·1	9·1	31 Dec
Germany	euro=100 cent	EUR	1·2	34,100	0·3	7·5	31 Dec
Greece	euro=100 cent	EUR	1·2	32,100	1·2	9·5	31 Dec
Haiti	Gourde=100 Centimes	HTG	58·9	1,300	0	—	30 Sep
Hong Kong	HK Dollar=100 Cents	HKD	11·5	42,700	−0·5	5·3	31 Mar
Hungary	Forint=100 Fillér	HUF	333·6	18,600	4·2	10·8	31 Dec
India	Rupee=100 Paise	INR	67·8	3,100	10·9	10·7	31 Mar
Indonesia	Rupiah=100 Sen	IDR	13,358·9	4,000	4·8	7·7	31 Dec
Iran	Rial(=100 Dinars)	IRR	14,825·9	12,900	13·5	11·8	20 Mar
Iraq	Iraqi Dinar (=1,000 Fils)	IQD	1,726·4	3,600	6·8	15·2	31 Dec
Ireland	euro=100 cent	EUR	1·2	42,200	−4·5	11·8	31 Dec
Israel	Shekel=100 Agorot	ILS	5·7	28,400	3·3	7·6	31 Dec
Italy	euro=100 cent	EUR	1·2	30,300	0·8	7·7	31 Dec
Japan	Yen=100 Sen	JPY	135·1	32,600	1·3	5·1	31 Mar
Jordan	Dinar=1,000 Fils	JOD	1·0	5,300	−1·4	12·9	31 Dec
Kazakhstan	Tenge=100 Tiyin	KZT	217·6	11,800	7·3	6·3	31 Dec
Kenya	Shilling=100 Cents	KES	119·1	1,600	9·3	40·0	30 Jun
Korea, North	NK Won=100 Chon	KPW	119·1	1,900	—	—	31 Dec
Korea, South	SK Won=100 Chon	KRW	1,736·7	28,000	2·8	3·7	31 Dec

Country	Currency	Currency code	£1 =	GDP per capita $	Inflation %	Unemployment %	Fiscal year end
United Kingdom	Pound=100 Pence	GBP	—	35,200	2·2	8·0	5 Apr
United States	Dollar=100 Cents	USD	1·5	46,400	−0·3	9·3	30 Sep
Kuwait	Dinar=1,000 Fils	KWD	0·4	54,100	4·0	2·2	31 Mar
Latvia	Lats=100 Santims	LVL	0·8	14,500	3·5	17·1	31 Dec
Lebanon	Pound=100 Piastres	LBP	2,224·3	13,100	3·4	9·2	31 Dec
Liberia	Dollar=100 Cents	LRD	103·7	500	11·2	85	31 Dec
Lithuania	Litas=100 Centas	LTL	4·1	15,400	4·5	13·7	31 Dec
Malaysia	Ringgit=100 Sen	MYR	4·7	14,800	0·6	3·7	31 Dec
Mexico	Peso=100 Centavos	MXN	18·5	13,500	3·6	5·5	31 Dec
Monaco	euro=100 cent	EUR	1·2	30,000	1·9	0	31 Dec
Morocco	Dirham=100 Centimes	MAD	13·2	4,600	1·2	9·1	31 Dec
Netherlands	euro=100 cent	EUR	1·2	39,200	1·2	4·9	31 Dec
New Zealand	Dollar=100 Cents	NZD	2·1	27,300	2·1	6·2	31 Mar
Nigeria	Naira=100 Kobo	NGN	224·4	2,400	12·4	4·9	31 Dec
Norway	Krone=100 Øre	NOK	9·4	58,600	2·1	3·2	31 Dec
Pakistan	Rupee=100 Paisa	PKR	126·6	2,600	13·6	14·0	30 Jun
Peru	New Sol=100 Centimos	PEN	4·2	8,600	2·9	8·1	31 Dec
Philippines	Peso=100 Centavos	PHP	67·4	3,300	3·3	7·5	31 Dec
Poland	Zloty=100 Groszy	PLN	4·8	17,900	3·5	8·9	31 Dec
Portugal	euro=100 cent	EUR	1·2	21,800	−0·8	9·5	31 Dec
Romania	Leu=100 Bani	RON	5·1	11,500	5·6	7·8	31 Dec
Russia	Ruble=100 Kopecks	RUB	45·6	15,100	11·7	8·4	31 Dec
Rwanda	Franc=100 Centimes	RWF	867·6	900	10·4	—	31 Dec
Saudi Arabia	Riyal=100 Halala	SAR	5·6	20,400	5·1	11·7	31 Dec
Singapore	Dollar=100 Cents	SGD	2	50,300	0·2	3·0	31 Mar
Slovakia	euro=100 cent	EUR	1·2	21,200	1·6	11·4	31 Dec
Slovenia	euro=100 cent	EUR	1·2	27,900	0·9	9·2	31 Dec
Somalia	Shilling=100 Cents	SOS	2,245·0	600	—	—	—
South Africa	Rand=100 Cents	ZAR	11·1	10,100	7·1	24	31 Mar
Spain	euro=100 cent	EUR	1·2	33,700	−0·8	18·0	31 Dec
Sudan	Pound=100 Piastres	SDG	3·3	2,300	11·2	18·7	31 Dec
Sweden	Krona=100 Øre	SEK	11·4	36,800	−0·3	8·3	31 Dec
Switzerland	Franc=100 Centimes	CHF	1·6	41,700	−0·5	4·4	31 Dec
Syria	Pound=100 Piastres	SYP	69·5	4,600	2·6	8·5	31 Dec
Taiwan	Dollar=100 Cents	TWD	69·5	29,800	−0·9	5·9	31 Dec
Thailand	Baht=100 Satang	THB	47	8,100	−0·9	1·5	30 Sep
Turkey	Lira=100 Kurus	TRY	47·8	11,200	6·3	14·1	31 Dec
Ukraine	Hryvnia=100 Kopiykas	UAH	11·7	6,400	12·3	8·8	31 Dec
Venezuela	Bolívar=100 Centimos	VEF	6·4	13,100	27·1	7·9	31 Dec
Vietnam	Dong=100 Xu	VND	28,110·7	2,900	7	6·5	31 Dec
Zimbabwe	Dollar=100 Cents	ZWD	560·9	<100	5·1	95·0	31 Dec

—— GAZETTEER · ALGERIA – SOUTH KOREA · [4/4] ——

Country	Voting age	Driving side	UN vehicle code	Internet country code	Military service	Death penalty	National Day
United Kingdom	18 U	L	GB	.uk	N	N	—
United States	18 U	R	USA	.us	N	Y	4 Jul
Algeria	18 U	R	DZ	.dz	Y	N*	1 Nov
Argentina	18 UC	R	RA	.ar	N	N	25 May
Australia	18 UC	L	AUS	.au	N	N	26 Jan
Austria	16 U	R	A	.at	Y	N	26 Oct
Belarus	18 U	R	BY	.by	Y	Y	3 Jul
Belgium	18 UC	R	B	.be	N	N	21 Jul
Brazil	16 U	R	BR	.br	Y	Y*	7 Sep
Bulgaria	18 U	R	BG	.bg	N	N	3 Mar
Burma/Myanmar	18 U	R	BUR	.mm	N	N	4 Jan
Cambodia	18 U	R	K	.kh	Y	N	9 Nov
Canada	18 U	R	CDN	.ca	N	N	1 Jul
Chile	18 UC	R	RCH	.cl	Y	Y*	18 Sep
China	18 U	R	–	.cn	Y	Y	1 Oct
Colombia	18 U	R	CO	.co	Y	N	20 Jul
Cuba	16 U	R	CU	.cu	Y	Y	1 Jan
Czech Republic	18 U	R	CZ	.cz	Y	N	28 Oct
Denmark	18 U	R	DK	.dk	Y	N	5 Jun
Egypt	18 UC	R	ET	.eg	Y	Y	23 Jul
Estonia	18 U	R	EST	.ee	Y	N	24 Feb
Finland	18 U	R	FIN	.fi	Y	N	6 Dec
France	18 U	R	F	.fr	N	N	14 Jul
Germany	18 U	R	D	.de	Y	N	3 Oct
Greece	18 UC	R	GR	.gr	Y	N	25 Mar
Haiti	18 U	R	RH	.ht	–	N	1 Jan
Hong Kong	18 U	L	–	.hk	N	N	1 Oct
Hungary	18 U	R	H	.hu	N	N	20 Aug
India	18 U	L	IND	.in	N	Y	26 Jan
Indonesia	17 U	L	RI	.id	Y	Y	17 Aug
Iran	18 U	R	IR	.ir	Y	Y	1 Apr
Iraq	18 U	R	IRQ	.iq	N	Y	14 Jul
Ireland	18 U	L	IRL	.ie	N	N	17 Mar
Israel	18 U	R	IL	.il	Y	Y*	14 May
Italy	18 U	R	I	.it	N	N	2 Jun
Japan	20 U	L	J	.jp	N	Y	23 Dec
Jordan	18 U	R	HKJ	.jo	N	Y	25 May
Kazakhstan	18 U	R	KZ	.kz	Y	Y*	16 Dec
Kenya	18 U	L	EAK	.ke	N	N*	12 Dec
Korea, North	17 U	R	–	.kp	Y	Y	9 Sep
Korea, South	19 U	R	ROK	.kr	Y	N*	15 Aug

—————— GAZETTEER · KUWAIT – ZIMBABWE · [4/4] ——————

Country	Voting age	Driving side	UN vehicle code	Internet country code	Military service	Death penalty	National Day
United Kingdom	18 U	L	GB	.uk	N	N	—
United States	18 U	R	USA	.us	N	Y	4 Jul
Kuwait	21 U	R	KWT	.kw	Y	Y	25 Feb
Latvia	18 U	R	LV	.lv	N	Y*	18 Nov
Lebanon	21 C	R	RL	.lb	N	Y	22 Nov
Liberia	18 U	R	LB	.lr	N	N*	26 Jul
Lithuania	18 U	R	LT	.lt	Y	N	16 Feb
Malaysia	21 U	L	MAL	.my	N	Y	31 Aug
Mexico	18 UC	R	MEX	.mx	Y	N	16 Sep
Monaco	18 U	R	MC	.mc	—	N	19 Nov
Morocco	18 U	R	MA	.ma	Y	N*	30 Jul
Netherlands	18 U	R	NL	.nl	N	N	30 Apr
New Zealand	18 U	L	NZ	.nz	N	N	6 Feb
Nigeria	18 U	R	WAN	.ng	N	Y	1 Oct
Norway	18 U	R	N	.no	Y	N	17 May
Pakistan	18 U	L	PK	.pk	N	Y	23 Mar
Peru	18 UC	R	PE	.pe	N	Y*	28 Jul
Philippines	18 U	R	RP	.ph	Y	N	12 Jun
Poland	18 U	R	PL	.pl	Y	N	3 May
Portugal	18 U	R	P	.pt	N	N	10 Jun
Romania	18 U	R	RO	.ro	N	N	1 Dec
Russia	18 U	R	RUS	.ru	Y	N*	12 Jun
Rwanda	18 U	R	RWA	.rw	N	N	1 Jul
Saudi Arabia	21	R	SA	.sa	N	Y	23 Sep
Singapore	21 UC	L	SGP	.sg	Y	Y	9 Aug
Slovakia	18 U	R	SK	.sk	N	N	1 Sep
Slovenia	18 U	R	SLO	.si	N	N	25 Jun
Somalia	18 U	R	SO	.so	N	Y	1 Jul
South Africa	18 U	L	ZA	.za	N	N	27 Apr
Spain	18 U	R	E	.es	N	N	12 Oct
Sudan	17 U	R	SUD	.sd	Y	Y	1 Jan
Sweden	18 U	R	S	.se	Y	N	6 Jun
Switzerland	18 U	R	CH	.ch	Y	N	1 Aug
Syria	18 U	R	SYR	.sy	Y	Y	17 Apr
Taiwan	20 U	R	—	.tw	Y	Y	10 Oct
Thailand	18 UC	L	T	.th	Y	Y	5 Dec
Turkey	18 U	R	TR	.tr	Y	Y	29 Oct
Ukraine	18 U	R	UA	.ua	Y	N	24 Aug
Venezuela	18 U	R	YV	.ve	Y	N	5 Jul
Vietnam	18 U	R	VN	.vn	Y	Y	2 Sep
Zimbabwe	18 U	L	ZW	.zw	Y	Y	18 Apr

Society & Health

Your prayers should be for a healthy mind in a healthy body. — JUVENAL

————————— ANIMAL TESTING —————————

3,619,540 scientific procedures on living animals were started in Britain in 2009 (a fall of 1% from 2008) – according to the latest Home Office data released in July 2010. Below is a table of the species of animal upon which tests were performed.

BIRD *No. of procedures*	– Other carnivore 995
– Domestic fowl 114,301	– Horse and other equids 8,747
– Turkey (*Gallus domesticus*) 2,896	– Pig 3,757
– Quail (*Coturnix coturnix*) 20	– Goat 133
– Quail (not *Coturnix coturnix*) 500	– Sheep 38,003
– Other bird 9,064	– Cattle 4,358
REPTILE 460	– Deer 71
AMPHIBIAN 20,715	– Camelid 0
FISH 398,101	– Other ungulate 22
CEPHALOPOD 0	– Primate
MAMMAL	· Prosimian 0
– Mouse 2,628,556	– New World monkey 619
– Rat 333,865	· Marmoset, tamarin 0
– Guinea pig 19,159	· Squirrel, owl, spider monkey 0
– Hamster 3,157	· Other New World monkey 0
– Gerbil 928	– Old World monkey
– Other rodent 2,504	· Macaque 3,644
– Rabbit 16,562	· Baboon 0
– Cat 275	· Other Old World monkey 0
– Dog	– Ape
· Beagle 5,864	· Gibbon 0
· Greyhound 0	· Great ape 0
· Other incl. cross-breeds 59	– Other mammal 1,315
– Ferret 890	TOTAL 3,619,540

Below are 'designated establishments' and the number of experiments performed:

Public health laboratories .... *procedures* 11,686		>1%
Universities, medical schools 1,615,842		45%
NHS hospitals 21,870		1%
Government departments 92,666		3%
Other public bodies 529,818		15%
Non-profit-making organisations 315,490		9%
Commercial organisations 1,032,168		29%

———— UK POPULATION CHANGE ————

Historically, the main influence on UK population has been 'net natural change' (i.e., the difference between births and deaths). In recent years, however, net inflow of immigrants has become the main driver of population growth. According to December 2009 figures from ONS Social Trends, 62% of the UK population growth between 2001–08 was accounted for by immigration. This trend is expected to begin to reverse by 2011–21, with projected population increases suggesting that 58% of population change will be due to natural change, and the rest will be due to inward migration. UK population change† 1951–2021 is tabulated below:

(000's) Period	population at start of period	live births	deaths	net natural change	net migration and other	overall change
1951–61	50,287	839	593	246	6	252
1961–71	52,807	962	638	324	–12	312
1971–81	55,928	736	666	69	–27	42
1981–91	56,357	757	655	103	5	108
1991–2001	57,439	731	631	100	68	167
2001–08	59,113	710	591	119	191	310
2008–11	61,383	781	561	221	198	419
2011–21	62,649	791	544	248	183	431

† Figures after 2008 are projections. All figures are in thousands and based on annual averages. ❦ The ONS forecasts that the UK's population will grow by more than 8m over the next two decades, reaching 70m around 2029. According to the BBC, this is equivalent to adding eight new cities, each with a population roughly the size of Birmingham. England is projected to absorb 90% of the growth, though the country is already among the most densely populated in the European Union.

———— MOST AND LEAST POPULATED UK AREAS ————

The ten most and least populated places in the UK by local authority area, 2008:

Most populated local authority	people	Least populated local authority	people
Birmingham	1,016,840	Isles of Scilly	2,130
Leeds	770,830	City of London	7,940
Glasgow city	584,240	Moyle	16,880
Sheffield	534,460	Orkney Islands	19,890
Bradford	501,650	Shetland Islands	21,980
City of Edinburgh	471,650	Teesdale	24,800
Manchester	464,190	Berwick-upon-Tweed	25,920
Liverpool	434,860	Eilean Siar	26,200
City of Bristol	421,320	Ballymoney	30,110
Kirklees	403,940	Larne	31,290

The most *densely* populated local authority in the UK is the London borough of Kensington & Chelsea, which has *c*.14,900 people per square kilometre. All of the top ten most densely populated local authorities are located in London. [Source: ONS Social Trends · Released December 2009]

———————————————— BIRTH TRENDS ————————————————

708,711 babies were born in England and Wales in 2008, according to ONS data released in December 2009. This represented an increase of 19,000 births since 2007, reflecting a growing fertility rate. 54% of all mothers were aged 25–34 at the time of birth; 25% were aged under 25; and 20% of mothers were aged >35. Fathers tended to be older than mothers – 47% of babies born had mothers aged >30, but 63% had fathers in this age group. The average age of a woman giving birth in England and Wales in 2008 was 29·3 years; the average age for fathers was 32·4. The majority of births (55%) registered in 2008 were within a marriage, but an increasing number were born to couples who were not married but living together. The percentages of live births by age of mother, and type of registration, are below:

Registration type (%)	age <20	20–24	25–29	30–34	35–39	>40
Within marriage	6·1	28·1	57·2	71·7	70·2	64·1
Joint reg. same address	38·6	44·1	30·6	21·4	22·4	25·0
– different address	33·9	17·0	7·0	3·8	4·0	5·7
Sole registrations	21·4	10·8	5·2	3·1	3·4	5·1
TOTAL (numbers)	44,691	135,971	192,960	192,450	116,220	26,419

48% of births to UK-born mothers were within marriage, compared to 76% to women who were born outside the UK. These figures do not simply show a higher rate of marriage for those mothers born outside Britain, since there are many disparities – for example, 98% of births to women born in India, Pakistan, or Bangladesh were within marriage, compared to just 39% of births to women born in the Caribbean. In 2008, 43% of all births were first births to previously child-less women; 33% were second births; 14% third births; and 9% were fourth or subsequent births. Live births by mother's age and birth order are tabulated below:

Birth order	age <20	20–24	25–29	30–34	35–39	≥40	total
First child	36,870	74,609	85,471	70,105	32,176	7,268	306,499
Second child	7,006	46,877	63,930	70,083	40,995	8,029	236,920
Third child	806	12,136	29,034	30,333	24,051	5,310	101,670
Fourth and higher	9	2,349	14,525	21,929	18,998	5,812	63,622

———————————————— CONTRACEPTION USE ————————————————

75% of women aged 16–49 in Great Britain used birth control in 2008/9, accord-ing to ONS data released in October 2009. The most popular non-surgical meth-ods, among those using any form of birth control, are shown below by age of user:

% using ...	age 16–19	20–24	25–29	30–34	35–39	40–44	45–49	all
Pill	54	54	41	46	27	10	13	34
Male condom	65	50	42	32	24	21	11	33
IUD	–	4	7	6	12	9	11	7
Withdrawal	3	7	5	8	5	6	4	6
Injection	4	6	9	3	2	2	4	4

—————————— TWINS & MULTIPLE BIRTHS ——————————

Parents of twins are more likely to suffer financially, are less likely to work, and are more likely to divorce, than parents of single babies, according to a study by Stephen McKay of the University of Birmingham. The research, published in March 2010, revealed that the incidence of multiple births had increased from 1:100 births in 1970, to 1:65 today – largely as a result of in vitro fertilisation (IVF). This trend means that twins or triplets are often born to older parents, who are more likely to be married – a status that should bestow a social advantage. However, the research found that 62% of parents of twins or triplets reported they had become financially worse-off since their children were born, compared to 40% of other parents. Mothers of twins and triplets were 20% less likely to have returned to work 9 months after giving birth, compared to mothers of single babies. The financial pressures of raising twins may also partly explain why married couples with twins or triplets were 17% more likely to divorce than couples who had a number of single births.

—————————— MOST POPULAR BABY NAMES · 2009 ——————————

The top UK baby names in 2009, according to surveys by parenting club Bounty:

Jack	*nickname for John*	1	*? feminine version of Oliver*	Olivia
Oliver	*? from Latin for 'olive tree'*	2	*from the gemstone*	Ruby
Harry	*pet form of Henry*	3	*flower, symbol of purity*	Lily
Charlie	*pet form of Charles*	4	*French form of Sophia*	Sophie
Alfie	*pet form of Alfred*	5	*from the Latin Aemilia*	Emily
Thomas	*Greek form of Aramaic for 'twin'*	6	*Greek for 'young green shoot'*	Chloe
Joshua	*Jehova saves*	7	*from the Latin Gratia*	Grace
James	*English form of Jacomus & Jacob*	8	*allegedly created by Shakespeare*	Jessica
William	*from German for 'protector'*	9	*pet form of Eve*	Evie
Daniel	*from Hebrew for 'God is my judge'*	10	*blend of medieval Emilia & Amalia*	Amelia

David and Samantha Cameron named their daughter (born 24/8) *Florence Rose Endellion*. St Endellion is a parish and village in N Cornwall, near where the Camerons had been holidaying at the time of the birth. The site is named after a C6th Cornish saint, who may have been King Arthur's foster daughter.

—————————— REGRETTABLE NAMES ——————————

A 2010 survey of parents by OnePoll found that one in five respondents regretted the names they had chosen for their children. 19% said they were annoyed at the sheer number of children sharing the name, while 10% said the novelty of their choice had worn off in time. Below are the most-regretted names for boys and girls:

Regrettable boy's names	(1) William (2) Oliver (3) Jack (4) Alfie (5) Thomas (6) Joshua (7) Daniel (8) Charlie (9) Harry (10) James
Regrettable girl's names	(1) Chloe (2) Ruby (3) Olivia (4) Emily (5) Grace (6) Jessica (7) Charlotte (8) Evie (9) Sophie (10) Daisy

Schott's Almanac 2011

GIRLS' ATTITUDES SURVEY

Results from a Girlguiding UK survey published in November 2009 provided insight into the way young British women aged 7–21 viewed life, school, their future and their bodies. Respondents were asked what they wanted to be when they grew up:

Job (%)	*age 7–11*	*11–16*	*16–21*				
Hairdresser	17	14	2	Child-carer	3	9	5
Teacher	7	10	16	Actor	10	7	1
Vet	13	10	1	Doctor/nurse	5	6	10
Artist/designer	12	10	3	Lawyer/solicitor	2	4	6
				Scientist/engineer	0	1	6

When questioned about body image, it emerged that girls became less satisfied with their looks as they got older. Satisfaction with appearance is tabulated below:

(%)	7–11	11–16	16–21				
Very happy	44	17	7	Not very happy	10	18	23
Quite happy	39	47	62	Not at all happy	2	11	7
				Don't know	6	7	1

Older girls (aged 11–21) were asked if they would ever consider having cosmetic surgery. 12% of 11–16s reported that they would, compared to 24% of 16–21s. All age groups were asked what they would like to change about their bodies:

Would change (%)	*7–11*	*11–16*	*16–21*				
Thinner	8	21	33	Skin/spots	10	10	9
Body shape	6	14	9	Face	4	7	7
Teeth	14	9	9	Nose	2	6	6
Taller	7	7	6	Hair	12	6	3
				Nothing	23	7	5

The survey also revealed that a high proportion of girls of all ages still consider marriage to be important. 83% of 7–11s thought marriage should be for life, as did 70% of 11–16s, and 84% of 16–21s. However, there was a certain amount of ambivalence about whether marriage should come before parenthood: 41% of 11–16s agreed that marriage should come before children, compared with 49% of 16–21s (the youngest children were not asked this question). The older age groups were asked if they thought it was acceptable to get married more than once – 26% of 11–16s thought it was acceptable to get married several times, compared to 31% of 16–21s. Girls of all ages were also asked who they thought of as suitable role models for their age group. The top three role models for each group are below:

7–11	%	11–16	%	16–21	%
Cheryl Cole†	31	Cheryl Cole	28	Michelle Obama	17
Rebecca Adlington	8	Katie Price	15	Cheryl Cole	15
Katie Price	7	Michelle Obama	8	Rebecca Adlington	12

It seems that as girls grow up they become less convinced that being a girl is better than being a boy: aged 7–11, 90% think it is better to be a girl, compared to 81% of 11–16s, and 78% of 16–21s. † Cole was named the top female role model in another Sep 2009 National Mentoring Initiative poll.

———————— CHILDREN'S FEARS ————————

When it comes to the safety of their children, parents most often fear strangers and paedophiles, while young people worry primarily about gangs and knife crime, according to December 2009 research by the Department for Children, Schools and Families. Below are the top safety fears listed by each group, without prompting†:

Parents & carers of 5–17s	*% worried*	*Young people 12–17*	*% worried*
Strangers/paedophiles	50	Gangs/knife crime	34
Bullying	39	Strangers/paedophiles	20
Accidents outside the home	37	Anti-social behaviour‡	20
Smoking/drinking/drugs	27	Bullying	16
Anti-social behaviour‡	24	Accidents outside the home	13
Harmful/inappropriate content	11	Stress/depression/self-harm	5
Sexual activity/STDs/pregnancy	10	Sexual activity/STDs/pregnancy	3
Internet safety	9	Harmful/inappropriate content	3
Accidents in the home	6	Internet safety	2
Stress/depression/self-harm	6	Accidents in the home	2

† When asked to name any fear. When researchers read out a list of potential fears, the portion of respondents saying they had such fears increased. ‡ Including fighting, threatening behaviour, &c.

———— CHARACTERISTICS OF BULLYING VICTIMS ————

Though children from minority ethnic groups are often assumed to be targets for bullies, a study of 14 and 16-year-olds released by the Department for Education in 2010 found little to support this idea. While the characteristics of bullying victims are complex, the study found that the following traits generally made children more prone to attack: being white; being female (except for physical bullying); having a religion the child felt was important to them; having lived in care; being a young carer; living with a step-family; or having recently switched schools. Overall, 47% of 14-year-olds reported being bullied, though this number fell to 41% at 15, and 29% at 16. At 16, those who had reported being bullied were significantly more likely to be NEET (Not in Education, Employment or Training) than other young people.

———————— VISITING PARENTS ————————

39% of British adults aged >40 don't visit their parents as often as they feel they should, according to a 2010 poll commissioned by live-in care agency Christies Care. The most common reasons cited for not visiting were: physical distance (42%), busy lives (36%), and work commitments (33%). Tabulated below are the number of times respondents said they visited their parents in an average year:

0–2 *visits* … 11% *adults*	11–20	10	101–200		8
3–5 … 11	21–50	14	201–300		7
6–10 … 11	51–100	12	301+		17

———— NUMBER OF SEXUAL PARTNERS IN PAST YEAR ————

Age	zero partners		one		two or three		≥four	
%	♂	♀	♂	♀	♂	♀	♂	♀
16–24	31	16	44	60	17	19	8	5
25–29	7	5	71	86	11	7	10	2
30–34	4	5	80	89	12	6	4	1
35–39	10	8	79	86	9	5	2	1
40–44	5	8	82	89	10	3	3	0
45–49	7	14	89	84	3	2	1	0
50–69	16	–	81	–	3	1	1	–
TOTAL	14	10	74	80	8	8	4	2

Source: ONS. Data are 2008/9, Great Britain only · Data for women ≥50 were not collected.

———————— (IN)DECENT PROPOSALS ————————

The 2009 Durex British Sex Survey explored whether Britons would be prepared to have sex for remuneration and – if so – how much they would expect to be paid:

Proposition for sex	% who'd say yes		
A drink	3·4	£100,000	15·0
Dinner	3·1	£1,000,000	29·7
Pair of designer shoes	3·3	Mortgage paid	13·1
£100	5·5	Year's rent on home	9·1
£1,000	10·8	World Cup tickets	5·4
£25,000	14·1	Do it for free	13·2
		No way	43·5

———————————— DIVORCE ————————————

Although the number of divorces in England and Wales has been decreasing over the past few years, the number of older couples choosing to separate (so-called 'silver splitters') has been on the rise. Below are the number of divorces granted in various recent years, and the median age at divorce for women and men during those years:

Year	divorce decrees (thousands)	age at divorce ♂	♀
1961	25·4	–	–
1966	39·1	36·4	33·6
1971	74·4	36·6	33·6
1976	126·7	35·4	33·1
1981	145·7	35·4	33·2
1986	153·9	36·2	33·6
1991	158·7	37·0	34·3
1996	157·1	38·1	35·6
1997	146·7	38·4	36·0
1998	145·2	38·7	36·3
1999	144·6	39·2	36·9
2000	141·1	39·7	37·3
2001	143·8	40·0	37·7
2002	147·7	40·4	38·2
2003	153·5	40·9	38·7
2004	153·4	41·4	39·2
2005	141·8	42·0	39·8
2006	132·6	42·4	40·1
2007	128·5	42·7	40·5

[Source: Office for National Statistics]

PROFESSIONS & DIVORCE

Research published in the *Journal of Police and Criminal Psychology* in December 2009 looked at the link between profession and likelihood of divorce. The study suggested that those employed in extrovert industries with unpredictable hours were more likely to separate. A list of professions with their chance of divorce is below:

Profession	% chance of divorce
Dancers/choreographers	43
Bartenders	38
Massage therapists	38
Nursing/carers	29
Entertainers/sports persons	28
Waiters/waitresses	27
Roofers	27
Cleaners/domestic help	26
Chefs	20
Journalists	18
Urban planners	18
Librarians	17
Dieticians/fitness instructors	17
Writers	16
Police officers	16
Travel agents	16
Judges	12
Chief executives	10
Agricultural engineers	2

THE EFFECTS OF DIVORCE

38% of children whose parents had separated said that the divorce made them feel isolated, and 19% felt 'used' by their parents, according to a study released by law firm Mishcon de Reya in November 2009. The report, commissioned to mark the twentieth anniversary of the 1989 Children Act, found that far from improving the welfare of children whose parents were going through divorce, the process was still highly damaging. 70% of the parents questioned said that their children's welfare was their main priority as they went through a separation, yet 25% thought that their child had been so scarred by the separation that they had self-harmed or contemplated suicide. 68% of parents confessed to using their children indiscriminately as 'bargaining tools' during a divorce, and 49% admitted deliberately drawing out the divorce process to secure their desired outcome. Disturbingly, 20% of separated parents confessed that they had deliberately made their partner's experience 'as unpleasant as possible', regardless of the impact on their children. The children surveyed painted an equally depressing picture: 42% reported that they had witnessed aggressive arguments; 24% were forced by one parent to lie to the other; and 15% were asked to 'spy' on their mother or father. Perhaps most tellingly of all, 38% of all children interviewed said they never saw their father again after the divorce.

In November 2009, Australian economist Paul Frijters used his ongoing research into the impact of major life events to calculate the value of marriage and divorce. Frijters asked some of the 10,000 people he has tracked since 2001 what lump sum of money they would have to receive to make them as happy as their marriage would over a lifetime. On average, men valued marriage at £18,000; women valued it at just £9,000. When it came to separation, respondents were asked to compare the feelings of devastation caused by divorce to the loss of a devastating amount of money. On average, men said getting divorced would feel as if they had lost £61,500, whereas women likened divorce to losing just £5,000. It is unclear how much these nominal figures relate to the emotional impact of marriage or divorce, since the perception of what constitutes a large sum of money may differ between the sexes.

—— ATTITUDES TO RELIGIOUS & ETHNIC GROUPS ——

Attitudes to religious minorities in Britain are mainly favourable, according to a 2009 report by the Pew Global Attitudes Project. The report surveyed views on key ethnic and religious groups in Western Europe and the US. The results are below:

BRITAIN	fav. %	unfav.	unsure[†]
Catholics	84	5	11
Jews	81	6	13
Hindus	69	15	16
Muslims	61	27	12

FRANCE			
Jews	87	10	3
N. Africans	72	26	2

ITALY			
Christians	81	11	8
Jews	52	29	19
Muslims	21	69	10
Roma	9	84	7

SPAIN	fav. %	unfav.	unsure[†]
Roma	44	45	11
Muslims	40	46	13

GERMANY			
Jews	78	9	14
Roma	46	31	23
Poles	71	23	7
Turks	65	30	6

USA			
Whites	89	5	6
Blacks	86	8	7
Asians	81	8	10
Hispanics	77	15	8

† 'Unsure' included 'don't know' and 'refused'.

—— PERCEPTIONS OF RACIAL DISCRIMINATION ——

30% of Britons reported that they expected public service organisations to treat their racial group worse than members of other races, according to the Communities and Local Government's latest *Citizenship Survey*, released in December 2009. Below are the ethnic groups that most Britons considered were given preferential treatment:

Asian people	42%	White people	13
Black people	26	Mixed race people	5
Eastern Europeans	24	Chinese people	5
New immigrants	23	Hindus	3
Asylum seekers/refugees	16	Sikhs	3
Muslims	15	Buddhists	2
Other group	14	Jews	2

56% of those questioned thought that there was more racial prejudice now than five years ago, and only 11% said there was less. 44% thought Muslims suffered the greatest increase in racial prejudice today compared to five years ago, followed by Asians (39%), and Eastern Europeans (29%). When asked which religious groups received too much or too little protection from the government, the vast majority mentioned Muslims: 84% of people said they thought Muslims received too much religious protection, and 60% thought Muslims received too little, reflecting the complicated relationship Britain has with its Muslim community.

———————— THE PINK LIST 2010 ————————

The *Independent on Sunday* annually compiles a 'Pink List' of the most influential gays and lesbians in British society. Listed below are the 2010 Pink List top 12:

1..Gareth Thomas.........*rugby player*
2..Mary Portas.........*'Queen of Shops'*
3..Stephen Fry....*broadcaster & writer*
4..Evan Davis..............*broadcaster*
5..Carol Ann Duffy..... *Poet Laureate*
6..Alan Carr.................*comedian*
7..Peter Tatchell..*human rights activist*
8..Michael Salter........*adviser to PM*
9..Nicholas Hytner.....*theatre director*
10.Sue Perkins ...*comedian and writer*
11.Simon Hughes............ *Lib Dems*
12.Scott Mills.............. *Radio 1 DJ*

———— RACIAL DISCRIMINATION IN RECRUITMENT ————

Job candidates with 'white British' names were far more likely to be invited for interview than equivalent candidates with 'ethnic minority' names, according to research released by the Department for Work and Pensions in 2009. Researchers created three fictional candidates with similar qualifications and experiences, all of whom had British education and job histories. One candidate was given the typically white British name 'Alison Taylor', another was given the typically Asian name 'Nazia Mahmood', and a third the typically African name 'Mariam Namagembe'. Using these false identities, the researchers submitted 2,961 job applications across a variety of sectors. The results suggested that a white applicant needed to send nine applications to receive a positive response from an employer (such as an interview request or a phone call of encouragement), whereas an ethnic minority candidate with the same skills needed to send 16 applications before receiving a positive response. The researchers discovered that none of the fake candidates experienced discrimination when applying for public sector roles, and suggested that this was because the public sector tended to use formal application forms.

— GYPSIES, TRAVELLERS, & TRAVELLING SHOWPEOPLE —

GYPSIES AND TRAVELLERS

'Persons of nomadic habit of life whatever their race or origin, including such persons who on grounds only of their own or their family's or dependants' educational or health needs or old age have ceased to travel temporarily or permanently, but excluding members of an organised group of travelling show people or circus people travelling together as such.'

[Source: Office of the Deputy PM]

TRAVELLING SHOWPEOPLE

'Members of a group organised for the purposes of holding fairs, circuses or shows (whether or not travelling together as such). This includes such persons who on the grounds of their own or their family's or dependants' more localised pattern of trading, educational or health needs or old age have ceased to travel temporarily or permanently.'

[Source: Communities and Local Govt]

————————— INTERNATIONAL MIGRATION —————————

About 590,000 people came from other countries to live in the UK in 2008, while *c.*427,00 left the country to live elsewhere, according to the Office for National Statistics. Overall, the UK gained 163,000 residents through migration in 2008, 70,000 fewer than in 2007. The decrease was due to the higher number of people leaving the UK, 60% of whom did not have British citizenship. A breakdown of immigrants coming to the UK, and emigrants leaving, is charted below by citizenship:

Immigrating to UK	citizenship	emigrating from UK
85,000	British	173,000
198,000	EU27†	134,000
90,000	EU15†	54,000
89,000	EU8 (see below)	69,000
165,000	Commonwealth	66,000
142,000	other foreign	55,000
590,000	TOTAL	427,000

The top countries of last and next residence for UK migrants are tabulated below:

Country of last residence		Country of next residence	
Poland	143,000 *immigrants*	Australia	115,000 *emigrants*
India	100,000	Poland	69,000
Australia	59,000	Spain	47,000
Pakistan	49,000	France	42,000
USA	47,000	USA	41,000

The top countries of last and next residence for migrants with British citizenship:

Country of last residence		Country of next residence	
Australia	21,000 *immigrants*	Australia	75,000 *emigrants*
Spain	18,000	Spain	39,000
USA	10,000	USA	23,000
Germany	8,000	France	22,000
France	8,000	Germany	21,000

Since the EU accession of eight Central and Eastern European countries in 2004, migration from those countries to the UK has greatly increased. In 2004, 167,000 people born in an EU8 country were living in the UK, compared to 689,000 in 2008. The list below shows EU8-born residents of the UK in 2008, by birth country:

Poland	497,000	Hungary	26,000
Lithuania	57,000	Czech Republic	26,000
Slovakia	48,000	Estonia	5,000
Latvia	28,000	Slovenia	1,000

Data include civilians changing residence for ≥1 year. † Does not include British citizens. ❦ Formal study was the top reason given for immigration; the main reason for emigration was employment.

──────── N IRELAND GOOD RELATIONS INDICATORS ────────

A report measuring indicators of 'good relations' inside Northern Ireland is produced regularly by the Office of the First Minister and Deputy First Minister of
Northern Ireland. The latest report – published in December 2009 – revealed
the progress made in each of the nine 'priority outcome' areas tabulated below:

[1] Northern Ireland society is free from racism, sectarianism and prejudice.
[2] All places are shared, safe, inclusive and welcoming for everyone.
[3] Positive and harmonious relationships exist between communities at
interface areas. [4] Increased sharing in education.
[5] Northern Ireland is a community where people of all backgrounds work, live,
learn, and play together. [6] All work places are safe and shared.
[7] Minority ethnic people participate in public, political, and economic life.
[8] Minority ethnic people will benefit from equality in health and welfare.
[9] N. Ireland is a place where cultural diversity is embraced, respected, and valued.

Some findings of the 2009 *Good Relations Indicators* report are enumerated below:

Sectarian incidents/crimes recorded

	incidents	crimes
2005/06	1,701	1,470
2006/07	1,695	1,217
2007/08	1,584	1,056
2008/09	1,595	1,017

No. attacks on symbolic premises

	2005	2008
Churches	83	35
GAA/AOH† properties	1	13
Orange halls	35	58
Schools	132	15

% of people who felt intimidated by
republican/loyalist murals, kerb
paintings, or flags in the last year:

	Republican	loyalist
2005	23	25
2006	13	17
2007	14	18
2008	13	15

Deaths p/a due to security situation:

2005	5	2007	3
2006	3	2008	1

No. casualties per annum as a result
of paramilitary-style shootings:

	Loyalist groups	Rep. groups
2005	74	11
2006	25	11
2007	1	5
2008	3	13

No. casualties per annum as a result
of paramilitary-style assaults

	Loyalist groups	Rep. groups
2005	60	29
2006	33	16
2007	39	7
2008	28	12

No. of security related incidents

	2005	2008
Shootings	167	42
Bombings	83	37
Incendiaries	9	5

% of children (<16) who think relations
between Protestants and Catholics are
better now than they were 5 years ago:

2005	43	2008	68

† GAA: Gaelic Athletic Association; AOH: Ancient Order of Hibernians.

──────── VOLUNTEERING & CHARITABLE GIVING ────────

27% of people in England took part in formal volunteering at least once a month in 2007–08, according to the *Citizenship Survey* released by the Department for Communities and Local Government in December 2009. 35% participated in informal volunteering at least once a month in 2007–08. Those who took part in regular formal volunteering spent on average 11 hours volunteering in the 4 weeks before interview for the survey. Informal volunteers spent an average of 7·8 hours. The most common regular formal volunteering[†] activities are listed below:

Activity	%		
Organising or helping to run an activity or event	55	Giving information/advice	24
Raising or handling money/taking part in sponsored event	52	Visiting people	24
		Secretarial/admin work	23
Leading group/cmtee member	37	Befriending/mentoring	21
Providing transport/driving	26	Representing someone	18
		Campaigning	10
		Other practical help	36

The most common regular and informal volunteering activities are listed below:

Giving advice	52%	Writing letters/filling in forms	30
Keeping in touch with someone	38	Cooking, cleaning	26
Transporting/escorting someone	38	Decorating, home improvement	17
Looking after property/pet	37	Representing someone	11
Babysitting/childcare	35	Sitting with, personal care	8
Doing shopping/collecting pension	33	Any other activities	6

The types of organisation helped by regular formal volunteers are listed below:

Sports/exercise	53%	Health/disability/social welfare	25
Hobbies/arts/social clubs	42	Local community/neighbourhood	24
Religion	36	Environment/animals	20
Children's education/schools	34	Education for adults	19
Youth/children's activities	32	The elderly	17

76% of people in England had donated money to charity in the four weeks before interview in 2007–08. The average amount donated was £16·13. The most popular way of making a donation was buying raffle tickets (27%), followed by buying goods from a charity shop or catalogue (23%), and donating via direct debit (23%). Analysis of the findings indicated that the following types of people were more likely to have given to charity in the previous four weeks: aged between 50–74; females; of Pakistani or Indian origin; regular formal or informal volunteers; and in the middle (£15,000–£49,999) or highest (>£75,000) income band.

† There were differences to be noted between the types of volunteering carried out by men and women: men were more likely to have led a group (43% compared to 32% of women), or provided transport (32% compared to 22%), whereas women were more likely to have been involved in raising or handling money (54% compared to 48%), or visiting people (28% compared to 19%).

──────── FAILING HOSPITALS ────────

In November 2009, 27 hospitals with unusually high mortality rates were uncovered by the *2009 Hospital Guide* published by Dr Foster, a part-private, part-NHS-run company. Some of the safety issues uncovered by the *Hospital Guide* are below:

12 trusts significantly under-performed on basic safety measures
27 trusts had significantly high death rates
39% of hospitals do not investigate all unexpected deaths or cases of serious harm that occur on their wards
82 incidents of 'wrong-site' surgery (operating on the wrong part of the body) were recorded last year
478 operations were cancelled in 2008/09 because patient notes were missing
5,024 people admitted with 'low-risk' conditions died in hospital last year
848 people who died after being admitted with 'low-risk' conditions were under the age of 65

The *Hospital Guide* rated hospitals on a range of 'safety indicators', which included infections rates, staffing levels and deaths. The 12 lowest-scoring hospitals were:

Hospital	safety rating (out of 100)
Basildon & Thurrock	0
Scarborough & NE Yorkshire	2·06
Lewisham	3·43
Coventry & Warwickshire	3·43
Weston Area	4·11
South Manchester	4·80
Tameside	4·80
South London	4·80
St Helens & Knowsley	5·48
Mid Yorkshire	6·16
Blackpool, Fylde, & Wyre	6·16
Hereford	6·85

The highest scoring hospital was University College London Hospital, which scored 100.

In July 2010, the new coalition Health Sec. Andrew Lansley announced another major NHS restructuring, involving the abolition of 10 strategic health authorities and the 152 primary care trusts, and a shift of power (and money) back to GPs.

──────── NHS PATIENT EXPERIENCES ────────

The NHS regularly surveys patients about their experiences with the health care system. The survey results are used to create 'patient experience scores' which rate NHS hospitals on key measures of quality, using a scale from 1–100. Average scores for adult inpatient and outpatient departments in England in 2009/10 were:

	adult inpatient depts	outpatient depts
'Access & waiting'	85·0	72·5
'Safe, high quality, coordinated care'	64·4	83·2
'Better information, more choice'	66·8	79·1
'Building closer relationships'	82·9	87·3
'Clean, friendly, comfortable place to be'	79·1	70·9
OVERALL	75·6	78·6

—————— SOME HEALTH STORIES OF NOTE ——————

{OCT 2009} · American ear, nose and throat experts warned that driving a convertible car with the roof down can seriously damage hearing. Cruising at 50–70mph in a convertible can expose drivers and passengers to sounds as loud as a pneumatic drill, and experts advised that ear protection should be worn. ❦ The Food Standards Agency found that two-thirds of all chicken on sale in the UK is contaminated with *Campylobacter*, a bacterium responsible for *c.*55,000 cases of food poisoning each year. {NOV} · A report in *Epidemiology & Community Health* warned that women who smoke while pregnant are at a greater risk of having children with behavioural problems. The scientists suggested that smoking during pregnancy may hamper the development of a baby's brain. {DEC} · Research published in the *Proceedings of the National Academy of Sciences* suggested that cancer may be more likely, and more deadly, in lonely people. Scientists studying rats noted that rodents kept in isolation tended to develop more tumours, and tumours of a more deadly type, than rats kept in a group. ❦ A University of Montreal study that sought to compare the views of men who watched pornography with those who had never seen it faltered when the school was unable to find a single male student in the latter category. {JAN} · A study of combat casualties in Iraq found that receiving a dose of morphine in the wake of a disaster could help alleviate post-traumatic stress. Researchers writing in the *New England Journal of Medicine* suggested the practice could be more widely used to help trauma victims mitigate psychological problems. ❦ A study in

The Lancet suggested that rising obesity rates may mean that doses of antibiotics need to be increased to have sufficient effect – ending the current 'one-dose-fits-all' method of prescribing some drugs. ❦ Research by scientists at Imperial College London indicated that ambidextrous children were more likely to be hyperactive or struggle at school. The study published in *Pediatrics* followed 8,000 children from Finland, 87 of whom were ambidextrous. The results suggested that, compared to their right-handed peers, mixed-handed children aged 7–8 were more likely to have difficulty with language, and at 15–16 were twice as likely to have ADHD. {FEB} · *The Lancet* retracted the highly controversial 1998 article by Dr Andrew Wakefield linking the MMR vaccine to autism. ❦ A study published in the *British Journal of Psychiatry* suggested that 'baby brain' is a myth. Although mothers often claim that they become more absent-minded while pregnant, the study – which followed hundreds of pregnant women – could find no evidence to support this popular belief. ❦ People who experience high levels of boredom in their job are at greater risk of dying from heart disease or stroke. Researchers from University College London followed >7,000 civil servants over 25 years, and found that those who had complained of being bored were 40% more likely to have died by the end of the study. {MAR} · A mental health outreach team assembled by University College London in the wake of the 7/7/2005 bombings reported that a third of the *c.*1,000 survivors they contacted required treatment for post-traumatic stress disorder – though only

——————— SOME HEALTH STORIES OF NOTE cont. ———————

4% were referred for treatment by their GP. ❦ Public health officials in Middlesbrough warned that cases of syphilis had increased fourfold in the area in the past year. It was suggested that online social networking sites were partly to blame because they were 'making it easier for people to meet up for casual sex'. ❦ A report from the House of Commons Environmental Audit Committee found that air pollution cuts the average Briton's life expectancy by 7–8 months, and could be contributing to 50,000 premature deaths each year in the UK. {APR} · Research published in the *Journal of the National Cancer Institute* found that eating more fruit and vegetables reduces cancer risk only slightly – an extra two portions per day was found to prevent 2·6% of cancers in men and 2·3% in women. ❦ A report in the *Archives of Dermatology* found that >30% of college students who used tanning beds appeared to be addicted to the practice. This conclusion was based on a questionnaire that measured how often those in the study thought about tanning, and the extent to which tanning affected their life. {MAY} · A *British Medical Journal* report on the risks of 'head-banging' found that the average heavy metal song could cause mild head injury if the headbanger's range of motion was >75°. To minimise the risk of trauma, head-bangers were advised to decrease their range of motion, replace heavy metal with adult-oriented rock, headbang to every second beat, or wear 'personal protective equipment'. ❦ University of North Carolina researchers won a $100,000 grant from the Gates Foundation to continue testing an ultrasound blast that, when

applied to the testes, can temporarily stop sperm production. The researchers hope to use the technology to create a low-cost, non-hormonal, reversible contraceptive for men. {JUN} · A study in the *Archives of Internal Medicine* suggested that Americans who ate two servings of brown rice a week reduced their risk of developing Type 2 diabetes by *c.*10%, compared to those who ate brown rice less than once a month. In contrast, eating white rice >5 times a week raised the risk of diabetes by 20%. ❦ A 13-year study by researchers in the Netherlands found that drinking several cups of tea or coffee daily can cut the risk of heart disease. Those who drank >6 cups of tea per day cut their risk by a third, and those who drank 2–4 coffees daily reduced their risk by 20%. {JUL} · A research project in Rhode Island found that changing school hours can have beneficial effects. For 9 weeks, a high school delayed its daily start from 08:00 to 08:30, during which time the number of students who got ≥8 hours of sleep rose from 16% to 55%, while reports of daytime sleepiness dropped from 49% to 20%, and incidents of lateness fell by almost half. {AUG} · A study in the *New England Journal of Medicine* found that fibromyalgia sufferers instructed in tai chi reported significant improvements in symptoms of pain, fatigue, and sleeplessness compared to sufferers given stretching exercises and wellness education. ❦ A study of *c.*1,200 girls in 3 US cities found that by age 7, 10·4% of the white girls studied had begun puberty, compared to *c.*5% in a similar study conducted in 1997. The report's authors suggested that obesity and hormones in the environment might be responsible.

———————————— TEMPERS, LOSS OF ————————————

Britons lose their tempers after an average of 8 minutes 22 seconds, according to a December 2009 survey by TalkTalk. The internet is reportedly to blame for diminishing levels of patience: 70% admit that they become frustrated if it takes more than a minute for a web page to load. TalkTalk investigated a number of rage-inducing scenarios and determined their corresponding 'points of impatience', viz:

Waiting...	*point of impatience*		
For an internet page to load...	3m 38s	For friends to arrive............	10m 1s
On hold on the telephone.......	5m 4s	For a tradesman to arrive.....	10m 43s
For the kettle to boil.............	5m 6s	For a response to a voice	
For food in a restaurant	8m 36s	or text message...............	13m 16s
		AVERAGE POINT	8m 22ss

People reacted to reaching their 'point of impatience' in a variety of ways: 37% had 'cancelled a service'; 35% 'demanded to speak to the manager'; 27% 'shouted at someone'; 26% 'slammed the phone down'; 24% 'pestered for a response'; 14% 'walked out'; 3% had 'thrown something across the room'; 1% had 'thrown a punch'.

———————— DUBIOUS ALTERNATIVE HEALTH THERAPIES ————————

32% of British women said they would try an alternative health therapy if a celebrity had used it, according to a November 2009 poll by insurance firm Aviva. The report on 'health hoaxes' indicated that the general public were heavily influenced by celebrity health fads – 94% of the women questioned believed that celebrities pay for the 'very best and most effective treatments'. The report went on to question 200 GPs, and found that 93% thought faddy health trends had no medical value. The top ten least effective alternative treatments according to the GPs were:

1	.........................cupping	6	.........................aromatherapy
2	......................colonic irrigation	7	...........................reflexology
3	...............food intolerance testing	8	.... vitamin B12 injections
4	.... detoxing	9	.... extreme yoga
5	......................macrobiotic diet	10	..........overnight health-farm stay

———————————— HOMEOPATHY & THE NHS ————————————

In February 2010 the House of Commons Science and Technology Committee recommended that the NHS stop funding homeopathic treatments. It was estimated that the NHS currently spends *c.*£4m a year on the complementary therapy. After hearing evidence from a variety of sources on the efficacy of homeopathic treatments, the committee concluded that 'the systematic reviews and meta-analyses conclusively demonstrate that homeopathic products perform no better than placebos'.

In January 2010 hundreds of homeopathy sceptics across Britain took part in a 'mass overdose' of homeopathic remedies to demonstrate that such 'medicines' are just the equivalent of sugar pills.

──────── ATTENDING ACCIDENT & EMERGENCY ────────

Those aged 20–29 are most likely to attend accident and emergency (A&E) in England, according to Hospital Episode Statistics 2008–09 released in January 2010 by the Dept of Health. A&E attendance by age group, 2008–09, is below:

Age group	number	%		number	%
0–9	1,937,963	14·0	50–59	1,182,733	8·6
10–19	1,916,610	13·9	60–69	1,035,865	7·5
20–29	2,281,334	16·5	70–79	983,427	7·1
30–39	1,742,829	12·6	80–89	865,588	6·3
40–49	1,597,425	11·6	90–99	214,734	1·6
			>100	9,377	0·1

Curiously, A&E departments are busiest not on Fridays or Saturdays, but Mondays and Tuesdays. Below is a breakdown of A&E visits, by day, between 2008–09:

Day	number	%		number	%
Monday	2,186,095	15·8	Thursday	1,916,262	13·9
Tuesday	2,000,358	14·5	Friday	1,918,415	13·9
Wednesday	1,916,703	13·9	Saturday	1,898,654	13·8
			Sunday	1,957,585	14·2

Tabulated below are A&E attendances by leading primary diagnosis, 2008–09:

Primary diagnosis description	%		%
Laceration	8·5	Soft tissue inflammation	6·1
Dislocation/fracture/joint injury/		Contusion/abrasion	5·7
amputation	8·3	Gastrointestinal conditions	5·3
Sprain/ligament injury	6·8	Respiratory conditions	4·6
		Cardiac conditions	3·6

In March 2010, 17 doctors, nurses, and health workers wrote to *The Times* criticising the public for visiting GPs for minor ailments. The signatories noted that in 2007, heartburn/indigestion accounted for 6·8m GP visits; nasal congestion 5·3m; constipation 4·3m; acne 2·4m; and headache 1·8m.

──────────────── ASSISTED SUICIDE ────────────────

In February 2010, Director of Public Prosecutions Keir Starmer QC released guidelines to clarify the law on assisted suicide [see *Schott's Almanac 2010*]. Starmer stressed that his advice was not a change in the law, and said 'nothing in this policy could be taken to amount to an assurance that a person will not be prosecuted if he assists the suicide or attempted suicide of another person'. Starmer suggested that prosecutors shift their focus from the victim's condition (e.g., terminal illness) to the motives of the suspect. Some of the factors that could mitigate against the prosecution of a suspect include: the victim clearly reached a voluntary decision to commit suicide; the suspect was solely motivated by compassion; and the suspect reported the suicide to the police and fully assisted with their inquiries. It remains an offence under the 1961 Suicide Act to encourage or assist a suicide or a suicide attempt in England and Wales; anyone found guilty could face up to 14 years in prison.

Schott's Almanac 2011

———————— HEALTH & SAFETY EXECUTIVE ————————

The roots of the Health & Safety Executive (HSE) lie in the C19th realisation that industrialisation needed to be tempered with care for the workforce – especially child labour. Her Majesty's Factory Inspectorate was founded in 1833; the first Inspector of Mines and Collieries was appointed in 1843; and the Quarry Inspectorate was established in 1895. A series of Acts in the C20th continued this trend (not least the foundation of the Nuclear Installations Inspectorate in 1959), and in 1975 the Health and Safety Commission was established by the Health and Safety at Work Act 1974. The HSE currently defines its mission as 'the prevention of death, injury and ill health to those at work and those affected by work activities'. ❧ Below are the injuries to employees by kind of accident, severity of injury, and type of industry, for 2008/09. These figures exclude incidents (such as road traffic accidents, deaths in police custody, &c.) which are usually within the remit of other organisations:

Kind of accident	fatal	major†	>3-day‡
Contact with moving machinery	14	1,174	3,109
Struck by moving, including flying/falling, object	22	3,223	11,981
Struck by moving vehicle	23	583	1,529
Strike against something fixed or stationary	7	953	4,348
Injured while handling, lifting or carrying	0	3,516	38,166
Slips, trips or falls on same level	4	10,368	23,797
Falls from a height	16	4,654	7,065
≤2 metres	*3*	*3,036*	*5,034*
>2 metres	*12*	*610*	*359*
not stated	*1*	*1,008*	*1,672*
Trapped by something collapsing/overturning	13	105	152
Drowning or asphyxiation	3	16	11
Exposure to, or contact with, a harmful substance	1	493	2,745
Exposure to fire	0	57	190
Exposure to an explosion	3	40	63
Contact with electricity or electrical discharge	4	95	316
Injured by an animal	0	311	833
Acts of violence	4	921	5,221
Other kind of accident	4	990	4,545
Injuries not classified by kind	11	95	230
TOTAL	129	27,594	104,301

† Major, but not fatal. ‡ >3-day means off work for more than this period. [Source: HSE *Reporting of Injuries, Diseases & Dangerous Occurrences Regulations*; some data are provisional.]

So-called 'elf 'n' safety' tends to get a bad press, and journalists delight in reporting on what some deride as the mollycoddling of society. Mindful of this, since April 2007, the HSE has published (in order to debunk) a health and safety 'myth of the month', including such erroneous beliefs as: 'Kids must wear goggles to play conkers'; 'Graduates are banned from throwing mortar boards'; 'New regulations would require trapeze artists to wear hard hats'; 'Egg boxes are banned in craft lessons as they might cause salmonella'; 'You can't wear flip-flops to work'; 'The HSE has banned stepladders'; 'Ice cream toppings have been banned for safety reasons'; 'Pancake races are banned'; and so on.

---------------------- SMOKING, DRINKING & CHILDREN ----------------------

The number of children reporting that they had ever tried a cigarette decreased from 17·7% in 1997 to 11·4% in 2008, according to statistics from the Health Survey for England released in December 2009. The percentage of boys and girls (aged 8–15) reporting that they had 'ever smoked' is provided in the table below:

♂ · 1997	2002	2008	age	2008	2002	1997· ♀
6·9	4·1	1·0	8	1·3	0·8	2·1
4·1	6·8	3·6	9	3·2	3·3	2·1
7·4	6·8	1·6	10	4·7	6·1	5·9
7·8	11·2	4·5	11	4·7	8·6	4·6
16·4	16·2	10·8	12	7·3	15·5	18·6
29·5	21·7	12·1	13	15·0	22·9	31·0
30·8	30·5	22·9	14	25·0	34·3	48·7
47·6	46·9	30·8	15	39·6	57·6	58·0

The % of boys and girls reporting they had 'ever drunk a proper alcoholic drink':

♂ · 1999	2002	2008	age	2008	2002	1999 · ♀
10·5	12·1	8·2	8	4·6	7·2	15·0
29·1	15·5	6·3	9	5·2	11·4	6·0
29·9	24·9	7·5	10	6·9	15·3	13·4
28·6	34·7	18·1	11	16·0	24·7	31·3
43·1	46·6	23·8	12	28·0	44·3	39·6
66·4	63·5	36·8	13	47·3	59·7	62·6
74·6	70·7	54·5	14	62·0	72·7	59·7
81·0	88·3	70·2	15	74·1	86·0	82·3

------------------------------- DRINKING -------------------------------

71% of men and 56% of women in England aged ≥16 reported having a drink on at least one day of the week prior to a 2010 ONS survey. 11% of men and 6% of women said they had a drink every day of the previous week. Curiously, Londoners were the least likely to report drinking at least once during the week:

	% who drank ... prior week	5 days/wk
England	63	15
– North-east	63	14
– North-west	63	13
– Yorkshire & Humber	67	16
– East Midlands	65	15
– West Midlands	60	16
– East of England	66	16
– London	51	14
– South-east	67	17
– South-west	66	18
Wales	57	13
Scotland	56	11

The average weekly alcohol consumption in England was 16·8 units for men and 8·6 units for women. A 'unit' is defined as 10ml pure alcohol, roughly equivalent to a half pint of normal strength beer, lager or cider; 25ml of spirits; or half a standard 175ml glass of wine. [Data are from 2008.]

——— SEIZURES OF DRUGS IN ENGLAND & WALES ———

A record 241,090 drug seizures were carried out by police and the UK Border Agency in England and Wales in 2008/09, according to October 2009 figures released by the Home Office. Seizures of Class A drugs decreased by 1% from 2007/08 to 2008/09, while Class B drugs seizures increased by 9% in the same period (probably reflecting the re-classification of cannabis from a Class C to a Class B drug in 2008/09). The most commonly seized drugs, by number of seizures in 2008/09, are below:

Drug	class	no. seizures				
Cannabis	B	185,890	Ketamine	C	1,266
Cocaine†	A	24,604	Methadone	A	1,063
Heroin	A	13,273	Anabolic steroids	C	802
Amphetamines	B	7,735	Temazepam	C	609
Crack	A	6,612	LSD	A	131
Ecstasy	A	5,206			
Benzodiazepines	C	4,029			

† Seizures of cocaine have risen sharply in recent years, roughly doubling since 2005.

97% of all drugs seizures in 2008/09 were made by the police, and the majority were for relatively small quantities. The other 3% were seized by the UK Border Agency, who tended to confiscate much larger quantities. The total weight of the drugs seized in 2008/09 were: 65 tonnes of cannabis (herbal and resin); 2·9 tonnes of cocaine; 2·9 tonnes of amphetamines; and 1·6 tonnes of heroin.

——— BUCKFAST & PROBLEM DRINKING IN SCOTLAND ———

An investigation by BBC Scotland, broadcast in January 2010, linked the popular drink Buckfast Tonic Wine to violent crime in Scotland. A Freedom of Information request revealed that Buckfast was mentioned in 5,638 Strathclyde Police crime reports between 2006–09 – an average of three incidents a day. One in ten of these reported incidents was violent, and on 114 occasions a Buckfast bottle was allegedly employed as a weapon. ❦ Buckfast Tonic Wine is made in Devon by Benedictine monks who remain true to a recipe brought over to England by French monks in the 1880s. A 75cl bottle of the 15% proof brew contains 11 units of alcohol and 281mg of caffeine (roughly equivalent to 8 cans of cola). A bottle of Bucky costs *c*.£5·49, and more than half of the £37m annual sales are made in Scotland. ❦ Such is Buckfast's belligerent reputation north of the border that the drink has a host of nicknames, including: 'Commotion Lotion', 'Wreck the Hoose Juice', 'Liquid Speed', and 'Bottle of Beat-the-Wife'. ❦ Jim Wilson, of J. Chandler & Co, the company which distributes Buckfast in Scotland, defended the Benedictine monks: 'Why should they accept responsibility? They're not up here pouring any of their Buckfast down somebody's throat. People take it by choice because they like it, because it's a good product'.

Data analysed by NHS Health Scotland in January 2010 indicated that, on average, adults in Scotland consume the equivalent of 46 bottles of vodka a year. Sales of alcohol suggested that each Scot over the age of 18 consumed 12·2 litres of pure alcohol annually – the equivalent of 537 pints of beer or 130 bottles of wine. Scots drank 25% more alcohol per head than residents of England and Wales.

——————— BRITISH CRIME STATISTICS ———————

Overall crime in England and Wales, as measured by the British Crime Survey (BCS), fell by 9% and police-recorded crime fell 8% between 2008/09–2009/10. The Home Office estimated there were *c*.9·6m crimes against adults resident in households (*c*.10·5m the year before), and the police recorded *c*.4·3m crimes (4·7m previously). The 2009/10 BCS also suggested that the risk of being a victim of crime was 21·5% – compared to 23% in 2008/09, and 39·7% in 1995. ❦ The annual BCS measures crime in England and Wales by interviewing people about crimes they have experienced in the past year, and their fear of crime. The BCS is widely seen as a useful partner to the police's recorded crime figures since, for a wide number of reasons, certain crimes often go unreported. ❦ Charted below are the changes in BCS and reported crimes from 2008/09–2009/10:

British Crime Survey	08/09–09/10	*Police Recorded Crime*	08/09–09/10
ALL BCS CRIME	↓9%	TOTAL RECORDED CRIME	↓8%
Vandalism	↓11%	Violence against the person	↓4%
Domestic burglary	↓9%	Sexual offences	↑6%
Vehicle-related theft	↓17%	Robbery	↓6%
Bicycle theft	↓9%	Domestic burglary	↓6%
Other household theft	↑1%	Other burglary	↓8%
Theft from person	↓28%	Offences against vehicles	↓16%
Theft of personal property	↓5%	Other theft	↓4%
All violence	↓1%	Fraud and forgery	↓7%
'The BCS does not measure homicide but it is well		Criminal damage	↓14%
covered by the police figures as it is likely that rela-		Drug offences	↓4%
tively few homicides do not come to police attention.'		Other misc. offences	↓2%

Charted below is a breakdown of BCS crime, from its peak in 1995 to 2009/10:

British Crime Survey	1995–09/10		
ALL BCS CRIME	↓50%	Bicycle theft	↓29%
Vandalism	↓28%	Other household theft	↓49%
Burglary	↓63%	Theft from person	↓23%
Vehicle-related theft	↓72%	Theft of personal property	↓50%
		All violence	↓50%

Below are some of the more unusual crimes recorded by the police in 2008/09:

Offence	*No. of offences recorded*		
Corporate manslaughter	1	Poisoning or female genital mutilation	141
Intentional destruction of viable unborn child	3	Perjury	186
Adulteration of food	4	Endangering railway passengers	231
Endangering life at sea	7	Rape of a male†	1,174
Abandoning a child >2	9	Blackmail	1,458
Unnatural sexual offences	15	Dishonest use of electricity	1,738
Aiding suicide	17	Kidnapping	1,868
Bigamy	60	Theft of mail	3,103
		(† Rape of a female	13,991)

— PRISON POPULATION —

Male............................80,722
Female............................4,233
TOTAL............................84,955
Usable Operational Capacity†..87,641
Number under Home Detention
Curfew supervision 2,383

† 'The operational capacity of a prison is the total number of prisoners that an establishment can hold taking into account control, security and the proper operation of the planned regime. Usable Operational Capacity of the estate is the sum of all establishments' operational capacity less 2,000 places. This is known as the operating margin and reflects the constraints imposed by the need to provide separate accommodation for different classes of prisoner i.e., by sex, age, security category, conviction status, single cell risk assessment and also due to geographical distribution.' As at 3·9·2010. [Source: Ministry of Justice]

— CELLS IN THE CELLS —

For obvious reasons, mobile phones are banned in prison, yet 8,648 phones or SIM cards were seized from prisons in England and Wales in the first 6 months of 2009 alone – including 255 found in maximum security jails. Mobiles can be purchased by inmates for as little as £400, and some criminals use them to ply their trade from behind bars. In the November 2009 Queen's Speech, Gordon Brown promised to criminalise the possession of a mobile phone in jail. However, David Jamieson, chairman of Wandsworth Prison's Independent Monitoring Board, urged the government to jam mobile signals: 'The technology ... does exist,' Jamieson told the BBC. 'It would cost about £250,000 to equip a prison to jam calls. That would pay for itself quite easily over time.'

— PRISONERS' PROPERTY —

Below are the items commonly allowed to be held by prisoners in England and Wales, subject to size and space limitations and the local rulings of governors:

Newspapers, magazines and books. ❦ A combined sound system, or a radio combined with a record, cassette or compact disc player, with records, cassettes or CDs, and earphones. ❦ A computer, floppy discs, &c. ❦ Smoking materials (where smoking is allowed), including up to 62·5g of loose tobacco, or 80 cigarettes or cigars or a combination of both for convicted prisoners, or 137·5g or 180 cigarettes for unconvicted prisoners. ❦ Locally approved games, including approved electronic games and players. ❦ Materials related to cell hobbies. ❦ One birdcage and one small bird, where birds are allowed. (Prisoners are responsible for the care of the bird, including feeding, cleaning of the cage, and any veterinary fees.) ❦ Writing and drawing materials (except those that pose a threat to security or good order or discipline). ❦ A wrist watch, excluding any with additional functions which may pose a risk to security (e.g., built-in camera, &c.). ❦ An electric shaver. ❦ Batteries for personal possessions, of an approved type and quantity. ❦ Toiletries for personal use. ❦ One wedding ring or other plain ring. ❦ One medallion or locket. ❦ Religious texts and artefacts, and incense. ❦ Photographs and pictures, in unglazed frames (excluding any considered offensive or inappropriate). ❦ Unpadded greetings cards. ❦ A calendar. ❦ A diary or personal organiser (electronic organisers subject to security checks). ❦ An address book. ❦ Postage stamps and envelopes. ❦ Approved medication. ❦ Disability aids (subject to security checks).

[Source: HM Prison Service Order 1250]

———————— UK TERROR THREAT ————————

In August 2006, the British government made public for the first time a simplified system of 'threat levels' that had been used covertly for some years. According to MI5, they were released to give the public a 'broad indication of the likelihood of a terrorist attack'. Below are the changes to this alert level since its introduction:

Date	reason for raising level	threat level
01·08·2006		set at SEVERE
10·08·2006	discovery of a transatlantic airline terror plot	↑ CRITICAL
14·08·2006		↓ SEVERE
30·06·2007	terrorist incidents in London and Glasgow	↑ CRITICAL
04·07·2007		↓ SEVERE
20·07·2009		↓ SUBSTANTIAL
22·01·2010	'broad range' of domestic and international threats	↑ SEVERE

——— ILLEGAL MIGRATION & HUMAN TRAFFICKING ———

The number of illegal immigrants attempting to enter Europe fell in 2009, in part because the economic crisis lessened labour demand, according to a 2010 report by EU border agency Frontex. 106,200 attempts to illegally cross the external borders of the EU were detected in 2009, 33% less than in 2008. Albanians accounted for the largest share of detections (38%), trailed by Afghans (14%) and Somalians (9%). Notably, detections of Iraqi nationals fell by 52%. Detections of Palestinian nationals rose by 77%, although Frontex speculated that false declarations of nationality may have inflated this total. According to the Serious Organised Crime Agency's (SOCA) *Threat Assessment of Organised Crime 2009/10*, the following routes are the most popular for illegal immigrants entering the EU:

from China, Indian subcontinent, parts of SE Asia > *to* Kiev (by air directly or via Moscow) > *to* EU (many through Slovakia or Poland)
from Sub-Saharan Africa and Indian subcontinent > *to* North Africa coast (mainly Egypt and Libya) > *to* Italy, Greece, and Malta
From various areas via the E Mediterranean and Balkans *to* Greece/Turkey border

A portion of illegal immigrants are victims of human trafficking. While forms of human trafficking vary, the UN defines the practice as 'the acquisition of people by improper means such as force, fraud or deception, with the aim of exploiting them'. 4,371 victims of human trafficking were identified by Frontex in 2008, although the real number is likely to be significantly higher. 90% of the trafficking victims identified by Frontex were female, and 10% were minors. Romanians were by far the most-represented nationality (50% of the trafficked minors reported were Romanian), followed by Nigerians and the Dutch. Sexual exploitation was reported as the main purpose of trafficking, followed by slavery or practices similar to slavery, and begging or associated activities. According to SOCA, victims of human trafficking in the UK are also frequently employed in areas where cheap labour is needed, including agriculture, horticulture, marine farming, textiles, and car washes.

———————— HOMICIDES ————————

651 deaths were recorded as homicide in England and Wales in 2008–09, according to Home Office figures released in January 2010. This showed a decrease of 14% (or 102 homicides) since 2007–08. Males were far more likely than females to be murdered: 459 men and 192 women were homicide victims in 2008–09. The most common method of killing was by sharp instrument – 39% of homicides were by this method. Homicides by method of killing and sex of victim are below:

♂ · Apparent method 2008–09 victims	♀ · Apparent method 2008–09 victims
Sharp instrument 180	Sharp instrument 75
Blunt instrument 40	Blunt instrument 17
Hitting, kicking, &c. 127	Hitting, kicking, &c. 25
Strangulation 13	Strangulation 34
Shooting 35	Shooting 4
Explosion 2	Explosion .... –
Burning 11	Burning 10
Drowning 2	Drowning 1
Poison or drugs 8	Poison or drugs 6
Motor vehicle 8	Motor vehicle 3
Other 22	Other 11
Not known 11	Not known 6

In 53% of all female homicides, the principal suspect was a partner or ex; 15% of suspects were another family member; and 12% a stranger. By comparison, male homicide victims were most likely to be the victim of a stranger (37%), followed by someone known to them (35%); in only 7% of cases was the principal suspect the victim's partner or ex. Where the victim was under 16, the most likely main suspect was one of the victim's parents (56%). Below are the number of homicides by apparent circumstances and relationship of victim to principal suspect, 2008–09:

Acquaintance	apparent circumstance	stranger
229	quarrel, revenge, loss of temper	117
21	in furtherance of theft or gain	24
5	the result of arson	1
22	other circumstances	39
19	irrational act	6
79	not known	89
375	total	276

The number of homicides per million population, by age of victim, 2008–09:

Age	rate ♂	♀		♂	♀		♂	♀
<1	36	17	11–15	4	2	50–69	14	5
1–4	6	6	16–20	35	6	>70	5	10
5–10	1	2	21–29	30	11			
			30–49	22	8	ALL AGES	17	7

[Source: Home Office · Homicides, Firearms Offences & Intimate Violence, 2008–09]

——————TERRORISM ARRESTS & OUTCOMES——————

There were 190 arrests relating to terrorism in Great Britain in 2008–09, according to Home Office figures released in November 2009. Since 11 September 2001 there have been 1,661 terrorism arrests – 66% of these resulted in charges being brought; 57% of those charged were subsequently convicted. In 2008–09 the majority of those arrested under s41 of the Terrorism Act 2000 were held in pre-charge detention for less than 7 days (78%), and 45% were held for <1 day. During this period no one was held for longer than 14 days, but since the extension of pre-charge detention to 28 days in 2006, 11 suspects have been held for >14 days, and 6 for the full 28. The principal offences for terrorism convictions since 9/11 were:

Possession of an article for terrorist purposes..................................21%
Membership of proscribed organisations 13%
Preparation for terrorist acts..13%
Collecting of information useful for a terrorism act 11%
Fundraising 10%

The 'ethnic appearance' of suspects arrested for terrorism (2005/06–2008/09) was:

	White	Black	Asian	other	total
Number arrested	185	123	374	237	919
% of total arrests	20	14	41	25	100
Number charged	43	46	90	31	210
% of all charged	22	22	43	11	100
% of arrests resulting in charge	25	37	24	–	23

As of 31 March 2009, 143 people were detained in British prisons for terrorist-related offences. Of these, 22 were classed as domestic extremists/separatists, and 8 are historic cases who were imprisoned before the Terrorism Act 2000. The self-declared nationalities of terrorist prisoners in Britain, as of 31 March 2009, were:

Nationality	No.				
British	80	Kuwaiti	2	Syrian	1
Somalian	6	Italian	2	Bangladeshi	1
Ethiopian	4	Egyptian	1	Albanian	1
Algerian	3	Gambian	1	Swedish	1
Pakistani	3	Ghanaian	1	Unrecorded	2
Moroccan	2	Sudanese	1		
		Jordanian	1	Total	113

104 of those imprisoned in Great Britain under terrorist legislation were Muslim, 4 were Church of England, 2 Catholic, and 2 had no religion. Of the 22 held as domestic extremists/separatists: 5 were Buddhist, 3 Catholic, 2 C of E, 1 Greek/Russian Orthodox, 1 Pagan, 1 Agnostic, and 9 no religion. Historic terrorist cases included: 2 Muslims, 2 Church of Scotland, 1 C of E, 1 Catholic, and 2 no religion.

[Source: Operation of Police Powers Under the Terrorism Act 2000 and Subsequent Legislation: Arrests, Outcomes and Stop & Searches, Great Britain 2008–09 · Released November 2009]

Media & Celebrity

The strongest poison ever known came from Caesar's laurel crown.
— WILLIAM BLAKE (1757–1827)

——————— HELLO! vs OK! COVER STARS ———————

Date	Hello!	OK!
04·01·10	Prince William	Peter Andre
11·01·10	Jude Law & Sienna Miller	Cheryl Cole
18·01·10	Robbie Williams & Ayda Field	Michelle Heaton
25·01·10	Prince William & Kate Middleton	Gary Barlow
01·02·10	David & Victoria Beckham	Samia Smith
08·02·10	Coleen Rooney	Katie Price & Alex Reid
15·02·10	John & Toni Terry	Peter Andre
22·02·10	Prince William	Cheryl Cole
01·03·10	Cheryl Cole	Simon Cowell
08·03·10	Kylie & Dannii Minogue	Cheryl Cole
16·03·10	Sandra Bullock (Oscar special)	Peter Andre
22·03·10	Victoria Beckham	Dannii Minogue
29·03·10	Prince William & Kate Middleton	Nadine Coyle
05·04·10	Queen Rania	Peter Andre & Kerry Katona
12·04·10	Coleen Rooney	Katie Price
19·04·10	Cheryl Cole	Charlotte Church & Gavin Henson
26·04·10	Melanie Griffith & Antonio Banderas	Katie Price
03·05·10	Prince William & Kate Middleton	Peter Andre
10·05·10	Sandra Bullock	Kerry Katona
17·05·10	Prince Harry & Chelsy Davy	Katie Price & Kerry Katona
24·05·10	David & Samatha Cameron	Katie Price
31·05·10	Cheryl Cole	Cliff Parisi marries Tara Wyer
07·06·10	Rod Stewart & family	Peter Andre
14·06·10	Wayne & Coleen Rooney	Kym Marsh
21·06·10	Kylie Minogue	Kerry Katona
29·06·10	Crown Princess Victoria of Sweden	Katie Price & Alex Reid
05·07·10	Eamonn Holmes marries Ruth Langsford	Alex Gerrard & Peter Andre
12·07·10	Brendan Cole marries Zoe Hobbs	Katie Price marries Alex Reid
19·07·10	Cheryl Cole	Cheryl Cole
26·07·10	Prince William & Kate Middleton	Sally Whittaker
02·08·10	Jennifer Aniston	Michelle Heaton's wedding
09·08·10	Weddings of Camilla Dallerup & Kirsty Gallacher	Kerry Katona
17·08·10	Robbie Williams marries Ayda Field	Katie Price & Alex Reid
23·08·10	Simon Cowell & Mezhgan Hussainy	Abbey Clancy
30·08·10	Cheryl Cole	Kerry Katona
06·09·10	Elin Nordegren	Josie Gibson [*Big Brother 11* winner]

———— SOME HATCHED, MATCHED, & DISPATCHED ————

HATCHED

Florence Rose Endellion [see p.97] *to* .... Samantha & David Cameron
Kai Wayne *to* .... Coleen & Wayne Rooney
Lou Sulola *to* .... Heidi Klum & Seal
Nelly May Lois *to* .... Zoe Ball & Norman 'Fatboy Slim' Cook
Ruby Tatiana *to* .... Carly & Joe Cole
Betsy *to* .... Denise Van Outen & Lee Mead
Cosima Violet Vaughn Drummond *to* .... Claudia Schiffer & Matthew Vaughn
Ethan Edward *to* .... Dannii Minogue & Kris Smith

MATCHED

Mark Owen & Emma Ferguson .... Cawdor, Scottish Highlands
Kevin Jonas & Danielle Deleasa .... Oheka Castle, Long Island
Katie Price & Alex Reid .... Las Vegas
Isla Fisher & Sacha Baron Cohen ..., ... Paris
Calista Flockhart & Harrison Ford .... Santa Fe
Penélope Cruz & Javier Bardem .... the Bahamas
Miranda Kerr & Orlando Bloom .... undisclosed†

† Bloom & Kerr wed in secret in July 2010. Their marriage was discovered when Kerr withdrew from an Australian department store appearance because of her honeymoon. Other highly secretive marriages in 2009–10 included Penélope Cruz & Javier Bardem and Harrison Ford & Calista Flockhart.

DISPATCHED

Jamelia & Darren Byfield (*married for* 17 months) .... divorcing
Avril Lavigne & Deryck Whibley (3 years) .... divorcing
Cheryl & Ashley Cole (3½ years) .... divorced
Kate Winslet & Sam Mendes (7 years) .... separated
Sandra Bullock & Jesse James (5 years) .... divorcing
Lenny Henry & Dawn French (25 years) .... separated
Tiger Woods & Elin Nordegren (6 years) .... divorced

———— SEXIEST WOMEN AND COOLEST MEN · 2010 ————

FHM's 'sexiest' women		*GQ*'s 'coolest' men
Cheryl Cole	1	Prince Harry
Megan Fox	2	Robert Pattinson
Marissa Miller	3	Reggie Love
Frankie Sandford	4	Dizzee Rascal
Keeley Hazell	5	Jason Schwartzman
Kristen Stewart	6	Usain Bolt
Kelly Brook	7	Ryan McGinley
Adriana Lima	8	Dustin Lance Black
Jessica Alba	9	Matt Helders
Abbey Clancy	10	Wells Tower

STRICTLY

BBC sports presenter Chris Hollins and his scantily clad partner Ola Jordan were the unlikely winners of 2009's *Strictly Come Dancing*. Hollins's journey from tentative hoofer to confident dancer enthralled the public, which rewarded his efforts by turning away from the strong favourite, Ricky Whittle. New judge and former winner Alesha Dixon did not boost the ratings, as had been hoped. The contestants were voted off in the following order:

16......................Martina Hingis
15................Richard Dunwoody
14...........................Rav Wilding
13..................Lynda Bellingham
12........................Joe Calzaghe
11...............................Jo Wood
10...........................Zoe Lucker
9.............................Craig Kelly
8.............................Phil Tufnell
7................................Ricky Groves
6..............Jade Johnson (injured)
5........................Natalie Cassidy
4...............................Laila Rouass
3..............................Ali Bastian
RUNNER-UP ....Ricky Whittle
WINNER ....Chris Hollins

X FACTOR

The early weeks of live *X Factor* shows were dominated by the guilty pleasure of Irish identical twins John & Edward. Each week, millions tuned in to see which song 'Jedward' would murder – and to savour Simon Cowell's withering put-downs. Once Jedward was dispatched, the serious singing contest began. Joe McElderry's consistently flawless performances marked him out as the most likely winner – and he did not disappoint. The acts were eliminated in the following order:

12...........................Kandy Rain
11...........................Rikki Loney
10.............................Miss Frank
9........................Rachel Adedeji
8...............................Lucie Jones
7............................Jamie Archer
6...........................John & Edward
5...........................Lloyd Daniels
4...........................Danyl Johnson
3...........................Stacey Solomon
RUNNER-UP ....Olly Murs
WINNER ....Joe McElderry

For the second year running, Cheryl Cole played mentor to the winning contestant.

OTHER REALITY TV SHOWS OF NOTE · 2010

Show	winner	prize
Big Brother	Josie Gibson	£100,000
I'm a Celebrity [2009]	Gino D'Acampo	a crown
Britain's Got Talent	Spellbound	£100,000 & Royal Variety Show gig
Dancing on Ice	Hayley Tamaddon	a trophy
Over the Rainbow	Danielle Hope[†]	role as Dorothy in Lloyd Webber's production of the *Wizard of Oz*
Got to Dance	Akai Osei	£100,000
Celebrity Masterchef	Lisa Faulkner	a trophy
Let's Dance for Sport Relief	Rufus Hound	a trophy

† The show also included a hunt for a dog to play Toto. A 1-year-old Mini Schnauzer – Dave – triumphed after a series of tasks; he was one of five potential Totos selected by Andrew Lloyd Webber.

—— VANITY FAIR 2010 HOLLYWOOD EDITION COVER ——

The 16th annual† *Vanity Fair* 'Hollywood edition' – with a cover shot by Annie Leibovitz – was published in February 2010. Film fans noted the absence of any young starlet of colour in the line-up of the hot young things to watch in 2010:

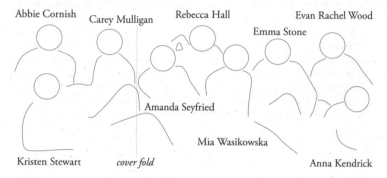

Abbie Cornish   Carey Mulligan   Rebecca Hall   Evan Rachel Wood

Emma Stone

Amanda Seyfried

Mia Wasikowska

Kristen Stewart   *cover fold*   Anna Kendrick

† Due to the recession, the 2009 Hollywood edition featured President Barack Obama on the cover.

—— CELEBRITY BODY PARTS AT AUCTION ——

A dozen singed strands of Michael Jackson's hair were sold for £1,140 at auction in London in October 2009. The hair was collected by producer Ralph Cohen after Jackson's barnet was accidentally set on fire while filming a Pepsi commercial in 1984. Below are some other celebrity body parts that have been sold at auction:

Celebrity	auctioned	item	price reached
Elvis Presley	2009	hair trimmed when the King enlisted	$15,000
Lord Nelson	2009	hair cut from his head after Btl. of Trafalgar	£2,500
John Lennon	2007	hair collected by band's hairdresser	£24,000
William Shatner	2006	a kidney stone	$25,000
Jack Nicholson	2001	baby teeth; provenance unknown	unsold
Judy Garland	1979	pair of false eyelashes	$125
Napoleon	1977	penis, removed and preserved after autopsy	$3,000

—— MOST 'POINTLESS' CELEBRITIES ——

The UK's most 'pointless' celebs, according to a 2010 poll by MyVoucherCodes:

Jedward [see p.122]	71% *agreed*	Michelle Heaton	57
Jodie Marsh	68	Calum Best	53
Kerry Katona	64	Danielle Lloyd	49
Jack Tweed	61	Chantelle Houghton	46
Tara Beckworth	59	Tara Palmer Tomkinson	44

——— CELEBRITY UN GOODWILL AMBASSADORS ———

Orlando Bloom was appointed a Goodwill Ambassador for the United Nations Children's Fund (UNICEF) in October 2009. This honour is given to celebrities who demonstrate a commitment to improving the rights of children worldwide. Below are some other celebrity ambassadors appointed by the United Nations:

Celebrity	ambassador for		
Angelina Jolie .... UNHCR · *refugees*	David Beckham.....UNICEF · *children*
Gisele Bündchen..UNEP · *environment*	George Clooney....messenger of peace
Nicole Kidman...... UNIFEM · *women*	Michael Douglas...messenger of peace
Roger Federer ......UNICEF · *children*	Drew Barrymore.........WFP · *hunger*
Vienna Phil. Orchestra ..WHO · *health*	Geri Halliwell..... UNFPA · *population*
Maria Sharapova . UNDP · *development*	Giorgio Armani..... UNHCR · *refugees*
	Whoopi Goldberg ..UNICEF · *children*

——— CELEBRITY COLUMN INCHES ———

Madonna's enduring fame ensured she was the most written-about celebrity of the noughties, according to an analysis of British national newspaper coverage released in December 2009 by online UK TV channel Liv. The celebrities who dominated gossip and garnered the most column inches in 2009, and across the decade, are below:

Most written-about celebs in 2009 total articles		*Most written-about celebs in the 2000s* total articles
Michael Jackson.....6,838	1	45,633 .... Madonna
Simon Cowell.......6,213	2	27,976 ...... Robbie Williams
Madonna............4,612	3	27,910 .... Britney Spears
Cheryl Cole 3,745	4	26,561 ....Posh & Becks
Katie Price...........3,700	5	26,494 .... Kate Moss
Susan Boyle 3,170	6	25,204 .... Victoria Beckham
Jade Goody............3,049	7	24,631 ...... David Beckham
Lily Allen............3,021	8	22,426 ......Michael Jackson
Peter Andre.........2,985	9	22,263 .... Simon Cowell
Kate Moss...........2,618	10	20,347 ......Paul McCartney

——— MOST-FOLLOWED PEOPLE ON TWITTER ———

In August 2010, pop star Lady Gaga overtook pop star Britney Spears to become the Twitter user with the most followers. Almost all of the top Twitterers are celebs:

	followers†		
Lady Gaga................... 5,769,841	Justin Bieber 4,726,078
Britney Spears.............. 5,713,747	Kim Kardashian............. 4,541,302
Ashton Kutcher............. 5,586,618	Oprah Winfrey............. 4,074,573
Ellen DeGeneres........... 5,086,156	Taylor Swift 3,991,330
Barack Obama 5,077,349	John Mayer.................. 3,616,053

[Source: twitaholic.com · † As of 24/8/10]

—— CELEBRITY INTRIGUE ——

{OCT 2009} · A record 25,000 people complained to the Press Complaints Commission after *Daily Mail* journalist Jan Moir wrote an article entitled, 'Why there was nothing natural about Stephen Gately's death' [see p.61]. {NOV} · Katie Price quit *I'm A Celebrity* and separated from her cross-dressing boyfriend Alex Reid live on air. ❦ Tiger Woods was found semi-conscious in the street outside his house after a minor car crash, fuelling speculation about his private life. He later released a statement apologising for his 'transgressions' [see p.303].

Lady Gaga

{DEC} · Joe McElderry was pipped to the Christmas number one spot by Rage Against the Machine after a Facebook campaign to prevent the *X Factor* winner topping the chart; Simon Cowell congratulated the couple behind the campaign, saying 'they turned this into a very exciting race' [see p.146]. {JAN 2010} · John Terry was stripped of the England captaincy after it was alleged he had conducted an affair with the ex-girlfriend of a former teammate. {FEB} · Sky reporter Kay Burley was criticised after she appeared to reduce Peter Andre to tears when she asked him how he would feel if Katie Price's new husband, Alex Reid, wanted to adopt his children. ❦ Vernon Kay made a public on-air apology to his wife Tess Daly after it was revealed he had exchanged 'racy' text messages with a number of women. {MAR} · Take That member Mark Owen publicly apologised to his partner for a series of affairs which took place prior to their 2009 marriage. ❦ Sandra Bullock's husband Jesse James

apologised to his wife and children following reports that he had had an affair; he said that the 'vast majority' of the allegations were 'untrue and unfounded'. {APR} · Sandra Bullock told *People* that she had secretly adopted an infant boy – named Louis Bardo Bullock – in January 2010; she also said that she was finalising the adoption as a single parent, and was filing for divorce. {MAY} · Russell Crowe walked out of a BBC radio interview after the presenter Mark Lawson asked whether it was true the actor had not wanted to say the famous *Gladiator* line: 'I will have my vengeance, in this life or the next.' Crowe also objected to Lawson's suggestion that his accent in *Robin Hood* sounded Irish. ❦ Lindsay Lohan was issued with an 'alcohol-monitoring anklet' as part of enhanced probation conditions that were imposed when she missed a probationary hearing because she had lost her passport and was stranded in France. {JUN} · US rapper Chris Brown was denied entry to the UK because he had been found guilty of a serious offence: assaulting singer Rihanna in 2009. ❦ Blogger Perez Hilton was much criticised for posting an 'upskirt' photo of 17-year-old Miley Cyrus. {JUL} · Lindsay Lohan was sentenced to 90 days in jail for violating the terms of her parole; she was ordered to attend a rehabilitation programme after her release. {SEP} · Lady Gaga caused bemusement when she wore a dress made of meat to the MTV Video Music Awards. ❦ George Michael was sentenced to 8 weeks in prison for driving under the influence of cannabis.

> *You've seriously got dead ears if you think that's an Irish accent.*
> — RUSSELL CROWE

—— CELEBRITY QUOTES ——

SARAH JESSICA PARKER (to the *Sun*) · I find doing karaoke incredibly depressing, really and seriously. ... I'd much rather be changing nappies – which I secretly love to do, so that's not a very good comparison. ❦ JAKE GYLLENHAAL (to BANG Showbiz) · Some people may say I am in many ways a princess so playing a prince was fitting. ❦ SUSAN BOYLE (on susanboylemusic.com) · If I had the chance I would like to have my teeth done but that would be it. I don't want to change too much of myself. Come on what do you think I'd become a Barbie doll? ❦ KATIE PRICE (on *I'm a Celebrity* ...) · I hold my hands up, for the last seven months I have acted like a right twit but that was the way I dealt with things. I'm sorry if I upset people. ❦ GUY RITCHIE (to *Esquire*) · It's okay to have beliefs, just don't believe in them. ❦ RUSSELL BRAND (to *Rolling Stone*) · The top of the hit parade would look very different if teenyboppers were exposed to heroin. It would weed a lot of them out. ❦ ROBERT PATTINSON (to *Nightline*, on fame) · I don't like people doing things for me, really, and that's the only thing that really changes. You get a lot of people offering to do things. ❦ TIGER WOODS (in a public statement) · I thought I could get away with whatever I wanted to. I felt that I had worked hard my entire life and deserved to enjoy all the temptations around me. I felt I was entitled. ❦ LADY GAGA (to the *Daily Mail*) · I can't believe I'm saying this – don't have sex. ... It's not really cool anymore to have sex all the time. It's cooler to be strong and independent. ❦ EMMA WATSON (on finishing the Harry Potter films) · I feel like someone is dying. ❦ SANDRA BULLOCK

Robert Pattinson

(after kissing Scarlett Johansson at the MTV Movie Awards; see also p.158) · Now that we have done that, can we please go back to normal? Because therapy is really expensive. ❦ KRISTEN STEWART (to British *Elle*) · What you don't see are the cameras shoved in my face and the bizarre intrusive questions being asked, or the people falling over themselves, screaming and taunting to get a reaction. ❦ JUSTIN BIEBER (via Twitter, after being mobbed by fans at the airport) · Not happy that someone stole my hat and knocked down my mama. Come on people. ❦ PRINCE (to the *Daily Mirror*) · The Internet's completely over. ... All these computers and digital gadgets are no good. They just fill your head with numbers and that can't be good for you. ❦ JULIA ROBERTS (on botox, to *Elle*) · Your face tells a story ... and it shouldn't be a story about your drive to the doctor's office. ❦ FERGIE (on how she stays thin, to *Elle*) · I'm not going to lie: There are times I play mind tricks on myself, like that the french fries are poison. ❦ KATY PERRY (to the *New York Times*, on how her younger self would see her today) · I think the 15-year-old me would be excited and flabbergasted ... and also say, 'Put on some clothes.' ❦ COURTNEY LOVE (to the *Guardian*) · I've got good social skills. Sometimes I'm a little bit weird, but never unpopular, never a bully and never a scapegoat. ❦ RUSSELL CROWE (to *GQ*) · I'm a guy who likes poetry, who writes songs. I put on make-up for a living. ... If I was a hard man, I wouldn't be any good at my job. ❦ DEMI MOORE (to *Harper's Bazaar*) · 'Cougar' has become so distasteful. I really hate that expression ... ['Puma'] has a sweeter quality, more elegant.

——CELEBRITY POLITICAL SUPPORT · ELECTION 20——

Supported the Conservatives
Kirstie Allsopp · Gary Barlow
Ian Botham · Michael Caine†
Brooke Kinsella · William Roche

Supported the Liberal Democrats
Floella Benjamin · Bella Freud
Richard Dawkins · Brian Eno
Colin Firth · Boy George
Armando Iannucci · Bianca Jagger
John Lloyd · Art Malik
Beth Orton · Daniel Radcliffe

Supported Labour
Duncan Bannatyne · Bill Bailey
Jo Brand · Antony Cotton
Alan Davies · Liz Dawn
Alex Ferguson · Eddie Izzard
Ross Kemp · Sean Pertwee
Dave Rowntree · Prunella Scales
Patrick Stewart · David Tennant
Richard Wilson

[Sources: the *Telegraph*, the *Guardian*, Sky News]
† Supported 'National Citizen Service' plans.

——————CELEBRITIES AND SCIENCE——————

In January 2010 the charity Sense About Science released its annual *Celebrities and Science* review, highlighting some of the more dubious scientific claims made by celebrities over the past year. The review also included responses from scientists and scientists-in-training, in an effort to encourage celebrities to check their facts before speaking out. A selection of celebrity quotes and scientist responses appear below:

I avoid carbonated drinks – they sap all the oxygen from your body and make your skin wrinkly – Shilpa Shetty
Carbonated drinks have no effect on oxygen levels in the body – Ron Maughan, physiologist, Loughborough University

There are even surveys suggesting that eating foie gras can lead to Alzheimer's, diabetes, and rheumatoid arthritis – Roger Moore
There is no scientific evidence that eating foie gras will directly cause Alzheimer's disease, diabetes or rheumatoid arthritis – Dr Stuart Rulten, molecular biologist, University of Sussex

[Meat] sits in your colon for 40 years and putrefies, and eventually gives you the illness you die of – Heather Mills
Meat proteins, like all other proteins, are digested by enzymes, and absorbed in the small bowel before they ever reach the colon – Dr Melita Gordon, gastroenterologist, U. of Liverpool

She is vague about her methods but I know she massages you using fluid from a placenta … I am going to try – Arsenal striker Robin Van Persie
Any benefits from the placenta treatment would more likely be due to the massage – Professor Greg Whyte, sports scientist, Liverpool John Moores University

[I] didn't believe in the theory that human beings … originated from fish that sprouted legs and crawled out of the sea – Sarah Palin, in *Going Rogue*
Evolution is not a matter of belief; the evidence is there in fossils, in embryology and in genetics – Richard Dawkins, evolutionary biologist & author

I was unaware [of] the dangerous chemicals antiperspirants contain, which have been linked to breast cancer – singer Natasha Hamilton
It is unlikely that these products would even enter the body – Dr Gary Moss, pharmaceutical scientist, U. of Keele

———— THE BBC'S SECRET TALENT LEAGUE TABLE ————

A leaked talent 'league table' reportedly compiled by managers at the Corporation's factual arm, BBC Knowledge, revealed what bosses supposedly thought of many of the network's stars. The document came to light in December 2009, when it was published by a number of papers. It was far from flattering to many of the stars it graded. The BBC declined to explain the existence of the 'talent table' but released a statement contradicting the gradings: 'The artists named are highly valued presenters and viewers will recognise that they appear regularly across our channels. Our schedules make it abundantly clear how important these presenters are to the BBC.' Some of the presenters in each of the four graded categories are tabulated below:

'Top tier – highly valued'
Alan Yentob · Stephen Fry
Nigella Lawson · Rick Stein
Richard Hammond · Andrew Marr
Jeremy Paxman · Jeremy Clarkson

'Mid-range – average appeal'
Ray Mears · Melvyn Bragg
Evan Davis · Emily Maitlis

'On the way up – worth investment'
Mark Kermode · Chris Packham
Sophie Dahl · Sue Perkins
Duncan Bannatyne · Levi Roots

'Occasional sparkle – but limited appeal'
Delia Smith · Giles Coren
Dr Robert Winston
Michael Palin · Sophie Raworth

In January 2010, Jonathan Ross announced that his 13-year relationship with the BBC would end. He was initially replaced by Claudia Winkleman (*Film 2010*) and Graham Norton (Friday nights on BBC1 and Saturday mornings on Radio 2). Ross said that he was planning a new chat show for ITV.

———————— THE BBC'S 'DEATH LISTS' ————————

In February 2010 the *Daily Mail* reported that the BBC had updated its policy for dealing with the death of high-profile figures. The system previously worked by listing major personalities as either Category 1† or Category 2, depending on their perceived significance. Those in Category 2 would merit an obituary procedure that included interrupting programmes with news flashes and the broadcast of special documentaries. From 2010, a new obituary category called 'other notables' was created to replace Category 2. Any death from this category would now be viewed as 'major breaking news stories with coverage on merit', allowing the corporation greater flexibility. The following people are said to be included in this new category:

Gordon Brown · David Cameron · Barack Obama · Nick Clegg
Muhammad Ali · Bob Dylan · Lech Walesa · Prince Harry
Princess Anne · Prince Andrew · Prince Edward · Countess of Wessex
Duchess of Cornwall · Archbishop of Canterbury · The Pope
The Dalai Lama · Margaret Thatcher · Nelson Mandela · Mikhail Gorbachev

† Category 1 apparently still exists, and is said to include only the Queen, the Duke of Edinburgh, Prince Charles, and Prince William. Should any of these people die there would be an immediate interruption of all broadcasts on BBC 1, BBC2, and BBC News channels for an official announcement.

—————————— THE TV BAFTAS · 2010 ——————————

Best actor... Kenneth Branagh · *Wallander* [BBC1]
Best actress ....Julie Walters · *Mo* [C4]
Entertainment performance...............Anthony McPartlin & Declan Donnelly
                                I'm A Celebrity ... Get Me Out Of Here! [ITV1]
Female comedy performance................Rebecca Front · *The Thick Of It* [BBC2]
Male comedy performance ....Peter Capaldi · *The Thick Of It* [BBC2]
Single drama ....*The Unloved* [C4/Revolution Films]
Drama serial...................................... *Occupation* [BBC1/Kudos Film & TV]
Drama series .... *Misfits* [E4/Clerkenwell Films]
Continuing drama............................... *EastEnders* [BBC/BBC Productions]
Feature ....*Masterchef: The Professionals* [BBC2/Shine Television]
Factual series .... *One Born Every Minute* [C4/Dragonfly Productions]
Specialist factual ....*Inside Nature's Giants* [C4/Windfall Films]
Single documentary.................................. *Wounded* [BBC1/BBC Productions]
Sport.................................... *World Athletics Championships* [BBC2/BBC Sport]
News coverage...................................... *ITV News at Ten – Haiti* [ITV1/ITN]
Current affairs.................. *Terror in Mumbai (Dispatches)* [C4/Quicksilver Media]
New Media.............................. *Virtual Revolution* [BBC2/BBC Productions]
Entertainment......................*Britain's Got Talent* [ITV1/Syco/Talkback Thames]
Sitcom.. *The Thick of It* [BBC2/BBC Productions]
International ....*Mad Men* [BBC4/Lionsgate]
Comedy programme............... *The Armstrong and Miller Show* [BBC1/Toff Media]
YouTube Audience Award ....*The Inbetweeners* [E4/Bwark Productions]

BAFTA IN QUOTES

DECLAN DONNELLY · I don't know what the hell we did wrong for the first eight series. ❦ ANTHONY McPARTLIN · You feed a couple of kangaroo testicles to a glamour model and you get a Bafta. ❦ SIMON COWELL · One of my happiest memories as a kid was when my Dad came home with a colour TV set ... So for me to be standing here tonight getting an award for making TV shows is the happiest feeling of my life. ❦ ARMANDO IANNUCCI [writer and director of *The Thick of It*] · I'd like to thank Nick Clegg for destroying our plans for the next series.

—————————— TV'S FUNNIEST CATCHPHRASE ——————————

'Yeah, but, no, but, yeah, but' – the refrain of *Little Britain*'s Vicky Pollard – was named Britain's funniest catchphrase in a 2010 survey by OnePoll.com. The top ten:

[1] Yeah, but, no, but, yeah, but · *Little Britain*
[2] D'oh! · *The Simpsons* [3] Am I bovvered? · *Catherine Tate Show*
[4] I don't believe it! · *One Foot in the Grave*
[5] Lovely jubbly! · *Only Fools & Horses* [6] I'm a laydee · *Little Britain*
[7] Deal or no deal? · *Deal or No Deal* [8] How you doin'? · *Friends*
[9] Here's one I made earlier · *Blue Peter*
[10] I am the only gay in the village · *Little Britain*

———————————— BBC iPLAYER ————————————

The BBC iPlayer received an average of 3·1m daily requests during July 2009 (0·9m for radio; 2·2m for TV). Below are the daily BBC iPlayer requests since January 2009:

———————————— TV ATTITUDES & HABITS ————————————

13% of Britons would rather give up their partner than their television, according to a 2010 survey by shopping channel QVC. In addition, the survey found that:

51% *of Britons*.................said watching TV was an integral part of their lives
42.......................watched TV as a way to relax after a stressful day
35.......................watched TV when they could not get to sleep
29.......................admitted they had the TV on for company
25.......................used the television for shopping
22.......................said they found TV therapeutic
21.......................reached for the remote control first thing in the morning
15.......................left the TV on overnight
11.......................felt safer with the TV on
10.......................used the television for gaming
10.......................used the television for education

———————————— TV TROPES ————————————

TvTropes.org is a website on which pop-culture fans from around the world catalogue the tropes (i.e., recurrent themes) employed on television and in other media. Since the site was launched in 2004, *c.*42,000 contributors ('tropers') have added entries that explain these motifs and track their (over)use. Tropes on the site include:

Boy Meets Girl · 'boy meets girl, boy loses girl, boy finds girl' (e.g., *Romeo & Juliet*) ❦ *Absent-Minded Professor* · 'a brilliant scientist, but … often forgetting things like the date, people's names, meetings, eating, people's names' (e.g., *Doctor Who*) ❦ *Chased By Angry Natives* · 'the not-so-noble savages are angry at [the hero] stealing their sacred idol and/or refusing to be dinner' (e.g., *Raiders of the Lost Ark*) ❦ *Exact Time To Failure* · 'Whenever a technological device is about to fail, the magical computer knows exactly how long it will take to fail and displays a timer counting down' (e.g., *Lost*) ❦ *I Got Better* · 'no one could survive that, yet apparently he did' (e.g., *Monty Python*).

———————————— TV & THE GENDER GAP ————————————

One woman appears on British television for every two men, according to research conducted by Dr Guy Cumberbatch for Channel 4 in March 2010. The researchers studied a sample of 386 hours of peak-time viewing on BBC1, BBC2, ITV1, C4, Five, and Sky1 and discovered that men have 65% of all roles on television – from drama to news. Older women are especially underrepresented on screen: women >40 are featured *c.*40% of the time, compared to men >40 who appear *c.*60% of the time. Women had nearly half of all roles in soap operas, but in light entertainment, drama, and comedy they make up just 40% of participants. In factual programming women account for one-third of all participants and in news broadcasting women are represented on screen just 31% of the time (although this jumps to 69% when 'softer' subjects such as health, education or cookery are featured).

——————— TV VIEWING BY GENRE AND GENDER ———————

The percent of men and women who say they watch TV programmes of various types:

Type of programme	% men	% women	% all aged >16
National or local news	73	71	72
Films	68	64	66
Comedy	64	54	59
Live sports coverage	72	37	54
Soaps	29	58	44
History	44	34	39
Food & cookery	30	46	39
Quiz shows	31	37	35
Current affairs or politics	36	29	33
Other sport	46	17	31

[Source: Taking Part: the National Survey of Culture, Leisure and Sport, Department for Culture, Media & Sport, 2007/08 England · ONS Social Trends 2010]

————————————— TV & ACTOR AGE —————————————

BBC2 is the terrestrial channel most likely to employ actors and presenters aged ≥50, according to a 2010 study commissioned by residential care provider Anchor. The percentage of actors and presenters aged ≥50 for each channel is shown below:

BBC2	ITV1	BBC1	Channel 4	Five
37%	27%	20%	12%	0%

[Based on an analysis of a week's worth of domestic, first-run programming.] 2010 research by the *Radio Times* found that the age gap between male and female TV personalities is narrowing: the average age of a woman on prime-time BBC1 and ITV1 today is 40·22, compared to 32·62 in 1950. In 1950 the average age for a man on TV was 46 – a number that remains unchanged today.

———— TELEVISION TECHNOLOGY TIMELINE ————

Nearly 30,000 people across the UK still watch television on black and white sets – according to figures released in 2009 by TV Licensing to celebrate the 40th anniversary of colour broadcasting. Below are some of the key dates in the history of TV:

1925............John Logie Baird gave the first public demonstration of television
1927.....................................the BBC was established by Royal Charter
1929..................................first television trials were made by the BBC
1931......................John Logie Baird's first outside broadcast – The Derby
1932............BBC started official broadcasts (in poor-quality 30-line pictures)
1936..... launch of 405-line high-definition transmissions from Alexandra Palace
1937....BBC chose the 405-line Marconi-EMI system over Logie Baird's system
1937.....George VI's coronation was televised – first use of outside broadcast van
1939.................television transmission suspended due to outbreak of WWII
1946.......................BBC resumed transmission, £2 licence fee introduced
1948...........................the Olympic Games were televised from Wembley
1953.........coronation of Queen Elizabeth broadcast; *c.*20m watched the event
1955...ITV began broadcasting
1962...................the first communications satellite, Telstar, was launched
1964...................BBC Two launched on higher-definition 625-line system
1966.............32m watched England beat West Germany in World Cup Final
1967....................BBC2 began first regular colour television transmissions
1969......................BBC1 and ITV began broadcasting in colour
1974......................Ceefax, the BBC's teletext service, was launched
1982......................................Channel Four began broadcasting
1984............Sky television started broadcasting to cable and satellite receivers
1988.............................ITV started broadcasting 24 hours a day
1990...Sky merged with BSB to form BSkyB
1995.....C4's quiz show *Fifteen to One* was first programme shown in widescreen
1996............BSkyB launched their first pay-per-view event – a boxing match
1997...Channel Five launched
1998............OnDigital (later ITV Digital) became first terrestrial digital service
1998.....................BBC Choice and ITV2 launched on digital platforms
2001.................E4 launched, taking an impressive 3·68% of audience share
2002..ITV Digital went into administration
2002.........................free-to-air digital TV platform Freeview launched
2006...................................first high-definition television broadcasts
2006.........................C4 became the first major broadcaster to launch a
                              computer-based video-on-demand service: 4OD
2007... Whitehaven became first British region to have analogue TV switched off
2007.................the BBC's on-demand catch-up TV service iPlayer launched
2008.........Freesat, the satellite version of free digital service Freeview, launched
2008....................ITV launched their ITV player video-on-demand service
2009...............................the United States ceased analogue broadcasting
2010..........first World Cup broadcast in H(igh) D(efinition) on terrestrial TV

[Sources: british-tv-history.co.uk, screenonline.org.uk, and various others]

———————— SESAME STREET'S 40TH ANNIVERSARY ————————

Sesame Street celebrated its 40th anniversary in November 2009. In the years since its inaugural broadcast, the show has undergone numerous changes, while maintaining its goal of preparing children across the socioeconomic spectrum for education and life. *Sesame Street* was first conceived at a New York dinner party in the 1960s, and the show drew critical acclaim almost as soon as it aired. Today *Sesame Street* is broadcast in 140 countries (though not in most of the UK since 2001), and 20 local productions exist. Below are some of the recent or current international editions:

Country/region	title	first aired	key characters include
N. Ireland	*Sesame Tree*	2008	Hilda, Potto, and Claribelle
Indonesia	*Jalan Sesama*	2008	Tantan, Momon, Putri, Jabrik
India	*Galli Galli Sim Sim*	2006	Chamki, Aanchoo, Googly, Boombah
France	*5, Rue Sésame*	2005	Nac, Griotte, Georges Le Pingouin
Bangladesh	*Sisimpur*	2005	Ikri Mikri, Halum, Shiku, Tuktuki
Japan	*Sesame Street Japan*	2004	Teena, Arthur & Pierre, Mojabo
South Africa	*Takalani Sesame*	2000	Moshe, Zuzu, Elmo, Zikwe, Kami
Egypt	*Alam Simsim*	2000	Filfil, Nimnim, Khokha
Palestine	*Shara'a Simsim*	1997	Karim, Haneen
Israel	*Rechov Sumsum*	1983	Brosh, Mahboub, Moshe Oofnik[†]
Netherlands	*Sesamstraat*	1976	Ieniemienie, Purk, Pino[‡], Tom
Germany	*Sesamstrasse*	1973	Feli Filu, Finchen, Wolle, Pferd, Gusta
Brazil	*Vila Sésamo*	1972	Garibaldo[†], Bel
Latin America	*Plaza Sésamo*	1972	Abelardo[†], Lola, Pancho

According to *Sesame Street*'s producers, the 'Sesame' in the show's title is an allusion to 'Open, Sesame!' from *The Arabian Nights*, which was chosen to convey 'excitement and adventure' ('Street' was chosen because it describes the setting). † Related to Oscar the Grouch. ‡ Related to Big Bird.

———————— UK TELEVISION EXPORTS ————————

The international sale of British television programmes (and associated activities) rose by 25% in 2008, to £980m, according to a November 2009 report by the industry body, Pact. America is the UK's largest market for television programmes and formats although, on occasion, export deals are frustrated by: the low number of episodes per series that is the norm in Britain (US TV favours longer runs); the highly UK-centric nature of our programming; and a bias towards slower, 'grittier' shows that are not as popular abroad. Export sales by territory are tabulated below:

Territory (£m)	2007	2008	±%	Territory (£m)	2007	2008	±%
USA	316	350	+11	Scandinavia	42	51	+21
Canada	28	40	+42	Rest of W Europe	65	90	+39
Germany	29	34	+17	Eastern Europe	31	44	+43
France	36	47	+29	Australia/NZ	77	127	+65
Spain	21	23	+8	Latin America	15	18	+21
Italy	22	25	+15	Asia	42	67	+57
				Other	58	67	+14

MOST COMPLAINED-ABOUT ADVERTS

The Advertising Standards Authority (ASA) received 28,978 complaints in 2009, which resulted in 2,397 advertisements being changed or withdrawn. According to the ASA's annual report, television remained the most complained-about medium, followed by the internet, posters, the national press, and transport. In broadcast media, the top complaint was offensiveness, while in non-broadcast media the top complaint was that ads were misleading. The six most complained-about ads were:

THE CHRISTIAN PARTY
The bus ad read, 'There definitely is a God' – a response to a bus ad by the British Humanist Association [see below]. Complainants argued that the statement could not be substantiated and was offensive to atheists. However, as a political-party ad it was deemed outside the ASA's remit.
1,204 complaints · Not investigated

VOLKSWAGEN
The television advert featured graphic, *Matrix*-esque scenes of a man fighting his clones alongside the slogan, 'Sometimes the only one you have to beat is yourself'. It was deemed not suitable to be shown before 9pm.
1,070 complaints · Upheld in part

HOMEPRIDE
A television advert for an oven cleaner included the tagline, 'So easy, even a man can do it'. Complainants said the ad was offensive, but the ASA said it was meant to be tongue-in-cheek.
804 complaints · Not upheld

ADVANCED MEDICAL INSTITUTE
A poster for a nasal spray asked, 'Want longer lasting sex?' Complainants found it offensive and unsuitable for public places. The ASA also found that it advertised an unlicensed medicine.
525 complaints · Upheld

ISRAELI GOV. TOURIST OFFICE
A poster headlined 'Experience Israel' showed a map of the nation that included the West Bank, Gaza Strip and Golan Heights. Complainants said this gave the impression the areas were part of the internationally recognised boundaries of Israel.
445 complaints · Upheld

BRITISH HUMANIST ASSOCIATION
A bus ad proclaimed, 'There's probably no God'. Complainants said it was offensive and could not be substantiated. The ASA said that it did not make claims about a specific faith, did not have a hostile tone, and was not capable of being objectively substantiated.
392 complaints · Not investigated

AD SPENDING

The share of global ad spending devoted to various media in 2009 is shown below:

Medium	% of global ad spending	Medium	% of global ad spending
Television	39·4	Internet	12·6
Newspapers	23·1	Magazines	10·3
		Radio	7·7

[Source: ZenithOptimedia April 2010.] ZenithOptimedia also forecast that TV would expand its share to 40·6% in 2012, while internet spending will likewise increase, to 17·1% in 2012.

OFFENSIVE LANGUAGE

The words 'cunt' and 'motherfucker' are among the most offensive that can be broadcast on radio and television, according to 2010 Ofcom research. The regulator commissioned discussion groups asking Britons whether they considered various terms acceptable for broadcast pre-watershed (before 9pm) or post-watershed (after 9pm). Ofcom discovered that the acceptability of these terms depended greatly on context, including whether they fit the audience's expectations for the character, programme, or time of broadcast; the intent with which the words were used; and whether the words were uttered by accident (i.e., on live television) or by design. Despite these considerations, Ofcom was able to group an assortment of potentially offensive terms into the following broad categories of acceptability:

Pre-watershed	*level of acceptability*	*post-watershed*
arse, breasts, bum, damn, tits	HIGHER	bitch, bloody, bollocks, crap, slag, shit, dick, bugger, goddam, wanker, piss/pissed, shag
bloody, bullocks, bugger, crap, goddam, piss/pissed	HIGHER/MEDIUM	cock, twat, bastard, shit
bitch, bastard, dick, wanker, shag, slag, shit	MEDIUM	pussy
cock, twat	MEDIUM/LOWER	fuck
pussy, fuck, motherfucker, cunt	LOWER	cunt, motherfucker

Ofcom also canvassed public opinion regarding some potentially discriminatory terms, and sorted them according to the following loose categories of acceptability:

Acceptable	*nutter, looney, mental, lezza, poof, queer, Jesus Christ, homo, gender-bender, chick with a dick, tranny*
Less acceptable	*nigger, paki, spastic, dyke, faggot, schizo, chink[1], yid, mong/mongoloid, fenian[2], towelhead, hun[3], nazi*
Polarising (divided views)	*retarded, gyppo, pikey[4], cripple*

Potentially derogatory or offensive terms for: 1. Chinese people; 2. Catholics; 3. Protestants; 4. Travellers.

PRODUCT PLACEMENT

The ban on product placement in British television programming was partially lifted in February 2010 by the SoS for Culture, Media & Sport. This relaxation of the law will allow the British television industry to remain competitive within Europe, where every country (except Denmark) allows or intends to allow product placement. Product placement will not be allowed in news, current affairs, consumer, or religious programming, and the following types of products may not be featured:

Alcoholic drinks · Food or drinks high in fat, salt or sugar
Gambling · Smoking accessories · Over-the-counter medicines
Infant formula and follow-on formula

———————— NEWSPAPER READERSHIP & ELECTIONS ————————

In October 2009, the *Sun* announced it would support the Conservatives at the 2010 general election. In the weeks following the announcement, a slew of articles attempted to forecast the effect of this switch of allegiance on the electorate. Statistics published on the *Guardian*'s Data Blog indicated that since 1992 the majority of *Sun* readers had backed the winner in each general election. Details are below:

Election year	1992			1997			2001			2005		
Newspaper (%)	Con	*Lab*	*LD*	*Con*	Lab	*LD*	*Con*	Lab	*LD*	*Con*	Lab	*LD*
Guardian	15...	55	...25	8 ...	.67	.. 22	6 ...	52	...34	7 ...	.48	.. 34
Sun	45...	36	...15	30 ...	.52	.. 12	29...	52	...11	35 ...	.44	.. 10
Telegraph	72...	11	...16	57 ...	.20	.. 17	65...	16	...14	64 ...	.14	.. 18
Express	68...	15	...15	49 ...	.29	.. 16	43...	33	...19	44 ...	.29	.. 20
Daily Mail	65...	14	...18	49 ...	.29	.. 14	55...	24	...17	57 ...	.24	.. 14
Times	64...	15	...19	42 ...	.28	.. 25	40...	28	...26	44 ...	.27	.. 24
Independent	25...	37	...35	16 ...	.47	.. 30	12...	38	...44	11 ...	.38	.. 43
Mirror	20...	63	...14	14 ...	.72	.. 11	11...	71	...13	13 ...	.66	.. 15
Star	32...	53	...12	17 ...	.66	.. 12	21...	56	...17	17 ...	.53	.. 13

[Election winner in Roman · Sources: *Guardian Guide to the House of Commons* (1992), *The Times*, Mori]

———————— DAILY NEWSPAPER READERSHIP ————————

% of adults† who read ...	1971	1978	1981	1991	2001	2009
Sun	17	29	26	22	20	16
Daily Mail	12	13	12	10	12	10
Daily Mirror	34	28	25	22	12	7
Daily Telegraph	9	8	8	6	5	4
Times	3	2	2	2	3	4
Daily Express	24	16	14	8	4	3
Daily Star	–	–	9	6	3	3
Guardian	3	2	3	3	2	2
Independent	–	–	–	2	1	1
Financial Times	2	2	2	2	1	1
Any national daily newspaper	–	72	72	62	53	42

[Source: ONS Social Trends 40, 2010 · † Adults in GB ≥15 years who read paper the day prior]

———————— BRITISH PRESS AWARDS · 2010 ————————

Newspaper of the year .... *Daily Telegraph*
Journalist of the year .... William Lewis · *Telegraph Media Group*
Reporter of the year .... Paul Lewis · *Guardian*
Photographer of the year .... Stefan Rousseau · Press Association Images
Scoop .... MPs' Expenses · *Daily Telegraph*

MAJOR BRITISH NEWSPAPERS

Title	editorial address	phone	editor	circulation	readership	cost	owner	found
Sun	1 Virginia St, Wapping, London E98 1SN	020 7782 4000	Dominic Mohan	3,042,406	7,751,000	30p	N	19[..]
Daily Mail	Northcliffe Ho., 2 Derry St, London W8 5TT	020 7938 6000	Paul Dacre	2,117,839	4,881,000	50p	A	1896
Daily Mirror	1 Canada Sq., Canary Wharf, London E14 5AP	020 7293 3000	Richard Wallace	1,242,466	3,381,000	45p	T	1903
Daily Star	10 Lower Thames St, London EC3R 6EN	020 8612 7000	Dawn Neesom	843,229	1,617,000	20p	S	1978
Daily Telegraph	111 Buckingham Palace Rd, London SW1W 0DT	020 7931 2000	Tony Gallagher	678,391	1,840,000	100p	H	1855
Daily Express	10 Lower Thames St, London EC3R 6EN	020 8612 7000	Peter Hill	663,871	1,529,000	30p	S	1900
Times	1 Virginia St, Wapping, London E98 1XY	020 7782 5000	James Harding	502,588	1,768,000	100p	N	1785
Financial Times	1 Southwark Bridge, London SE1 9HL	020 7873 3000	Lionel Barber	378,497	418,000	200p	P	1888
Guardian	Kings Place, 90 York Way, London N1 9GU	020 3353 2000	Alan Rusbridger	277,246	1,124,000	100p	G	1821
Independent	2 Derry St, London W8 5HF	020 7005 2000	Simon Kelner	183,975	635,000	100p	I	1986
Evening Standard	2 Derry St, London W8 5TT	020 3367 7000	Geordie Greig	–	1,348,000	Free	E	1827
News of the World	1 Virginia St, Wapping, London E98 1SN	020 7782 1001	Colin Myler	2,890,523	7,642,000	100p	N	1843
Mail on Sunday	Northcliffe Ho., 2 Derry St, London W8 5TT	020 7938 6899	Peter Wright	1,954,616	5,213,000	150p	A	1982
Sunday Mirror	1 Canada Sq., Canary Wharf, London E14 5AP	020 7293 3000	Tina Weaver	1,155,101	3,826,000	100p	T	1915
Sunday Times	1 Virginia St, Wapping, London E98 1XY	020 7782 5000	John Witherow	1,068,158	3,219,000	200p	N	1821
Sunday Express	10 Lower Thames St, London EC3R 6EN	020 8612 7000	Martin Townsend	568,740	1,622,000	130p	S	1918
People	1 Canada Sq., Canary Wharf, London E14 5AP	020 7293 3000	Lloyd Embley	539,692	1,331,000	95p	T	1881
Sunday Telegraph	111 Buckingham Palace Rd, London SW1W 0DT	020 7931 2000	Ian MacGregor	505,214	1,677,000	190p	H	1961
Daily Star Sunday	10 Lower Thames St, London EC3R 6EN	020 8612 7424	Gareth Morgan	370,032	950,000	90p	S	2002
Observer	Kings Place, 90 York Way, London N1 9GU	020 3353 2000	John Mulholland	314,602	1,212,000	200p	G	1791
Independent on Sun.	2 Derry St, London W8 5HF	020 7005 2000	John Mullin	155,565	600,000	180p	I	1990
Scotland on Sunday	108 Holyrood Rd, Edinburgh EH8 8AS	0131 620 8620	Ian Stewart	42,850	190,000	160p	J	1988

Ownership: [N]ews Corporation · [I]ndependent News & Media · Press [H]oldings Ltd · [A]ssociated Newspapers · [G]uardian Media Group · [J]ohnston Press · [T]rinity Mirror [E]vening Press Ltd · Northern & [S]hell Media · [P]earson · Circulation: ABC [Jul 2010] · Readership: NRS [Mar 2010] · Founded dates relate to the paper's earliest incarnation.

———————————— TOP RADIO STATIONS ————————————

A record 90·6% of the adult British population listened to the radio in January–March 2010, according to Rajar. Listed below are the BBC Radio and national commercial radio networks with the greatest share of listeners during those months:

BBC network	% reach†	Commercial network	% reach†
BBC Radio 2	28	Heart Network (UK)	14
BBC Radio 1	23	Classic FM	11
BBC Radio 4	20	Galaxy Network (UK)	8
BBC Radio 3	4	Total Magic/ Total Kiss [tie]	7
BBC Radio 5 Live	13	Total Smooth Radio/talkSPORT [tie]	5

† % of British adults >15 who listened for ≥5 mins in an average week. Source: Rajar

In March 2010, a BBC review recommended, among other cost-cutting measures, the closure of two radio stations: Asian Network and 6 Music. Although supporters of both these stations reacted with dismay, the threat to 6 Music – which champions independent and underplayed bands – became a national story. A Facebook campaign was supported by high-profile artists such as Coldplay and Jarvis Cocker, and the station's audience figures soared on the consequent publicity. In July, the BBC Trust announced that 6 Music had been saved, though Asian Network would close.

———————————— UK RADIO HALL OF FAME ————————————

The Radio Academy Hall of Fame pays tribute to 'those legendary voices who make and have made an outstanding contribution to the sound of British radio and to British cultural life'. In 2009, the academy inducted just one performer into the Hall of Fame – Sir Terry Wogan. At a lunch celebrating the induction, Sir Terry was also awarded the Performing Rights Society's John Peel Outstanding Contribution To Music Award in recognition of his 27 years at the helm of Radio 2's breakfast show. The timing of the award, a week before Wogan handed over to Chris Evans, ensured it was an emotional event – Wogan admitted, 'I don't really want to go.'

———————————— THE SONY AWARDS · 2010 ————————————

Since 1983, the Sony Radio Academy has rewarded excellence in British radio with bronze, silver, and gold awards. Some of the golds awarded in 2010 are listed below:

Breakfast show of the year [>10m listeners] ...... Today [BBC Radio News for BBC Radio 4]
Music radio personality of the year .... Scott Mills [BBC Radio 1]
Music broadcaster of the year .... Zane Lowe [BBC Radio 1]
Speech broadcaster ..Sir David Attenborough [Natural History Unit Radio, BBC Radio 4]
News journalist .... Lyse Doucet [BBC World Service News and Current Affairs]
Digital station of the year .... Planet Rock
UK station of the year .... BBC Radio 5 live

NOTABLE DESERT ISLAND DISCS · 2009–10

Castaway	luxury	favourite Desert Island Disc
Dame Ellen MacArthur	a fluffy purple worm (which she has taken everywhere)	The Boys of Summer (Don Henley)
Steve Coogan	a fully restored Morris Minor Traveller with wooden detail	We Have All the Time in the World (Louis Armstrong)
Jan Pienkowski	an audiobook of Martin Jarvis reading Just William by Richmal Crompton	Eleanor Rigby (The Beatles)
Colin Pillinger	a picture of the Clifton Suspension Bridge	As Time Goes By (Johnnie Ray)
Jerry Springer	a cheeseburger machine	Wind Beneath My Wings (Bette Midler)
Anthony Julius	San Pellegrino water on tap	The Promise of Living (Aaron Copland)
Morrissey	a comfy bed with lots of pillows	(There's Gonna Be A) Showdown (New York Dolls)
Baroness Scotland	a luxurious bathroom	Pie Jesu (Andrew Lloyd Webber, performed by Sarah Brightman)
Sebastian Coe	a piano and guide to playing it	The Closest Thing to Crazy (Katie Melua)
Sir Michael Caine	a large bed with 50% goose down and 50% feather pillows	My Way (Frank Sinatra)
David Tennant	a solar DVD player loaded with the seven series of The West Wing	White Wine in The Sun (Tim Minchin)
John Copley	his 49-year-old double bed	Dopo Notte (Handel)
June Spencer	a Scrabble board	Concierto de Aranjuez (Rodrigo)
Frank Cottrell-Boyce	a ferris wheel	Miserere (Allegri)
Emma Thompson	a saucepan (heavy bottomed with a removable handle)	Corsarsik (Patrick Doyle)
Fay Weldon	a shotgun	Rockin' My Life Away (Jerry Lee Lewis)
Dame Stephanie Shirley	Mother and Child by Henry Moore	Sonata in C, K. 545 (Mozart)
Gyorgy Pauk	a Nespresso coffee machine	Andante from the Second Sonata in A Minor (Handel)
Frank Skinner	a ukulele	The Fall (Rowche Rumble)
Lewis Gilbert	a football	I'll String Along with You (Al Bowlly with Ray Noble & His Orchestra)
Dame Fanny Waterman	a grand piano and a stool	Piano Concerto No. 3 (Beethoven)
Tim Robbins	a surfboard	A Case of You (Joni Mitchell)
Lynn Barber	a cyanide pill	Macushla (John McCormack)
Jimmy Mulville	a solar-powered espresso machine	In My Life (The Beatles)
Kathy Burke	a life-size laminated photo of entrepreneur James Caan (from BBC's Dragon's Den)	Bad Romance (Lady Gaga)

———————————— BITS VS BOXES ————————————

Britons still prefer media in physical packages over digital downloads, according to the results of a May 2010 Hewlett-Packard study. The survey of 1,000 Brits aged 16–60 years old found that the following percentages preferred hard copies of …

Books	95%	Photographs	68%
Films	75%	Music	64%

86% said they regularly accessed digital media of some kind – the average value respondents placed on their collections was £482. Only 73% of respondents said they could envision a time when they'd completely switch over to subscription-based models to purchase their digital film and music.

———————————— STATE OF THE BLOGOSPHERE ————————————

In September 2009, the blog search engine company Technorati asked 2,800 bloggers from around the world about why they blog, how their blog is run, and their thoughts on the future of blogging. The results were released in the report *State of the Blogosphere 2009*, and the answers to selected questions are presented below:

Top reasons for blogging	% of respondents
'In order to speak my mind on areas of interest'	71
'To share my expertise and experiences with others'	68
'To meet and connect with like-minded people'	49
'To keep friends and family updated on my life'	24
'To attract new clients for my business'	24

Top blog topics	% of respondents	*Top blog styles*	% of respondents
Personal musings	45	Sincere	75
Technology	41	Conversational	63
Politics	32	Expert	54
News	30	Humorous	44
Computers	28	Journalistic	41

46% of respondents said 'blogs are just as valid' as traditional media, and 69% said 'blogs are getting taken more seriously as sources of information'. 52% said 'more people will be getting their news and entertainment from blogs than from traditional media in the next five years'. 34% said they blogged 'for fun', and did not make or plan to make a profit. 48% of respondents were from the US, 26% from the EU, and the rest from elsewhere. ❦ Technorati also ranks the 100 most influential blogs, based on links and other factors. The top ten in August 2010 were:

1	The Huffington Post	6	Gawker
2	Mashable!	7	TMZ.com
3	TechCrunch	8	The Daily Beast
4	Gizmodo	9	Boing Boing
5	Engadget	10	ReadWriteWeb

———————————— TOO MUCH INFORMATION? ————————————

The total amount of information consumed in the US in 2008 was estimated to be:

1·3 trillion hours · 10,845 trillion words · 3·6 zettabytes†

This is according to a December 2009 report *How Much Information?* – released by the Global Information Industry Center at the University of California San Diego. The report was an ambitious attempt to quantify the information Americans consumed in 2008 during all non-work hours. Information was defined as 'data delivered for use by a person', as opposed to by a machine, and was measured in hours, words, and bytes. The estimates were based on a wide variety of academic, government, and corporate studies of information consumption in previous years. The report also listed the amount of information consumed daily, by media type:

Medium	hours per day	gigabytes per day	words per day
TV	4·91	11·75	45,100
Radio	2·22	0·1	10,645
Phone	0·73	0·01	5,269
Print	0·6	0·01	8,659
Computer	1·93	0·08	27,122
Computer games	0·93	18·46	2,459
Movies	0·03	3·3	198
Recorded music	0·45	0·08	1,112
TOTAL	11·8	33·8	100,564

To bring these numbers into perspective, some comparison figures are listed below‡:

Average YouTube clip ... 2 mins 46 secs	Hi-res digital picture... *c*.10 megabytes
Average film ... 110 mins	*War and Peace* .... *c*.460,000 words
One hour of hi-def video .*c*.7 gigabytes	English language ... *c*.1,000,000 words

According to the report, Americans consume 6% more information each year. As this 'info explosion' continues, very large units of measurement for digital data have become more common. The largest appear below, with examples of their capacity:

Terabyte	10^{12} *bytes*	1,000,000,000,000	*size of largest hard drive*
Petabyte	10^{15}	1,000,000,000,000,000	*799m copies of Moby-Dick*
Exabyte	10^{18}	1,000,000,000,000,000,000	*200,000 British Libraries*
Zettabyte	10^{21}	1,000,000,000,000,000,000,000	*all data created in 2009§*
Yottabyte	10^{24}	1,000,000,000,000,000,000,000,000	*essentially incomprehensible*

† According to *How Much Information?*, 3·6 zettabytes printed as text in paperback books would stretch in a 7ft layer across the continental United States and Alaska. ‡ YouTube length according to the Digital Ethnography project at Kansas State University. Film length calculated by Slashfilm.com based on the top 50 movies of 2008. Number of words in the English language according to Global Language Monitor. Other measurements according to *How Much Information?* and *The New York Times*. § Zettabyte equivalent according to a September 2009 speech by Google CEO Eric Schmidt.

Music & Cinema

Lady Gaga ... New York's answer to Su Pollard.
— PETER KAY at the Brit Awards [see p.146]

——— UK NUMBER ONES · 2009–10 ———

W/ending	weeks	artist	song
29·08·09	1	David Guetta *ft.* Akon	*Sexy Chick*
05·09·09	1	Dizzee Rascal	*Holiday*
12·09·09	1	Jay-Z *ft.* Rihanna & Kanye West	*Run This Town*
19·09·09	1	Pixie Lott	*Boys & Girls*
26·09·09	3	Taio Cruz	*Break Your Heart*
17·10·09	1	Chipmunk	*Oopsy Daisy*
24·10·09	1	Alexandra Burke *ft.* Flo Rida	*Bad Boys*
31·10·09	2	Cheryl Cole	*Fight For This Love*
14·11·09	1	JLS	*Everybody in Love*
21·11·09	1	Black Eyed Peas	*Meet Me Halfway*
28·11·09	1	X Factor Finalists 2009	*You Are Not Alone*
05·12·09	2	Peter Kay's Animated All Star Band	*BBC Children in Need*
19·12·09	1	Lady Gaga	*Bad Romance*
26·12·09	1	Rage Against The Machine	*Killing in the Name*
02·01·10	1	Joe McElderry	*The Climb*
09·01·10	1	Lady Gaga	*Bad Romance*
16·01·10	2	Iyaz	*Replay*
30·01·10	3	Owl City	*Fireflies*
20·02·10	2	Helping Haiti	*Everybody Hurts*
06·03·10	1	Jason Derulo	*In My Head*
13·03·10	2	Tinie Tempah	*Pass Out*
27·03·10	2	Lady Gaga *ft.* Beyoncé	*Telephone*
10·04·10	2	Scouting for Girls	*This Ain't a Love Song*
24·04·10	1	Usher *ft.* Will I Am	*OMG*
01·05·10	1	Diana Vickers	*Once*
08·05·10	3	Roll Deep	*Good Times*
29·05·19	1	B.o.B. *ft.* Bruno Mars	*Nothin' on You*
05·06·10	1	Dizzee Rascal	*Dirtee Disco*
12·06·10	1	David Guetta *ft.* Chris Willis	*Gettin' Over You*
19·06·10	2	Shout *ft.* Dizzee Rascal & James Corden	*Shout for England*
03·07·10	2	Katy Perry ft Snoop Dogg	*California Gurls*
17·07·10	1	JLS	*The Club is Alive*
24·07·10	1	B.o.B. *ft.* Hayley Williams	*Airplanes*
31·07·10	1	Yolanda be Cool *vs* D Cup	*We No Speak Americano*
07·08·10	1	Wanted	*All Time Low*
14·08·10	1	Ne-Yo	*Beautiful Monster*

MOST-VIEWED YOUTUBE VIDEOS

Videos by Justin Bieber, Lady Gaga, and amusing babies all made inroads on YouTube in 2010. The top-viewed videos on the site as of July 2010 are listed below:

Justin Bieber · *Baby* ft. *Ludacris* ....*views* – 255m
Lady Gaga · *Bad Romance* 249m
Charlie bit my finger – again! [†] 212m
Evolution of Dance by Judson Laipply [‡] 147m
Miley Cyrus · *Party In The USA* 140m

[†] Home video of infant biting another child's finger. [‡] Comedian acting out C20th dance crazes.

FANTASY DUETS

A duet between Lady Gaga and Elvis Presley was the fantasy musical pairing the British would most like to see, according to a March 2010 poll commissioned by the dating site Match.com. The nation's favourite fantasy musical couples are below:

(1) Lady Gaga & Elvis Presley · (2) Michael Bublé & Nina Simone
(3) Aretha Franklin & Luther Vandross · (4) Barbra Streisand & Will Young
(5) Bonnie Tyler & Meat Loaf

FAVOURITE ROCK SONG

Stairway To Heaven was voted the nation's most-loved rock song in a 2010 poll by digital station Absolute Classic Rock. The nation's top rock anthems were said to be:

1 . *Stairway To Heaven* · Led Zeppelin[†]
2 ... *Won't Get Fooled Again* · The Who
3 .... *Bohemian Rhapsody* · Queen
4 ..... *Whole Lotta Love* · Led Zeppelin
5 .. *Smoke On The Water* · Deep Purple
† Led Zep took three spots in the top 10.

TOP KARAOKE SONGS

Abba's 1974 Eurovision Song Contest winner – *Waterloo* – was named the nation's favourite karaoke track by the Performing Right Society in a 2009 survey. The list was compiled using data from the mid-1990s (when the karaoke craze took off in Britain) to the present day. The top ten most popular karaoke classics were:

1 .... *Waterloo* · Abba
2 .... *Bohemian Rhapsody* · Queen
3 .... *My Way* · Frank Sinatra
4 .... *I Will Survive* · Gloria Gaynor
5 .... *Dancing Queen* · Abba
6 .... *Angels* · Robbie Williams
7 .... *Like A Virgin* · Madonna
8 ...... *It's Raining Men* · Weather Girls
9 .... *Summer Nights*
Olivia Newton John & John Travolta
10 .... *I Should Be So Lucky*
Kylie Minogue

———— MOST-PLAYED MUSICIANS OF THE DECADE————

Madonna was the artist whose music was most often played in public in the UK during the noughties, according to figures released by licensing body PPL. The organisation tracked tunes played on radio and TV, as well as in pubs, clubs, restaurants, and shops, between 2000–09. The ten most-played acts appear in the list below:

(1) Madonna · (2) The Beatles · (3) Robbie Williams
(4) Queen · (5) Take That · (6) Sugababes · (7) Elton John
(8) Elvis Presley · (9) Abba · (10) Coldplay

In addition, the following songs were the most-played in public during the decade:

(1) *Chasing Cars*, Snow Patrol (released 2006) · (2) *Shine*, Take That (2006)
(3) *I Don't Feel Like Dancin'*, Scissor Sisters (2006) · (4) *Love It When You Call*,
The Feeling (2005) · (5) *About You Now*, Sugababes (2007)

———————— NME ALBUM OF THE DECADE————————

The top ten best albums of the decade, as proposed by *NME* at the close of 2009:

1 ... The Strokes .... *Is This It* (released 2001)
2 ... The Libertines .... *Up The Bracket* (2002)
3 ... Primal Scream .... *XTRMNTR* (2000)
4 ... Arctic Monkeys .... *Whatever People Say I Am, That's What I'm Not* (2006)
5 ... Yeah Yeah Yeahs .... *Fever To Tell* (2003)
6 ... PJ Harvey .... *Stories From The City, Stories From The Sea* (2000)
7 ... Arcade Fire .... *Funeral* (2005)
8 ... Interpol .... *Turn On The Bright Lights* (2002)
9 ... The Streets .... *Original Pirate Material* (2002)
10.. Radiohead .... *In Rainbows* (2007)

———————— GLOBAL BEST-SELLING ALBUMS · 2009————————

Album	*artist*
I Dreamed a Dream	Susan Boyle
The E.N.D. (The Energy Never Dies)	Black Eyed Peas
This Is It	Michael Jackson
Fearless	Taylor Swift
The Fame	Lady Gaga
Crazy Love	Michael Bublé
No Line on the Horizon	U2
Thriller	Michael Jackson
Number Ones	Michael Jackson
My Christmas	Andrea Bocelli

[Source: IFPI · physical albums & downloads]

—— BANDS WE WOULD MOST LIKE TO SEE REFORM ——

PRS for Music asked the British public in November 2009 to name the band (with the majority of original members still alive) they would most like to see reform:

Band	year of split	%
ABBA	1983	25
The Police	1984	13
Pink Floyd	1985/95†	11
The Smiths	1987	11
Oasis	2009	10
The Jam	1982	9

Band	year of split	%
Dire Straits	1995	8
The Clash	1986	6
Spice Girls	2001	4
Sex Pistols	1978	3

† Roger Waters left in 1985, but the group continued recording without him until 1995.

To the delight of fans, 2010 saw several musical groups reunite. Soundgarden announced their reunion in January 2010, while Pavement embarked upon a reunion tour in March. In June, Bush announced their reunion, and in July, Robbie Williams confirmed that he had rejoined Take That.

—————— HERITAGE PLAQUES ——————

In 2009 the Performing Right Society announced a scheme to install Heritage Plaques at the locations where famous UK bands first performed. The inaugural plaque was unveiled on 30 November at the East Anglian Railway Museum's Goods Yard, to commemorate the location of Blur's first gig in 1989. The Society plans to install the plaques around the UK, and to create a database and interactive map charting their locations. After Blur, the first five Heritage Plaques honoured:

Dire Straits.............*first performed* outside flats in Deptford, London, 1977
Jethro Tull.................Holy Family RC Church, Blackpool, Lancashire, 1964
Squeeze...Greenwich Dance Hall, London, 1975
Sir Elton John...............................The Northwood Hills, London, 1962
Snow Patrol....................Duke of York pub, Belfast, Northern Ireland, 1998

—————— MUSICAL INSTRUMENT MUSEUM ——————

In April 2010, the Musical Instrument Museum in Phoenix, Arizona, opened its doors. The $250m project claims to be the first museum devoted to musical instruments from around the world, and its collection of 12,000 instruments represents every nation on the globe (3,000 objects have been put on display). The brainchild of US businessman Bob Ulrich, the collection was assembled by five curators who consulted ethnomusicologists and local experts. Instruments on view include:

Nigerian trumpet made of food cans · Appalachian dulcimer, sousaphone & ukulele
Hanging drum from Japan's Edo period · Piano on which Lennon wrote 'Imagine'
C17th English bentside spinet · Apache fiddle · 1725 Bohemian viola d'amore
Benin Vodun drums · Uighur bowed lute · Italian octobasse · Indonesian sasandu
Giant drum played at the 2008 Chinese Olympics

THE BRIT AWARDS · 2010

The 30th-anniversary Brit Awards were hosted by the affable comedian Peter Kay, whose down-to-earth style proved a welcome contrast to the glitz and egos of the assembled musicians. Cheryl Cole was praised by the press for her 'bravery' in performing an energetic (some said defiant) rendition of her hit single *Fight For This Love* in the wake of lurid tabloid allegations involving her footballer husband, Ashley Cole. The flamboyantly idiosyncratic Lady Gaga gave the awards some edge with a stand-out acoustic performance. The 2010 Brit Awards winners are below:

British male solo artist .... Dizzee Rascal
British female solo artist .... Lily Allen
British group .... Kasabian
British album .... Florence + the Machine · *Lungs*
British single .... JLS · *Beat Again*
British breakthrough act .... JLS
International male solo artist .... Jay-Z
International female solo artist .... Lady Gaga
International album .... Lady Gaga · *The Fame*
International breakthrough act .... Lady Gaga
Critics' choice .... Ellie Goulding
Brits best album of 30 years .... Oasis · *(What's the Story) Morning Glory?*
Best performance of 30 yrs . The Spice Girls · *Wannabe/Who Do You Think You Are*
Outstanding contribution to music .... Robbie Williams

IN QUOTES: PETER KAY (introducing Lady Gaga) · New York's answer to Su Pollard. ❧ LADY GAGA (tearfully) · I was really excited to win the first two awards. This award means even more to me because I worked so hard on this album for so long. ❧ LILY ALLEN · I only wore this orange wig because I thought it would be hard for the cameramen to find me to catch my disappointed face. ❧ DIZZEE RASCAL · It's about time as well. ❧ LIAM GALLAGHER (on Oasis) · The best band in the fucking world.

CHRISTMAS NUMBER ONE · 2009

After four consecutive Christmas number ones, Simon Cowell's yuletide *X Factor* spell was finally broken in December 2009, when Rage Against The Machine's rebellious anthem *Killing in the Name* triumphed over *X Factor* winner Joe McElderry, selling *c*.500,000[†] copies to McElderry's *c*.450,000. McElderry was the obvious candidate to take the festive top spot – even with a somewhat lacklustre version of Miley Cyrus's syrupy 2009 ballad, *The Climb*. However, a Facebook group, established by husband and wife Jon and Tracy Morter, urged 'real' music fans to rage against the corporate machine by purchasing the 1992 single *Killing in the Name* – chosen because of its anarchic refrain: 'Fuck you, I won't do what you tell me.' This unholy chart battle kept the nation enthralled and amused – though for all the anti-establishment aspirations of the Morters' campaign, the real winner appeared to be the corporate giant Sony, the record label behind both singles. († This was the first time a band had hit the British number one spot based solely on download sales.)

OTHER NOTABLE MUSIC AWARDS · 2010

Awards	prize	*winner*
	Best British band	Bullet For My Valentine
Kerrang!	*Hall of fame*	Mötley Crüe
	Best live band	Bullet For My Valentine
	Best British band	Muse
	Best solo artist	Jamie T
NME	*Best new band*	Bombay Bicycle Club
	Best album	Kasabian · *West Ryder Pauper Lunatic Asylum*
	God-like genius award	Paul Weller
	Best female video	Lady Gaga · *Bad Romance*
MTV	*Video of the year*	Lady Gaga · *Bad Romance*
	Best new artist	Justin Bieber
	Record of the year	Kings Of Leon · *Use Somebody*
Grammys	*Album of the year*	Taylor Swift · *Fearless*
	Song of the year	Beyoncé · *Single Ladies (Put A Ring On It)*
	Best new artist	Zac Brown Band
	Best song	Lily Allen & Greg Kurstin · *The Fear*
Ivor Novello	*Songwriter of the year*	Lily Allen & Greg Kurstin
	Most performed work	Lily Allen & Greg Kurstin · *The Fear*
	Best contemporary song	Daniel · *Natasha Khan*
	Best UK act	N-Dubz
	Best newcomer	JLS
MOBO [2009]	*Best R&B/soul*	Keri Hilson
	Best hip hop	Chipmunk
	Best African act	Nneka
	Icon award	Duane Eddy
MOJO	*Maverick*	Hawkwind
	Song of the year	Kasabian · *Fire*
	Best album	Richard Hawley · *Truelove's Gutter*

THE MERCURY MUSIC PRIZE · 2010

The 2010 Mercury Music Prize was won by the 3-piece band The xx for its album *xx* – described by the *Guardian* as 'lustrous, nagging, near-lubricious goth'n'b', and by the *NME* as 'the perfect sound-track for wandering aimlessly along rainy London streets'. The Mercury judges encapsulated the thinking behind The xx's award with one word – 'atmosphere'. The xx's singer and guitarist Ollie Sim said, 'it's felt a bit like a haze to us, being here has been a weird moment of clarity. It just means so much.'

The other 2010 Mercury nominees	
Biffy Clyro .... *Only Revolutions*	Kit Downes Trio .... *Golden*
Corinne Bailey Rae .... *The Sea*	Laura Marling... *I Speak Because I Can*
Dizzee Rascal.......... *Tongue n' Cheek*	Mumford & Sons........ *Sigh No More*
Foals.................. *Total Life Forever*	Paul Weller...... *Wake Up the Nation*
I Am Kloot............... *Sky at Night*	Villagers..............*Becoming a Jackal*
	Wild Beasts............... *Two Dancers*

——————— THE EUROVISION SONG CONTEST · 2010 ———————

The UK went into Eurovision 2010 with the bold hope that it could match or even improve upon 2009's performance, when a song written by Andrew Lloyd Webber came in a respectable fifth. In January, the BBC announced that the UK entry would be penned by Pete Waterman and Mike Stock, of 1980s hit factory Stock Aitken Waterman. In March, six unknown acts vied on BBC 1's *Your Country Needs You!* for the chance to sing *That Sounds Good To Me* at the Eurovision finals in Oslo:

Alexis Gerred · Esma Akkilic · Josh Dubovie · Karen Harding · Miss Fitz · Uni5

19-year-old Essex lad Josh Dubovie was chosen by a public vote to represent the UK.

Paddy Power's odds for Eurovision winner
Azerbaijan 2/1 · Germany 3/1 · Armenia 6/1 · Israel 10/1 · UK 150/1

THE FINAL · 29·05·10 · OSLO, NORWAY

The European economic crisis obliged the hosts Norway to scale back the final stage show, and budgetary constraints forced a number of countries (Hungary, Andorra, the Czech Republic, and Montenegro) to remain at home. Yet even the near collapse of the euro could not dampen the all too familiar admixture of soaring ballads, energetic dance moves, and industrial-strength hair product. Unscripted entertainment was provided by a stage-crasher who briefly danced with the Spanish entrants before scarpering. ❦ Amidst the spandex and spangles, Lena, a sprightly 19-year-old representing Germany, proved refreshingly uncomplicated. (She was not hindered by the fact that her contemporary pop song, *Satellite*, was already a hit across Europe.) In contrast, the UK was not a hit. As the points rolled in (a fifty-fifty mix of votes from the public and judging panels), it became clear that Dubovie would not escape the ignominy of last place. Although Dubovie managed to scrape just 10 points, many in the press were more critical of Waterman and Stock's cheesy pop confection than its unfortunate performer. The UK's disastrous showing – the third time it had ranked last in eight years – prompted some to question why the country perseveres in participating in a contest to which it is so patently ill-suited. ❦ The top three acts at Eurovision 2010, with their points, are tabulated below:

Country	artist	song	score
Germany	Lena	*Satellite*	246
Turkey	maNga	*We Could Be The Same*	170
Romania	Paula Seling & Ovi	*Playing With Fire*	162

SONG LYRICS OF NOTE

GERMANY · *Love my aim is straight and true, Cupid's arrow is just for you, I even painted my toenails for you, I did it just the other day.* ❦ ARMENIA · *Kisses of the earth, Fruits of the sun, Apricot stone, Hidden in my hand, Given back to me, From the motherland.* ❦ UK · *So if you bring the sunshine, I'll bring the good times, Just add your laughter, It's happy ever after.* ❦ IRELAND · *Look straight ahead, Hold on to your dreams, Believe in this magic, Open your eyes, Open your mind, And it's there.* ❦ SWITZERLAND · *Pampadadam padadam padadadada, pam pada dam pada dam.*

─────────── ILLEGAL MUSIC DOWNLOADS ───────────

Only 9% of British adults admit to downloading music illegally from the internet, although 33% say they have used search engines to find 'unofficial' music services where they can download tracks for free. This 2009 research, released by the think tank Demos, indicated that illegal downloaders have the following characteristics:

57% are male · 70% are under 35
90% own an iPod, iPhone, or other MP3 player
80% have bought CDs, vinyl, or downloads in the past 12 months
66% also download movies, games or software illegally

Interestingly, Demos's research indicated that those who download music illegally spend the most on legal music – on average, £77 a year on legitimate music purchases. This contrasts to adults who claim never to download music illegally, who spend on average just £44 a year on music. Those who used unofficial music downloading services were asked how this affected their music buying habits; their responses are below:

Buy a lot more music	10%	Buy a little less music	8%
Buy a little more music	16%	Buy a lot less music	11%
Buy about the same	47%	Don't know	9%

When asked why they downloaded music illegally, the following reasons were given:

Because I can/it's available	46%	Already own song on CD/vinyl	25
To try before I buy	42	Spend enough money on	
To find things not available on		music already	20
commercial legal services	32	Don't see anything wrong with it	19
Don't have enough money to pay	27	Nobody ever gets caught/fined	9
Because lots of people do it	27	I don't care about copyright	9

72% of those who admit to illegally downloading music said they would be interested in an official paid-for download subscription service[†] (compared to just 47% of all British adults), indicating that a dearth of appealing legal sites may be deterring people from paying for music. Respondents who admitted downloading illegally were asked which of the following would deter them from the practice:

The availability of new appealing legal music services 64%
The threat of having their internet service suspended for one month 61
The threat of receiving a fine 61
Concerns about getting a virus/spyware 58
Receiving a warning letter from their internet service provider 57
The threat of internet speed being significantly reduced for a month 41
The threat of having internet service suspended for an hour 33
Publicity about impact on the music industry 25
Disapproval of friends and family 23

† The research suggested revenue would be maximised at £5/month for unlimited legal downloads.

——————— CHILDREN'S FAVOURITE CLASSICAL TUNE ———————

Children's top ten classical tunes, according to a November 2009 poll by *Classic FM*:

[1] *Harry Potter theme* · John Williams · [2] *Walking in the Air* (The Snowman)
· Howard Blake [3] *Peter's Theme* (Peter and the Wolf) · Sergei Prokofiev
[4] *Dance of the Sugar Plum Fairy* (The Nutcracker) · Tchaikovsky
[5] *The Duck Scene* (Peter and the Wolf) · Sergei Prokofiev
[6] *The Sorcerer's Apprentice* (Fantasia) · Paul Dukas
[7] *Pomp and Circumstance Op. 39, No. 4* (Fantasia) · Edward Elgar
[8] *Canon* · Johann Pachelbel [9] *Romeo and Juliet* · Sergei Prokofiev
[10] *Flight of the Bumblebee* · Nikolai Rimsky-Korsakov

——————— MOST LISTENED-TO CLASSICAL PIECE ———————

Carl Orff's *O Fortuna* from *Carmina Burana* was named the most listened-to classical track of the past 75 years according to a December 2009 list compiled by
royalties collection body PPL. The top ten most listened-to classical pieces were:

#	piece	composed by	conducted by
1	*O Fortuna*	Carl Orff	Kurt Eichhorn
2	*Fantasia on a Theme*	Ralph Vaughan Williams	Bernard Haitink
3	*Scheherazade*	Nikolai Rimsky-Korsakov	Charles Mackerras
4	*The Sleeping Beauty*	Pyotr Tchaikovsky	Mikhail Pletnev
5	*Romance in F Sharp Major*	Robert Schumann	Joseph Cooper
6	*Sylvia*	Léo Delibes	Richard Boynge
7	*Symphony No. 2*	Sergei Rachmaninov	Vladimir Ashkenazy
8	*The Planets*	Gustav Holst	James Loughran
9	*The Sleeping Beauty*	Pyotr Tchaikovsky	Valery Gergiev
10	*Symphony No. 5*	Franz Schubert	Neville Marriner

——————— CLASSIC FM HALL OF FAME · 2010 ———————

Each year *Classic FM* asks listeners to vote for their favourite classical pieces, and
the top 300 are inducted into the station's 'Hall of Fame'. The 2010 top ten were:

	[2009:1]	Ralph Vaughan Williams	*The Lark Ascending*
1	[2009:1]	Ralph Vaughan Williams	*The Lark Ascending*
2	[2]	Sergei Rachmaninov	*Piano Concerto No. 2*
3	[3]	Ralph Vaughan Williams	*Fantasia on a Theme by Thomas Tallis*
4	[4]	Ludwig van Beethoven	*Piano Concerto No. 5 ('Emperor')*
5	[8]	Edward Elgar	*Cello Concerto*
6	[6]	Wolfgang Amadeus Mozart	*Clarinet Concerto*
7	[5]	Ludwig van Beethoven	*Symphony No. 6 ('Pastoral')*
8	[10]	Edward Elgar	*Enigma Variations*
9	[9]	Ludwig van Beethoven	*Symphony No. 9 ('Choral')*
10	[7]	Max Bruch	*Violin Concerto No. 1*

BBC PROMS · 2010

The 116th Proms season (16/7–11/9) featured 31 major new commissions and premieres (including 17 new works from British composers), as well as celebrations of Stephen Sondheim, Rodgers and Hammerstein, and the event's founder-conductor, Henry Wood. Dr Who returned to the Proms for two performances featuring music from the show, a selection of classical favourites, and Matt Smith, the new Time Lord. ☙ The BBC announced that the 2010 Proms had been record-breaking; the total audience had grown 5% (on 2009), and 39,600 people bought tickets for the first time.

PROM 76 · THE LAST NIGHT OF THE PROMS · 11·9·2010

Jonathan Dove (BBC commission, world premiere)	*A Song of Joys*
Pyotr Ilyich Tchaikovsky	*Capriccio Italien*
Pyotr Ilyich Tchaikovsky (arr. Maxim Rysanov)	*Rococo Variations*
Hubert Parry	*Blest Pair of Sirens*
Richard Strauss	*Verführung, Op. 33 No. 1*
	Freundliche Vision, Op. 48 No. 1; Ständchen, Op. 17 No. 2
	Winterweihe, Op. 48 No. 4; Zueignung, Op. 10 No. 1
Emmanuel Chabrier	*Joyeuse marche*
Bedřich Smetana	*Dalibor – Dobrá! Já mu je dám! ... Jak je mi?*
Antonín Dvořák	*Rusalka – Song to the Moon*
Vaughan Williams	*Suite for viola and small orchestra – Prelude; Galop*
Richard Wagner	*Lohengrin – Bridal Chorus*
Richard Rodgers & Oscar Hammerstein	*Carousel – You'll never walk alone*
Trad. (arr. Nic Raine)	*Fisher's Hornpipe*
Thomas Arne (arr. Malcolm Sargent)	*Rule, Britannia!*
Hubert Parry (orch. Edward Elgar)	*Jerusalem*
Edward Elgar	*Pomp and Circumstance March No. 1, Land of Hope and Glory*
Henry Wood (arr.)	*The National Anthem*

ROYAL PHILHARMONIC SOCIETY AWARDS · 2009

Chamber-scale composition	Kevin Volans · *viola:piano*
Large-scale composition	Kaija Saariaho · *Notes on Light*
Conductor	Oliver Knussen
Instrumentalist	Stephen Hough
Singer	Philip Langridge
Ensemble	London Sinfonietta

THE CLASSICAL BRITS · 2010

Best album	Only Men Aloud · *Band Of Brothers*
Female artist of the year	Angela Gheorghiu
Male artist of the year	Vasily Petrenko
Young British classical performer or group	Jack Liebeck
Lifetime achievement award	Dame Kiri Te Kanawa

—————— PLACIDO DOMINGO & CHANGING REGISTER ——————

Plácido Domingo took on his first baritone role in more than 50 years in October 2009, performing the title role in Verdi's *Simon Boccanegra* at the State Opera in Berlin. Famous as one of the Three Tenors, Domingo began his singing career as a baritone, but switched to tenor at the behest of the Mexican National Opera in 1959. Critics have previously delighted in the rich tones at the lower end of Domingo's vocal register, and the move has been seen as an effort to prolong the 68-year-old's career. (Domingo is booked to appear both as a tenor and a baritone as far in advance as the 2013–14 season.) In January 2007, when it was confirmed that Domingo would appear as Simon Boccanegra, Tim Ashley noted in the *Guardian*: 'Voices are notoriously tricky things. They change with age, time and training, and a shift in type or register, whether upwards or downwards, is not uncommon in the operatic world.' Other notable opera singers to have switched registers include:

Singer	singing voice	also performed as
Lorraine Hunt Lieberson	mezzo-soprano	soprano
Christa Ludwig	mezzo-soprano	soprano
Lauritz Melchior	tenor	baritone
James Morris	bass	baritone
Leonie Rysanek	soprano	mezzo-soprano
Ramón Vinay	tenor	baritone

—————— QUEEN'S MEDAL FOR MUSIC ——————

The Queen's Medal for Music is awarded annually to those who have had 'a major influence on the musical life of the nation'. The nomination process is overseen by a committee under the chairmanship of the Master of the Queen's Music[†], currently Sir Peter Maxwell Davies. In November 2009, the award was presented to the president of the London Symphony Orchestra, SIR COLIN DAVIS. ❦ Sir Colin began his musical career as a clarinettist; he attended the Royal College of Music and subsequently played in the band of the Household Cavalry while completing national service. Yet Davis's passion was conducting and he spent his early years amassing freelance work. In 1957, he was appointed assistant conductor to the BBC Scottish Orchestra. Two years later, he was made Principal Conductor at Sadler's Wells. Davis rapidly expanded his conducting credits with guest spots across America, from the New York Philharmonic to the Boston Symphony Orchestra. During this time he became known for tackling modern atonal works (such as those by Michael Tippet) with as much gusto as the classics. Davis's star continued to rise, affording him opportunities to work with many of the world's greatest orchestras, including the Royal Opera at Covent Garden, the Bavarian Radio Symphony Orchestra, the BBC Symphony Orchestra, and the London Symphony Orchestra, with which he has had a fifty-year association.

† Committee members include: *The Times's* critic Richard Morrison; composer Michael Berkeley; MD of the Barbican Nicholas Kenyon; and former chair of the Royal Opera House, Lord Moser.

———————— CLASSICAL ANNIVERSARIES · 2011 ————————

2011 marks 200 years since the birth of Hungarian composer and pianist FRANZ LISZT (22·10·1811) and 100 years since the death of Austrian composer and conductor GUSTAV MAHLER (18·5·1911). Some other notable anniversaries are below:

b.1561.....................Jacopo Peri
b.1661........Giacomo Antonio Perti
b.1711.................William Boyce
b.1711.............. Ignaz Holzbauer
b.1711... Jean-Joseph de Mondonville
b.1811................Ferdinand Hiller
b.1811.............. Ambroise Thomas
b.1861........Marco Enrico Bossi
b.1861...............Pierre de Bréville
b.1861........Charles Martin Loeffler
b.1911.............. Jehan-Ariste Alain
b.1911...Bernard Herrmann [see p.163]
b.1911................Alan Hovhaness
b.1911............ Gian Carlo Menotti

b.1911........Gustaf Allan Pettersson
b.1911.............. Franz Reizenstein
b.1911......................Nino Rota
b.1911........ Phyllis (Margaret) Tate
b.1911.......... Vladimir Ussachevsky
d.1361............... Philippe de Vitry
d.1611........Tomás Luis de Victoria
d.1761....................Francesco Feo
d.1861......Anthony Philip Heinrich
d.1861............. Heinrich Marschner
d.1911......Félix-Alexandre Guilmant
d.1911....... Johan Severin Svendsen
d.1961.................Percy Grainger
d.1961................. Carlos Salzédo

———————— OPERA ANNIVERSARIES · 2011 ————————

The following operas celebrate the anniversary of their original premieres in 2011:

Opera	composer	premiered	anniversary
The Death of Klinghoffer	John Adams	1991, Brussels	20th
Gawain	Harrison Birtwistle	1991, London	20th
Amahl & the Night Visitors	Gian Carlo Menotti	1951, New York	60th
Billy Budd	Benjamin Britten	1951, London	60th
The Pilgrim's Progress	Ralph Vaughan Williams	1951, London	60th
The Rake's Progress	Igor Stravinsky	1951, Venice	60th
The Love for Three Oranges	Sergei Prokofiev	1921, Chicago	90th
Der Rosenkavalier	Richard Strauss	1911, Dresden	100th
L'heure espagnole	Maurice Ravel	1911, Paris	100th
Rusalka	Antonín Dvořák	1901, Prague	110th
Hérodiade	Jules Massenet	1881, Brussels	130th
Libuše	Bedřich Smetana	1881, Prague	130th
The Maid of Orleans	Pyotr Tchaikovsky	1881, St Petersburg	130th
The Tales of Hoffmann	Jacques Offenbach	1881, Paris	130th
Aïda	Giuseppe Verdi	1871, Cairo	140th
Norma	Vincenzo Bellini	1831, Milan	180th
The Magic Flute	Wolfgang A. Mozart	1791, Munich	220th
Rinaldo	George Frideric Handel	1711, London	300th
Calisto	Francesco Cavalli	1651, Venice	360th

[Source: *The New Kobbé's Opera Book*, edited by the Earl of Harewood & Anthony Peattie, 1997.]

THE RETURN OF 3-D

In cinematic terms, 2010 may be remembered as the fruition of 3-D's third golden age. The release of James Cameron's *Avatar* in December 2009 ushered in a parade of stereoscopic spectaculars, from *Alice in Wonderland* and *Clash of the Titans* to the box-office smash *Toy Story 3*. Despite European ticket surcharges of *c.*£2–£3, customers flocked to 3-D screenings, generating $1·42bn globally in the first five months of 2010. This surge of enthusiasm came just in time for an industry battling piracy, recession, and an ever-better home-viewing experience. ❦ As its name implies, 3-D provides the illusion of a third dimension (depth) in addition to the height and width experienced in 2-D. 3-D films are produced by cameras that record two perspectives of the same image, which are later conjoined using projection hardware and special glasses that 'trick' the brain into perceiving depth. Though such techniques were patented in the 1890s, it was not until 1922 that the first 3-D film (*The Power of Love*) was shown to a paying audience. 3-D's first 'golden age' is said to have begun in 1952 with *Bwana Devil*, which paved the way for a host of multidimensional thrillers whose novelty helped cinema fight the threat posed by TV. Interest in 3-D declined in the later 1950s, however, largely due to distaste for the clunky technology, and the introduction of new wide-screen formats. 3-D again found itself in the spotlight in the 1970s and '80s, usually for gory horror flicks and remakes. The latest wave of 3-D films is often traced to *The Polar Express* (2004) – the first full-length, animated IMAX 3-D feature – which reportedly earned 14 times more when screened in 3-D. By 2009, 3-D films had become a bona fide trend, with the release of *My Bloody Valentine*, *Monsters vs. Aliens*, *Up*, and *Coraline*. (According to the UK Film Council, 3-D films took 16% of the UK and Irish box office in 2009, compared to 0·4% in 2008.) After the stunning success of *Avatar*, studios rushed to create as many 3-D releases as possible – in part by retrofitting 2-D films. In 2010 Dreamworks and Disney/Pixar stated that all their future animations would be released in 3-D, and directors unveiled a slew of 3-D remakes, including *Titanic* and *The Wizard of Oz*. ❦ The appeal of 3-D has not been limited to film. 3-D TVs, gaming consoles, laptops, magazines, and books all made their debut during 2010, driving demand for content suitable for the format. Trend-spotters even noted the student fad of wearing 3-D glasses with the lenses popped out. Yet not everyone was convinced. For one thing, *c.*15% of viewers report that 3-D triggers headaches or nausea, according to *Consumer Reports*. And, for struggling cinemas, the cost of upgrading to 3-D equipment can be prohibitive. Then there are the critics: both Roger Ebert and Mark Kermode were savage in their attack on 3-D, arguing that the format adds little to the cinematic experience – especially for films aimed at adults. As Ebert asked, 'What would *Fargo* gain in 3-D? *Precious*? *Casablanca*?' ❦ If 2010 is the third golden age of 3-D, it remains to be seen whether it will be longer lasting than the previous two. But with the breadth of media involved, and the format's proven commercial draw, it seems that 3-D may have finally outgrown its creature–feature roots and entered the mainstream.

———————— TOP-GROSSING FILMS OF ALL TIME ————————

In January 2010, James Cameron's *Avatar* beat James Cameron's *Titanic* to become the highest-grossing film ever made. Analysts noted that the film's earnings were lifted both by its 3-D technology, which commands higher ticket prices, and by inflation (if inflation is taken into account, *Gone With The Wind* is still the top-grossing film). According to Box Office Mojo, the highest-grossing films ever released (as of 1/2010) were:

Title	director	$bn gross	year
Avatar	James Cameron	1,878	2009
Titanic	James Cameron	1,843	1997
TLOTR: The Return of the King	Peter Jackson	1,119	2003
Pirates of the Caribbean: Dead Man's Chest	Gore Verbinski	1,066	2006
The Dark Knight	Christopher Nolan	1,002	2008
Harry Potter and the Sorcerer's Stone	Chris Columbus	975	2001
Pirates of the Caribbean: At World's End	Gore Verbinski	961	2007
Harry Potter and the Order of the Phoenix	David Yates	938	2007
Harry Potter and the Half-Blood Prince	David Yates	934	2009
The Lord of the Rings: The Two Towers	Peter Jackson	925	2002

———————— UK TOP-GROSSING FILMS · 2009 ————————

Film	UK box office gross (£m)	Director
Harry Potter and the Half-Blood Prince	50·72	David Yates
Avatar	41·00	James Cameron
Ice Age III	35·02	Carlos Saldanha/Mike Thurmeier
Up	34·42	Pete Docter/Bob Peterson
Slumdog Millionaire	31·66	Danny Boyle/Loveleen Tandan
The Twilight Saga: New Moon	27·08	Chris Weitz
Transformers: Revenge of the Fallen	27·06	Michael Bay
The Hangover	22·12	Todd Phillips
Star Trek	21·40	J.J. Abrams
Monsters vs. Aliens	21·37	Rob Letterman/Conrad Vernon

[Source: Nielsen EDI, UK Film Council · Box office gross as at 10·1·2010]

———————— 2009 FILM GENRES ————————

The most popular genres for films released in the UK and Ireland in 2009 were:

	% of releases	% box office
Comedy	24·1	19·8
Drama	20·7	6·9
Documentary	11·3	1·1
Action	10·9	13·1
Horror	7·0	5·9
Crime	6·4	3·6
Thriller	3·8	3·0
Biopic	3·8	2·0
Animation	2·8	14·2
Romance	2·0	3·4

[Source: UK Film Council]

─────── 82ND ACADEMY AWARDS · 2010 ───────

Director Kathryn Bigelow triumphed over her ex-husband, James Cameron, at the 82nd Academy Awards, held on 7 March 2010 in Los Angeles. Bigelow's critically acclaimed Iraq War drama, *The Hurt Locker*, beat Cameron's *Avatar* to take Best Picture, while Bigelow also bested Cameron for Best Director – the first time the prize had been awarded to a woman. 41·3m Americans tuned in to the ceremony (the most since 2005), yet many found the evening predictable – hosts Steve Martin and Alec Baldwin relied heavily on old-fashioned one-liners, and the prizes primarily rewarded front-runners established earlier in the awards' season. And the winners were ...[†]

Leading actor.. Jeff Bridges · *Crazy Heart*
Leading actress ....Sandra Bullock · *The Blind Side*
Supporting actor...............................Christoph Waltz · *Inglourious Basterds*
Supporting actress ...... Mo'Nique · *Precious: Based on the Novel 'Push' by Sapphire*
Best picture.. *The Hurt Locker*
Director ....Kathryn Bigelow · *The Hurt Locker*
Animated feature..Pete Docter · *Up*
Art direction ....Rick Carter, Robert Stromberg, Kim Sinclair · *Avatar*
Cinematography ....Mauro Fiore · *Avatar*
Costume design................................. Sandy Powell · *The Young Victoria*
Doc. feature..............................Louie Psihoyos & Fisher Stevens · *The Cove*
Doc. short subject......Roger Ross Williams & Elinor Burkett · *Music by Prudence*
Film editing........................ Bob Murawski & Chris Innis · *The Hurt Locker*
Foreign language film................ *The Secret in Their Eyes* (*El Secreto de Sus Ojos*)
Make-up....................Barney Burman, Mindy Hall & Joel Harlow · *Star Trek*
Music (score)..Michael Giacchino · *Up*
Music (song) ... Ryan Bingham & T Bone Burnett · *The Weary Kind* · *Crazy Heart*
Short film (animated)...............................Nicolas Schmerkin · *Logorama*
Short film (live) .... Joachim Back & Tivi Magnusson · *The New Tenants*
Sound mixing.................Paul N.J. Ottosson & Ray Beckett · *The Hurt Locker*
Sound editing................................. Paul N.J. Ottosson · *The Hurt Locker*
Visual effects ....Joe Letteri, Stephen Rosenbaum, Richard Baneham
                                              & Andrew R. Jones · *Avatar*
Screenplay (adapted)..................................... Geoffrey Fletcher · *Precious*
Screenplay (original)...................................Mark Boal · *The Hurt Locker*

QUOTES ❦ SANDRA BULLOCK · Did I really earn this, or did I just wear you all down? ❦ JEFF BRIDGES · Thank you mum and dad for turning me on to such a groovy profession. ❦ MO'NIQUE · I would like to thank the Academy for showing it can be about the performance and not the politics. ❦ KATHRYN BIGELOW · It's the moment of a lifetime. ❦ STEVE MARTIN · Anyone who has ever worked with Meryl Streep always ends up saying the exact same thing: 'Can that woman act!' And, 'What's up with all the Hitler memorabilia?' ❦ SANDY POWELL · I already have two of these.

† For the first time since 1988, Oscar presenters were asked to announce victors with the phrase, 'And the winner is ...'. Since 1989, presenters had been told to say, 'And the Oscar goes to ...', apparently to lessen the sting for losers. There was no word on why producers switched back to the older phrase.

———————— OSCAR NIGHT FASHION · 2010 ————————

Star	dress	*designer*
Cameron Diaz	*gold, beaded, fifties-style full-length gown*	Oscar de la Renta
Kate Winslet	*silver, structured strapless bodice, silk skirt*	Yves Saint Laurent
Sandra Bullock	*gold mermaid dress with embroidered lace bodice*	Marchesa
Helen Mirren	*silver/grey gown with beaded chiffon overlay*	Badgley Mischka
Mo'Nique	*royal blue silk, draped asymmetric bodice*†	Tadashi Shoji
Maggie Gyllenhaal	*strapless column dress in blue printed silk*	Dries Van Noten
Carey Mulligan	*black, strapless, embellished with tiny cutlery, keys, &c.*	Prada
Charlize Theron	*two-tone lilac silk with rosettes at the bosom*	Christian Dior
Vera Farmiga	*fuchsia strapless gown with a riot of large ruffles*	Marchesa
Penélope Cruz	*maroon silk, strapless, gathered bodice, full skirt*	Donna Karan
Kathryn Bigelow	*pewter silk column dress, embellished bodice*	Yves Saint Laurent
Anna Kendrick	*pale pink, off-the-shoulder, chiffon, full, draped skirt*	Elie Saab

† Mo'Nique revealed that she wore this shade of dress and a gardenia in her hair to mirror the attire worn by Hattie McDaniel in 1940 when she became the first black woman to win an Oscar.

———————— OSCAR STAGE-CRASHERS ————————

Although some bemoaned a lack of drama at the 82nd Oscars, there was at least one moment of surprise. As director Roger Ross Williams began his acceptance speech for Best Documentary Short (for *Music by Prudence*), the film's producer, Elinor Burkett, bounded on-stage with the phrase, 'Let the woman talk!' before delivering her own speech. (The two had reportedly been feuding.) This puzzling interlude wasn't the first time the Oscar podium had hosted an unexpected guest. In 1973, Marlon Brando sent activist Sacheen Littlefeather to refuse his Best Actor award for *The Godfather* (she delivered a screed against the industry's treatment of Native Americans). The next year, a San Francisco artist streaked across the stage wearing only a peace sign, prompting host David Niven to quip: 'Probably the only laugh that man will ever get in his life is by stripping off and showing his shortcomings.'

———————— OSCAR HOSTS ————————

Steve Martin also hosted the Oscars in 2001 and 2003, giving him membership in an elite group of emcees who have hosted more than twice. The group includes:

Bob Hope	*host in* 1940, 1942, 1943, 1945, 1946, 1953, 1955, 1958, 1959, 1960, 1961, 1962, 1965, 1966, 1967, 1968, 1975, 1978 (18 *times*)
Billy Crystal	1990, 1991, 1992, 1993, 1997, 1998, 2000, 2004 (8)
Johnny Carson	1979, 1980, 1981, 1982, 1984 (5)
Whoopi Goldberg	1994, 1996, 1999, 2002 (4)
Jack Lemmon	1958, 1964, 1972, 1985 (4)
Jerry Lewis	1956, 1957, 1959 (3)
David Niven	1958, 1959, 1974 (3)

MOVIE AWARDS OF NOTE

BAFTAs 2010

Best film.. *The Hurt Locker*
Outstanding British film .... *Fish Tank*
Best actor in a leading role .... Colin Firth · *A Single Man*
Best actress in a leading role....................... Carey Mulligan · *An Education*
Best actor in a supporting role................ Christoph Waltz · *Inglorious Basterds*
Best actress in a supporting role............................... Mo'Nique · *Precious*

MTV MOVIE AWARDS 2010

Best movie .... *The Twilight Saga: New Moon*
Best male performance............ Robert Pattinson · *The Twilight Saga: New Moon*
Best female performance...........Kristen Stewart · *The Twilight Saga: New Moon*
Biggest badass star ....Rain
Best villain.................... Tom Felton · *Harry Potter and the Half-Blood Prince*

GOLDEN GLOBES 2010

Best dramatic film ....*Avatar*
Best dramatic actor .... Jeff Bridges · *Crazy Heart*
Best dramatic actress..............................Sandra Bullock · *The Blind Side*
Best director.. James Cameron · *Avatar*
Best actor in musical or comedy..............Robert Downey Jr. · *Sherlock Holmes*
Best actress in musical or comedy...................... Meryl Streep · *Julie & Julia*

BRITISH INDEPENDENT FILM AWARDS 2009

Best British independent film ....*Moon*
Best actor.. Tom Hardy · *Bronson*
Best actress .... Carey Mulligan · *An Education*
Best director.. Andrea Arnold · *Fish Tank*

GOLDEN RASPBERRIES 2010

Worst picture......................................*Transformers: Revenge Of The Fallen*
Worst actor(s) .... Jonas Brothers · *Jonas Brothers: The 3-D Concert Experience*
Worst actress .... Sandra Bullock · *All About Steve*

EMPIRE AWARDS 2010

Best actor......................................Christoph Waltz · *Inglourious Basterds*
Best actress .... Zoe Saldana · *Avatar*
Best director.. James Cameron · *Avatar*
Best British film..*Harry Brown*
Best film..*Avatar*

EVENING STANDARD BRITISH FILM AWARDS 2010

Best film.. *Fish Tank*
Best actor....................................Andy Serkis · *Sex & Drugs & Rock & Roll*
Best actress ....Anne-Marie Duff · *Nowhere Boy*
Most promising newcomer ..Peter Strickland (writing & directing) · *Katalin Varga*

OSCAR CURSE

In March 2010, the two most recent winners of the Best Actress Oscar both found themselves in the spotlight for romantic troubles, continuing an unfortunate tradition that some have dubbed the 'Oscar curse'. Within the last dozen years, a host of Best Actress winners have seen their marriages end soon after winning the award:

actress	year of award	break-up
Helen Hunt	1998	*filed for divorce from Hank Azaria in 1998*
Halle Berry	2002	*separated from Eric Benet in 2003*
Hilary Swank	2005	*filed for divorce from actor Chad Lowe in 2006*
Reese Witherspoon	2006	*filed for divorce from Ryan Philippe in 2006*
Kate Winslet	2009	*separated from Sam Mendes in 2010*
Sandra Bullock	2010	*filed for divorce from Jesse James in 2010*

A number of other Best Actress winners are reported to have split from their boyfriends soon after their awards. In American sports, there are several other curses said to follow success, including hexes rumoured to befall athletes on the cover of *Sports Illustrated*, or featured on cans of Campbell's Soup.

BEST VALUE-FOR-MONEY ACTRESSES

Naomi Watts offers studios the best 'return on investment' of any Hollywood actress, according to Forbes magazine. In 2009, Forbes calculated that Watts's last three major films made $44 for every dollar that she earned. Forbes considered only those actresses who had starred in at least three widely released films ($\geq$500 cinemas) in the last five years. The actresses' estimated earnings for their last three films were weighed against the films' revenues to calculate a 'return on investment' score. The five best value-for-money actresses in Hollywood were thus said to be:

Actress	$ made per $ earned		
Naomi Watts	44	Rachel McAdams	30
Jennifer Connelly	41	Natalie Portman	28
		Meryl Streep	27

In November 2009, Forbes calculated that comedian Will Ferrell offered studios the least value for money – with his films making just $3·29 for every dollar he was paid (though see the list below).

HARDEST-WORKING ACTORS

Seth Rogen is the hardest-working man in show business, according to Forbes. In 2010 the magazine released a list of the A-list actors who had acted in the most starring or significant roles from January 2005–December 2009, and whose films had earned the highest US box office totals in that period. The five busiest actors were:

	films	total box office		films	total box office
Seth Rogen	12	$892m	Matt Damon	8	$696m
Morgan Freeman	9	$1·1bn	Will Ferrell	8	$607m
			Robert Downey Jr.	7	$788m

─────HOLLYWOOD WALK OF FAME─────

The Hollywood Walk of Fame celebrated its 50th birthday in 2010. The 18 blocks along Hollywood Boulevard and Vine Street in Los Angeles have been called 'the most famous sidewalk in the world', and *c*.12m visitors come each year to see >2,400 terrazzo-and-brass stars commemorating Hollywood greats of past and present. The idea for the walk emerged in the early 1950s as a scheme to bring tourism to the area, which had fallen on hard times after the 1920s boom. The concept was proposed by Hollywood Chamber of Commerce president E. M. Stuart, who may have been inspired by the decorations on the dining room ceiling at the Hollywood Hotel. In 1958, eight prototype stars were installed to stir interest, though construction on the rest of the walk did not begin for two more years. The initial stars honoured:

Olive Borden · Ronald Colman · Louise Fazenda · Preston Foster
Burt Lancaster · Edward Sedgwick · Ernest Torrence · Joanne Woodward

New stars can be suggested by any member of the public, as long as the submission is accompanied by written permission from the celebrity. Names are voted on by the Hollywood Walk of Fame Committee, which considers achievement, longevity, contributions to the community, and whether the star guarantees they will attend the dedication ceremony. Celebrities who are selected must contribute $25,000 to the ceremony and their star's upkeep. Stars can be awarded in one of five categories, each with its own insignia that appears in a brass circle below the honouree's name:

Motion pictures (a film camera) · *television* (a TV set) · *radio* (a microphone)
recording (a phonograph record) · *live theatre/performance* (theatrical masks)

In 2010, the following people were scheduled to receive stars on the Walk of Fame:

Motion pictures: James Cameron, Russell Crowe, John Cusack, Colin Firth, Gale Ann Hurd, Alan Menken, Randy Neuman, Adam Sandler, Emma Thompson, Mark Wahlberg · *Television*: Chris Berman, Jon Cryer, Peter Graves, Jimmy Kimmel, Julia Louis-Dreyfuss, Bill Maher, Sam Waterston *Recording* · Bryan Adams, The Funk Brothers, Alan Jackson, Chaka Khan, Van Morrison, Marco Antonio Solis, Ringo Starr, Roy Orbison, ZZ Top *Live theatre/performance*: Andrea Bocelli, Cirque Du Soleil/Guy Laliberté

─────THE HOLLYWOOD SIGN─────

In April 2010, *Playboy* mogul Hugh Hefner came to the rescue of the famous Hollywood sign in LA. An investment group had planned to sell 138 acres near the sign to developers, but residents became concerned that homes destined for the site would block the view of the iconic letters. In response, a non-profit group mounted a $12·5m fund-raising campaign to purchase the land. Hefner provided the final $900,000, saying the sign was 'Hollywood's Eiffel Tower'. (Hefner also aided the sign in 1978, when he ceremonially bought the 'H'.) Gov. Schwarzenegger noted, '*The Hollywood sign will welcome dreamers, artists and Austrian bodybuilders for generations to come.*'

———————— GAFFES OF THE YEAR ————————

Eagle-eyed contributors to the Internet Movie Database regularly report errors they have discovered in films. Some of the gaffes spotted in 2009–10 films include these:

Robin Hood　　a title card identifies the historical period as 'turn of the C12th', but the story takes place at the turn of the C13th

The Karate Kid　　the film shows an Air China flight from Detroit–Beijing; no such route exists on Air China, and the airport filmed is in Hong Kong

Sex and the City 2　　Carrie says her first day in NYC was Tuesday June 11, 1986, which was actually a Wednesday

Avatar　　during one scene Jake's watch suddenly skips from 2:19 to 2:57

The Twilight Saga: Eclipse　　a local newscast is shot at night, though characters watching it live are clearly in daylight

Inception　　sticky tape and a blood pack are visible on Saito's chest wound

Alice in Wonderland　　Alice's father mentions Jakarta; it was then called Batavia

———————— THE VATICAN'S FILM REVIEWS ————————

The epic science fiction film *Avatar* [see p.154] was a 'facile anti-imperialist and antimilitarist parable which doesn't have the same bite as other more serious films', according to a review in the Vatican's semi-official newspaper *L'Osservatore Romano* in January 2010. *L'Osservatore Romano* has published a variety of film reviews over the last few years, and although the Church cautions that the write-ups don't carry the weight of Papal edict, they do provide a fascinating insight into the intersection of the Vatican City and Hollywood. Selections from some recent reviews are below:

Harry Potter & the Half-Blood Prince†　　*draws a 'clear line of demarcation between good and evil, making clear that good is right'*

Angels & Demons　　*offers 'harmless entertainment, which hardly affects the genius and mystery of Christianity'*

The Da Vinci Code‡　　*contains 'allegories and suggestive symbols of a third-rate neo-medievalism'*

The Golden Compass　　*viewers will find the movie 'devoid of any particular emotion apart from a great chill'*

The Simpsons (TV show)　　*'realistic and intelligent writing ... a mirror of the indifference and the need that modern man feels toward faith'*

In November 2009 the Pontifical Council of Culture declared that the vampire movie *New Moon* was 'a moral vacuum with a deviant message', and warned viewers away from it. † This positive review came as a surprise to many, since it followed a 2008 *L'Osservatore Romano* article attacking Harry Potter as the 'wrong kind of hero' and warning that the series contained a 'grave and deep lie'. Furthermore, in 2003 then-Cardinal Joseph Ratzinger (now Pope Benedict XVI) wrote a letter encouraging a critic of the Harry Potter books, saying: 'It is good that you explain the facts of Harry Potter ... because this is a subtle seduction, which has deeply unnoticed and direct effects in undermining the soul of Christianity'. ‡ While *The Da Vinci Code* drew anger from a variety of cardinals, the *L'Osservatore Romano* review was even-tempered, and headlined 'Much Ado About Nothing'.

─────── TOP-GROSSING BRITISH DIRECTORS ───────

Below are the UK directors whose films earned the most at the international box office in the years 2001–09, according to a 2010 ranking by the UK Film Council:

Director	film(s)	total gross ($m)
David Yates	*Harry Potter and the Order of the Phoenix, Harry Potter and the Half-Blood Prince*	1,871
Christopher Nolan	*Batman Begins, The Dark Knight*	1,370
Mike Newell	*Harry Potter and the Goblet of Fire*	896
Ridley Scott	*American Gangster, Hannibal, Kingdom of Heaven*	826
Paul Greengrass	*The Bourne Supremacy, The Bourne Ultimatum*	731
Phyllida Lloyd	*Mamma Mia!*	585
Guy Ritchie	*Sherlock Holmes*	417
Danny Boyle	*Slumdog Millionaire*	362
Beeban Kidron	*Bridget Jones: The Edge of Reason*	261
Sharon Maguire	*Bridget Jones's Diary*	254

Orlando Bloom was the most commercially successful UK actor of the period 2001–09, according to the UK Film Council – he appeared in 8 of the 200 top-grossing films released during those years.

─────── FELLOWS OF THE BRITISH FILM INSTITUTE ───────

Since 1983, prominent film and programme-makers from around the world have been awarded honorary fellowship of the BFI. In October 2009 John Hurt became the latest luminary to be awarded a fellowship. Some other BFI fellows include:

Robert Altman · Lord Attenborough · Bernardo Bertolucci
Dirk Bogarde · Michael Caine · Bette Davis · Gérard Depardieu
Clint Eastwood · Graham Greene · Alec Guinness · Derek Jarman
Lynda La Plante · Mike Leigh · Ken Loach · Michael Parkinson
Lord Puttnam · Vanessa Redgrave · Martin Scorsese · Ridley Scott
Maggie Smith · Elizabeth Taylor · Bob & Harvey Weinstein · Orson Welles

─────── FILM FESTIVAL PRIZES · 2010 ───────

Sundance · World Cinema Jury Prize Dramatic. *Animal Kingdom* · David Michôd
Berlin · Golden Bear..*Bal* · Semih Kaplanoglu
Tribeca · Best Narrative Feature.........................*When We Leave* · Feo Aladag
Cannes · Palme d'Or.................*Uncle Boonmee Who Can Recall His Past Lives*
Apichatpong Weerasethakul
Moscow · Golden St George........................*Hermano* · Marcel R. Venezuela
Edinburgh · Audience Award............................*Get Low* · Aaron Schneider
Venice · Golden Lion.....................................*Somewhere* · Sofia Coppola
Toronto · People's Choice Award...................*The King's Speech* · Tom Hooper
London · Sutherland Trophy [OCT '09]..... *Ajami* · Scandar Copti & Yaron Shani

─────────────── SCARIEST FILM MUSIC ───────────────

The violin score written for *Psycho*'s shower scene is the most frightening film music ever – according to a survey released in 2009 by the royalty collection group PRS for Music. The organisation canvassed its membership of composers, songwriters, and music publishers to reveal the five most harrowing film tunes ever composed:

No.	song	film	composer
1	Psycho Theme	Psycho	Bernard Herrmann
2	Ave Satani	The Omen	Jerry Goldsmith
3	Samara's Song	The Ring	Hans Zimmer
4	Phantom of the Opera	Phantom of the Opera	Andrew Lloyd Webber
5	Tubular Bells	The Exorcist	Mike Oldfield

The Shining is the best horror film ever made, according to a 2009 ranking by Total Sci-Fi Online. *Rosemary's Baby* was No. 2, followed by *The Wicker Man* (3), *Bride of Frankenstein* (4), *Psycho* (5), *Alien* (6), *Night of the Living Dead* (7), *The Texas Chainsaw Massacre* (8), *Halloween* (9), and *Jaws* (10).

─────────────── SOME MOVIE TAGLINES OF NOTE · 2010 ───────────────

There is no plan B	*The A-Team*
Just like real spies ... only furrier	*Cats & Dogs: The Revenge of Kitty Galore*
Titans will clash	*Clash of the Titans*
Arriving this summer (hopefully)	*Get Him to the Greek*
Your mind is the scene of the crime	*Inception*
I can't fly. But I can kick your ass	*Kick-Ass*
Who's your nanny?	*Nanny McPhee Returns*
Defy the future	*Prince of Persia: The Sands of Time*
It ain't ogre ... til it's ogre	*Shrek Forever After*
Carrie on	*Sex and the City 2*

─────────────── WORST MOVIES OF THE DECADE ───────────────

In 2009, the website Metacritic.com released a list of the movies that suffered the worst critical receptions of the decade. Since 1999, Metacritic has been tracking reviews of films, books, music, and games written by critics at major American publications. The reviews are combined in weighted averages known as 'metascores', which range from 1–100. The films below received the lowest metascores 2000–09:

Film (year)	metascore
The Singing Forest (2003)†	1
Chaos (2005)	3
Strippers (2000)	5
Vulgar (2002)	5
Ntnl Lampoon's Gold Diggers (2004)	6
The Hottie and the Nottie (2008)	7
Screwed (2000)	7
Miss March (2009)	7
Transylmania (2009)	8
State Property (2002)	9

† *Variety* said the gay romance 'provides scant entertainment value, intentional or otherwise'.

Books & Arts

Art, like morality, consists of drawing the line somewhere.
— G.K. CHESTERTON (1874–1936)

THE RISE OF E-BOOKS

While the death of the 'dead tree' book is still far from inevitable, several developments in 2010 certainly helped expand the e-book market from geeky 'first adopters' to mainstream book buyers and readers. In May, Apple released its eagerly-awaited iPad – a tablet capable of providing the audio, video, and general computing power missing from 'traditional' e-readers. (Some publishers nicknamed the iPad the 'Jesus tablet', so hopeful were they that it would miraculously resurrect their trade.) In the same month, Google announced its own digital bookstore, Google Editions, which allows readers to purchase texts that can be read on a variety of devices. In August, Amazon launched a dedicated UK e-bookstore, alongside cheaper upgrades of its own e-reader, the Kindle. 2010 also saw an explosion of e-book 'apps' – from Apple's own iBooks store to one-off programs created for specific titles. These developments, among many others, intensified the scramble to develop e-texts for the market – even as authors, agents, publishers, and booksellers struggled to adapt to the new format. At issue are questions concerning the rights to digital works, royalty splits, distribution models, copyright protection, and consumer pricing. Publishers are anxious to avoid the fate of the music industry – which saw profits plummet when audio went digital – and, at the time of writing, some authors and agents were exploring ways of bypassing traditional publishing houses altogether. However, at least in the UK, media interest in e-books is outpacing demand: a March 2010 *Bookseller* survey found that just 2·4% of readers owned an e-reader, though 7·3% said they will 'probably' buy one. (Only 60% had heard of the iPad, and 26% of the Kindle.) ❦ Below, by way of perspective, is a time-line of the book:

6,000–3,000 BC .... writing develops	1473–4 .... first book with pagination
2,400 ... date of oldest papyrus found in Egypt	1476.............. first book printed in English
300 .... wood/bamboo books created in China	1479.............. first author portrait in book
200 .. parchment use spreads in Mediterranean	1798...................... lithography invented
100 ....earliest bookbindings, in India	1822................cloth bindings introduced
150 AD .... paper invented in China	1829................earliest known dust jacket
150–450..............shift from scroll to codex	1856...... first book printed with photographs
300 ....shift from papyrus to parchment	1935........paperbacks introduced in England
354 ....first book signed by author	1971... first digital library (Project Gutenberg)
600–1200s ... book production in monasteries	1986...........first e-book (by some accounts)
868 .. earliest complete printed book, in China	2000..... most prepress (layout &c.) go digital
1040...... Chinese begin to use moveable type	2004...........Google Books announced
1100s..... paper starts to spread across Europe	2006...................... Sony Reader released
1400s...wood block printing begins in Europe	2007..................Amazon Kindle released
1455............Gutenberg completes his Bible	2010..............................iPad released
1457.......................first colour printing	2010... e-books outsell hardcovers on Amazon

SEQUELS WRITTEN BY OTHER PEOPLE

In March 2010, the former Poet Laureate Sir Andrew Motion revealed that he was writing a sequel to *Treasure Island*, the pirate classic penned by Robert Louis Stevenson in 1883. *Return to Treasure Island* will follow the adventures of Jim Junior, son of the original protagonist Jim Hawkins, as he searches for the remaining silver. The book is due to be published in 2012. Sir Andrew admitted that writing the sequel to a beloved work was a challenge: 'A large part of me thinks "crikey, this is *Treasure Island*" and there is always a risk that a national treasure will be interfered with.' However, Motion may take comfort from the fact that he is not the first to attempt such a task: in October 2009, Eoin Colfer, author of the Artemis Fowl series, published a sixth volume in Douglas Adams's *The Hitchhiker's Guide to the Galaxy* trilogy in five parts'. (Adams had sketched a plan for the sixth novel but, due to his untimely death in 2001, the book was never written.) Some other sequels penned by different authors are listed below:

Sequel	original
Devil May Care · Sebastian Faulks (2008)	James Bond series · Ian Fleming
Return to Hundred Acre Wood · David Benedictus (2009)	*The House at Pooh Corner* · A.A. Milne (1928)
Mrs de Winter · Susan Hill (1993)	*Rebecca* · Daphne du Maurier (1938)
The Willows in Winter · William Horwood (1994)	*Wind in the Willows* · Kenneth Grahame (1908)
Scarlett · Alexandra Ripley (1991)	*Gone with the Wind* · Margaret Mitchell (1936)
Dracula: The Un-Dead · Dacre Stoker and Ian Holt (2009)	*Dracula* · Bram Stoker (1897)
Peter Pan in Scarlet · Geraldine McCaughrean (2006)	*Peter Pan* · J.M. Barrie (1911)
The Godfather Returns · Mark Winegardner (2004)	*The Godfather* · Mario Puzo (1969)
Heathcliff: The Return to Wuthering Heights · Lin Haire-Sargeant (1992)	*Wuthering Heights* · Emily Brontë (1847)
Jane Rochester · Kimberly A. Bennett (2000)	*Jane Eyre* · Charlotte Brontë (1847)
Ebenezer: The Final Years of Scrooge · Donna Lee Howell (2008)	*A Christmas Carol* · Charles Dickens (1843)
Later Days at Highbury · Joan Aiken (1996)	*Emma* · Jane Austen (1815)
Mansfield Revisited · Joan Aiken (1986)	*Mansfield Park* · Jane Austen (1814)
Pemberley · Emma Tennant (1993)	*Pride & Prejudice* · Jane Austen (1813)
Presumption · Julia Barrett (1993)	*Pride & Prejudice* · Jane Austen (1813)
Mr Darcy Takes A Wife · Linda Berdoll (2004)	*Pride & Prejudice* · Jane Austen (1813)

In July 2009 a judge banned the publication in America of a sequel to J.D. Salinger's classic *The Catcher in the Rye*. The sequel, *60 Years Later: Coming Through the Rye*, by Swedish writer Fredrik Colting, was said to bear too close a resemblance to the original without sufficient parody or critique to allow publication. The book had already been published in the UK.

—————————— CHILDREN & READING ——————————

34% of British parents said that their bookshelves were increasingly filled with DVDs and computer games rather than books. The research, published in October 2009 by the charity Booktrust, revealed that the shift towards digital forms of entertainment was particularly prevalent among older children (74% of parents of 11–12-year-olds said that books in their bedrooms were mainly being replaced by shelves of DVDs and computer games). 57% of parents admitted that their child (aged between 4–12) spent more time playing video games or watching films than they did reading. Parents of boys were much more likely to find their children preferred computer games to reading (69%) than were parents of girls (45%). Despite the distractions of digital entertainment, 96% of children surveyed (aged 5–12) said they enjoyed reading for pleasure. The type of books most enjoyed were:

Story books	75%	Picture books	30
Fact books	47	Joke books	27
Books linked to TV series	45	Young adult novels	23
Fairy tales	42	Graphic novels/comics	22
School books	39	Nursery rhymes	18

60% of children questioned said that their mother was most likely to read to them, and 18% said it was their father. 79% said they would most *like* their mother to read to them, and 56% said their father was their favourite reading partner (45% said they would like their dad to read with them more). Despite the preponderance of mother as reading partner, 76% of children said they principally chose their own reading matter. Their top ten favourite characters are listed below:

1 .... Harry Potter	6 .... Doctor Who	† School reading scheme characters. ‡ From *Charlie and the Chocolate Factory*. · Roald Dahl had four of his characters feature in the top 20.
2 .... Horrid Henry	7 .... Ben 10	
3 .... Tracy Beaker	8 ..... Winnie the Pooh	
4 . Biff, Chip & Kipper†	9 .. Captain Underpants	
5 ..... Hannah Montana	10 .... Charlie‡	

—————————— BEST BEDTIME STORIES ——————————

The 1969 tale of a caterpillar and his voracious appetite, *The Very Hungry Caterpillar*, was voted the best children's bedtime story ever written, in a 2010 survey of parents, commissioned by Munch Bunch. The ten best night-time reads were said to be:

(1) *The Very Hungry Caterpillar*, by Eric Carle (2) *The Lion, The Witch and The Wardrobe*, by C.S. Lewis (3) *The BFG*, by Roald Dahl (4) *Winnie the Pooh*, by A.A. Milne (5) *The Gruffalo*, by Julia Donaldson (6) *Famous Five*, by Enid Blyton (7) *Matilda*, by Roald Dahl (8) *The Tales of Peter Rabbit*, by Beatrix Potter (9) *Alice in Wonderland*, by Lewis Carroll (10) *The Secret Garden*, by Frances Hodgson Burnett

The survey also revealed that 70% of parents read to their children, on average five times a month.

─────── NOBEL PRIZE IN LITERATURE ───────

In 2009, the Nobel Prize in Literature was awarded to Herta Müller (1953–),

who, with the concentration of poetry and the frankness of prose,
depicts the landscape of the dispossessed

Biographies of Herta Müller have depicted her as a permanent outsider. Born in 1953 in a German-speaking region of Romania, Müller's family was persecuted under Nicolae Ceaușescu's dictatorship for its German roots. At university, Müller aligned herself with a group of German-speaking writers seeking freedom of speech, a move that did little to endear her to the authorities. After university she endured years of harassment for refusing to cooperate with the secret police, and when she began publishing in the early 1980s, Müller found herself ostracised by both the Romanian majority and the German minority. ❦ The announcement of Müller's award surprised the press and publishing industry – not least because it followed the 2008 award to another relatively obscure writer, J.M.G. Le Clézio. (Some speculated that Müller's honour recognised the 20th anniversary of Communism's fall.)

Nonetheless, in German literary circles Müller's work has been hailed as a uniquely poetic and personal exploration of totalitarianism. Her first book, *Niederungen* (published in censored form in Romania in 1982) told of life in a Romanian village from the view of a child. Her 1994 novel *Herztier* (*The Land of the Green Plums*) won the German Kleist and Irish IMPAC award for its account of a group of friends targeted by the secret police. Müller has also published essays dealing with language and identity, as well as collage poems. Her most recent work, 2009's *Atemschaukel* (*Everything I Possess I Carry With Me*) describes the plight of German Romanians in the gulags. Müller's work is not unrelentingly bleak: her December 2009 Nobel lecture used the question 'Do you have a handkerchief?' to illustrate the small gestures of human kindness and resilience that can persist even amidst repression.

─────── BULWER-LYTTON FICTION CONTEST ───────

In 1982, the Department of English and Comparative Literature at San José State University inaugurated a literary contest in honour of E.G.E. Bulwer-Lytton (1803–73), who opened his book *Paul Clifford* with the now-famous line, 'It was a dark and stormy night'. The contest rewards the best 'bad' opening line to a nonexistent novel. 2010's winner was Molly Ringle of Seattle, Washington, a novelist who claims that she 'only writes bad fiction when she fails at good fiction'. Her entry is below:

For the first month of Ricardo and Felicity's affair, they greeted one another at
every stolen rendezvous with a kiss – a lengthy, ravenous kiss, Ricardo lapping
and sucking at Felicity's mouth as if she were a giant cage-mounted
water bottle and he were the world's thirstiest gerbil.

———————— NEGLECTED CLASSICS ————————

The Snow Goose by Paul Gallico was selected by BBC Radio 4 listeners in November 2009 as the neglected classic they would most like to see reintroduced to the nation's bookshelves. Radio 4's *Open Book* programme asked respected authors to act as advocates for ten long-forgotten books that deserved new attention. The winning book was later dramatised for the network. The books and their advocates were:

Advocate	*neglected classic (year of publication)*
William Boyd	*The Polyglots* · William Gerhardie (1925)
Susan Hill	*The Rector's Daughter* · F.M. Mayor (1924)
Hari Kunzru	*A Hero of Our Time* · Mikhail Lermontov (1840)
Ruth Rendell	*Many Dimensions* · Charles Williams (1931)
Cólm Toibín	*Esther Waters* · George Moore (1894)
Beryl Bainbridge	*The Quest for Corvo* · A.J.A. Symons (1934)
Howard Jacobson	*Rasselas* · Samuel Johnson (1759)
Val McDermid	*Carol* · Patricia Highsmith (1953)
Michael Morpurgo	WINNER: *The Snow Goose* · Paul Gallico (1941)
Joanna Trollope	*Miss Mackenzie* · Anthony Trollope (1865)

———————— QUEEN'S MEDAL FOR POETRY ————————

Scottish poet Don Paterson was awarded the Queen's Gold Medal for Poetry in January 2010 for his anthology *Rain*. The medal was the first to be awarded during the laureateship of Carol Ann Duffy, who praised Paterson's work as 'poetry of bravery and conviction'. Paterson has received a variety of awards since his first book of poems, *Nil Nil*, won the Forward Poetry Prize for Best First Collection in 1993, including the T.S. Eliot Prize for Poetry, the Geoffrey Faber Memorial Prize, the Forward Poetry Prize for Best Collection (for *Rain*), and the OBE in 2008. Although the Gold Medal for Poetry is usually awarded on 23 April, Shakespeare's birthday, in 2010 it was for the first time bestowed alongside the New Years Honours.

———————— ODDEST BOOK TITLE OF THE YEAR · 2009 ————————

The Diagram Prize for Oddest Book Title of the Year is administered by the *Bookseller* and voted on by the book trade. The 2009 winner and runners-up were:

Crocheting Adventures with Hyperbolic Planes · Dr Daina Taimina – WINNER

RUNNERS-UP: *What Kind of Bean is this Chihuahua?* .... Tara Jansen-Meyer
Collectible Spoons of the Third Reich .... James A. Yannes
Afterthoughts of a Worm Hunter .... David Crompton
Governing Lethal Behaviour in Autonomous Robots .... Ronald C. Arkin
The Changing World of Inflammatory Bowel Disease ...... E. Scherl & M. Dubinsky

Memorable previous winners have included *How to Avoid Huge Ships* and *Living with Crazy Buttocks*.

--- MOST ROMANTIC HEROES ---

Mr Rochester is the most romantic literary hero, according to an October 2009 survey by Mills & Boon. The brooding hero (and almost-bigamist) of Charlotte Brontë's 1847 novel, *Jane Eyre*, beat literary eminents and lovable rogues such as Mr Darcy and Rhett Butler to the top spot. The ten most romantic heroes were:

1 ... Mr Rochester .... *Jane Eyre* .... Charlotte Brontë
2 ... Richard Sharpe .... The *Sharpe* books .... Bernard Cornwell
3 ... Fitzwilliam Darcy .... *Pride and Prejudice* .... Jane Austen
4 ... Heathcliff .... *Wuthering Heights* .... Emily Brontë
5 ... Rhett Butler .... *Gone with the Wind* .... Margaret Mitchell
6 ... Mark Darcy .... *Bridget Jones's Diary* .... Helen Fielding
7 ... Captain Corelli .... *Captain Corelli's Mandolin* ...... Louis de Bernières
8 ... Henry DeTamble .... The *Time Traveller's Wife* .... Audrey Niffenegger
9 ... Gabriel Oak .... *Far from the Madding Crowd* ...... Thomas Hardy
10 .. Rupert Campbell-Black .... The *Rutshire Chronicles* .... Jilly Cooper

--- OTHER BOOK PRIZES OF NOTE · 2010 ---

Carnegie Medal	Neil Gaiman · *The Graveyard Book*
Kate Greenaway Medal	Freya Blackwood · *Harry & Hopper*
Commonwealth Writers' Prize	Rana Dasgupta · *Solo*
Forward Prize: best poetry collection [2009]	Don Paterson · *Rain*
Guardian children's fiction [2009]	Mal Peet · *Exposure*
First book award	Petina Gappah · *An Elegy for Easterly*
Man Booker [2009]	Hilary Mantel · *Wolf Hall*
Orange Prize	Barbara Kingsolver · *The Lacuna*
Samuel Johnson Prize for non-fiction	Barbara Demick *Nothing to Envy: Real Lives in North Korea*
T.S. Eliot Prize for poetry [2009]	Philip Gross · *The Water Table*
Costa Book Awards: novel [2009]	Colm Tóibín · *Brooklyn*
Children's prize	Patrick Ness · *The Ask and the Answer*
Biography	Graham Farmelo · *The Strangest Man*
Poetry	Christopher Reid · *A Scattering*
First Novel	Raphael Selbourne · *Beauty*
Blue Peter Book Awards	
Book I couldn't put down	Ali Sparkes · *Frozen in Time*
Best book with facts	Mitchell Symons · *Why Eating Bogeys is Good For You*
Most fun story w. pictures	Guy Bass · *Dinkin Dings & the Frightening Things*

In May 2010, J.G. Farrell won the Lost Man Booker Prize for his novel set on the eve of the Irish war of Independence, *Troubles*, the first in his *Empire* trilogy. The Lost Booker was awarded to address a gap that occurred when the Booker shifted its schedule, in 1971, to honour books published in the year of the award, instead of the year prior. A shortlist of books was selected by a panel of judges born *c.*1970, and the winner was chosen by the public voting on the Man Booker Prize website.

————————— UK MEMORY OF THE WORLD —————————

Ten documents and collections held at libraries and archives across the United Kingdom became the first items inscribed in the UK Memory of the World Register, in July 2010. The Register is a component of UNESCO's Memory of the World Programme, which seeks to promote the preservation of – and access to – historically and culturally significant documents around the globe. Items on the UK Memory of the World Register were chosen for their cultural significance to the nation by the UK Memory of the World Committee, from nominations submitted by museums, archives, and libraries in early 2010. The first ten items on the register were:

Charter of King William I to the City of London · *1067 charter granted by William the Conqueror recognising the rights of the inhabitants of the City*
The Peterloo Relief Fund Account Book · *record of payments made to those wounded, and dependants of those killed, in the 1819 Peterloo Massacre*
WVS/WRVS Narrative Reports 1939–1996 · *monthly reports of the activities of the Women's Royal Voluntary Service (later the Women's Voluntary Service)*
Letter from George Stephenson · *1827 letter from the engineer to his son, discussing construction of the world's first passenger railway (from Liverpool to Manchester)*
Peniarth Manuscript Collection · *most important manuscript collection in Wales, comprising 561 C12th–C19th works in Welsh, English, Latin, French, & Cornish*
Company of Scotland Trading to Africa & the Indies 1695–1707 · *trade records that provide insight into the economics behind the creation of modern Scotland*
The Life Story of David Lloyd George · *1918 film that is thought to be the world's first feature-length biopic of a living politician*
The Chapman and Myllar Prints · *11 pieces of printing, including the earliest surviving dated book printed in Scotland (The Complaint of the Black Knight, 1508)*
St Kilda, Britain's Loneliest Isle · *film depicting a voyage from Glasgow to St Kilda, shot in the 1920s – St Kilda's last decade of human habitation*
The Pont Manuscript Maps · *earliest surviving maps of Scotland (1583–1614)*

UNESCO also maintains a global Memory of the World Register, with treasures such as Anne Frank's diaries, the League of Nations archives 1919–46, and the archives of the Dutch East India Company.

————————— OLD BOOK SMELL —————————

In November 2009, researchers published a scientific analysis of the smell of old books, in the hope that such olfactory knowledge may one day aid conservationists. Chemist Matija Strlic of University College London's Centre for Sustainable Heritage led a team of researchers who analysed 72 historical documents from the C19th and C20th. The researchers discovered that certain components, including wood fibre and pine tar resin, produced distinctive patterns of volatile organic compounds (and thus distinctive aromas) as they aged. Strlic described the overall smell of old books as '*a combination of grassy notes with a tang of acids and a hint of vanilla over an underlying mustiness*'. The research may pave the way for a hand-held gadget that can 'sniff' books to assess their condition – an improvement over current methods which often require touching or even destroying a portion of the book to be preserved.

THE TURNER PRIZE · 2009

Founded in 1984, the Turner Prize is awarded each year to a British artist (defined, somewhat loosely, as an artist working in Britain or a British artist working abroad) under 50, for an outstanding exhibition or other presentation in the twelve months prior to each May. The winner receives £25,000 – and three runners-up £5,000.

Glasgow-based fresco painter Richard Wright was announced as the winner of the Turner Prize in December 2009. In their prize announcement, the judges (chaired by Director of Tate Britain Stephen Deuchar) praised Wright's work as 'rooted in fine art tradition yet radically conceptual in impact'. Critics and the art world alike were happy to applaud the success of a 'traditional' artist whose working techniques mimic those of the great Renaissance fresco painters. Wright's stunning showcase exhibition at the Tate consisted of a vast and elaborate gold fresco painted directly onto the gallery wall. The piece was produced by tracing an abstract design on paper, pricking holes in its surface, and then using chalk dust, adhesive, and gold leaf to transfer the design to the wall. As critics have noted, the beauty of Wright's work lies partly in its evanescence – all of his work is painted directly onto walls, with the proviso that once the show closes the work will be painted over. Wright has said, 'I am interested in placing painting in the situation where it collides with the world; the fragility of that existence. Being here for a short period of time, I feel, heightens the experience of it being here. ... Sometimes I feel a sense of loss because I can't repeat the work ... but maybe that sense of loss is part of the point'. ❦ Wright was awarded the Turner for frescos exhibited at the 55th Carnegie International in Pittsburgh, and the Ingleby Gallery in Edinburgh. At 49 years old, he took his last opportunity to claim the prize, reflecting his long road to recognition. In fact, Wright was 40 before he staged his first exhibition at a commercial gallery. He began his artistic career painting figurative works on canvas before retraining as a sign-painter. He returned to art in the early 1990s, re-imagining himself as an abstract fresco artist. Despite struggling financially due to the intangible nature of his work, Wright claims it gives him great satisfaction: 'There's already too much stuff in the world. And it buys you a kind of freedom. Not having [paintings] come back to haunt you is a kind of liberation. You make something, and a month later it is gone.'

Richard Wright

Year	winner				
'01	........Martin Creed	'03	.... Grayson Perry	'06	.........Tomma Abts
'02	..........Keith Tyson	'04	........Jeremy Deller	'07	......Mark Wallinger
		'05	...... Simon Starling	'08	.........Mark Leckey

The runners-up for the 2009 Turner Prize were: sculptor Roger Hiorns, contemporary surrealist Enrico David, and multimedia artist Lucy Skaer. ❦ In May 2010, the following were short-listed for the 2010 Turner: painter Dexter Dalwood, painter/sculptor Angela de la Cruz, sound installation artist Susan Philipsz, and film and installation artists The Otolith Group. The winner will be announced on 6 December.

LONDON 2012 ARTWORKS

In October 2009, the Arts Council announced the results of a competition to find a dozen artworks that would showcase British culture in the run-up to the Olympic games in London 2012. More than 2,000 entries were received from across the United Kingdom, from which the following were selected to share the £5·4m prize:

East of England · The Pacitti Theatre Company will make a feature film from a series of 'spectacular' outdoor events across the region.

East Midlands · Three hand-crocheted 30ft lions will be displayed in a taxidermy case in Nottingham.

London · LED panels will be affixed to the roofs of bus stops allowing Londoners to express what is special about their city.

North-east · A sustainable watermill containing an interactive arts space will be floated down the River Tyne.

North-west · A huge spinning cloud of light will rise from Birkenhead's disused Morpeth dock.

Northern Ireland · Donated items will be displayed in a warehouse to inspire a musical composition by the largest chorus ever assembled in N Ireland.

Scotland · A full-size football pitch hosting games for Scottish amateurs will be created in woodland in the Scottish Borders.

South-east · A boat will be created from 'significant' wooden objects donated by the public.

South-west · An island discovered by the artist Alex Hartley in the High Arctic will be towed to the South-west, addressing issues of land ownership and climate change.

Wales · A wingless silver bird made from a recycled DC9 aeroplane will nest in various locations across Wales.

West Midlands · Lady Godiva will be recreated as a giant human puppet to lead a procession to London.

Yorkshire · The buildings, streets and people of Leeds will be used as a giant canvas.

Plans to build the ArcelorMittal Orbit, a spiralling crimson sculpture to be located in London's Olympic Park, were announced by steel giant ArcelorMittal and artist Anish Kapoor in March 2010. The £19·1m project, which is to be completed in late 2011, will join a host of other mammoth structures built for world events – most famously the Eiffel Tower, unveiled at the 1889 World's Fair.

THE ART FUND PRIZE · 2010

The £100,000 Art Fund Prize celebrates 'originality and excellence' in UK museums and galleries. In 2010, the prize was awarded to the Ulster Museum, Belfast. Tim Cooke, Director of National Museums Northern Ireland, commented, 'this is the first time in Northern Ireland's history that a prestigious cultural prize of this nature has been awarded to an institution in the region. This prize will encourage us as we endeavour to play a meaningful role at the heart of our changing society.'

— SOME GREAT ART MUSEUMS —

Museum, location	opened	objects	visitors	focus	famous pieces of note
Alte Pinakothek, Munich	1836	c.800	–	C14–18th European painting	Giotto's The Last Supper
Art Institute of Chicago	1893	260,000	1.8m	world art & artefacts	Edward Hopper's Nighthawks
British Museum, London	1759	7m	5.6m	world art & artefacts	Rosetta Stone, Parthenon sculptures
Centre Pompidou, Paris	1977†	c.60,000	3.5m	modern & contemporary art	Pablo Picasso's The Guitarist
The Hermitage, St Petersburg	1852	c.3m	2.4m	world art & artefacts	Rembrandt's The Return of the Prodigal Son
Kunsthistorisches Museum, Vienna	1891	c.800,000	1.1m	world art & artefacts	Pieter Bruegel's The Tower of Babel
Louvre, Paris	1793	35,000	8.5m	European & Mideast art & artefacts	Leonardo da Vinci's Mona Lisa
Metropolitan Museum of Art, NY	1872	c.2m	4.9m	world art & artefacts	John Singer Sargent's Madame X
Musée d'Orsay, Paris	1986	83,000	3m	French Art 1848–1914	Paul Gauguin's Tahitian Women
Museum of Fine Arts, Boston	1876	450,000	0.9m	world art & artefacts	J.S. Sargent's The Daughters of Edward Darley Boit
Museum of Modern Art, NY	1939	150,000	2.7m	modern art	Salvador Dalí's The Persistence of Memory
National Gallery, London	1838	c.2,300	4.8m	W Europe painting C13–20th	Vincent van Gogh's Sunflowers
National Gallery, Washington	1941	116,000	4.6m	American & European art	Edgar Degas's The Dance Lesson
Philadelphia Museum of Art	1877	c.225,000	0.8m	world art & artefacts	Salvador Dalí's Soft Construction with Boiled Beans
Prado, Madrid	1819	c.17,300	2.8m	European art	Hieronymus Bosch's The Garden of Earthly Delights
Rijksmuseum, Amsterdam	1800	c.1m	0.9m	Netherlandish, European & Asiatic art	Vermeer's The Kitchen Maid
Tate Galleries	1897	c.66,000	6.8m	British art 1500–, world art 1900–	J.W. Waterhouse's The Lady of Shalott
Uffizi, Florence	c.1591	4,800	1.5m	European painting 1200–, statuary	Botticelli's The Birth of Venus
Vatican Museums, Rome	c.1506	–	4.4m‡	European art & artefacts	Michelangelo's Sistine Chapel Ceiling

Britain's oldest museum, the Ashmolean in Oxford, reopened in November 2009 after a £61m redevelopment which added a new 5-storey building and doubled the overall exhibition space. The Ashmolean, which first opened to the public in 1683, was formed out of a great cabinet of curiosity assembled by the naturalist, gardener, and collector John Tradescant the Elder (c.1570–1638). According to the Ashmolean's website, it was the first museum in the world to be open to the public. † The Musée National d'Art Moderne first opened in 1947; it was moved to the Centre Pompidou in 1977. ‡ 2008 attendance; all other attendance figures are for 2009. [Sources for attendance include The Art Newspaper.]

———— MOST POWERFUL PEOPLE IN ART ————

Each year an international panel of experts assembled by *Art Review* magazine assesses the most powerful players in the art world. Rankings are based on global influence over the production of art, activity in the past year, and 'sheer financial clout' – though the magazine's editors noted that this factor counted less in 2009 than in previous years. The 2009 list also reflected a shake-up in global influence, as names that were once inevitable in the top 10, such as artist Damien Hirst and collector Charles Saatchi, plunged down the list. The top ten of the 2009 Power 100 were:

No.	name	position	2008
1	Hans Ulrich Obrist	*Director, Serpentine Gallery*	35
2	Glenn D. Lowry	*Director, MoMA, New York*	3[†]
3	Sir Nicholas Serota	*Director, Tate Gallery*	4
4	Daniel Birnbaum	*Director, Venice Biennale*	13
5	Larry Gagosian	*owner, Gagosian Gallery*	2
6	François Pinault	*owner of Christie's, collector*	8
7	Eli Broad	*founder of The Broad Art Foundation, collector*	10
8	A. Vidokle, J. Aranda, & B.K. Wood	*creators of website* e-flux.com	–
9	Iwona Blazwick	*Director, Whitechapel Art Gallery*	76
10	Bruce Nauman	*artist*	45

41% of those on the list were American, 16% British, 13% German, 5% French, 5% Italian, and 5% Swiss. † In 2008 this ranking was actually held by MoMA Associate Director Kathy Halbreich.

———— TOP EXHIBITIONS · 2009 ————

An exhibition of Buddhist treasures in Tokyo drew more visitors than any other museum show in the world in 2009, according to an annual ranking of museum attendance compiled by the *Art Newspaper*. An exhibition by graffiti artist Banksy took second place in the UK rankings, marking the Bristol City Museum and Art Gallery's first appearance on the list. The best-attended exhibitions in 2009 were:

GLOBAL TOP FIVE

Exhibition, museum	*daily attendance*
Ashura & Masterpieces from Kohfukuji, Tokyo National Museum	15,960
61st Annual Exhibition of Shoso-in Treasures, Nara National Museum	14,965
Treasures of the Imperial Collections, Tokyo National Museum	9,473
C17th Painting from the Louvre, National Museum of Western Art, Tokyo	9,267
2nd Photoquai Biennale, Musée Quai Branly, Paris	7,868

UK TOP FIVE

The Revolution Continues, Saatchi Gallery, London	4,139
Banksy vs *Bristol Museum*, City Museum and Art Gallery	3,859
Unveiled: New Art from the Middle East, Saatchi Gallery, London	3,828
Anish Kapoor, Royal Academy of Arts, London	3,604
BP Portrait Award, National Portrait Gallery, London	3,141

--------------------- MADE FROM SALVAGE ---------------------

The *USS New York* – a warship built using 7·5 tonnes of steel salvaged from the remains of the World Trade Center – sailed into New York City in November 2009. The ship passed up the Hudson River to a point near Ground Zero, where a 21-gun salute was fired in honour of those who died in the terror attacks of 11 September 2001. ❦ Other items made from historically significant salvage include:

The Resolute Desk · An ornate desk was made from the remains of British ship the HMS *Resolute*. The ship was sent to search for the missing explorer Sir John Franklin, but became wedged in Arctic sea ice. The Americans salvaged and refitted the ship, returning it to Britain as a gift in 1856. Once the ship was decommissioned in 1879, Queen Victoria had the remains made into two desks, one of which she gave to President Hayes – the other is in Buckingham Palace. The desk has been used by most US Presidents since then, and currently has pride of place in the Oval Office of President Obama.

Victoria Cross · Victoria Cross medals (Britain's highest military honour) are fashioned from the bronze salvaged from two cannons captured from the Russians at Sevastopol during the Crimean war (1853–56). The remains of the cannons (rumoured to now weigh just 358 ounces) are kept under guard at the Royal Logistics Corps in Donnington. Only Royal jewellers and official medal makers, Hancock & Co., are allowed to remove samples of the metal in order to cast new medals.

Novara Cross · A wooden cross in the chapel at Castle Miramere in Trieste, Italy, was fashioned from the remains of the celebrated ship SMS *Novara*. The

Novara carried Maximillian (brother of Austrian Emperor Franz Josef) on his voyage to become Emperor of Mexico in 1864. In 1867, the Mexican revolutionary Benito Juarez seized power, and Maximillian was executed. His body was sent home to Italy on the *Novara*, and when the ship was scrapped, a cross was fashioned from the remains and erected in the chapel of Saint Canciano at the family castle.

The Place Vendôme Column · Erected to celebrate Napoleon's victory at Austerlitz in 1805, the highly decorative bronze bas-relief column was made from hundreds of cannons captured from the defeated Russo-Austrian armies.

Nelson's Column · Built 1840–43 to mark the death of Nelson at the Battle of Trafalgar in 1805, the column incorporates a number of salvaged items. The acanthus leaves at the top of the column are made of bronze from cannons taken from the Woolwich Arsenal. The pedestal is surrounded by four panels, depicting Nelson's four most famous naval victories, which were cast in bronze from captured armaments at the battles of St Vincent, Nile, Copenhagen, and Trafalgar. The base includes the remains of 29 cannons salvaged from the HMS *Royal George* (sister ship of Nelson's HMS *Victory*).

The medals for the 2010 Winter Olympics in Vancouver were made from precious metals salvaged from old circuit boards found in discarded televisions, computers, and other electronic waste. ❦ The photographer Luis Marden, who discovered the ruined wreck of the HMS *Bounty* off the Pitcairn Islands in 1957, is said to have sported cuff links made from nails salvaged from the famous ship.

—————— THE CRITICAL YEAR · 2009–10 ——————

{OCT 2009} · Dominic West's return to the London stage after a successful run as Detective McNulty in the US TV series *The Wire* was greeted with delight. West starred as the ill-fated prince in Pedro Calderón de la Barca's 1635 play *Life is a Dream* at the Donmar. In *The Times* Dominic Maxwell said West 'impresses throughout. He roars when he needs to, softens when he has to and eventually finds that real freedom is about living with limitations'. ❧ Damien Hirst's collection of paintings at the Wallace Collection was largely greeted with dismay. Adrian Searle in the *Guardian* called the works 'deadly dull'; Tom Lubbock added in the *Independent*, 'they're thoroughly derivative. Their handling is weak. They're extremely boring. I'm not saying that he's absolutely hopeless. But I'm not saying he's any good either'. {NOV} · British-Asian dancer-choreographer Akram Khan opened the 13-day Svapnagata festival at Sadler's Wells with an exemplary performance of classical N Indian Kathak dancing. Mark Monahan in the *Telegraph* almost ran out of superlatives, summing up the show as 'simply astonishing'. {DEC} · *Cat on a Hot Tin Roof* at the Novello, London, was notable for being performed by an all-black cast, but for reviewers it was the performances that impressed. Michael Billington wrote in the *Guardian*, 'The real bonus is the presence of the titanic James Earl Jones as Big Daddy; and his second-act, father-son confrontation with Adrian Lester's Brick is one of the high water-marks of the London year'. ❧ The casting of starlet Keira Knightley in Martin Crimp's updated version of Molière's

Keira Knightley

The Misanthrope at the Comedy Theatre raised a number of issues for the critics. In the *Independent,* Paul Taylor said that the production had seemed 'in danger of breaking the play's own implied moral code'. But Taylor, like many other critics, found his concerns unfounded: 'it's a tonic to report that Knightley finesses all this ethical fussing by turning in a performance that is not only strikingly convincing but, at times, rather thrilling in its satiric aplomb'. {JAN} · Cirque de Soleil's *Varekai* at the Royal Albert Hall was given a lukewarm reception. In the *Guardian* Michael Billington summed up what many felt: 'What I had not quite expected was a show that, for all the skills involved, combined corporate soullessness with spiritual pretension'. ❧ The critics were reluctantly won over by the musical *Legally Blonde* (a Broadway confection based on the film of the same name) at the Savoy Theatre. Benedict Nightingale said in *The Times*, 'What redeems this flamboyantly preposterous show – though why must a Broadway musical be anything else? – is that its tongue stays permanently in its cheek'. {FEB} · The Henry Moore retrospective at Tate Britain raised questions about the degree to which the volume of Moore's output had blunted its impact. Laura Cumming noted in the *Observer,* 'Moore made far too much to be consistently original. His work became as repetitive as it has become familiar; this tends to neutralise whatever power it may have'. However, Richard Dorment in the *Telegraph* disagreed: 'Almost a quarter of a century on, we are far enough away to see it [Moore's work] in perspective. It no longer

THE CRITICAL YEAR · 2009–10 cont.

looks passé, but eternal.' {MAR} · The *Independent*'s Charles Darwent was confounded by the critical response to the British Museum's exhibition of C12–15th W African Sculpture, *Kingdom of Ife*: 'Critics from other papers have lavished unanimous praise on the figures in the British Museum's show – "unmissable", "extraordinary", "exceptional" – but, worryingly, I can't join in. While I find the Ife torso of a king interesting as an artefact and useful as information, I also find it uninventive and unmoving as an artwork.' ❦ The *Telegraph*'s Charles Spencer was ebullient in his praise of the Adelphi Theatre's *Love Never Dies* – Andrew Lloyd Webber's sequel to *Phantom of the Opera*. Spencer called it Webber's 'finest show since the original *Phantom*, with a score blessed with superbly haunting melodies and a yearning romanticism that sent shivers racing down my spine'. Michael Billington gave a more tepid assessment in the *Guardian*, saying the lyrics were 'no more than serviceable'. {APR} · In the *Telegraph*, Mark Brown enthused about the Scottish Ballet's revival of Krzysztof Pastor's *Romeo and Juliet* at the Glasgow Theatre Royal. Praising the staging, which relocated the love story to C20–21st Italy, he remarked: 'The production's concept holds up beautifully in its 80-year span, from Il Duce to the present day. It also finds powerful and gorgeous choreographic expression.' {MAY} · Reviewing ENO's production of *Tosca* at the Coliseum for the *Independent*, Anna Picard was full of praise for the musical director and orchestra, but unimpressed by the direction: 'This, then, is "singers' opera": a style in which no performer

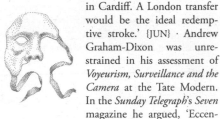

Love Never Dies

hinders the arm movements of another, and henchmen cluster in formation like entrants in a Dick Dastardly lookalike competition'. ❦ Calling *The Devil Inside Him* at Cardiff's New Theatre 'revelatory', the *Telegraph*'s Dominic Cavendish was wholly complimentary about the acting and observed: 'What a shame this Welsh coup on behalf of an old English master has such a short run in Cardiff. A London transfer would be the ideal redemptive stroke.' {JUN} · Andrew Graham-Dixon was unrestrained in his assessment of *Voyeurism, Surveillance and the Camera* at the Tate Modern. In the *Sunday Telegraph*'s *Seven* magazine he argued, 'Eccentric, thoughtless or slapdash selection fatally compromises the show at every turn'. {JULY} · In the *Independent*, Michael Coveney raved about a 'brilliant little revival' of *Aspects of Love* at the Menier Chocolate Factory, calling it 'a musical mini-masterpiece'. ❦ In a five-star review, Clement Crisp of the *Financial Times* pronounced the Bolshoi Ballet's production of *Coppélia* at the Royal Opera House an 'unabashed delight'. Discussing Natalia Osipova's performance, he said, 'her integrity of means, the sweetness of her dramatic playing, even at her naughtiest with old Coppélius, illuminate this masterpiece'. {AUG} · In the *Telegraph*, Dominic Cavendish described Howard Brenton's *Anne Boleyn* at Shakespeare's Globe as a 'shrewd, funny, drop-dead inventive account of [Boleyn's] rise and decapitating fall from grace'. {SEP} · The *Guardian*'s Jonathan Jones said Jeremy Deller's *Baghdad, 5 March 2007* at the Imperial War Museum prompted the terrible question: 'If the bomb did this to metal, what did it do to flesh?'

─────────────── THE ROYAL SHAKESPEARE COMPANY ───────────────

The Royal Shakespeare Company was officially formed in 1960, when Peter Hall created a new company based at the Royal Shakespeare Theatre (formerly the Memorial Theatre) in Stratford-Upon-Avon. However, the roots of the prestigious company can be traced back to 1875, when Stratford brewer Charles Edward Flower began a campaign to have a theatre built in Shakespeare's birthplace. Flower donated the land for the two-acre site on which the Shakespeare Memorial Theatre was built, and the Victorian gothic building opened to the public in 1879 with a performance of *Much Ado About Nothing*. In 1925, a Royal Charter recognising continued excellence was granted to the company, but a year later the company suffered a setback when the theatre burned down. The new Shakespeare Memorial Theatre, designed in Art Deco splendour by Elisabeth Scott, opened in 1932 and hosted thousands of productions before it was closed in 2007 for a radical overhaul. At the time of writing, the theatre was scheduled to reopen in late 2010. Some of the most noteworthy members of the Company have included:

Francesca Annis · Kenneth Branagh · Judi Dench · Ralph Fiennes · Jeremy Irons
Derek Jacobi · Ben Kingsley · Vivien Leigh · Ian McKellen · Helen Mirren
Vanessa Redgrave · Patrick Stewart · Juliet Stevenson · David Tennant

─────────────────── DOUBLE FALSEHOOD ───────────────────

In March 2010, *Double Falsehood* was published in the respected Arden Shakespeare series – and credited to William Shakespeare. The event was a triumph for scholars who claim the Bard is at least partially responsible for the play, the authorship of which has been contested for *c.*300 years. *Double Falsehood* was first staged under that title in 1727, by the writer Lewis Theobald. Theobald claimed to have based his work on a lost Shakespeare play (often called *Cardenio*) which he said he had found. At first the drama enjoyed popular support, but was soon savaged by critics as a fraud. Arden's publication was prompted by the research of Professor Brean Hammond, who argued that early parts of the play contain unmistakable Shakespeare 'DNA'.

─────────────────────── TWEET SEATS ───────────────────────

In 2010, several theatres experimented with the concept of 'tweet seats' – designated areas of the playhouse in which theatre-goers are free to share thoughts about the performance they are watching (or anything else) via the micro-messaging service Twitter. Theatres with 'tweet seats' for some 2010 performances included Broadway San Jose and the SF Playhouse, both in California. The West Yorkshire Playhouse also considered the idea in April, before rejecting it. Other venues, such as the Sydney Opera House, have made a point of inviting popular tweeters to their opening performances. Such moves ignited passionate debate within the theatre community – some argued that typing on brightly illuminated screens during a play is tantamount to heckling, while others maintained that in-performance tweets could serve as good publicity, and potentially attract much-needed younger audiences.

THEATRE'S MOST POWERFUL

The most powerful people in British theatre, listed by the *Stage* in December 2009:

1 ....Howard Panter & Rosemary Squire.............Ambassador Theatre Group
2 ....Sir Cameron Mackintosh.........................producer and theatre owner
3 ....Andrew Lloyd Webber....................composer, producer, theatre owner
4 ....Michael Grandage...Donmar Warehouse
5 ....Nicholas Hytner..National Theatre
6 ....Nica Burns & Max Weitzenhoffer......................................Nimax
7 ....Dominic Cooke..Royal Court Theatre
8 ....Bill Kenwright..Bill Kenwright Ltd
9 ....Michael Boyd.....................................Royal Shakespeare Company
10...Kevin Spacey & Sally Greene................................Old Vic Theatre

LAURENCE OLIVIER AWARDS · 2010

The Mountaintop was a surprise win at the 2010 Laurence Olivier Awards, earning Katori Hall the first Best New Play prize for a black woman. Other top winners:

Best actor.. Mark Rylance · *Jerusalem*
Best actress .... Rachel Weisz · *A Streetcar Named Desire*
Best actor in a supporting role..............................Eddie Redmayne · *Red*
Best actress in a supporting role............Ruth Wilson · *A Streetcar Named Desire*
Best new play ....*The Mountaintop* · Katori Hall
Best new musical...*Spring Awakening*
Best actor (musical or entertainment)   Aneurin Barnard *Spring Awakening*
Best actress (musical or entertainment) ....Samantha Spiro · *Hello Dolly!*
Best new comedy ....*The Priory* · Michael Wynne
Best director..Rupert Goold · *Enron*

THE TONY AWARDS · 2010

The 2010 Tony Awards were an especially good night for British actors and productions, as John Logan's *Red* swept the prizes with six trophies. Winners included:

Best play...*Red* · John Logan
Best musical...*Memphis*
Best leading actor in a play..............................Denzel Washington · *Fences*
Best leading actress in a play....................................Viola Davis · *Fences*
Best leading actor in a musical ....Douglas Hodge · *La Cage aux Folles*
Best leading actress in a musical........Catherine Zeta-Jones · *A Little Night Music*
Best featured actor in a play....................................Eddie Redmayne · *Red*
Best featured actress in a play........... Scarlett Johansson · *A View from the Bridge*
Best direction of a play ....Michael Grandage · *Red*
Best direction of a musical.......................Terry Johnson · *La Cage aux Folles*

─────────────── PRIMA BALLERINAS ───────────────

Prima Ballerina is an Italian ballet term used to denote an exceptional female lead. The first *Prima Ballerina* is generally agreed to have been Mademoiselle de la Fontaine, who appeared in Jean-Baptiste Lully's ballet *Le Triomphe de l'Amour* at the Paris Opera in 1681 (the event is said to be the first time women performed as professional ballerinas). The only rank higher than *Prima Ballerina* is that of *Prima Ballerina Assoluta* [absolute], but this is rarely conferred. The title is essentially honorary and is generally bestowed by a ballet company's director or ballet master. Dancers who have been named *Prima Ballerinas Assolutas* include: Pierina Legnani, Alicia Alonso, Eva Evdokimova, Margot Fonteyn, Mathilde Kschessinska, Alicia Markova, Maya Plisetskaya, Phyllis Spira, and Galina Ulanova. The male equivalent of a *Prima Ballerina* is usually referred to as a *Premier Danseur*. Although most modern ballet companies now use non-gender specific terms to denote lead dancers, the terms *Prima Ballerina* and *Premier Danseur* are still used occasionally – usually by the media. At most ballet companies, decisions on a ballet dancer's rank are made by the company's director or ballet master. It is not unheard of for ascendent dancers to skip a rank and, when moving from one company to another (usually a more prestigious one), it is not unusual for a dancer to accept a demotion. The Paris Opera Ballet is unique in requiring that dancers seeking a promotion compete in an annual competition. The only Paris Opera Ballet rank not obtained in this way is that of *Étoile*, which is awarded on the recommendation of the company's director. The dancer hierarchy at four major ballet companies is provided below:

The Royal Ballet · Artists → First Artists → Soloists → First Soloists → Principal Character Artists → Principals.

The Mariinsky (Kirov) Ballet · Corps de Ballet → Coryphées[†] → Principal Character Artists → Second Soloists → First Soloists → Principals.

American Ballet Theatre · Corps de Ballet → Soloists → Principals.

Paris Opera Ballet · Quadrilles → Coryphées → Sujets → Premiers Danseurs → Étoiles.

[†] From the Ancient Greek for leader.

─────────────── NATIONAL DANCE AWARDS · 2009 ───────────────

The Critics' Circle National Dance Awards are judged and presented by 50 critics and journalists who review dance productions. The winners for 2009 included:

Outstanding achievement	Alexander Grant
Best male dancer	Paul Liburd · *Scottish Ballet*
Best female dancer	Leanne Benjamin · *The Royal Ballet*
Outstanding company	*Ballet Black*
Best choreography: classical	Wayne McGregor · *Infra*
– modern	Christopher Bruce · *Hush*
Dance UK industry Award	Marie McCluskey · *Swindon Dance*
Patron's Award	Richard Bonynge
Best foreign dance company	Merce Cunningham Dance Company

—— EDINBURGH FRINGE COMEDY AWARDS · 2010 ——

30-year-old Russell Kane won the 2010 Foster's Edinburgh Comedy Award, and
£10,000, for his show *Smokescreens and Castles* – in which he explored, room by
room, the council house in which he grew up. The Best Newcomer award was
presented to Roisin Conaty (for *Hero, Warrior, Fireman, Liar*), and the Panel Prize –
for the act that embodies the spirt of the Fringe – went to Bo Burnham (for *Words,
Words, Words*). The other nominated acts were: Josie Long; Greg Davies; Sarah Millican; Asher
Treleaven; Imran Yusuf; The Boy with Tape on His Face; Gareth Richards; and Late Night Gimp Fight!

—————— FUNNIEST ONE-LINERS ——————

Below are the funniest gags at the Fringe, as selected by judges from Dave TV:

TIM VINE (winner)	*I've just been on a once-in-a-lifetime holiday. I'll tell you what, never again.*
David Gibson	*I'm currently dating a couple of anorexics. Two birds, one stone.*
Emo Philips	*I picked up a hitchhiker. You gotta when you hit them.*
Jack Whitehall	*I bought one of those anti-bullying wristbands when they first came out. I say 'bought' – I actually stole it off a short, fat ginger kid.*
Gary Delaney	*As a kid I was made to walk the plank. We couldn't afford a dog.*
John Bishop	*Being an England supporter is like being the over-optimistic parents of the fat kid on sports day.*
Bo Burnham	*What do you call a kid with no arms and an eye patch? Names.*
Gary Delaney	*Dave drowned. So at the funeral we got him a wreath in the shape of a lifebelt. Well, it's what he would have wanted.*
Robert White	*For Vanessa Feltz, life is like a box of chocolates empty.*
Gareth Richards	*Wooden spoons are great. You can either use them to prepare food, or if you can't be bothered with that, just write a number on one and walk into a pub.*

—————— BRITISH COMEDY AWARDS · 2009 ——————

Best TV comedy actor	Simon Bird · *The Inbetweeners*
Best TV comedy actress	Katherine Parkinson · *The IT Crowd*
Best TV comedy	*Outnumbered*
Best comedy entertainment programme	*Harry Hill's TV Burp*
Best male comedy newcomer	Charlie Brooker · *You Have Been Watching*
Best female comedy newcomer	Ramona Marquez · *Outnumbered*
Best new British TV comedy	*Psychoville*
Best TV comedy drama	*Pulling*
Best live stand-up	Michael McIntyre
Best comedy panel show	*Have I Got News For You*
Best sitcom	*Outnumbered*
Best sketch show	*Harry & Paul*
Lifetime achievement award	Sir Terry Wogan
Outstanding contribution to comedy	Peter Kay

AGE & MALE WAISTBAND HEIGHT

An online survey of 1,000 men, conducted by Debenhams, found that the height of a man's waistband changes dramatically as he ages: from the low-slung styles favoured by teenagers to the 'armpit-huggers' worn by pop impresarios. The retailer calculated the average height of male waistbands for various ages, based on survey responses:

Age	influences	trousers worn
≤12	parents	at waist
16	trends, American rappers and prison culture	5" below waist
27–36	job searching, impressing prospective in-laws	return to waist
39	encroaching middle age	last age at natural waist
45	weight gain	2" above waist
57	weight gain	all-time high: 5" above waist
65	onset of old-age shrinkage	3" above waist
75	old-age shrinkage	1" above waist

PHOTOSHOP & RETOUCHING

Adobe Photoshop celebrated its twentieth anniversary in 2010. The image-editing software has become a staple in fashion photography, where it is used to 'airbrush' away wrinkles, spots, or extra weight. However, in 2009–10 there were increasing calls for the limiting or monitoring of photo retouching. In September 2009, the Liberal Democrats called for a ban on retouched images in adverts aimed at under-16s, and encouraged people to report cases of 'extreme airbrushing' to advertising watchdogs. In February 2010, the Royal College of Psychiatrists called for labels on retouched images – an idea supported by Girlguiding UK in August. Such controversies have also led to a new sport. In 2010 several websites (such as photoshopdisasters.blogspot.com) began collecting examples of clumsy retouching – from the unnatural contours of Katy Perry's stomach on the cover of *Rolling Stone*, to the apparent peregrinations of Lindsay Lohan's navel in German *GQ*. [Adobe, quite reasonably, objects to the use of its trademark Photoshop® being used as generic slang.]

FASHION ACRONYMS

An amusing *Guardian* article by Hadley Freeman in January 2010 reported on the proliferation of novel fashion acronyms – the most recent being LSD (Little Sequined Dress), a popular choice during the 2009–10 winter holidays. Below are other fashion acronyms, some quite dubious, reported by Hadley and others:

BCBG	*Bon Chic, Bon Genre*†	TFFF	Too Fat For Fashion
LBD	Little Black Dress	VBL	Visible Bra Line
NFFP	Not For Fashion People	VBS	Visible Bra Strap
OTK	Over The Knee	VPL	Visible Panty Line
OTT	Over The Top		† French expression meaning
RTW	Ready To Wear		'Good Style, Good Attitude'.

───── READY-TO-WEAR FASHION WEEKS ─────

NEW YORK
February & September
Who shows: *Ralph Lauren, Vera Wang,*
Diane Von Furstenberg, Calvin Klein,
Zac Posen, Narcisco Rodriguez,
Michael Kors, Donna Karan

MILAN
February & September
Who shows: *Gucci, Giorgio Armani,*
Prada, Dolce & Gabbana, Moschino,
Versace, Roberto Cavalli,
Max Mara, Fendi

LONDON
February & September
Who shows: *Aquascutum, Erdem,*
Paul Smith, Nicole Farhi,
Jasper Conran, Betty Jackson,
Marios Schwab, House of Holland

PARIS
March & September/October
Who shows: *Stella McCartney, Chanel,*
Vivienne Westwood, Jean Paul Gaultier,
John Galliano, Issey Miyake,
Christian Dior, Chloé, Lanvin

According to *Vogue*, key trends for autumn/winter 2010/11 included: camel coats, shearling jackets, nipped-in waists, full skirts, ladylike accessories, red lips, faded florals, and high-heeled hiking boots.

─── BEST DRESSED ───

Stella McCartney topped *Harper's Bazaar's* Britain's best dressed woman list in November 2009. The top ten were:

1 .... Stella McCartney
2 .... Tilda Swinton
3 .... Alexa Chung
4 .... Yasmin Le Bon
5 .... Florence Welch
6 .... Kate Moss
7 .... Agyness Dean
8 .... Rachel Weisz
9 .... Natalia Vodianova
10 .... Tracey Emin

─── ELLE STYLE AWARDS ───

Best	*winner*
Actor	Colin Firth
Actress	Carey Mulligan
Music	Florence And The Machine
Style icon ..	Ashley & Mary-Kate Olsen
Woman of the year	Kristen Stewart
Model	Claudia Schiffer
Breakthrough talent	Nicholas Hoult
Editor's choice	Alexa Chung
Outstanding contribution	Naomi Campbell†
TV star	Dannii Minogue

† For her work as patron of the White Ribbon Alliance, which promotes safe pregnancy.

─── BRITISH FASHION AWARDS · 2009 ───

Designer of the year	Christopher Bailey for Burberry
Designer brand	Christopher Bailey for Burberry
Menswear designer	Kim Jones for Dunhill
Accessory designer	Katie Hillier
Model of the year	Georgia May Jagger
Emerging talent award for Ready-to-Wear	Peter Pilotto
British collection of the year	Christopher Kane
Outstanding achievement in fashion	John Galliano

———————— WORLD'S UGLIEST BUILDINGS · 2009 ————————

The Morris A. Mechanic Theatre in Baltimore, USA, is the world's 'ugliest building', according to members and editors of VirtualTourist.com. The theatre, which is currently boarded up, was deemed to be 'grim' and 'impersonal', and is considered by some locals to be long overdue for demolition. The 10 'ugliest buildings' listed in VirtualTourist.com's November 2009 rank of architectural eyesores were:

[1] Morris A. Mechanic Theatre · *Baltimore, USA*
[2] Žižkov TV Tower · *Prague, Czech Republic*
[3] 'The Beehive' (Parliament Building) · *Wellington, New Zealand*
[4] Centre Pompidou · *Paris, France*
[5] Federation Square · *Melbourne, Australia*
[6] Petrobras Headquarters · *Rio de Janeiro, Brazil*
[7] Markel Building · *Richmond, Virginia, USA*
[8] Royal Ontario Museum · *Toronto, Canada*
[9] National Library · *Pristina, Kosovo*
[10] Ryugyong Hotel · *Pyongyang, North Korea*

———————— THE STIRLING PRIZE · 2009 ————————

Richard Rogers's architecture practice, Rogers Stirk Harbour + Partners, won the annual RIBA Stirling Prize for the second time, in October 2009, with Maggie's Centre – a cancer support centre in west London. RIBA described the building as 'truly, unquestionably a haven for those who have been diagnosed with cancer', stating that it 'expresses in built form compassion, sensitivity and a deep sense of our common humanity'. The other nominees for the 2009 RIBA Stirling Prize were:

Nominated building	*architect*
5 Aldermanbury Square, London	Eric Parry Architects
Bodegas Protos, Spain	Rogers Stirk Harbour + Partners
Fuglsang Kunstmuseum, Denmark	Tony Fretton Architects
Kentish Town Health Centre, London	Allford Hall Monaghan Morris
Liverpool One Masterplan, Liverpool	BDP

———————— WORLD'S MOST IMPORTANT BUILDINGS ————————

A June 2010 survey by *Vanity Fair* magazine asked 52 leading architects, critics, and deans of architecture schools to name the most important buildings, bridges, or monuments constructed since 1980. The structures said to be most significant are:

Guggenheim Museum, Bilbao, Spain	*designed by* Frank Gehry, 1997
Menil Collection, Houston	Renzo Piano, 1987
Thermal Baths, Vals, Switzerland	Peter Zumtho, 1996
HSBC Building, Hong Kong	Sir Norman Foster, 1985
Seattle Central Library	Rem Koolhaas (Office for Metropolitan Architecture), 2004

————— THE ARCHAEOLOGICAL YEAR 2009–10—————

{OCT 2009} · *c.*150m-year-old dinosaur footprints were uncovered by French palaeontologists in the Jura near Switzerland. The 1·5m-wide prints were said to have been made by herbivorous sauropods, *c.*25m long, weighing some 30 tonnes. ❦ Archaeologists from the University of Southampton discovered an ancient Roman amphitheatre near Fiumicino airport in Italy. Because the building was constructed from highly expensive materials, it is thought to have been used to entertain nobles.

{NOV} · A study of extinct giant deer which roamed Europe >10,000 years ago revealed that the species probably became extinct when climate change killed off its food supply. {DEC} · Archaeologists reported in the journal *Antiquity* that remains of *c.*500 humans, discovered in a 7,000-year-old burial site in SW Germany, had been 'intentionally mutilated' in a manner indicative of mass cannibalism. {JAN} · A report on the location of workers' tombs near the pyramids of Khufu and Khafre, Egypt, suggested that these structures had not been built by slaves. The 4,500-year-old-tombs were found very close to a king's pyramid, indicating that those buried inside were not of low status. ❦ Analysis of the skeleton of a high-status neolithic male in France revealed that the man had his forearm amputated cleanly and survived – suggesting 'surgeons' of the time were able to anaesthetise, use flint tools to amputate, and create sterile conditions. {FEB} · A DNA study of King Tutankhamun's remains published in the *Journal of the American Medical Association* suggested that he was the product of an incestuous relationship, and had been a sickly child with a club foot. The

latter condition may explain why >130 walking sticks were found in King Tut's tomb. {MAR} · Archeologists writing in *BMC Biology* said that DNA analysis of 4,000-year-old mummies with Western features, found in China's Tarim Basin, suggested that the group had mixed Siberian and European ancestry. The mummies had piqued scientific interest in part because they had been buried underneath boats, despite being laid to rest in the desert. {APR} · An arrangement of 9 megaliths found in a remote part of N Dartmoor were carbon-dated to 3,500 BC. This was the first prehistoric stone row to be reliably carbon-dated, thanks to peat growing above and below the rocks. {MAY} · Palaeontologists announced that an amateur fossil hunter in Texas had discovered the lower jawbone of a flying dinosaur that lived 95m years ago – and boasted 100 teeth. {JUN} · The world's oldest leather shoe was uncovered in SE Armenia. Archeologists estimated the footwear to be 5,500 years old. {JUL} · Researchers at the British Museum announced that 78 flint tools discovered in Norfolk were >800,000 years old. The tools provided the first substantial evidence of early humans in Northern Europe. ❦ Workers digging at the site of the September 11 attacks in New York unearthed the 10-metre hull of a C18th ship. Archeologists speculated that the vessel had been buried as part of the debris used to extend the lower Manhattan shoreline into the Hudson River during the C18th and early 19th. {AUG} · Geoscientists discovered what may be the earliest-known sign of animal life – minuscule fossils, perhaps of sponges, in rocks that are *c.*650m years old.

Sci, Tech, Net

Science is but an image of the truth. — FRANCIS BACON (1561–1626)

———— SUBSTANCE OF THE YEAR · 'UNOBTAINIUM' ————

In James Cameron's 2009 sci-fi blockbuster *Avatar*, 'Unobtainium' is a precious mineral mined on the moon 'Pandora'. Unfortunately for Pandora's natives, deposits of Unobtianium (valued at $20,000,000/ kg) lie just under their most sacred site. While some giggled at the term 'Unobtainium' (long-used by aerospace engineers to describe hard-to-procure materials), others drew uncomfortable parallels between the fictional dilemmas of Pandora and real-life issues concerning increasingly vital 'rare earth elements' (REEs). ❦ REEs are 17 metallic elements, usually found together in the same mineral deposits, which share similar properties – for example, high electrical conductivity. Once thought to be rare, REEs have now been found across the Earth's crust – although locating exploitable concentrations is problematic, and separating REEs from the minerals in which they occur is complex and costly. In recent decades, REEs have proved crucial to the burgeoning high-tech, defence, and green energy sectors. *Neodymium* is used in the magnets inside hard drives, cell phones, wind turbines, and hybrid cars. *Lanthanum* is a prime component in the battery of the Toyota Prius. (Each Prius is said to contain some 25lbs of REEs.) *Terbium* is critical for low-energy light bulbs; *Samarium* for precision-guided weaponry; *Dysprosium* for lasers, nuclear reactors, compact discs, and hard

drives; and *Erbium* for fibre optics. Every new vehicle uses *Yttrium* for fuel efficiency, and all new TVs rely on *Europium* to produce the colour red. ❦ More than 90% of the world's REE supply is mined in China – a dominance that results from Beijing's controversial efforts in the 1980s and '90s to flood the market with cheap REEs, forcing out competition. In 2009 China mooted an export ban on some REEs because of growing domestic demand. Beijing later backed down, but has since imposed tight regulations and export quotas. Fearing that China's own REE supply may be dwindling, several countries (e.g., Japan and S Korea) are stockpiling REEs, and interest has spiked in Canadian, Australian, and S African mines – though these will take some years to develop. ❦ The lesson of REEs seems to be that, as with nuclear power and oil, the world is again becoming reliant on hazardous-to-source materials found, often, in unstable places. In Africa, *Tantalum* (used in missiles, surgical implants, &c.) is financing the blood-soaked Second Congo War – alongside other 'conflict minerals' such as tin, tungsten, and gold. ❦ As the gap widens between our shiny high-tech toys and the grind of their production, we may be forced to scrutinise the 'ingredients' of our electronics, in the same way that we increasingly scrutinise the ingredients of our food.

—————— MOST IMPORTANT SCIENTIFIC DISCOVERIES ——————

X-rays were voted the most important modern scientific discovery in a November 2009 poll conducted by the Science Museum. Nearly 50,000 people voted on a shortlist of scientific achievements chosen by the museum's curators. X-rays, discovered in 1895 by German physicist Wilhelm Röntgen, were deemed to have had more impact on the past, present, and future than penicillin or the manufacture of the Model T Ford. The ten most important discoveries and inventions were:

1... X-ray .... *(invented/discovered)* 1895
2... Penicillin 1928
3... DNA double helix........... 1953
4... Apollo 10 capsule............ 1969
5... V2 rocket engine 1944

6... Stephenson's Rocket 1829
7... Pilot ACE computer......... 1950
8... Steam engine................. 1712
9... Model T Ford................ 1908
10 . Electric telegraph 1837

In December 2009, *New Scientist* readers voted the microprocessor the discovery that has made the biggest impact on the world in the last 50 years. 'We are fascinated with creating machines built in our image. The microprocessor is arguably the greatest of them all', wrote Federico Faggin (part of the team that created the Intel 4004, the first commercial microprocessor) in a piece for the magazine.

————————— 'EDGE' ANNUAL QUESTION · 2010 —————————

Each year, the online science and culture magazine *Edge* invites scientists, artists and others to answer one open-ended question. The 2010 question was, 'How is the internet changing the way you think?' Excerpts from some answers appear below:

STEVEN PINKER (psychologist, author) · *Not at all. Electronic media aren't going to revamp the brain's mechanisms of information processing.* ❦ TOM STANDAGE (editor, *The Economist,* author) · *It has sharpened my memory. A quick search with a few well chosen keywords is usually enough to turn a decaying memory ... into perfect recall.* ❦ JAMES CROAK (artist) · *For me the internet made art-making rural, not centred in cities as it had been for centuries.* ❦ VIRGINIA HEFFERNAN (columnist, *The New York Times*) · *Philosophers and critics must only be careful, as we are trained to be careful, not to mistake this new, highly stylized and artificial order, the Internet, for reality itself.* ❦ PETER H. DIAMANDIS (CEO, X Prize Foundation) · *I'm realising that even complex questions can be answered (with* *embarrassment) with little more work than a digital prayer cast into the social-verse.* ❦ DOUGLAS COUPLAND (writer, artist) · *The internet has made me very casual with a level of omniscience that was unthinkable a decade ago. I now wonder if God gets bored knowing the answer to everything.* ❦ MARISSA MAYER (VP Search & User Experience, Google) · *It's not what you know, it's what you can find out. The internet has put at the forefront resourcefulness and critical-thinking and relegated memorization of rote facts to mental exercise or enjoyment.* ❦ BRIAN ENO (musician, artist) · *I notice that more of my time is spent in words and language – because that is the currency of the Net – than it was before. My notebooks take longer to fill.* ❦ STEVE QUARTZ (neuroscientist) · *We know less about thinking than we think.*

—————————— THE ROYAL SOCIETY ——————————

The Royal Society celebrated its 350th anniversary in 2010. The oldest scientific academy in the world, the Society dates back to the 1640s, when a group of 'natural philosophers' met regularly to discuss the ideas of Francis Bacon. In November 1660, 12 group members decided to found 'a Colledge for the Promoting of Physico-Mathematicall Experimentall Learning'. The following were founding members:

William Balle (*c*.1627–90) · Robert Boyle (1627–91) · Sir William Petty (1623–87)
Sir Paul Neile (*c*.1613–*c*.86) · Jonathan Goddard (1617–75)
John Wilkins (1614–72) · Abraham Hill (1633–1721)
Sir Robert Moray (1608–73) · Lawrence Rooke (1622–62)
William Brouncker, 2nd Viscount Brouncker (1620–84)
Alexander Bruce, 2nd Earl of Kincardine (1629–80)
Sir Christopher Wren (1632–1723)

In 1660, the group met once a week to conduct experiments and discuss scientific topics. In 1661, the Society was presented with its first book, and thereafter began to amass a significant library and collection of specimens. In 1662, King Charles II granted the Society a Charter of Incorporation; a second Charter granting further privileges was granted in 1663. In 1662, the Society also published its first books: Robert Hooke's *Micrographia*, and John Evelyn's *Sylva*. In 1665, the first issue of *Philosophical Transactions*, edited by the Society's secretary, appeared in print. ♥ Nowadays the Royal Society is engaged in funding research, advising the government, sponsoring events, and awarding honours (12 medals, eight prizes, and seven lectureships). The Society also publishes the following highly respected journals:

Philosophical Transactions A (maths, physical, engineering science) and *B* (biological sciences)
Proceedings A (maths, physical, engineering science) and *B* (biological research)
Journal of the Royal Society Interface (cross-disciplinary physical & life sciences)
Notes and Records of the Royal Society (history and philosophy of science)
Biology Letters (life sciences)

From its earliest days, fellowships awarded on the basis of an election have been the cornerstone of the Royal Society. Four types of memberships exist (all are for life):

Fellows · ≤44 citizens or residents per year of the Commonwealth or Ireland may be awarded fellowships for 'substantial' contributions to science; they may use the post-nominal letters 'FRS'. *Foreign Members* · ≤8 people ineligible for regular fellowships who are 'eminent for scientific discoveries' may be awarded foreign memberships per year; they may use the letters 'ForMemRS'.

Honorary Members · ≤1 non-scientist who has 'rendered signal service to the cause of science, or whose election would significantly benefit the Society by their great experience' may be awarded such a membership per year. *Royal Fellows* · as recommended by The Council of the Royal Society; currently Prince Philip, the Prince of Wales, the Princess Royal, and the Duke of Kent.

The motto of the Royal Society, taken from Horace, is *Nullius In Verba* – 'take nobody's word for it'.

———————— PUBLIC PERCEPTION OF SCIENCE ————————

The public's perception of science is decidedly mixed, according to members of science academies from around the world surveyed by the *New Scientist* in January 2010. The magazine interviewed 70 members of science academies meeting in London for the InterAcademy Panel – a group that helps science academies (such as the Royal Society) advise the public on the scientific aspects of global issues. The respondents painted the following portrait of the public's attitudes to science:

TRUST IN SCIENCE		UNDERSTANDING OF SCIENCE	
People in my country ...	%	People in my country ...	%
Have a high degree of trust	.26	*Have a great understanding*	.6
Trust science to some extent	.53	*Have a reasonable understanding*	.26
Are divided on the issue	.20	*Have medium understanding*	.26
Are mistrustful to some extent	.1	*Have some understanding*	.33
Have a high degree of mistrust	.0	*Have little understanding*	.10

———————— MUSICAL TRIBUTES TO SCIENCE ————————

In February 2010, the official choir of the European Organisation for Nuclear Research (CERN) performed a song dedicated to the Large Hadron Collider (LHC), the world's largest particle accelerator. *The Particle Physicists' Song*, written by amateur songwriter Danuta Orlowska, is sung to the tune of *The Hippopotamus Song* by Flanders and Swann. It includes the lyrics: '*Higgs, Higgs, glorious Higgs / The theory told them these thingumajigs / Were so fundamental ...*'. Splendidly, this song was not the first musical tribute to the LHC. In 2008, an enterprising CERN press officer created a rap video about the accelerator. The track began, '*Oh yeah, I'm about to drop some particle physics in da club ...*'. (Predictably, the video was a smash hit on YouTube.) Taking the concept further, in 2009 Buzz Aldrin joined professional musicians, including Snoop Dogg, to release a rap commemorating the 1969 lunar landing. *Rocket Experience* featured the octogenarian Aldrin rapping lines such as, '*I've been there, now I say it's your turn; all we've got to do is make the engine burn ...*'.

In an August 2010 interview with *Vibe* magazine, hip-hop pioneer Dr Dre announced that he was working on an instrumental album entitled *The Planets*. 'It's just my interpretation of what each planet sounds like,' Dre revealed. ❦ Several US universities boast science-themed bands. At New York University, a group of neuroscientists called The Amygdaloids play 'heavy mental', while cell biologists and other scientists at Yale have formed The Cellmates. The Northwestern maths department is home to the Klein Four group, described as 'the premier *a cappella* group of the world of higher mathematics'.

———————— THE DARWIN AWARDS · 2009 ————————

The Darwin Awards commemorate 'those who improve our gene pool by removing themselves from it'. The 2009 prize was a rare 'Double Darwin' awarded to two men in Dinant, Belgium, who tried to blast open an ATM. The pair misjudged the amount of dynamite necessary and blew up the building – including themselves.

—————— NOBEL PRIZES IN SCIENCE · 2009 ——————

THE NOBEL PRIZE IN PHYSICS

One half to Charles K. Kao, *Standard Telecommunication Laboratories/ Chinese University of Hong Kong*

'for groundbreaking achievements concerning the transmission of light in fibers for optical communication'

One half jointly to Willard S. Boyle, *Bell Laboratories, and* George E. Smith, *Bell Laboratories*

'for the invention of an imaging semi-conductor circuit – the CCD sensor'

In 1966, Kao and his team discovered that using cables made of pure glass dramatically increased the transmission capabilities of fibre optics. Today, such cables form the backbone of the entire global communications system. In 1969, Boyle and Smith invented the 'eye' that later made digital cameras possible. Their device, called a CCD sensor, uses an array of photosensitive cells that emit electrons in proportion to incoming light, thereby transforming an optical image into a digital one. The sensor makes use of Albert Einstein's photoelectric effect, for which he was awarded a Nobel in 1921.

THE NOBEL PRIZE IN CHEMISTRY

Venkatraman Ramakrishnan, *MRC Laboratory of Molecular Biology, Cambridge*

Thomas A. Steitz, *Yale University*

Ada E. Yonath, *Weizmann Institute of Science, Israel*

'for studies of the structure and function of the ribosome'

Ramakrishnan, Steitz, and Yonath all made major contributions towards understanding the structure and function of the ribosome, by using a technique called X-ray crystallography to map the composition of the ribosome's atoms. The ribosome is the part of the cell responsible for 'translating' DNA into protein; understanding its inner workings has been central to developing a new class of antibiotics that work by blocking the ribosomes inside bacteria.

THE NOBEL PRIZE IN PHYSIOLOGY OR MEDICINE

Elizabeth H. Blackburn, *University of California, San Francisco*

Carol W. Greider, *Johns Hopkins University*

Jack W. Szostak, *Harvard Medical School/Howard Hughes Medical Inst.*

'for the discovery of how chromosomes are protected by telomeres and the enzyme telomerase'

The work of Blackburn, Greider, and Szostak solved the mystery of how chromosomes are copied without degradation during cell division. While it was known that the ends of the chromosomes, the telomeres, played a protective role, Blackburn et al. were able to show exactly how the telomere functions. Blackburn and Greider also discovered the enzyme that creates the telomere, called telomerase. The group's insights have enhanced our understanding of how cells operate, and have raised hopes for new treatments that target ageing and cancer.

――――― ABEL PRIZE ―――――

The Abel Prize, awarded by the Norwegian Academy of Science and Letters for extraordinary contributions in the mathematical sciences, was presented in 2010 to John Tate of the University of Texas at Austin. The committee noted that 'many of the major lines of research in algebraic number theory and arithmetic geometry are only possible' because of Tate's work. The prize carries a NOK 6,000,000 (*c.*£600,000) award.

――――― COPLEY MEDAL ―――――

The Copley Medal, presented by the Royal Society, is the world's oldest prize for scientific achievement. Two medals were presented in 2010, in honour of the Society's 350th year [see p.188]. One medal was presented to Sir David Cox for his contributions to statistics. The other medal was given to Dr Tomas Lindahl for his work on the biochemistry of DNA repair. The silver gilt medal is accompanied by a gift of £5,000.

――― GRIGORY PERELMAN & THE MILLENNIUM PRIZE ―――

In June 2010, notoriously reclusive Russian mathematician Grigory Perelman announced that he would not accept the $1m Millennium Prize. Perelman had been awarded the prize in March 2010 for solving the Poincaré Conjecture, which had bedevilled mathematicians since 1904. Perelman first posted a solution to the problem online in 2002, but after a flurry of publicity withdrew from public life, and is said to live in a spartan flat with his mother. Perelman told reporters his main reason for refusing the award was his 'disagreement with the organized mathematical community', whom he considered 'unjust'. The Millennium Prizes were created in 2000 to highlight the biggest mysteries of mathematics, and the prize to Perelman was the first to be awarded. Perelman also refused the Fields Medal in 2006.

――――――――― Ig NOBEL PRIZES ―――――――――

Some highlights of the 2009 Ig Nobel prizes, which award scientific 'achievements that cannot or should not be reproduced':

PUBLIC HEALTH · Elena N. Bodnar, Raphael C. Lee, and Sandra Marijan (Chicago, Illinois) *for inventing a brassiere that, in an emergency, can be quickly converted into a pair of protective face masks, one for the brassiere wearer and one to be given to some needy bystander.*

BIOLOGY · Fumiaki Taguchi, Song Guofu, and Zhang Guanglei (Kitasato University Graduate School of Medical Sciences, Japan) *for demonstrating that* *kitchen refuse can be reduced more than 90% in mass by using bacteria extracted from the feces of giant pandas.*

MATHEMATICS · Gideon Gono (governor of Zimbabwe's Reserve Bank) *for giving people a simple, everyday way to cope with a wide range of numbers ... by having his bank print bank notes with denominations ranging from one cent ($·01) to one hundred trillion dollars.*

MEDICINE · Donald L. Unger (Thousand Oaks, California) *for investigating a possible cause of arthritis of the fingers, by diligently cracking the knuckles of his left hand ... every day for more than 60 years.*

—— SOME NOTABLE SCIENTIFIC RESEARCH · 2009–10 ——

{OCT 2009} · Evolutionary biologists at Yale predicted that women, on average, will stand *c*.2cm shorter and weigh 1kg more by the year 2409. The researchers based their conclusion on a multi-generational study of 14,000 Massachusetts residents, which found that shorter, heavier women consistently had more children, and passed on their physical traits to their daughters. {NOV} · NASA's LCROSS mission confirmed the presence of water on the Moon, after sending a rocket to collide with the lunar surface. A spectral analysis of the resulting plume of debris clearly showed particles of H_2O among the moon dust. ❦ Scientists in Brazil discovered that volunteers who played the computer game *Doom* before bed scored higher on the game the next day if they reported dreaming about playing the game. Researchers said the results lent credence to the idea that dreaming is linked to learning. {DEC} · Scientists at the UK's Wellcome Trust Sanger Institute sequenced for the first time the genomes of lung cancer and skin cancer cells. After comparing the cells with normal tissue, the geneticists found 23,000 mutations in the lung cancer cells (most triggered by smoking), and 33,000 mutations in the skin cancer cells (most activated by sunlight). {JAN 2010} · Psychiatry researchers at Columbia University Medical Center in New York found that teenagers whose parents set them a bedtime of midnight or later were 24% more likely to suffer from depression than those whose bedtimes were set at or before 10pm. ❦ Geneticists at the University of Utah estimated that 1.2m years ago the human population numbered only *c*.55,500 – roughly twice the

number of gorillas then living on the planet. {FEB} · Scientists in the UK and Belgium established communication with several severely brain-damaged patients who were living in a 'vegetative state'. Using functional magnetic resonance imaging (fMRI) scans, the scientists were able to detect brain activity wilfully generated in response to questions. In one case, the scientists obtained correct answers to biographical questions by asking a patient to think about motor imagery for 'yes', and spatial imagery for 'no'. ❦ Biological anthropologists at the University of Illinois at Urbana-Champaign analysed the maximum life-spans of 776 mammal species and found that tree-dwellers live almost twice as long as earth bound species – probably because it is easier for tree-dwellers to escape predators. ❦ Oceanographers at the Sea Education Association in Massachusetts reported on a concentration of rubbish in the Atlantic Ocean between 22°–38° N. In some areas, students discovered 200,000 items of trash per km^2. Reports likened this area to a vast concentration of rubbish in the ocean between California and Hawaii, which is known as the 'Great Pacific Garbage Patch'. {MAR} · An international panel of scientists concluded that an asteroid was responsible for killing off the dinosaurs. After combing through 20 years' worth of multidisciplinary research, the experts decided that the evidence suggested a 10–15km-wide space rock struck Mexico's Yucatan Peninsula 65m years ago – causing earthquakes, vast fires, and a global winter that killed more than half the Earth's species. ❦ A study of genetic material from dog breeds and wild grey wolves around

— SOME NOTABLE SCIENTIFIC RESEARCH · 2009–10 cont. —

the world suggested that dogs were first domesticated in the Middle East and not East Asia, as earlier research had suggested. ❦ A team of scientists at Cornell University, New York, examined 52 'Last Supper' paintings created over the past two millennia, and discovered that the portion sizes had increased dramatically. The size of meals was found to have grown by 69%, plate size by 66%, and bread size by 23%. {APR} · Russian and American scientists created the long-theorised element 117 by smashing together isotopes of calcium and berkelium in a Russian particle accelerator. The scientists said that element 117 would be added to the periodic table if independently confirmed. ❦ Researchers at the University of Cologne found that people playing on a putting green sank 35% more putts when told they were playing with a 'lucky' ball. {MAY} · German biologists reported that comparisons of Neanderthal and human DNA pointed to interbreeding between the two groups *c.*100,000–60,000 years ago. As a result, 1–4% of the genome of non-Africans today probably comes from Neanderthals. ❦ Physicists at the Tevatron particle accelerator in Illinois announced that the behaviour of some mysterious subatomic particles could provide a clue to the existence of the universe. Physics has long been unable to explain why the equal amounts of matter and anti-matter produced at the Big Bang did not destroy one another. The Tevatron researchers discovered that particles called 'neutral B mesons' decaying in their accelerator produced 1% more matter than antimatter – mirroring what may have happened at the birth of the universe. {JUN} ·

Researchers from New Zealand and Fiji who compared aerial photos of 27 low-lying Pacific islands from the past 60 years found that only 4 of the islands had diminished in size, while the rest had grown or stayed stable. The researchers cautioned that while the islands appeared to be responding well to sea level rises, they could still become uninhabitable within the next century. ❦ A study at the University of Exeter found that young Ugandan mongooses [or mongeese, if you like] adopt the specific foraging techniques used by elder mentors, even when these differed from other animals in the group. The study supported the idea that certain animals enjoy some form of tradition. {JUL} · At the 18th International Aids Conference in Vienna, researchers unveiled study results showing that South African women who used a vaginal gel containing the drug tenofovir reduced their chances of contracting HIV via sex by 39%. (Those who used the gel consistently reduced their chances by 54%.) The study was the first to show promising results for an anti-HIV microbicide, and was hailed as a 'game-changer' in allowing women to protect themselves from HIV/Aids. ❦ A study comparing isotopes in the Earth's mantle with those in meteorites estimated that the Earth is 4·467bn years old – *c.*70m years younger than previously thought. {AUG} · The decade-long Census of Marine Life released data showing that crustaceans are the most common creatures in the oceans, followed by molluscs. {SEP} · Oxford University researchers revealed that falling in love causes the average individual to lose two relationships from their innermost circle of friends.

——————— DARK SKY PARKS & THE BORTLE SCALE ———————

In November 2009, Galloway Forest Park, in south-west Scotland, was named the UK's first 'Dark Sky Park' by the International Dark-Sky Association (IDA). Dark Sky Parks are publicly accessible areas that are relatively free from light pollution, from which the natural phenomena of the night sky can be enjoyed. The IDA selects such parks for the darkness of their night skies and for their commitment to preserving darkness as a scenic and scientific resource. Galloway Forest Park joined the Natural Bridges National Monument, Utah; Cherry Springs State Park, Pennsylvania; and Geauga Park, Ohio [all in the US], as the world's only IDA-designated Dark Sky Parks. ❦ About two-thirds of the world's population live in areas with light pollution, according to the *World Atlas of the Artificial Night Sky Brightness*, published by US and Italian researchers in 2001. In 2000, the Campaign to Protect Rural England mapped night-time light pollution using satellite measurements of artificial light. These measurements employed a scale of 0–255, where 0 meant no light was detected and 255 meant the detector was fully saturated. Charted below is the breakdown of England's night-time light pollution levels:

Light reading	% of England		
0–1·70 – *truly dark*	11	50·01–150 – *bright*	52
1·71–50 – *dark*	16	150·01–240 – *brighter*	14
		240·01–255 – *saturated*	7

In 2001, the astronomer John E. Bortle created the Bortle Dark Skies Scale as a way for astronomers to gauge the quality of their observation sites. (The scale is also used by the IDA to establish Dark Sky Parks.) A summary of the scale appears below:

1 · Excellent dark-sky site   *Zodiacal light, gegenschein[†], zodiacal band visible; surroundings basically invisible; Triangulum Galaxy seen by naked eye*

2 · Typical truly dark site   *airglow visible near horizon; clouds as dark holes; Triangulum Galaxy seen with direct vision; surroundings barely visible*

3 · Rural sky   *some light pollution on horizon; clouds may appear illuminated; Milky Way is detailed; M4, M5, M15 and M22[‡] visible to naked eye*

4 · Rural/suburban   *light pollution over population centres; zodiacal light doesn't extend halfway to zenith at beginning or end of twilight; Milky Way lacks detail*

5 · Suburban sky   *Milky Way very weak; light sources in most directions*

6 · Bright suburban sky   *no trace of zodiacal light; sky glows greyish white within 35° of horizon; Triangulum Galaxy impossible to see without binoculars*

7 · Suburban/urban transition   *entire sky greyish white; strong light sources in all directions; Milky Way is nearly invisible*

8 · City sky   *sky glows whitish or orange; newspaper headlines would be visible; Triangulum Galaxy and Cancer constellation may be seen on good nights*

9 · Inner-city sky   *entire sky is bright, even at zenith; many familiar constellations invisible; the only pleasing telescopic objects are Moon, planets, and brightest stars*

† Literally 'counter-glow' in German, the gegenschein is a faint light seen opposite the sun at dawn or dusk under good conditions. [Source for scale: *Sky & Telescope* magazine] ‡ The prefix 'M' denotes a 'Messier object' included in the catalogue of deep-sky objects compiled by French comet-hunter Charles Messier (1730–1817). More information on these objects may be found at messier.obspm.fr.

─── SOME INVENTIONS OF NOTE · 2009–10 ───

{OCT 2009} · Engineers in Mexico developed a 'smart' speed bump that collapses into the ground when drivers are obeying the speed limit, but stays elevated when cars approach too quickly. Its developers said their goal was both to reduce pollution generated when drivers brake and accelerate, and also to offer an incentive for drivers who follow the rules. ❦ Inventors at the University of California created the 'Transborder Immigrant Tool' – a GPS-enabled mobile phone designed for illegal immigrants trying to enter America. The phone comes with tools to help migrants navigate, and locate supplies and assistance. {NOV} · Researchers in the US demonstrated a new model for implantable medical devices – thin, flexible, silicon electronics backed by silk. The silk conforms to living tissue and dissolves harmlessly, leaving electrodes well integrated in the body. {JAN} · At the 9th British Invention Show in London, a Spanish entrepreneur touted bedsheets impregnated with Viagra. The inventor claimed his product would help those couples who are too tired for sex. {FEB} · The UK government unveiled two prototypes of shatterproof pub glasses designed to reduce the injuries inflicted when beer glasses are used as weapons. One prototype featured a strengthening bioresin coating, the other employed two bonded layers of glass. ❦ An event at the MoD's Centre for Defence Enterprise showcased a liquid polymer that can be moulded around the body yet turns into a rigid shell when hit. Previously used in sports, the material has applications in military helmets and body armour. ❦ A man in Louisiana developed a chastity belt for female dogs. The 'Pet Anti-Breeding Device' locks over the dog's groin only when the animal is in heat, and was advertised as a way to spare dogs from surgery. {MAR} · Scientists at Surrey University and the space company Astrium unveiled a design for massive sails to help clean up debris in outer space. Called CubeSails, the devices unfurl from nanosatellites and drag 'space junk' down through the Earth's atmosphere, where it is incinerated. {APR} · A graduate student in Spain developed contact lenses that temporarily correct vision defects by re-shaping the cornea. The lenses, which are worn at night, were said to be as effective as surgery for problems like myopia and astigmatism. {MAY} · Scientists in Colorado announced that human trials would soon begin in India on a powdered form of the measles vaccine, which can be inhaled from a plastic sack. Developers said a vaccine without needles would make it much easier to immunise children. {JUN} · At the Glastonbury Festival, the telecoms company Orange debuted wellies capable of charging mobile phones by collecting heat from the wearer's feet and converting it into electricity. 12 hours of stomping charged a mobile phone for an hour. {JUL} · Microsoft unveiled a technology that enables devices to accept batteries regardless of how they are loaded. The 'Instaload' contains positive and negative terminals in each end of the battery compartment, eliminating the need for '+' and '–' signs. {AUG} · A bottle that uses UV light to sterilise water was awarded top honours at the UK finals of the James Dyson Award. In tests, it took just 90 seconds for the bottle to remove 99·9% of bacteria and viruses.

———————— UK & GLOBAL SPACE AGENCIES ————————

The UK Space Agency (UKSA) was launched in April 2010. The goal of the agency is to manage UK space budgets (currently £270m) and policies, and represent the UK in international space negotiations. Prior to the creation of the UKSA, these roles were divided among a variety of different government departments. The UKSA will first assume responsibility for Britain's European Space Agency (ESA) subscriptions, and then other major EU projects, such as the satellite system Galileo. ❦ In December 2009 the British National Space Centre released a report on the options for the UK's space programme. The *Space Exploration Review* considered whether to reduce UK involvement in the mandatory ESA science programmes; continue with the status quo (participation in mandatory ESA activities and robotic exploration of Mars); increase investment in robotic-only exploration; or invest in both human and robotic space exploration. The report concluded that a mix of robot and human exploration would offer the best financial return. The report also included a look at the programmes of other space-faring nations, noting that space exploration is increasingly coordinated in a global strategy. Notes on some of these programmes are below:

USA · *NASA has more funding than any other space programme ($18·7bn in 2010). Its goals include pioneering space exploration, scientific discovery, and aeronautics research.*

Japan · *The Japan Aerospace Exploration Agency is focused on developing launch vehicles and satellites, and aims to take a leading role in creating a lunar base.*

Canada · *The Canadian Space Agency is focused on space exploration for science and innovation, and has developed a speciality in creating robotic arms.*

China · *The National Space Admin. has made vast strides in the last 15 years, and China became the third nation to put astronauts in space (in 2003).*

Russia · *Roscosmos focuses on the use of space to enhance quality of life, economic growth, and national security; exploration of the Moon is a top priority.*

India · *The Indian Space Research Organisation has been launching science missions to space, and is planning robotic missions to the Moon and Mars, as well as an eventual human mission to Mars.*

Doctor Who fans noted a resemblance between the UKSA logo (a stylised Union Jack pierced by a red arrow) and the logo of the British Rocket Group – a fictional agency created for the 2005 *Doctor Who* Christmas special. The creators of the UKSA logo said there was only a passing resemblance.

———————————— THE MoD AND UFOs ————————————

In December 2009, the MoD withdrew the dedicated answer-phone and email service it operated to record public sightings of unidentified flying objects – reportedly saving £44,000 a year. The Ministry said: 'The MoD has no opinion on the existence or otherwise of extra-terrestrial life. However, in over fifty years, no UFO report has revealed any evidence of a potential threat to the United Kingdom'. An MoD spokesman told the BBC, 'Any legitimate threat to the UK's airspace will be spotted by our 24/7 radar checks and dealt with by RAF fighter aircraft'.

————————— KEY SPACE MISSIONS OF 2009–10 —————————

SMOS · The Soil Moisture and Ocean Salinity (SMOS) satellite – the second of ESA's Earth Explorer satellites – is designed to provide information about Earth's water cycle. The satellite aims to use an interferometric radiometer to measure microwave emissions that reflect changes in the saltiness of the oceans and the moisture in the soil. This information will help meteorologists better understand the climate and predict the weather. The SMOS launch, in November 2009, also carried the satellite Proba 2, which was designed to demonstrate 17 satellite technologies and four scientific instruments.

SDO · NASA's Solar Dynamics Observatory (SDO) was launched in February 2010 to study the Sun's activity in minute detail. Telescopes aboard the SDO will transmit images of the Sun back to Earth every 0·75 seconds. These images will help scientists learn more about how the Sun impacts our climate, and will also help keep track of solar weather that can disrupt power grids and GPS technology.

CRYOSAT-2 · Launched in April 2010, ESA's CryoSat-2 is the first European mission to study the Earth's ice. CryoSat-2 will use an SAR/Interferometric Radar Altimeter (SIRAL) to provide detailed measurements of the thickness of the ice sheets over Antarctica and Greenland, as well as in the polar oceans. The information will help scientists understand how ice is responding to climate change, and the role that ice plays within the Earth's climate systems.

STS-132 · The final mission for NASA's Atlantis shuttle carried a Russian-built research module to the International Space Station, where it was slated to provide storage space and a docking port for Soyuz and Progress spacecraft. The 12-day mission, in May 2010, also included three space walks to maintain equipment outside the station.

NASA's venerable space shuttle programme, which began in 1981, was scheduled for retirement in 2010 – after 36 missions to the International Space Station.

————————— PLANETARY EVENTS · 2011 —————————

3 January . . . . *Perihelion: Earth is at orbital position closest to the Sun*
4 January . . . . *partial solar eclipse visible in northern Africa, Europe, and Asia*
20 March . . . . *Equinox: the Sun passes northward over the equator at 23:31 GMT*
3 April . . . . *Saturn at opposition*
1 June . . . . . . *partial solar eclipse visible in E Asia, Alaska, N Canada, and Greenland*
15 June . . . . *total lunar eclipse visible in S America, Europe, Africa, Asia, Australia*
21 June . . . . *Solstice: the Sun directly above the Tropic of Cancer at 17:16 GMT*
22 August . . . . *Neptune at opposition*
4 July . . . . *Aphelion: Earth is at orbital position farthest from the Sun*
23 September . . . . . . *Equinox: the Sun passes southward over the equator at 9:04 GMT*
25 September . . . . *Uranus at opposition*
29 October . . . . *Jupiter at opposition*
25 November . *partial solar eclipse visible over Antarctica, part of S Africa, Tasmania*
21 December . . . . *Solstice: Sun directly above Tropic of Capricorn at 5:30 GMT*

——————— SCI, TECH, NET WORDS OF NOTE ———————

SOSOS · Switch On to Switch Off · people who can only feel relaxed with their personal communication devices turned on.

MESSTING · text messaging that messes up your life. *Also* CHEXTING · cheating + texting. *Also* METROTEXTUALS · men who sign text messages to other men with an 'x' for 'kiss'.

THUMBO · a text message typo made with the thumb. *Also* THUMB TRIBE · a term reported in Asia for young people who prefer text messaging to talking.

INFORMATION CURTAIN · Hillary Clinton's Churchillian term for the effects of internet censorship in China and elsewhere.

SYNTHIA · a nickname for the computer-created cell developed by J. Craig Venter in 2010, which some hailed as the first form of synthetic life.

HELLA · Californian slang for 'a lot', and the subject of a campaign by a California physics student to make the term the official SI prefix for 10^{27} [see p.206].

CHAOTIAN · proposed name for a newly demarcated eon of geologic time, which stretches from the origin of the Solar System to the collision of proto-planets that formed the Moon and the Earth at its current size.

SINGLE SERVING SITES · websites which fulfil an extremely narrow purpose – such as IsItChristmas.com (the answer is 'no' 364 days a year).

JI-HOBBYISTS · internet users who 'self-radicalise' by seeking out jihadist content online.

YAKA-WOW · a mistaken transcription of the words 'yuck' + 'wow' that briefly became an internet meme after an April 2010 *Times* interview quoted neuroscientist Susan Greenfield as saying, 'if you have a load of breezy people who go around saying yaka-wow … Is that the society we want?'

ILLEGAL FLOWER DONATION · flowers left by Chinese Google users at the search engine's headquarters in Beijing, after the company announced plans to withdraw. The phrase is said to have been coined by security staff.

SEDIBA · a new hominid species discovered in South Africa and announced in 2010. The word means 'fountain' or 'wellspring' in the Sotho language.

SUPERTASKERS · a nickname given in a University of Utah study to the 2·5% of participants who were able to drive competently while text messaging.

HALFALOGUE · the irritating half-conversations shared by mobile users.

ZOMBIE-SAT · nickname for the 'dead but alive' satellite Galaxy-15, which failed in 2010 and required intervention from other satellites.

NEXTING · skipping to a new session on the webcam chat site Chatroulette, which randomly matches up strangers from around the world.

HOURGLASS SYNDROME · stress and frustration caused by slow computers – which often display an hourglass symbol while processing data.

VOOKS · books with embedded video content, often for display on an iPad.

———————— COMPUTING IN CLOUD ————————

In a splendid article for the *Wall Street Journal*, Max Colchester shed light on the pitfalls associated with France's efforts to keep English out of the French language. Discussing the challenge facing a team of experts charged with translating into French the term 'cloud computing', Colchester noted, 'keeping the French language relevant isn't easy in the Internet age. For years, French bureaucrats have worked hard to keep French up-to-date by diligently coming up with equivalents for English terms. … But technological advancements mean new Anglicisms are spreading over the Internet at warp speed, leaving the French scratching their heads'. Translating 'cloud computing' was challenging because the word 'cloud' in French is commonly associated with daydreaming. In October 2009, France's General Commission of Terminology and Neology rejected the literal translation of the term, '*informatique en nuage*' (computing in cloud) because they considered it too vague. At the time of writing, no official translation of the term had been decided upon. Below is a list of English computing terms, and their French translations, as approved by the Commission of Terminology and Neology:

English term	French equivalent	literally
Chipset	*jeu de puces*	game of chips
Hotkey	*raccourci au clavier*	keyboard shortcut
Joystick	*manche à balai*	broom handle
Netlist	*liste d'interconnexions*	list of interconnections
Podcasting	*diffusion pour baladeur*	diffusion for personal stereo
Touch pad	*pavé tactile*	tactile pad
World Wide Web	*toile d'araignée mondiale*	global spider web

In March 2010, the French government announced the results of a student contest to find replacements for C21st words invading the French language. As a substitute for '*le buzz*', the judges chose '*ramdam*' – an Arab term for the hubbub that arises when fasting ends at night during Ramadam. '*Le tuning*' (modifying cars to make them faster) may be replaced by '*bolidage*', an invented term from French slang '*le bolide*' (literally fireball or meteorite, and often used to refer to a fast car). Instead of '*le talk*' (used for talk radio), the judges favoured '*débat*'; for the English '*chat*' they chose '*éblabla*' and '*tchatche*'; and for '*newsletter*' the winner was the rather uninspired term '*infolettre*'.

———————— SCIENTIFIC NAMES OF THE YEAR · 2009–10 ————————

Some odd and unusual names for the plant and animal species discovered this year:

Crikey steveirwini · Australian snail named for naturalist Steve Irwin.
PancakeCroc, BoarCroc, and RatCroc · ancient crocodile cousins from the Sahara.
Leviathan melvillei · extinct whale named for *Moby-Dick* author Herman Melville.
Fedexia striegeli · fossil amphibian named for FedEx, owners of the discovery site.
Elysia manriquei · sea slug named in honour of artist César Manrique.
Csiromedusa medeopolis · Tasmanian jellyfish named for the Commonwealth Scientific & Industrial Research Organisation [CSIRO]; 'Medeopolis' is Latin for 'city of gonads' – a reference to the species' external reproductive glands.

―――― iPHONE APPS――――

'Apps' are mini computer programs designed for a specific device (e.g., an iPhone) and often with a very narrow purpose (e.g., checking the weather or sending virtual farm animals to Facebook friends). The apps on Apple's App Store, designed for iPods, iPhones, and iPads, have proved particularly popular. According to London-based consulting firm AppManifesto, at the end of the first quarter of 2010 there were 152,065 apps for sale on the UK App Store, at an average price of £1·51. Below are the top iPhone app categories in the store during 2010 Q1:

	apps for sale QI 2010
Games	23,997
Books	20,745
Entertainment	19,889
Education	11,862
Utilities	9,729
Travel	9,170
Lifestyle	8,825
Reference	6,129
Sports	5,983
Music	5,928

―――――― TOP GAMES――――――

The best-selling videogames of 2009 (across all formats) are listed below:

1 ....*Call of Duty: Modern Warfare 2*
2 ....*FIFA 10*
3 ....*Wii Sports Resort*
4 ....*Wii Fit*
5 ....*Wii Fit Plus*
6 ....*Assassin's Creed II*
7 ....*Mario Kart Wii*
8 ....*Mario & Sonic At Olympic Winter Games*
9 ....*Call Of Duty: World At War*
10 ....*FIFA 09*

[Source: ELSPA/GfK Chart-Track]

―――SOCIAL NETWORKING―――

44% of UK internet users had a social networking profile as of 2010, according to Ofcom. Facebook was by far the most popular site, and accounted for 90% of profiles (compared to 18% for MySpace, and 17% for Bebo). 41% of those with a profile said they visited their social networking site of choice at least once a day, and just 8% visited less often than once a week. Some of the many crazes that swept Facebook in 2010:

Women updating status messages with the colour of their bras (aimed at raising awareness about breast cancer) · Replacing profile pictures with an image of a celebrity 'Doppelgänger' · Changing status messages to the Urbandictionary.com definition of one's name · Calculating a 'fine' for one's misspent youth · Committing 'Facebook suicide' (deleting one's profile)

―――TOP SUPERCOMPUTERS―――

The TOP500 project biannually rates the world's fastest supercomputers. The top ten as of June 2010 are listed below:

Name	country	max teraflops[†]
Jaguar	US	1759·00
Nebulae[‡]	China	1271·00
Roadrunner	US	1042·00
Kraken	US	831·70
JUGENE	Germany	825·50
Pleiades	US	772·70
Tianhe-1	China	563·10
BlueGene/L	US	478·20
Intrepid	US	458·61
Red Sky	US	433·50

† Flops (FLoating point Operations Per Second) is the unit used to measure the speed of computer calculation. A teraflop is equal to one trillion calculations per second. ‡ The highest rank ever reached by a Chinese computer on the list.

———————————— CHILDREN & THE INTERNET ————————————

In December 2009, the British government launched a campaign to help keep children safe online. The strategy – *Click Clever, Click Safe* – was unveiled by the Council for Child Internet Safety, and it featured a variety of initiatives, including: the addition of internet safety as a compulsory subject in the National Curriculum from age 5 in England (beginning September 2011); an independent review of the Council's standards for online services, to be used by the government to review websites; and a new awareness campaign featuring the online 'Green Cross Code'[†]:

ZIP IT	BLOCK IT	FLAG IT
Keep your personal stuff private and think about what you say and do online	*Block people who send nasty messages and don't open unknown links and attachments*	*Flag up with someone you trust if anything upsets you or if someone asks to meet you offline*

As part of the launch, the government released a report on parent and child attitudes to online safety, entitled the *Staying Safe Survey 2009*. The survey found that parents were generally more concerned about online safety than their children:

	parents of kids aged 5–11	parents of kids 12–17	kids 12–17
Had internet at home	82%	90%	90%
Had internet in child's room	17	45	51
Had concerns about internet use	86	83	61
Concerned about inappropriate contact	44	47	30
Concerned about inappropriate content	52	42	9
Concerned about computer security	12	14	24
Concerned about cyber-bullying	14	13	8
(Kids) had come across harmful content	12	13	18

Other research released by the Council in 2009 found that children spend much more time online than their parents believe: children aged 8–17 estimated that they spent *c.*44 hours online per month, while their parents believed they spent only about 19 hours online. Indeed, an October 2009 report by the charity Youth-Net labelled young people 16–24 'digital natives', because of their constant exposure to the high technology (including the internet) from the nursery onwards. The YouthNet survey revealed some attitudes to the internet held by UK 16–24s:

80%	*agreed 'new technology is making my life simpler'*
77	*agreed 'on the internet you can never know if someone is who they say they are'*
76	*agreed 'the internet is a safe place as long as you know what you're doing'*
75	*agreed 'I couldn't live without the internet'*
45	*agreed 'I feel happiest when I'm online'*

† Based on the Green Cross Code for road safety, which long included the advice 'Stop, Look, Listen.'
❡ In July 2010, Facebook and the Child Exploitation and Online Protection Centre (CEOP) agreed to a Facebook application that will allow children to report inappropriate behaviour, such as by suspected paedophiles. The addition of a so-called 'panic button' followed similar moves by Bebo and MySpace.

─────────── INTERNET USERS WORLDWIDE ───────────

There are about 1·4bn internet users in the world, according to the UN's *Information Economy Report 2009*. The greatest number of users are in China (298m) followed by the US (191m), and Japan (88m). The nations below have the highest and lowest internet penetration, as measured by the number of internet users per 100 people:

Most users per 100 pop., 2008		*Fewest users per 100 pop., 2008*	
Bermuda	78·1	Niger	0·27
Monaco	76·4	Sierra Leone	0·42
South Korea	72·7	DR Congo	0·46
Andorra	71·0	Ethiopia	0·47
Japan	69·2	Chad	0·63

Over the past few years, the number of internet users in the developing world has grown five times faster than in the developed world. However, large gaps in accessibility remain, and some nations that have access to the internet may be hampered by insufficient speed and bandwidth. The list below shows the average international internet data capacity in 2008 for various world regions, as expressed in *bits per capita*:

Europe & Central Asia	20,712	Middle East and N Africa	478
Americas	7,991	South Asia	58
East Asia and Pacific	1,182	Sub-Saharan Africa	30

─────── UK INTERNET ACCESS & TIME SPENT ONLINE ───────

18·3m UK households had access to the internet in 2009 (about 70%), according to the ONS. The table below shows the share of households with net access by region:

England	71%	– South-west	72	– North-east	66
– London	80	– East Midlands	67	– Yorks & Humber	64
– East of England	77	– West Midlands	67	Wales	68
– South-east	75	– North-west	67	Scotland	62

Britons are spending an increasing amount of time online and are devoting a growing share of that time to social networking and blogs, according to a 2010 report by the UK Online Measurement Company. The report analysed UK time spent online in April 2007 (536m hours) and April 2010 (884m hours; a rise of 65%). A breakdown of time spent on various online activities in the two months is below:

Activity (%)	04/07	04/10	±		04/07	04/10	±
Blogs/social[†]	8·8	22·7	+159	Search	4·1	4·0	–3
Email	6·5	7·2	+11	Software info &c.	5·3	3·4	–36
Games	5·9	6·9	+15	News	1·5	2·8	+84
Instant messaging	14·2	4·9	–66	Adult	2·8	2·7	–3
Classifieds/auction	5·0	4·7	–6	Other	42·2	36·8	–13
Portals	3·7	4·0	+10				

† Social networking

—— INTERNATIONALISED TOP LEVEL DOMAINS ——

In May 2010, the Internet Corporation for Assigned Names and Numbers (ICANN†) announced that the first URLs ending in non-Latin characters were available for use. Since the creation of the internet in 1969, the suffixes that end web addresses – such as *.com*, *.org*, and *.uk* – have been limited to the letters A–Z in upper and lower case, the digits 0–9, and the hyphen. (For technical reasons, non-Latin characters, such as those in Hindi or Chinese, were not allowed, though certain tricks were used to include them in earlier parts of the web address.) Such suffixes are known as Top Level Domains (TLDs), and are of two types: Country Codes‡ (CCs) such as .uk [see pp.92–93], and Generic Top Level Domains (gTLDs) such as .com. The first Internationalised Top Level Domains to come online were the Country Codes for Egypt, Saudi Arabia, and the United Arab Emirates, all written in Arabic. Plans were also afoot to allow non-Latin gTLDs. Currently, the following gTLDs exist:

Domain	reserved for	sponsor
.AERO	*air-transport industry*	Société Internationale de Téléc. Aeronautique
.ARPA	*operationally critical infrastructural identifier spaces*	IANA†
.ASIA	*Pan-Asia and Asia Pacific community*	DotAsia Organisation Ltd
.BIZ	*Business*	NeuStar, Inc.
.CAT	*Catalan linguistic and cultural community*	Fundacio puntCAT
.COM	*generic*	VeriSign Global Registry Services§
.COOP	*cooperative associations*	DotCooperation LLC
.EDU	*accredited post-secondary institutions*	EDUCAUSE
.GOV	*US government*	General Services Administration
.INFO	*generic*	Afilias Limited
.INT	*organisations established by international treaties*	IANA†
.JOBS	*human resource managers*	Employ Media LLC
.MIL	*US military*	DoD Network Information Center
.MOBI	*mobile content creators/users*	mTLD Top Level Domain Ltd
.MUSEUM	*museums*	Museum Domain Management Association
.NAME	*individuals*	The Global Name Registry Ltd
.NET	*generic*	VeriSign Global Registry Services§
.ORG	*generic*	Public Interest Registry (PIR)
.PRO	*professionals and related entities*	Registry Services Corp.
.TEL	*for businesses and individuals to publish contact data*	Telnic Ltd
.TRAVEL	*the travel industry*	Tralliance Registry Management Company, LLC

The first generic TLDs, created in 1984, were *.com*, *.edu*, *.gov*, *.mil*, and *.org*. Today, *.com* has by far the most registrations of any TLD (about 80m), followed by *.cn* (China), *.de* (Germany) and *.net*. † ICANN is a non-profit organisation based in California. A sub-body, the Internet Assigned Numbers Authority (IANA) is in charge of assigning administrative responsibility for TLDs and maintaining their technical and administrative details. IANA was the responsibility of one man, Jon Postel of the Information Sciences Institute at the University of Southern California, from IANA's creation in the 1970s until Postel's death in 1998. ‡ Country Codes are based on the International Organization for Standardisation standard ISO 3166, first published in 1974 and taken from a list of countries and 'areas of geopolitical interest' from the Statistical Office of the UN. § VeriSign is an American company based in California, which reportedly answers ≤50bn Domain Name System queries each day.

— DECADE IN GOOGLE—

Top Google search terms, UK   *year*
Nostradamus† 2001
Spiderman 2002
Prince Charles 2003
Big Brother 2004
James Blunt 2005
Steve Irwin 2006
iPhone 2007
iPlayer 2008
Stephen Gately 2009

† The French doctor and seer whose real name was Michel de Nostredame (1503–66). ❦ In March 2010, *Yahoo!* revealed that the most-searched news topics of the past 15 years had been: (1) September 11 · (2) Cloning · (3) Iraq war · (4) Saddam Hussein · (5) Harry Potter book releases · (6) Michael Jackson death · (7) Steve Irwin death · (8) Tsunami · (9) Enron scandal · (10) The Millennium.

——— GOOGLE UK A–Z ———

The first search result offered by Google UK when a user types a single letter of the alphabet into the search box:

A – *Argos* · B – *BBC* · C – *Currys*
D – *Debenhams* · E – *eBay*
F – *Facebook* · G – *Google Maps*
H – *Hotmail* · I – *Ikea*
J – *John Lewis* · K – *KLM*
L – *Lotto* · M – *MSN*
N – *Next* · O – *O2*
P – *PayPal* · Q – *Quidco*
R – *Rightmove* · S – *SkyNews*
T – *Tesco* · U – *UCAS*
V – *Vodafone* · W – *Weather*
X – *XE* · Y – *YouTube* · Z – *Zara*

As of 8·09·10 · According to Google's website, the company's predictive results come from a blend of past personal searches (when signed in), searches performed by other users, sites in the search index, and ads in Google's network.

— MOST POPULAR SITES—

The websites with the greatest number of unique users during January 2010, according to the Nielsen company:

Site	*unique users*
Google	349,758,716
MSN/WindowsLive/Bing	271,929,865
Yahoo!	233,479,611
Microsoft	220,410,208
Facebook	218,860,914
YouTube	203,258,182
Wikipedia	154,174,390
AOL	128,146,575
eBay	121,740,943

[Source: BBC.] Covers UK, France, Germany, Italy, Spain, Switzerland, Brazil, US, Australia.

— 2010 WEBBY AWARDS—

Celebrity/fan .... *jimcarrey.com*
Activism .... *makeitrightnola.org*
Best practices .... *twitter.com*
Breakout .... *Chatroulette*
Mobile app .... *evernote.com*
Personal site .... *thisisindexed.com*
Humour .... *theonion.com*
Copy/writing .... *newyorker.com*
Community .... *flickr.com*
Education .... *wechoosethemoon.org*
Fashion .... *bluebelljeans.com*
Food/beverage *www.asylum626.com*
Games .... *recordtripping.com*
Green .... *loveletterstothefuture.com*
Law .... *bitterlawyer.com*
Magazine .... *newyorker.com*
Music .... *pandora.com*
News .... *nytimes.com*
Person of the Year .... *Roger Ebert*
Tourism .... *snapshotsofprovence.com*

Webby Award winner speeches are limited to 5 words. In 2010 Roger Ebert said, 'veni vidi vici', while Snapshots of Provence's representative said, 'Finally, the French win something'.

STN SIGNIFICA

Some (in)significa(nt) Sci, Tech, Net footnotes to the year. ❦ In November 2009, the first 'worm' to target iPhones hit Australian users. The virus switched victims' phone 'wallpaper' to an image of 1980s popstar Rick Astley. ❦ A California man brought a $1m lawsuit against the makers of *World of Warcraft*, saying the online role-playing game had left him 'sad, lonely and alienated', and that he had become dependent on the game for 'the little ongoing happiness' in his life. ❦ Egypt's telecommunications regulatory body released a 16-point 'Ethics Code' for the use of mobile phones. Users were advised to avoid speaking loudly in public, to be patient when encountering wrong numbers, and to choose 'non-annoying' ring tones. ❦ The Royal Society of Chemistry launched a competition to find an octogenarian as 'well preserved' as the actor Sean Connery, in an attempt to highlight the role of British science in preserving the health of the nation. The winner was Edinburgh resident Bill Lamond, who received a collection of Connery's films, a designer tracksuit, £300 in cash, and a 20-year subscription to *Chemistry World* magazine. ❦ Facebook announced that it would give users the option to 'memorialise' profiles of family members and friends who have passed away, shutting off status updates and wiping contact information but leaving a 'wall' for loved ones to share memories. ❦ Google ignited a frenzy of competition among US cities after announcing that it was seeking locations to test its new ultra-fast broadband service. The mayor of Topeka, Kansas, temporarily re-named his town 'Google', while the mayor of Duluth, Minnesota, announced that all firstborn males there would be named 'Google Fiber' and girls, 'Googlette'. ❦ Scientists at NASA said the 8·8 magnitude earthquake that struck Chile [see p.21] had shortened the length of an Earth day by 1·26 milliseconds. The change was said to be due to the effect of the earthquake on the Earth's rotation, which will now spin slightly faster. ❦ Mattel added the title 'Computer Engineer' to Barbie's lengthy résumé. The 'I Can Be … Computer Engineer' Barbie wore a tunic patterned with binary code, sported a pink BlueTooth headset, and carried a pink laptop. ❦ The market intelligence firm IDC estimated that, in 2009, the total amount of digital information in the world grew 62%, to 800,000 petabytes – and that by the end of 2010 the total would reach 1·2 zettabytes [see p.206]. ❦ The Hay Festival in Wales announced the winner of a contest to find 'the most beautiful Tweet'. The winning tweet, by Marc MacKenzie from Edmonton, was: 'I believe we can build a better world! Of course, it'll take a whole lot of rock, water & dirt. Also, not sure where to put it.' ❦ The US state of Wisconsin named a bacterium used in cheese-making, *Lactococcus lactis*, as its official state microbe. ❦ A Bulgarian mobile number was reportedly decommissioned after 3 of its owners died. (The first of cancer, and the latter two after being shot.) People who call 0888 888 888 get a message saying the phone is 'outside network coverage'. ❦ A tourist who became lost on the ice off N Germany was rescued after a woman admiring the scenery via a webcam noticed him flashing his camera for help and phoned the police.

——————————— SI PREFIXES ———————————   — °C – °F —

Below are the SI prefixes and symbols for the decimal
multiples and submultiples of SI Units from 10^{24} to 10^{-24}.

10^{24}	yotta	Y	1 000 000 000 000 000 000 000 000
10^{21}	zetta	Z	1 000 000 000 000 000 000 000
10^{18}	exa	E	1 000 000 000 000 000 000
10^{15}	peta	P	1 000 000 000 000 000
10^{12}	tera	T	1 000 000 000 000
10^{9}	giga	G	1 000 000 000
10^{6}	mega	M	1 000 000
10^{3}	kilo	k	1 000
10^{2}	hecto	h	100
10	deca	da	10
1			1
10^{-1}	deci	d	0.1
10^{-2}	centi	c	0.01
10^{-3}	milli	m	0.001
10^{-6}	micro	μ	0.000 001
10^{-9}	nano	n	0.000 000 001
10^{-12}	pico	p	0.000 000 000 001
10^{-15}	femto	f	0.000 000 000 000 001
10^{-18}	atto	a	0.000 000 000 000 000 001
10^{-21}	zepto	z	0.000 000 000 000 000 000 001
10^{-24}	yocto	y	0.000 000 000 000 000 000 000 001

——————— SOME USEFUL CONVERSIONS ———————

A	A *to* B *multiply by*	B *to* A *multiply by*	B
inches	25.4	0.0397	millimetres
inches	2.54	0.3937	centimetres
feet	0.3048	3.2808	metres
yards	0.9144	1.0936	metres
miles	1.6093	0.6214	kilometres
acres	0.4047	2.471	hectares
square feet	0.0929	10.76	square metres
square miles	2.5899	0.3861	square kilometres
UK pints	0.5682	1.7598	litres
UK gallons	4.546	0.2199	litres
cubic inches	16.39	0.0610	cubic centimetres
ounces	28.35	0.0353	grams
pounds	0.4536	2.2046	kilograms
stones	6.35	0.157	kilograms
miles/gallon	0.3539	2.825	kilometres/litre
miles/US gallon	0.4250	2.353	kilometres/litre
miles/hour	1.609	0.6117	kilometres/hour

°C	°F	°C	°F
		49	120.2
100	212	48	118.4
99	210.2	47	116.6
98	208.4	46	114.8
97	206.6	45	113
96	204.8	44	111.2
95	203	43	109.4
94	201.2	42	107.6
93	199.4	41	105.8
92	197.6	40	104
91	195.8	39	102.2
90	194	38	100.4
89	192.2	37	98.6
88	190.4	36	96.8
87	188.6	35	95
86	186.8	34	93.2
85	185	33	91.4
84	183.2	32	89.6
83	181.4	31	87.8
82	179.6	30	86
81	177.8	29	84.2
80	176	28	82.4
79	174.2	27	80.6
78	172.4	26	78.8
77	170.6	25	77
76	168.8	24	75.2
75	167	23	73.4
74	165.2	22	71.6
73	163.4	21	69.8
72	161.6	20	68
71	159.8	19	66.2
70	158	18	64.4
69	156.2	17	62.6
68	154.4	16	60.8
67	152.6	15	59
66	150.8	14	57.2
65	149	13	55.4
64	147.2	12	53.6
63	145.4	11	51.8
62	143.6	10	50
61	141.8	9	48.2
60	140	8	46.4
59	138.2	7	44.6
58	136.4	6	42.8
57	134.6	5	41
56	132.8	4	39.2
55	131	3	37.4
54	129.2	2	35.6
53	127.4	1	33.8
52	125.6	0	32
51	123.8	-1	30.2
50	122	-2	28.4

Normal body temp.
= 37°C (98.6°F)
range 36.1–37.2°C
(97.7–98.9°F)

Travel & Leisure

It is most important that we should keep in this country a certain leisured class. I am of the opinion of the ancient Jewish book which says 'there is no wisdom without leisure'.
— WILLIAM BUTLER YEATS (1865–1939)

'NAKED' AIRPORT SCANNERS

On 5 January, the government announced that full-body scanners would be introduced into all British airports. This was a response to an attempted attack on an Amsterdam–Detroit flight on Christmas Day 2009 – allegedly by a Nigerian man who tried to detonate plastic explosives concealed in his underwear. ❦ Full-body (or 'naked') scanners use 'backscatter X-ray' or 'active millimetre waves' to produce detailed images of the entire body. They were installed at Manchester airport in January 2010, Heathrow in February, Gatwick in May, and an eventual nationwide roll-out is planned. According to the Dept for Transport (DfT), full-body scanners will be used on randomly selected passengers and those who trigger other security 'red flags'. Screeners are prohibited from selecting passengers on the basis of personal characteristics such as age, ethnicity, or sex. ❦ Advocates of full-body scanners note that they can detect contraband material – including plastics – missed by metal detectors. Critics argue that the machines represent an affront to personal dignity and human rights, and a threat to children and human health. Furthermore, there is a lively debate as to how accurate the scanners actually are. ❦ Privacy campaigners and the press gleefully pointed out that

full-body scanners display 'explicit' images of genitalia, breasts, and medical implants. (Passengers may request a screener of the same sex, but forfeit their right to fly if they refuse to be scanned.) In response, the DfT argued that the scanners blur all faces, and noted that scanning takes place in private rooms, with no opportunity to copy, transfer, or store any images. Nevertheless, in February 2010 the Equality and Human Rights Commission warned that the government must do more to ensure that this new technology complies with privacy and nondiscrimination laws. (In March, a male worker at Heathrow was disciplined for taking a picture of a scan of a female employee – proving, at least, the potential for abuse.) Children's rights advocates have also questioned whether full-body scanners violate the Protection of Children Act 1978, which makes it illegal to create indecent images or 'pseudo-images' of a child. The government responded that the Act contains provisions for the detection of a crime, and maintained that staff must pass background checks. ❦ At the time of writing, the DfT was conducting a public consultation on the new scanners. And, despite the initial furore, it seemed that most passengers were coming to terms with 'naked' scanning as just another sacrifice for safety.

———————————————— CARS ON THE ROAD ————————————————

31,035,791 cars were in use in Britain at the end of 2009 – 0·7% fewer than at the end of 2008, according to the Society of Motor Manufacturers and Traders (SMMT). The decline was the first recorded in 64 years, and the first during peacetime since 1904. The SMMT noted that while the recession was the most obvious factor behind the fall, the government's scrappage scheme, as well as stricter enforcement of rules on unlicensed vehicles, had also contributed.

1,994,999 *new* cars were registered in 2009, a drop of 6·4% from 2008. The most popular models in 2009 were:

Ford Fiesta · Ford Focus
Vauxhall Corsa · Vauxhall Astra
Volkswagen Golf · Peugeot 207
MINI · BMW 3 Series
Vauxhall Insignia · Ford Mondeo

The Ford Fiesta remained the most popular new car in Britain as of August 2010.

The SMMT found that silver was the top hue for all cars on the road, followed by blue, black, and red.

———————————————— MOTORING ETIQUETTE ————————————————

In April 2010, the publishers of Debrett's and the car brand Astra released *Thoroughly Modern Motoring Manners*. Below are some of their pearls of polite wisdom:

On music: *Music should be carefully chosen and kept at a sociable volume … avoid singing along.* ❦ For men: *A chivalrous passenger is as well-behaved and polite in the car as he is when he's out and about. He realises that jokes about women drivers are clichéd and is never a backseat driver.* ❦ For women (exiting a car): *Keeping your knees together, swivel your body and swing your legs outwards. Place one foot down, keeping your knees together. Dip your head and shoulders forward and slide and glide out of the car.* ❦ On being the perfect host: *Sometimes your passengers will want to doze or daydream. Always respect their wishes – if they want to stay in their own world for the duration of the journey, let them.* ❦ For hat-wearers: *It's good manners to remove your hat in the car, just as you would when entering a building.*

———————————————— SEX DIFFERENCES IN CAR INSURANCE ————————————————

Men pay on average 71% more for car insurance than women, according to a November 2009 analysis of 6m quotes, released by the price-comparison website moneysupermarket.com. According to the site's head of motor insurance, women are charged less because they are considered to be 'safer and more mature motorists'. The table below lists the average cost of car insurance, by gender and age:

Age	men (£)	women (£)	Age	men (£)	women (£)
18	2,319	1,237	40s	331	261
19	1,873	1,007	50s	249	204
20s	1,004	598	60s	200	171
30s	473	349	70s	218	200
			80s	309	237

2010 CONCEPT CARS

'Concept cars' are one-off vehicles built to demonstrate new design ideas and technology. They often serve as the *pièce de résistance* for a manufacturer's exhibit at an auto show, and provide a useful method for gauging customer reaction to a new feature (power windows, cruise control, and folding roofs all first appeared on concept cars). While many concept vehicles never make it past the auto-show floor, others (like Chrysler's PT Cruiser or the Porsche Boxer) do eventually hit the road. The first concept car is generally said to have been the Y-Job, created in 1938 by GM designer Harley Earl, which took a bold stand against the boxy designs of its day with streamlined curves and convertible top. A few of 2010's concept cars include:

Rinspeed UC? [sic] .... *2·5 metre electric 2-seater designed to be loaded onto trains*
Aston Martin Cygnet .... *smart car based on Toyota IQ with classic Aston details*
MINI Beachcomber ...... *4-wheeler with removable doors and roof and elevated seats*
Pininfarina 2uettottanta ... *Alfa Romeo 2-seater Red Spider, homage to 1960s Duetto*
Renault Twizy Z.E. .... *2·3 metre electric 2-seater with open bodywork*
GM EN-V ... *1·5 metre electric 2-seater that 'senses' traffic & can drive autonomously*
Honda 3R .... *3-wheel, single-seat electric with futuristic clear canopy*
Porsche 918 Spyder .... *hybrid supercar with 'eco', 'hybrid', 'sport', and 'race' modes*

CAR NAME MEANINGS

When Renault unveiled the *Zoe Z.E.* concept car at the Frankfurt auto show in September 2009, the vehicle's name provoked an uproar in France. Zoe is the 17th most popular girl's name in France, and many feared their daughters would for ever be associated with a car. Parents flooded Renault with complaints, but Renault was unmoved, stating that Zoe 'is a name that evokes values of femininity, of youth, a playful spirit and vivacity'. The meanings of some other car names are below:

Car maker	model	derived from
Volkswagen....	Touareg.......	*the Tuareg, a North African tribe native to the Sahara*
Lamborghini ..	Murciélago	*celebrated fighting bull, survived 28 sword strokes†*
Toyota.........	Prius	*Latin for 'to go before' to reflect its eco innovation*
Chevrolet......	Corvette	*anti-submarine warship*
Ford	Cortina	*Italian 1956 Olympic ski resort Cortina d'Ampezzo*
Vauxhall.......	Zafira	*Arabic word meaning 'success'*
Fiat	Punto.........	*Spanish word meaning 'direct hit' or 'point'*
Skoda..........	Fabia..........	*Italian girl's name, apparently meaning 'bean farmer'*
Renault........	Clio..........	*in Greek mythology the 'muse of history'*
Porsche	Carrera	*Spanish for 'race'*
Bugatti........	Veyron......	*Bugatti driver Pierre Veyron, won 1939 24 hrs Le Mans*
Ferrari	Testarossa.......	*Italian for 'redhead'*

In May 2010, a 23-year-old Parisian woman named Zoe Renault said she was considering suing the car company. † Nearly all Lamborghinis are named after bulls or bullfighting terms. One notable exception is the Countach, an Italian colloquial expression for something that is stunning or striking.

——————————— MOT FAILURE RATES ———————————

In January 2010, the Vehicle and Operator Services Agency (VOSA) released detailed data on MOT failure rates after the BBC lodged a freedom of information request. The BBC compiled a table created from VOSA raw data of MOTs undertaken in 2007, which revealed the failure rate for the most popular models of vehicles†. The five models with the highest and lowest failure rates are below:

Highest failure rate			Lowest failure rate		
Make	model	failure rate	Make	model	failure rate
Ford	Transit Connect	30·5%	Toyota	Corolla	11·2
Renault	Megane	28·1	Honda	Jazz	13·3
Ford	Transit	26·3	Honda	Civic	14·1
Peugeot	307	24·7	Toyota	Yaris	14·2
Vauxhall	Corsa	24·7	Ford	Fiesta	15·6

† Those with >20,000 MOTs. Figures relate to models of car made in 2004. Caution should be applied when examining the table, since the mileage of the vehicles in question was not taken into account.

——————— BRITAIN'S MOST INTIMIDATING JUNCTIONS ———————

Spaghetti Junction in Birmingham is Britain's most intimidating junction, according to a November 2009 survey by road rescue firm Britannia Rescue. The top ten:

[1] Gravelly Hill (Spaghetti Junction), Birmingham [2] M8 junctions, Glasgow
[3] Marble Arch, London [4] Magic Roundabout, Swindon
[5] Hanger Lane Gyratory, London [6] M5/M6 intersection, Birmingham
[7] Piccadilly Circus, London [8] Five Ways junction, Birmingham
[9] Magic Roundabout, Hemel Hempstead [10] Kingston Bridge, Glasgow

——————————— MOTOR VEHICLE OFFENCES ———————————

Below are the number of motoring offences (verdicts of guilt, penalty notices, and written warnings) recorded by the DfT in England and Wales for some recent years:

Offence (thousands of offences)	1998	2002	2007
Dangerous, careless, or drunk driving	190	171	267
Accident offences	21	18	16
Speed limit offences	962	1,538	1,591
Unauthorised taking or theft of car	37	32	23
Licence, insurance, or record-keeping offences	817	819	641
Vehicle test & condition offences	277	228	116
Neglect of traffic signs and pedestrian rights	271	213	239
Obstruction, parking, and waiting offences	2,139	1,180	453
Other offences	353	239	344
ALL OFFENCES	5,066	4,439	3,690

—————— MOTORCYCLISTS & ATTITUDES TO RISK ——————

In October 2009, the Department for Transport released a report titled 'Passion, Performance, Practicality: Motorcyclists' Motivations and Attitudes to Safety', which examined the complex relationship motorbike riders have with risk. After a series of interviews, the researchers proposed the following list of seven types of motorcyclists, each classified and defined by their motivation for riding:

LOOK-AT-ME ENTHUSIASTS · *young (or never-grew-up) riders with limited experience but limitless enthusiasm — riding is all about self-expression and looking cool* ... 24·8% of those interviewed

RIDING DISCIPLES · *passionate riders for whom riding is a way of life, built on a strong relationship with the bike itself and membership of the wider fraternity of riders* .... 16·3%

PERFORMANCE HOBBYISTS · *solitary, summer-only riders, for whom riding is all about individual experiences and sensations — not concerned about what other riders are doing* .... 14·7%

RIDING HOBBYISTS · *older, summer-only riders who enjoy the social interac-tion with other riders almost as much as the riding itself — and who like to look the part* .... 14·5%

CAR ASPIRANTS · *young people looking forward to getting their first car when age/finances allow — but for the time being are happy to have got their own wheels* .... 11·2%

CAR REJECTERS · *escapees from traffic, fuel costs, and other problems with cars — who don't care for motorcycles, but do care for low-cost mobility (more women than other segments)* .... 10·1%

PERFORMANCE DISCIPLES · *commit-ted, all-year riders with a total focus on high performance riding, dislike for anything that gets in its way* ...... 8·3%

The researchers further explored how each of these seven groups thought about and managed the risks of riding a motorbike. The findings are summarised below:

Look-at-me enthusiasts blasé confidence: recognise risks but see themselves as relatively safe; strong tendency to see risk as part of what makes riding fun

Riding disciples active management of risks: highly conscious of potential risk, take active steps to manage it by responsible riding behaviour and use of gear

Performance hobbyists cautious attraction: see risk as part of the fun, but very circumspect about own abilities to deal with risks, leading to caution in behaviour

Riding hobbyists personal responsibility for avoiding risk: highly conscious of risk, tendency to avoid potentially risky situations altogether

Car aspirants low awareness but high educability: tend not to think about the risks and may not take steps to manage them; but signs that they will take steps when the risks are pointed out to them

Car rejecters high awareness and high unhappiness: very sensitive to the risks of riding, and see this as a strong argument against riding

Performance disciples precautionary fatalism: see risk as unavoidable negative of riding — emphasis on personal skill and armour as responses to risk

———————————— AIR PASSENGER EXPERIENCE ————————————

The experiences of passengers at six airports across Britain (Heathrow, Gatwick, Stansted, Manchester, Luton, and Edinburgh) were canvassed by the Civil Aviation Authority for a Department for Transport survey. The first phase of results, published December 2009, reflected passenger opinions from January–June 2009. The results below show passenger answers to questions about satisfaction with check-in:

Airport	% very/fairly satisfied	neither	very/fairly dissatisfied	av. queue time
Heathrow	94	3	3	4·7 minutes
Stansted	88	5	6	6·7
Manchester	92	4	4	6·0
Gatwick	93	3	3	7·2
Luton	93	5	3	6·2
Edinburgh	93	5	2	4·5

Passengers were also questioned about their satisfaction with security screenings:

Airport	% very/fairly satisfied	neither	very/fairly dissatisfied	av. queue time
Heathrow	87	8	6	6·6 minutes
Stansted	87	8	5	7·0
Manchester	93	4	3	4·2
Gatwick	87	8	5	5·6
Luton	88	7	4	4·3
Edinburgh	91	6	3	5·1

Passengers were asked how far they agreed with the following statement: 'any inconvenience caused by the security screening was acceptable'; responses are below:

Airport	% strongly agree/agree	neither	strongly disagree/disagree
Heathrow	89	7	4
Stansted	88	7	5
Manchester	91	3	6
Gatwick	90	5	4
Luton	90	7	2
Edinburgh	91	5	4

———————————— WORLD'S HIGHEST AIRPORT ————————————

In January 2010, China announced plans to build the world's highest airport, in Nagqu, Tibet. At 4,436 metres above sea level, Nagqu Dagring Airport will be 764 metres below the Chinese base camp on Mt Everest. Construction is due to begin in 2011, and will take three years to complete. The airport is part of ambitious (and controversial) plans by China to build new infrastructure in the once-isolated area: a railway connecting Tibet to the rest of China opened in 2006, and six new railway lines were planned at the time of writing. Since 1994, the world's highest airport has been Bamda airport, also in Tibet, located at an elevation of 4,334 metres.

──── DISRUPTIVE BEHAVIOUR ON UK AIRCRAFT ────

3,529 reports of disruptive behaviour onboard UK aircraft were received by the Civil Aviation Authority in 2008/09. 44 of these incidents were 'serious', 29 caused a passenger to be restrained, and 13 resulted in an aircraft diverting (one incident involved both restraint and diversion). 73% of disruptive passengers in 2008/09 were male, and 27% female. Incidents of disruption generally fell into one or more of the following categories: verbal abuse (37%); passengers disobeying cabin crew (28%); general disruptiveness (28%); passenger seating, use of seat belts, or passengers refusing to be seated (18%); arguments between passengers – often caused by seats being reclined (13%); mobile phone or laptop use (5%); stowage of hand luggage (3%). 7% of all incidents resulted in violence, 44% of which were directed towards cabin crew. Alcohol was involved in 37% of all disruptive incidents, and smoking was a factor in 21% (of which 95% involved smoking in a lavatory).

In February 2010, Manchester airport temporarily changed security procedures to avoid spoiling passengers' Valentine's Day proposal plans. According to the airport, in previous years, engagement rings have been prematurely discovered during security checks. From 12–15 February, ring-wielding would-be proposers were able to request a private search by saying 'be my Valentine' to security checkers.

──── INTERNATIONAL AIR TRAFFIC STATISTICS ────

The airline industry saw fewer international customers in 2009 than at any time since WWII, according to figures from the International Air Transport Association. The table below compares passenger and freight air traffic during 2009 and 2008:

(2009 vs 2008)	passenger traffic ±%	freight traffic ±%
Africa	−6·8	−11·2
Asia/Pacific	−5·6	−9·2
Europe	−5·0	−16·1
Latin America	+0·3	−4·0
Middle East	+11·2	+3·9
North America	−5·6	−10·6
TOTAL INDUSTRY	−3·5	−10·1

──── UK AIRPORT TRAFFIC · 2009 ────

218m passengers travelled through UK airports in 2009, 7·3% fewer than in 2008 – the largest annual decline since WWII. The drop was most pronounced at regional airports, where the number of passengers fell by 10·7%, whereas London airports experienced a 4·9% decline. The busiest airports in the UK in 2009 are listed below:

	passengers†		
Heathrow	65,846,990	Manchester	12,679,916
Gatwick	26,040,881	Edinburgh	8,844,151
Stansted	19,304,531		

† Scheduled terminal passengers

——————————— THE FIRST >£1,000 TRAIN FARE ———————————

The first >£1,000 train fare was uncovered by rail expert Barry Doe, in a November 2009 survey of UK fares. The train ticket – from Newquay, Cornwall, to the Kyle of Lochalsh in the Scottish Highlands – was for a 'turn-up-and-go' first-class return; it cost a staggering £1,002. Doe's research revealed that many turn-up-and-go fares had risen 100% since the mid-1990s. A standard London–Manchester return cost £33 in 1995, but was £66·10 in 2009; a ticket from London to Newcastle upon Tyne had increased by 84%, to £105. Passengers opting for the 1,700 mile journey from Newquay to the Kyle of Lochalsh would spend over 20 hours on a train yet, despite the first-class billing, both the beginning and end of the journey would be made in trains without first-class carriages. The train company selling the ticket, CrossCountry, pointed out that no one had actually purchased the >£1,000 fare; most opted instead for a first-class advance saver return that cost a mere £561.

——————————— RAILWAY PASSENGER SATISFACTION ———————————

81% of British railway passengers were satisfied with their journey and rail facilities in 2009. Further findings from the 2009 *National Passenger Survey* are below:

%	satisfactory or good	neither satisfactory nor unsatisfactory	unsatisfactory or poor
Punctuality/reliability	80	9	7
Frequency of trains on that route	75	9	15
Upkeep and repair of train	72	16	12
Comfort of seating area	69	18	13
Sufficient room for passengers	66	14	20
Station facilities and services	50	20	30
Car parking facilities	44	18	38
Availability of staff	41	29	30
Value for money	40	21	39
Toilet facilities	36	24	40

[Source: National Passenger Survey, Great Britain · ONS Social Trends, February 2010]

——————————— LONDON STATION DESTINATION GUIDE ———————————

Charing Cross..*serves* South & South-east
Euston................................. Midlands, North-west of England & Scotland
King's Cross............................... Midlands, North of England & Scotland
Liverpool Street.................. East of England & East Anglia · Stansted Express
Marylebone ....Chilterns
Paddington............................West of England & Wales · Heathrow Express
St Pancras ....East Midlands & Yorkshire · Eurostar
Victoria..South & South-east · Gatwick Express
Waterloo.. South & South-west

———————— THE ORIENT EXPRESS ————————

In December 2009, the celebrated Orient Express made its last (and much reduced) journey from Strasbourg to Vienna. After 125 years the train service, which inspired many a literary icon (Agatha Christie, Ian Fleming, and Graham Greene, to name but three), has been overtaken by high-speed train links and cheap flights. The original service began in 1883 and travelled from Paris to Istanbul on a glamorous route that took in Vienna, Budapest, and Bucharest and involved catching a ferry between Varna, Bulgaria, and Istanbul (then called Constantinople). In 1919, after the opening of the Simplon Tunnel, a more southerly Orient Express route was inaugurated. This route, known as the Simplon Orient Express, ran from Paris to Istanbul via Milan,

Venice, Belgrade, and Sofia. At the height of its fame in the 1930s, the Orient Express left Paris daily, and the journey took three days. The blue and gold-liveried train comprised four S-type sleeping cars, each containing 10 wood-panelled compartments, and a restaurant car. By 1977, both the southerly and northerly Orient Express routes stopped travelling all the way to Istanbul: the Orient Express confined itself to Paris–Vienna, and the Simplon Orient Express to Paris–Venice. Although the original Orient Express service has now come to an end, the Simplon Orient Express still runs a luxury service travelling from London–Paris–Venice–Budapest–Bucharest–Istanbul, and costs at least £1,200 per person for a one-way journey with meals.

———————— THE WORST ENGLISH TRAIN STATIONS ————————

The ten worst train stations in England were named and shamed by Station Champions Chris Green and Sir Peter Hall in November 2009. Each station across the country was visited by a team of 'mystery shopper'-style inspectors who rated the stations on their cleanliness, ease of access, passenger information and facilities. The ten stations that received the lowest passenger satisfaction ratings are below:

Station	passenger satisfaction (%)		
Manchester Victoria	32	Wigan North Western	47
Clapham Junction	39	Luton	48
Crewe	42	Liverpool Central	49
Warrington Bank Quay	44	Stockport	50
Barking	45		
Preston	46		

The report recommended that stations aim to get a passenger satisfaction rating of at least 80%.

In January 2010, Network Rail teamed up with the Samaritans to launch a 5-year-plan to reduce the number of railway suicides by 20%. There are *c.*200 suicides on the railways every year, costing Network Rail >£15m in compensation to train operators. The Samaritans plan to work with railway staff on how to spot and talk to potentially suicidal people, offer support in the aftermath of a suicide, and work with the media to ensure responsible reporting, which can reduce the risk of copycat deaths.

——————————————— NEW ROUTEMASTER ———————————————

In May 2010, Mayor of London Boris Johnson unveiled the design for a new class of red double-decker buses inspired by the venerable and much-loved Routemaster. Routemasters were introduced to London in the mid-1950s, and served as a metonym for the capital until they were withdrawn from regular service in 2005 amidst concerns about safety and accessibility. In 2008, Johnson made the revitalisation of the Routemaster a cornerstone of his election campaign. The aerodynamic new design features 3 doors, 2 staircases, a wheelchair-accessible open platform, room for 87 riders, and a hybrid engine that is 40% more efficient than diesel double-deckers. The new models are being manufactured by Wrightbus and are set to debut in 2012.

——————————— PUBLIC TRANSPORT JOURNEYS ———————————

A breakdown of passenger journeys by mode of public transport in 2008 is below:

Local buses	5,236m	Other rail & metro	200
National rail	1,274	Air passengers	21
London Underground	1,089	All passenger journeys	7,820

[Source: Department for Transport · ONS Social Trends, February 2010]

——————————————————— FREIGHT ———————————————————

The volume of goods lifted by freight in the UK during 2008 is tabulated below:

mode	*tonnes (m)*	Rail	103	Pipeline	147
Road	1,868	Water	123	All modes	2,241

Domestic freight moved in 2008 is shown below by commodity type, expressed as the weight of the load multiplied by the distance it is carried (billion tonne kms):

Commodity group	pipeline	rail	road
Agricultural products/live animals	–	–	13·4
Foodstuffs/animal fodder	–	–	37·5
Solid mineral fuels	–	7·9	1·1
Petroleum products	10·2	1·5	6·5
Ores/metal waste	–	–	1·8
Metal products	–	1·5	5·7
Crude minerals/building materials	–	2·7	22·4
Fertilisers	–	–	1·9
Chemicals	–	–	7·3
Machinery, manufactured articles & misc	–	–	66·0
ALL COMMODITIES	10·2	20·6	163·5

[Source: Department for Transport · Transport Statistics Great Britain 2009]

——————— ENERGY USE & TRADE ———————

The UK consumed 152·7m tonnes of energy in 2009, as measured in 'tonnes of oil equivalent' (TOE). Shown below is the share of energy consumption by *type of fuel*:

Petroleum	natural gas	electricity	other[†]
47·5%	30·5%	18%	

Below is the share of energy consumption in 2009 shown by the *sector of final user*:

Transport	domestic	industry	other
37%	28·5%	17·5%	17%

A breakdown of the energy use within each sector during 2009 is tabulated below:

Transport.........56,512 *thousand* TOE
– road...........................40,704
– air.............................12,730
– national navigation 1,570
– rail.............................1,507
Industry..........................26,671
– chemicals.......................4,388
– food, beverages, &c. 2,929
– unclassified....................2,955
– mineral products...............2,789
– paper, printing, &c............2,254
– iron and steel..................1,157
– mechanical engineering, &c...1,289
– vehicles........................1,190

– electrical engineering, &c........871
– textiles, leather, &c..............832
– non-ferrous metals...............822
– construction......................450
– other industry.................4,744
Other 60,697
– domestic.......................43,590
– commercial.....................8,962
– public administration..........5,712
– miscellaneous 1,522
– agriculture......................909
Non energy use[‡]...................8,866

‡ Fuels used as feedstocks, lubricants, &c.

The UK imported 148·1m tonnes of oil equivalent in 2009, and exported 98·3m. The table below shows the amount and type of fuel imported and exported in 2009:

	imports (TOE)	exports (TOE)
Crude oil	55·4m	47·3m
Natural gas	39·2	11·8

	imports (TOE)	exports (TOE)
Coal/other solid fuel	25·2	0·5
Petroleum products	27·7	38·3
Electricity	0·3	0·1

Below are the top places the UK imports crude oil from, and exports crude oil to:

Imports		Exports	
Norway	35,007 *thousand* (TOE)	Netherlands	17,016 *thousand* (TOE)
Russia	4,068	US	10,289
Libya	1,872	Germany	7,782
Nigeria	1,842	France	2,671
Algeria	1,194	Spain	1,101

Source: Department of Energy and Climate Change (DECC)

† 4% of UK energy consumption comes from coal, manufactured fuels, renewables, and other fuels.

──────── SHIPPING FORECAST GLOSSARY ────────

Below is an explanation of the terms commonly used in the shipping forecast:

GALE WARNINGS
Gale ....*winds ≥Beaufort force 8 (34–40 knots) or gusts reaching 43–51 knots*
Severe gale................ *winds of force 9 (41–47 knots) or gusts reaching 52–60 knots*
Storm.....................*winds of force 10 (48–55 knots) or gusts reaching 61–68 knots*
Violent storm .... *winds of force 11 (56–63 knots) or gusts of ≥69 knots*
Hurricane force† ....*winds of force 12 (≥64 knots)*
Imminent ....*expected within 6 hours of time of issue*
Soon...................................... *expected within 6–12 hours of time of issue*
Later... *expected >12 hours from time of issue*

VISIBILITY
Very poor.. *<1,000 metres*
Poor ....*between 1,000 metres and 2 nautical miles*
Moderate.. *2–5 nautical miles*
Good .... *>5 nautical miles*

MOVEMENT OF PRESSURE SYSTEMS | Rather quickly .... *25–35 knots*
Slowly .... *<15 knots* | Rapidly.................... *35–45 knots*
Steadily.................... *15–25 knots* | Very rapidly.................. *>45 knots*

PRESSURE TENDENCY IN STATION REPORTS
Rising (or falling) more slowly ....*pressure rising (or falling) at a progressively slower rate through the preceding three hours*
Rising (or falling) slowly................*pressure change of 0·1–1·5 hPa‡*
Rising (or falling) ....*pressure change of 1·6–3·5 hPa‡*
Rising (or falling) quickly ....*pressure change of 3·6–6·0 hPa‡*
Rising (or falling) very rapidly .... *pressure change of >6·0 hPa‡*
Now rising (or falling)................... *pressure has been falling (rising) or steady‡ but at the time of observation was definitely rising (falling)*

WIND
Wind direction................*indicates the direction from which the wind is blowing*
Becoming cyclonic....................*indicates that there will be considerable change in wind direction across the path of a depression within the forecast area*
Veering.. *the wind direction changing clockwise*
Backing........ *the wind changing in the opposite direction to veering (anticlockwise)*

SEA STATE · Smooth... *wave height >0·5m* | Very rough ....4·0–6·0m
Slight........................ 0·5–1·25m | High..........................6·0–9·0m
Moderate................... 1·25–2·5m | Very high.................. 9·0–14·0m
Rough ....2·5–4·0m | Phenomenal....................>14·0m

† The term used is 'hurricane force'; the term 'hurricane' on its own means a true tropical cyclone, not experienced in British waters. ‡ In the preceding 3 hours. (1hPa=1mb) [Source: The Met Office]

OFFSHORE SHIPPING AREAS

[Map adapted from the Met Office]

─────── VISITS TO AND FROM BRITAIN───────

Travel between Britain and the rest of the world fell markedly in 2009, after years of growth. According to the ONS report, *Travel Trends*, UK residents made 58·6 million trips abroad in 2009, a fall of 15% from 2008. Residents of other countries paid 29·9m visits to the UK in 2009, down 6·3% from 2008. Business travel was the sector hit hardest, while holiday visits from overseas visitors increased by 0·5m The most popular destinations in Britain for overseas visitors are tabulated below:

visits (000s)	± '08–'09 (000s)		*visits (000s)*	± '08–'09 (000s)
London	14,211 ... –542	Liverpool	458 ... –95
Edinburgh	1,324 ... +133	Bristol	421 ... –71
Manchester	800 ... –89	Oxford	416 ... –21
Birmingham	709 ... –54	Cambridge	400 ... +18
Glasgow	623 ... –6	Brighton & Hove	330 ... –1
		Cardiff	313 ... –29

The most popular international destinations for British residents in 2009 were:

visits (000s)	± '08–'09 (%)		*visits (000s)*	± '08–'09 (%)
Spain	11,582 ... –16·2	Germany	2,127 ... –21·3
France	9,764 ... –10	Greece	1,881 ... –10·2
Irish Rep.	3,549 ... –9·5	Netherlands	1,840 ... –8·4
US	3,187 ... –20·4	Portugal	1,809 ... –28·5
Italy	2,610 ... –22·6	Turkey	1,622 ... –16·2

[Mexico visits fell 41%, likely due to 'flu fears.]

─────── MOST ATTRACTIVE MEN & SEXIEST ACCENTS───────

Italian men are the most attractive in Europe, according to an October 2009 poll released by the travel website Zoover. The poll asked (male and female) site visitors to judge which country had Europe's most attractive males. British respondents said:

Most attractive	*Least attractive*
Italy (25% of votes) · Turkey (15%)	Switzerland (3%) · Germany (4%)
Spain (14%)	France (6%)

Irishmen have the world's sexiest accent, according to an international survey by OnePoll.com in November 2009 – perhaps because of the popularity of Irish actors such as Colin Farrell and James Nesbitt. The French – who came fourth – might blame their president for their ranking, according to a OnePoll.com spokesman: 'The French accent is nowhere near as popular as it used to be ... You can probably blame Nicolas Sarkozy for that, he has single-handedly changed the perception of how the world sees French men.' The ten top sexiest accents were said to be:

[1] Irish　[2] Italian　[3] Scottish　[4] French　[5] Australian
[6] English　[7] Swedish　[8] Spanish　[9] Welsh　[10] American

60% of the 5,000 women polled confessed they had been seduced by someone due to their accent.

—— WORLD EXPOS ——

Between May and October 2010, Shanghai hosted World Expo 2010, billed as the largest world expo ever, and the first held in a developing country. 192 nations participated, hosting 20,000 events in a 5·3km² site built at a rumoured cost of $58bn. The theme of the expo was sustainable development (using the slogan *Better City, Better Life*), although it also served to celebrate China's place on the world stage. Highlights included Saudi Arabia's $164m pavilion, a Spanish pavilion constructed of handwoven wicker, and Britain's Seed Cathedral – a glowing orb of fibreglass rods encasing a collection of seeds from around the world. ❦ The first world expo is generally said to have been the 'Great Exhibition of the Works of Industry of All Nations', held in London in 1851. This 'Great Exhibition' drew *c*.6m people to see 100,000 objects arrayed in the iron-and-glass Crystal Palace. Since then, some of the most notable world expos and their highlights have been:

WELTAUSSTELLUNG 1873 WIEN
Vienna 1873 · *Rotunda with world's largest dome, Japanese buildings and garden, Turkish coffee house*

CENTENNIAL EXPOSITION
Philadelphia 1876 · *Moorish glass palace, Corliss steam engine, telephone demonstrated*

EXPOSITION UNIVERSELLE
Paris 1889 · *Eiffel Tower unveiled, 111-metre long 'Galerie des Machines', Buffalo Bill's Wild West show*

WORLD'S COLUMBIAN EXPOSITION
Chicago 1893 · *Edison's 'cinematoscope', amusement park with Ferris Wheel, all-white façades*

PANAMA–PACIFIC INTL EXPOSITION
San Francisco 1915 · *Panama Canal opened, 'Tower of Jewels' covered in glass gems, giant typewriter*

CENTURY OF PROGRESS INTL EXPO.
Chicago 1933–34 · *Snake show, flea circus, 'Sky Ride' cable railway*

EXPO '58 BRUSSELS · *Molecule-shaped 'Atomium' building, Le Corbusier-designed pavilion, 'electronic poem'*

EXPO '67 MONTREAL · *Buckminster Fuller-designed geodesic dome, astronaut ephemera, Le Ronde amusement park*

EXPO '98 LISBON · *Aquarium with 15,000 fish, Utopia Pavilion with multimedia show, funicular*

EXPO 2000 HANNOVER · *Dutch pavilion with six eco-systems, 400ft glass structure with giant busts of 47 famous Germans*

EXPO 2005 AICHI JAPAN · *Live feed of images from Mars Rover, recreation of a building from the film My Neighbor Totoro, plentiful robots*

—— THE WORLD'S BEST YOUTH HOSTELS ——

Each January, Hostelworld.com awards the 'Hoscars' for the world's best youth hostels. To select the winners, 900,000 customers rate 23,000 hostels on character, security, location, staff, 'fun', and cleanliness. The top ten hostels in 2010 were:

1 ...Travellers House............ Lisbon	6 ...Riverhouse Backpackers....Cardiff
2 ...Rossio Hostel................Lisbon	7 ...Lisbon Lounge ....Lisbon
3 ...Living Lounge Hostel...... Lisbon	8 ...Greg & Tom Hostel....... Krakow
4 ...Academy Hostel.......... Florence	9 ...The Naughty Squirrel.........Riga
5 ...Carpe Noctem.......... Budapest	10..Lisboa Central Hostel..... Lisbon

———— MOST THREATENED WORLD WONDERS ————

In January 2010, *Wanderlust* magazine listed eight heritage-rich locations around the world that are under threat. The most threatened world wonders are below:

Destination	threatened by
Wadi Rum, Jordan	*lack of centralised protection; overrun by 4×4 tours*
Yangshuo, China	*karst limestone scenery spoiled by overcrowding & pollution*
Tulum, Mexico	*local Mayan culture overshadowed by large tourist developments*
Stonehenge, UK	*the tranquillity of the site marred by the busy A303*
Machu Picchu, Peru	*hordes of tourists*
Jaisalmer, India	*visitors putting pressure on an aged infrastructure*
Timbuktu, Mali	*threat of terrorism and kidnap*
Bay of Fires, Tasmania, Australia	*Aborigines & state dispute ownership*

———— NATIONAL TRUST'S MOST POPULAR WALKS ————

The National Trust has >130 downloadable walks and trails featured on its website; these were downloaded >250,000 times in 2009. In February 2010, the Trust revealed the walks which were most frequently downloaded. The top five were:

No.	*walk*		
1	Bath Skyline	3	Ashridge, Hertfordshire
2	Clumber Park, Nottinghamshire	4	Formby, NW England
		5	Flatford Mill, Suffolk

———— NEWLY INSCRIBED WORLD HERITAGE SITES · 2010 ————

Cultural sites: Bikini Atoll, Marshall Islands · Australian Convict Sites
At-Turaif District in ad-Dir'iyah, Saudi Arabia
Camino Real de Tierra Adentro, Mexico
Central Sector of the Imperial Citadel of Thang Long, Hanoi, Vietnam
Episcopal City of Albi, France · Historic Monuments of Dengfeng, China
Historic Villages of Korea: Hahoe and Yangdong · Jantar Mantar, India
Prehistoric Caves of Yagul and Mitla in the Central Valley of Oaxaca, Mexico
Proto-urban site of Sarazm, Tajikistan · Tabriz Historic Bazaar Complex, Iran
São Francisco Square in the Town of São Cristóvão, Brazil
C16th–C17th canal ring area of Amsterdam inside the Singelgracht, Netherlands
Sheikh Safi al-din Khānegāh and Shrine Ensemble in Ardabil, Iran
Natural sites: Central Highlands of Sri Lanka · China Danxia, China
Phoenix Islands Protected Area, Kiribati · Putorana Plateau, Russian Federation
Pitons, cirques and remparts of Reunion Island, France
Mixed cultural & natural site · Papahānaumokuākea, Hawaii

The following sites were added to the World Heritage in Danger list in 2010:
Bagrati Cathedral and Gelati Monastery, Georgia · Everglades National Park, US
Atsinanana Rainforests, Madagascar · Tombs of Buganda Kings, Uganda

——————— 'ISTANBUL WAS CONSTANTINOPLE' ———————

In December 2009, Venezuelan president Hugo Chavez called for the renaming of the world's highest waterfall, Angel Falls, which plunges for 979 metres in the southeast of the country. The falls had been named after US aviator Jimmy Angel who, in 1933, was the first foreigner to see them. Chavez said the falls should now be called by their indigenous name, *Kerepakupai-Meru,* or 'waterfall of the deepest place'. Toponymic changes are nothing new for Chavez: after taking office in 1999 he changed the name of his country to the 'Bolivarian Republic of Venezuela', in honour of the patriot Simón Bolívar. ❦ Other notable name changes of recent years include:

Current name	*formerly known as*	*changed*
Beijing, China	Beiping	1949
Burkina Faso	Upper Volta	1984
Chemnitz, Germany	Karl-Marx-Stadt	1990
Chennai, India	Madras	1996
Cóbh, Ireland	Queenstown	1922
Democratic Republic of the Congo	Zaire	1997
Democratic Socialist Republic of Sri Lanka	Ceylon	1972
Gdańsk, Poland	Danzig	1945
Harare, Zimbabwe	Salisbury	1980
Ho Chi Minh City, Vietnam	Saigon	1975
Islamic Republic of Iran	Persia	1935
Istanbul, Turkey	Constantinople	1930
Jakarta, Indonesia	Batavia	1949
Kingdom of Cambodia	Kampuchea	1989
Kingdom of Thailand	Siam	1939
Kitchener, Ontario, Canada	Berlin	1916
Kolkata, India	Calcutta	1999
Mumbai, India	Bombay	1995
Oslo, Norway	Kristiania	1925
Republic of Indonesia	Netherlands East Indies, Dutch East Indies	1945
Republic of Malawi	Nyasaland	1964
Republic of Suriname	Dutch Guiana	1975
Republic of Zimbabwe	Rhodesia	1980
St Petersburg, Russia	Leningrad	1991
Turkmenbashi, Turkmenistan†	Krasnovodsk	1993
Union of Myanmar‡	Burma	1989
Yangon, Myanmar	Rangoon	1988

† Turkmenbashi ('leader of all Turkmen') was the self-proclaimed title of Turkmenistan's former President for Life Saparmurat Niyazov, who renamed the city after himself. ‡ This name change is controversial, because it was instated by the country's military junta; many (including the UK & US) persist in calling the nation Burma. ❦ Bangkok, Thailand, may have the longest place name in the world. In English, its full name reads: *The City of Gods, the Great City, the Residence of the Emerald Buddha, the Impregnable City (of Ayutthaya) of the God Indra, the Grand Capital of the World Endowed with Nine Precious Gems, the Happy City Abounding in Enormous Royal Palaces Which Resemble the Heavenly Abode Wherein Dwell the Reincarnated Gods, a City Given by Indra and Built by Vishnukarm.*

————————— BRITISH WILD BIRD POPULATION —————————

Defra has been tracking the UK wild bird population since 1970. In October 2009, the department released data showing that while the 'all bird species' index (114 species) has increased by 3% since 1970, many bird sub-populations have been on the decline. The breeding farmland birds index (19 species) was 47% lower in 2008 than in 1970, while the breeding woodland birds index (38 species) was 14% lower. However, the breeding seabirds index (19 species) was 27% above the number measured in 1970, and the breeding water and wetland birds index (26 species) was 1% higher than in 1975 (the year these populations were first counted). Below are the species that have seen the greatest rise and the biggest loss since 1970:

Greatest increase in population	*Greatest decrease in population*
Avocet · Buzzard · Collared Dove	Corn Bunting · Spotted Flycatcher
Great Spotted Woodpecker	Willow Tit · Grey Partridge
Peregrine · Great Skua · Woodlark	Lesser Redpoll · Tree Sparrow
Cetti's Warbler · Dartford Warbler	Turtle Dove

————————————— INVASIVE SPECIES —————————————

In December 2009, Defra and the Welsh Assembly Government added 62 species to Schedule 9 of the *Wildlife and Countryside Act*, which lists the animals, birds, and plants that cannot be introduced into the wild in Britain. The species on Schedule 9 are deemed invasive and harm biodiversity by preying upon wildlife, competing with it for resources, or spreading disease. Some of the species added in 2009 are below:

American oyster drill · Australian flatworm · Bar-headed goose · Barnacle goose
Curly waterweed · Duck potato · Emperor goose · Green seafingers
False virginia creeper · Giant rhubarb · Giant knotweed · Giant salvinia
Hottentot fig · Himalayan balsam · Hybrid knotweed · Monk parakeet
New Zealand pygmyweed · Red-billed chough · Red-crested pochard · Snow goose
Spiny-cheek crayfish · Water lettuce · Wild boar · Virginia creeper · Yellow azalea

Introducing one of the above species into the wild can result in two years in jail or a £5,000 fine. ❦ The most invasive mammal in Europe is the brown rat, according to a 2010 analysis by Swiss researchers.

————————————— TOY OF THE YEAR —————————————

Since 1965, the Toy of the Year Award has been presented by the Toy Retailers Association to celebrate the top market performers. In 2009, the overall winner was Character Option's Go Go Hamsters. Other notable winners in 2009 included:

Category	*winner*		
Boys' range	Ben 10	Creative	Bendaroos Megapack
Girls' range	Sylvanian Families	Active	Smart Trike
Game of the Year	Monopoly City	Pre-school range	Kidizoom
		Construction	Lego

——————— FLOURISHING FAST FOOD ———————

A report released by the Local Data Company in November 2009 indicated that fast food outlets in major UK cities are flourishing. The number of takeaway outlets has increased by 8·2% from 2007/08–2008/09. The report illustrated that central London hosts by far the most fast food outlets, boasting in 2009; 20 branches of Burger King;19 KFCs; 42 McDonald's; 1 Wimpy; 67 EATs; 64 Subways; and a staggering 122 Pret A Mangers. The UK cities with the most takeaways are:

Rank	Centre	No. of takeaways
1	London	847
2	Edinburgh	192
3	Glasgow	94
4	Manchester	74
5	Liverpool	64
6	Bristol	60
7	Newcastle	60
8	Leeds	53
9	Birmingham	51
10	Cardiff	24

Of branded outlets, EAT had seen the biggest expansion (34% increase) in the past 12 months.

——————— CLIMATE DECLARATIONS ON FOOD ———————

It is estimated that, in the developed world, 25% of an individual's CO_2 emissions are directly attributable to the food they eat. Consequently, in autumn 2009, Sweden drew press attention for becoming the first country to introduce 'food climate labelling' – ensuring that foodstuffs are marked with stickers stating the total amount of CO_2 emissions involved in their manufacture and transport. Although such data can be problematic to calculate accurately, advocates of climate labelling hope that providing this information will encourage consumers to choose products with smaller CO_2 footprints. ❧ In 2008, the Swedish food producer Lantmännen began placing climate declaration stickers on its chilled chickens (1·7kg CO_2 per kg, regardless of the chicken), and later on its rolled oats and breakfast foods. Several other Swedish manufacturers and restaurant chains followed suit, and it seems likely that producers across Europe might catch on – especially if encouraged by consumer pressure. The carbon declarations for some Swedish foods are below:

	CO_2 kgs produced		
1 kg beef	15–25	1 kg oatmeal	0·87
1 kg pork	5	1 kg wheat flour	0·52
One hamburger	1·7	One chicken sandwich	0·4
1 kg white bread	1	1 kg carrots	0·1
		[Source: Lantmännen, *The New York Times*]	

According to the *Guardian* and author Mike Berners-Lee, bananas have a carbon footprint of 80g CO_2 each, while black tea or coffee (if made by boiling only the water needed) uses 235g CO_2. A large cappuccino requires 340g CO_2, and a local bottled beer from a shop or foreign beer in a pub 500g CO_2. ❧ In November 2009 Lord Stern, former chief economist of the World Bank and author of a much-publicised 2006 review of the economics of climate change, predicted that attitudes towards eating meat would evolve to the point where carnivorousness could be seen as ecologically unacceptable. Meat puts 'enormous pressure on the world's resources', Stern told *The Times*, noting how views on other injurious practices, such as drinking and driving, had evolved over the past few decades.

———————— FRENCH vs BRITISH COOKING ————————

The British may be better cooks than the French – they at least spend more time in the kitchen – according to a 2010 poll by BBC food magazine *Olive* and French magazine *Madame Le Figaro*. 2,061 British readers and 1,345 French readers answered questions about their culinary habits and values. Selected results are below:

Respondents who ...	*British* (%)	*French* (%)
Cook at home each day	72	59
Spend at least 30 minutes cooking each night	50	27
Usually cook two courses or more	18	47
Say they never cook	1	4
Use family recipes	20	40
Use internet recipes	17	29

French respondents rated their cooking abilities an average 6/10, close to the British rating of 5·6/10.

———————— THE WORLD'S BEST RESTAURANTS ————————

A Danish restaurant that uses only local ingredients won the top spot in *Restaurant* magazine's 2010 rankings of the world's best eateries, knocking the avant-garde El Bulli[†] from the spot it had held since 2006. Only three British restaurants were on the list, one fewer than in 2009. The ten best restaurants in the world were said to be:

1..*Noma*[‡] ....Copenhagen	6..*Osteria Francescana*..Modena, Italy
2..*El Bulli*..........Costa Brava, Spain	7..*Alinea* .... Chicago
3..*The Fat Duck* ...... Bray, Berkshire	8..*Daniel*..............New York City
4..*El Celler de Can Roca*.......Girona	9..*Arzak*.......... San Sebastián, Spain
5..*Mugaritz*...... San Sebastián, Spain	9..*Per Se* .... New York City

† In 2010, the chef-owner of El Bulli, Ferran Adrià, announced that the restaurant would close in 2012 and re-emerge as a foundation for culinary study in 2014. Although the details of the foundation had yet to be decided at the time of writing, Adrià has said it will be 'a place for free thinking and kicking around ideas' about food. ‡ Menu items at Noma include cooked barley and birch syrup served with 'herbs and frozen milk', and a dessert ominously named 'the snowman from Jukkasjärvi'.

———————— LIFE'S LITTLE PLEASURES ————————

Having a really good night's sleep was voted life's greatest little pleasure in a December 2009 poll by Batchelors Cup-a-Soup. The top ten little pleasures were:

1 .... a good night's sleep	6 ....freshly laundered bed linen
2 ....finding a forgotten £10 in pocket	7 ....getting a bargain
3 ....cuddling with partner in bed	8 .... making someone smile
4 .... crying with laughter	9 ....catching up with an old friend
5 ....having a lie-in	10 ....laughing over old memories

—— NEW UK MICHELIN STARS · 2010 ——

The UK now has more Michelin-starred restaurants than ever before, after 140 establishments earned the accolade in the 2010 Michelin Guide. 17 restaurants earned one star, and one eatery was awarded two stars. Alain Ducasse at The Dorchester secured the highly coveted three stars, the fourth establishment in the UK to have warranted the honour. The UK restaurants awarded new stars in 2010 are below:

* *The Samling*.........................Ambleside, Cumbria..........modern eclectic
* *The Pipe & Glass Inn*..............Beverley, Yorkshire......................British
* *The Royal Oak*.....................Bray-on-Thames.......................British
* *The Goose*..........................Britwell Salome, Oxfordshire...........British
* *Sienna*.............................Dorchester, Dorset.............modern British
* *21212*..............................Edinburgh.....................modern French
* *The Peat Inn*.......................Fife..............................modern French
* *Kinloch Lodge*†.....................Isle of Skye.............................Scottish
* *The Walnut Tree*....................Abergavenny, Monmouth...modern European
* *Tyddyn Llan*........................Llandrillo, Denbighshire.......modern British
* *Ynyshir Hall*.......................Machynlleth, Powys...........modern British
* *The Harwood Arms*.................Fulham, London............modern European
* *Bingham Restaurant*................Richmond-upon-Thames...............British
* *Apsleys at The Lanesborough*.......Belgravia, London.......................Italian
* *Galvin at Windows*.................Mayfair, London.......................French
* *Tamarind*...........................Mayfair, London.......................Indian
* *Texture*............................Marylebone, London........modern European
** *The Ledbury*......................Kensington, London....................French
****Alain Ducasse at The Dorchester*..Mayfair, London..............modern French

† Isabella Eveling, who runs Kinloch with her husband Tom and chef Marcello Tully, called the star 'a fantastic recognition', and told *The Herald*: 'We're having a big takeaway curry tonight to celebrate.'

—— ENDANGERED EXPORTS ——

During the December 2009 climate change conference in Copenhagen [see p.27], *Time* magazine published a list of the top exports endangered by global warming, based on a survey of current research. The top ten most-threatened exports were:

Italian pasta	*higher temperatures & less rain mean durum wheat crops could vanish*
French wine	*warming temperatures are giving wine a heavier, more 'jammy' taste*
Argentine honey	*wetter weather preventing bees from leaving hives to collect nectar*
German beer	*weather is becoming inhospitable for hop crops*
Vietnamese rice	*rising sea levels are destroying low-lying croplands*
Spanish fruit and vegetables	*warmer temps could turn country into a desert*
Maldivian tourism	*tourist spots are disappearing beneath the ocean*
Northern European vodka	*higher temperatures are hostile to potatoes and wheat*
Colorado ski resorts	*snow season could decrease by a month*
Malian cotton	*7-month rainy season has become 3 months; cotton drying out*

CRUFTS BEST IN SHOW · 2010

A Hungarian Vizla named Yogi became the first of his breed to take the Best in Show title at Crufts 2010. 22,000 dogs from 187 different breeds were shown over four days at the Birmingham NEC, before just seven dogs were selected to compete for the coveted Best in Show title. Yogi beat a Scottish Terrier, a Rottweiler, a Maltese, a Welsh Corgi, a Pharaoh hound, and an Akita to claim the dog world's biggest prize. Crufts was broadcast on More4 for the first time, after the BBC dropped coverage of the show because of concerns raised over the health of pedigree dogs.

CATS vs DOGS

Dogs really are man's best friend, and cats are more of an acquaintance, according to a December 2009 study by *New Scientist* magazine. 'The great pet showdown', as it was dubbed, compared the results from a variety of recent scientific research to see whether cats or dogs were superior as pets. The contest went to the dogs (in a good way), though *New Scientist* admitted that it is impossible to quantify the cuddliness of each unique 'furry family member'. Details of the fur fight appear below:

Category	results	winner
Brains...*cats have more neurons (300m) than dogs (160m) in their cortices* ..		cats (+1)
Shared history............................. *dogs have lived with us longer* ..		dogs (+1)
Bonding.............*dogs are descended from pack animals; cats are loners* ..		dogs (+1)
Popularity ..... *more cats (c.204m) than dogs (c.173m) are pets worldwide* ..		cats (+1)
Understanding................................*dogs work better with people* ..		dogs (+1)
Problem solving..... *not enough is known, but dogs are more collaborative* ..		dogs (+1)
Vocalisation ....*dogs have more flexibility, but cats more guile* ..		cats (+1)
Tractability............. *dogs are easy to train; people barely try it with cats* ..		dogs (+1)
Super senses.......*the average cat can see, hear, and smell more than a dog* ..		cats (+1)
Eco-friendliness...............*dogs have bigger carbon footprints* [see p.229] ..		cats (+1)
Utility ....*dogs can do more for, and with, humans* ..		dogs (+1)
FINAL WINNER...*dogs* (6 pts)		

A golden retriever caused panic in an American jewellery store in May 2010 when he swallowed a $20,000 diamond that had fallen to the floor. (The gem reappeared after nature had taken its course.)

THE SUPREME CAT SHOW · 2009

The annual Supreme Cat Show (the world's largest cat show) is organised by the Governing Council of the Cat Fancy (GCCF). To be eligible, a cat must have qualified by winning a certificate at an ordinary GCCF championship show. A knock-out competition selects the Supreme Kitten, the Supreme Adult, and the Supreme Neuter, who then battle it out to be crowned Supreme Exhibit. The 2009 Show was held at Birmingham's NEC in November 2009. The Supreme Exhibit was awarded to Supreme UK Imperial Grand Champion MAINMAN KISSCHASE, a female brown Burmese, owned and bred by Ms J. Mooney & Miss S. Reid.

───────────── BLUE PETER PETS ─────────────

A former stray dog named Barney became the latest pet to join the *Blue Peter* menagerie, in October 2009. The nine-month-old cross-breed was donated to the show by the Dogs Trust. Other animals that have found a home on the show include:

Petra – dog [appeared on the show 1962–77] · *Freda* – tortoise [1963–79]
Jason – cat [1964–76] · *Patch* – dog (son of Petra) [1965–71] · *Shep* – dog [1971–78]
Maggie & *Jim* – tortoises [1974–82] · *Jack* & *Jill* – cats [1976–83]
Goldie – dog [1978–86] · *George* – tortoise [1982–2004]
Bonnie – dog (daughter of Goldie) [1986–99] · *Willow* – cat [1986–91]
Kari & *Oke* – cats [1991–2004] · *Mabel* – dog [1996–2010] · *Lucy* – dog [1998–]
Shelley – tortoise [2004–] · *Smudge*† – cat [2005] · *Socks*‡ – cat [2005–]
Cookie – cat [2007–] · *Barney* – dog [2009–]

† *Smudge* was the shortest-lived *Blue Peter* pet; the kitten was run over outside his house after only a few months on the show. ‡ *Blue Peter* apologised when it emerged that the programme had ignored the results of a competition to name the cat. The public chose the name *Cookie*, but the team preferred *Socks*. To make amends, another kitten was brought onto the show, and named *Cookie*.

───────────── ECOLOGICAL PAW-PRINTS ─────────────

It takes more land to produce enough food to feed a medium-sized dog for a year than it does to keep an SUV running, according to a 2009 book *Time to Eat the Dog? The Real Guide to Sustainable Living*, by Brenda and Robert Vale. The Vales calculated the ecological 'paw-prints' of various domestic companions, based on the land needed to grow the meat and cereals in common brands of pet food. Below are some examples, which were highlighted in a 2009 *New Scientist* article:

hectares per year to feed/fuel	
Large dog (German Shepherd).........1·1	Cat................................. 0·15
Medium-sized dog (Alsatian)....... 0·84	Hamster..........................0·014
SUV (Toyota Land Cruiser†) .... 0·41	Goldfish........................0·00034
	† Driven 10,000 km per year

───────────── UK CATS & DOGS ─────────────

A snapshot of UK pet cat and dog ownership appears below, based on research conducted by the University of Bristol and reported in *The Veterinary Record* in 2010:

CATS	DOGS
Total pets in UK · 10·3m	*Total pets in UK* · 10·5m
% of households own · 26%	*% of households own* · 31%
Most likely to be owned by · households with gardens, semi-urban/rural households, households where someone has a degree, females, those aged <65	*Most likely to be owned by* · households with gardens, larger households, rural households, females, those aged <55
	(Research conducted in 2006)

ANIMALS IN THE NEWS · 2009–10

Some of the year's more unusual animal stories. ❧ Paul the Octopus – an actual octopus, resident in Germany's Oberhausen Sea Life Aquarium – became a global star during the 2010 World Cup after he accurately forecast the winner of every German game, and the final. Paul made his predictions by selecting a mussel from one of two boxes marked with flags. In the glare of media interest and, reportedly, death threats from angry fans, Paul was retired from his disturbingly accurate bivalve-based prognostication. ❧ Canadian Conservatives at a dinner in Toronto were shocked when a text message from Transport Minister John Baird reported: 'Thatcher has died'. As the assembled dignitaries began to mourn, an aide composed a message of condolence before ringing Buckingham Palace and No. 10 – who informed him that Margaret Thatcher was still very much alive. After some confusion, it emerged that Baird had been texting about his pet cat, who he named after his political heroine. ❧ Indian police detained a pigeon suspected of spying for Pakistan. The bird was caught in the Punjab state with a ring around its foot and a Pakistani phone number stamped on its body. Police said they were keeping the pigeon under armed guard, and would not allow visitors. ❧ The world's oldest sheep, 'Lucky', died aged 22 after a spate of hot weather in her home country, Australia. Her owners admitted that in her final years Lucky suffered from increasingly angry mood swings, and had to be hand-fed crushed grain after her teeth fell out. ❧ An article in *Current Biology* described octopuses in Indonesia prying coconut shells from the ocean bed, scurrying away with the shells in their arms, and then hiding beneath them. Scientists said the behaviour was an astonishing example of tool use, once thought the exclusive domain of humans. ❧ A woman in Florida reported seeing a monkey falling into her swimming pool before absconding with some of her grapefruits. Authorities admitted that the monkey had been on the loose for nearly a year, and had been spotted scaling walls and digging through rubbish. ❧ University of Australia scientists searching for a new method to combat the invasive (and hideous) cane toad discovered that cat food placed near breeding ponds lured hordes of meat ants, which then attacked and killed the baby toads. Cane toads have been the scourge of Australia since they were introduced in the 1950s to control beetles. Previous eradication techniques have involved carbon dioxide, cricket bats, and/or golf clubs. ❧ A US geriatrician published a book about the uncanny abilities of a cat named Oscar, who lived at a nursing home. Oscar was said only to visit patients very close to death – his prescience was so unerring that staff began alerting the relatives of any patient with whom he chose to sit. ❧ A German student caused a traffic jam after he threw a puppy at a group of Hells Angels before escaping on a bulldozer. No motive for his attack was given; the puppy escaped unharmed. ❧ The first study into the vision of hammerhead shark – reported in *Experimental Biology* – concluded that the animal's peculiarly-placed eyes give them 360° vision. ❧ A man in County Durham lost his driving licence after he was caught 'walking' his dog by extending its lead out of the window of his moving car.

Money

Rule No. 1: Never lose money. Rule No. 2: Never forget rule No. 1.
— WARREN BUFFETT (1930–) [Attrib.]

———————SOVEREIGN CREDIT RATINGS———————

Countries, like individuals and corporations, have credit ratings. These ratings offer forward-looking opinions about risk, helping to answer the question, will a country be able to pay back its debts in full and on time? Lenders pay close attention to nations' credit scores. Indeed, some banks and investment organisations are prohibited from lending to countries with all but the best ratings. The creditworthiness of entire countries has become increasingly thorny as governments around the world face tough choices about how much money to borrow (or print) to secure their economies. For example, it is currently considered less risky to lend to McDonald's than to Brazil. ❦ Credit ratings are offered by various agencies, each of which employs different methods to calculate and define risk, usually using an alphabetical scale. Below are the credit rating definitions used by the agency Standard & Poor's:

Rating	opinion
AAA	*Extremely strong capacity to meet debts.*
AA	*Very strong capacity to meet debts.*
A	*Strong capacity to meet debts but somewhat more susceptible to adverse changes in economic conditions*
BBB	*Adequate capacity to meet debts, but adverse economic conditions or changing circumstances are more likely to lead to a weakened capacity.*
BB	*Faces major ongoing uncertainties – exposure to adverse business, financial or economic conditions could lead to an inadequate capacity to meet debts.*
B	*Currently has the capacity to meet its debts, but adverse business, financial or economic conditions will be likely to impair its capacity or willingness to do so.*
CCC	*Currently vulnerable, and dependent upon favourable business, financial and economic conditions to meet debts.*
CC	*Currently highly vulnerable.*
SD/D	*Selective [i.e., partial] default / Default.*
+/–	*The ratings AA to CCC may be modified with plus or minus signs to indicate relative standing within the categories.*

Below are Standard & Poor's domestic ratings for a range of states, as of 3/9/2010:

Argentina	B–	India	BBB–	Russian Fed.	BBB+
Brazil	BBB+	Ireland	AA–	Saudi Arabia	AA–
China	A+	Italy	A+	Spain	AA
Greece	BB+	Japan	AA	UK	AAA
Iceland	BBB	Pakistan	B–	USA	AAA

——— BEYOND GDP & ODD ECONOMIC INDICATORS ———

For some time, Gross Domestic Product (GDP) has been criticised as too narrow an indicator of economic well-being and prosperity. Consequently, in 2008, French President Nicolas Sarkozy asked several leading economists to form The Commission on the Measurement of Economic Performance and Social Progress, and charged them with considering what data might form a more rounded economic index. In autumn 2009, this commission proposed a series of 'key dimensions' of well-being that should be considered simultaneously in any new economic measure:

Material living standards (income, consumption, and wealth) · *Health*
Education · *Personal activities* (including work) · *Political voice and governances*
Social connections and relationships · *Environment* (present and future)
Insecurity (economic and physical)

Crucially, the committee concluded that no single indicator can adequately measure all of the above dimensions, and consequently any assessment must use a 'dashboard' of tools. One such dashboard that already exists is the European Commission's Sustainable Development Indicators (SDIs), created in 2005. The SDIs use ten overall themes and three indicator levels to address economic, social, environmental, and institutional dimensions. In 2009, the top-level indicators were:

Sustainable Development Indicator	EU27	UK
GDP per inhabitant growth rate, 2010 forecast	−0.3	−0.2
Resource productivity (GDP÷consumption), 2005	1.30	2.58
% at risk of poverty, by gender, 2007	♂16 ♀18	♂18 ♀20
% older workers employed, 2008	45.6	58.0
Number of healthy life years expected, 2007	62.30	66.2
Greenhouse gas emissions (% of Kyoto year), 2007	90.7	82.0
% of renewables in energy consumption, 2007	7.8	2.1
Transport energy use (1,000 tons oil equiv.), 2007	377,249	56,210
Common bird index (pop. + diversity), 2006	75.0†	68.7
% fish catches outside safe biological limits, 2006	21‡	–
Official Dev. Assistance as % of Gross Nat. Income, 2008	0.4	0.43

Most recent data available; some years are estimates. ‡ Includes all EU-managed waters.

The recent world economic turmoil has prompted economists (and journalists) to assess unusual measures of economic activity. Some of these are merely anecdotal – how easily one can hail a taxi, or the length of a coffee shop's queue. Others were hitherto used only by insiders – such as the Baltic Dry Index, which tracks international cargo shipping prices. Below are some of the more curious economic measures of note:

THE TUNNEL INDEX · according to the *LA Times*, the city's 2nd Street Tunnel is so popular a location for car adverts that the number of location permits granted acts as a barometer of confidence in the US auto industry.

THE HEMLINE INDEX · the economist George Taylor is credited with the idea that skirts get longer as the economy declines: a kind of frock-market index.

— BEYOND GDP & ODD ECONOMIC INDICATORS cont. —

THE SHOE SHINE INDEX · legend has it that Joseph P. Kennedy (father of John, Bobby, &c.) said that it was time to get out of the market when the shoe-shine boy started discussing stocks and shares.

THE HOT WAITRESS INDEX · writing in *New York* magazine in August 2009, Hugo Lindgren observed: 'The hotter the waitresses, the weaker the economy. In flush times, there is a robust market for hotness. Selling everything from condos to premium vodka is enhanced by proximity to pretty young people (of both sexes) who get paid for providing this service. That leaves more-punishing work, like waiting tables, to those with less striking genetic gifts. But not anymore.'

THE R-WORD INDEX · the *Economist's* informal method of tracking economic activity: counting how many stories in the *New York Times* and the *Washington Post* include the word 'recession'. The magazine claims, 'over the past two decades the R-count has been pretty good at spotting economic turning-points'.

LATVIAN HOOKER INDEX · in May 2009, the economist John Hempton posited a link between the price of prostitutes in Latvia and the country's economic well-being, noting the unusual flexibility in the pricing of prostitution and low barriers to entry: 'Well, I want a reasonable cross-border comparison of labour costs of labour of roughly equal skill. I guess I could use the price of an electrician – but I don't know how to find that. So instead I use the price of prostitutes.'

LUGGAGE SALES · Merrill Lynch proposed that tracking the sales of luggage might indicate consumer confidence.

PLAYBOY GIRLS · 2004 research by Pettijohn and Jungeberg suggested when social and economic times were tough *Playboy* selected 'older, heavier, taller Playmates of the Year with larger waists, smaller eyes, larger waist-to-hip ratios, smaller bust-to-waist ratios, and smaller Body Mass Index values'.

THE CREDIT CRUNCH BEARD · observed in 2009 – as the recession hit spending on expensive shaving requisites, and rising unemployment meant that fewer people had to shave for work.

POPCORN INDEX · in 2009, the cinema chain Odeon mapped consumer spending on popcorn against the FTSE and found that sweet and salty sales tracked, and, on occasion, predicted the market.

THE BIG MAC INDEX · published by the *Economist*, the index tracks the price of a McDonald's Big Mac (available in *c.*120 countries) as a way of assessing the purchasing-power parity of various currencies.

COUPON REDEMPTION INDEX · when times are tough, more people clip coupons and redeem them for discounts. The *New York Times* reported that coupon redemption had increased by 23% in the first 6 months of 2009.

In 2004, President Hu Jintao announced that China would begin trials of 'Green GDP', which sought to subtract the cost of pollution from GDP. The first report, released in 2006, estimated that pollution had cost China 3% of its GDP in 2004. Environmental activists had expected the total to be far higher (8–12%), but the figures nevertheless panicked some officials, especially in provinces where growth rates were reduced to zero. The project was scrapped, and a second report planned for 2007 never appeared.

———————— BUDGET MARCH 2010 · KEY POINTS ————————

Alistair Darling's third Budget, on 24 March 2010, was set against the background of a looming election and disagreement between the parties on how fast and severely to cut government expenditure. 'I know there are some demanding immediate cuts to public spending,' Darling said, 'I believe such a policy would be both wrong and dangerous'. The Chancellor reported that his tax on bank bonuses had raised £2bn in 2009–10, twice as much as forecast, and he drew cheers from the Labour benches when he announced a new 5% stamp duty rate for houses worth >£1m to fund a doubling of the stamp duty threshold from £125,000 to £250,000. Although the Chancellor claimed 'we have not raised … taxes out of dogma or ideology', most commentators were in little doubt that Darling had chosen to 'soak the rich' in an attempt to set political dividing lines before the upcoming election.

Forecasts	British economy shrank by 6% over the recession; growth forecast for 2010, 1–1·25%; and for 2011, 3–3·5%
Borrowing	2009–10, £167bn (£11bn lower than predicted); 2010–11, £163bn; 2011–12, £131bn; 2012–13, £110bn; 2013–14, £89bn; and in 2014–15, £74bn
Public sector net debt	54% of gross domestic product in 2010, increasing to 75% in 2014–15
Income tax	personal allowances to be reduced for those earning >£100,000
National Insurance	no new announcements
VAT	no new announcements
Inheritance tax	threshold frozen at £325,000 for 4 years
Pensions	tax relief restricted from 2011 for those earning >£130,000
Small businesses	£2·5bn package for skills and innovation; one year business rate cut from October; investment allowance doubled to £100,000; doubling capital gains tax relief for entrepreneurs
Basic bank accounts	guaranteed for *c.*1m people
Employment	6 month work/training guarantee for >24s extended to 2012
ISAs	annual limits raised from £7,200 to £10,200
Afghanistan	£4bn funds allocated
Tax information agreements	with Dominica, Grenada, & Belize
(this was interpreted as a not-so-subtle dig at the Tory backer and Belize resident, Lord Ashcroft)	
Civil Service	15,000 civil servants relocated, including 1,000 Ministry of Justice posts to outside London
Stamp Duty	scrapped for homes >£250,000 for first-time buyers, for 2 years; duty on residential homes >£1m raised to 5% from April 2011
Public sector pay	rises held at 1% for 2 years from 2011
Fuel duty	increase to be staggered; +1p in April; +1p in October; and the remainder of the increase in January 2011
Off-shore wind farms	£60m funds allocated
Green investment bank	with £2bn in equity, funded partly by asset sales
Internet	50p tax on landlines to fund superfast broadband
Roads	£100m to repair roads, £285m to repair motorways
Tobacco	1% above inflation rise in 2010; 2% rise thereafter to 2014
Beer, wine, and spirits	increase as planned
Cider	increase by 10% above inflation

—— EMERGENCY BUDGET JUNE 2010 · KEY POINTS——

George Osborne unveiled his 'emergency' Budget on 22 June 2010, emphasising the need to tackle 'decisively' Britain's 'record debts'. Conceding that the Budget was 'tough', Osborne argued, 'but it is also fair'. The Chancellor pledged to balance the structural deficit by 2015–16, and argued that the bulk of savings should come from spending cuts rather than tax rises. 'The country has overspent; it has not been under-taxed', he said, announcing that in his Budget 77% of the deficit reduction would be delivered in the form of spending cuts, and 23% would come from increased taxes. His announcement of a 2·5% rise on VAT drew jeers from opposition politicians, as did his assertion that the Budget was 'progressive'. Commentators seemed broadly to agree that the Budget would hit the middle classes hardest.

Forecasts	growth forecast to be 1·2% in 2010; 2·3% in 2011; 2·8% in 2012; 2·9% in 2013 and 2·7 % in 2014–15
Borrowing	2009–10, £154·7bn; 2010–11, £149bn; 2011–12, £116bn; 2012–13, £89bn; 2013–14, £60bn; 2014–15, £37bn; 2015–16, £20bn
Public sector net debt	to peak at 70·3% of Gross Domestic Product in 2013–14; it will be reduced to 67·4% in 2015–16
Spending	average real cuts of 25% over four years to departments other than health and overseas aid
Income tax	personal allowance to rise by £1,000 in April 2011
Capital Gains tax	increased to 28% for higher rate taxpayers; threshold for entrepreneurs' relief rate of 10% rose to £5m
Small companies	small profits rate to be reduced to 20% from April 2011
National Insurance	threshold for employer NI contributions to rise by £21/week above inflation
VAT	increased to 20%, effective 4 January 2011
Inheritance tax	threshold frozen at £325,000 until 2014–15
Council tax [England]	to be frozen in 2011–12
Pensions	basic state pensions will rise in line with earnings, prices or by 2·5% – whichever is highest
Corporation tax	reduced from 28% to 24% over the course of four years
Child benefit & child tax credit	benefit frozen for three years; child element of tax credit to rise £150 above inflation rate in April 2011, but eligibility to be reduced for families earning >£40,000
Disability Living Allowance	medical assessments to be introduced for claimants
Banks	levy to be introduced in January 2011 at an initial rate of 0·04%
Unemployment	predicted to peak at 8·1% by the end of 2010
Housing benefit	caps will be introduced, starting at £250/wk for a one bedroom property to £400/wk for ≥four bedrooms; from 2013, benefit will be cut by 10% after 12 months for Jobseekers Allowance claimants
Enterprise Finance Guarantee	lending facility for small businesses to be increased by £200 million in 2010/11
Public sector pay	frozen for 2 years from 2011 for staff earning >£21,000
Fuel duty	no increases planned; discount for rural areas to be considered
Beer, wine, and spirits	no planned changes
Cider	planned 10% increase on duty to be scrapped

—————————————— INCOME TAX 2010–11 ——————————————

Income tax was first levied in 1799 by Pitt the Younger as a 'temporary measure' to finance the French Revolutionary War. The initial rate was 2 shillings in the pound. The tax was abolished in 1816, only to be re-imposed in 1842 by Robert Peel (again temporarily) to balance a fall in customs duties. By the end of the C19th, income tax was a permanent feature of the British economy. The current rates are:

Income tax allowances	2009–10	2010–11
Personal allowance‡	6,475	6,475
Personal allowance (65–74)† ‡	9,490	9,490
Personal allowance (>75)† ‡	9,640	9,640
Income limit for age-related allowances	22,900	22,900
Married couple's allowance (aged ≥75)	6,965	6,965
Minimum amount of married couple's allowance	2,670	2,670
Blind person's allowance	1,890	1,890

The rate of relief for married couple's allowance remains 10%. † These allowances are reduced by £1 for every £2 of income that exceeds the income limit, not falling below the basic personal allowance or minimum amount of married couple's allowance in 2009–10. ‡ From 2010–11, the personal allowance is reduced by £1 for every £2 of income above £100,000, and is applicable irrespective of age.

Income tax rates	*threshold*	%
Basic rate	£0–£37,400	20
Higher rate	£37,401–150,000	40
Additional rate	>150,000	50

Additionally, there is a 10% starting rate for savings income only, with a limit of £2,440. Where an individual has non-savings income in excess of this limit, the 10% savings rate will not be applicable. The tax rates payable on dividends in 2009–10 are the 10% ordinary rate and the 32·5% upper rate. For 2010–11, in addition to these ordinary and upper rates, there will be an additional rate of 42·5%.

—————————————— STAMP DUTY ——————————————

The thresholds below (in £) represent the 'total value of consideration' of the deal. The rate that applies to any given transfer applies to the whole value of that deal.

rate %	*Residential* not *in a disadvantaged area*	*Residential in a disadvantaged area*	*Non-residential*
0	0–125,000	0–150,000	0–150,000‡
1	125,001–250,000†	150,001–250,000†	150,001–250,000
3	250,001–500,000	250,001–500,000	250,001–500,000
4	>500,000	>500,000	>500,000

The rate of stamp duty on the transfer of SHARES and SECURITIES is set at 0·5%.
† From March 2010–12, first-time buyers pay no duty on properties <£250,000.
‡ Stamp duty of 1% is levied where the annual rent of a property is ≥£1,000.

───────── NATIONAL INSURANCE 2010–11 ─────────

Although National Insurance dates from 1911, modern funding of social security was proposed by Beveridge and established by the National Insurance Act (1946).

Lower earnings limit, primary Class 1	£97/w
Upper earnings limit, primary Class 1	£844/w
Primary threshold	£110/w
Secondary threshold	£110/w
Employees' primary Class 1 rate	11% of £110–£844/w · 1% >£844/w
Employees' contracted-out rebate	1·6%
Married women's reduced rate	4·85% of £110–£844/w · 1% >£844/w
Employers' secondary Class 1 rate	12·8% on earnings above £110/w
Employers' contracted-out rebate, salary-related schemes	3·7%
Employers' contracted-out rebate, money-purchase schemes	1·4%
Class 2 rate	£2·40/w
Class 2 small earnings exception	£5,075/y
Special Class 2 rate for share fishermen	£3·05/w
Special Class 2 rate for volunteer development workers	£4·85/w
Class 3 rate	£12·05/w
Class 4 lower profits limit	£5,715/y
Class 4 upper profits limit	£43,875/y
Class 4 rate	8% of £5,715–£43,875/y · 1% >£43,875/y

───────── CAPITAL GAINS TAX ─────────

Annual exemptions 2010–11 Individuals &c. = £10,100 · Other trustees = £5,050

From June 2010, Capital Gains Tax for individuals will be charged at a basic rate of 18% (for gains ≤£37,400) and 28% thereafter; trustees, or representatives of those who have died, will be charged at a rate of 28%. A 10% rate will apply to gains qualifying for entrepreneurs' relief, subject to a maximum lifetime limit of £5 million.

───────── INHERITANCE TAX ─────────

Annual exemptions 2010–11 Individuals = £325,000 · Couples &c. = £650,000

Inheritance Tax is charged at 40% on the value of estates over the allowance limit.

───────── CORPORATION TAX ON PROFITS ─────────

2010	2011	£ per year
Small profits rate: 21%	20%	0–300,000
Marginal relief		300,001–1,500,000
Main rate: 28%	27%	≥1,500,001

—— BANK OF ENGLAND INTEREST RATES & THE MPC ——

The Monetary Policy Committee (MPC) has kept the BoE base rate at 0·5% since
5 March 2009. Tabulated below are all of the base rate changes since May 2007:

Date	change	rate		Date	change	rate		Date	change	rate
05·03·09	−0·50	0·50%		04·12·08	−1·00	2·00%		07·02·08	−0·25	5·25%
05·02·09	−0·50	1·00%		06·11·08	−1·50	3·00%		06·12·07	−0·25	5·50%
08·01·09	−0·50	1·50%		08·10·08	−0·50	4·50%		05·07·07	+0·25	5·75%
				10·04·08	−0·25	5·00%		10·05·07	+0·25	5·50%

—— INCOME TAX PAYABLE · 2009–10 ——

Annual income (£)	No. of taxpayers (000s)	Total tax liability (£m)	Average rate of tax (%)	Average amount of tax (£)
£6,475–7,499	990	92	1·3	93
£7,500–9,999	2,650	1,030	4·4	387
£10,000–14,999	6,290	6,090	7·8	967
£15,000–19,999	5,060	9,900	11·3	1,960
£20,000–29,999	6,680	22,200	13·6	3,320
£30,000–49,999	5,270	30,700	15·5	5,820
£50,000–99,999	1,800	26,500	22·4	14,700
£100,000–149,999	304	10,500	28·6	34,500
£150,000–199,999	117	6,190	30·8	52,800
£200,000–499,999	134	12,700	33·0	94,900
£500,000–999,999	26	6,060	34·5	234,000
≥£1,000,000	11	8,680	36·0	781,000
ALL INCOMES	29,300	141,000	17·3	4,790

[Source: HM Revenue & Customs, Social Trends 40. Total income of the individual for income
tax purposes including earned and investment income. Figures relate to taxpayers only.]

—— UK HOUSEHOLD SAVINGS ——

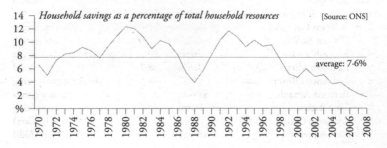

─────────── SUNDAY TIMES RICH LIST · 2010 ───────────

No.	billionaire (UK)	£ billion	activity	'09
1	Lakshmi Mittal and family	22·5	steel	1
2	Roman Abramovich	7·4	oil, industry	2
3	The Duke of Westminster	6·8	property	3
4	Ernesto and Kirsty Bertarelli	6·0	pharmaceuticals	4
5	David and Simon Reuben	5·5	property, internet	9=
6	Alisher Usmanov	4·7	steel, mines	18=
7	Galen and George Weston and family	4·5	retailing	47
8	Charlene and Michel de Carvalho	4·4	banking, brewing	7
9	Sir Philip and Lady Green	4·1	retailing	6
10	Anil Agarwal	4·1	mining	70=

The wealth of the 1,000 richest on the 2010 *Sunday Times* Rich List rose £77·3bn to £335·5 billion.

─────────── THE UK'S 'HIDDEN DEBT' ───────────

On average, UK adults are £9,731·51 in debt, according to an April 2010 poll by the Post Office, which also found that 31% of those with debts lie about them to their family. Below are the reported effects of hiding debts from one's partner or family:

Sleepless nights....... *% reporting*	43	Drinking more alcohol 12	
Higher anxiety 32		Couldn't do my job properly 12	
Mood swings.........................21		Volatile nerves.........................12	
Comfort eating......................15		Loss in trust from partner 6	

─────────── FORBES MAGAZINE RICH LIST · 2010 ───────────

Mexican telecom magnate Carlos Slim Helu took the top spot on *Forbes* magazine's 2010 list of the world's richest people, marking the first time a tycoon from a developing country has ranked number one. Overall, the list showed the world's richest men bouncing back from the recession, as the tally expanded from 793 billionaires in 2009 to 1,011 in 2010. The top ten richest people in the world were said to be:

No.	billionaire	citizenship	$bn	business
1	Carlos Slim Helu & family	Mexico	53·5	communications &c.
2	William Gates III	US	53·0	software
3	Warren Buffett	US	47·0	investing
4	Mukesh Ambani	India	29·0	petrochemicals, oil, gas
5	Lakshmi Mittal	India	28·7	steel
6	Lawrence Ellison	US	28·0	database computing
7	Bernard Arnault	France	27·5	luxury goods
8	Eike Batista	Brazil	27·0	mining
9	Amancio Ortega Gaona	Spain	25·0	retail (Zara)
10	Karl Albrecht	Germany	23·5	retail (Aldi)

─────────── WHAT WOULD YOU DO FOR £400? ───────────

To highlight people's reticence in applying for rewarding financial products, moneysupermarket.com polled what individuals were prepared to do to earn £400 – the amount a cash-back credit card repays someone who spends *c.*£2,500 a year.

Would do for £400	all %	♂ %	♀ %
Fill out a form to enter a competition	75	73	78
Wait in a queue for 4 hours	57	61	53
Write a 1,000 word essay question	54	54	53
Lick the pavement	25	31	20
Take part in a medical experiment	24	27	20
Sky dive	22	31	15
Be a crash test dummy	6	9	3

─────────────── CHARITIES ───────────────

The Charity Commission reported that the 162,194 registered charities in England and Wales have a combined annual income of some £52·5bn. Tabulated below is a breakdown of charities in England and Wales, by income bracket, as of June 2010:

No. of charities	%	annual income bracket	%	income £bn
73,172	45	£0–10,000	1	0·245
50,588	31	£10,001–£100,000	3	1·771
16,828	10	£100,001–£500,000	7	3·815
7,725	5	£500,001–£5,000,000	22	11·555
1,759	1	>£5,000,000	67	35·128
150,072	93	Sub-total	100	52·514
12,122	7	Not yet known	–	–
162,194	100	TOTAL	100	52·514

In July 2010, the Charity Commission asked Ipsos Mori to explore the public's trust and confidence in charities – building on similar research undertaken in 2005 and 2008. The public was asked to give an overall trust and confidence rating using a scale of 0–10, where 0 means they do not trust charities at all, and 10 means they trust charities completely. In 2010, average trust was 6·6 – unchanged from 2008:

On a scale of 0–10, how much trust and confidence do you have in charities?

Trust	0–4	5–7	8–10	?	mean
2010	12	46	41		6·6
2008	12	51	36		6·6
2005	14	52	31		6·3

The research found that charities ranked third in the list of most trusted organisations, behind doctors and the police, but ahead of social services, ordinary men and women on the street, banks, private companies, local councils, and newspapers.

—— SOME MAJOR INTERNATIONAL PRIZES · RANKED BY MONETARY VALUE ——

Award	task	cash prize
Google Lunar X Prize†	building a robot that can land on the moon, travel 500 metres, and transmit data	$30m
Archon X Prize†	sequencing 100 human genomes in 10 days	$10m
Progressive Automotive X Prize†	the development of viable, superefficient vehicles	$10m
Ibrahim Prize	excellence in African governance by a former leader	$5m over 10 years; $200,000/year for life
Templeton Prize	exceptional contributions affirming life's spiritual dimension [see p.292]	£1m
Nobel Prizes	achievements in physics, chemistry, physiology/medicine, literature, and peace	SEK 10m (£905,000) each
Abel Prize	outstanding contributions to mathematics	NOK 6,000,000 (£678,000)
Clay Maths Institute Problems†	solving any of seven important maths questions [see p.191]	$1m each
Kavli Prizes	outstanding research in astrophysics, nanoscience, and neuroscience	$1m each
Dan David Prize	scientific, cultural, or social achievements (past, present, and future categories)	$1m each
Shaw Prize	outstanding contributions in astronomy, life science/medicine, and mathematics	$1m each
Planeta Prize	Spanish-language novel	€601,000
Postcode Lottery Green Challenge	viable inventions that reduce greenhouse gas emissions	€500,000
MacArthur Fellowships	highly dedicated, original, and creative individuals	$500,000 over 5 years
Lasker Awards	breakthroughs in medical research (in basic, clinical, and public service categories)	$250,000 each
World Food Prize	improving the quality, quantity, or availability of food in the world	$250,000
Goldman Prize	grassroots environmental 'heroes' from each of the six inhabited continents	$150,000 each
World's Children's Prize	outstanding efforts for the rights of the child	SEK 1m (£90,600)
IMPAC Dublin Literary Award	fictional works of 'high literary merit' nominated by libraries	$100,000
Nansen Refugee Award	extraordinary and dedicated service to refugees	$100,000
Loebner Prize†	first team to develop a computer whose responses are indistinguishable from a human's	$100,000
Pritzker Prize	contributions to humanity and the built environment through architecture	$100,000
Man Booker Prize	best novel of the year by a citizen of the Commonwealth or the Rep. of Ireland [see p.169]	£50,000

Sources include the *Economist*. † Prizes each awarded only once, as a result of a specific achievement.

——————— FINANCIAL SNAP·SCHOTT · 2010 ———————

Item (£)	09·2005	09·2010
Church of England · marriage service (excluding certificate)	198·00	260·00
– funeral service (excluding burial and certificate)	84·00	99·00
Season ticket · Arsenal FC (2009/10; centre, E & W upper tiers)	1,825·00	1,825·00
– Grimsby Football Club (2009/10; Upper Findus)	325·00	299·00
Annual membership · MCC (full London member)	334·00	388·00
– Stringfellows, London	600·00	600·00
– Groucho Club, London (+35; London member)	550·00	695·00
– Trimdon Colliery & Deaf Hill Workmen's Club	3·00	8·50
– The Conservative Party (>22)	15·00	25·00
– The Labour Party (banded by income from 2009)	24·00	19·50–132·00
– The Liberal Democrats (minimum required)	5·00	10·00
– UK Independence Party	20·00	20·00
– Royal Society for the Protection of Birds (adult)	30·00	36·00
Annual television licence[†] · colour	121·00	145·50
– black & white	40·50	49·00
Subscription, annual · *Private Eye*	21·00	28·00
– *Vogue*	28·50	26·49
– *Saga Magazine*	22·80	17·95
New British Telecom line installation (subject to survey)	74·99	127·99
Entrance fee · Thorpe Park (12+ purchased on the day)	30·00	38·00
– Buckingham Palace State Rooms (adult)	13·50	17·00
– Eden Project, Cornwall (adult, day)	12·50	17·50
'Pint of best bitter' · Railway Inn, Honiton, Devon	1·90	2·80
– Railway Inn, Banff, Scotland	–	2·90
– Railway Inn, Trafford, Manchester	1·65	2·00
– Railway Inn, Coleshill, Birmingham	2·25	2·80
– Railway Inn, Putney, London, SW15	–	1·55
Fishing rod licence · Salmon and Sea Trout (full season)	63·75	72·00
List price of the cheapest new Ford (Ford Ka 'on the road')	7,095·00	7,995·00
British naturalisation (includes ceremony fee)	268·00	735·00
Manchester United home shirt (2009/10 season)	39·99	44·99
Tea at the Ritz, London (afternoon, per person)	34·00	39·00
Kissing the Blarney Stone (admission to Blarney Castle)	€7·00	€10·00
Hampton Court Maze (adult)	3·50	3·85
Ordinary London adult single bus ticket (cash)	1·20	2·00
Mersey Ferry (adult return)	2·10	2·45
Passport · new, renewal, or amendment (3-week postal service)	42·00	77·50
Driving test (practical + theory; cars, weekday)	66·50	93·00
Driving licence (first · car, motorcycle, moped)	38·00	50·00
NHS dental examination (standard)	5·84	16·50
NHS prescription charge (per item)	6·50	7·20
Moss Bros three-piece morning suit hire (weekend, basic 'Lombard')	45·00	49·00
FedEx Envelope (≤0·5kg) UK–USA	27·00	47·46

† The blind concession is 50%. Those ≥75 may apply for a free licence.

———— RPI & CPI ————

Some 2010 changes to the RPI basket:	CPI & RPI % change over 12 months:

items removed · pitta bread; baby food; fruit drink carton; fizzy canned drink; men's training shoe – casual footwear; gas call out charge; gas service charge; eyesight test charge; disposable camera; squash court hire; lipstick (replaced by lip gloss); individual bar of toilet soap; hairdryer.

items added† · garlic bread; cereal bars; frozen fish in breadcrumbs/batter; powdered baby formula; fruit drink, bottle; still mineral water, small bottle (added to represent water in the 'on the go' drinks market); allergy tablets (reflects increased expenditure); blu-ray disc players; computer games with accessory; electrical hair straighteners/tongs; lip gloss; liquid soap; household services maintenance policy (e.g., extended warranty for central heating system)

Year	month	CPI	RPI
2010	Aug	3·1	4·7
	Jul	3·1	4·8
	Jun	3·2	5·0
	May	3·4	5·1
	Apr	3·7	5·3
	Mar	3·4	4·4
	Feb	3·0	3·7
	Jan	3·5	3·7
2009	Dec	2·9	2·4
	Nov	1·9	0·3
	Oct	1·5	−0·8
	Sep	1·1	−1·4
	Aug	1·6	−1·3
	Jul	1·8	−1·4
	Jun	1·8	−1·6
	May	2·2	−1·1
	Apr	2·3	−1·2
	Mar	2·9	−0·4
	Feb	3·2	0·0
	Jan	3·0	0·1
2008	Dec	3·1	0·9

† According to information gleaned from a BBC Freedom of Information request, tattoos, ear piercings, iPhone applications, eyebrow waxings, and herbal tea bags were also considered for inclusion.

———— VALUE ADDED TAX RECEIPTS ————

Tabulated below are the domestic VAT receipts for recent months, and the 'live trader population' – i.e., the number of traders registered for Value Added Tax:

Date		(£m) receipts	repayments	net	registered traders
2009	Oct	10,200	−3,559	6,641	1,952,507
	Nov	8,422	−4,398	4,024	1,954,808
	Dec	7,020	−3,811	3,209	1,946,688
2010	Jan	9,992	−3,106	6,886	1,943,784
	Feb	9,522	−4,533	4,989	1,941,432
	Mar	7,437	−4,715	2,722	1,942,349
	Apr	11,547	−3,960	7,587	1,944,183
	May	9,622	−5,811	3,811	1,940,188
	Jun	7,801	−4,589	3,212	1,936,317

[Source: HM Revenue & Customs; the most recent figures are provisional.]

─────────────────── 500 EURO NOTES ───────────────────

In May 2010, the Serious Organised Crime Agency (SOCA) announced that the
€500 banknote would no longer be available in the UK, since more than 90%
of the demand for such notes came from the criminal fraternity. The €500 bill –
the second-highest denomination note in the world, after the Swiss 1,000 Franc
– has been nicknamed 'Bin Laden' because of its notorious elusiveness. The banknote's function in organised crime is explained by the fact that £1m in £20 notes
weighs 50kg, whereas the same sum in €500 bills weighs just 2·2kg. Furthermore,
as Reuters reported, 'an adult male "mule" could stuff and swallow 150,000 euros ... while 20,000 euros could be hidden in a cigarette packet'. SOCA noted
that the €500 note had not been 'criminalised', and that the notes could still be
paid into UK bank accounts if legitimately brought into the country from abroad.

── INTERNATIONAL LETTER-WRITING COMPETITION ──

In November 2009, the Universal Postal Union and UNESCO announced that
14-year-old Czech Dominika Koflerová had won the 38th annual International
Letter-Writing Competition for Young People. The contest, which began in 1972,
is designed to make young people aware of the importance of postal services and
foster an appreciation for the art of letter-writing. Each year's competition is
assigned a theme, and in 2009 entrants were asked to 'explain how decent working
conditions can lead to a better life'. Ms. Koflerová won with her letter about the
importance of fair trade chocolate. Some previous competition themes have been:

1972	*To a friend*	1995	*Even little letters travel far*
1976	*If I were a letter*	1996	*The pleasure of writing a letter*
1978	*The postman, my best friend*	1998	*My views on human rights*
1981	*A day in the life of a postman*	2004	*How young people can*
1984	*What if the post did not exist*		*help reduce poverty*
1988	*How do you imagine*	2008	*Why the world needs tolerance*
	the journey of a letter?	2010	*Why it is important to talk*
1990	*What can we young people do to*		*about AIDS and to protect yourself*
	help fight hunger in the world?		[Winners receive a gold medal and certificate]

─────────── GREAT BRITAIN POSTAL STATISTICS ───────────

Total number of staff	172,245	Letter post items, domestic	19·9bn
No. post offices	13,756	Intl letters dispatched	456m
No. mobile post offices	88	Intl letters received	390m
No. letter boxes	116,000	Intl parcels dispatched	416,000
No. post boxes	113,000	Intl parcels received	2·4m
Avg. No. letter post items/person	335	[Source: Universal Postal Union; 2007 figures]	

There are >600,000 post offices in total around the world, which employ more than 5m people and
operate somewhere around 1m postal vehicles, according to figures from the Universal Postal Union.

───── POSTAL PRICING IN PROPORTION ─────

Category	size (mm)	thickness (mm)	weight (g)	1st	2nd
Letter	≤240×165	≤5	0–100	41p	32p
Large Letter	≤353×250	≤25	0–100	66p	51p
			101–250	96p	81p
			251–500	132p	111p
			501–750	187p	159p
Packet	>353 long or >250 wide	or >25	0–100	139p	117p
			101–250	172p	151p
			251–500	224p	195p
			501–750	275p	236p
			751–1,000	335p	284p
			1,001–1,250	450p	—

Items >1,250g cost an extra 70p for each additional 250g or part thereof, up to 2,000g.

Recorded Signed For = postage + 74p · Special Delivery (9am) = £11·35 for up to 100g

───── AIRMAIL RATES ─────

AIRMAIL	Letters Europe	Rest of World			
Postcards	0·60	0·67			
≤10g	0·60	0·67			
≤20	0·60	0·97			
≤40	0·88	1·46			
≤60	1·14	1·98			
≤80	1·39	2·51			
≤100	1·65	3·04			
≤120	1·92	3·54			
≤140	2·19	4·08			

To find a postcode call 09063 021 222 peak or 08457 111 222 off-peak. For further information see royalmail.com

Small packets / Printed papers

	Europe	RoW
	1·31	1·82
	1·42	2·10
	1·57	2·38

A universal stamp can be used to send letters up to 40g to Europe (60p), or worldwide (£1·12).

───── 2010 SPECIAL STAMPS ─────

The Royal Mail's Stamp Programme issued the following Special Stamps in 2010:

7 January	*Classic Album Covers*
26 January	*Smilers 2010*
2 February	*Girl Guiding UK*
25 February	*The Royal Society*
11 March	*Battersea Dogs & Cats*
23 March	*House of Stewarts*
13 April	*Mammals* (Action for Species 4)
6 & 8 May	*London 2010 Stamp Fest.*
13 May	*Britain Alone*
15 June	*House of Stuarts*
27 July	*The London 2012 Olympic & Paralympic Games*
19 August	*Musicals*
16 September	*Great British Railways*
12 October	*Children's Books*
2 November	*Christmas*

——————————— JOBS BY INDUSTRY ———————————

Statistics from ONS Social Trends released in December 2009 revealed the percentage of people employed in the United Kingdom by industry, 1978–2009:

Industry	(%) 1978	1988	1998	2008	2009	1978–2008
Agriculture & fishing	1·7	1·4	1·3	1·0	1·0	–0·7
Energy & water	2·8	1·8	0·8	0·7	0·7	–2·1
Manufacturing	28·5	20·7	17·0	10·5	10·0	–18·0
Construction	5·7	5·1	4·4	4·8	4·8	–0·8
Distribution, hotels, restaurant	19·5	21·3	23·8	23·6	23·5	4·1
Transport & communications	6·5	5·9	5·7	5·9	5·8	–0·7
Finance & business services	10·5	14·8	18·1	21·4	20·8	10·9
Public admin, educ., health	21·1	24·5	24·2	26·9	28·1	5·8
Other services	3·8	4·5	4·7	5·3	5·4	1·5

——————————— JOBS OF THE FUTURE ———————————

Below are some of the 'jobs of 2030' as predicted by Fast Future, which interviewed a global sample of futurists on behalf of Dept. for Business, Innovation, & Skills:

Job　　　　　　　　　　　　　　　　　　　　　　　　　　job description
Body part maker ..... *create living body parts (salespeople and repairmen also needed)*
Nano-medic .... *administer sub-atomic devices, inserts, and procedures*
'Pharmer' .... *raise genetically engineered crops and livestock*
Old age wellness manager/consultant .... *address health of ageing population*
Memory augmentation surgeon ....*add memory capacity or erase memories as needed*
'New science' ethicist ......*sort out issues raised by cloning, nanotech, and other fields*
Space pilot, tour guide, or architect ....*ferry, guide, and design for space tourists*
Vertical farmers ....*grow city-based, hydroponically fed vertical farms*
Climate change reversal specialist ......*reduce/reverse climate change in specific areas*
Quarantine enforcer ....*enforce quarantine in case of a deadly virus*
Weather modification police ....*control the use of cloud-seeding and other techniques*
Virtual lawyer .... *resolve legal disputes that arise online*
Avatar manager/devotee/virtual teacher.....*employ avatars as teachers in classrooms†*
Alternative vehicle developer .... *develop vehicles using new materials and fuels*
'Narrowcaster'...........*create and 'broadcast' specialised content for individual needs*
Waste data handler................................*provide secure data disposal service*
Virtual clutter organiser ....*help people organise their electronic lives*
Time broker/time bank trader. *manage 'time banks' and other alternative currencies‡*
Social 'networking' worker ....*help those marginalised by social networking*
Personal brander .....*create and manage personal 'brands' through blogs, Twitter, &c.*

† Avatars are representations of a user's self or alter ego in a computer-generated world, as in Wii games, for example. 'Devotees' are humans that match a teacher's avatar to appropriate students.
‡ Time banks are a system of exchange in which members of a community trade services, with each hour of labour valued as one 'time credit' that can be exchanged for an hour of another's labour.

HISTORICAL ECONOMIC INDICATORS

Indicator	2009	2008	2007	2006	2005	2004	2003	2002	2001	2000	1999
FTSE 100 share index	4,593	5,257	6,425	5,941	5,168	4,520	4,030	4,566	5,541	6,348	6,313
Dow Jones Industrial Average	8,876	11,253	13,170	11,409	10,548	10,317	8,994	9,226	10,189	10,735	10,465
CBI business optimism survey	-14.0	-4.3	-1.5	-8.0	-18.5	6.5	-7.5	-3.2	-27.0	-3.0	-7.0
RPI inflation (% year-on-year)	-0.5	4.0	4.3	3.2	2.8	3.0	2.9	1.6	1.8	2.9	1.6
Real GDP (% year-on-year)	-4.9	-0.1	2.7	2.8	2.2	3.0	2.8	2.1	2.5	3.9	3.5
Average mortgage rate (%)	4.05	6.30	7.44	6.51	6.53	6.15	5.47	5.66	6.81	7.55	6.92
Number of taxpayers (million)	31.3	33.3	31.8	31.1	30.3	28.5	28.9	28.6	29.3	27.2	26.9
Highest rate of income tax (%)	40	40	40	40	40	40	40	40	40	40	40
Employment rate (%)	72.8	72.5	74.6	74.6	74.7	74.7	74.6	74.5	74.4	74.4	74.0
Unemployed (millions)	2.39	1.78	1.65	1.67	1.47	1.42	1.49	1.53	1.49	1.59	1.73
Unemployment rate (%)	7.7	5.7	5.3	5.4	4.8	4.8	5.0	5.2	5.1	5.4	6.0
Growth in consumer credit (% year-on-year)	1.6	6.3	6.0	7.6	12.5	14.2	14.9	15.9	13.4	14.5	15.8
Credit cards in issue (millions)	62.0	67.4	68.2	67.7	70.6	71.4	66.4	60.4	53.9	49.7	43.5
Outstanding credit card balance (£bn)	64.5	66.3	65.7	66.4	67.5	63.8	54.2	47.5	40.7	35.6	29.7
Total goods exports (% change year-on-year)	-11.7	1.3	-10.3	11.5	8.9	1.5	-0.2	-1.2	2.1	12.2	3.2
Total goods imports (% change year-on-year)	-12.8	-1.8	-2.7	10.5	7.0	7.0	1.8	4.7	5.2	9.3	6.6
Retail sales volume (% change year-on-year)	1.4	2.2	3.9	3.9	1.8	6.0	3.3	6.3	4.6	3.9	2.2
Change in average earnings (%)	2.1	3.7	3.6	3.7	4.0	4.2	3.6	4.0	4.9	4.5	3.6
GfK consumer confidence aggregate [see p.24]	-25	-29	-7	-5	-3	-3	-5	3	1	0	2
UK current account balances ($bn)	-28.7	-39.8	-75.3	-81.1	-59.2	-45.6	-30.0	-27.9	-30.4	-38.9	-35.4
New car registrations (thousands)	1,994	2,131	2,390	2,340	2,444	2,599	2,646	2,682	2,578	2,337	2,242
US Dollar/GB Pound ($/£)	1.56	1.83	2.00	1.84	1.82	1.83	1.63	1.50	1.44	1.51	1.62
Euro/GB Pound (€/£)	1.12	1.25	1.46	1.47	1.46	1.47	1.44	1.59	1.61	1.64	1.52
Gold price per Troy ounce (£)	622	472	347	328	245	223	222	206	188	184	172
Oil US Dollar/barrel (Brent futures close)	62.7	98.5	72.7	66.1	55.2	38.0	28.5	25.0	24.9	28.5	18.0

[Sources: Bank of England; ONS; OECD; SMMT; HM Treasury; British Bankers' Association · Many figures have been rounded]

———— METHOD OF NON-CASH TRANSACTIONS ————

Below are the various methods of non-cash transactions for UK households:

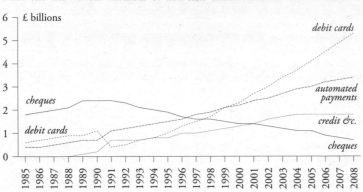

[Debit cards include Debit, Switch, Electron, Solo, &c. Automated payments include direct debits, standing orders, &c. Credit cards include Visa, MasterCard, store cards, &c. Source: Social Trends]

———— HIGHEST & LOWEST PAID PROFESSIONS ————

Average annual salary

Directors and chief executives of major organisations (CEO, MD, &c.).... £115,576
Medical practitioners (GP, physician, psychiatrist, &c.)............................ £78,366
Senior officials in national government (diplomat, MEP, MP, &c.) £68,283
Brokers (insurance broker, shipbroker, stockbroker, &c.) £61,117
Air traffic controllers (controller of aircraft, flight planner, &c.) £60,548
Financial managers and chartered secretaries (company registrar, &c.) £58,295
Senior officials in local government (town clerk, &c.) £55,921
Police officers (inspectors and above).. £53,937
IT strategy and planning professionals (computer/software consultant, &c.)..... £50,143
Solicitors, lawyers, judges, coroners... £48,908
* *Average national wage for a full-time employee*.............................. £25,800
Nursery nurses (crèche assistant, nursery assistant, &c.)........................... £13,872
Cleaners, domestics (car valeter, chambermaid, &c.) £13,807
Hairdressers and related occupations (barber, beautician, manicurist, &c.)...... £13,194
Leisure and theme park attendants (fairground worker, usher/usherette, &c.) ... £12,767
Retail cashiers and check-out operators (petrol pump attendant, &c.) £12,736
Launderers, dry cleaners, pressers (carpet cleaner, laundry worker, &c.) £12,657
Travel and tour guides (coach guide, escort, guide, &c.)........................... £12,561
Kitchen and catering assistants (canteen assistant, washer-up, &c.).............. £12,410
Waiters and waitresses £11,930
Bar staff £11,930

[Source: Office for National Statistics, *Annual Survey of Hours & Earnings*, 2009]

———————— PERCEPTIONS OF WEALTH ————————

2·5m British households earn an annual gross income of >£92,936, according to the *Hiscox Wealth Review 2009* published in December 2009 – yet 95% of these high-earners[†] do not consider themselves to be wealthy. The report revealed that 26% of those earning >£92,000 had savings of >£25,000, 25% went on two or more foreign holidays a year, 11% owned valuable jewellery, and 10% owned art. Despite these trappings of wealth, the respondents claimed that to feel *truly* rich they would need an average household income of £152,865, as well as the following:

Required to feel wealthy	%
>£20,000 in disposable income	48
Owning more than one property	35
Mortgage free	31
Owning a holiday home	27

Driving a luxury car 26
Owning original pieces of art 13

[†] The national average household income in the United Kingdom is roughly £35,000.

— THE CHANGING FACE OF BRITAIN'S HIGH STREETS —

Since 1997, Britain has lost 7,500 post offices, 3,460 pubs and 1,310 public toilets but gained 1,270 betting shops and 276 lapdancing clubs. The data comes from the Valuation Office Agency who, in February 2010, carried out a survey of British services and businesses since 1997 in order to revalue business rates. The businesses and services showing the greatest increase and most significant falls are below:

Greatest increase	1997	2010	±	% ±
Lapdancing clubs	24	300	+276	+1,150
Drive-through restaurants	990	1,510	+520	+53
Large supermarkets	1,420	2,120	+700	+49
Betting shops	3,270	4,540	+1,270	+39
Casinos	110	140	+30	+27
Nightclubs	1,050	1,320	+270	+26
Hypermarkets (>27,000 sq. ft)	1,420	1,780	+360	+25
Charity shops	5,000	6,500	+1,500	+20
Wine bars	850	990	+140	+16
Greatest decrease				
Sport & social clubs	21,130	9,450	−11,680	−55
Petrol stations	11,870	5,650	−6,220	−52
Livestock markets	180	110	−70	−39
Post offices	19,000	11,500	−7,500	−39
Hospitals and clinics	1,840	1,260	−580	−32
Bingo halls	650	460	−190	−29
Public toilets	5,610	4,300	−1,310	−23
Swimming pools	720	570	−150	−21
Schools	23,850	21,470	−2,380	−10
Police stations	2,000	1,840	−160	−8
Pubs	49,520	46,060	−3,460	−7
Public libraries	3,066	2,870	−196	−6

Parliament & Politics

Always vote for principle, though you may vote alone, and you may cherish the sweetest reflection that your vote is never lost. — JOHN QUINCY ADAMS (1767–1848)

───── HOUSE OF COMMONS · STATE OF THE PARTIES ─────

Conservative 305
Labour............................ 256
Liberal Democrat 57
Scottish National Party 6
Plaid Cymru 3
Democratic Unionist 8
Sinn Féin† 5
Social Democratic & Labour......... 3
Alliance (Naomi Long) 1

Green (Caroline Lucas) 1
Independent (Lady Sylvia Hermon)...... 1
Speaker 1
Deputy Speakers 3
GOVERNMENT MAJORITY 83
TOTAL (as at 30·7·10) 650

† Have not taken their seats and cannot vote.
There are 143 female MPs – 22% of the total.

───── PARLIAMENTARY SITTING TIMES ─────

Normal hours	Commons†	Westminster Hall	Lords
Monday	14:30–22:30	—	14:30–22:00
Tuesday	14:30–22:30	9:30–14:00	14:30–22:00
Wednesday	11:30–19:30	9:30–17:00	15:00–22:00
Thursday	10:30–18:30	2:30–17:30	11:00–19:30
Friday	9:30–15:00	—	10:00 (occasionally)

† The House may sit beyond these hours (or occasionally finish earlier). Since January 2003, the House sits on Fridays only when there are Private Members' bills to discuss. Previously, there were only ten Fridays in a session on which the House did not sit. There are plans to reform these hours.

───── GENDER, RACE, & THE DESPATCH BOX ─────

On 9 December 2009, Dawn Butler, the then Cabinet Office Minister for Young Citizens and Youth Engagement, became the first black woman ever to speak at the House of Commons despatch box. Butler, Labour MP for Brent South, was already the first black female Minister, and the third black female MP, yet her debut at the despatch box drew warm praise in the House. Butler responded by saying: 'While I am honoured to be the first black woman Minister to answer questions at the despatch box, I expect and hope to be the first of many. This historic moment sends a clear message that equality and opportunity is for everyone no matter what their background. I am confident that through my role I can encourage individuals, especially young people, to become involved in the political process.'

———————— 2010 ELECTION MANIFESTOS ————————

LABOUR · 12 April · 76pp
A Future Fair for All

Under Labour's economic plans, the deficit would be halved by 2014, banking regulations toughened and a global banking tax introduced. Banks in which the government has a controlling stake would be broken up. Income tax rates would not be increased. ❦ The minimum wage would increase in line with average earnings; and a 'better off in work' top-up would be introduced to encourage people off benefits. ❦ Families would benefit from a toddler tax credit and increased paternity leave; parents could request new school leaders. Struggling primary school children would be entitled to one-to-one tuition. ❦ Plans for the NHS include guaranteed specialist treatment within 18 weeks, and cancer test results within 1 week; all hospitals would become foundation trusts. ❦ Failing police forces could be taken over, and police officers would spend more time on the beat. ❦ 400,000 green jobs would be created and a 40% low-carbon electricity target would be set for 2015. ❦ MPs would not be allowed to work for lobbyists; a referendum would be held on electoral reform, and the House of Lords would be made fully elected. ❦ The English test for migrants would be toughened; benefits would be increasingly reserved for citizens and residents.

CONSERVATIVE · 13 April · 131pp
An Invitation to Join the Government of Britain

£6bn would be saved in 2010–11 by reducing waste, freezing public sector pay, and cutting the number of MPs. ❦ City supervision would be returned to the Bank of England. ❦ The rise in National Insurance would be scrapped and the inheritance tax threshold increased to £1m. ❦ The long-term unemployed would have to work for their benefits; 20,000 apprenticeships would be created. ❦ Tax credits and child trust fund contributions to wealthy families would end; marriage and civil partnerships would be recognised in the tax system. ❦ Parents, charities, &c. could set up their own schools within the state system. ❦ NHS waiting list targets would be scrapped; A&E and maternity ward closures would be halted; patients could choose their health provider. ❦ Police and councils could shut shops and pubs selling alcohol to <18s. ❦ A National Citizen Service would be introduced for 16-year-olds. ❦ Heathrow's third runway would be scrapped in favour of a high speed rail line; low carbon energy schemes would be promoted. ❦ The electorate would be able to recall MPs. ❦ A cap would be set on non-EU migrants. ❦ A free vote would be held on repealing the Hunting Act.

LIBERAL DEMOCRAT · 4 April · 112pp
Change That Works For You

The income tax threshold would be raised to £10,000, the tax credit system reformed and a 'mansion tax' introduced. ❦ A banking levy would be introduced; retail banks would be separated from investment banks. ❦ ID cards and the like-for-like Trident renewal would be scrapped. ❦ Low-ranking personnel in the Armed Forces would be paid more. ❦ Class sizes would be cut and university tuition fees scrapped. ❦ Patients could choose their GP. ❦ 3,000 police officers would be recruited. ❦ A 100% clean energy target would be set for 2050. ❦ The single transferable vote system would be introduced. ❦ An amnesty would be given to illegal immigrants who have been in the UK for many years.

─────────── POLITICAL WORDS OF THE YEAR ───────────

BULLYGATE · the furore surrounding allegations (not least those in Andrew Rawnsley's *The End of the Party*) that Brown presided over an intimidatory atmosphere in No. 10. ❦ The *Sun*'s front page headline was: THE PRIME MONSTER.

THE FORCES OF HELL · Alistair Darling reported that, after he predicted the worst recession for 60 years, in 2008, 'the forces of hell were unleashed' against him by both the Tories and No. 10. *Also* THE FORCES OF HULL · Andrew Rawnsley's description of John Prescott, formerly MP for Hull East.

DAMP RAG · MEP Nigel Farage's caustic description of EU President Herman Van Rompuy: 'I don't want to be rude but, really, you have the charisma of a DAMP RAG and the appearance of a LOW-GRADE BANK CLERK.'

OIK · Reportedly, George Osborne's Oxford 'Bullingdon Club' nickname (because he was schooled at St Paul's, not Eton).

CAB FOR HIRE · MP Stephen Byers's description of himself, secretly filmed by Channel 4's *Dispatches* as part of an investigation into political lobbying.

BIGOTGATE · see p.32.

BALANCED PARLIAMENT · euphemistic term for hung parliament. *Also* CONFIDENCE & SUPPLY · see p.16.

LABSERVATISM · a Lib Dem campaign idea designed to portray Labour and the Tories as agents of a seamless electoral duopoly. *For more of the same* ran the spoof LABSERVATIVE slogan.

CHIHUAHUAS · Conservatives In their Head, UKIP At Heart.

GET REAL · Brown's put-down of Clegg during the second debate, concerning the Lib Dems' plan to scrap Trident.

ED BALLS'S PORTILLO MOMENT · the campaign against Ed Balls to create a defining election-night moment akin to Michael Portillo's ousting in 1997. George Osborne reportedly called it the CASTRATION STRATEGY – a pun on the party's DECAPITATION strategy of targeting senior Labour MPs [see p.18].

#GORDONWHO · a Twitter tag established to track down 'rare examples' of Labour candidates using photos of Brown in their election material. *Also* CYANIDE ON THE DOORSTEP · a description of Brown from one Labour candidate, reported in *The Times*.

THE ELEPHANT IN THE ROOM · the Lib Dems' description of the Lab-Con reluctance to discuss the national debt.

TOM, DICK, HARRY · nicknames for Cameron's three election battle buses.

SECOND DIVISION · a note Yvette Cooper wrote to her colleague Liam Byrne (during a press conference addressed by her husband Ed Balls) was caught on camera: YC: *It's clearly second division today – presumably that's why we're allowed to do this?* LB: *Sort of like being allowed to play in the sand pit.*

LONG TOFFEE NOSE · Peter Mandelson's description of Cameron; he also called Cameron and Osborne JUST A COUPLE OF KIDS IN SCHOOL TROUSERS. *Also* RADIO FACE · Neil Kinnock's description of Brown. *Also* COMETH THE HOUR, COMETH THE TAN · quip about Tony Blair's pre-vote return to Britain to campaign for Brown.

───── POLITICAL WORDS OF THE YEAR ─────

ILLEGAL LAUGH · reference to the ban on audience reaction during the three televised leaders' debates [see p.19].

I AGREE WITH NICK · a refrain from the first leaders' debate [see p.19], when Brown, especially, was eager to associate himself with Clegg. *Also* CLEGG-MANIA *and* CLEGGISM · the surge in popularity for Nick 'Obama' Clegg who, according to a poll days after the first debate, was the most popular party leader since Winston Churchill, with an approval rating of 72%. (Hence VOTE CHURCHILL GET STALIN – the Tory assertion that a vote for Clegg would let in Brown.) In the *Telegraph*, Simon Heffer called Clegg THE NATION'S FAVOURITE SON-IN-LAW. *Also* THE CLEGG BUBBLE. *Also* THE YELLOW SURGE. *Also* THE GLIB DEMS · Trevor Kavanagh's sceptical nickname for the resurgent third party. *Also* #NICKCLEGGSFAULT· Twitter tag collecting absurd things for which Clegg is to blame (e.g., 'I have an awful cold') created in response to a series of press attacks on the Lib Dem leader.

THE WORM · a real-time focus-group tracker used to gauge the party leaders' popularity during the debates [see p.19].

THE NEW POLITICS · essentially meaningless term used by all three parties.

SCRAMBLED CLEGG AND TOAST (BUT CAMERON'S FULL OF BEANS)· the *Sun's* headline take on Clegg and Brown after the third debate [see p.19].

THE LONG GORDBYE · the *Sun's* take on Brown's reluctance to quit office. *Also* CEAUSESCU MOMENT · threat by some Labour supporters of what would happen should Brown cling to power.

RAINBOW *or* TRAFFIC LIGHT COALITION · nickname for a possible deal between the 'reds, yellows, and greens', i.e., Labour, Lib Dems, various N Irish MPs, and the Greens' Caroline Lucas. *Also* COALITION OF THE LOSERS. *Also* PROGRESSIVE ALLIANCE. *Also* CLUNK-CLEGG · nickname for a possible Lib-Lab coalition deal [Blair once described Brown as a 'great clunking fist'.] *Also* CON-DEM · supposedly arch description of the Tory-Lib Dem coalition. *Also* BROKEBACK COALITION · a description of the uneasy relationship between Clegg and Cameron.

I'M AFRAID THERE IS NO MONEY. KIND REGARDS – AND GOOD LUCK · the text of a 'joke' letter left by the outgoing Chief Sec. to the Treasury, Liam Byrne to whomever would replace him.

STUPID, SANCTIMONIOUS DWARF · the Health Minister Simon Burns's description of Speaker John Bercow; reported in Hansard as 'interruption'. *Also* SCRUTINY BY SCREECH · Speaker Bercow's description of PMQs.

MAD, BAD, AND DANGEROUS · Blair's description of Brown, according to Mandelson's memoirs.

ILLEGAL WAR · Clegg's description of the Iraq invasion, notable as he used the term at the despatch box during PMQs.

JUNIOR PARTNER · David Cameron's controversial description of Britain's role in the US-UK 'special relationship'.

BIG SOCIETY · a central component of Cameron Conservatism which aims to 'empower' individuals and communities; derided by critics as DIY POLITICS and GOVERNMENT ON THE CHEAP.

——————— 2010 ENGLISH LOCAL COUNCIL ELECTIONS ———————

The English 2010 council elections were overshadowed by the uncertain result of the general election held on the same day. Yet they offered some hope for Labour supporters that the party might not have lost as much support as some feared:

Party	Councils		Councillors	
	total	±	total	±
Conservative	66	–4	3,447	–119
Labour	37	+17	2,945	+412
Liberal Democrat	14	–4	1,714	–129
Others	0	0	286	–107
Residents Association	0	0	63	0
Green	0	0	35	–9
British National Party	0	0	19	–27
Liberal	0	0	12	0
UK Independence Party	0	0	9	–4
Independent Health Concern	0	0	8	–2
Respect	0	0	4	–8
No Overall Control	45	–7	–	–

——————————————— @EYESPYMP ———————————————

Although many MPs eagerly embraced social networks, not all were amused by the launch of the crowd-sourced political Twitter site 'eyespymp' – which publishes irreverent gossip about the eating, meeting, social, and sartorial habits of those inside the Westminster village. ('eyespymp' originally tweeted as 'parliament_spy'). The editor(s) of 'eyespymp' was anonymous at the time of writing, though it was speculated that 'bored parliamentary researchers' may be behind the site. In response to criticism, eyespymp noted: 'Our crowd sources include lackeys, flunkeys, front benchers and cabbies. Many are the people whom MPs push in front of in queues.' A selection of tweets from 'eyespymp' gives a flavour of the site, and an indication why some MPs are a little irked:

Phyllis Starkey looking stern and barking into her phone at the doors to Portcullis House. [01·02·10]

Osborne standing on the left hand side of the escalator. Oh George, when will you learn? [23·03·10]

Former Deputy PM & MP for Hull East John Prescott enjoying civilian life in the Humberside sunshine. [14·05·10]

MP for Spelthorne, Kwasi Kwarteng ordering two sandwiches, then goes to sit on his own. [14·06·10]

Rare spotting indeed! Gordon Brown seen rushing through Portcullis House.
[04·07·10]

The Hain in Spain. [12·08·10]

Michael Gove cycling through Westminster on a Boris bike. [02·09·10]

On 12 July 2010, the site tweeted: *So according to the Sunday Times MPs want EyeSpyers banned. How? We are too many and everywhere.*

—————————————— THE CABINET ——————————————

David Cameron's first Cabinet was a dramatic illustration of the brave 'new politics' of coalition government. Five Lib Dem MPs were included in the Cabinet – not the least of whom was Nick Clegg, who became Deputy PM and Lord President of the Council with special responsibility for political and constitutional reform. Cameron also continued Gordon Brown's early efforts at bipartisanship by appointing the respected Labour MP Frank Field as an advisor on reducing poverty.

Prime Minister; First Lord of the Treasury	David Cameron
Deputy Prime Minister, Lord President of the Council	Nick Clegg†
First Secretary of State, Foreign Secretary	William Hague
Chancellor of the Exchequer	George Osborne
Lord Chancellor, SoS Justice	Kenneth Clarke
SoS Home Department; Minister for Women & Equalities	Theresa May
SoS Defence	Liam Fox
SoS Business, Innovation and Skills	Vincent Cable†
SoS Work and Pensions	Iain Duncan Smith
SoS Energy and Climate Change	Chris Huhne†
SoS Health	Andrew Lansley
SoS Education	Michael Gove
SoS Communities and Local Government	Eric Pickles
SoS Transport	Philip Hammond
SoS Environment, Food and Rural Affairs	Caroline Spelman
SoS International Development	Andrew Mitchell
SoS Northern Ireland	Owen Paterson
SoS Scotland	Danny Alexander†
SoS Wales	Cheryl Gillan
SoS Culture, Olympics, Media, & Sport	Jeremy Hunt
Chief Secretary to the Treasury	David Laws†*
Leader of Lords, Chancellor of the Duchy of Lancaster	Lord Strathclyde
Minister without Portfolio	Baroness Warsi‡

Also attending Cabinet meetings

Minister for the Cabinet Office, Paymaster General	Francis Maude
Minister of State, Cabinet Office	Oliver Letwin
Minister of State (Universities and Science)	David Willetts
Leader of the House of Commons, Lord Privy Seal	George Young
Parliamentary Secretary to the Treasury & Chief Whip	Patrick McLoughlin
Attorney-General	Dominic Grieve§

† Indicates a Lib Dem. ‡ Indicates an unpaid position. § Attends Cabinet when requested. * David Laws resigned from the Cabinet on 29 May when it was revealed that he had claimed on expenses c.£40,000 for rent that he had paid to his homosexual partner; he denied any wrongdoing. Laws was replaced by Danny Alexander, who in turn was replaced as SoS for Scotland by Michael Moore. ❦ Cameron said that the Cabinet would meet each Tuesday at 9am for up to an hour and a half, and stated that he intended to continue the Blairite tradition of convening the Cabinet in regions across the country. One Cameron innovation was to make Ministers surrender their mobiles and PDAs before each meeting. At the first Cabinet meeting in May 2010, Ministers agreed to accept a 5% pay cut.

---------------------------- THE SCOTTISH PARLIAMENT ----------------------------

The current state of parties (as at 8 September 2010)

Number of MSPs	Constituency	Regional	Total
Scottish National Party	21	26	47
Scottish Labour	37	9	46
Scottish Conservative and Unionist	3	13	16
Scottish Liberal Democrat	11	5	16
Scottish Green Party	0	2	2
Independent	0	1	1
Presiding Officer (Alex Fergusson)	1	0	1

In September 2010, the Scottish National Party confirmed it had scrapped plans to introduce a bill on holding a referendum on independence before the 2011 elections.

---------------------------- THE NATIONAL ASSEMBLY FOR WALES ----------------------------

The current state of parties (as at 8 September 2010)

Number of AMs	Constituency	Regional	Total
Labour	24	2	26
Plaid Cymru	7	7	14
Conservative	5	8	13
Liberal Democrat	3	3	6
Independent	1	0	1
Presiding Officer (Lord Dafydd Elis-Thomas)	1	0	1

Plaid Cymru member Mohammad Asghar defected to the Conservatives in late 2009, saying that he felt 'out of tune with the views and policies of Plaid Cymru'.

---------------------------- THE NORTHERN IRELAND ASSEMBLY ----------------------------

The current state of parties (as at 3 June 2010)

DUP.................36	SDLP................16	Green Party 1
Sinn Féin.............27	Alliance................ 7	Independent........... 3
Ulster Unionists......17	Ind. Health Coalition. 1	Speaker: William Hay

---------------------------- THE LONDON ASSEMBLY ----------------------------

The current state of parties (as at 8 September 2010)

Conservative 11	Liberal Democrat 3	Independent........... 1
Labour................ 8	Green.................. 2	(May 2008 turnout, 45·3%)

THE HOUSE OF LORDS

State of the parties (as at 1 July 2010)

Conservative	188
Labour	225
Liberal Democrat	75
Crossbench	182
Bishops	26
Other	26
Total	722

Excludes 16 Members who are on leave of absence, 16 senior judiciary members and 1 disqualified as an MEP.

Archbishops and Bishops	26 [0]
Life Peers under the Appellate Jurisdiction Act 1876	23 [1]
Life Peers under the Life Peerages Act 1958	614 [151]
Peers under the House of Lords Act 1999	92 [2]

[Numbers within brackets indicate the number of women included in the figure.]

TOP TEN MOST FANCIABLE MPs · 2010

Below are the 'most fanciable' members of parliament, according to *Sky News*'s political editor Adam Boulton, who publishes a list on his blog each Valentine's Day:

# MP (age)	party
1 .. Lynne Featherstone† (58)	LD
2 .. Caroline Flint (48)	LAB
3 .. Julie Kirkbride (49)	CON
4 .. Adam Afriyie (44)	CON
5 .. Julia Goldsworthy (31)	LD
5 .. Nick Clegg (43)	LD
7 .. Jeremy Hunt (43)	CON
7 .. Andy Burnham (40)	LAB
9 .. Theresa May (53)	CON
10. Ed Vaizey (41)	CON

† 'For a woman who stopped counting her age several decades ago, I am very flattered by the compliment.'

SCOTS GUIDE TO THE SCOTTISH PARLIAMENT

In November 2009, a handbook to the workings of the Scottish Parliament was published in a Scots translation – to some mockery by the English press (the *Mail on Sunday* called it 'Rab C. Nesbitt dialect'). The handbook – 'Garrin the Scottish Pairlament wark for ye' – contains a wealth of information, including a glossary:

BILL · A set o proposals that micht become law gin the Scottish Pairlament cairries it. ❦ CANDIDATE · A person that stauns for election as a memmer o a political pairty or as a lane independent. ❦ COMATEE · A comatee is a sma group o MSPs that looks at specific issues in detail. MSPs are waled in sic a wey as tae reflect the balance o the sindry political pairties and independent MSPs in the Pairlament. ❦ CONSTITUENCY · Scotland is dividit intae 73 local areas for elections; ilkane o thae areas is kent as a constituency, and ilka constituency elects yin MSP kent as a constituency MSP. ❦ DEBATE · A collogue atween MSPs that aften leads tae a vote. Debates ordinarly gets held in the Debatin Chaumer. ❦ HALYRUDE · The Scottish Pairlament is aften cried Halyrude efter the pairt o Embra whaur it stauns. The Scottish Pairlament biggin at Halyrude wis officially handselt on 9 October 2004.

—————PARLIAMENTARY SALARY & ALLOWANCES—————

Members of Parliament

Members' Parliamentary salary .... £65,738 (from 1·4·2010)
Staffing expenditure (maximum) £105,265
IT equipment (centrally provided) .... worth c.£3,000
Pension provision for members' staff .... Group Stakeholder Arrangement
Administrative and Office Expenditure (AOE) £22,930
Communications expenditure £10,400
London costs allowance £7,500
Personal Additional Accommodation Expenditure (PAAE) £24,803
Winding up allowance £42,732
Car mileage, first 10,000 miles .... 40p per mile
– thereafter .... 25p per mile
Motorcycle allowance .... 24p per mile
Bicycle allowance .... 20p per mile

Position

Prime Minister[†] .... £132,923 (from 1·4·2010)
Cabinet Minister[†] £79,754
Cabinet Minister (Lords) £108,253
Minister of State[†] £41,370
Minister of State (Lords) £84,524
Parliamentary Under Secretary[†] £31,401
Parliamentary Under Secretary (Lords) £73,617
Government Chief Whip[†] £79,754
Government Deputy Chief Whip[†] £41,370
Government Whip[†] £26,624
Leader of the Opposition[†] £73,617
Leader of the Opposition (Lords) £73,617
Opposition Chief Whip[†] £41,370
Speaker[†] £79,754
Attorney General (Lords) £113,248
Chairman of Ways and Means[†] £41,370

[† Ministers in the Commons, and others, additionally receive their salaries as MPs, as above.]

MEMBERS OF THE HOUSE OF LORDS

In November 2009, a review of financial support for Members of the House of Lords found that the system then in place 'did not meet the standards of governance, precision and transparency now demanded for the use of public funds'. In July 2010, the House of Lords approved a motion to replace this system with a simpler one. Previous allowances for day and night subsistence, and office costs, were consolidated into a single daily rate of £300, with a reduced rate of £150, payable to those with Parliamentary business away from Westminster, or to those preferring not to receive the full rate. Lords members will also be able to reclaim their own travel expenses and up to 6 journeys a year for spouses, civil partners, or dependants.

——— SALARIES FOR DEVOLVED LEGISLATURES &c. ———

Scottish Parliament (from 1·4·2010)	*total salary*
Member of the Scottish Parliament (MSP)	£57,520
First Minister	£140,847
Cabinet Secretary	£100,748
Scottish Minister	£84,598
Presiding Officer	£100,748
Solicitor General	£98,358

National Assembly for Wales (from 1·4·2010)	*total salary*
Assembly Member (AM)	£53,852
Assembly First Minister	£134,723
Assembly Minister	£95,802
Presiding Officer	£95,802
Leader of the largest non-cabinet party	£95,802
Deputy Presiding Officer	£80,232

Northern Ireland Assembly (from 1·4·2010)	*total salary*
Members of the Legislative Assembly (MLA)	£43,101
Presiding Officer	£80,902

European Parliament (as at 8·9·2010)	*total salary*
UK Members of the European Parliament	as MPs or *c.*€7,000/month

† Since July 2009, MEPs receive a common salary. UK MEPs elected before June 2009 may choose to receive this flat rate or opt to receive the same remuneration as an MP, as they did previously.

Members of Parliament who are also members of a devolved legislature receive their full parliamentary salary [see above] and one-third of the salary due to them for their other role. Since 2004, Westminster MPs are ineligible to serve additionally as MEPs. The devolved legislatures control their own expenses and allowances.

London Assembly (from 1·4·2010)	*total salary*
Member of the London Assembly (MLA)	£53,439
Mayor of London	£143,911
Deputy Mayor	£96,092

——————— 'COALITION SPEAK' ———————

In August 2010, the *Daily Mail* reported that the Dept for Education had issued a note on the 'language of the new Government', to replace New Labour's jargon:

Old jargon	new jargon		
Delivery model	getting things done	*State*	(big/stronger) society
Safeguarding	predictability	*State control*	social responsibility
Targets & outcomes	results & impact	*Stakeholders*	people, practitioners, volunteers, professional organisations

——————— THE COST OF PARLIAMENT & MPs ———————

The combined cost of the Commons and Lords in 2007/08 was just over half a billion pounds – a dramatic increase since 1992/93, when Parliament cost 'just' £184m. Below are the costs of [a] the administration of the House of Commons, [b] expenditure of MPs, and [c] Peers' expenses and general Lords administration:

Fiscal year (£000s)	Commons administration	Commons Members	Lords expenditure	Total
1992/93	84,670	67,038	32,217	183,925
1993/94	94,162	68,502	36,260	198,924
1994/95	98,091	69,467	37,381	204,939
1995/96	112,239	72,125	39,846	224,210
1996/97	130,149	81,728	38,519	250,396
1997/98	145,228	95,819	39,407	280,454
1998/99	173,550	86,175	43,240	302,965
1999/00	164,583	91,799	45,267	301,649
2000/01	214,409	94,322	66,828	375,559
2001/02	165,426	120,159	71,449	357,034
2002/03	180,006	128,523	85,817	394,346
2003/04	178,217	133,902	81,119	393,238
2004/05	189,881	141,501	90,766	422,148
2005/06	320,559	156,598	106,382	583,539
2006/07	210,608	155,990	98,622	465,220
2007/08	227,885	159,310	121,500	508,695

Below are total and per-MP expenditures, in both actual sums and 2007/08 prices:

Total MPs' expenditure	2007/08 prices	fiscal year (£)	expenditure per MP	2007/08 prices
67,038,000	97,300,000	1992/93	103,000	149,000
68,502,000	96,777,000	1993/94	105,000	149,000
69,467,000	96,627,000	1994/95	107,000	148,000
72,125,000	97,502,000	1995/96	111,000	150,000
81,728,000	106,544,000	1996/97	126,000	164,000
95,819,000	121,720,000	1997/98	145,000	185,000
86,175,000	107,188,000	1998/99	131,000	163,000
91,799,000	111,983,000	1999/00	139,000	170,000
94,322,000	113,571,000	2000/01	143,000	172,000
120,159,000	141,525,000	2001/02	182,000	215,000
128,523,000	146,649,000	2002/03	195,000	223,000
133,902,000	148,552,000	2003/04	203,000	225,000
141,501,000	152,827,000	2004/05	215,000	232,000
156,598,000	165,738,000	2005/06	242,000	257,000
155,990,000	160,765,000	2006/07	241,000	249,000
159,310,000	159,310,000	2007/08	247,000	247,000

[Source: House of Commons Library, *Parliamentary Trends, Statistics About Parliament*, 2009]

─────────── THE NUMBER OF MPs ───────────

A popular component of David Cameron's election campaign [see p.251] was reducing the cost of politics. To this end, he pledged to cut the number of MPs by 10% should he win – a move that would, he claimed, save *c*.£12m a year, and make the electoral system fairer, by equalising the number of voters in each constituency. Below are the number of Westminster MPs, broken down by country, since 1832:

Year	England	Wales	Scotland	(N) Ireland	Total No. of seats
1832	468	32	53	105	658
1844	466	32	53	105	656
1852	464	32	53	105	654
1861	466	32	53	105	656
1865	468	32	53	105	658
1868	460	33	60	105	658
1870	456	33	60	103	652
1885 (Jun)	452	33	60	103	648
1885 (Nov)	461	34	72	103	670
1918	492	36	74	105	707
1922	492	36	74	13	615
1945	517	36	74	13	640
1950	506	36	71	12	625
1955	511	36	71	12	630
1974	516	36	71	12	635
1983	523	38	72	17	650
1992	524	38	72	17	651
1997	529	40	72	18	659
2005	529	40	59	18	646
2010	533	40	59	18	650

In August 2010, Nick Clegg announced that new maps would be drawn up by the independent Boundary Commissions, equalising constituency sizes and cutting the number of Members by 50.

The House of Commons has the most seats of any lower parliamentary chamber in Europe. Below is a comparison of the number of constituents that each elected member represents in a variety of lower assemblies in countries across the world:

Country	population per Member	Country	population per Member
Ireland	24,000	Canada	107,000
Sweden	26,000	France	111,000
Norway	30,000	Netherlands	113,000
New Zealand	33,000	Spain	129,000
Italy	94,000	Australia	133,000
UK	94,000	Germany	134,000
		USA	696,000

[Source: House of Commons Library, *Parliamentary Trends, Statistics About Parliament*, 2009 quoting *Rallings & Thrasher, British Electoral Facts 1832–2006*, Ashgate Publishing Ltd, and Review Body on Senior Salaries, *Review of Parliamentary Pay Pensions and Allowances 2007*]

———— ACTIVITIES OF THE HOUSE OF COMMONS ————

Sittings of the House of Commons   *2009/10*
Number of sitting days...146
   Average length of sitting days 7hr 44min
Westminster Hall sitting days...94
   Average length of Westminster Hall sitting days 3hr 52min
Hansard · Total columns of debate reported (Chamber and Westminster Hall) .. 26,622
   Average columns published per sitting day...................................182
   Debate report columns per significant error (target=13) ....26·7
   Average daily print run 1,335
   Daily vote bundle · Average number of pages per sitting day...............324
Questions, motions, & answers
Average number of questions dealt with by the Table Office per sitting day....455
Number of Members who have used e-tabling facility...........................266
Percentage of questions e-tabled ....57·8%
Total number of written answers published 55,615
Early Day Motions: Average number tabled per week...........................75
   Average number of signatures per week...................................3,704
Legislation
Government bills 33
Private Members' bills 115
Private bills..10
General Committee meetings...413
Total number of new amendments, new clauses, and new schedules tabled. 4,882
Average per sitting day..33·7
Hansard (Public bill and general committees)
Total number of pages of debates published................................. 4,758
Columns per significant error (target=13) 32
Statutory Instruments
Considered by Joint or Select Committee on Statutory Instruments 1,737
Special attention of the House drawn to 64
Regulatory reform
Draft Legislative Reform Orders reported on 3
European Scrutiny Committee
EU Documents scrutinised...915
Reported as legally or politically important 416
Debates in European Standing Committee...33
Debates on the floor of the House...1
Joint Committee on Human Rights
Bills considered 30
Special attention of the House drawn to 17
Select Committees
Meetings...1,237
Reports (departmental committees only)...364

[Source: 32nd Report of the House of Commons Commission, Financial Year 2009/10]

──── GENERAL ELECTION BREAKDOWN 1979–2005 ────

Date	3.5.79	9.6.83	11.6.87	9.4.92	1.5.97	7.6.01	5.5.05
Winning party	Con	Con	Con	Con	Lab	Lab	Lab
Seat majority	43	144	102	21	179	167	67
PM	Thatcher	Thatcher	Thatcher	Major	Blair	Blair	Blair
Leader of Op.	Callaghan	Foot	Kinnock	Kinnock	Major	Hague	Howard
Lib (Dem) leader	Steel	Steel	Steel	Ashdown	Ashdown	Kennedy	Kennedy

Conservative

Seats	339	397	375	336	165	166	198
Votes (m)	13.70	13.01	13.74	14.09	9.60	8.36	8.78
Share of votes (%)	43.9	42.4	42.2	41.9	30.7	31.7	32.4
% of seats	53.4	61.1	57.8	51.6	25.0	25.2	30.5

Labour

Seats	268	209	229	271	418	412	355
Votes (m)	11.51	8.46	10.03	11.56	13.52	10.72	9.55
Share of votes (%)	36.9	27.6	30.8	34.4	43.2	40.7	35.2
% of seats	42.4	32.2	35.2	41.6	63.6	62.7	55.2

Liberal Democrat (&c.)

Seats	11	23	22	20	46	52	62
Votes (m)	4.31	7.78	7.34	6.00	5.24	4.81	5.99
Share of votes (%)	13.8	25.4	22.6	17.8	16.8	18.3	22.0
% of seats	1.7	3.5	3.4	3.1	7.0	7.9	9.6

Monster Raving Loony

Candidates	–	11	5	22	24	15	19
Average vote (%)	–	0.7	0.7	0.6	0.7	1.0	–
Lost deposits	–	11	5	22	24	15	19

Women MPs	19	23	41	60	120	118	127
– as %	3.0	3.5	6.3	9.2	18.2	17.9	19.7

Turnout (%)	76.0	72.7	75.3	77.7	71.4	59.4	61.4
– England (%)	75.9	72.5	75.4	78.0	71.4	59.2	61.3
– Wales (%)	79.4	76.1	78.9	79.7	73.5	61.6	62.6
– Scotland (%)	76.8	72.7	75.1	75.5	71.3	58.2	60.8
– N. Ireland (%)	67.7	72.9	67.0	69.8	67.1	68.0	62.9

Postal vote (%)	2.2	2.0	2.4	2.0	2.3	5.2	14.6
Spoilt ballots (%)	0.38	0.17	0.11	0.12	0.30	0.38	0.7
– av./constituency	186	79	57	61	142	152	291
Deposit to stand	£150	£150	£500	£500	£500	£500	£500
– threshold (%)	12½	12½	5	5	5	5	5

Some figures (e.g., that of a winning party's majority) are disputed. Source: House of Commons.

BRITISH PRIME MINISTERS

Prime Minister	date of birth	star sign	position in family	siblings	child of MP	at Eton	at Harrow	at Oxbridge	in the forces	party as PM	age when first PM	time as PM	Admins.	date of death	age at death
David Cameron	09.10.1966	♎	3rd of 4	1b 2s	•	♦	•	O	•	Con	43y 214d	—	—	—	—
Gordon Brown	20.02.1951	♓	2nd of 3	2b	•	•	•	•	•	Lab	56y 129d	2y 318d	1	—	—
Tony Blair	06.05.1953	♉	2nd of 3	1b 1s	•	•	•	O	•	Lab	43y 361d	10y 56d	3	—	—
John Major	29.03.1943	♈	4th of 4	2b 1s	•	•	•	•	•	Con	47y 245d	6y 154d	2	—	—
Margaret Thatcher	13.10.1925	♎	2nd of 2	1s	•	•	•	O	•	Con	53y 204d	11y 209d	3	—	—
James Callaghan	27.03.1912	♈	2nd of 2	1s	•	•	•	•	♦	Lab	64y 9d	3y 29d	1	26-03-2005	92
Edward Heath	09.07.1916	♋	1st of 2	1b	•	•	•	O	♦	Con	53y 335d	3y 259d	1	17-07-2005	89
Harold Wilson	11.03.1916	♓	2nd of 2	1s	•	•	•	O	•	Lab	48y 219d	7y 279d	4	24-05-1995	79
Alec Douglas-Home	02.07.1903	♋	1st of 7	4b 2s	•	♦	•	O	•	Con	60y 109d	363d	1	09-10-1995	92
Harold Macmillan	10.02.1894	♒	3rd of 3	2b	•	♦	•	O	♦	Con	62y 335d	6y 281d	2	29-12-1986	92
Anthony Eden	12.06.1897	♊	4th of 5	3b 1s	•	♦	•	O	♦	Con	57y 299d	1y 279d	1	14-01-1977	79
Clement Attlee	03.01.1883	♑	7th of 8	4b 3s	•	•	•	O	♦	Lab	63y 205d	6y 92d	2	08-10-1967	84
Winston Churchill	30.11.1874	♐	1st of 2	1b	♦	•	♦	•	♦	Con	65y 163d	8y 240d	3	24-01-1965	90
Neville Chamberlain	18.03.1869	♓	3rd of 6	1b 4s	♦	•	•	•	•	Con	68y 71d	2y 343d	1	09-11-1940	71
Ramsay MacDonald	12.10.1866	♎	only child	0	•	•	•	•	•	Lab	57y 102d	6y 289d	4	09-11-1937	71
Stanley Baldwin	03.08.1867	♌	only child	0	•	•	♦	C	•	Con	55y 292d	7y 82d	4	13-12-1947	80
Andrew Bonar Law	16.09.1858	♍	4th of 7	3b 3s	•	•	•	•	•	Con	64y 37d	209d	1	30-10-1923	65
David Lloyd George	17.01.1863	♑	3rd of 4	1b 2s	•	•	•	•	•	Lib	53y 325d	5y 317d	2	26-03-1945	82
Herbert Henry Asquith	12.09.1852	♍	2nd of 5	1b 3s	•	•	•	O	•	Lib	55y 198d	8y 244d	4	15-02-1928	75
Henry Campbell-Bannerman	07.09.1836	♍	6th of 6	1b 4s	•	•	•	C	•	Lib	69y 89d	2y 122d	1	22-04-1908	71
Arthur James Balfour	25.07.1848	♌	3rd of 8	4b 3s	♦	♦	•	C	•	Con	53y 352d	3y 145d	1	19-03-1930	81
Earl of Rosebery	07.05.1847	♉	3rd of 4	1b 2s	♦	♦	•	O	•	Lib	46y 302d	1y 109d	1	21-05-1929	82
Marquess of Salisbury	03.02.1830	♒	5th of 6	3b 2s	♦	♦	•	O	•	Con	55y 144d	13y 252d	4	22-08-1903	73
William Ewart Gladstone	29.12.1809	♐	5th of 6	3b 2s	♦	♦	•	O	•	Lib	58y 340d	12y 126d	4	19-05-1898	88
Benjamin Disraeli	21.12.1804	♐	2nd of 5	3b 1s	•	•	•	•	•	Con	63y 68d	6y 339d	2	19-04-1881	76
Viscount Palmerston	20.10.1784	♎	1st of 5	1b 3s	♦	•	♦	C	•	Lib	71y 109d	9y 141d	2	13-10-1865	81
Earl of Aberdeen	28.01.1784	♒	1st of 7	5b 1s	♦	•	♦	C	•	Con	68y 326d	2y 42d	1	14-12-1860	76

—— BRITISH PRIME MINISTERS cont. ——

Prime Minister	date of birth	star sign	position in family	siblings	child of MP	at Eton	at Harrow	at Oxbridge	in the forces	party as PM	age when first PM	time as PM	Admins.	date of death	age at death
Earl of Derby	29·03·1799	♈	1st of 7	2b 1s	◈	◈		O		Con	52y 331d	3y 280d	3	23·10·1869	70
Lord John Russell	18·08·1792	♌	3rd of 7	6b	◈			C		Lib	53y 316d	6y 11d	2	28·05·1878	85
Robert Peel	05·02·1788	♒	3rd of 11	5b 3s	◈		◈	O		Con	46y 308d	5y 57d	2	02·07·1850	62
Lord Melbourne	15·03·1779	♓	2nd of 6	3b 2s		◈		C		Whig	55y 123d	6y 255d	2	24·11·1848	69
Earl Grey	13·03·1764	♓	2nd of 9	6b 2s	◈			C		Whig	66y 254d	3y 229d	1	17·07·1845	81
Duke of Wellington	01·05·1769	♏	6th of 9	6b 2s		◈			◈	Tory	58y 266d	2y 320d	2	14·09·1852	83
Viscount Goderich	01·11·1782	♏	2nd of 3	2b	◈		◈	C		Tory	44y 305d	130d	1	28·01·1859	76
George Canning	11·04·1770	♈	2nd of 13	7b 5s		◈		O		Tory	57y 1d	119d	1	08·08·1827	57
Earl of Liverpool	07·06·1770	♊	1st of 3	1b 1s	◈			O		Tory	42y 1d	14y 305d	1	04·12·1828	58
Spencer Perceval	01·11·1762	♏	5th of 9	2b 6s	◈		◈	C		Tory	46y 338d	2y 221d	1	11·05·1812	49
Lord Grenville	24·10·1759	♏	6th of 9	3b 5s	◈	◈		O		Whig	46y 110d	1y 42d	1	12·01·1834	74
Henry Addington	30·05·1757	♊	4th of 6	1b 4s				O		Tory	43y 291d	3y 54d	1	15·02·1844	86
William Pitt	28·05·1759	♊	4th of 5	2b 2s	◈			C		Tory	24y 205d	18y 343d	2	23·01·1806	46
Duke of Portland	14·04·1738	♈	3rd of 6	1b 4s		◈		O		Whig	44y 335d	3y 82d	2	30·10·1809	71
Earl of Shelburne	02·05·1737	♉	1st of 5	1b 3s	◈			O	◈	Whig	45y 63d	266d	1	07·05·1805	68
Lord North	13·04·1732	♈	1st of 6	1b 4s	◈	◈		O		Tory	37y 290d	12y 58d	1	05·08·1792	60
Duke of Grafton	28·09·1735	♎	2nd of 3	2b	◈	◈		C		Whig	33y 16d	1y 106d	1	14·03·1811	75
Earl of Chatham	15·11·1708	♏	4th of 7	1b 5s	◈	◈		O	◈	Whig	57y 257d	2y 76d	1	11·05·1778	69
Marquess of Rockingham	13·05·1730	♉	8th of 10	4b 5s	◈	◈				Whig	35y 61d	1y 113d	2	01·07·1782	52
George Grenville	14·10·1712	♎	2nd of 7	5b 1s	◈	◈			◈	Whig	50y 184d	2y 85d	1	13·11·1770	58
Earl of Bute	25·05·1713	♊	2nd of 8	2b 5s	◈	◈		O		Tory	49y 1d	317d	1	10·03·1792	78
Duke of Devonshire	1720	?	2nd of 7	3b 3s	◈					Whig	c.36	225d	1	02·10·1764	c.44
Duke of Newcastle	21·07·1693	♋	8th of 11	2b 8s	◈			C		Whig	60y 238d	7y 205d	2	17·11·1768	75
Henry Pelham	26·09·1694	♎	9th of 11	2b 8s	◈			O	◈	Whig	48y 336d	10y 191d	1	06·03·1754	59
Earl of Wilmington	?1673	?	5th of 5	3b 1s	◈			O		Whig	c.69	1y 136d	1	02·07·1743	c.70
Robert Walpole	26·08·1676	♍	5th of 17	9b 7s	◈	◈		C		Whig	44y 107d	20y 314d	1	18·03·1745	60

—— COMMONS SITTINGS OF MORE THAN 24 HOURS ——

Listed below are the occasions that the Commons has sat for longer than 24 hours:

Date	main item of business	total sitting time hours:minutes
31·07·1877	South Africa Bill	26:15
	Established a S African Union & the annexation of the Transvaal	
31·01·1881	Protection of Person & Property (Ireland) Bill	41:30
	Authorised the detention of criminal suspects without trial	
30·06·1882	Prevention of Crime (Ireland) Bill	30:00
	Creation of juryless tribunals; more power for police to search & arrest	
19·07·1904	Finance Bill	25:35
	Enacted the 1904 budget which called for increased indirect taxes	
20·03·1907	Consolidated Fund Bill	26:51
	Parliamentary authorisation on government expenditure	
22·07·1936	Unemployment Assistance Regulations	34:19
	Opposition objected to retention of means-tested assistance	
11·06·1951	Finance Bill	31:46
	Debate centred on alterations to profit tax regulations	
13·07·1967	Medical Termination of Pregnancy Bill	24:29
	Established legal grounds for performing an abortion	
12·06·1969	Divorce Reform Bill	24:11
	Permitting divorce in instances of irretrievable marital breakdown	
24·07·1975	Remuneration Charges and Grants Bill	26:26
	Amendments to pay limit regulations, aimed at curbing inflation	
21·06·1977	Price Commission Bill	31:03
	Powers granted to the Price Commission to investigate & freeze prices	
28·07·1977	Consolidated Fund (Appropriation) Bill	24:09
	Parliamentary authorisation on government expenditure	
04·08·1980	Consolidated Fund (Appropriation) (No. 2) Bill	24:21
	Delayed by opposition to stop proceedings on another scheduled bill	
01·04·1981	British Telecommunications Bill	25:00
	Reducing British Telecom's monopoly & debate on phone tapping	
22·05·1984	Local Government (Interim Provisions) Bill	32:12
	Abolishing Greater London Council & six other metropolitan councils	
05·03·1985	Water (Fluoridation) Bill	30:16
	Granting water companies the power to add fluoride	
10·12·1986	Teachers' Pay and Conditions Bill	26:08
	Increased teachers' salaries & ended their right to bargain over pay	
10·11·1987	Felixstowe Dock & Railway Bill (Private Bill)	30:25
	Expansion of the dock & creation of a nature reserve	
14·06·1988	Housing Bill	29:31
	Altered role of housing authorities & strengthened landlords' rights	
25·01·2000	Disqualifications Bill	29:21
	Allowing members of the Irish parliament to be elected to Westminster	
10·03·2005	Prevention of Terrorism Bill	32:22
	Introduction of 'control orders' such as house arrest & electronic tagging	

[Source: House of Commons Information Office, *Sittings of the House*; *The Times* archive]

SALARIES OF HEADS OF STATE

Tabulated below are the annual salaries of Heads of Government in various countries, and a comparison of each salary with that of the British Prime Minister.

Country	position	annual salary	£ equivalent	% of UK
UK	Prime Minister	£188,848	£188,848	100
Australia	Prime Minister	Aus $330,356	£146,825	78
Canada	Prime Minister	Can $301,600	£151,558	80
France	Prime Minister	€242,472	£168,383	89
Germany	Chancellor	€189,990	£133,796	71
Ireland	Prime Minister	€271,822	£167,791	89
Italy	Prime Minister	€196,452	£141,332	75
Netherlands	Prime Minister	€128,000	£91,429	48
New Zealand		NZ $360,000	£151,261	80
Norway		NKr 1,115,000	£79,473	42
Spain	Prime Minister	€89,304	£72,019	38
Sweden	Prime Minister	SKr 1,512,000	£101,955	54
USA	President	$400,000	£246,914	131

[Source :Review Body on Senior Salaries, *Review of parliamentary pay, pensions & allowances*, 2007/08]

DENNIS SKINNER & THE QUEEN'S SPEECH

Dennis Skinner, the Labour MP for Bolsover since 1970, is known for his bold approach to Parliamentary etiquette and the caustic one-liners he delivers from a sedentary position on the back-benches. His most famous quips are at the expense of the monarchy, and come just before the Queen's Speech, when Black Rod enters the Commons to summon MPs to the Lords†. Below are some of Skinner's finest:

Year　quip　　　　　　　　　　　　　　　　　　　　　　　　　　reference to
2010.. No royal commissions this week? .... *Sarah Ferguson's recent scandal* [see p.277]
2009.. Royal expenses are on the way!......................... *The MPs' expenses scandal*
2008.. Any Tory moles at the palace?‡............... *the arrest of Tory MP Damian Green*
2007.. Who shot the harriers? .... *the shooting of two hen harriers near the Sandringham estate*
2006.. Is Helen Mirren on standby?................... *Mirren's TV portrayal of the Queen*
2005.. Has she brought Camilla with her? ..... *Charles's marriage to Camilla Parker-Bowles*
2000.. Tell 'er to read the *Guardian*!.......... *the newspaper's questioning of the monarchy*
1997.. New Labour, new Black Rod!................... *the election of Blair's New Labour*
1992.. Tell her to pay her taxes!.................................. *the 'her' was the Queen*
1991.. I bet he drinks Carling Black Label! .... *a popular television advert for lager*
1990.. It tolls for thee, Maggie!.............. *Margaret Thatcher's approaching defenestration*

† Skinner remains in the Commons chamber during the Queen's Speech; he told *The New York Times*: 'I'm not one of those people that ring up the press and say, "Look what I'm doing", but I decided when I was elected to Parliament that I wouldn't be involved in crawling or grovelling to the monarchy'.
‡ To which the outgoing Black Rod, Sir Michael Willcocks, quietly replied, 'I shall miss you, Dennis'.

———————— RECALL OF PARLIAMENT ————————

The process by which the Commons is recalled is laid down in Standing Order 13:

Whenever the House stands adjourned and it is represented to the Speaker by Her Majesty's Ministers that the public interest requires that the House should meet at a time earlier than that to which the House stands adjourned, the Speaker, if he is satisfied that the public interest does so require, may give notice that, being so satisfied, he appoints a time for the House to meet, and the House shall accordingly meet at the time stated in such notice.

This Order means that the Speaker can only recall the House once he or she has received a request from the government – a situation that some regard as problematic. As the Hansard Society Commission on Parliamentary Scrutiny argued in 2001: 'If Parliament is to be an effective forum at times of crisis, and retain its significance to political debate, there must be an alternative mechanism for the recall of Parliament.' In 2007, the Labour government indicated its support for allowing the Speaker to recall the Commons 'where a majority of members of Parliament request a recall'. At the time of writing, the Modernisation Committee had yet to report on its examination of this issue. Below are the 23 Parliamentary recalls since 1948:

Day/month	*year*	*reason for recall*
27–29/9	1949	devaluation of the pound by 30·5%
12–19/9	1950	the Korean War and its impact on the British economy
4/10	1951	so that a general election could be called
12–14/9	1956	the 'Suez Crisis'
18/9	1959	so that a general election could be called
17–23/10	1961	the 'Berlin Crisis'
16/1	1968	Harold Wilson on government expenditure cuts
26–27/8	1968	the Soviet invasion of Czechoslovakia; Nigeria & Biafra
26–29/5	1970	so that a general election could be called
22–23/9	1971	internment and the crisis in Northern Ireland
9–10/1	1974	the fuel crisis and Britain's economic turmoil
3–4/6	1974	Northern Ireland & the collapse of power sharing
3/4 (Saturday)	1982	Argentina's invasion of the Falkland Islands
14/4	1982	Argentina's invasion of the Falkland Islands
6–7/9	1990	Iraq's invasion of Kuwait & the 'Gulf Crisis'
24–25/9	1992	Government economic policy on the European exchange rate mechanism; UN operations in Yugoslavia, Iraq, Somalia
31/5	1995	the crisis in Bosnia & Britain's military involvement
2–3/9	1998	the Omagh bombing & emergency terror legislation
14/9; 4 & 8/10	2001	9/11 attacks & military action in Afghanistan
3/4	2002	death of the Queen Mother
24/10	2002	Iraq and 'Weapons of Mass Destruction'

The Scottish Parliament can be recalled by its Presiding Officer without any ministerial request, and has been recalled thrice: on Donald Dewar's death (2000); on the Queen Mother's death (2002); and on the release of Abdelbaset al-Megrahi (2009). The assemblies in N Ireland and Wales use the same recall procedure as Westminster, but have not yet been recalled. [Source: House of Commons]

—THE SPECTATOR PARLIAMENTARIAN AWARDS · 2009—

Newcomer of the Year ....Kenneth Clarke [CON]
Inquisitor of the Year .... Paul Farrelly [LAB]
Peer of the Year.. Baroness Warsi [CON]
Speech of the Year.....................................Daniel Hannan† [CON, MEP]
Resignation of the Year ....James Purnell [LAB]
Minister to Watch .... Lord Adonis [LAB]
Campaigner of the Year........................... Joanna Lumley and the Gurkhas
Survivor of the Year..Alistair Darling [LAB]
Backbencher of the Year ....Andrew Tyrie [CON]
Parliamentarian of the Year...............................Harriet Harman [LAB]
Politician of the Year.......................................Lord Mandelson [LAB]

† In March 2009, Hannan delivered a 3½-minute speech at the European Parliament aimed at Gordon Brown, who was sitting in the chamber. In a brazenly personal attack, Hannan criticised the PM for being 'pathologically incapable of accepting responsibility', concluding: 'You are a devalued Prime Minister, of a devalued government'. One YouTube clip of the speech has been viewed >2·7m times.

—————— THINK TANK OF THE YEAR · 2009——————

In 2009, *Prospect* gave its 'Think Tank of the Year' jointly to the Centre for Social Justice ('the moderate social-policy friendly right wingers') and the Institute for Fiscal Studies ('the financial wizards'). The 'One to Watch' think tank was Demos; the 'Foreign Policy Think Tank of the Year' was The Royal United Services Institute.

——————— MPs' STAFFING LEVELS———————

2,694 members of MPs' staff were on the payroll at the end of the 2007/08 financial year – in addition to a number of volunteers and interns working in Westminster or constituency offices – according to the House of Commons Commission. Below are the number of Members and Members' staff per Session:

Year	MPs	staff	per MP
1997–98	659	1,753	2·66
1998–99	659	1,849	2·81
1999–00	659	1,867	2·83
2000–01	659	1,850	2·81
2001–02	659	2,179	3·31
2002–03	659	2,280	3·46
2003–04	659	2,446	3·71
2004–05	659	2,584	3·92
2005–06	646	2,577	3·99
2006–07	646	2,493	3·86
2007–08	646	2,694	4·17

——————— WESTMINSTER DOG OF THE YEAR · 2009———————

The Westminster Dog of the Year contest is open to all MPs and Lords, and, since 2005, parliamentary journalists. In October 2009, the award was won by Molly, a Welsh springer spaniel belonging to MP for Sutton Coldfield, Andrew Mitchell.

─────────────── THE EUROPEAN UNION ───────────────

The European Union (EU) has its roots in the European Coal & Steel Community (ECSC), formed in 1951 between Belgium, France, Germany, Italy, Luxembourg, and the Netherlands, who united to co-operate over production of coal and steel: the two key components of war. Since then, through a series of treaties, Europe as an economic and political entity has developed in size, harmonisation, and power. For some, the expansion in EU membership [see below] and the introduction of the euro (in 2002) are welcome developments in securing co-operation and peace; for others, the growth of the EU is a threat to the sovereignty of member nations.

MAJOR EU INSTITUTIONS

European Parliament · the democratic voice of the people of Europe, the EP approves the EU budget; oversees the other EU institutions; assents to key treaties and agreements on accession; and, alongside the Council of Ministers, examines and approves EU legislation. The EP sits in Strasbourg and Brussels, and its members are directly elected every 5 years.

Council of the EU · the pre-eminent decision-making body, the Council is made up of ministers from each national government. The Council meets regularly in Brussels to decide EU policy and approve laws, and every three months Presidents and PMs meet at European Councils to make major policy decisions.

European Commission · proposes new laws for the Council and Parliament to consider, and undertakes much of the EU's day-to-day work, such as overseeing the implementation of EU rules. Commissioners are nominated by each member state, and the President of the Commission is chosen by the national governments. It is based in Brussels.

European Court · ensures EU law is observed and applied fairly, and settles any disputes arising. Each state sends a judge to the Court in Luxembourg.

EU MEMBERSHIP

Country	entry	members
Belgium		
France		
Germany	1952	6
Italy		
Luxembourg		
Netherlands		
Denmark	1973	9
Ireland		
UK		
Greece	1981	10
Portugal	1986	12
Spain		
Austria		
Finland	1995	15
Sweden		
Cyprus		
Czech Rep.		
Estonia		
Hungary		
Latvia		
Lithuania	2004	25
Malta		
Poland		
Slovakia		
Slovenia		
Romania		
Bulgaria	2007	27
Turkey, Iceland		
Croatia	*in accession talks*	
Macedonia		
Serbia, Albania		
Bosnia-Herzegovina	*candidates*	
Montenegro		
Kosovo (UNSCR Resolution 1244)		

THE EUROPEAN PARLIAMENT

Below are MEPs by state and political group, for the seventh parliamentary term:

	European People's Party	Prog. Alliance of Socialists & Dems	Alliance of Liberals & Dems	Greens/European Free Alliance	European Conservatives & Reformists	E. United Left – Nordic Green Left	Europe of Freedom & Democracy	Non-attached members	TOTAL
Belgium	5	5	5	4	1	·	·	2	22
Bulgaria	6	4	5	·	·	·	·	2	17
Czech Rep.	2	7	·	·	9	4	·	·	22
Denmark	1	4	3	2	·	1	2	·	13
Germany	42	23	12	14	·	8	·	·	99
Estonia	1	1	3	1	·	·	·	·	6
Ireland	4	3	4	·	·	1	·	·	12
Greece	8	8	·	1	·	3	2	·	22
Spain	23	21	2	2	·	1	·	1	50
France	29	14	6	14	·	5	1	3	72
Italy	35	21	7	·	·	·	9	·	72
Cyprus	2	2	·	·	·	2	·	·	6
Latvia	3	1	1	1	1	1	·	·	8
Lithuania	4	3	2	·	1	·	2	·	12
Luxembourg	3	1	1	1	·	·	·	·	6
Hungary	14	4	·	·	1	·	·	3	22
Malta	2	3	·	·	·	·	·	·	5
Netherlands	5	3	6	3	1	2	1	4	25
Austria	6	4	·	2	·	·	·	5	17
Poland	28	7	·	·	15	·	·	·	50
Portugal	10	7	·	·	·	5	·	·	22
Romania	14	11	5	·	·	·	·	3	33
Slovenia	3	2	2	·	·	·	·	·	7
Slovakia	6	5	1	·	·	·	1	·	13
Finland	4	2	4	2	·	·	1	·	13
Sweden	5	5	4	3	·	1	·	·	18
UK	·	13	12	5	25	1	11	5	72
TOTAL	265	184	85	55	54	35	30	28	736

EURO MYTHS

The European Commission in the UK maintains a blog to debunk some of the persistent 'Euro myths' reported in the press. For example: 'Suggestions from some papers over the Easter holiday that "EU officials" want to change the name of the English Channel to the "Anglo-French Pond" are as untrue as they are ridiculous.' And, 'Despite numerous news reports in the past 48 hours, there are no EU plans to ban the sale of eggs sold by the dozen, or even by the half-dozen for that matter!'

———————— UK OPINION ON THE EU ————————

The latest Eurobarometer Survey (Spring 2010) shows just how Eurosceptic the UK is. Charted below are some UK opinions and comparisons with the EU27 average:

Generally speaking, do you think that (our country's) membership of the EU is

%	EU	UK
A good thing	49	29
A bad thing	18	33
Neither good nor bad	29	31
Don't know	4	7

Taking everything into account, would you say that (our country) has on balance benefited from being in the EU?

%	EU	UK
Benefited	53	36
Not benefited	35	50
Don't know	12	14

What are the two most important issues you are facing at the moment?

%	EU	UK
Rising prices/inflation	38	29
Economic situation	25	21
Unemployment	21	19
Healthcare system	18	18
Pensions	16	18
Taxation	14	14
Education system	10	12
Crime	8	13
Housing	6	7
Energy	6	8
The environment	5	5
Immigration	3	8
Terrorism	1	3

Which of the following would best strengthen your feeling about being a European citizen?

% (maximum of four answers)	EU	UK
A European social welfare system harmonised between the member States (health, pensions, &c.)	34	17
A president of the EU directly elected by all EU citizens	18	12
EU embassies in non-EU countries	7	6
Being able to vote in all elections organised where you live even if you are not a citizen of that member state	17	12
European emergency response to international natural disasters	23	22
A European civic education course for primary school children	18	11
Being able to use your mobile across the EU at the same price	19	19
Being able to shop online from all EU countries at the same price and with the same consumer protection legislation	14	11
Seeing a European researcher winning a Nobel prize	3	2
Seeing the president of the EC on TV delivering a 'general policy speech' in front of the European Parliament	7	8
A European Parliament that had the right to decide on taxes raised in the European Union	12	5
Being able to move to any EU country after your retirement and to take your pension with you	27	26
A European ID card in addition to national ID cards	21	11
A European army	10	9
You do not want to be, or feel that you are, a European citizen[†]	5	5
Other/None[†] († spontaneous answer)	8	20

—————————— THE LISBON TREATY ——————————

The Lisbon Treaty became law on 1 December 2009, after it had been ratified by all 27 EU member states. (This process was by no means smooth. The Irish rejected the treaty in a June 2008 referendum, only to approve it in October 2009 – no doubt influenced by the scale of the economic meltdown.) Depending on your political persuasion, the Lisbon Treaty is either a much-needed tool of bureaucratic reform, or another ratchet click towards a federal Europe. Some argue that the treaty is simply a reformulation of the European Constitution rejected in 2005 by the French and the Dutch. ❦ Below are some of the Libson Treaty's many elements:

Creation of the post of President of the European Council (awarded to Herman Van Rompuy), elected for 2½ years; creation of the post of High Representative of the Union for Foreign Affairs and Security Policy (awarded to Baroness Ashton) and the creation of a European External Action Service (i.e., an EU foreign office); creation of a single EU 'legal personality'; the European Parliament given more power over EU laws; EU assembly membership cut to 751 from 785; the EU executive cut from 27 members to 18, from 2014; Commissioners, selected by rotation among states, to have 5-year terms; legal establishment of the EU Charter of Fundamental Rights, though some countries have opt-outs; establishment of the right of ≥1m citizens to call on the Commission to introduce a specific legislative proposal; recognition, for the first time, that a member state can withdraw from the EU.

—————————— THE COMMONWEALTH ——————————

The Commonwealth of Nations is a voluntary association of 53 sovereign states – all of which, excepting Mozambique, have experienced British rule. The Commonwealth has no formal constitution; its goal is to promote 'democracy and good governance, respect for human rights and gender equality, the rule of law, and sustainable economic and social development'. The Commonwealth Nations are:

Antigua & Barbuda* · Australia* · Bahamas* · Bangladesh · Barbados*
Belize* · Botswana · Brunei Darussalam · Cameroon · Canada* · Cyprus
Dominica · Fiji Islands† · The Gambia · Ghana · Grenada* · Guyana · India
Jamaica* · Kenya · Kiribati · Lesotho · Malawi · Malaysia · Maldives · Malta
Mauritius · Mozambique · Namibia · Nauru‡ · New Zealand* · Nigeria · Pakistan
Papua New Guinea* · St Kitts & Nevis* · St Lucia* · St Vincent* · Samoa
Seychelles · Sierra Leone · Singapore · Solomon Islands* · South Africa
Sri Lanka · Swaziland · Tanzania · Tonga · Trinidad & Tobago
Tuvalu* · Uganda · United Kingdom · Vanuatu · Zambia

In December 2003, Zimbabwe withdrew its membership after its suspension was not lifted.
* The Queen is not only Queen of the UK and its overseas territories, but also of these realms.
† Following the decisions taken by the Commonwealth Ministerial Action Group on 31 July 2009, Fiji Islands was suspended from membership on 1 September 2009. ‡ Nauru is a Member in Arrears (i.e., it has not contributed to the Commonwealth Secretariat's funds) and, as such, does not benefit from technical assistance from the Secretariat and cannot attend the Heads of Government meeting.

Establishment & Faith

Once you touch the trappings of monarchy, like opening
an Egyptian tomb, the inside is liable to crumble.
— ANTHONY SAMPSON (1926–2004)

---------------------------- THE SOVEREIGN ----------------------------

ELIZABETH II
by the Grace of God, of the United Kingdom of Great Britain
and Northern Ireland and of her other Realms and Territories Queen,
Head of the Commonwealth, Defender of the Faith

Born at 17 Bruton Street, London W1, on 21 April 1926, at *c.*2:40am
Ascended the throne, 6 February 1952 · Crowned 2 June 1953

In August, *Jeeves.com* said that one of the most popular celebrity searches concerned the Queen's age.

---------------------------- ROYAL FLICKR ----------------------------

In June 2010, Buckingham Palace opened an account on photo-sharing site Flickr. The website – flickr.com/photos/britishmonarchy – contains thousands of archive images, as well as regularly updated shots of the Royal family 'at work'.

---------------------- THE ROYAL ORDER OF SUCCESSION ----------------------

Sovereign · The Prince of Wales · Prince William of Wales · Prince Henry of Wales · The Duke of York · Princess Beatrice of York · Princess Eugenie of York · The Earl of Wessex · Viscount Severn · The Lady Louise Windsor · The Princess Royal · Mr Peter Phillips · Miss Zara Phillips · Viscount Linley · The Hon Charles Armstrong-Jones · The Hon Margarita Armstrong-Jones · The Lady Sarah Chatto · Master Samuel Chatto · Master Arthur Chatto · The Duke of Gloucester · The Earl of Ulster · Lord Culloden · The Lady Davina Lewis · The Lady Rose Windsor · The Duke of Kent · The Lady Amelia Windsor · The Lady Helen Taylor · Master Columbus Taylor · Master Cassius Taylor · Miss Eloise Taylor · Miss Estella Taylor · The Lord Frederick Windsor · The Lady Gabriella Windsor · Princess Alexandra, the Hon. Lady Ogilvy · Mr James Ogilvy · Master Alexander Ogilvy · Miss Flora Ogilvy · Miss Marina Ogilvy · Master Christian Mowatt · Miss Zenouska Mowatt · The Earl of Harewood

The eldest son of the monarch is heir to the throne followed by his heirs, after whom come any other sons of the monarch and their heirs, followed by any daughters of the monarch and their heirs. Roman Catholics are barred from succession under the Act of Settlement (1701).

ROYAL GREENWICH

As part of the preparations for her Diamond Jubilee [see below], in January 2010, the Queen bestowed the status of Royal Borough upon Greenwich, London, to take effect in 2012. The then President of the Privy Council, Lord Mandelson, declared: 'This rare honour is to be bestowed in recognition of the historically close links forged between Greenwich and our Royal family, from the Middle Ages to the present day, and the Borough's global significance as the home of the Prime Meridian, Greenwich Mean Time, and a UNESCO World Heritage Site.' Greenwich will become the fourth Royal Borough, after Windsor & Maidenhead [in 1277]; Kensington & Chelsea [in 1901]; and Kingston-upon-Thames [in 1927]. (In 1963, the Welsh Borough of Caernarvon was made a Royal Borough; it subsequently became the Royal Town of Caernarvon.) The status of Royal Borough is purely honorific, and confers no additional powers.

ROYAL CHOCOLATE

Cadbury manufactures unique bars of chocolate for the Royal family, according to a December 2009 report in the *Daily Mail*. The secret recipe, apparently tailored to the Queen's taste, 'is said to contain more cocoa solids than many other dark chocolates, making it ideal for both eating and cooking'. Indeed, the chocolate is labelled simply 'CADBURY'S SUPERIOR CULINARY DARK CHOCOLATE'. The *Mail* reported that only three or four batches of 'Royal Household chocolate' are made each year – on specially dedicated production equipment. A Cadbury spokesman told the newspaper: 'We do make the Queen a bar of dark chocolate. It's not for sale to the public. We make this for her, under the terms of the royal mark. ... We've been providing chocolates to the Royal family since Victorian times but I cannot discuss the recipe.'

DIAMOND JUBILEE

Celebrations for Queen Elizabeth II's Diamond Jubilee will take place around the first week of June, 2012, according to Buckingham Palace and the Dept. for Culture, Media, and Sport. The Diamond Jubilee will mark 60 years of the Queen's reign: she ascended the throne in 1952, although her Coronation took place in 1953. The Queen celebrated her Silver Jubilee [25 years] in 1977 and her Golden Jubilee [50 years] in 2002. The only other British monarch to celebrate a Diamond Jubilee was Queen Victoria, in 1897. To mark the Diamond Jubilee, the late spring bank holiday will be delayed until Tuesday 5 June, and a special bank holiday will be declared on Monday 4 June – creating a 4-day weekend. (According to the OED, the word jubilee derives from the Latin words *jubilum* – a wild cry – and *jubilare* – to shout, halloo, huzza, &c.)

AUSTRALIAN REPUBLICANISM

Australia's PM Julia Gillard caused a ripple of controversy in August 2010, when she suggested that the Queen's death would be an 'appropriate time' for Australia to become a republic. Gillard, who was speaking days before a tight general election, added, 'obviously I'm hoping for Queen Elizabeth that she lives a long and happy life, and having watched her mother I think there's every chance that she will'.

———————————————— ROYAL FINANCES ————————————————

The Queen receives income from public funds to meet expenditure that relates to her duties as Head of State and the Commonwealth. This derives from 4 sources:

Source (year ending 31 March)	2009	2010
The Queen's Civil List†	£13·9m	£14·2m
Parliamentary Annuities	£0·4m	£0·4m
Grants-in-Aid	£22·6m	£19·7m
Expenditure met directly by Government Departments and the Crown Estate	£4·6m	£3·9m
TOTAL	£41·5m	£38·2m

† Figures are for 2008–09. ❦ Reporting the above figures, Buckingham Palace noted: 'Head of State support reduced for 2009–10 by more than £3 million – a decrease in real terms of 12·2%. ... This cut is due mainly to a reduction in commercial charter flights and a refund of lease rentals arising from the sale of The Queen's helicopter, which was replaced last year. ... The Treasury contributed the equivalent of just 62 pence per person in the country to enable The Queen to carry out her duties as Head of State. ... The Royal Household is acutely aware of the difficult economic climate and took early action to reduce its Civil List expenditure by 2·5% in real terms in 2009. We are implementing a headcount freeze and reviewing every vacancy to see if we can avoid replacement.'

——————————— ROYAL FAMILY ENGAGEMENTS · 2009 ———————————

Mr Tim O'Donovan annually compiles a list of official engagements undertaken by the Royal family during the year – as reported in the pages of the Court Circular – which is subsequently published as a letter to *The Times*. Below is 2009's listing:

	Official visits, openings, &c.	Receptions, lunches, dinners, &c.	Other, e.g., investitures, meetings	Total official engagements UK	Total official engagements abroad
The Queen	105	62	188	355	20
Duke of Edinburgh	140	134	52	326	21
Prince of Wales	163	94	163	420	109
Duchess of Cornwall	118	41	20	179	78
Duke of York	81	61	103	245	280
Earl of Wessex	112	50	45	207	134
Countess of Wessex	77	35	27	139	29
Princess Royal	305	113	80	498	75
Duke of Gloucester	156	36	42	234	8
Duchess of Gloucester	82	28	18	128	2
Duke of Kent	164	30	14	208	26
Princess Alexandra	66	27	15	109	2

Prince William carried out 30 official engagements and Prince Harry 16, including 8 overseas.

———————— MONARCHY & TOURISM ————————

Britain's monarchy generates >£500 million a year, directly and indirectly, from overseas tourists, according to July 2010 data from VisitBritain. This figure is expected to soar during the Queen's Jubilee Year in 2012 [see p.275]. Below are the most popular 'monarchy related' attractions – ranked by visitor numbers in 2009:

Attraction	visits	charge/free	±%
Tower of London	2,389,548	C	+11
National Maritime Museum, Greenwich	2,367,904	F	+15
Victoria and Albert Museum, London	2,269,880	F	+10
St Paul's Cathedral	1,821,321	F/C	+8
Westminster Abbey	1,449,593	F/C	−2
Edinburgh Castle	1,196,481	C	+6
Windsor Castle	987,000	C	+6
Leeds Castle	646,801	C	+12
Hampton Court Palace	541,646	C	+10
Portsmouth Historic Dockyard	532,158	F/C	−5
Buckingham Palace	402,000	C	+2
V&A Museum of Childhood, London	387,823	F	+10
Stirling Castle	383,293	C	+2
Dover Castle	304,513	C	+4
Urquhart Castle, Loch Ness	282,203	F/C	+4
Kensington Palace	272,606	C	+11
Royal Armouries	271,513	F	+3
HMS Belfast, London	260,423	C	+7
Osborne House, Isle of Wight	238,931	C	+10
The Palace of Holyroodhouse	237,000	C	+9
Castle Howard, Yorkshire	232,871	C	+15
Penrhyn Castle, Llandygai	228,820	F/C	+22

——————— FERGIE & THE NEWS OF THE WORLD ———————

On 23/5/2010, the *News of the World* published details of a 'sting operation' against Sarah Ferguson, the Duchess of York, during which, for £500,000, she appeared to offer to introduce a 'businessman' to her former husband, Prince Andrew, the UK's special representative for trade and investment. The Duchess of York was filmed accepting a cash payment of $40,000, and saying, 'look after me and he'll look after you … you'll get it back tenfold. I can open any door you want'. In the aftermath of the exposé, Buckingham Palace 'categorically' denied that Prince Andrew had any knowledge of his ex-wife's actions – a position supported by the Duchess, who apologised for 'a serious lapse in judgement'. Some days later, Ferguson appeared on Oprah Winfrey's US talk show, where, in a somewhat confused confessional, she claimed to have been motivated by a desire to find $38,000 for a friend. However, the Duchess also admitted that she had been drinking at the time of the sting and said, 'I think I've been like a huge over-trusting, idiotic, stupid woman'.

—————— THE QUEEN'S CHRISTMAS BROADCAST · 2009 ——————

'Each year that passes seems to have its own character. Some leave us with a feeling of satisfaction, others are best forgotten. 2009 was a difficult year for many, in particular those facing the continuing effects of the economic downturn. ❦ I am sure that we have all been affected by events in Afghanistan and saddened by the casualties suffered by our forces serving there. Our thoughts go out to their relations and friends who have shown immense dignity in the face of great personal loss. But, we can be proud of the positive contribution that our servicemen and women are making, in conjunction with our allies. Well over 13,000 soldiers from the United Kingdom, and across the Commonwealth – Canada, Australia, New Zealand and Singapore – are currently serving in Afghanistan. The debt of gratitude owed to these young men and women, and to their predecessors, is indeed profound. ❦ It is 60 years since the Commonwealth was created and today, with more than a billion of its members under the age of 25, the organisation remains a strong and practical force for good. ... For many, the practical assistance and networks of the Commonwealth can give skills, lend advice and encourage enterprise. It is inspiring to learn of some of the work being done by these young people, who bring creativity and innovation to the challenges they face. ... The Commonwealth is not an organisation with a mission. It is rather an opportunity for its people to work together to achieve practical solutions to problems. In many aspects of our lives, whether in sport, the environment, business or culture, the Commonwealth connection remains vivid and enriching. It is, in lots of ways, the face of the future. And with continuing support and dedication, I am confident that this diverse Commonwealth of nations can strengthen the common bond that transcends politics, religion, race and economic circumstances. ❦ We know that Christmas is a time for celebration and family reunions; but it is also a time to reflect on what confronts those less fortunate than ourselves, at home and throughout the world. Christians are taught to love their neighbours, having compassion and concern, and being ready to undertake charity and voluntary work to ease the burden of deprivation and disadvantage. We may ourselves be confronted by a bewildering array of difficulties and challenges, but we must never cease to work for a better future for ourselves and for others. ❦ I wish you all, wherever you may be, a very happy Christmas.

2009 was a difficult year for many, in particular those facing the continuing effects of the economic downturn.

When the Queen's Christmas broadcast is entered into Microsoft Word's 'Auto Summarise' feature and is condensed down to two sentences, the result is:

Recently I attended the Commonwealth Heads of Government Meeting in Trinidad and Tobago and heard how important the Commonwealth is to young people. For many, the practical assistance and networks of the Commonwealth can give skills, lend advice and encourage enterprise.

—— ROYAL GIFTS RECEIVED ON OVERSEAS TOURS ——

In January 2010, Clarence House published the official gifts received by the Prince of Wales and the Duchess of Cornwall while on overseas official visits during 2009:

{Chile} Prince of Wales Country Club Tie; Framed reproduction of traditional Mapuche silver jewellery; Shield; Sample of wood; pair of cuff links; Rose gold box; Leather photograph album; 3 bottles of red wine; Framed photograph; Brochure on SWM wood; Set of 6 silver & lapis lazuli tea spoons; 2 crates teabags, toiletries, snacks. {Brazil} Watercolour; Beaded necklace; Pestle & mortar; Brown leather & wild rubber bag; Brazilian football shirt; Ceramic dish; Plaque; Canvas bag; Jar of honey; Raffia basket with 3 T-shirts, poster, blowpipe; Certificate; Wild rubber embroidered sheet, folder; Wooden box, folder; Wild rubber hat; Photograph album made from tree-free paper; Folder; Box of jams & chocolates; Wild rubber satchel; Silver & leather necklace & earring set; Native Spa products; T-shirt; Bouquet of flowers; Wild rubber handbag, raffia handbag; Pink hat & handbag made from recycled bottles; 3 T-shirts; Model of Santa Claus; Plastic photograph holder; 3 raffia baskets of sweets & chocolates; Raffia basket with 2 T-shirts, poster, necklace; Box of jams & chocolates; Wild rubber satchel; Silver & leather necklace & earring set; Native Spa products; T-shirt; Bouquet of flowers; Wild rubber handbag, raffia handbag; Pink hat & handbag made from recycled bottles; 3 T-shirts [yes, ×2: one each]; Woven table mats & napkins; Guitar, wooden bowl; Box of personalised stationery; Wooden fruit bowl; 3 rubber samples; Silver tray; Ceramic model of a bride & groom riding a bull; Set of silver coffee spoons; 2 pamphlets; Box of chocolates; Ceramic model of a man cooking over a fire; Box of biscuits & chocolates; Pamphlet; T-shirt; Wild rubber & raffia bag; Necklace; 2 keyrings; Wooden box; Wild rubber satchel; Raffia basket; Wooden box; 2 calendars; 2 Panama DVDs; Panama hat; Folder & CD; Red tie; T-shirt; Baseball hat; Bottle of Churchill's 1985 vintage port; Panama hat; Floppy hat; Cream hat; Silver brooch; 2 embroidered handkerchiefs; Onyx model of a turtle; Wooden carving of a seal & cub; Framed relief of a blue-footed boobie bird; 2 plastic flags; 4 T-shirts; Framed painting; 2 canvas bags of Galapagos coffee; 2 polo shirts. {Italy} 3 silver commemorative coins; Leg of prosciutto ham; Framed print; Map of Wales; Framed photograph; Glass vase; Official Annual gold medal of the year III of the Pope Benedict XVI; Portfolio; Papal rosaries; 2 scrolls; Murano glass model of an anchor; Selection of colour photographs; Wooden shield with crest; Necklace; Gold ring; Glass vase. {Germany} German Sustainability Award; Fairtrade football; T-shirt; Football pennant; Framed photograph; Framed photograph. {Canada} Ceramic teapot, wooden tray, & tea caddy; 3 certificates; Birthday card; Box of organic chocolates; Business card holder; 2 booklets; BlackBerry 9500; Limited edition commemorative coin: Toronto Scottish Regiment; Limited edition commemorative coin: The Royal Regiment of Canada; Cashmere scarf; Blue hooded jumper; Wood & amethyst pin brooch; Hard hat; Birthday card; Basket of biscuits & jar of damson jam; Gift packet: Teas; Swiss cheese; Jar of organic cider; Cloth bag, apron; Selection of jams & maple syrup; Booklet; Black & white photographs & correspondence; Blue & grey Vancouver Winter Olympics branded scarf, 2 pairs of red woollen mittens; Carved 'Talking Stick'; Indigenous headdress; Samples of watercolours & letter; Bottle of Victoria Gin; Information pack & lapel pin: Keroul; Pair of cast glass sculptures; 2 paperweights; 2010 Calendar: *Island Paradise*; Birthday card; Wooden box: 'Royal Canadian Dragoons'; Blazer badge; Cuff links & shirt studs; Framed photograph; Pin badges; CD; Pen; Green wicker basket: Selection of honey, maple syrup, & boxed metal badges; Inuit tapestry: *Brother & Sister of The Moon*; Carved 'Talking Stick'; Stretched canvas: *Autumn Feast*; Blanket; Embroidered pillowcase; Soapstone sculpture of an otter; Wooden box of herbal tea; Leather pouch; CDs; CD: *Cape Breton Symposium*; Calendar; Note cards; Wine; Booklet; Polar bear soft toy, seal cub soft toy; Pink & lilac hand-knitted jumpers; Framed photograph; CD; Textile wall hanging; Ceramic mug: *TRH's Royal Wedding 8-4-2005*; BlackBerry 9500; 3 CD's; Booklet; 2 commemorative white metal discs; Pin brooch: Toronto Scottish Regiment; Pin brooch: The Royal Regiment of Canada; Limited edition commemorative coin: The Royal Regiment of Canada; Cashmere wrap; Limited edition commemorative coin: Toronto Scottish Regiment; Ceramic plate; Ceramic pot; Necklace & earrings; Certificate; Painting on stone: *Dundurn Castle*; Street sign; Information pack; Fascinator; Vancouver Winter Olympics branded thermos flask; Black umbrella; Black crocheted scarf; Pale blue & white Vancouver Winter Olympics branded scarf; 2 pairs of red woollen mittens; Indigenous headdress; 'Safe Hip' garment; Greetings card; Ceramic sculpture: Polar bear; Children's black saddle; Boxed stone sculpture: *High Kick*; Framed lithograph; 2 sepia posters; Tartan tie & shawl with 2 pin badges on red inscribed book marks; Cotton embroidered pouch: 6 packets of seeds; Framed etching; Framed photograph; Illustrator's information pack; 3 ceramic plates; Painting: *Dundurn Castle* [sic]; photograph album & greetings card; Chocolate fondue set; Purple bag: 5 bibs, wrist bands, 2 baby jumpers, packets of poppy seeds; Framed portrait: TRH The Prince of Wales & The Duchess of Cornwall; Homemade greetings card; Musquram design blanket; Set of pictured correspondence cards; British Columbian stone & carved wooden eagle; 2 blankets; Photograph; Correspondence cards & poem; CD; Cowichan sweaters; Colour photographs; Greetings card; Business & greetings card; Green stone sculpture; Bronze sculpture: *L'homme De La Paix*; 2 signed prints; Welcome greetings card; Selection of clothing; 2 bags of Vancouver Winter Olympics branded clothing; Food hamper; Cirque du Soleil memorabilia; 2 masks & stands; 2 watercolour paintings; Hooded top, baseball cap, 2 T-shirts: Canadian Rangers (2 sets, for William & Harry); as well as some 93 unidentified books, and more than 20 unidentified DVDs.

——————— WHO'S NEW IN WHO'S WHO ———————

Published annually since 1849, *Who's Who* is one of the world's most respected bio-graphical reference books. Below are some of the *c.*1,000 new entries in the 2010 *Who's Who* (those who have died during the year enter the companion *Who Was Who*):

Katherine Allenby...............*athlete*
Sara Arber....................*sociologist*
Mark Avery.......*director, conservation,
                                      RSPB*
Amanda Berry.. *chief executive, BAFTA*
Ivor Braka....................*art dealer*
Anthony Buzan .. *founder Buzan World*
Tanya Byron.........*clinical psychologist*
Margaret Chan. *director-general, WHO*
Sarah Chang ....*violinist*
Paulo Coelho....................*writer*
Jason Cowley.... *editor, New Statesman*
Declan Donnelly.... *television presenter*
Penelope Dyer. *voice & dialect specialist*
Alan Edwards ....*publicist*
Martin Elliott ....*cardiothoracic surgeon*
Roger Federer ....*tennis player*
Robert Flowerdew ....
                      horticultural consultant
Anna Friel.........................*actress*
Ricky Gervais ....*comedian & writer*
Liam Gillick.......................*artist*
Edward (Bear) Grylls .... *adventurer*
Mary Hammond........*singing teacher*
Ivan Harbour..................*architect*
Valentine (Ruthie) Henshall..... *actress*
Ian Hutchings..*manufacturing engineer*
Conn Iggulden...................*writer*
Isobel (Chrissie) Iles ....*curator*
Alison Jarvis....*management consultant*
Andrew Jefford....*broadcaster & writer*

Robert Joseph...............*wine expert*
Richard Klein .....*controller, BBC Four*
Jeff Koons ....*artist*
Felicity Lawrence.............*journalist*
Trevor Leighton...........*photographer*
Valerie Lund ....*rhinologist*
Jonathan Mant..*primary care researcher*
John Mather...............*astrophysicist*
Anthony McPartlin . *television presenter*
Mohamed Nasheed *President, Maldives*
Cathy Newman ...*Channel 4 journalist*
Michelle Ogundehin...*magazine editor*
Neil Oliver ....*broadcaster & writer*
John Oxford...................*virologist*
Orhan Pamuk.....................*writer*
Jennifer Plane-Te Paa ....*theologian*
Jeremy Rawkins...................*judge*
Margaret (Meg) Rosoff ....*writer*
Dorothy Rowe ....*psychologist*
Stephan Shakespeare....................
                      co-founder, YouGov
Keith Shine....... *physical meteorologist*
Mark Stephens ....*broadcaster & writer*
Claire (Samantha) Taylor ......*cricketer*
Sophie Thomas.................*designer*
Jennifer Ullman......*landscape designer*
Susan Ward.......... *immigration judge*
Edward Watson ....*dancer, Royal Ballet*
Robert Woods................*economist*
Marina Yannakoudakis ....*politician*
Nadhim Zahawi.... *co-founder, YouGov*

A few recreations: IVOR BRAKA 'impersonating Alice Cooper' · ANTHONY BUZAN 'breeding three-spined sticklebacks' · IAN HUTCHINGS 'not gardening' · ROBERT JOSEPH 'travel, photography, cooking, collecting irony, tortoise husbandry' · JONATHAN MANT 'amassing unread novels, untidy desks, Tintin memorabilia' · NEIL OLIVER 'drinking tea, drinking wine, fantasising about one day moving the whole family to a small holding' · JEREMY RAWKINS 'spending frequent days in hot pursuit of sea and freshwater fish and endlessly analysing the reasons for absence of success' · MARGARET ROSOFF 'horse riding, misplacing things' · MARK STEPHENS 'bees, badinage and dandyism' · SOPHIE THOMAS 'collecting plastic flotsam, screen printing, growing vegetables, cheating at crosswords'

SOME HONOURS OF NOTE · 2010

New Year Honours

KNIGHT BACHELOR
Nicholas Hytner .... director
Patrick Stewart .... actor

DBE
Claire Bertschinger.... nurse & activist

CBE
Sarah Connolly .... opera singer
George Daniels.............. horologist
Peter Donohoe .... pianist
George Ferguson .... architect
Maggi Hambling... painter & sculptor
Dyfrig John .... banker
Phyllida Lloyd .... director
Tessa Ross .... Channel 4 executive
Margaret Tyzack .... actor

OBE
Craig Armstrong .... composer
Gareth Hoskins .... architect
Stephen Jones .... milliner
Michelle Mone .... businesswoman
David Nixon .... choreographer
Rick Parfitt .... musician
Francis Rossi .... musician
Dick King-Smith................. writer

MBE
Mohammed Aslam................. chef
Norman Barrett ...... circus ringmaster
Luella Bartley .... designer
Jenson Button............. racing driver
Lauren Child....... writer & illustrator
Timothy Everest .... tailor
Rose Gray .... restaurateur
Anna Hemmings.............. canoeist
Catherine Kidston .... designer
Catriona Matthew .... golfer
Maurice Murphy............. trumpeter
Ruth Rogers............... restaurateur
Lemn Sissay...................... writer
(Samantha) Claire Taylor ..... cricketer
Elizabeth Tweddle............ gymnast

Queen's Birthday Honours

KNIGHT BACHELOR
(Theodore) Wilson Harris .... writer
Ronald Harwood .... writer
Donald Insall................. architect

DBE
Paula Rego .... artist

CBE
George Benjamin .... composer
Catherine Zeta Jones.............. actor
Prudence Leith............. food writer
Robin Millar .... record producer
Harold Tillman .... businessman

OBE
Brian Clemens .... screenwriter
Wendy Cope .... poet
Bonnie Greer................ playwright
Nick Knight.............. photographer
Anthony (Tony) McCoy........ jockey
John Nettles...................... actor
Julian Pettifer................. journalist

MBE
David Coulthard.......... racing driver
Eileen Derbyshire................. actor
Fred Dinenage .... TV presenter
Michael Garrick.............. musician
Lubaina Himid................... artist
Mike Ingham.... football commentator
Anne Reid........................ actor
Amy Williams........... skeleton racer

979 people were honoured in the New Year Honours list, 441 (45%) of whom were women. 6% of those honoured were from ethnic minorities. 73% were commended for work in their local community. In the Queen's Birthday Honours 975 people were rewarded, 47% of whom were women. 7·3% came from ethnic minorities. 10% of honours went to those working in education. Health accounted for 9% of the awards. Sport made up 3% of the total.

— REMEMBRANCE SUNDAY · CENOTAPH CEREMONY —

Although services marking Remembrance Sunday (the second Sunday in November) are held across the world, the focus of British mourning is the Cenotaph in Whitehall. Here, the Royal family is joined by the country's political, spiritual, and military leaders – as well as *c.*45 High Commissioners, *c.*7,500 ex-Service men and women, and *c.*1,600 civilians. At 11:03, after the Two Minutes' Silence and the Last Post, 63 wreaths are laid on the top and bottom steps of the Portland stone memorial in a carefully choreographed (and rigidly ranked) display. The Queen lays her wreath first. Below is a schematic of the order and position of wreaths at the 2009 service:

THE CENOTAPH

Designed by Sir Edwin Lutyens at the request of PM, Lloyd George, the Cenotaph (*kenos* [empty] and *taphos* [tomb] in Greek) was originally the temporary centrepiece for a victory parade in July 1919. However, the sombre elegance of Lutyens' geometry endeared his construction to the British public, and later that year it was decided to make the Cenotaph a permanent memorial to the 'Glorious Dead' of WWI.

Letters refer to members of the Royal family, numbers to other dignitaries; see key opposite. Italic characters indicate where each person stands, bold roman characters the position of each wreath.

—————— REMEMBRANCE SUNDAY · CENOTAPH cont. ——————

The Royal family

A.................................. HM The Queen
B.................HRH The Duke Of Edinburgh
C................HRH Prince Henry Of Wales†
D ....HRH Prince William Of Wales
E.......................HRH The Duke Of York
F.......................HRH The Earl Of Wessex
G ....HRH The Princess Royal
H ....HRH The Duke Of Kent
★................................ Equerries In Waiting

Politics

1 ....The Prime Minister
2 .... Leader of the Opposition
3 ....Leader of the Liberal Democrats
4 .....Leader of the Democratic Unionist Party
5 .. Representative of the Scottish Nationalists‡
6 .... SoS Foreign And Commonwealth Affairs
7 .....The Speaker of the House Of Commons
8 ....The Lord Speaker
9 ....SoS For Culture, Media And Sport
10. Former Prime Ministers; Cabinet Ministers
    & Other Ministers; The Mayor Of London

High Commissioners or their representatives

11 ....Canada
12 ....Australia
13 .... New Zealand
14 .... South Africa
15 ....India
16 ....Pakistan
17 ....Sri Lanka
18 ....Ghana
19 ....Malaysia
20 ....Cyprus
21 ....Nigeria
22 ....Sierra Leone
23 ....Tanzania
24 ....Jamaica
25 ....Trinidad & Tobago
26 ....Uganda
27 ....Kenya
28 ....Malawi
29 ....Malta
30 ....Zambia
31 ....The Gambia

32 ....Maldives
33 ....Singapore
34 ....Guyana
35 ....Botswana
36 ....Lesotho
37 ....Barbados
38 ....Mauritius
39 ....Swaziland
40 ....Tonga
41 ....Fiji
42 ....Bangladesh
43 ....Bahamas
44 ....Grenada
45 ....Papua New Guinea
46 ....Commonwealth of Dominica
47 ....St Lucia
48 ....St Vincent & The Grenadines
49 ....Belize
50 ....Antigua & Barbuda
51 .... St Christopher & Nevis
52 ....Brunei
53 ....Namibia
54 ....Cameroon
55 ....Mozambique

Military &c

56 ....Chief of the Defence Staff
57 ....Chief of the Naval Staff
58 ....Chief of the General Staff
59 ....Chief of the Air Staff
60 ....Merchant Navy and Fishing Fleets
61 ....Merchant Air Service
62 .... HM Chief of Constabulary
    – on behalf of the civilian services

Religious

63 ....Members of Faith Communities
64 .... The Bishop of London
65 .... The Chaplain-General, the Sub-Dean of
    Her Majesty's Chapels Royal and the Choir

† Laid a wreath on behalf of the Prince of
Wales who was on an official visit to Canada. ❦
Only leaders of parties with ≥6 parliamentary
seats lay wreaths. ‡ On behalf of Plaid Cymru/
SNP Parliamentary group. [Source: DCMS]

AN ELEMENTARY GUIDE TO FORMS OF ADDRESS

Personage	envelope	start of letter	verbal address
The Queen	The Queen's Most Excellent Majesty[†]	Madam/May it please your Majesty	Your Majesty/Ma'am
The Duke of Edinburgh	HRH The Duke of Edinburgh[†]	Sir	Your Royal Highness/Sir
The Queen Mother	Her Majesty Queen ——— The Queen Mother[†]	Madam	Your Majesty/Ma'am
Royal Prince	HRH The Prince ——— (The Prince of ———)[†]	Sir	Your Royal Highness/Sir
Royal Princess	HRH The Princess (of) ———[†]	Your Royal Highness	Your Royal Highness/Madam
Royal Duke	HRH The Duke of ———[†]	Your Royal Highness	Your Royal Highness/Sir
Royal Duchess	HRH The Duchess of ———[†]	Your Royal Highness	Your Royal Highness/Madam
Duke	His Grace The Duke of ———	My Lord Duke/Dear Duke	Your Grace/Duke
Duchess	Her Grace The Duchess of ———	Dear Madam/Dear Duchess	Your Grace/Duchess
Marquess	The Most Honourable The Marquess of ———	My Lord/Dear Lord	My Lord/Lord
Marchioness	The Most Honourable The Marchioness of ———	Madam/Dear Lady	Madam/Lady
Earl	The Rt Hon. The Earl of ———	My Lord/Dear Lord	My Lord/Lord
Earl's wife	The Rt Hon. The Countess of ———	Madam/Dear Lady	Madam/Lady
Countess	The Rt Hon. The Countess of ———	Madam/Dear Lady	Madam/Lady
Viscount	The Rt Hon. The Viscount ———	My Lord/Dear Lord	Lord
Viscount's wife	The Rt Hon. The Viscountess ———	Madam/Dear Lady	Lady
Baron	The Rt Hon. Lord ———	My Lord/Dear Lord	Lord
Baron's wife	The Rt Hon. Lady ———	My Lady/Dear Lady	Lady
Baroness	The Rt Hon. The Lady (*or* The Baroness) ———	My Lady/Dear Lady	Madam/Lady
Baronet	Sir Bertie Wooster Bt (*or* Bart)	Dear Sir Bertie	Sir Bertie
Baronet's wife	Lady ———	Dear Madam/Dear Lady	Lady
Knight of an Order	Sir Bertie Wooster (*and order*)	Dear Sir Bertie	Sir Bertie
Knight Bachelor	Sir Bertie Wooster	Dear Sir Bertie	Sir Bertie
Knight's wife	Lady ———	Dear Madam/Dear Lady	Lady
Dame	Dame ———	Dear Madam/Dear Dame	Dame

—— AN ELEMENTARY GUIDE TO FORMS OF ADDRESS cont. ——

Personage	envelope	start of letter	verbal address
Life Peer	The Rt Hon. Lord —— (of ——)	My Lord/Dear Lord ——	Lord ——
Life Peeress	The Rt Hon. The Lady (or Baroness) —— (of ——)	My Lady/Dear Lady ——	Lady ——
Archbishop	The Most Rev. & Rt Hon. The Lord Archbishop of ——	Dear Archbishop ——	Your Grace/Archbishop
Bishop	((The Rt Rev.) (and Right Hon.)) The Bishop of ——	Dear Bishop	Bishop
Lord Chancellor	The Rt Hon. The Lord Chancellor	by rank	by rank
Prime Minister	The Rt Hon. The Prime Minister PC MP	Dear Prime Minister	Prime Minister/Sir
Deputy PM	The Rt Hon. The Deputy Prime Minister PC MP	Dear Deputy Prime Minister	Deputy Prime Minister/Sir
Chancellor of the Exchequer	The Rt Hon. The Chancellor of the Exchequer PC MP	Dear Chancellor	Chancellor/Sir
Foreign Secretary	The Rt Hon. The SoS for Foreign & Comwlth Affairs.	Dear Foreign Secretary	Foreign Secretary/by rank
Home Secretary	The Rt Hon. The SoS for the Home Department	Dear Home Secretary	Home Secretary/by rank
Secretary of State	The Rt Hon. The SoS for ——	Dear Secretary of State.	Secretary of State/by rank
Minister	(The Rt Hon.) Bertie Wooster Esq. (PC) MP	Dear Minister	Minister/by rank
MP†	Bertie Wooster Esq. MP	Dear Mr Wooster.	Mr Wooster
MP Privy Councillor	The Rt Hon. Bertie Wooster PC MP	Dear Mr Wooster.	Mr Wooster
Privy Councillor	The Rt Hon. Bertie Wooster PC	Dear Mr Wooster.	Mr Wooster
High Court Judge	The Hon. Mr Justice ——	Dear Sir ——/Dear Judge	Sir/My Lord/Your Lordship
Ambassador (British)	His Excellency —— HM Ambassador to ——	by rank	Your Excellency
Lord Mayor	The Rt Hon. The Lord Mayor of ——	My (Dear) Lord Mayor	Lord Mayor
Mayor	The Worshipful Mayor of ——	(Dear) Mr Mayor.	Mr Mayor

It is hard to overstate the complexity of 'correct' form which (especially in the legal and clerical fields, as well as chivalry) can become extremely rococo, and is the subject of considerable dispute between sources. Consequently, the above tabulation can only hope to provide a very elementary guide. ☞ Readers interested in the correct formal styling of the wives of younger sons of earls, for example, are advised to consult specialist texts on the subject. † It is usual to address correspondence to members of the Royal family in the first instance to their Private Secretary. ‡ A similar styling is used for Members of the European Parliament [MEP]; Scottish Parliament [MSP]; National Assembly for Wales [AM]; and Northern Ireland Assembly [MLA]. From the moment Parliament is dissolved there are no Members of Parliament, and consequently the letters MP should not be used. By convention medical doctors are styled Dr ——, whereas surgeons use the title Mr ——; many gynaecologists, although surgeons, are styled Dr ——.

———————— THE UK SUPREME COURT ————————

On 1 October 2009, the Supreme Court of the United Kingdom came into existence and, in replacing the Appellate Committee of the House of Lords, became the highest court in the land. Established through Part 3 of the Constitutional Reform Act 2005, the Supreme Court hears *criminal* appeal cases from England, Wales, and N Ireland, and *civil* appeal cases from England, Wales, N Ireland, and Scotland. (The High Court of Judiciary remains the ultimate court of appeal in *Scottish criminal* law. The Supreme Court also took over the devolution jurisdiction of the Judicial Committee of the Privy Council [JCPC] as it relates to Scotland, N Ireland, and Wales – although the JCPC remains the final court of appeal for certain Commonwealth countries, as well as Crown Dependencies, &c.) ❦ Below are the first 12 Supreme Court justices – 11 men, and one woman. Most cases will be heard by five judges, though the most consequential will involve nine.

The Right Hon the Lord Phillips of Worth Matravers (President)
The Right Hon the Lord Hope of Craighead (Deputy President)
The Right Hon the Lord Saville of Newdigate
The Right Hon the Lord Rodger of Earlsferry
The Right Hon the Lord Walker of Gestingthorpe
The Right Hon the Baroness Hale of Richmond
The Right Hon the Lord Brown of Eaton-under-Heywood
The Right Hon the Lord Mance
The Right Hon the Lord Collins of Mapesbury
The Right Hon the Lord Kerr of Tonaghmore
The Right Hon the Lord Clarke of Stone-cum-Ebony
The Right Hon Sir John Anthony Dyson†

Although the creation of the Supreme Court had little dramatic impact on the actual judicial process, the abolition of the Appellate Committee in favour of an independent court had significant constitutional ramifications, as Lord Phillips noted: 'This is the last step in the separation of powers in this country. We have come to it fairly gently and gradually, but we have come to the point where the judges are completely separated from the legislature and executive.' ('Fairly gently and gradually' was an elegant understatement: until 2009, the Law Lords had sat within Parliament since 1399.) ❦ The Supreme Court is located in Middlesex Guildhall – an early C20th neo-Gothic mass of Portland stone which stands on Parliament Square opposite the Palace of Westminster. This central position, close to but separate from the two other constitutional branches, was selected in part to emphasise a new era of independence. As Lord Bingham of Cornhill said in 2003, 'The creation of a Supreme Court is driven by the need for transparency and clarity in our constitutional arrangements. Its setting should reflect the public right to come and see an institution which belongs to them, in action'. This desire for accessibility was behind the decision to open the court to the public and, for the first time in British legal history, to television cameras. The then Justice Secretary, Jack Straw, observed: 'In this place we now have this court – public, accessible, visible – situated in this square at the heart of our nation's history over a millennium.'

† Sworn in on 19·4·10, filling a vacancy left by Lord Neuberger's appointment to Master of the Rolls.

—————————— THE JUDICIAL OATH ——————————

When judges are sworn in, they take the Oath of Allegiance and the Judicial Oath:

I, ____ , do swear by Almighty God that I will be faithful and bear true allegiance to Her Majesty Queen Elizabeth the Second, her heirs and successors, according to law.

I, ____ , do swear by Almighty God that I will well and truly serve our Sovereign Lady Queen Elizabeth the Second in the office of ____ , and I will do right to all manner of people after the laws and usages of this realm, without fear or favour, affection or ill will.

Most forms of religious belief can be incorporated into these two oaths, for example: Hindus may use the words, 'I swear by Gita', Muslims the words, 'I swear by Allah', and Sikhs the words, 'I swear by Guru Nanak'. Judges may also elect to affirm.

————— CRACKED, INEFFECTIVE, & VACATED TRIALS —————

CRACKED TRIAL · When, on the date of the trial, a defendant offers acceptable pleas or the prosecution offers no evidence. A cracked trial requires no further court time, but as a consequence the time allocated has been wasted, and witnesses have been unnecessarily inconvenienced thus impacting confidence in the system.

INEFFECTIVE TRIAL · When, on the day, a trial does not proceed because of action or inaction by one of the parties and a further trial date is needed.

VACATED TRIAL · When a trial is cancelled before it has begun.

[Source: HM Court Service]

————————— 'SUPER-INJUNCTIONS' —————————

Injunctions are court orders requiring an individual, corporation, or other body to perform or, more commonly, desist from performing a specified action. In the media world, injunctions are commonplace and are usually sought to prevent or limit the publication of information argued by a party to be damaging or untrue. In recent months, the emergence of more restrictive injunctions – known colloquially as 'super-injunctions' – has caused considerable disquiet in the press. A super-injunction performs the same function as an injunction except that its very existence must be kept a secret. In 2009, the Lord Chief Justice argued that there were instances where super-injunctions had a valid legal purpose – for example, to prevent associates of an injuncted fraudster from disposing of their assets or fleeing the country. Yet super-injunctions are more problematic when they are used by celebrities or corporations to 'gag' entirely the dissemination of a story – which it seems is increasingly the case. In October 2009, the *Guardian* reported that it had been served with at least 12 super-injunctions that year, compared with 6 in 2006, and 5 in 2005. In 2010, an example of the still uncertain reach of super-injunctions emerged when, for a brief period, it seemed that the *Guardian* was barred from reporting on a question tabled in Parliament by a Labour MP.

———————————— MoD ANNUAL REPORT ————————————

SERVICE & CIVILIAN PERSONNEL · AT 1·4·2009

TOTAL PERSONNEL (thousands).. 275·0	*Women % ethnic minority*
– Service................................. 188·4	9·5......... ALL SERVICES ....6·5
– Civilian Level ....86·6	*12·1............ Officers ....2·5*
Naval Service ....38·3	*8·9............ Other ranks...........7·2*
– Officers................................7·4	9·6....... NAVAL SERVICE ....3·3
– Other ranks ....30·9	*9·7............ Officers ....1·6*
Army ....106·5	*9·5...........Other Ranks...........3·7*
– Officers.............................14·5	7·8.............ARMY..............9·4
– Other Ranks ....92·0	*11·2............ Officers ....3·0*
Royal Air Force ....43·6	*7·3...........Other Ranks ....10·4*
– Officers ....9·8	13·5.....ROYAL AIR FORCE.......2·2
– Other Ranks ....33·8	*15·2............ Officers ....2·6*
Civilian Level 0 ....86·6	*13............ Other ranks...........2·0*
– Non-industrial ....53·1	36·6...........CIVILIAN...........3·2
– Industrial ....11·1	*42·3........ Non-industrial ....3·5*
– Trading Funds ....9·6	*20·2............Industrial.............2*
– Royal Fleet Auxiliaries ....2·3	*23·8........ Trading fund ....2·5*
– Locally Engaged Civilians ....10·5	(Some figures are provisional)

LAND AND FORESHORE HOLDINGS AND RIGHTS · AT 1·4·2009

The MoD had access to 372,000 hectares of land, of which 219,000 was freehold.

SERVICE (thousand hectares)	*freehold*	*leasehold*	*rights held*
Royal Navy...............................	15·0	3·0	26·0
Army......................................	151·0	6·0	88·0
Royal Air Force	28·0	8·0	9·0
The Centre†	24·0	1·0	10·0
Other.....................................	1·0	3·0	–
COUNTRY			
England	171·0	17·0	34·0
Wales	21·0	–	2·0
Scotland..................................	25·0	3·0	96·0
Northern Ireland........................	3·0	–	–
USAGE			
Training areas and ranges...............	148·0	15·0	128·0
Airfield	24·0	–	2·0
Barracks and camps.....................	11·0	–	1·0
Storage and supply depots..............	11·0	–	–
Research and Development..............	16·0	1·0	1·0
Radio and W/T stations.................	5·0	1·0	1·0
Naval bases..............................	1·0	–	–
Miscellaneous	2·0	3·0	2·0

† The Centre includes Defence Equipment & Support, and Central Staff. [Source: DASA]

UK SERVICE RANKS

service	ROYAL NAVY	ROYAL MARINES†	ARMY	ROYAL AIR FORCE	NATO
OFFICERS					
	Admiral of the Fleet	—	Field Marshal	Marshal of the RAF	OF-10
	Admiral	General	General	Air Chief Marshal	OF-9
	Vice Admiral	Lieutenant General	Lieutenant General	Air Marshal	OF-8
	Rear Admiral	Major General	Major General	Air Vice-Marshal	OF-7
	Commodore	Brigadier	Brigadier	Air Commodore	OF-6
	Captain	Colonel	Colonel	Group Captain	OF-5
	Commander	Lieutenant Colonel	Lieutenant Colonel	Wing Commander	OF-4
	Lieutenant Commander	Major	Major	Squadron Leader	OF-3
	Lieutenant	Captain	Captain	Flight Lieutenant	OF-2
	Sub-Lieutenant	Lieutenant/2nd Lieutenant	Lieutenant/2nd Lieutenant	Flying Officer/Pilot Officer	OF-1
	Midshipman	—	Officer Cadet	Officer Designate	OF-(D)
OTHER RANKS					
	Warrant Officer Class 1	Warrant Officer Class 1	Warrant Officer Class 1	Warrant Officer	OR-9
	Warrant Officer Class 2	Warrant Officer Class 2	Warrant Officer Class 2		OR-8
	Chief Petty Officer	Colour Sergeant	Staff Sergeant	Flight Sergeant/Chief Technician	OR-7
	Petty Officer	Sergeant	Sergeant	Sergeant	OR-6
	Leading Rate	Corporal	Corporal	Corporal	OR-4
			Lance Corporal		OR-3
	Able Rating	Marine	Private (Class 1–3)	Junior Technician/ Leading & Senior Aircraftman	OR-2
			Private (Class 4)/Junior	Aircraftman	OR-1

[Source: DASA] The Naval rank of Warrant Officer Class 2 was introduced in 2004. † The Royal Marines were established in 1664 as a corps of sea soldiers to be raised and disbanded as required. In 1755, they became a permanent part of the Navy, trained as soldiers and seamen to fight and to maintain discipline on ships. The Royal Marines gained their tough fighting reputation during the capture of Gibralar in 1704, and have since played a decisive role in military deployments across the world.

—————— MILITARY AWARDS FOR GALLANTRY ——————

Military awards for gallantry were introduced in 1854, when the Distinguished Conduct Medal (DCM) was first struck to recognise acts of extraordinary courage by the lower ranks during the bloodbath of the Crimean War (October 1853–February 1856). (Prior to this the Order of the Bath was awarded – but only to officers of field rank or higher.) In 1855, the Navy introduced the equivalent Conspicuous Gallantry Medal (CGM). In 1856, the Victoria Cross (VC) was introduced as the highest award for gallantry for which officers and other ranks in both services were eligible. ❦ In 1993, the government simplified the system of awards for gallantry, introducing a two-tier system of medals that could be awarded to all ranks across the forces:

Hierarchy of gallantry, leadership, and bravery awards for active operations (in presence of the enemy)		
Level 1	*Victoria Cross* (VC)	
Level 2	*Distinguished Service Order* (DSO) For command and leadership	*Conspicuous Gallantry Cross* (CGC) For gallantry
Level 3	*Distinguished Service Cross* (DSC) At sea	*Military Cross* (MC) On land ‖ *Distinguished Flying Cross* (DFC) In the air
Level 4	*Mention in Despatches*†	
Hierarchy of gallantry and bravery awards for non-active operations (not in presence of the enemy)		
Level 1	*George Cross* (GC)	
Level 2	*George Medal* (GM)	
Level 3	*Queen's Gallantry Medal* (QGM)	*Air Force Cross* (AFC)
Level 4	*Queen's Commendation for Bravery*	*Queen's Commendation for Bravery in the Air*

Recipients of Level 1–3 awards may use the post-nominal abbreviations in parentheses. [Source: MoD] In November 2009, Medical Assistant Able Seaman Class 1, Kate Nesbitt, became the first woman in the Royal Navy to be awarded the MC, for assisting an injured comrade while under fire in Afghanistan.

† A despatch is a report from a senior commander detailing military operations; it includes the names of any personnel who have distinguished themselves. Being mentioned in despatches is the lowest level commendation for gallantry in the British Armed Forces; it is also the oldest such recognition. Those mentioned in despatches have their name published in the London Gazette, are issued with a certificate, and are entitled to wear a silver oak-leaf emblem on the ribbon of their campaign medal, or on their jacket if no medal has been awarded. The oak-leaf emblem, which was initially bronze, was introduced in 1920 as a means of identifying those personnel who were mentioned in despatches during WWI.

———————————— ARMED FORCES COMPENSATION ————————————

In January 2010, the MoD updated its compensation scheme tariff, which details how much members of the Armed Forces will be paid if they are injured in the course of service. Below are the levels of lump-sum compensation, with examples:

1 .... £570,000 .... Brain injury with persistent vegetative state
2 .... £402,500 .... Loss of eyes
3 .... £230,000 .... Loss of both legs at or above knee
4 .... £172,500 .... Loss of both arms below elbow
5 .... £115,000 .... Hemiplegia
6 .... £92,000 .... Total deafness in both ears
7 .... £63,825 .... Loss of both thumbs
8 .... £48,875 .... Infertility
9 .... £34,100 .... Permanent mental disorder, causing moderate
                                       functional limitation and restriction
10 ... £23,100 .... Serious permanent damage to, or loss of, one kidney
11 ... £13,750 .... Severe facial scarring which produces
                                       a poor cosmetic result despite camouflage
12 ... £9,075 .... Persistent phantom limb pain
13 ... £5,775 .... Loss of two or more front teeth
14 ... £2,888 .... Simple skull fracture
15 ... £1,155 .... Loss of one toe, other than great toe, from one foot

Those with the most severe injures receive an additional index-linked, tax-free annual payment for the rest of their life. A government review is expected to increase these payments from Spring 2011.

———————— ILLEGAL USE OF MILITARY DECORATIONS ————————

In January 2010, a 62-year-old man pleaded guilty to an offence under section 197(1)(b) of the Army Act 1955, which makes it an offence for any person who:

(a) without authority uses or wears any military decoration, or any badge, wound stripe or emblem supplied or authorised by the Defence Council, or
(b) uses or wears any decoration, badge, wound stripe, or emblem so nearly resembling any military decoration, or any such badge, stripe or emblem as aforesaid, as to be calculated to deceive, or
(c) falsely represents himself to be a person who is or has been entitled to use or wear any such decoration, badge, stripe or emblem as is mentioned in (a)

The man had been photographed marching in a 2009 Armistice Day parade wearing: Distinguished Service Order (with bar signifying Queen's Commendation for Valuable Service); Military Cross (with bar signifying mentioned in despatches); Queen's Commendation Medal; Military Medal; Distinguished Service Medal; Meritorious Service Medal; Campaign Service Medal; South Atlantic Medal; Gulf Medal; Accumulated Campaign Service Medal; Saudi Arabian Medal (for the liberation of Kuwait); Kuwaiti Liberation Medal; Army Long Service & Good Conduct Medal; Nato Medal; the beret and insignia of the SAS; Veteran's badge of UK Armed Forces; and 3 unidentified foreign medals.

———————————— MORALITY & CLEANLINESS ————————————

'Clean smells might not only regulate physical cleanliness, but may also motivate virtuous behaviour,' was the bold suggestion made by psychologists at Brigham Young University, Utah, in October 2009. The researchers performed two experiments. In the first, subjects were given $12 (reportedly sent by an anonymous partner in another room) and were asked to divide it fairly. Those performing this test in a room that had been sprayed with the cleaning fluid Windex returned almost twice as much money as those in the 'normal smelling' room. In the second experiment, subjects were asked about their interest in volunteering with and donating money to the charity Habitat for Humanity. As before, those in the Windex-wafted room were significantly more willing to volunteer and more generous in their donations. Writing in *Psychological Science*, the researchers said, 'the current findings suggest there is some truth to the claim that cleanliness is next to godliness; clean scents summon virtue, helping reciprocity prevail over greed, and charity over apathy'.

———————————— THOU SHALT (NOT) STEAL ————————————

In December 2009, Father Tim Jones of St Lawrence and St Hilda in York gave a sermon suggesting that hardship offered some leeway with the eighth Commandment: 'My advice, as a Christian priest, is to shoplift ... I do not offer such advice because I think that stealing is a good thing, or because I think it is harmless, for it is neither.' He added, 'I would ask that they do not steal from small, family businesses, but from large national businesses, knowing that the costs are ultimately passed on to the rest of us in the form of higher prices'. Inevitably, this advice caused a storm of controversy – and both the Church and the police questioned its wisdom. However, Father Jones maintained that his aim was simply to raise awareness of those who have fallen through the net of social services: 'If one has exhausted every legal opportunity to get money and you're still in a desperate situation it is a better moral thing to do to take absolutely no more than you need for no longer than you need.'

———————————— THE TEMPLETON PRIZE ————————————

The evolutionary geneticist and molecular biologist Francisco J. Ayala won the £1m Templeton Prize in March 2010. The prize, established by Sir John Templeton in 1972, annually honours 'a living person who has made an exceptional contribution to affirming life's spiritual dimension'. Ayala is known for his work on the parasites that cause tropical diseases (including malaria), and his discoveries have been heralded for their potential to lead to new vaccines. He is also a former Dominican priest, and has been a vocal proponent of the view that science and religion should be kept separate. In 1981, Ayala was an expert witness in a US court challenge that overturned a state law mandating the teaching of creationism alongside evolution. Three years later, he was asked by the US National Academy of Sciences to be lead author of *Science, Evolution, & Creationism*, a key refutation of 'intelligent design'. In a statement, Ayala said that science and religion 'cannot be in contradiction because ... [they] concern different matters, and each is essential to human understanding'.

—————————— SAINTS' RELICS ——————————

In September 2009, the relics of Saint Thérèse arrived in Britain for a tour of more than 20 churches. Thousands of Britons flocked to venerate the remains of one of the Catholic faith's most popular saints. The majority of Saint Thérèse's relics are based in Liseaux, France, but two extra caskets exist to allow more people access to the holy remains. One casket permanently travels around France, and the other tours the world – visiting such disparate places as Iraq, Burkina Faso, and Kazakhstan. ❦ St Thérèse was born in Alençon, France, in 1873, but her family moved to Lisieux in 1877 after the death of her mother. St Thérèse (known as the 'Little Flower' because of her love of nature) always had a deep faith, and at the age of 15 she became a Carmelite nun. After writing a popular account of her spiritual childhood, *Story of a Soul*, St Thérèse died of tuberculosis aged just 24. She was canonised by Pope Benedict XV in 1925, and has been named the patron saint of florists, aviators, and Aids sufferers. She is also co-patroness of France, alongside Joan of Arc. ❦ Relics have been an important part of the Catholic faith since its inception. One of the first recorded cases of relic veneration was of St Polycarp (AD 69–155) who was burnt to death by the Romans. His charred remains were salvaged from the pyre and secretly worshipped in Rome's catacombs. During the Second Council of Nicea (AD 787) it was decreed that every church should have a relic at its altar. This order was official rescinded in 1969, yet many churches continue the tradition nevertheless. Relics are generally split into three classifications:

1st class.........*part of a saint (bones, hair, teeth, &c.) or remnants of the True Cross*
2nd class............*an item owned by the saint or the instrument of their martyrdom*
3rd class..........................*an object that has touched a first or second class relic*

The locations of some of the most venerated first-class relics are listed below:

Relic	*location*
Skull of St Elizabeth of Hungary.........Convent of St Elizabeth, Vienna, Austria
The Venerable Bede..Durham Cathedral
St Edward the Confessor† .... Westminster Abbey, London
St John Southworth (within a silver effigy).......... Westminster Cathedral, London
St Bernadette†............................... Convent of St Gildard, Nevers, France
Crown of Thorns and a piece of the True Cross........Notre Dame, Paris, France
St Vincent de Paul† ....Church of St Vincent de Paul, Paris, France
The Three Magi..................................... Cathedral of Cologne, Germany
St Walburga‡ .... Church of St Walburga, Eichstätt, Germany
The right hand of King Saint Stephen.. Saint Istvan's Basilica, Budapest, Hungary
St Francis Xavier†................................... Basilica Bom Jesus, Goa, India
St Valentine .... The Carmelite Whitefriar Church, Dublin, Ireland
St Francis of Assisi.....Lower Church of the Basilica of Saint Francis, Assisi, Italy
The hearts of all the popes from Sixtus V to Pius IX...Piazza di Trevi, Rome, Italy

† Indicates a saint who is 'incorrupt' – this refers to a phenomenon whereby the body of the saint has not decomposed. ‡ St Walburga's relics excrete a special 'oil of saints' which is said to have healing properties. For some reason this oil only appears between 12 October and 25 February each year.

———————————— MUSLIMS WORLDWIDE ————————————

*c.*23% of the world's population is Muslim, according to October 2009 survey by the Pew Forum on Religion and Public Life. The research, which was conducted in 232 countries and territories, estimated that there are 1·57bn Muslims around the world. The list below shows the number and percentage of Muslims by world region:

Region	no. Muslims	% pop Muslim	% of global Muslims
Asia-Pacific	972,537,000	24·1	61·9
Middle East/North Africa	315,322,000	91·2	20·1
Sub-Saharan Africa	240,632,000	30·1	15·3
Europe	38,112,000	5·2	2·4
Americas	4,596,000	0·5	0·3

The nations listed below are home to the greatest number of Muslims in the world:

WORLD			EUROPE		
Country	no. Muslims	% Muslim	Country	no. Muslims	% Muslim
Indonesia	202,867,000	88·2	Russia	16,482,000	11·7
Pakistan	174,082,000	96·3	Germany†	4,026,000	≈5·0
India	160,945,000	13·4	France†	3,554,000	≈6·0
Bangladesh	145,312,000	89·6	Albania	2,522,000	79·9
Egypt	78,513,000	94·6	Kosovo	1,999,000	89·6
Nigeria	78,056,000	50·4	UK	1,647,000	2·7
Iran	73,777,000	99·4	Bosnia-Herz.†	1,522,000	≈40·0
Turkey†	73,619,000	≈98·0	Netherlands	946,000	5·7
Algeria	34,199,000	98·0	Bulgaria	920,000	12·2
Morocco†	31,993,000	≈99·0	Rep. of Mac.	680,000	33·3

317m (20%) of the world's Muslims live in countries where they are religious minorities. The countries with the largest Muslim minority populations are below:

Country	no. Muslims	% Muslim
India	160,945,000	13·4
Ethiopia	28,063,000	33·9
China	21,667,000	1·6
Russia	16,482,000	11·7
Tanzania	13,218,000	30·2
Ivory Coast	7,745,000	36·7
Mozambique	5,224,000	22·8

Country	no. Muslims	% Muslim
Philippines	4,654,000	5·1
Germany†	4,026,000	≈5
Uganda	3,958,000	12·1

Muslim 'minorities' in some areas are still quite sizeable. China is home to more Muslims than Syria, Germany to more than Lebanon, and Russia to more than Jordan and Libya combined.

Only 10–13% of the world's Muslims are Shias, while 87–90% are Sunnis. Three-quarters of all Shias live in Asia (including Iran), and a quarter in the Middle East/North Africa. 68–80% live in just four countries: Iran, Pakistan, India, and Iraq. The two groups differ in opinion on political leadership and some areas of practice.

† Data from Turkey, Morocco, Germany, France, and Bosnia-Herzegovina are from general population surveys, which are considered less reliable than censuses, and so numbers are rounded upwards.

—————— CHOOSING THE DALAI LAMA ——————

The 14th Dalai Lama, Tenzin Gyatso, celebrated his 75th birthday in July 2010. A global figure known for his spiritual teachings and advocacy of non-violent resistance, the Dalai Lama is both the senior monk in Tibetan Buddhism and also, by tradition, Tibet's head of state. Yet, since Tibet has been controlled by China since 1951, the Dalai Lama now leads his Tibetan government-in-exile from Dharamsala, India. Relations between the Dalai Lama and China are far from warm, a state of affairs that has caused concern over the naming of the Dalai Lama's successor. Traditionally, the search for a new Dalai Lama begins shortly after the previous Dalai Lama's death. A party of High Lamas and Tibetan officials scours the land for a young boy who they consider is the reincarnation of the previous Dalai Lama. This quest is highly intuitive and mystical, and may include one or more of the following techniques:

Following clues from a High Lama's dream · Looking for signs in a sacred lake
Watching the direction of the smoke from the cremation of the last Dalai Lama

Once the search party has located a promising child, he is presented with a series of objects that belonged to the previous Dalai Lama. If the child recognises these as his own, he may be taken to a monastery and raised as the new Dalai Lama. This process is flexible, however, and the current Dalai Lama has said his successor might be named in an entirely new fashion (perhaps by searching outside Tibet, while he is still alive, or by including females). Perhaps ironically, the Chinese government has insisted on following the traditional process, leading some to raise the possibility of two Dalai Lamas – one chosen by China and one by the government-in-exile. The Dalai Lama has even speculated that he may be the last to hold the position, if the Tibetan people decide it has outlived its usefulness. The previous Dalai Lamas are:

No.	name (birth–death)	highlights of reign
1	Gedun Drupa (1391–1474)	*developed the Gelugpa School of Buddhism in Tibet*
2	Gedun Gyatso (1475–1542)	*abbot of Drepung, the largest Gelugpa monastery*
3	Sonam Gyatso (1543–88)†	*established Namgyal monastery*
4	Yonten Gyatso (1589–1617)	*abbot of Drepung and Sera monasteries*
5	Lobsang Gyatso (1617–82)	*united Tibet, created links with China & Mongols*
6	Tsangyang Gyatso (1682–1706)	*unconventional Lama who wrote love songs*
7	Kelsang Gyatso (1708–57)	*sovereign of Tibet by Chinese decree*
8	Jamphel Gyatso (1758–1804)	*built Norbulingka Park & Summer Palace*
9	Lungtok Gyatso (1805–15)	*died at age nine*
10	Tsultrim Gyatso (1816–37)	*reconstructed the Potala Palace, died young*
11	Khedrup Gyatso (1838–56)	*third Dalai Lama to die young*
12	Trinley Gyatso (1856–75)	*fourth Dalai Lama to die young*
13	Thupten Gyatso (1876–1933)	*kept Tibet together amid turbulence, enhanced role of the Dalai Lama, instituted modernisations and reforms*

† The first to be given the 'Dalai Lama' title; the previous were so named posthumously. All Dalai Lamas are seen as the reincarnation of Chenrezig, Bodhisattva of Compassion and patron deity of Tibet, as well as reincarnations of their predecessors. *Dalai* is Mongolian for 'ocean' and *lama* is Tibetan for 'teacher' or 'guru'. Dalai Lama is often translated as 'Ocean Teacher' or 'Ocean of Wisdom'.

———————— BIBLE KNOWLEDGE ————————

Knowledge of the Bible in England and Wales was explored by The National Biblical Literacy Survey, released in 2010 by CODEC at St John's College in Durham:

Knew something accurate about	%		%
– Abraham	79	Own a Bible	75
– Moses	75	*– traditional Bible*	*46*
– Judas	68	*– modern Bible*	*18*
– Thomas	42	*– both*	*36*
– Mary Magdalene	43	Were read Bible stories as a child	39
– The Crucifixion	83	Had read a Bible in the last week	18
– The Good Samaritan	40	Had never read a Bible	13
– Abraham and Isaac	21	The Bible was significant to them	31
		– not significant	47

When it came to people's knowledge of the Ten Commandments, the survey found that just 5% knew all ten; 57% knew three or more; and 16% could not name any. Curiously, 41% of non-church goers knew the 'golden rule' (*Do unto others as you would have them do to you*) compared to just 31% of self-declared churchgoers.

———————— THE FOREIGN OFFICE & THE POPE ————————

The Foreign & Commonwealth Office was embarrassed in April 2010 when the *Sunday Telegraph* published the results of an internal 'brainstorming' session to plan for Pope Benedict XVI's visit to Britain [see p.37]. Some of the (one assumes sarcastic) ideas included: 'launch of Benedict condoms', 'open an abortion ward', 'bless a civil partnership', 'sacking dodgy bishops', and 'launch helpline for abused children'.

———————— ON LYING ————————

On average, British men lie some 1,092 times year, and women 728 times, according to a survey of 3,000 adults conducted by the Science Museum. Below are the most popular lies told by British men and women to their romantic partners:

Top ten lies MEN *tell to their partner*	*Top ten lies* WOMEN *tell their partner*
1 ..... I didn't have that much to drink	1 .... Nothing's wrong, I'm fine
2 .... Nothing's wrong, I'm fine	2 .... I don't know where it is,
3 .... I had no signal	I haven't touched it
4 .... It wasn't that expensive	3 .... It wasn't that expensive
5 .... I'm on my way	4 ..... I didn't have that much to drink
6 .... I'm stuck in traffic	5 .... I've got a headache
7 .... No, your bum doesn't	6 .... It was in the sale
look big in that	7 .... I'm on my way
8 .... Sorry, I missed your call	8 .... Oh, I've had this ages
9 .... You've lost weight	9 .... No, I didn't throw it away
10 ..... It's just what I've always wanted	10 .... It's just what I've always wanted

———————— HUNGER STRIKES ————————

The origins of the hunger strike have been lost to time, although the idea of fasting as a means of seeking redress is found in both ancient Ireland and India – two areas where hunger strikes became a prominent feature of C20th politics. The earliest modern hunger strikes were undertaken by suffragettes in the early 1900s, first in England and then Ireland, and the tactic was swiftly adopted by Irish nationalists [see below]. Since then, hunger strikes have become a well-known, if high-risk, strategy for the powerless to protest against an injustice. Commentators have pointed out that the success of hunger strikes depends on a moral and ethical system in which letting others starve is seen as morally wrong, and on a media environment in which such acts are publicised. In *Promoting Health in Prisons,* a 2007 document designed for health workers, the World Health Organization differentiates between two types of hunger strikes, and details the physical effects of the latter:

DRY FASTING · refusing all solid or fluid intake · *death after 4–10 days*	TOTAL FASTING · consuming only water · *death after c.40–75 days*

1st week ....*feelings of hunger and fatigue, stomach cramps*
2nd–3rd week.......... *weakness, dizziness, hunger & thirst disappear, feeling of cold*
3rd–4th week ....*worsening of symptoms above, intellectual powers slow*
5th week....*change in consciousness, lack of motor coordination, difficulty swallowing, uncontrollable eye movements, loss of vision and hearing*

Tabulated below are just a few of the many notable hunger strikes of the C20th:

Date	striker(s)	location	cause	duration
1909	*Marion Dunlop*	England	suffrage‡	91 hours
1912	*Lizzie Barker*	Ireland	suffrage‡	several days
1917	*Thomas Ashe†*	Ireland	*Irish Republicanism*‡	5 days
1920	*Terence MacSwiney†*	England	*Irish Republicanism*‡	74 days
1968	*Cesar Chavez*	California	*migrant farm workers*	25 days
1972	*Pedro Luis Boitel†*	Cuba	*anti-Castro*	53 days
1981	*Bobby Sands§*	Ireland	*Irish Republicanism*‡	66 days
1987	*Thileepan†*	Sri Lanka	*Tamil rights*	12 days
1989	*c.1,000 students*	Tiananmen Sq	*democratic reform*	various
1996	*c.2,000 prisoners†*	Turkey	*mistreatment*	<69 days
2005–	*Inmates*	Guantánamo Bay	*mistreatment*	various
2009	*P. Subramaniam*	England	*Sri Lankan war*	24 days
2009	*Roxana Saberi*	Iran	*prison sentence*	c.2 weeks

Gandhi undertook at least 17 fasts during his life, some of which sought to obtain particular ends; however, some scholars are wary of viewing these as 'hunger strikes', because of their spiritual dimension. ❧ The Malta Declaration, adopted by the World Medical Association in 1991, advises that doctors should respect the wishes of a mentally competent person to refuse food, and states that force-feeding is morally unacceptable. ❧ Some strikers above undertook multiple hunger strikes. † Strike resulted in death(s). ‡ Strike to protest detainment and seek status as a political prisoner. § Sands was one of 10 Republicans who starved themselves to death during the notorious H-Block prison protests.

Sport

I don't understand the [lack of] technology. With it we don't stand here and talk about 'goal' or 'no goal', I can't understand why. — FABIO CAPELLO, *England manager*

———— FIFA WORLD CUP 2010 · ENGLAND & MISC. ————

England went into the World Cup with expectations only a touch below the usual hysteria. John Terry's February sacking from the captaincy (over allegations concerning his private life) was compounded by injuries to David Beckham and new captain Rio Ferdinand. After England performed poorly in its opening games (1–1 *vs* USA; 0–0 *vs* Algeria), rumours emerged of divisions in the camp and dissatisfaction at Capello's strict regime. Hopes raised by qualification for the second stage (beating Slovenia 1–0) were dashed by a controversial 4–1 humiliation by a young German side. With this game poised delicately at 2–1, Frank Lampard had a goal disallowed – despite replays showing the ball 2ft over the line after it bounced off the crossbar. (Some saw this as divine retribution for Hurst's disputed 1966 goal against W Germany, which was allowed in very doubtful circumstances.) Although Capello and some of his team blamed their exit on this refereeing blunder, England's shambolic concession of goals – and its sub-par performance throughout the World Cup – prompted the inevitable outpouring of anguish as well as calls for the manager to be sacked. Resilient to this pressure, the FA decided to retain Capello for the remaining two years of his contract.

The defining sound of the tournament came from the 'vuvuzela' – a traditional S African plastic horn that emits a piercing, monotone, B-flat rasp. So pervasive and annoying was this drone that FIFA was said to have considered banning the instruments following complaints from broadcasters and TV-viewers alike. ❦ The defining animal of the tournament was Paul the Octopus – to learn more, turn to p.230. ❦ N Korea produced one of the few surprises of the tournament when it managed to scrape a 2–1 defeat against the mighty Brazil. Delighted by this performance, Pyongyang relaxed its strict censorship and allowed N Korea's second game to be televised live. Sadly, this allowed the citizens of N Korea to see their boys spanked 7–0 by Portugal. (The N Korean coach was reportedly sent to work on a building site on his team's return.) ❦ Although there were fears that S Africa would not be able to cope with hosting an event as complex as the World Cup, concerns that poor infrastructure and high crime would derail the event happily proved misplaced. Indeed, more than 450,000 people were estimated to have travelled to S Africa – fewer than the 1m who journeyed to Germany in 2006, but more than the 250,000 who went to Japan and Korea in 2002. Sadly the host nation was not able to make it past the group stages [see p.299].

Golden Ball .... Diego Forlan [URG]
Golden Boot ... Thomas Mueller [GER]
(5 goals, 3 assists)
Golden Glove .... Iker Casillas [SPA]
Young Player ... Thomas Mueller [GER]
FIFA Fair Play .... Spain

FIFA WORLD CUP SOUTH AFRICA · 2010

Group A

South Africa	1–1	Mexico
Uruguay	0–0	France
South Africa	0–3	Uruguay
France	0–2	Mexico
Mexico	0–1	Uruguay
France	1–2	South Africa

Group B

Korea Rep	2–0	Greece
Argentina	1–0	Nigeria
Argentina	4–1	Korea Rep
Greece	2–1	Nigeria
Nigeria	2–2	Korea Rep
Greece	0–2	Argentina

Group C

England	1–1	United States
Algeria	0–1	Slovenia
Slovenia	2–2	United States
England	0–0	Algeria
Slovenia	0–1	England
United States	1–0	Algeria

Group D

Serbia	0–1	Ghana
Germany	4–0	Australia
Germany	0–1	Serbia
Ghana	1–1	Australia
Ghana	0–1	Germany
Australia	2–1	Serbia

Group E

Netherlands	2–0	Denmark
Japan	1–0	Cameroon
Netherlands	1–0	Japan
Cameroon	1–2	Denmark
Denmark	1–3	Japan
Cameroon	1–2	Netherlands

Group F

Italy	1–1	Paraguay
New Zealand	1–1	Slovakia
Slovakia	0–2	Paraguay
Italy	1–1	New Zealand
Slovakia	3–2	Italy
Paraguay	0–0	New Zealand

Group G

Ivory Coast	0–0	Portugal
Brazil	2–1	Korea DRP
Brazil	3–1	Ivory Coast
Portugal	7–0	Korea DRP
Portugal	0–0	Brazil
Korea DRP	0–3	Ivory Coast

Group H

Honduras	0–1	Chile
Spain	0–1	Switzerland
Chile	1–0	Switzerland
Spain	2–0	Honduras
Chile	1–2	Spain
Switzerland	0–0	Honduras

2nd Round

Netherlands	2	
Slovakia	1	
Brazil	3	
Chile	0	
United States	1	
Ghana (aet)	2	
Korea Rep	1	
Uruguay	2	
	1	Spain
	0	Portugal
	0 (5) *penalties*	Paraguay
	0 (3)	Japan
	1	Mexico
	3	Argentina
	1	England
	4	Germany

QUARTER-FINAL

2 July · Port Elizabeth — Netherlands 2, Brazil 1

2 July · Johannesburg — Ghana 1 (2), Uruguay *penalties* 1 (4)

3 July · Johannesburg — Spain 1, Paraguay 0

3 July · Cape Town — Argentina 0, Germany 4

SEMI-FINAL

6 July · Cape Town — Netherlands 3, Uruguay 2

7 July · Durban — Spain 1, Germany 0

FINAL ·
11 July 2010
Johannesburg

Spain
bt
Netherlands
1–0

10 July · Port Elizabeth, Germany *bt* Uruguay 3–2 for 3rd place

──────── THE PREMIER LEAGUE · 2009/10 ────────

Team	won	drew	lost	goals for	goals against	goal difference	points
Chelsea	27	5	6	103	32	+71	86
Man. Utd	27	4	7	86	28	+58	85
Arsenal	23	6	9	83	41	+42	75
Tottenham	21	7	10	67	41	+26	70
↑ CHAMPIONS LEAGUE ↑							
Man. City	18	13	7	73	45	+28	67
Aston Villa	17	13	8	52	39	+13	64
Liverpool	18	9	11	61	35	+26	63
↑ EUROPA LEAGUE ↑							
Everton	16	13	9	60	49	+11	61
Birmingham	13	11	14	38	47	–9	50
Blackburn	13	11	14	41	55	–14	50
Stoke City	11	14	13	34	48	–14	47
Fulham	12	10	16	39	46	–7	46
Sunderland	11	11	16	48	56	–8	44
Bolton	10	9	19	42	67	–25	39
Wolverhampton	9	11	18	32	56	–24	38
Wigan Athletic	9	9	20	37	79	–42	36
West Ham Utd	8	11	19	47	66	–19	35
↓ RELEGATION ↓							
Burnley	8	6	24	42	82	–40	30
Hull City	6	12	20	34	75	–41	30
Portsmouth	7	7	24	34	66	–32	19†

† Pompey had 9 points deducted when it became the first Premier League club to enter administration.
❡ Didier Drogba (Chelsea) was the league's top scorer: 29 goals; Wayne Rooney (Man U) scored 26.

──────── OTHER DIVISIONS – UP & DOWN ────────

Up	*2009/10*	*Down*
Newcastle Utd, West Brom. Albion, Blackpool	*Championship*	Sheffield Wed.†, Plymouth Argyle, Peterborough Utd
Norwich City, Leeds Utd, Millwall	*League One*	Gillingham, Wycombe Wdrs, Southend Utd, Stockport Cty
Notts County, Bournemouth, Rochdale, Dag. & Redbridge	*League Two*	Grimsby Town, Darlington
Stevenage Oxford United	*Blue Square Premier*	Salisbury City, Ebbsfleet, Grays Athletic, Chester City‡

† At the time of writing, Sheffield Wed. had been saved from going into administration. ‡ Chester City was expelled from the Conference for various breaches of the rules and their results were expunged.

THE FA CUP FINAL · 2010

15/5/2010 · Wembley Stadium
CHELSEA – 1 (Drogba 59), PORTSMOUTH – 0
Attendance: 88,335 · Referee: Chris Foy

Chelsea became only the 7th club to achieve a league and FA Cup double[†] when they beat relegated (and nearly bankrupt) Portsmouth to win the FA Cup for the 6th time. Chelsea was superior throughout an open and exciting match, hitting the post five times in the first half alone. It looked like they might pay for this goalmouth profligacy, however, when Pompey was awarded a penalty after 56 minutes. The controversial Kevin Prince Boateng (who had earlier fouled the Blues' Michael Ballack in an incident which was to cause the German captain to miss the World Cup) hit a poor penalty into the legs of Chelsea keeper, Petr Cech, and Portsmouth's chances of an 'against all odds' victory at the end of a troubled season seemed to fade. Two minutes later, Didier Drogba hit in a 25-yard free kick off the left-hand post to score his 6th goal in 6 Wembley appearances. Despite a rare Frank Lampard penalty miss late in the game, Chelsea held on for victory. ❦ Ashley Cole became the most decorated player in FA Cup history, picking up his 6th winner's medal.

† The other 6 clubs to achieve this are: Preston North End (1889); Aston Villa (1897); Spurs (1961); Arsenal (1971, 1998, 2002); Liverpool (1986); and Manchester United (1994, 1996, 1999).

THE CHAMPIONS LEAGUE FINAL · 2010

22/5/2010[‡] · Estadio Santiago Bernabeu, Madrid
INTER MILAN – 2 (Milito 34, 70), BAYERN MUNICH – 0
Attendance: 80,100 · Referee: Howard Webb [ENG]

José Mourinho joined an exclusive club when he led Inter Milan to its first European Cup victory in 45 years. In so doing, he became only the 3rd manager to win the trophy with two clubs (he won with Porto in 2004). Despite being criticised for an overly defensive style in reaching the finals, Mourinho stuck to his tried and tested tactics, and Bayern failed to dent Inter's rock-solid defence, despite dominating for long periods. Bayern's Dutch winger, Arjen Robben, who played under Mourinho at Chelsea, was particularly threatening. Just after the half hour, against the run of play, Inter's Argentine striker Diego Milito collected the ball from Wesley Sneijder and hit a clipped shot into the roof of the Bayern net, to take the lead 1–0. Bayern started the second half brightly, and Thomas Mueller should have equalised shortly after the interval. Yet Inter held firm and, in the 70th minute, Milito again caught the German side on the break, turning the defence to side-foot his 30th goal of the season, thereby putting the game beyond reach. At the final whistle Mourinho embraced Bayern manager Louis Van Gaal, his former mentor at Barcelona, and went on to salute the adoring Nerazzurri fans. This game proved Mourinho's last as manager of Inter before his move to take charge of Real Madrid.

‡ The final was played on a Saturday for the first time – instead of the traditional Wednesday.

———————— PREMIERSHIP WAGE BILL ————————

Premier League clubs spent 67% of their revenues, a total of £1·3bn, on player wages in 2008/09, up 11% (£132m) from the previous season. Deloitte's Annual Review of Football Finance, published in June 2010, also revealed that Premier League operating profits fell by more than half to £79m, the lowest level for over a decade. (The Premier League was overtaken by Germany's Bundesliga as the world's most profitable league.) The wage bills for Premier League teams in 2008/09 were:

Team	2008/09 wages · £'000s		
Chelsea	167,179	Tottenham Hotspur	62,567
Manchester United	123,120	Sunderland	49,530
Liverpool	107,206	Everton	49,069
Arsenal	103,978	Fulham	46,232
Manchester City	82,633	Blackburn Rovers	46,143
Newcastle United	73,312	Wigan Athletic	42,198
Aston Villa	70,577	Bolton Wanderers	40,892
West Ham United	70,048	Middlesbrough	34,052
* Premier League average	66,400	Hull City	33,598
Portsmouth	65,187	West Bromwich Albion	30,709
		Stoke City	29,749

———— SOME FOOTBALL AWARDS OF NOTE · 2009/10 ————

FIFA world player of the year	Lionel Messi [Barcelona]
European footballer of the year	Lionel Messi [Barcelona]
Prof. Footballers' Assoc. player of the year	Wayne Rooney [Man. Utd]
PFA young player award	James Milner [Aston Villa]
Football Writers' Assoc. player of the year	Wayne Rooney [Man. Utd]
FA women's football awards: players' player of the year	Kim Little [Arsenal]
LMA manager of the year	Roy Hodgson [Fulham]

— PREMIER LEAGUE · CHANGES OF OWNERSHIP 2009/10 —

Premier League football clubs are increasingly the playthings of wealthy individuals and sovereign funds, taking them further from their (increasingly alienated) traditional fan bases. Below are some of the clubs that have recently changed hands.

Club	previous owner	new owner	Date
Sunderland	Drumaville Consortium	Ellis Short	5/2009
West Ham	Björgólfur Guðmundsson	CB Holdings	6/2009
Portsmouth	Alexandre Gaydamak	Sulaiman Al-Fahim	8/2009
Brum City	Davids Sullivan & Gold	Grandtop Int.	10/2009
Portsmouth	Sulaiman Al-Fahim	Ali al-Faraj	10/2009
West Ham	CB Holdings	Sullivan & Gold	01/2010
Portsmouth	Ali al-Faraj	Balram Chainrai	2/2010
Liverpool	G. Gillett & T. Hicks	*not known*	*pending*

─────── GOLF MAJORS · 2010 ───────

♂	course	winner	score
MASTERS	Augusta, Georgia	Phil Mickelson [USA]	–16
US OPEN	Pebble Beach, California	Graeme McDowell [NIR]	E
THE OPEN	St Andrews, Scotland†	Louis Oosthuizen [RSA]	–16
US PGA	Whistling Straits, Wisconsin	Martin Kaymer [GER]	–11‡

♀

KRAFT NABISCO	Mission Hills, California	Yani Tseng [TAI]	–13
LPGA	Locust Hill CC, New York	Cristie Kerr [USA]	–19
US OPEN	Oakmont CC, Pennsylvania	Paula Creamer [USA]	–3
BRITISH OPEN	Royal Birkdale, England	Yani Tseng [TAI]	–11

† The Open's 150th anniversary was notable for its benign conditions, soft greens, and low scores.
‡ Kaymer finished level with American Bubba Watson after 72 holes, before winning the 3-hole play-off by one shot. Kaymer followed McDowell and Oosthuizen in winning a major for the first time.

─────── TIGER TIGER ───────

Tiger Woods shocked the sporting (and celebrity) world when, in late 2009, he admitted a string of extra-marital affairs, belying his 'squeaky clean' family-man image. As Woods withdrew from all golf 'indefinitely', many of his marquee sponsors – Accenture, Gillette, Gatorade, Tag Heuer – scaled back or terminated their relationship, denting his estimated $100m annual income. In February 2010, Woods stage-managed a public apology as a prelude to his return at the US Masters in Augusta. Despite sitting only four stokes off the lead going into the final round, Woods failed to achieve the fairy-tale return for which many had hoped, and he finished tied-4th, five shots behind eventual winner, Phil Mickelson. ❦ Woods finished the US Open tied-4th, three shots off the lead; the Open Championship tied-23rd, thirteen shots back; and the US PGA tied-28th, nine shots back.

─────── OFFICIAL WORLD GOLF RANKINGS ───────

Phil Mickelson narrowly missed taking Woods' World No. 1 ranking in August 2010 – almost adding insult to Tiger's self-inflicted injuries. The Official World Golf Rankings were first released in April 1986; they were based on unofficial rankings published from 1968 by the original 'super agent' Mark McCormack†. Initially, the rankings were calculated over a three-year period using a point system that graded different tournaments into categories. (The winner of a major championship, for example, would receive 50 points.) Nowadays, the rankings are designed to reward recent form by 'holding' the points accrued at every event for 13 weeks before tapering them incrementally each week over a two-year period. Thirteen players have been ranked as the Official World No. 1 – the first was Germany's Bernhard Langer. Tiger Woods still holds the longest consecutive streak as No. 1 – 276 weeks, and counting. [† Under the McCormack rankings, Jack Nicklaus was year-end World No. 1 from 1968–77, Tom Watson from 1978–82, and Seve Ballesteros from 1983–85.]

———————— RUGBY UNION SIX NATIONS · 2010 ————————

France won its 9th Grand Slam, beating England 12–10 at the Stade de France in the tournament's final game (held, unusually, on a Saturday night). England produced its best display of the Championship in the final, but failed to convert its chances.

Date		result		venue
06·02·10	Ireland	29–11	Italy	Croke Park
06·02·10	England†	30–17	Wales	Twickenham
07·02·10	Scotland	9–18	France	Murrayfield
13·02·10	Wales	31–24	Scotland	Millennium Stadium
13·02·10	France	33–10	Ireland	Stade de France
14·02·10	Italy	12–17	England	Stadio Flaminio
26·02·10	Wales	20–26	France	Millennium Stadium
27·02·10	Italy	16–12	Scotland	Stadio Flaminio
27·02·10	England	16–20	Ireland	Twickenham
13·03·10	Ireland	27–12	Wales	Croke Park
13·03·10	Scotland	15–15	England	Murrayfield
14·03·10	France	46–20	Italy	Stade de France
20·03·10	Wales	33–10	Italy	Millennium Stadium
20·03·10	Ireland	20–23	Scotland	Croke Park
20·03·10	France	12–10	England	Stade de France

FINAL TABLE 2010 　　　　　　　　　　　　　　　　TOTAL HONOURS EVER

points	w	d	l	pd	country	triple crowns	grand slams	titles
10	5	0	0	+66	France	N/A	9	17
6	3	0	2	+11	Ireland	10	2	11
5	2	1	2	+12	England	23	12	25
4	2	0	3	–4	Wales	19	10	24
3	1	1	3	–17	Scotland	10	3	14
2	1	0	4	–68	Italy	N/A	0	0

† England's kit paid homage to that sported in 1910, with an old-style red rose and no sponsor's logo.

———————— HEINEKEN EUROPEAN CUP FINAL · 2010 ————————

TOULOUSE 21–19 BIARRITZ · 22·05·10 · Stade de France, Paris
TOULOUSE – *pens:* Fritz, Skrela *drop:* Fritz, Skrela (3)
BIARRITZ – *tries:* Hunt; *cons:* Courrent; *pens:* Yachvili (4)

———— INTERNATIONAL RUGBY BOARD AWARDS · 2009 ————

International player of the year .... Richie McCaw [NZL]
International team of the year... South Africa
International coach of the year................................ Declan Kidney [IRE]
International sevens player of the year.......................... Ollie Phillips [ENG]

——————— MAN OF STEEL & SUPER LEAGUE · 2009 ———————

Huddefield's Australian full-back Brett Hodgson was named the Man of Steel in October 2009. Only the fourth Australian to win the award since its inception in 1977, Hodgson ended a run of four successive St Helen's Man of Steel winners. ❦ Leeds Rhinos won the Super League grand final at Old Trafford in Manchester, beating St Helen's 18–10. Kevin Sinfield won the Harry Sunderland Trophy, awarded to the man of the match by the Rugby League Writers' Association.

——————— RUGBY LEAGUE CHALLENGE CUP · 2010 ———————

LEEDS RHINOS 6–30 WARRINGTON WOLVES
28·8·10 · Wembley Stadium
LEEDS – *tries:* Smith · *goals:* Sinfield
WARRINGTON – *tries:* Atkins (2), Hicks (3), L. Anderson *goals:* Westwood (3)

Warrington retained the Challenge Cup with a devastating display against out-classed Leeds. A hat-trick of tries from Chris Hicks, and a brace from Ryan Atkins, caught the headlines. Yet it was the clever display of tactical kicking from Wolves' Lee Briers which made the difference, and earned the veteran half-back the Lance Todd Trophy, awarded to the final's man of the match. Warrington's victory was a personal triumph for coach (and Leeds old-boy) Tony Smith, who celebrated in front of a sell-out 85,217 crowd – the highest for a Challenge Cup final since the 1980s.

——————— COURT OF ARBITRATION FOR SPORT ———————

An international arbitral body, based in Lausanne, the Court of Arbitration for Sport (CAS) presides, as its name suggests, over disputes related to sport. The court was founded in 1984 by the International Olympic Committee (IOC) to resolve contro-versies arising out of the Olympics. But by the early 1990s, its remit had expanded to cover a wide range of sports and a host of related issues – from employment con-tracts and television rights to sponsorship and, increasingly, drugs and doping. ❦ In 1994 the Swiss Federal Tribunal held that, should the IOC ever be party to pro-ceedings, CAS's independence would be called into question. As a result, the CAS is now independent from the IOC. ❦ Today, the court operates in all areas of sport, and the majority of its cases relate to disputes over doping and football transfer fees. Its arbitrators are respected lawyers and administrators from a wide variety of countries, many of whom have some form of connection with the world of sport.

N Irish FA appealed against players playing for the Republic.....................2010
US ♂ 4×100m 2000 Olympic relay squad appealed for return of gold medals ..2010
Togo appealed exclusion from 2012 & 2014 Africa Cup of Nations.............2010
Adrian Mutu lost appeal against payment of €17m fine to Chelsea.............2009
Oscar Pistorius won appeal against IAAF ban due to his artificial limbs........2008
Gibraltar held to have valid grounds for its application to join UEFA...........2006
Alain Baxter lost a bid for the return of his 2002 Olympic slalom bronze.......2002

———TOUR DE FRANCE · 2010———

Spain's Alberto Contador won his second consecutive (and third overall) Tour when he narrowly beat Luxembourg's Andy Schleck in somewhat controversial circumstances. During Stage 15, Schleck was ahead by 31 seconds when his chain came loose and jammed his wheel. Contador rode on, taking the Yellow Jersey and establishing a lead he was not to relinquish. This prompted complaints that the Spaniard had disregarded cycling etiquette by challenging a Yellow Jersey wearer who had fallen or suffered a mechanical failure. Contador said he had been una-ware of Schleck's difficulties, although after he was booed at the podium at the end of the stage he explained: 'At a time like that all you think about is riding as fast as you can ... to me, fair play is very important.' Britain's Mark Cavendish again rode well, winning 5 stages (taking his tally to 15), including the prestigious finale in Paris[†]. However, for the second year in a row, Cavendish just missed the top sprint-er's Green Jersey. Lance Armstrong also hit the headlines – this time for announc-ing his (second) retirement from the Tour. Armstrong finished well off the pace, having suffered several crashes, and he was denied a stage win for the first time in 5 years after he was edged out in a sprint finish on the 16th Stage, from Bagnères-de-Luchon to Pau. Below are the final standings in the 2010 Tour de France:

1	Alberto Contador	ESP	Astana	91 hours 58 mins 48s
2	Andy Schleck	LUX	Team Saxo Bank	+39s
3	Denis Menchov	RUS	Radobank	+2 min 1s

Green Jersey (points classification) – Alessandro Petacchi [ITA], Lampre-Farnese, 243pts | Polka Dot Jersey (King of the Mountains) – Anthony Charteau [FRA] – Bbox Bouygues Telecom 143pts. | White Jersey (best young rider) – Andy Schleck [LUX], Team Saxo Bank, 91:59:27. | Team – Team Radioshack, 276:02:03. † Cavendish became the first man to win two years in a row on the Champs-Élysées when he outsprinted Green Jersey winner Petacchi in the last 100m.

——— TRACK CYCLING WORLD CHAMPIONSHIP · 2010———

For the second year running, Britain failed to dominate the Track Cycling World Championships held in March 2010 at Copenhagen's Ballerup Super Arena, this despite the return of four-time Olympic gold medallist Chris Hoy. Australia again topped the table, wining 10 medals (6 of which were gold). Britain's 9 medals are below:

event	medallist	medal
♂ ...Men's Keirin	Chris Hoy	G
♂ ...Men's Omnium	Ed Clancy	G
♀ ....Women's Sprint	Victoria Pendleton	G
♂ ...Men's Team Pursuit	Great Britain	S
♀ ....Women's Individual Pursuit	Wendy Houvenaghel	S
♀ ....Women's Team Pursuit	Great Britain	S
♀ ... Women's Keirin	Victoria Pendleton	S
♀ ....Women's Omnium	Lizzie Armitstead	S
♂ ...Men's Team Sprint	Great Britain	B

———————FORMULA ONE TEAMS & DRIVERS · 2010———————

McLaren............................ Jenson Button [GBR] & Lewis Hamilton [GBR]
Mercedes .... Michael Schumacher [GER] & Nico Rosberg [GER]
Red Bull............................ Sebastian Vettel [GER] & Mark Webber [AUS]
Ferrari .... Fernando Alonso [ESP] & Felipe Massa [BRA]
Williams..................... Rubens Barrichello [BRA] & Nico Hülkenberg [GER]
Renault................................ Robert Kubica [POL] & Vitaly Petrov [RUS]
Force India..........................Adrian Sutil [GER] & Vitantonia Liuzzi [ITA]
Toro Rosso .... Sebastien Buemi [SWI] & Jaime Alguersuari [ESP]
Lotus ....Jarno Trulli [ITA] & Heikki Kovalainen [FIN]
Hispania Racing .... K Chandhok [IND], B Senna [BRA] & S Yamamoto [JPN]
BMW Sauber ....Pedro de la Rosa [ESP] & Kamui Kobayahi [JPN]
Virgin Racing........................ Timo Glock [GER] & Lucas di Grassi [BRA]

———————FORMULA ONE WORLD CHAMPIONSHIP · 2010———————

Date	Grand Prix	track	winning driver	team
14·03·10	Bahrain	Sakhir	Fernando Alonso	Ferrari
28·03·10	Australian	Albert Park	Jenson Button	McLaren
04·04·10	Malaysian	Sepang	Sebastian Vettel	Red Bull
18·04·10	Chinese	Shanghai	Jenson Button	McLaren
09·05·10	Spanish	Barcelona	Mark Webber	Red Bull
16·05·10	Monaco	Monte Carlo	Mark Webber	Red Bull
30·05·10	Turkish	Istanbul	Lewis Hamilton	McLaren
13·06·10	Canada	Montreal	Lewis Hamilton	McLaren
27·06·10	European	Valencia	Sebastian Vettel	Red Bull
11·07·10	British	Silverstone	Mark Webber	Red Bull
25·07·10	German	Hockenheim	Fernando Alonso	Ferrari
01·08·10	Hungarian	Hungaroring	Mark Webber	Red Bull
29·08·10	Belgian	Spa	Lewis Hamilton	McLaren
12·09·10	Italian	Monza	Fernando Alonso	Ferrari
26·09·10	Singaporean	Singapore		
10·10·10	Japanese	Suzuka		
24·10·10	Koren	Yeongam		
07·11·10	Brazilian	Sao Paulo		
14·11·10	Abu Dhabi	Yas Marina		

———————SUPERBIKES, RALLY & MOTORSPORT———————

Isle of Man TT (Superbike) [2010] .... Ian Hutchinson (Honda)
Moto GP [2009]...Valentino Rossi (Yamaha)
British Superbikes [2009]................................... Leon Camier (Yamaha)
World Superbikes [2009]....................................... Ben Spies (Yamaha)
World Rally [2009] .... Sébastien Loeb (Citroën)
Le Mans [2010] .... Mike Rockenfeller, Timo Bernhard, Romain Dumas (Audi)

TWENTY20 WORLD CUP · 2010

England beat Australia to win the third World Twenty20, held in the West Indies. It was their first victory in an ICC international competition after four previous finals defeats [see below]. Paul Collingwood's side dominated the tournament with a mix of aggressive batting and disciplined bowling, although the selectors caused some controversy by picking four foreign-born players (including an Irishman). Kevin Pietersen was named player of the tournament, although Sri Lankan Mahela Jayawardene was the leading scorer (302), and Australia's Dirk Nannes took the most wickets (14). The competition was also notable for the presence of a team from war-torn Afghanistan. As before, the women's tournament was played alongside the men's.

Women's competition	Men's competition
SEMI-FINAL 1 *Beausejour St, St Lucia*	SEMI-FINAL 1 *Beausejour St, St Lucia*
India 119/5 (20 ov)	Sri Lanka 128/6 (20 ov)
Australia 123/3 (18·5 ov)	England 132/3 (16 ov)
Australia won by 7 wickets	England won by 7 wickets
SEMI-FINAL 2 *Beausejour St, St Lucia*	SEMI-FINAL 2 *Beausejour St, St Lucia*
New Zealand 180/5 (20 ov)	Pakistan 191/6 (20 ov)
West Indies 124/8 (20 ov)	Australia 197/7 (19·5 ov)
New Zealand won by 56 runs	Australia won by 3 wickets
FINAL *Kensington Oval, Barbados*	FINAL *Kensington Oval, Barbados*
Australia 106/8 (20 ov)	Australia 147/6 (20 ov)
England 103/6 (20 ov)	England 148/3 (17 ov)
Australia won by 3 runs	England won by 7 wickets

ENGLAND DEFEATS IN WORLD CRICKET FINALS

Year	tournament	venue	opposition & result
1979	World Cup	Lord's	West Indies won by 92 runs
1987	World Cup	Eden Gardens, Calcutta	Australia won by 7 runs
1992	World Cup	Melbourne CG	Pakistan won by 22 runs
2004	Champions Trophy	The Oval	West Indies won by 2 wickets

WISDEN CRICKETERS OF THE YEAR

The 2010 Wisden Cricketers of the Year (awarded to the players who exerted the greatest influence on the English season) were Stuart Broad [ENG], Michael Clark [AUS], Graham Onions [ENG][†], Matt Prior [ENG], and Graeme Swann [ENG]. For the second year running Wisden's Leading Cricketer in the World was Virender Sehwag [IND].

† A name that demanded a good headline: *Onions Sizzled at Lord's*, and *Onions Put W. Indies in a Pickle* were two suggested by Simon Barnes in *The Times*. Onions's partnership at Durham with keeper Phil Mustard added to the fun: >10 batsmen succumbed to the eye-watering dismissal, *c.* Mustard *b.* Onions.

―――――――――― TWENTY20 CUP FINAL DAY · 2010 ――――――――――

Hampshire clinched a narrow victory in the Twenty20 Cup, beating Somerset by virtue of having lost fewer wickets in the final. Chasing a challenging 173/6, Hampshire looked on course for the win when they reached 163/3 with two overs remaining. Two wickets, a dropped catch, a pulled hamstring, and a runner later, it took a scrambled leg bye off the final ball to secure the narrowest of wins.

Semi-final 1 .... Hampshire (157/4, 19·2 ov) *bt* Essex (156/7, 20 ov) by 6 wickets
Semi-final 2 .... Somerset (182/5, 20 ov) *bt* Notts (117/4,13 ov) (D/L) by 3 runs
CUP FINAL ... Hampshire (173/5, 20 ov) *bt* Somerset (173/6, 20 ov) lost fewer wickets

――――――――――― INDIAN PREMIER LEAGUE · 2010 ―――――――――――

The Indian Premier League returned to India after it had decamped to South Africa in 2009 for security reasons. However, the tournament was quickly mired in scandal, politicking, backbiting and intrigue. Accusations flew of corruption, money laundering, illegal betting, and sleaze, and tax officials searched the offices of several teams and officials. The tournament was eventually won by the Chennai Super Kings who beat the Mumbai Indians (led by the legendary Sachin Tendulkar) by 22 runs.

―――――――――――― PAKISTANI CRICKET ――――――――――――

Following the attack on the Sri Lankan touring team in Karachi in March 2009, all international cricket in Pakistan was suspended until the security situation improved. ❦ After a humiliating defeat in Australia in early 2010, a number of senior Pakistani players were reprimanded and fined for their behaviour, and a new captain, Shahid Afridi, was named for the 2010 tour of England (which included a rearranged 'home' test series against Australia). Bizarrely, Afridi resigned after the first Test defeat by Australia at Lord's, seemingly leaving his team in disarray. However, Pakistan bounced back to beat the Aussies in the 2nd Test under a new captain – their fourth in 8 months. ❦ The rollercoaster continued with two heavy defeats in the next two Tests against England in July, after which some commentators called for two divisions in Test cricket. Pakistan bounced back yet again with an unlikely victory in the third Test at The Oval. ❦ The final Test at Lord's in August was no less extraordinary. England was reduced to 102/7, before Trott and Broad put on a world-record 8th-wicket partnership of 332 to take the home side to 446 all out. Pakistan then collapsed twice, to lose by an innings and 225 runs. ❦ Off the field, the action was no less dramatic. On 29/8, the *News of the World* alleged that Pakistani players had agreed to fix matches and individual aspects of games (e.g., the timing of no-balls) in collusion with betting syndicates. ❦ At the time of writing, the police and the International Cricket Council were investigating these accusations, and 3 Pakistani players had flown home early – though all denied any wrongdoing. It remains to be seen what damage the *News of the World*'s allegations do to the Pakistani side, and the game in general.

—————— EUROPEAN CHAMPIONSHIP ATHLETICS · 2010 ——————

Great Britain amassed its largest-ever medal haul at a European Athletics Championships – securing an impressive 19 medals (6 of which were gold) at the meeting held in Barcelona between July–August, 2010. The team easily exceeded coach Charles van Commenee's bullish target of 10–15 medals, and mustered several stand-out performances. Jessica Ennis won the women's heptathlon with a points total only 8 shy of Denise Lewis's British record, and Mo Farah became the first Briton ever to win the 5,000m and 10,000m double. Farah, who was born in Somalia and moved to England with his father at the age of 8, said, 'you have to believe in yourself, it doesn't come overnight … I want to thank everyone who's helped me and believed in me'. Britain's medal winners are tabulated below:

event	medallist	medal
♂ .... 110m hurdles	Andy Turner	G
♂ .... 400m hurdles	Dai Greene	G
♂ ... 5,000m	Mo Farah	G
♂ ... 10,000m	Mo Farah	G
♂ .... triple jump	Phillips Idowu	G
♀ ..... heptathlon	Jessica Ennis	G
♂ 100m	Mark Lewis-Francis	S
♂ 200m	Christian Malcolm	S
♂ 400m	Michael Bingham	S
♂ ... 800m	Michael Rimmer	S
♂ .... 400m hurdles	Rhys Williams	S
♂ ... 10,000m	Chris Thompson	S
♂ ... 4×400m relay	Great Britain	S
♂ ... 400m	Martyn Rooney	B
♂ .... long jump	Chris Tomlinson	B
♀.... 400m hurdles	Perri Shakes-Drayton	B
♀.... 800m	Jenny Meadows	B
♂ .... high jump	Martyn Bernard	B
♀..... 4×400m relay	Great Britain	B

————————————————— BULLFIGHTING —————————————————

In July 2010, an historic vote in the parliament of Catalonia saw the traditional 'sport' of bullfighting banned by 68 votes to 55, with 9 abstentions. This followed a long campaign by animal rights groups, who drew comparisons with Britain's 2005 ban on fox hunting with dogs. (The city of Barcelona had originally banned bullfighting in 2004 – although, through lack of enforcement, this was regarded as a symbolic gesture.) Many traditionalists expressed outrage at the 2010 vote, calling bullfighting an 'art form' to be preserved. But a member of the campaign group *Prou* ['*enough*' in Catalan] said, 'there is incredible suffering in a bullfight … it's not right to pay money to go and watch that kind of cruelty'. However, some believe that the impetus for the ban came from Catalonia's desire to forge a separate identity from the rest of Spain as much as from any concerns over animal welfare.

─────────── LONDON MARATHON · 2010 ───────────

Some 36,000 runners took part in the 30th London Marathon in damp conditions in April 2010, including HRH Princess Beatrice, who became the first member of the Royal family to complete the race. In doing so, HRH helped to set a record for the highest number of interlinked runners to finish, as one of the 34 members of a human caterpillar, which crossed the line in 5h 15m 57s. The key results were:

♂ *race results*
T. Kebede [ETH] 2h 5m 19s
E. Mutai [KEN].............. 02:06:23
J. Gharib [MOR]............. 02:06:55

♂ *wheelchair race results*
J. Cassidy [CAN]............. 01:35:21
M. Hug [SWI] 01:36:06
D. Weir [GBR]............... 01:37:01

♀ *race results*
L. Shobukhova [RUS] 02:22:00
I. Abitova [RUS]..............02:22:19
A. Mergia [ETH]..............02:22:38

♀ *wheelchair race results*
W. Tsuchida [JPN]............01:52:33
S. Graf [SWI] 01:52:34
A. McGrory [USA] 01:52:36

─ OTHER MARATHONS OF NOTE · 2009/10 ─

BERLIN.................*first run* 1974
2009 · 20 Sep ....fine, warm
♂ .....H. Gebrselassie [ETH] · 2:06:08
♀.A. Habtamu Besuye [ETH] · 2:24:47
Purse.........................$340,000

NEW YORK..............*first run* 1970
2009 · 1 Nov................fine, mild
♂ ....M. Keflezighi [USA] · 2:09:15
♀............. D. Tulu [ETH] · 2:28:52
Purse......................>$600,000

CHICAGO...............*first run* 1977
2009 · 11 Oct.....................cool
♂ .... S. Wanjiru [KEN] · 2:05:41
♀......L. Shobukhova [RUS] · 2:25:56
Purse.........................$485,000

BOSTON ....*first run* 1897
2010 · 19 Apr.....................cool
♂ .. R. Kiprono Cheruiyot [KEN] · 2:05:52
♀...........T. Erkesso [ETH] · 2:26:11
Purse.........................$806,000

─────────── THE LAUREUS AWARDS · 2010 ───────────

World sportsman of the year.................................Usain Bolt[†] (sprinter)
World sportswoman of the year...........................Serena Williams (tennis)
World team of the year..............................Brawn GP Formula One Team
World breakthrough of the year....................Jenson Button (Formula One)
World comeback of the year ....Kim Clijsters (tennis)
World sportsperson of the year with a disability ......Natalie du Toit (swimming)
World action sportsperson of the year.................Stephanie Gilmore (surfing)

[†] Bolt won the top Laureus award for the second year running after becoming the first man to hold simultaneously the 100m and 200m World and Olympic titles. He also beat his own world records in the two events, taking (coincidentally) 0·11s off both his previous times. Bolt ran the 100m in 9·58s – the greatest margin of improvement since the introduction of electronic timing – and the 200m in 19·19s.

──────── DARTS · PDC ────────

Phil 'The Power' Taylor secured his 15th World title at Alexandra Palace in January 2010, with a three-dart tournament average of 104·63 – a World Championship record. In the final, Taylor fought back from 1–2 down, winning 5 straight sets, before going on to beat Australian Simon 'The Magician' Whitlock 7–3. The match was of the highest quality with both men's three-dart averages over 100, and both scoring maximum 170 checkouts. But it was 49-year-old Taylor who eventually took the winner's cheque made out for a record £200,000. His feat was described as 'Bradmanesque' by one paper; another wondered if he should be ranked alongside Tiger Woods and Roger Federer as one of the sportsmen of the decade. The tournament was also notable for Dutchman Raymond 'Barney' van Barneveld throwing his second 'nine-dart finish' in consecutive years at the PDC event.

──────── DARTS · BDO ────────

Perennial crowd favourite Martin 'Wolfie' Adams won his second Lakeside World Darts title, fighting off a brave challenge from unseeded Dave 'Chizzy' Chisnall in the final. Adams stormed into a 4–2 lead, but Chisnall, as he had done in his quarter and semi-final matches, fought back to level the match, 4–4. Adams took the lead again with a 170 checkout and a 10-dart finish, and he resisted another Chisnall fightback to win 7–5, claiming the £100,000 first prize on his 17th appearance at Frimley Green. The trend for musical 'oche walks' continued this year, with Adams walking on to *Hungry Like a Wolf* by Duran Duran, and Chisnall to *I Predict a Riot* by the Kaiser Chiefs. Other notable themes included *One Step Beyond* by Madness (Darryl 'The Dazzler' Fitton), *Be On Your Way* by DJ Zany (Ted 'The Count' Hankey), and *Sandstorm* by Darude (Alan 'Chuck' Norris).

NINE-DART FINISH · Barneveld's achievement at Alexandra Palace was something quite special. A 'nine-darter' is the name given to the completion of a leg of 501 darts in the fewest number of throws (i.e., nine). Such is the rarity of the achievement that, until 2002, there had only been two televised nine-dart finishes and only one, by American Paul Lim in 1990, in a World Championship match. The traditional scoring sequence for a nine-dart finish (which 'Barney' matched in both years) is; treble 20 ~ treble 20 ~ treble 20 (180); treble 20 ~ treble 20 ~ treble 20 (180) (360); treble 20 ~ treble 19 ~ double 12 (141) (501) – although there are many other possible variations.

──────────────── PEA SHOOTING ────────────────

In July 2010, Ian Ashmeade won the 40th World Pea Shooting Championships, which are held annually in Witcham, Cambridgeshire. (The contest was created in 1971 by a local teacher, John Tyson, who was inspired by the weapons he confiscated from his pupils.) ❦ The world of pea shooting was rocked a decade ago when avionics experts from nearby US Air Force bases introduced electronic sights and laser targeting to the traditionally Heath Robinson-esque sport. Controversy still rages as to whether such technology should be allowed but, for the time being at least, old and new techniques of pea propulsion coexist. Contestants have to hit from 12 yards a target constructed from putty, to which the peas stick or make an indentation. Only legumes provided by the event's organisers may be used – presumably to prevent pea tampering.

———— WORLD BOXING CHAMPIONS · AT 30·8·2010 ————

Weight	WBC	WBA	IBF	WBO
Heavy	Klitschko V. [UKR]	Haye [GBR]	Klitschko W. [UKR]	Klitschko W. [UKR]
Cruiser	Wlodarczyk [POL]	Jones [PAN]	Cunningham [USA]	Huck [GER]
Light heavy	Pascal [CAN]	Shumenov [KAZ]	Cloud [USA]	Brähmer [GER]
Super middle	Kessler [DEN]	Ward [USA]	Bute [ROM]	Stieglitz [GER]
Middle	Martinez [ARG]	Sturm [GER]	Sylvester [GER]	Pirog [RUS]
Super welter	*vacant*	Cotto [PUE]	Bundrage [USA]	Dzindziruk [UKR]
Welter	Berto [USA]	Senchenko [UKR]	Zavec [SVN]	Pacquiao [PHI]
Light welter	Alexander [USA]	Khan [GBR]	Alexander [USA]	Bradley [USA]
Light	Soto [MEX]	Marquez [MEX]	Vazquez [MEX]	Marquez [MEX]
Super feather	Tajbert [GER]	Uchiyama [JPN]	*vacant*	Martinez [PUE]
Feather	Rojas [DOM]	John [IND]	Salido [MEX]	López [PUE]
Super bantam	Nishioka [JPN]	Caballero [PAN]	Molitor [CAN]	Vázquez Jr [PUE]
Bantam	Montiel [MEX]	Moreno [PAN]	Pérez [COL]	Montiel [MEX]
Super fly	*vacant*	Darchinyan [ARM]	Rosas [MEX]	Navarez [ARG]
Fly	Wonjongkam [THA]	Kameda [JPN]	Mthalane [RSA]	Miranda [MEX]
Light fly	Romero [MEX]	Segura [MEX]	Lazarte [ARG]	Segura [MEX]
Straw	Sithsamerchai [THA]	Gonzalez [NIC]	Joyi [RSA]	Nietes [PHI]

The Ring magazine, the self-proclaimed 'bible of boxing', creates a ranking of the best boxers across all weight divisions, which many fans regard as an authoritative source of the best 'pound-for-pound' boxers in the world. At 29/8/2010, *The Ring* top 10 were: [1] *Manny 'Pac Man' Pacquiao* (Welterweight); [2] *Floyd 'Pretty Boy' Mayweather Jr* (Super Welterweight); [3] *Juan Manuel Marquez* (Super Featherweight); [4] *Nonito Donaire* (Super Flyweight); [5] *'Sugar' Shane Moseley* (Super Welterweight); [6] *Paul Williams* (Welterweight); [7] *Sergio Martinez* (Middleweight); [8] *Pongsaklek Wonjongkam* (Flyweight); [9] *Fernando Montiel* (Bantamweight); [10] *Wladimir 'Dr Steelhammer' Klitschko* (Heavyweight).

———————————— DAVID HAYE ————————————

Londoner David 'Haymaker' Haye, the former undisputed World Cruiserweight Champion, became only the fourth Briton in history to become Heavyweight Champion of the World when he won a majority decision to claim Russian giant Nikolai 'The Beast from the East' Valuev's WBA title in November 2009. Haye successfully defended his title against American John Ruiz in Manchester in April 2010, after which he stated his intention to unify the division's multiple titles.

Britain's other heavyweight kings, in the order in which they first won the title, are: Bob 'The Freckled Wonder' Fitzsimmons (1896); Lennox Lewis (1993); and Frank 'Bomber' Bruno (1995).

———————————— WEMBLEY PITCH ————————————

In 2010, the pitch at Wembley was relaid for the twelfth time after players and managers complained that the poor surface led to injuries. The Desso GrassMaster surface combines '100% natural grass reinforced with synthetic Desso grass fibres'.

———————————— WIMBLEDON 2010 ————————————

I want to say thank you to the crowd because I was playing the local player
on Friday, and the respect on the court was amazing, and that doesn't happen
on every court in the world, so thank you very much. — RAFAEL NADAL

Rafael Nadal won his second Wimbledon in a super summer for Spanish sport, having been prevented by injury from defending his first title in 2009. Nadal beat Tomáš Berdych in straight sets in an anticlimactic final, although the Czech runner-up had already made his mark by stopping Roger Federer from reaching the final for the first time since 2002. ❦ In her first visit to Wimbledon since 1977 (her Jubilee), the Queen saw Andy Murray beat Finland's Jarkko Nieminen. Both players bowed before the Royal Box – a tradition that had not been observed since 2003. ❦ Serena Williams won her fourth ladies' title with characteristic aplomb – taking her grand slam tally to thirteen. She didn't drop a set throughout the tournament, and her victory meant that the coveted title had been held by one of the two Williams sisters for 9 of the past 11 years (they have met in the final four times). ❦ The results were:

MEN'S SINGLES
Rafael Nadal [SPA]
bt Tomáš Berdych [CZE]
6–3, 7–5, 6–4

————

LADIES' SINGLES
Serena Williams [USA]
bt Vera Zvonareva [RUS]
6–3, 6–2

————

At the end of the day, I'd love
to open more schools in Africa
or the United States.
I would love to help people
and be remembered.
– Serena Williams

MEN'S DOUBLES
Jürgen Melzer [AUS]
& Philipp Petzschner [GER]
bt Robert Lindstedt [SWE]
& Horia Tecau [ROM]
6–1, 7–5, 7–5

LADIES' DOUBLES
Vania King [USA]
& Yaroslava Shvedova [KAZ]
bt Elena Vesnina [RUS]
& Vera Zvonareva [RUS]
7–6 (8–6), 6–2

MIXED DOUBLES
Leander Paes [IND]
& Cara Black [ZIM]
bt Wesley Moodie [RSA]
& Lisa Raymond [USA]
6–4, 7–6 (7–5)

BOYS' SINGLES
Márton Fucsovics [HUN]
bt Benjamin Mitchell [AUS]
6–4, 6–4

GIRLS' SINGLES
Kristýna Plíšková [CZE]
bt Sachie Ishizu [JPN]
6–3, 4–6, 6–4

BOYS' DOUBLES
Liam Broady [GBR]
& Tom Farquharson [GBR]
bt Lewis Burton [GBR]
& George Morgan [GBR]
7–6 (7–4), 6–4

GIRLS' DOUBLES
Tímea Babos [HUN]
& Sloane Stephens [USA]
bt Irina Khromacheva [RUS]
& Elina Svitolina [UKR]
6–7 (7–9), 6–2, 6–2

—————————— ISNER vs MAHUT ——————————

In any other Wimbledon year, Federer losing before the final, and a visit by the Queen, would have been enough to satisfy the headline writers. But those stories were eclipsed by a first-round encounter between American John Isner and Frenchman Nicolas Mahut. This match became the longest in tennis history, both in terms of time and the number of games. The match began at 6:13pm on Tuesday 22 June and ended at 4:48pm on Thursday 24, after 11h 5m and 183 games. Play was suspended on the first evening at 9:07pm, due to fading light, with the match tied at 2 sets all. It resumed at 2:05pm the next day. The record for the longest match was broken at 5:45pm that afternoon, before bad light again stopped play, at 9:10pm. The match continued on Thursday, at 3:43pm, and ended when Isner hit a backhand down the line to win 6–4, 3–6, 6–7

(7–9), 7–6 (7–3), 70–68[†]. ♛ The final tally of 183 games easily beat the previous records of 122 (set during a Davis Cup doubles match between the USA and Chile in 1973) and 112 (set during a Wimbledon singles match between Pancho Gonzales and Charlie Pasarell in 1969). The fifth set alone lasted 8h 11m – 90m longer than the previous longest-ever *match*. Both players and the umpire, Sweden's Mohammed Lahyani, were presented with crystal bowls in recognition of their endurance. Although his second-round match was postponed for a day, Isner could not recover in time, and he lost to Thiemo de Bakker of Holland 0–6, 3–6, 2–6, in just 74 minutes.

† The scoreboard froze at 47–47 and had to be jiggered by an IBM technician. It then reached 50–50 before resetting to 0–0. The IBM team worked on the scoreboard until late into the night so that it would function for the final day.

————— TENNIS GRAND SLAM TOURNAMENTS · 2010 —————

Event	*month*	*surface*	♂	*winner*	♀
Australian Open	Jan	Plexicushion	Roger Federer		Serena Williams
French Open	May/Jun	clay	Rafael Nadal[†]		Francesca Schiavone
Wimbledon	Jun/Jul	grass	Rafael Nadal		Serena Williams
US Open	Aug/Sep	DecoTurf	Rafael Nadal		Kim Clijsters

† Rafael Nadal became only the 7th player to win all four Grand Slam tournaments – the 'Career Slam'.

————————— DAVIS CUP FINAL · 2009 —————————

4–6 December · World Group Final, Palau Sant Jordi, Barcelona
Clay (indoor) SPAIN *bt* CZECH REPUBLIC 5–0

Rafael Nadal [SPA] *bt* Tomáš Berdych [CZE] 7–5, 6–0, 6–2
David Ferrer [SPA] *bt* Radek Štěpánek [CZE] 1–6, 2–6, 6–4, 6–4, 8–6
F López & F Verdasco [SPA] *bt* T Berdych & R Štěpánek [CZE] 7–6 (9–7), 7–5, 6–2
Rafael Nadal [SPA] *bt* Jan Hájek [CZE] 6–3, 6–4
David Ferrer [SPA] *bt* Lukáš Dlouhý [CZE] 6–4, 6–2

—————— BBC SPORTS PERSONALITY OF THE YEAR · 2009 ——————

Sports personality of the year . . . . Ryan Giggs
Team of the year . . . . England men's cricket
Overseas personality . . . . Usain Bolt
Coach of the year . . . . Fabio Capello, England football
Lifetime achievement . . . . Seve Ballesteros
Young personality . . . . Tom Daley (diving world champion)
Unsung hero . . . . Doreen Adcock (Milton Keynes swimming teacher)
Helen Rollason Award 'for courage and achievement in the face of adversity' . . . Major Phil Packer

—————— WORLD SNOOKER CHAMPIONSHIP · 2010 ——————

Neil Robertson became the first Australian to win the snooker world title when he
beat the 2006 champion, Graeme Dott, by 18 frames to 13. (Robertson was the first winner
from outside the UK since 1980, when Canada's Cliff Thorburn beat Hurricane Higgins [see p.63].)
The tense, error-strewn final was completed at 00:54, equalling the latest-ever finish.

THE FINAL · 2–3 May 2010 · FRAME-BY-FRAME
Neil Robertson [AUS] 18–13 Graeme Dott [SCO]

Frame	*tally*						
10–87	0–1	47–74	3–5	113–23	9–7	116–13	13–11
65–55	1–1	66–5	4–5	23–87	9–8	36–72	13–12
1–93	1–2	90–6	5–5	69–56	10–8	69–15	14–12
35–62	1–3	79–72	6–5	82–1	11–8	63–49	15–12
68–56	2–3	79–53	7–5	31–66	11–9	53–78	15–13
62–56	3–3	52–11	8–5	89–12	12–9	74–23	16–13
24–73	3–4	4–71	8–6	2–116 (112)	12–10	58–10	17–13
		27–70	8–7	12–81	12–11	94–1	18–13

The tournament was overshadowed by allegations published in the *News of the World* that three-times
world champion John Higgins had been involved in 'match-fixing' negotiations. In May, Higgins was
suspended by the World Professional Billiards and Snooker Assoc. pending an investigation, although
he strenuously denied any wrongdoing. In September, a tribunal banned Higgins for 6 months and
fined him £75,000 for 'giving the impression to others that they were agreeing to act in breach of the
betting rules', although the principal charges of match fixing, bribery, and corruption were all dropped.

—————— THE TIMES SPORTING POWER TOP TEN ——————

In March 2010, *The Times* compiled its Sporting Power 100. The top 10 were:

1 . . Fabio Capello . . . manager, England
2 . . Sepp Blatter . . . . president, FIFA
3 . . Lord Coe . . . . London 2012
4 . . Jeremy Darrock . . . . CEO, BSkyB
5 . . Wayne Rooney . . . . footballer
6 . . Sheikh Mansour . . . . owner, Man C
7 . . Alex Ferguson . . . . manager, Man U
8 . . Richard Scudamore . . . . Premier Lg
9 . . Lord Triesman . . . (ex-)chairman, FA
10 . Bernie Ecclestone . . . . Formula 1

——— 2010 VANCOUVER WINTER OLYMPICS ———

The death of the 21-year-old Georgian luger, Nodar Kumaritashvili, who crashed at high speed during a practice run only hours before the opening ceremony, cast a shadow over the February 2010 Winter Olympics in Vancouver. Elements of the media blamed the tragedy on Canada's 'Own the Podium' initiative, which sought to make the host nation the game's leading medal-winner. It was alleged that non-Canadians had been restricted in their use of the luge track (and other venues) in the run-up to the event. ❦ Kumaritashvili's death began a war of words between local organisers and sections of the British media, who had already condemned the games as the 'worst ever'. (This followed the cancellation of events due to unseasonably warm weather, the return of more than 28,000 tickets, and long queues for spectators.) The event's CEO John Furlong hit back at the critics, saying, 'they don't appear to be attending the same Olympic Games as everyone else'. London's 2012 chief, Lord Coe, defended the Canadian committee, thanked it for its counsel, and praised the games' success. ❦ In the end, Canada shared the podium – winning more golds than any other nation, but ranking third in the total medals table. Britain's only gold (indeed, only medal) came in the women's skeleton, when Amy Williams bested her more

Medals	G	S	B	all
United States	9	15	13	37
Germany	10	13	7	30
Canada	14	7	5	26
Norway	9	8	6	23
Austria	4	6	6	16
Russian Fed.	3	5	7	15
Korea	6	6	2	14
China	5	2	4	11
Sweden	5	2	4	11
France	2	3	6	11
Switzerland	6	0	3	9
Netherlands	4	1	3	8
Czech Rep.	2	0	4	6
Poland	1	3	2	6
Italy	1	1	3	5
Japan	0	3	2	5
Finland	0	1	4	5
Australia	2	1	0	3
Belarus	1	1	1	3
Slovakia	1	1	1	3
Croatia	0	2	1	3
Slovenia	0	2	1	3
Latvia	0	2	0	2
Great Britain	1	0	0	1
Estonia	0	1	0	1
Kazakhstan	0	1	0	1

celebrated compatriot Shelley Rudman – Britain's only medal winner at the 2006 Winter Games. ❦ Perhaps the most talked-about event of the games was the newly introduced sport of ski cross, where four skiers race simultaneously down an action-packed course. The aggressive overtaking, thrilling speed, and inevitable collisions made some of the more traditional alpine events appear quaint in comparison. ❦ Below are some other highlights of the games: Alex Bilodeau won the men's mogul to become the first Canadian to win an Olympic gold on home turf, catalysing an outpouring of emotion and relief from the host nation. ❦ In the final of the men's ice hockey, and in sudden death overtime, Canada beat its fierce rival America, to whom it had lost earlier in the tournament. ❦ Lindsey Vonn became the first American to win gold in the women's alpine downhill skiing, despite nursing a shin injury she described as 'excruciating'. ❦ Joannie Rochette won bronze for Canada in the women's figure skating, despite her mother's sudden death only two days before the start of the competition. ❦ American Bode Miller finally won gold in the Super Combined alpine skiing, four years after his failure in Turin, where he had been criticised for his comment that he had 'partied at an Olympic level'.

—— READY RECKONER OF OTHER RESULTS · 2009/10 ——

AMERICAN FOOTBALL · Superbowl	New Orleans Saints 31–17 Indianapolis Colts
ANGLING · National Coarse Ch. Div.1	Steve Collett 56·02kg
BADMINTON · World. Ch.	♂ Chen Jin [CHI] *bt* Taufik Hidayat [IND] 21–13, 21–15
	♀ Wang Lin [CHI] *bt* Wang Xin [CHI] 21–11, 19–21, 21–13
BASEBALL · World Series [2009]	New York Yankees 4–2 Philadelphia Phillies
BASKETBALL · NBA finals	Los Angeles Lakers 4–3 Boston Celtics
BBL Trophy final	Newcastle Eagles 111–95 Cheshire Jets
THE BOAT RACE	Cambridge *bt* Oxford [by 1·33 lengths, in 17m, 35s]
BOG SNORKELLING	♂ Dan Morgan [WAL] ♀ Dineka Maguire [NIR]
BOWLS · World Matchplay	Ian Bond [ENG] *bt* Jason Greenslade [ENG] 9–5, 5–6, 2–0
CHEESE ROLLING · Cooper's Hill	*official event cancelled*
CHESS · British Championship	♂ GM Mickey Adams ♀ IM Jovanka Houska
FIDE World Championship [2009]	Vishwanathan Anand [IND]
COMPETITIVE EATING · Int. Hot Dog	Joey 'Jaws' Chestnut [USA] [54 dogs in 10 mins]
World Nettle Eating Championship	Sam Cunningham [ENG] [74' of raw leaves]
CRICKET · Test series – South Africa *vs* England (in SA)	South Africa *dr* England 1–1
One day series (in South Africa)	England *bt* South Africa 2–1
Test series – Bangladesh *vs* England (in Bangladesh)	England *bt* Bangladesh 2–0
One day series (in Bangladesh)	England *bt* Bangladesh 3–0
Test series – England *vs* Bangladesh	England *bt* Bangladesh 2–0
Test series – Pakistan *vs* Australia (in England)	Pakistan *dr* Australia 1–1
One day series – England *vs* Australia	England *bt* Australia 3–2
Test series – England *vs* Pakistan	England *bt* Pakistan 3–1
Women's One day series	England *bt* New Zealand 3–2
Women's T20 Series	New Zealand *bt* England 2–1
Clydesdale Bank 40	Warwickshire
County Championship	Nottinghamshire
CROQUET · World Team Championship (MacRobertson Shield)	Great Britain
CYCLING · Tour de France	Alberto Contador [ESP] [see p.306]
Tour of Britain	Michael Albasini (Team HTC – Columbia)
DARTS · Lakeside World Ch. [BDO]	Martin Adams *bt* Dave Chisnell [see p.312]
Ladbrokes World Ch. [PDC]	Phil Taylor *bt* Simon Whitlock [see p.312]
ELEPHANT POLO · Kings' Cup	Audemars Piguet 10–6 King Power
ENDURANCE RACES · Marathon des Sables	♂ Mohamad Ahansal [MOR] 19:45·08
	♀ Monica Aguilera Viladomiu [ESP] 29:44·11
Devil o' the Highlands	♂ Craig Stewart 5:30·58 · ♀ Joanna Zabrzewski 6:51·30
EQUESTRIANISM · Badminton	Inonothing *ridden by* Paul Tapner [AUS] 44·9 pen
Burghley	Lenamore *ridden by* Caroline Powell [NZL] 38·7 pen
FOOTBALL · FA Cup Women's	Everton 3–2 Arsenal
UEFA Europa League	Athletico Madrid 2–1 Fulham
Community Shield	Manchester Utd 3–1 Chelsea
Carling Cup	Manchester Utd 2–1 Aston Villa
Johnstone's Paint Trophy	Southampton 4–1 Carlisle Utd
Premier League	Chelsea
Championship	Newcastle Utd
League 1	Norwich City

— READY RECKONER OF OTHER RESULTS · 2009/10 cont. —

FOOTBALL (cont.) · League 2   Notts County
   Scottish Premier League   Rangers
   Scottish Cup   Dundee Utd 3–0 Ross County
FORMULA ONE · World Drivers' Ch. [2009]   Jenson Button [GBR] · Brawn GP
   World Constructors' Championship [2009]   Brawn GP [GBR]
GOLF · Solheim Cup   USA
   Mission Hills World Cup [2009]   Italy
GREYHOUND RACING · Blue Square Greyhound Derby   Bandicoot Tipoki
HOCKEY · Hockey World Cups   ♂ Australia *bt* Germany 2–1
                                            ♀ Argentina *bt* Holland 3–1
HORSE RACING · Grand Ntnl   Don't Push It *trained by* Jonjo O'Neill *ridden by* Tony McCoy
   Vodafone Epsom Derby   Workforce *trained by* Sir Michael Stoute *ridden by* Ryan Moore
   Chelt. Gold Cup Imperial Commander *trained by* Nigel Twiston-Davies *ridden by* Paddy Brennan
   1,000 Guineas   Special Duty *trained by* Criquette Head-Maarek *ridden by* Stephane Pasquier
   2,000 Guineas   Makfi *trained by* Mikel Delzangles *ridden by* Christophe Lemaire
   The Oaks   Snow Fairy *trained by* Ed Dunlop *ridden by* Ryan Moore
   St Leger   Arctic Cosmos *trained by* John Gosden *ridden by* William Buick
ICE HOCKEY · Stanley Cup   Chicago Blackhawks *bt* Philadelphia Flyers 4–2
MOBILE PHONE THROWING · UK Champ   Jeremy Gallop [GBR] 88·51m
NETBALL · Superleague title [2009]   Team Bath
RUGBY LEAGUE · Super League [2009]   Leeds Rhinos
   Challenge Cup   Warrington Wolves 30–6 Leeds Rhinos
   League Leaders' Shield   Leeds Rhinos
   World Club Challenge   Melbourne Storm 18–10 Leeds Rhinos
RUGBY UNION · Women's World Cup · Final   New Zealand 13–10 England
   Guinness Premiership   Leicester Tigers [top of table]
   Guinness Premiership Championship   Leicester Tigers 33–27 Saracens
   LV= Anglo-Welsh Cup   Northampton 30–24 Gloucester
   Magners Celtic League   Ospreys
   Heineken Cup   Toulouse 21–19 Biarritz
   European Challenge Cup   Cardiff Blues 28–21 Toulon
   Varsity Match [2009]   Cambridge 31–27 Oxford
RUNNING · Great North Run   ♂ Haile Gebrselassie [ETH] 0·59·33
                                     ♀ Berhane Adere [ETH] 1·08·49
SNOOKER · UK Ch. [2009]   Ding Junhui [CHI] *bt* John Higgins [SCO] 10–8
SUDOKU · World Sudoku Championship   Jan Mrozowski [POL]
TENNIS · Oz Open   R. Federer [SWI] *bt* A. Murray [GBR] 6–3, 6–4, 7–6 (13–11)
                      S. Williams [USA] *bt* J. Henin [BEL] 6–4, 3–6, 6–2
   French Open   R. Nadal [ESP] *bt* R. Söderling [SWE] 6–4, 6–2, 6–4
                      F. Schiavone [ITA] *bt* S. Stosur [ESP] 6–4, 7–6 (7–2)
   US Open   R. Nadal [ESP] *bt* N. Djokovic [SER] 6–4, 5–7, 6–4, 6–2
                      K. Clijsters [BEL] *bt* V. Zvonereva [RUS] 6–2, 6–1
   Fed Cup [2009]   Italy *bt* USA 4–0
   Davis Cup [2009]   Spain *bt* Czech Rep. 5–0
TRIATHLON · European Championships   ♂ Alistair Brownlee [GBR] 1:44·24
                                          ♀ Nicola Spirig [SWI] 1:57·58

Ephemerides

For everybody makes Almanacks now, and with very few exceptions,
they are all stupid affairs. — PUNCH, 1858 [see p.344]

---------------------------------- 2011 ----------------------------------

Roman numerals............... MMXI	Indian (Saka) year...... 1933 (22 Mar)
English Regnal year[1] ......59th (6 Feb)	Sikh year ....543 Nanakshahi Era (13 Apr)
Dominical Letter[2].....................B	Jewish year ....5772 (29 Sep)
Epact[3] XXV	Roman year [AUC] ...... 2764 (14 Jan)
Golden Number (Lunar Cycle)[4] .XVII	Masonic year.................6011 AL[5]
Chinese New Year. Rabbit 4709 (3 Feb)	Knights Templar year........ 893 AO[6]
Hindu New Year.........2067 (4 Apr)	Baha'i year................168 (21 Mar)
Islamic year.............1433 (26 Nov)	Queen bee colour................ white

[1] The number of years from the accession of a monarch; traditionally, legislation was dated by the Regnal year of the reigning monarch. [2] A way of categorising years to facilitate the calculation of Easter. If January 1 is a Sunday, the Dominical Letter for the year will be A; if January 2 is a Sunday, it will be B; and so on. [3] The number of days by which the solar year exceeds the lunar year. [4] The number of the year (1–19) in the 19-year Metonic cycle; it is used in the calculation of Easter, and is found by adding 1 to the remainder left after dividing the number of the year by 19. [5] Anno Lucis, the 'Year of Light' when the world was formed. [6] Anno Ordinis, the 'Year of the Order'.

---------------------- TRADITIONAL ZODIAC RHYME ----------------------

Behold our orbit as through twice six signs
Our central Sun apparently inclines:
The Golden Fleece his pale ray first adorns,
Then tow'rds the Bull he winds and gilds his horns;
Castor and Pollux then receive his ray;
On burning Cancer then he seems to stay;
On flaming Leo pours the liquid shower;
Then faints beneath the Virgin's conquering power;
Now the just Scales weigh well both day and night;
The Scorpion then receives the solar light;
Then quivered Chiron clouds his wintry face,
And the tempestuous Sea-Goat mends his pace;
Now in the water Sol's warm beams are quench'd,
Till with the Fishes he is fairly drench'd.
These twice six signs successively appear,
And mark the twelve months of the circling year.

RED-LETTER DAYS

Red-letter days are those days of civil and ecclesiastical importance – so named because they were marked out in red ink on early religious calendars. (The Romans marked unlucky days with black chalk, and auspicious days with white.) When these days fall within law sittings, the judges of the Queen's Bench Division sit wearing elegant scarlet robes. The Red-letter days in Great Britain are tabulated below:

Conversion of St Paul	25 Jan	St Barnabas	11 Jun
Purification	2 Feb	Official BD HM the Queen†	11 Jun
Accession of HM the Queen	6 Feb	St John the Baptist	24 Jun
Ash Wednesday†	9 Mar	St Peter	29 Jun
St David's Day	1 Mar	St Thomas	3 Jul
Annunciation	25 Mar	St James	25 Jul
BD HM the Queen	21 Apr	St Luke	18 Oct
St Mark	25 Apr	SS Simon & Jude	28 Oct
SS Philip & James	1 May	All Saints	1 Nov
St Matthias	14 May	Lord Mayor's Day†	12 Nov
Ascension†	2 Jun	BD HRH the Prince of Wales	14 Nov
Coronation of HM the Queen	2 Jun	St Andrew's Day	30 Nov
BD HRH Duke of Edinburgh	10 Jun	(† *indicates the date varies by year*)	

TRADITIONAL WEDDING ANNIVERSARY SYMBOLS

1st	Cotton	10th	Tin	35th	Coral
2nd	Paper	11th	Steel	40th	Ruby
3rd	Leather	12th	Silk, Linen	45th	Sapphire
4th	Fruit, Flowers	13th	Lace	50th	Gold
5th	Wood	14th	Ivory	55th	Emerald
6th	Sugar	15th	Crystal	60th	Diamond
7th	Wool, Copper	20th	China	70th	Platinum
8th	Pottery	25th	Silver	75th	Diamond
9th	Willow	30th	Pearl	*American symbols differ.*	

KEY TO SYMBOLS USED OVERLEAF

[★ BH]	UK Bank Holiday	[§ *patronage*]	Saint's Day
[☽]	Clocks change (UK)	[WA 1900]	Wedding Anniversary
[❤]	Hunting season (traditional)	●	New Moon [GMT]
[ND]	National Day	☺	Full Moon [GMT]
[NH]	National Holiday	[☄]	Annual meteor shower
[ID 1900]	Independence Day	[UN]	United Nations Day
[BD1900]	Birthday	[◉]	Eclipse
[†1900]	Anniversary of death	[£]	Union Flag to be flown (UK)

Certain dates are subject to change, estimated, or tentative at the time of printing.

——————————————— JANUARY ———————————————

Capricorn [♑] *Birthstone* · GARNET *Aquarius* [♒]
(Dec 22–Jan 20)   *Flower* · CARNATION (Jan 21–Feb 19)

1 ....New Year's Day · J. Edgar Hoover [BD1895] ....Sa
2 ....St Munchin [§ *Limerick*] · Sir Michael Tippett [BD1905] ....Su
3★..........★BH · St Genevieve [§ *Paris*] · Lord Haw-Haw [†1946 *executed*] ....M
4 ....☻ · Quadrantids [♆] · T.S. Eliot [†1965]....................Tu
5 .... Twelfth Night · Diane Keaton [BD1946] ....W
6 ....Epiphany · Rudolf Nureyev [†1993] ....Th
7 ....Magnus Magnusson [†2007] · Lewis Hamilton [BD1985]............. F
8 ....: Giotto [†1337] · Elvis Presley [BD1935] ....Sa
9 ....Gracie Fields [BD1898] · Simone de Beauvoir [BD1908]............Su
10..................... Pope Gregory X [†1276] · Samuel Colt [†1862].................M
11.........................Albert Hoffman [BD1906]...........................Tu
12.............Hermann Goering [BD1893] · Agatha Christie [†1976].............W
13......... St Hilary of Poitiers [§ *snake-bites*] · Salmon P. Chase [BD1808]..........Th
14.............Edmond Halley [†1742] · Humphrey Bogart [†1957].............. F
15.....................Martin Luther King [BD1929].........................Sa
16.................Carole Lombard [†1942] · Kate Moss [BD1974]................Su
17....... St Anthony of Egypt [§ *basket-makers*] · Benjamin Franklin [BD1706].......M
18.............................Cary Grant [BD1904]............................Tu
19.........☺ · St Henry of Finland [§ *Finland*] · Edgar Allan Poe [BD1809].........W
20.............St Sebastian [§ *archers, soldiers & athletes*] · George V [†1936] ....Th
21............. Benny Hill [BD1925] · Cecil B. DeMille [†1959]................ F
22.............. Lord Byron [BD1788] · Malcolm McLaren [BD1946]..............Sa
23............. St John the Almsgiver · William Pitt the Younger [†1806]..........Su
24.........St Francis de Sales [§ *journalists*] · Edith Wharton [BD1862] ....M
25......Scotland – Burns' Night · Conversion of St Paul · St Dwyn [§ *lovers*].....Tu
26........Australia – Australia Day [NH] · Andrew Ridgeley [BD1963]..........W
27..............Holocaust Memorial Day · Lewis Carroll [BD1832] ...:.........Th
28...... St Thomas Aquinas [§ *universities and students*] · Jackson Pollock [BD1912]....... F
29.................Edward Lear [†1888] · Germaine Greer [BD1939]...............Sa
30.........Charles I [†1649 *executed*] · Mahatma Gandhi [†1948 *assassinated*].........Su
31.............Anna Pavlova [BD1882] · Justin Timberlake [BD1981]..............M

French Rev. calendar......*Nivôse* (snow)	Dutch month ......*Lauwmaand* (frosty)
Angelic governor................*Gabriel*	Saxon month....... *Wulf-monath* (wolf)
Epicurean calendar..... *Marronglaçaire*	Talismanic stone ....*Onyx*

❦ The Latin month *Ianuarius* derives from *ianua* ('door'), since it was the opening of the year. It was also associated with *Janus* – the two-faced Roman god of doors and openings who guarded the gates of heaven. Janus could simultaneously face the year just past and the year to come. ❦ *If January Calends be summerly gay,'Twill be winterly weather till the calends of May.* ❦ *Janiveer – Freeze the pot upon the fier.* ❦ *He that will live another year, Must eat a hen in Januvere.* ❦ On the stock market, the *January effect* is the trend of stocks performing especially well that month. ❦

---— FEBRUARY ——---

Aquarius [♒]	*Birthstone* · AMETHYST	*Pisces* [♓]
(Jan 21–Feb 19)	*Flower* · PRIMROSE	(Feb 20–Mar 20)

1 .... Partridge & pheasant shooting season ends [❦] .... Tu
2 .... Candlemas · Groundhog Day, USA · Sid Vicious [†1979] .... W
3 .... ☻ · St Blaise [§ *sore throats*] · Buddy Holly [†1959] .... Th
4 .... Sri Lanka [ID 1948] · Karen Carpenter [†1983] .... F
5 .... St Agatha [§ *bell founders*] · William S. Burroughs [BD1914] .... Sa
6 ... Accession of HM Queen Elizabeth II [£] · New Zealand – Waitangi Day ... Su
7 .... Grenada [ID 1974] · Laura Ingalls Wilder [BD1867] .... M
8 .... Jack Lemmon [BD1925] · Gary Coleman [BD1968] .... Tu
9 .... St Apollonia [§ *dentists*] · Mia Farrow [BD1945] .... W
10 .... Alexander Pushkin [†1837] .... Th
11 ...... Scottish salmon fishing season opens [❦] · Mary Quant [BD1934] .... F
12 .... Immanuel Kant [†1804] · Abraham Lincoln [BD1809] .... Sa
13 .... St Modomnoc [§ *bee-keepers*] · Christabel Pankhurst [†1958] .... Su
14 .... St Valentine [§ *lovers*] · Captain James Cook [†1779 *murdered*] .... M
15 .... Ernest Shackleton [BD1874] · Nat King Cole [†1965] .... Tu
16 .... Sonny Bono [BD1935] · Kim Jong-il [BD1942] .... W
17 .... Ruth Rendell [BD1930] .... Th
18 .... ☽ · Nepal [ND] · Martin Luther [†1546] .... F
19 .... Prince Andrew [BD1960] [£] · Smokey Robinson [BD1940] .... Sa
20 .... Cindy Crawford [BD1966] .... Su
21 .... Int. Mother Language Day [UN] · Robert Mugabe [BD1924] .... M
22 .... Feast of Chair of St Peter · Bruce Forsyth [BD1928] .... Tu
23 .... Brunei [ND] · Stan Laurel [†1965] .... W
24 .... Estonia [ID 1918] · Alain Prost [BD1955] .... Th
25 .... Kuwait [ND] · Tennessee Williams [†1983] .... F
26 .... Levi Strauss [BD1829] · Johnny Cash [BD1932] .... Sa
27 .... Dominican Republic [ID 1844] · Paddy Ashdown [BD1941] .... Su
28 .... Hind stalking season closes [❦] · Henry James [†1916] .... M

French Rev. calendar ..... *Pluviôse* (rain)	Dutch month *Sprokelmaand* (vegetation)
Angelic governor .... *Barchiel*	Saxon month .... *Solmonath* (Sun)
Epicurean calendar .... *Harrengsauridor*	Talismanic stone .... *Jasper*

❦ Much mythology and folklore considers February to have the most bitter weather: *February is seldom warm.* ❦ *February, if ye be fair, The sheep will mend, and nothing mair; February, if ye be foul, The sheep will die in every pool.* ❦ *As the day lengthens, the cold strengthens.* ❦ That said, a foul February is thought to predict a fine year: *All the months in the year, Curse a fair Februeer.* ❦ The word *February* derives from the Latin *februum* – which means cleansing, and reflects the rituals undertaken by the Romans before spring. ❦ Having only 28 days in non-leap years, February was known in Welsh as *y mis bach* – the little month. ❦ February is traditionally personified in pictures either by an old man warming himself by the fireside, or as 'a sturdy maiden, with a tinge of the red hard winter apple on her hardy cheek'. ❦

— MARCH —

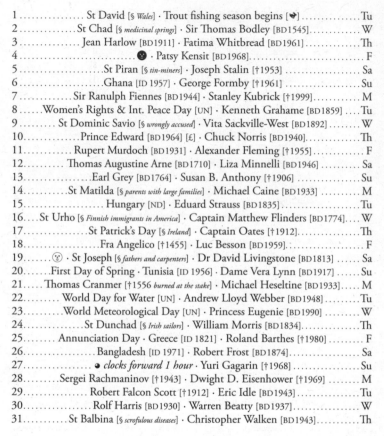

Pisces [♓]
(Feb 20–Mar 20)

Birthstone · BLOODSTONE
Flower · JONQUIL

Aries [♈]
(Mar 21–Apr 20)

1 .... St David [§ *Wales*] · Trout fishing season begins [➜] .... Tu
2 .... St Chad [§ *medicinal springs*] · Sir Thomas Bodley [BD1545] .... W
3 .... Jean Harlow [BD1911] · Fatima Whitbread [BD1961] .... Th
4 .... 😊 · Patsy Kensit [BD1968] .... F
5 .... St Piran [§ *tin-miners*] · Joseph Stalin [†1953] .... Sa
6 .... Ghana [ID 1957] · George Formby [†1961] .... Su
7 .... Sir Ranulph Fiennes [BD1944] · Stanley Kubrick [†1999] .... M
8 ..... Women's Rights & Int. Peace Day [UN] · Kenneth Grahame [BD1859] .... Tu
9 .... St Dominic Savio [§ *wrongly accused*] · Vita Sackville-West [BD1892] .... W
10 .... Prince Edward [BD1964] [£] · Chuck Norris [BD1940] .... Th
11 .... Rupert Murdoch [BD1931] · Alexander Fleming [†1955] .... F
12 .... Thomas Augustine Arne [BD1710] · Liza Minnelli [BD1946] .... Sa
13 .... Earl Grey [BD1764] · Susan B. Anthony [†1906] .... Su
14 .... St Matilda [§ *parents with large families*] · Michael Caine [BD1933] .... M
15 .... Hungary [ND] · Eduard Strauss [BD1835] .... Tu
16 .... St Urho [§ *Finnish immigrants in America*] · Captain Matthew Flinders [BD1774] .... W
17 .... St Patrick's Day [§ *Ireland*] · Captain Oates [†1912] .... Th
18 .... Fra Angelico [†1455] · Luc Besson [BD1959] : .... F
19 ...... ☺ · St Joseph [§ *fathers and carpenters*] · Dr David Livingstone [BD1813] ...... Sa
20 ...... First Day of Spring · Tunisia [ID 1956] · Dame Vera Lynn [BD1917] ...... Su
21 ..... Thomas Cranmer [†1556 *burned at the stake*] · Michael Heseltine [BD1933] ..... M
22 .... World Day for Water [UN] · Andrew Lloyd Webber [BD1948] .... Tu
23 .... World Meteorological Day [UN] · Princess Eugenie [BD1990] .... W
24 .... St Dunchad [§ *Irish sailors*] · William Morris [BD1834] .... Th
25 .... Annunciation Day · Greece [ID 1821] · Roland Barthes [†1980] .... F
26 .... Bangladesh [ID 1971] · Robert Frost [BD1874] .... Sa
27 .... ◑ *clocks forward 1 hour* · Yuri Gagarin [†1968] .... Su
28 .... Sergei Rachmaninov [†1943] · Dwight D. Eisenhower [†1969] .... M
29 .... Robert Falcon Scott [†1912] · Eric Idle [BD1943] .... Tu
30 .... Rolf Harris [BD1930] · Warren Beatty [BD1937] .... W
31 .... St Balbina [§ *scrofulous diseases*] · Christopher Walken [BD1943] .... Th

French Rev. calendar..... *Ventôse* (wind)	Dutch month ..*Lentmaand* (lengthening)
Angelic governor............. *Machidiel*	Saxon month..... *Hrèth-monath* (rough)
Epicurean calendar.... *Oeufalacoquidor*	Talismanic stone .... *Ruby*

❦ The first month of the Roman year, March is named for Mars, the god of war but also an agricultural deity. ❦ The unpredictability of March weather leads to some confusion (*March has many weathers*), though it is generally agreed that March *comes in like a lion, and goes out like a lamb*. Yet, because March is often too wet for crops to flourish, many considered *a bushel of Marche dust* [a dry March] *is worth a ransom of gold*. ❦ March hares are 'mad' with nothing more than lust, since it is their mating season. ❦ The *Mars* bar is named after its creator, Frank Mars. ❦

APRIL

 Aries [♈]
(Mar 21–Apr 20)

Birthstone · DIAMOND
Flower · SWEET PEA

Taurus [♉]
(Apr 21–May 21)

1 . . . . .April Fool's Day [except in Scotland] · Roebuck season opens [♥] . . . . F
2 . . . . . .St Urban of Langres [§ *vine dressers*] · Hans Christian Andersen [BD1805]. . . . . Sa
3 . . . . ☻ · Washington Irving [BD1783] · Tony Benn [BD1925] . . . . .Su
4 . . . . Senegal [ID 1960] · Sir Charles Siemens [BD1823] . . . . .M
5 . . . . .St Vincent Ferrer [§ *builders*] · Bette Davis [BD1908] . . . . .Tu
6 . . . . Paul Daniels [BD1938] · Rory Bremner [BD1961] . . . . W
7 . . . . World Health Day [UN] · William Wordsworth [BD1770] . . . . .Th
8 . . . . .Japan – Flower festival · Pablo Picasso [†1973] . . . . F
9 . . . . Isambard Kingdom Brunel [BD1806] . . . . Sa
10. . . . . .Joseph Pulitzer [BD1847] · Omar Sharif [BD1932] . . . . .Su
11. . . . . .St Stanislaw of Krakow [§ *Poland*] · Primo Levi [†1987] . . . . M
12. . . . . .St Zeno [§ *Verona*] · Franklin D. Roosevelt [†1945]. . . . . .Tu
13. . . . . Chad [ND] · Alan Clark [BD1928]. . . . . W
14. . . . . Abraham Lincoln [†1865 *assassinated*] · Julie Christie [BD1940] . . . . .Th
15. . . . . Emma Thompson [BD1959] · Samantha Fox [BD1966] . . . . F
16. . . . . .St Drogo [§ *shepherds*] · Spike Milligan [BD1918] . . . . Sa
17. . . . . .Syria [ID 1946] · Benjamin Franklin [†1790]. . . . . .Su
18. . . . . . .☺ · St Mary of the Incarnation [§ *widows*] · Albert Einstein [†1955] . . . . . . M
19. . . . . .Sue Barker [BD1956] · Frankie Howerd [†1992]. . . . . .Tu
20. . . . . Adolf Hitler [BD1889] · Bram Stoker [†1912] . . . . W
21. . . Queen Elizabeth II [BD1926] [£] · Lyrids [☄] · Charlotte Brontë [BD1816] . . .Th
22★ . . . . ★BH · Richard Nixon [†1994] . . . . F
23. . . . . St George [§ *England*] · World Book & Copyright Day [UN]. . . . . Sa
?4 . . . . .Daniel Defoe [†17?1] · Wallis Simpson [†1906]. . . . . Su
25★ . . . . ★BH · Australia & New Zealand – Anzac Day · Al Pacino [BD1940] . . . . . . M
26. Tanzania [ND] · Marcus Aurelius [BD121] . . . . .Tu
27. . . . . St Zita [§ *bakers*] · Socrates [†399 BC] . . . . W
28. . . . . .Benito Mussolini [†1945 *executed*] · Terry Pratchett [BD1948]. . . . . .Th
29. . . . . . St Peter the Martyr [§ *midwives & inquisitors*] · Alfred Hitchcock [†1980] . . . . F
30. . . . . Stag stalking season closes [♥] · Adolf Hitler [†1945 *suicide*]. . . . . Sa

French Rev. cal. . . . . . *Germinal* (budding)	Dutch month . . . . *Grasmaand* (grass)
Angelic governor . . . .*Asmodel*	Saxon month . . . . , . . . *Eastre-monath*
Epicurean calendar. . . . .*Petitpoisidor*	Talismanic stone . . . . *Topaz*

❦ April, T.S. Eliot's 'cruellest month', heralds the start of spring and is associated with new growth and sudden bursts of rain. ❦ Its etymology might derive from the Latin *aperire* ('to open') – although in Old English it was known simply as the *Eastre-monath*. ❦ *April with his hack and his bill, Plants a flower on every hill.* ❦ The custom of performing pranks and hoaxes on April Fool's Day (or *poisson d'avril*, as it is known in France) is long established, although its origins are much disputed. ❦ *If it thunders on All Fools' day, it brings good crops of corn and hay.* ❦ Cuckoos used to appear in letters to *The Times* c.8 April; the last was on 25 April, 1940. ❦

MAY

Taurus [♉]   *Birthstone* · EMERALD   *Gemini* [♊]
(Apr 21–May 21)   *Flower* · LILY OF THE VALLEY   (May 22–Jun 21)

1	May Day · Joseph Heller [BD1923]	Su
2★	★BH · Donatella Versace [BD1955] · David Beckham [BD1975]	M
3	● · World Press Freedom Day [UN] · St James the Lesser [§ *hatmakers*]	Tu
4	St Florian [§ *invoked against fire & water*] · International Firefighters Day	W
5	Eta Aquarids [☄] · Karl Marx [BD1818]	Th
6	Rudolph Valentino [BD1895] · Tony Blair [BD1953]	F
7	Robert Browning [BD1812] · Eva Peron [BD1919]	Sa
8	VE Day · Paul Gauguin [†1903]	Su
9	Europe Day – European Union [£] · Glenda Jackson [BD1936]	M
10	St Catald [§ *invoked against plagues, drought & storms*] · Paul Revere [†1818]	Tu
11	Spencer Perceval [†1812 *assassinated*] · Irving Berlin [BD1888]	W
12	St Pancras [§ *children*] · Perry Como [†2001]	Th
13	Daphne du Maurier [BD1907] · Harvey Keitel [BD1939]	F
14	St Matthias [§ *alcoholics & carpenters*] · Henry John Heinz [†1919]	Sa
15	International Day of Families [UN] · St Isidore [§ *rural life*]	Su
16	Liberace [BD1919] · Jim Henson [†1990]	M
17	☺ · Norway [ND] · Sandro Botticelli [†1510]	Tu
18	International Museum Day · Betrand Russell [BD1872]	W
19	St Yves [§ *lawyers & Brittany*] · William Ewart Gladstone [†1898]	Th
20	Cameroon [ND] · Cher [BD1946]	F
21	St Eugene de Mazenod [§ *dysfunctional families*] · Barbara Cartland [†2000]	Sa
22	International Day for Biological Diversity [UN]	Su
23	Bonnie Parker & Clyde Barrow [†1934 *ambushed*]	M
24	Gabriel Fahrenheit [BD1686] · Queen Victoria [BD1819]	Tu
25	Venerable Bede [†735]	W
26	Georgia [ID 1918] · Zola Budd [BD1966]	Th
27	Henry Kissinger [BD 1923] · Duncan Goodhew [BD 1957]	F
28	Azerbaijan [ND] · Ian Fleming [BD1908]	Sa
29	International Day of United Nations Peacekeepers [UN]	Su
30★	★BH · St Walstan [§ *agriculture*] · Voltaire [†1778]	M
31	The Visitation of the Blessed Virgin Mary · John Prescott [BD1938]	Tu

French Rev. calendar... *Floréal* (blossom)	Dutch month ...... *Blowmaand* (flower)
Angelic governor............... *Ambriel*	Saxon month....... *Trimilchi* [see below]
Epicurean calendar........... *Aspergial*	Talismanic stone .... *Garnet*

❦ Named after *Maia*, the goddess of growth, May is considered a joyous month, as Milton wrote: 'Hail bounteous May that dost inspire Mirth and youth, and warm desire'. ❦ However, May has long been thought a bad month in which to marry: *who weds in May throws it all away*. ❦ Anglo-Saxons called May *Trimilchi*, since in May cows could be milked three times a day. ❦ May was thought a time of danger for the sick; so to have *climbed May hill* was to have survived the month. ❦ Kittens born in May were thought weak, and were often drowned. ❦

━━━━━━━━━━━━━JUNE━━━━━━━━━━━━━

| **Gemini** [♊] | **Birthstone** · PEARL | **Cancer** [♋] | |
| (May 22–Jun 21) | **Flower** · ROSE | (Jun 22–Jul 22) | |

1 .... ● · Samoa [ID 1962] · Gerald Scarfe [BD 1936] .... W
2 .... Coronation of Elizabeth II [1953] [£] · Marquis de Sade [BD 1740] .... Th
3 ...... St Kevin [§ *blackbirds*] · Duke of Windsor & Wallis Simpson [WA 1937] ...... F
4 .... Tonga [ID 1970] · Kaiser Wilhelm II [†1941] .... Sa
5 .... World Environment Day [UN] · O. Henry [†1910] .... Su
6 .... D-Day · Robert Kennedy [†1968 *assassinated*] .... M
7 .... Malta [ND] · Robert the Bruce [†1329] .... Tu
8 .... St Medard [§ *good weather, prisoners & toothache*] · Cochise [†1874] .... W
9 .... Nero [†68 *suicide*] · Peter the Great [BD 1672] .... Th
10 .... HRH Prince Philip [BD 1921] [£] · Judy Garland [BD 1922] .... F
11 .... Jackie Stewart [BD 1939] · Catherine Cookson [†1998] .... Sa
12 .... Philippines [ID 1898] · Anne Frank [BD 1929] .... Su
13. St Anthony of Padua [§ *horses, mules, & donkeys*] · Harriet Beecher Stowe [BD 1811] . M
14 .... Jerome K. Jerome [†1927] .... Tu
15 .... ☽ · St Vitus [§ *epileptics*] · Ella Fitzgerald [†1996] .... W
16 .... Freshwater fishing season opens [🐟] · Stan Laurel [BD 1890] .... Th
17 .... St Botulph [§ *agricultural workers*] · Ken Livingstone [BD 1945] .... F
18 .... Seychelles [ND] · Delia Smith [BD 1941] .... Sa
19 .... St Gervase [§ *haymakers*] · Boris Johnson [BD 1964] .... Su
20 .... Longest Day · First Day of Summer · Lionel Richie [BD 1949] .... M
21 .... St Aloysius Gonzaga [§ *youth*] · Jean-Paul Sartre [BD 1905] .... Tu
22 .... Prunella Scales [BD 1932] · Meryl Streep [BD 1949] .... W
23 .... Midsummer Eve · Luxembourg [ND] · Alan Turing [BD 1912] .... Th
24 .... Midsummer Day · W.H. Smith [BD 1825] .... F
25 .... Mozambique [ID 1975] · George Orwell [BD 1903] .... Sa
26 .... United Nations Charter Day [UN] · Madagascar [ID 1960] .... Su
27 .... Djibouti [ID 1977] · Jack Lemmon [†2001] .... M
28 .... Peter Paul Rubens [BD 1577] · Mel Brooks [BD 1927] .... Tu
29 .... St Paul [§ *authors*] · Jayne Mansfield [†1967] .... W
30 .... St Theobald [§ *bachelors*] · Mike Tyson [BD 1966] .... Th

French Rev. calendar.. *Prairial* (meadow)	Dutch month ... *Zomermaand* (Summer)
Angelic governor .... *Muriel*	Saxon month .... *Sere-monath* (dry)
Epicurean calendar .... *Concombrial*	Talismanic stone .... *Emerald*

🌿 *June* is probably derived from *iuvenis* ('young'), but it is also linked to the goddess *Juno*, who personifies young women. In Scots Gaelic, the month is known as *Ian t-òg-mbìos*, the 'young month'; and in Welsh, as *Mehefin*, the 'middle'. 🌿 According to weather lore, *Calm weather in June, Sets corn in tune.* 🌿 To 'june' a herd of animals is to drive them in a brisk or lively manner. 🌿 Wilfred Gowers-Round asserts that 'June is the reality of the Poetic's claims for May'. 🌿 In parts of South Africa the verb 'to june-july' is slang for shaking or shivering with fear – because these months, while summer in the north, are mid-winter in the south. 🌿

——— JULY ———

Cancer [♋] (Jun 22–Jul 22)	*Birthstone* · RUBY *Flower* · LARKSPUR	*Leo* [♌] (Jul 23–Aug 23)

1 .... ● · Canada – Canada Day [NH] · Princess Diana [BD1961].......... F
2 .... Nostradamus [†1566] · Betty Grable [†1973] .... Sa
3 ....St Thomas [§ *architects*] · Franz Kafka [BD1883] .... Su
4 .... USA – Independence Day [NH] · Thomas Barnardo [BD1845] .... M
5 .... Algeria [ID 1962] · Thomas Stamford Raffles [†1826] .... Tu
6 ..... Kenneth Grahame [†1932] · Sylvester Stallone [BD1946]............ W
7 .... Gustav Mahler [BD1860] · Ringo Starr [BD1940] ....Th
8 ....Percy Bysshe Shelley [†1822 *drowned*] .... F
9 .... Edward Heath [BD1916] · Tom Hanks [BD1956] .... Sa
10 .... Camille Pissarro [BD1830] · Virginia Wade [BD1945].............. Su
11 .... World Population Day [UN] · St Benedict [§ *inflammatory diseases*] .... M
12 ....Kiribati [ID 1979] · Julius Caesar [BD100BC]................... Tu
13 .... St Henry [§ *the childless*] · Frida Kahlo [†1954] .... W
14 ....France – Bastille Day · Gustav Klimt [BD1862] ....Th
15 .... ☺ · St Swithin's Day · Rembrandt [BD1606] .... F
16 .... Feast of Our Lady of Mount Carmel · Ginger Rogers [BD1911]........ Sa
17 .... Duchess of Cornwall [BD1947] [£] · David Hasselhoff [BD1952] .... Su
18 ....Jane Austen [†1817] · Richard Branson [BD1950]............ M
19 .... Samuel Colt [BD1814] · Thomas Cook [†1892] .... Tu
20 ....St Wilgefortis [§ *difficult marriages*] · Sir Edmund Hillary [BD1919]......... W
21 ....Belgium [ND] · Robert Burns [†1796].......................Th
22 ....St Mary Magdalene [§ *hairdressers & repentant women*] · John Dillinger [†1934] ..... F
23 ....St Bridget of Sweden [§ *Sweden*] · Michael Foot [BD1913] .... Sa
24 .... Simón Bolívar Day – Venezuela & Ecuador.................. Su
25 ....St James [§ *labourers*] · Samuel Taylor Coleridge [†1834] .... M
26 .... St Ann [§ *women in labour*] · Helen Mirren [BD1946] .... Tu
27 ....St Pantaleon [§ *physicians*] · Alexandre Dumas Fils [BD1824] .... W
28 ....Delta Aquarids (South) [☄] · J.S. Bach [†1750]................Th
29 ....St Martha [§ *cooks*] · David Niven [†1983] .... F
30 ....Henry Ford [BD1863] · Otto von Bismarck [†1898]............... Sa
31 .... St Ignatius of Loyola [§ *those on spiritual exercises*] · Primo Levi [BD1919] .... Su

French Rev. calendar.. *Messidor* (harvest)	Dutch month ....*Hooymaand* (hay)
Angelic governor.............. *Verchiel*	Saxon month....*Mæd-monath* (meadow)
Epicurean calendar........... *Melonial*	Talismanic stone .... *Sapphire*

❧ July was originally called *Quintilis* (from *Quintus* – meaning 'fifth'), but it was renamed by Mark Antony to honour the murdered Julius Caesar, who was born on 12 July. ❧ *A swarm of bees in May is worth a load of Hay; A swarm of bees in June is worth a silver spoon; But a swarm of bees in July is not worth a fly.* ❧ *If the first of July be rainy weather, 'Twill rain mair or less for forty days together.* ❧ *Bow-wow, dandy fly – Brew no beer in July.* ❧ July used to be known as the thunder month, and some churches rang their bells in the hope of driving away thunder and lightning. ❧

———————————AUGUST———————————

Leo [♌]　　　*Birthstone* · PERIDOT　　　*Virgo* [♍]
(Jul 23–Aug 23)　　　*Flower* · GLADIOLUS　　　(Aug 24–Sep 23)

1 ..... Stag & buck stalking seasons begin [❦] · Yves Saint Laurent [BD1936].... M
2 ....Alexander Graham Bell [†1922] · Louis Blériot [†1936] ....Tu
3 .................P.D. James [BD1920] · Joseph Conrad [†1924].................. W
4 ....St Sithney [§ *mad dogs*] · Queen Mother [BD1900]................Th
5 ....Oyster Day, UK · Neil Armstrong [BD1930] .... F
6 ....Delta Aquarids (North) [☄] · Diego Velázquez [†1660] .... Sa
7 .... St Cajetan [§ *the unemployed*] · Oliver Hardy [†1957].............Su
8 .... St Dominic [§ *astronomers*] · Dustin Hoffman [BD1937].............. M
9 ....International Day of the World's Indigenous People [UN]........Tu
10 ....St Lawrence [§ *cooks*] · Herbert Hoover [BD1874].................. W
11 ....St Clare [§ *television & sore eyes*] · Edith Wharton [†1937] ....Th
12 .... Glorious Twelfth – grouse season begins [❦] · Perseids [☄] .... F
13 .... ☻ · William Caxton [BD1422] · Alfred Hitchcock [BD1899] .... Sa
14 ....Pakistan [ID 1947] · William Randolf Hearst [†1951]...........Su
15 ....VJ Day · Assumption Day · Princess Anne [BD1950] [£]........... M
16 ....St Stephen the Great [§ *bricklayers*] · Babe Ruth [†1948]...........Tu
17 ....Gabon [ID 1960] · Robert De Niro [BD1943] .... W
18 .... Genghis Khan [†1227] · Robert Redford [BD1937]...............Th
19 ....Afghanistan [ID 1919] · Ogden Nash [BD1902] .... F
20 ......St Oswin [§ *the betrayed*] · Leon Trotsky [†1940 *murdered*] .... Sa
21 ....Aubrey Beardsley [BD1872] ....Su
22 ....Claude Debussy [BD1862] · Dorothy Parker [BD1893] .... M
23 ....Gene Kelly [BD1912] · Keith Moon [BD1947].................Tu
24 ....St Bartholomew [§ *tanners*] · Stephen Fry [BD1957]............... W
25 ....St Genesius [§ *actors*] · Friedrich Nietzsche [†1900]...............Th
26 ....Robert Walpole [BD1676] · Charles Lindbergh [†1974].............. F
27 ......St Monica [§ *housewives & alcoholics*] · Lord Mountbatten [†1979 *assassinated*]...... Sa
28 ....St Augustine of Hippo [§ *brewers*] · John Huston [†1987]............Su
29★ ......★ BH · ☻ · Edmund Hoyle [†1769] · Michael Jackson [BD1958] .... M
30 ....Mary Wollstonecraft Shelley [BD1797] · Cameron Diaz [BD1972] ......Tu
31 ....Kyrgyzstan [ID 1991] · Van Morrison [BD1945] .... W

French Rev. calendar... *Thermidor* (heat)	Dutch month ..... *Oogstmaand* (harvest)
Angelic governor ....*Hamaliel*	Saxon month...... *Weod-monath* (weed)
Epicurean calendar...........*Raisinose*	Talismanic stone .... *Diamond*

❦ Previously called *Sextilis* (as the sixth month of the old calendar), August was renamed in 8BC, in honour of the first Roman Emperor, Augustus, who claimed this month to be lucky, as it was the month in which he began his consulship, conquered Egypt, and had many other triumphs. ❦ *Greengrocers rise at dawn of sun, August the fifth – come haste away, To Billingsgate the thousands run, Tis Oyster Day! Tis Oyster Day!* ❦ *Dry August and warme, Dothe harvest no harme.* ❦ *Take heed of sudden cold after heat.* ❦ *Gather not garden seeds near the full moon.* ❦ *Sow herbs.* ❦

SEPTEMBER

Virgo [♍]
(Aug 24–Sep 23)

Birthstone · SAPPHIRE
Flower · ASTER

Libra [♎]
(Sep 24–Oct 22)

1 ....Partridge shooting season opens [♥] · St Giles [§ *cripples, lepers, & nursing mothers*] .. Th
2 .... Jimmy Connors [BD1952] · J.R.R. Tolkein [†1973] .... F
3 ....Oliver Cromwell [†1658] · Ho Chi Minh [†1969] .... Sa
4 .... St Ida of Herzfeld [§ *widows*] · Beyoncé Knowles [BD1981]........... Su
5 ....Jesse James [BD1847] · Freddie Mercury [BD1946]................ M
6 .... Swaziland [ID 1968] · James II [†1701]..................... Tu
7 ....Brazil [ID 1822] · Buddy Holly [BD1936] .... W
8 ...... International Literacy Day [UN] · Nativity of Blessed Virgin Mary ......Th
9 ....Tajikistan [ND] · Mao Zedong [†1976] .... F
10 ....St Nicholas of Tolentino [§ *sick animals*] · Colin Firth [BD1960]..........Sa
11 ....New Year – Ethiopia · Nikita Khrushchev [†1971]..............Su
12 ....☺ · Elizabeth Barrett & Robert Browning [WA 1846] ....M
13 ....St John Chrysostom [§ *orators*] · Titus [†81]....................Tu
14 ....Exaltation of the Holy Cross · Grace Kelly [†1982] .... W
15 ....Battle of Britain Day · Isambard Kingdom Brunel [†1859] ....Th
16 ....International Day for the Preservation of the Ozone Layer [UN] .... F
17 .... Tobias Smollett [†1771] .... Sa
18 ....Chile [ID 1810] · Jimi Hendrix [†1970] .... Su
19 ....St Januarius [§ *blood banks*] · Kate Adie [BD1945]................. M
20 ....Jakob Grimm [†1863] · Sophia Loren [BD1934]................Tu
21 .... International Day of Peace [UN] · St Matthew [§ *accountants*] ....W
22 .... First Day of Autumn · Shaka Zulu [†1828]...................Th
23 .... Sigmund Freud [†1939] · Bruce Springsteen [BD1949] ....F
24 .... Guinea-Bissau [ID 1973] · F. Scott Fitzgerald [BD1896] .... Sa
25 ....St Cadoc of Llancarvan [§ *cramps*] · Ronnie Barker [BD1929]..........Su
26 ...St Cosmas & St Damian [§ *pharmacists & doctors*] · George Gershwin [BD1898]... M
27 ....● · St Vincent de Paul [§ *charitable societies*] ....Tu
28 .... Louis Pasteur [†1895] · Harpo Marx [†1964] .... W
29 .... Michaelmas Day · Billy Butlin [BD1899] ....Th
30 .... Botswana [ID 1966] · Truman Capote [BD1924]................ F

French Rev. calendar....*Fructidor* (fruit)	Dutch month ....*Herstmaand* (Autumn)
Angelic governor.................. *Uriel*	Saxon month......*Gerst-monath* (barley)
Epicurean calendar............*Huîtrose*	Talismanic stone ....*Zircon*

❧ September is so named as it was the seventh month in the Roman calendar. ❧ *September blows soft, Till the fruit's in the loft. Forgotten, month past, Doe now at the last.* ❧ *Eat and drink less, And buy a knife at Michaelmas.* ❧ To be 'Septembered' is to be multihued in autumnal colours, as Blackmore wrote: 'His honest face was Septembered with many a vintage'. ❧ *Poor Robin's Almanack* (1666) states: 'now *Libra* weighs the days and nights in an equal balance, so that there is not an hairs breadth difference betwixt them in length; this moneth having an R in it, Oysters come again in season'. ❧ The Irish name *Meán Fómhair* means 'mid-autumn'. ❧

─────────── OCTOBER ───────────

♎ *Libra* [♎]   *Birthstone* · OPAL   *Scorpio* [♏]   ♏
(Sep 24–Oct 22)   *Flower* · CALENDULA   (Oct 23–Nov 22)

1 ...... Int. Day of Older Persons [UN] · Pheasant shooting season opens [➹] .... Sa
2 .... Groucho Marx [BD 1890] · Graham Greene [BD 1904] .... Su
3 .... Germany [ND] · William Morris [†1896] .... M
4 .... St Francis of Assisi [§ *animals & birds*] · Buster Keaton [BD 1895] .... Tu
5 .... International Teacher's Day [UN] · Kate Winslet [BD 1975] .... W
6 .... Habitat Day [UN] · Alfred Lord Tennyson [†1892] .... Th
7 .... St Sergius [§ *Syria*] · Edgar Allan Poe [BD 1849] .... F
8 .... Chevy Chase [BD 1943] .... Sa
9 .... St Denis [§ *France & diabolical possession*] · Che Guevara [†1967 *executed*] .... Su
10 .... Fiji [ID 1790] · Harold Pinter [BD 1930] .... M
11 .... St Gummarus [§ *glove-makers*] · Bobby Charlton [BD 1937] .... Tu
12 .... ☻ · Spain [ND] · James Ramsay MacDonald [BD 1866] .... W
13 .... Margaret Thatcher [BD 1925] · Edwina Currie [BD 1946] .... Th
14 .... Errol Flynn [†1959] · Bing Crosby [†1977] .... F
15 .... St Teresa of Avila [§ *headache sufferers*] · Mata Hari [†1917 *executed*] .... Sa
16 .... World Food Day [UN] · St Hedwig [§ *brides*] .... Su
17 ..... Int. Day for the Eradication of Poverty [UN] · Evel Knievel [BD 1938] ..... M
18 .... St Luke [§ *artists & doctors*] · Martina Navratilova [BD 1956] .... Tu
19 .... John le Carré [BD 1931] .... W
20 .... St Acca [§ *learning*] · Christopher Wren [BD 1632] .... Th
21 .... St Hilarion [§ *hermits*] · Orionids [✧] .... F
22 .... Vatican [ND] · Paul Cézanne [†1906] .... Sa
23 .... St John of Capistrano [§ *jurors*] · Al Jolson [†1950] .... Su
24 .... United Nations Day [UN] · Zambia [ID 1964] .... M
25 .... Kazakhstan [ND] · Georges Bizet [BD 1838] .... Tu
26 .... ☻ · Domenico Scarlatti [BD 1685] .... W
27 .... Turkmenistan [ID 1991] · Dylan Thomas [BD 1914] .... Th
28 .... St Simon the Zealot [§ *sawyers*] · Czech Republic [ND] .... F
29 .... Turkey [ND] · Walter Raleigh [†1618 *executed*] .... Sa
30 .... ● *clocks back 1 hour* · Henry Winkler [BD 1945] .... Su
31 .... Hallowe'en · Indira Gandhi [†1984 *assassinated*] .... M

French Rev. cal. ... *Vendémiaire* (vintage)	Dutch month .... *Wynmaand* (wine)
Angelic governor .... *Barbiel*	Saxon month .... *Win-monath* (wine)
Epicurean calendar .... *Bécassinose*	Talismanic stone .... *Agate*

❦ October was originally the eighth month of the calendar. ❦ *Dry your barley land in October, Or you'll always be sober.* ❦ October was a time for brewing, and the month gave its name to a 'heady and ripe' ale: 'five Quarters of Malt to three Hogsheads, and twenty-four Pounds of Hops'. Consequently, *often drunk and seldom sober falls like the leaves in October.* ❦ In American politics, an *October surprise* is an event thought to have been engineered to garner political support just before an election. ❦ Roman Catholics traditionally dedicated October to the devotion of the rosary. ❦

———————————— NOVEMBER ————————————

    Scorpio [♏]   *Birthstone* · TOPAZ   *Sagittarius* [♐]
    (Oct 23–Nov 22)   *Flower* · CHRYSANTHEMUM   (Nov 23–Dec 21)

1 . . . . All Saints' Day · Hind and doe stalking season opens [❧] . . . . Tu
2 . . . . All Souls' Day · George Bernard Shaw [†1950] . . . . W
3 . . . . St Martin de Porres [§ *barbers*] · Annie Oakley [†1926] . . . . Th
4 . . . . . . St Charles Borromeo [§ *learning and the arts*] · Felix Mendelssohn [†1847] . . . . . . F
5 . . . . Guy Fawkes Night · Taurids [⚷] · Robert Maxwell [†1991] . . . . Sa
6 . . . . . St Leonard of Noblac [§ *against burglars*] · Pyotr Tchaikovsky [†1893 *? suicide*] . . . . Su
7 . . . . Albert Camus [BD1913] · Steve McQueen [†1980] . . . . M
8 . . . . John Milton [†1674] · Ken Dodd [BD1931] . . . . Tu
9 . . . . Cambodia [ID 1953] · Neville Chamberlain [†1940] . . . . W
10 . . . . ☺ · St Tryphon [§ *gardeners*] · Martin Luther [BD1483] . . . . Th
11 . . . . Remembrance Day · USA – Veterans Day · Angola [ID 1975] . . . . F
12 . . . . Roland Barthes [BD1915] · Grace Kelly [BD1929] . . . . Sa
13 . . . . St Homobonus [§ *clothworkers*] . . . . Su
14 . . . . Prince Charles [BD1948] [£] · Harold Larwood [BD1904] . . . . M
15 . . . . St Albert the Great [§ *scientists*] · William Herschel [BD1738] . . . . Tu
16 . . . . Int. Day for Tolerance [UN] · Tiberius [BD 42BC] . . . . W
17 . . . . Leonids [⚷] · Rock Hudson [BD1925] . . . . Th
18 . . . . St Odo of Cluny [§ *rain*] · Louis Daguerre [BD1789] . . . . F
19 . . . . Monaco [ND] · Calvin Klein [BD1942] . . . . Sa
20 . . . . Queen Elizabeth II & Prince Philip [WA 1947] [£] . . . . Su
21 . . . . Presentation of the Blessed Virgin Mary in the Temple . . . . M
22 . . . . Charles de Gaulle [BD1890] · C.S. Lewis [†1963] . . . . Tu
23 . . . . St Felicity [§ *martyrs*] · Boris Karloff [BD1887] . . . . W
24 . . . . John Knox [†1572] · Lee Harvey Oswald [†1963 *murdered*] . . . . Th
25 . . . . . ☻ · St Catherine of Alexandria [§ *philosophers*] · Joe DiMaggio [BD1914] . . . . . . F
26 . . . . . . St John Berchmans [§ *altar boys & girls*] · Charles M. Schultz [BD1922] . . . . Sa
27 . . . . Anders Celsius [BD1701] · Jimi Hendrix [BD1942] . . . . Su
28 . . . . East Timor [ND] · Nancy Mitford [BD1904] . . . . M
29 . . . . C.S. Lewis [BD1898] · Cary Grant [†1986] . . . . Tu
30 . . . . St Andrew [§ *Scotland & Russia*] · Jonathan Swift [BD1667] . . . . W

French Rev. calendar . . . . . *Brumaire* (fog)	Dutch month . . *Slaghtmaand* [see below]
Angelic governor . . . . *Advachiel*	Saxon month . . . . . . *Wind-monath* (wind)
Epicurean calendar . . . . *Pommedetaire*	Talismanic stone . . . . *Amethyst*

❧ Originally the ninth (*novem*) month, November has long been associated with slaughter, hence the Dutch *Slaghtmaand* ('slaughter month'). The Anglo-Saxon was *Blotmonath* ('blood' or 'sacrifice month'). ❧ A dismal month, November has been the subject of many writers' ire, as J.B. Burges wrote: 'November leads her wintry train, And stretches o'er the firmament her veil Charg'd with foul vapours, fogs and drizzly rain'. ❧ Famously, Thomas Hood's poem *No!* contains the lines 'No warmth, no cheerfulness, no healthful ease ... No shade, no shine, no butterflies, no bees, No fruits, no flowers, no leaves, no birds —— November!' ❧

— DECEMBER —

Sagittarius [♐]
(Nov 23–Dec 21)

Birthstone · TURQUOISE
Flower · NARCISSUS

Capricorn [♑]
(Dec 22–Jan 20)

1 .... World AIDS Day [UN] · Stephen Poliakoff [BD1952] .... Th
2 ....United Arab Emirates [ID 1971] · Philip Larkin [†1985] .... F
3 ..... International Day of Disabled Persons [UN] · Joseph Conrad [BD1857] .... Sa
4 ....········ St Ada [§ *nuns*] · Benjamin Britten [†1976] .... Su
5 .... Thailand [ND] · Wolfgang Amadeus Mozart [†1791].............. M
6 .... St Nicholas [§ *bakers & pawnbrokers*] · Don King [BD1932].............Tu
7 .... USA – Pearl Harbor Day · St Ambrose [§ *protector of bees & domestic animals*] ...... W
8 ....The Immaculate Conception · Lucien Freud [BD1922]............Th
9 ....Kirk Douglas [BD1916] .... F
10 .... ☺ · Nobel Prizes awarded · Human Rights Day [UN].............. Sa
11 ....St Damasus [§ *archaeologists*] · Marco Pierre White [BD1961]............Su
12 ....Edvard Munch [BD1863] · Robert Browning [†1889].............. M
13 .... St Lucy [§ *the blind*] · Dick Van Dyke [BD1925].................Tu
14 .... Geminids [♐] · St Agnellus [§ *invoked against invaders*] .... W
15 ....USA – National Bill of Rights Day · Frankie Dettori [BD1970].........Th
16 ....Glenn Miller [†1944 *missing presumed dead*]........................ F
17 ....Bhutan [ND] · Humphrey Davy [BD1778]................... Sa
18 ....International Migrants Day [UN] · Keith Richards [BD1943].......... Su
19 .... Emily Brontë [†1848] · Leonid Brezhnev [BD1906].............. M
20 .... St Ursicinus of Saint-Ursanne [§ *against stiff neck*] · John Steinbeck [†1968] ....Tu
21 .... Shortest Day · First Day of Winter · Benjamin Disraeli [BD1804]....... W
22 ....Beatrix Potter [†1943] ....Th
23 .... Ursids [♐] · St Dagobert [§ *kings, orphans & kidnap victims*] .... F
24 ....● · Christmas Eve · William Makepeace Thackeray [†1863] .... Sa
25 .─...............Christmas Day [NH] · Quentin Crisp [BD1908]...............Su
26★ ....★BH · Boxing Day [NH] · St Stephen [§ *stonemasons & horses*] .... M
27★ ....★BH · St John [§ *Asia Minor*] · Marlene Dietrich [BD1901].............Tu
28 .... Childermass · Maggie Smith [BD1934] .... W
29 ...... Madame de Pompadour [BD1721] · Thomas Becket [†1170 *murdered*] ......Th
30 ....Our Lady of Bethlehem · Rudyard Kipling [BD1865] .... F
31 .... New Year's Eve · Scotland – Hogmanay · Ben Kingsley [BD1943] .... Sa

French Rev. calendar.... *Frimaire* (frost)	Dutch month ... *Wintermaand* (Winter)
Angelic governor................*Hanael*	Saxon month......*Mid-Winter-monath*
Epicurean calendar..........*Boudinaire*	Talismanic stone .... *Beryl*

❦ *If the ice will bear a goose before Christmas, it will not bear a duck afterwards.* ❦
Originally the tenth month, December now closes the year. ❦ *If Christmas Day be bright and clear there'll be two winters in the year.* ❦ The writer Saunders warned in 1679, 'In December, Melancholy and Phlegm much increase, which are heavy, dull, and close, and therefore it behoves all that will consider their healths, to keep their heads and bodies very well from cold'. ❦ Robert Burns splendidly wrote in 1795 – 'As I am in a complete Decemberish humour, gloomy, sullen, stupid'. ❦

––––––––––––– THE COMIC ALMANACK –––––––––––––

JANUARY · Another new year! Something will probably happen before long. If it does not something else will. Look round corners as much as possible; and don't go to the end of the world, for fear of falling over the edge. Begin new undertakings which promise to be profitable. A bad month for marrying a shrew.

FEBRUARY · Give no bills in which February is included, in respect of its being so short. Never pull your shirt collars so high as to run the risk of the nether man's catching cold. A bad month for hanging yourself, put it off. Eat as much as you can. If anybody make you a handsome present, take it, and fear not. One of your friends will cut himself shaving – seek not to know which; pry not into the secrets of destiny.

MARCH · Never take hold of the poker by the wrong end. Go forth into the streets and gather a bushel of March dust; it is worth a king's ransom. Take it to the Goldsmiths' Hall, and they will pay you for it – (a king's ransom is 30,000 *l.*, which will be at once handed to you). Spring commences. Cut the pearl buttons off your shirts and sow them in the flower-pot; they will come up oysters. Avoid the vanities of dress, but do not go abroad without your pantaloons.

APRIL · Lie in bed all this month for fear of being made an April Fool. Many things happen in April. A good month to receive a large legacy in, but don't reject a small one. Clouds will gather in the social horizon. You will have a quarrel with your wife, which will be brought to an amicable conclusion by means of a shawl. Avoid bonnet shops. A bad month to be bankrupt in.

MAY · A merry month. Gather May dew (query: what are you to do with it when you get it?) Dance round the maypole. On no account dance round the north pole, or the south. Get your friends to do bills – it promotes generosity and liberality, which are virtues. Your hat will be blown off – if it be windy enough, and you don't hold it on. Be obliging; give anybody who asks, free permission to run pins into anybody else – innocent amusement ought to be encouraged.

JUNE · A bad month for your house to be burnt down – unless, indeed, it be insured for double its value, or your wife be in it. When you ride in the Park and the boys tell you to get inside the horse and draw down the blinds, don't – it's not seemly. Make money – Pass your bad half crowns. Give your clean-picked bones to the poor – charity covers a multitude of sins. If a comet appears, let it alone; and when it is tired of appearing it will disappear. If you see a ghost, tell it to stay there; and come for us, and we will go and look at it.

JULY · Walk about in armour for fear of mad dogs. The planetary system this month will go on as usual; distrust anybody who tells you to the contrary. Be a philosopher, and have as few wants as possible – cut off your legs, and then you won't require boots, which you will find to be a saving. When you sleep in church do not snore; it is disrespectful to the establishment. If you go to the opera and drop a double-barrelled lorgnette from the fifth tier, and it cracks a man's skull below, bring an action against his representatives for the value of the glass. Make yourself comfortable.

THE COMIC ALMANACK cont.

AUGUST · Events will take place and circumstances will happen; also things will come to pass. Beware, therefore, and trust the stars. You may have a cold in the head, and you may not. Tace is Latin for a candle, and things must be as they may. Avoid apoplexy, give no encouragement to rheumatism, and, if you are taken ill with typhus fever, don't stand it. Drink not physic slowly, and take chloroform when you're having your hair cut or sitting for your daguerreotype.

SEPTEMBER · Go out a shooting; but shoot not the moon, unless you find it convenient. A good month for drinking beer, but avoid salts. Recollect what the man sayeth: a bush in the hand is worth two in the bin! Be sage, stuffed with sage. The time for travelling. If you let your moustaches grow, you will immediately begin to speak French and German. Get a passport from the beadle of your parish, *viséd* by the turncock. Avoid sea-sickness by never ceasing eating and drinking when at sea. If you see the devil have nothing to say to him; he is very far from respectable; cut him.

OCTOBER · The harvest is gathered, and the barns are full. The best month for brewing – domestic storms and natural convulsions brewing as well as porter. Get all you can out of your friends. Make love to pretty women with money. If you go to California take care you don't dig up brass for gold. Take heed, the world will come to an end some day; pay your rent if you are obliged – not otherwise. Avoid breaking your leg in three places, five of your ribs, putting your collarbone out, and fracturing your skull.

NOVEMBER. The month for committing suicide; avoid it, however, for yourself. Give your friends presents of rope; if you give them enough, the sage sayeth, they will hang themselves. Fogs are thick; but the wise man sees through them. Roads are muddy; but the rich man rideth in a cab. In this month your hair will grow. Do not be alarmed. Buy the *Comic Almanack*.

DECEMBER · Winter commences. Bills come pouring in. Trust yet to the stars. Do the Income Tax – so sayeth the moral philosopher. All flesh is grass – but beef is not water cresses. Make moral reflections, and pay no bills. A bad month for paying bills. Give no Christmas dinner; but go to some one's who does. Receive presents of turkeys, geese, pickled salmon, and cod, with oysters for sauce. Look out for Saturn in the ascendant in the house of Mars; and when you see a comet with a green tail, send an express to the astronomer royal, with a lock of your hair.

— *The Comic almanack: an ephemeris in jest and earnest, containing merry tales, humorous poetry, quips, and oddities*, William Makepeace Thackeray, Albert Smith, Gilbert Abbott À Beckett, Horace Mayhew, &c., 1852

BRITISH SUMMER TIME

BST starts and ends at 1am on these Sundays (*'spring forward – fall back'*):
2011 .... clocks forward 1 hour, 27 March · clocks back 1 hour, 30 October
2012 .... clocks forward 1 hour, 25 March · clocks back 1 hour, 28 October

———————— PUBLIC & BANK HOLIDAYS ————————

England, Wales, & N. Ireland	2011	2012
New Year's Day	3 Jan	2 Jan
[NI *only*] St Patrick's Day	17 Mar	17 Mar
Good Friday	22 Apr	6 Apr
Easter Monday	25 Apr	9 Apr
Early May Bank Holiday	2 May	7 May
Spring Bank Holiday	30 May	4 Jun
Queen's Diamond Jubilee [see p.275]	–	5 Jun
[NI *only*] Battle of the Boyne	12 Jul	12 Jul
Summer Bank Holiday	29 Aug	27 Aug
Christmas Day	26 Dec	25 Dec
Boxing Day	27 Dec	26 Dec

Scotland	2011	2012
New Year's Day	3 Jan	2 Jan
2nd January	4 Jan	3 Jan
Good Friday	22 Apr	6 Apr
Early May Bank Holiday	2 May	7 May
Spring Bank Holiday	30 May	28 May
Summer Bank Holiday	1 Aug	6 Aug
Christmas Day	26 Dec	25 Dec
Boxing Day	27 Dec	26 Dec

These are the expected dates of holidays; some are subject to proclamation by the Queen.

———————— ANNIVERSARIES OF 2011 ————————

25th Anniversary (1986)
The space shuttle *Challenger* exploded in flight · Prince Andrew married Sarah Ferguson · The Chernobyl nuclear disaster occurred

50th Anniversary (1961)
Walt Disney's *One Hundred and One Dalmatians* was released
The Bay of Pigs invasion of Cuba

75th Anniversary (1936)
Gone With the Wind was published
King Edward VIII abdicated

100th Anniversary (1911)
Britain's first seaplane, *Water Bird*, made its inaugural voyage

150th Anniversary (1861)
The American Civil War began
Russia abolished serfdom

200th Anniversary (1811)
Franz Liszt was born · The Luddites began attacking industrial machinery

250th Anniversary (1761)
The British captured Pondicherry, India, from the French

500th Anniversary (1511)
Afonso de Albuquerque of Portugal conquered Malacca

800th Anniversary (1211)
The Mongols invaded Jin China

—————————— NOTABLE CHRISTIAN DATES · 2011 ——————————

Epiphany · *manifestation of the Christ to the Magi*......................................6 Jan
Presentation of Christ in the Temple (Candlemas) ....2 Feb
Ash Wednesday · *1st day of Lent*...9 Mar
The Annunciation · *when Gabriel told Mary she would bear Christ* ....25 Mar
Good Friday · *Friday before Easter; commemorating the Crucifixion* ....22 Apr
Easter Day (Western churches) · *commemorating the Resurrection* ....24 Apr
Easter Day (Eastern Orthodox) · *commemorating the Resurrection* ....24 Apr
Rogation Sunday · *the Sunday before Ascension Day*...............................29 May
Ascension Day · *commemorating the ascent of Christ to heaven*..........................2 Jun
Pentecost (Whit Sunday) · *commemorating the descent of the Holy Spirit* ....12 Jun
Trinity Sunday · *observed in honour of the Trinity* ....19 Jun
Corpus Christi · *commemorating the institution of the Holy Eucharist*.................23 Jun
All Saints' Day · *commemorating all the Church's saints collectively*......................1 Nov
Advent Sunday · *marking the start of Advent* ....27 Nov
Christmas Day · *celebrating the birth of Christ*....................................25 Dec

A few other terms from the Christian Calendar:

Bible Sunday................2nd in Advent	Palm Sunday..................before Easter
	Passion Sunday.................5th in Lent
Black/Easter Monday ..... the day after Easter	Plough Monday..............after Epiphany
Collop/Egg Monday..... first before Lent	Quadragesima............1st Sunday in Lent
Egg Saturday..... day prior to Quinquagesima	Quinquagesima..........Sunday before Lent
Fig/Yew Sunday ....Palm Sunday	Refreshment.............4th Sunday in Lent
Holy Saturday..................before Easter	Septuagesima .... 3rd Sunday before Lent
Holy Week ....before Easter	Sexagesima ....2nd Sunday before Lent
Low Sunday .... Sunday after Easter	Shrove Tuesday ('pancake day').... before Lent
Maundy Thursday,,,,,,,,,,, before Easter	Shrovetide.............period preceding Lent
	St Martin's Lent ....Advent
Mothering Sunday..............4th in Lent	Tenebrae .... last 3 days of Holy Week

——————— CHRISTIAN CALENDAR MOVEABLE FEASTS ———————

Year	Ash Wednesday	Easter Day	Ascension	Pentecost	Advent Sunday
2011	9 Mar	24 Apr	2 Jun	12 Jun	27 Nov
2012	22 Feb	8 Apr	17 May	27 May	2 Dec
2013	13 Feb	31 Mar	9 May	19 May	1 Dec
2014	5 Mar	20 Apr	29 May	8 Jun	30 Nov
2015	18 Feb	5 Apr	14 May	24 May	29 Nov
2016	10 Feb	27 Mar	5 May	15 May	27 Nov
2017	1 Mar	16 Apr	25 May	4 Jun	3 Dec
2018	14 Feb	1 Apr	10 May	20 May	2 Dec
2019	6 Mar	21 Apr	30 May	9 Jun	1 Dec
2020	26 Feb	12 Apr	21 May	31 May	29 Nov
2021	17 Feb	4 Apr	13 May	23 May	28 Nov
2022	2 Mar	17 Apr	26 May	5 Jun	27 Nov

NOTABLE RELIGIOUS DATES FOR 2011

HINDU

Makar Sankrant · *Winter festival* .... .14 Jan
Vasant Panchami · *dedicated to Saraswati and learning* .... .8 Feb
Maha Shivaratri · *dedicated to Shiva* .... 3 Mar
Holi · *spring festival of colours dedicated to Krishna* .... .19 Mar
Varsha Pratipada (Chaitra) · *Spring New Year* .... 4 Apr
Hindu New Year & Ramayana Week .... 4 Apr
Rama Navami · *birthday of Lord Rama* .... 12 Apr
Hanuman Jayanti · *birthday of Hanuman, the Monkey God* .... 18 Apr
Raksha Bandhan · *festival of brotherhood and love* .... .13 Aug
Janmashtami · *birthday of Lord Rama* .... .22 Aug
Ganesh Chaturthi · *birthday of Lord Ganesh* .... .1 Sep
Navarati & Durga-puja · *celebrating triumph of good over evil* .... *starts* 28 Sep
Saraswati-puja · *dedicated to Saraswati and learning* .... *starts* 3 Oct
Dassera (Vijay Dashami) · *celebrating triumph of good over evil* .... 6 Oct
Diwali (Deepvali) · *New Year festival of lights* .... .26 Oct
New Year .... .27 Oct

JEWISH

Purim (Feast of Lots) · *commemorating defeat of Haman* .... .20 Mar
Pesach (Passover) · *commemorating exodus from Egypt* .... 19 Apr
Shavuot (Pentecost) · *commemorating revelation of the Torah* .... .8 Jun
Tisha B'Av · *day of mourning* .... 9 Aug
Rosh Hashanah (New Year) .... 29 Sep
Yom Kippur (Day of Atonement) · *fasting and prayer for forgiveness* .... 8 Oct
Sukkoth (Feast of Tabernacles) · *marking the time in wilderness* .... .13 Oct
Simchat Torah · *9th day of Sukkoth* .... .21 Oct
Chanukah · *commemorating re-dedication of Jerusalem Temple* .... .21 Dec

ISLAMIC

Milad Al-Nabi · *birthday of Muhammad* .... 15 Feb
Ramadan · *the month in which the Koran was revealed* .... *starts* 1 Aug
Eid al-Fitr · *marks end of Ramadan* .... .30 Aug
Eid al-Adha · *celebrating the faith of Abraham* .... .6 Nov
Al Hijra (New Year) .... 26 Nov
Ashura · *celebrating Noah leaving the Ark, the saving of Moses, & Hussein's martyrdom* ...... 5 Dec

SIKH

Birthday of Guru Gobind Singh · *founder of the Khalsa* .... 5 Jan
Sikh New Year (Nanakshahi calendar) .... 13 Apr
Vaisakhi (Baisakhi) · *founding of the Khalsa* .... 13 Apr
Hola Mahalla · *festival of martial arts* .... 14 Apr
Birthday of Guru Nanak (founder of Sikhism) .... 14 Apr
Martyrdom of Guru Arjan .... 16 Jun
Diwali · *festival of light* .... .26 Oct
Martyrdom of Guru Tegh Bahadur .... 24 Nov

——— NOTABLE RELIGIOUS DATES FOR 2011 ———

BAHA'I

Nawruz (New Year)............ 21 Mar	Day of the Covenant.......... 26 Nov
Ridvan............................21 Apr	Ascension of Abdu'l-Baha ..... 28 Nov
Declaration of the Báb........23 May	*World Religion Day*.............. 18 Jan
Ascension of Baha'u'llah ......29 May	*Race Unity Day*.................. 12 Jun
Martyrdom of the Báb............ 9 Jul	*International Day of Peace*...... 21 Sep
Birth of the Báb................20 Oct	*In addition, the eve of each of the*
Birth of Baha'u'llah .... 12 Nov	*nineteen Baha'i months is celebrated.*

JAIN

Mahavira Jayanti · *celebrates the day of Mahavira's birth* ....16 Apr
Paryushan · *time of reflection and repentance*...26 Aug
Diwali · *celebrated when Mahavira gave his last teachings and attained ultimate liberation* . . 26 Oct
New Year ....27 Oct
Kartak Purnima · *time of pilgrimage* ....Oct/Nov

BUDDHIST

Parinirvana Day · *marks the death of the Buddha* ....8 Feb
Sangha Day (Magha Puja Day) · *celebration of Buddhist community* .... 18 Feb
Losar · *Tibetan New Year*...5 Mar
Wesak (Vesak) · *marks the birth, death, & enlightenment of the Buddha*.............. 17 May
Dharma Day · *marks the start of the Buddha's teaching* ....15 Jul

RASTAFARIAN

Ethiopian Christmas..............7 Jan	Birthday of Marcus Garvey.....17 Aug
Ethiopian Constitution.......... 16 Jul	Ethiopian New Year's Day...... 11 Sep
Haile Selassie birthday ....23 Jul	Crowning of Haile Selassie ......2 Nov

PAGAN

Imbolc · *fire festival anticipating the new farming season*...............................2 Feb
Spring Equinox · *celebrating the renewal of life* ....20 Mar
Beltane · *fire festival celebrating Summer and fertility*....................................1 May
Summer Solstice (Midsummer; Litha) · *celebrating the sun's power*................ 21 Jun
Lughnasadh · *harvest festival*...1 Aug
Autumn Equinox (Harvest Home; Mabon) · *reflection on the past season*......... 23 Sep
Samhain (Halloween; All Hallows Eve) · *Pagan New Year*.......................31 Oct
Winter Solstice (Yule) · *celebrating Winter*...22 Dec

CHINESE LUNAR NEW YEAR · 3 Feb

[Every effort has been taken to validate these dates. However, readers should be aware that there is a surprising degree of debate and dispute. This is caused by the interplay of: regional variations; differing interpretations between religious authorities; seemingly arbitrary changes in dates when holidays conflict; avoidance of days considered for one or other reason inauspicious; as well as the inherent unpredictability of the lunar cycle. Many festivals, especially Jewish holidays, start at sundown on the preceding day.]

—————————— DECADE NAMES ——————————

Both journalists and the general public struggled to agree on a name for the first decade of the C21st. By 2009, the still-slightly-awkward 'noughties' seemed to be the preferred British term – perhaps helped by the fact that it was pleasing to say out loud. But, as the credit crunch bit in May 2008, Dan Roberts noted in the *Telegraph*, 'Until now, [noughties] felt slightly crass: a bit frivolous for a decade that started with 9/11 and global warming. Suddenly, it makes perfect sense: the cheeky symbol of a debauched epoch, gorged on cheap debt and unearned wealth'. ❦ Decades that do not herald a new century have had an easier time. Below are some of the nicknames for other decades, and the cultural features they supposedly described:

1890s	Naughty Nineties	*new lightheartedness & laxity as Victorian mores faded*
1920s	Roaring Twenties†	*cultural and technological explosions of jazz, film, Art Deco, flappers, &c.*
1930s	Threadbare Thirties‡	*the poverty and shabbiness of the Great Depression (said to have been coined by Groucho Marx)*
1950s	Fabulous Fifties	*ascendancy of 'cool' culture & rock 'n' roll*
1960s	Swinging Sixties	*optimistic, psychedelic, youth-oriented fashion, music, and popular culture, centred in London*
1980s	Me Decade, Greedy Eighties	*individualism, materialism (coined by Tom Wolfe to describe the US in the 1970s)*
1990s	We Decade	*shift to communal values, focus on thrift, &c.*

Some other phrases used to describe recent decades around the world are below:

1890s	Gay Nineties	US	*same as the Naughty Nineties*
1890s	Mauve Decade	US	*after the popularity of an early synthetic dye*
1927–37	Nanjing Decade	China	*semi-dictatorship of Chiang Kai-shek, with Nanjing as capital; also 'Strenuous Decade'*
1930s	Década Infame	Argentina	*depression & discontent after 1930 coup*
1940s	Flying Forties	US	*the growth of aviation*
1950s	Haunting Decade	Romania	*repression under Gheorghiu-Dej*
1950s	Bland Decade	US	*stifling conformity (also the Plastic Decade, &c.)*
1973–82	Oil Decade	Middle East	*wealth & power after 1973 price hike*
1980s	NGO Decade	Global	*rise of non-governmental organisations*
1990s	Lost Decade	Japan	*end to expansion after asset price bubble burst*
1990s	Black Decade	Algeria	*Civil War that killed c.200,000*

In May 2008, Bank of England governor Mervyn King called the early 2000s 'the N.I.C.E. decade'. King was primarily referring to 'Non-Inflationary Consistent Expansion', but the phrase nevertheless captured the sense that the early 2000s had seen an overall rise in prosperity. Of course, some felt the need to dispute the term, calling these years 'the nasty decade'. † In France, the interwar years are called the *années folles* ('crazy years'), because of their exuberance and celebration. ‡ Other terms for the 1930s include the Devils Decade, the Hungry Thirties, and the Red (or Pink) Decade – the latter because of the spread of left-leaning politics. ❦ The large number of sporting events to be hosted by the UK in the 2010s (including the 2012 Olympics, 2014 Commonwealth Games, and 2015 Rugby World Cup) has led some to predict (hope?) that the 2010s will be a 'Golden Decade' for British sport.

— PHASES OF THE MOON · MMXI —

	1	2	3	4	5	6	7	8	9	10	11	12	13	14	15	16	17	18	19	20	21	22	23	24	25	26	27	28	29	30	31
January																															
February																															
March																															
April																															
May																															
June																															
July																															
August																															
September																															
October																															
November																															
December																															

Key: ● New Moon · ◑ First Quarter · ○ Full Moon · ◐ Last Quarter · Dates are based on Universal Time (Greenwich Mean Time)

MATRIMONIAL WEATHER TABLE

TO BE HUNG UP IN ALL PANTRIES AND SERVANTS' HALLS.

Constructed by a Butler of twenty-nine years' standing behind his Master's and Missus's chair.

CAUSES OF CHANGE	INDICATIONS	RESULTS & DREADFUL CONSEQUENCES
Cold meat for dinner	Very Sharp and Cutting; dead calm; horizon very black.	A visit, directly after dinner, to the club.
Money for the housekeeping: weekly expenses produced	Very Stormy; repeated thunderstorms about 10a.m.; violent explosion at 'Sundries'.	The puddings are cut off, and the servants' beer.
A proposal to go up the Rhine, or to Baden Baden	N N N N N N N N o or N N N N N N N N N O	A trip to Ramsgate or Broadstairs, and master goes down on Saturdays and returns on Mondays.
Hint of an evening or dinner party	Extremely Close; heavy clouds on master's brow; gloomy depression; mistress and the young ladies Rainy.	The old Mr and Mrs Glumpy are asked to dinner, and the Misses and young Mr Glumpy and a few friends are asked to drop in in the evening.
A box for the Opera	The same, with additional closeness.	Tickets for the Horticultural, or seats taken at the Lyceum.
No one down to breakfast at 10 o'clock to make tea	Regular Storm, blowing up everybody, and which makes the bells ring all over the house.	Missus unwell; cannot come down to breakfast; the young ladies 'suddenly indisposed', and do not show themselves; master goes out, and slams the door fit to shake the house down.
Boys home for the holidays	Unsettled; continual hurricane for six weeks.	Repeated thrashings.
New baby, or a new pair of boots	Squally and changeable.	Dines out; home very late. (Let him take care to whom it falls to pull off master's boots on a night like this!)

MATRIMONIAL WEATHER TABLE cont.

CAUSES OF CHANGE	INDICATIONS	RESULTS & DREADFUL CONSEQUENCES
Dividend day	Fair.	Theatre; oysters for supper (perhaps); a new bonnet.
Series of contradictions	High wind; very Stormy; air charged with thunder.	Nervous headache; mistress dines in her bedroom; no pudding for dinner, or dessert.
Taxes	Foul; every symptom of a Storm, but carried off towards the evening by a timely cheque.	Finding fault with everything; cook blown up for dinner, and one or two servants discharged.
Washing day	Very Rainy, pours buckets from morning to night: up to your ankles in water.	Master dines at club; not home till late; smokes a cigar in the evening; mistress faints.
Grand dinner party	Sharp, Frosty and Unsettled in the morning; very Hot before dinner; exceedingly Fair at dinner; pointing to Wet after, and frequent Storms towards 12 pm.	Abusing the servants, and counting the spoons, and running through the guests as soon as they are gone. Cold meat next day, carried off with pickles.
Grand evening party	Strange singing in the ears and dancing before the eyes all night; curious noise over head, and a fearful famine that devours everything about I am; blows dreadful cornet-a-pistons till the next morning.	Nothing but barley-sugar temples for breakfast, and blanc-manges for dinner for days afterwards.

When it is Fair, the servants and guests in the house can move about with the greatest safety; but if it is at all Cloudy, or the weather looks in the least Unsettled, then he had better look twice at the above table before he takes the smallest step, or else he will have the matrimonial storm breaking over his head. If missus is out, then the atmosphere is generally Fair; but it is invariably Stormy when master goes out and does not come home for dinner. If master and missus are both in, look out for a change or a sudden squall; and the eyes of the missus will probably point to Wet.

– *The Comic Almanack: an ephemeris in jest and earnest, containing merry tales, humorous poetry, quips, and oddities*
William Makepeace Thackeray, Albert Smith, Gilbert Abbott À Beckett, Horace Mayhew, Henry Mayhew, 1848

——————— MR PUNCH: 'REFORM YOUR ALMANACKS' ———————

'For everybody makes Almanacks now, and with very few exceptions, they are all stupid affairs. The Meteor which appeared to announce the publication of *Mr. Punch's Own*, and about which so many letters were written by astounded sky-gazers, was a very appropriate tribute to the single work of the kind that can be pronounced perfect. But though perfection is not to be expected elsewhere than at 85, Fleet Street, why need a thousand calendar-makers do their work so badly? ❦ What is the use of sticking against certain dates, that Horn Tooke died – that Barbarossa was born – that Partridge Shooting begins – that the Battle of Ravenna was fought – that Pickles were invented – that Cicero was murdered – that Garrick appeared – that the Granicus was crossed – that the Monument was finished – and so forth? Two-thirds of the dates which are usually commemorated nobody cares about, except those who will not be satisfied with such a barren record. Next, the jumble of things makes these memoranda more absurd, for the person who cares about Barbarossa does not care either for Garrick or pickles, and the Garrick fancier is not likely to be much interested in the Battle of Ravenna. As for the sporting entries, they are simply idiotic. What sportsman needs to be told when he may blaze at grouse, and when at pheasant? And who else wants to know anything about the matter? ❦ Instead of a ridiculous mixture of uselessness and incongruities, why not have *Class Almanacks*? Let everybody have his record of matter appertaining to his own sphere. Don't tell the burglar when Martin Luther was born; don't tell the lawyer about Howard the philanthropist; and don't remind an honest man and woman of the execution of the Mannings. But let us have Almanacks prepared in this fashion, and then folks can please themselves. Here are specimen weeks: —'

The Young Lady's Almanack

Tu. 14 ....St Valentine.
W. 15....................Polka invented.
Th. 16 .... Cellarius born.[1]
Fr. 17 ....Crinoline came in.
Sa. 18............Mario first appeared.[2]
Su. 19.............. New bonnet usual.
Mo. 20 ..... Doctor's Commons abol.

The Wife's Almanack

W. 3 .... Buttons invented.
Th. 4......... Cold mutton discovered.
Fr. 5....... Mother in laws prohibited.
Sa. 6 ....Latch-keys first used.
Su. 7...... Church clock before ready.
Mo. 8......Howell discovered James.[3]
Tu. 9........... Swan first met Edgar.[3]

The Author's Almanack

Mo. 13 .... Magazine article due.
Tu. 14 .... Sea air pleasant.
W. 15...........Bushy Chestnuts out.
Th. 16 ....Scriberus d. of overexertion.
Fr. 17 ......Napoleon shot a publisher.
Sa. 18.......Last day for Magazine art.
Su. 19.........Begin Magazine article.

The MP's Almanack

Fr. 1......................Pitt got tipsy.
Sa. 2 ....Fox got tipsy.
Su. 3 ....Castlereagh hit Canning.
Mo. 4..................Sadlier expelled.[4]
Tu. 5.....Althorp taken into custody.[5]
W. 6 ....Bribery Act passed.
Th. 7........... Disraeli spoke 5 hours.

From *Punch, or The London Charivari*, 8 January, 1858. (Notes: 1. Henri Cellarius, a c19th dancing master and pioneer of the waltz-mazurka. 2. The most famous Italian tenor of the day. 3. Two notable London emporia. 4. John Sadlier, the fraudulent and disgraced MP for Sligo who committed suicide on Hampstead Heath. 5. Lord Viscount Althorp, who was arrested after accusing MPs of dissembling.)

Index

Indexing is not a popular profession by any stretch of the imagination. Not only is it almost completely unknown in lay circles, but let's be honest: Writing indexes sounds about as exciting as cleaning the house, but a hundred times harder.
— SETH MAISLIN, *President of the American Society of Indexers* (2006–07)

@EYESPYMP – BEYOND GDP

———— BFI FELLOWS – DECADE NAMES ————

── DECEMBER EPHEMERIDES – GREENWICH, ROYAL ──

—————— MOAT, RAOUL – PRIZE, NOBEL PEACE ——————

—— PRIZE, NOBEL SCIENCE – SUPERLATIVES, WORLD ——

SUPREME CAT SHOW – ZODIAC RHYME

'Indexers are interesting people, partly because they are interested in everything. Approach an indexer at a party (perhaps that fellow over by the bookcase, his head tilted so he can read the spines of the host's books, or the woman who has been engaged all evening in animated conversation with diverse groups of people about obscure subjects) and ask, "What kind of indexing do you do?" The response you get is likely to be an extended one.'

— CAROLYN McGOVERN
President of the American
Society of Indexers, 1994–95

ERRATA, CORRIGENDA, &c.

In keeping with many newspapers and journals, *Schott's Almanac* will publish in this section any significant corrections from the previous year. Below are some errata from *Schott's Almanac 2010* – one of which was kindly noted by a reader.

[p.197 *of the 2010 edition*] The time of the Moon landing should have been given as 2:56 GMT not the impossible 2:65 GMT. [p.206] The micro sign (µ) was inexplicably omitted from the list of SI symbols; it has been reinstated, again on p.206. [p.259] The salary for Deputy Mayor of London from 1/4/2009 was £95,141, not £127,784 as stated; this has been updated, again on p.259.

'In the year 1501, was printed a work, entitled the *Anatomy of the Mass*. It is a thin octavo, of 172 pages, and it is accompanied by an Errata of 15 pages! The editor, a pious monk, informs us that a very serious reason induced him to undertake this task: for it is, says he, to forestall the artifices of Satan. He supposes that the Devil, to ruin the fruit of this work, employed two very malicious frauds: the first before it was printed, by drenching the manuscript in a kennel, and having reduced it to a most pitiable state, rendered several parts illegible: the second, in obliging the printers to commit such numerous blunders, never yet equalled in so small a work. To combat this double machination of Satan he was obliged carefully to reperuse the work, and to form this singular list of the blunders of printers under the influence of the Devil. All this he relates in an advertisement prefixed to the Errata.' – ISAAC DISRAELI, *Curiosities of Literature*, Vol. I, 1834

ACKNOWLEDGMENTS

The author would like to thank:

Pavia Rosati · Jonathan, Judith, Geoffrey, Oscar, & Otto Schott, Anette Schrag
Jenny Album, Catherine Best, Martin Birchall, Keith Blackmore,
Julia Clark, Andrew Cock-Starkey, James Coleman, Aster Crawshaw,
Jody & Liz Davies, Will Douglas, Mary Duenwald, Stephanie Duncan,
Jennifer Epworth, Kathleen Farrar, Minna Fry, Alona Fryman, Tobin Harshaw,
Mark & Sharon Hubbard, Nick Humphrey, Max Jones, Amelia Knight,
Snigdha Koirala, Alison Lang, Annik Le Farge, John Lloyd, Ruth Logan,
Chris Lyon, Mark Lotto, Jess Manson, Michael Manson, Susannah McFarlane,
Sara Mercurio, David Miller, Polly Napper, Nigel Newton, Sarah Norton,
Alex O'Connell, Cally Poplak, Dave Powell, Alexandra Pringle, Leanne Shapton,
David Shipley, Bill Swainson, Caroline Turner, Greg Villepique, & Rett Wallace

Reference books are a great place to get the facts you need.
That's because reference books specialise in facts.
– LAURIE ROZAKIS, *The Complete Idiot's Guide to Research Methods*, 2004